THE ENVIRONMENTAL CONSEQUENCES OF WAR
Legal, Economic, and Scientific Perspectives

Over the last three decades we have witnessed the environmental devastation caused by military conflict in the wake of the Vietnam War, the Gulf War, and the Kosovo conflict. This book brings together leading international lawyers, military officers, scientists, and economists to examine the legal, political, economic, and scientific implications of wartime damage to the natural environment and public health.

The book considers issues raised by the application of humanitarian norms and legal rules designed to protect the environment, and the destructive nature of war. Contributors offer an analysis and critique of the existing law of war framework, lessons from peacetime environmental law, means of scientific assessment and economic valuation of ecological and public health damage, and proposals for future legal and institutional developments.

This book provides a contemporary forum for interdisciplinary analysis of armed conflict and the environment, and explores ways to prevent and redress wartime environmental damage.

Jay E. Austin is Senior Attorney with the Environmental Law Institute, Washington, D.C.

Carl E. Bruch is Staff Attorney with the Environmental Law Institute, Washington, D.C.

THE ENVIRONMENTAL
CONSEQUENCES OF WAR

Legal, Economic,
and Scientific Perspectives

EDITED BY

JAY E. AUSTIN AND
CARL E. BRUCH

CAMBRIDGE
UNIVERSITY PRESS

PUBLISHED BY THE PRESS SYNDICATE OF THE UNIVERSITY OF CAMBRIDGE
The Pitt Building, Trumpington Street, Cambridge, United Kingdom

CAMBRIDGE UNIVERSITY PRESS
The Edinburgh Building, Cambridge CB2 2RU, UK   www.cup.cam.ac.uk
40 West 20th Street, New York, NY 10011–4211, USA   www.cup.org
10 Stamford Road, Oakleigh, Melbourne 3166, Australia
Ruiz de Alarcón 13, 28014 Madrid, Spain

First published 2000

Printed in the United Kingdom at the University Press, Cambridge

Typeface 10.5/13.5pt Minion   [GC]

A catalogue record for this book is available from the British Library

Library of Congress Cataloguing in Publication data

The environmental consequences of war: legal, economic, and scientific perspectives/
Jay E. Austin & Carl E. Bruch, editors.
p.   cm.
ISBN 0 521 78020 9 (hb)✔
1. War (International law)   2. Environmental law, International.   I. Austin, Jay.
II. Bruch, Carl (Carl E.), 1967–
KZ6385.E58 2000
341.6 – dc21   99–087919

ISBN 0 521 78020 9   hardback

CONTENTS

v

vii

B · Public health damages

Part V · Prospects for the future

ILLUSTRATIONS

TABLES

List of tables

CONTRIBUTORS

Mahmood Y. Abdulraheem
Regional Director for West Asia
United Nations Environment
Programme

Adel A. S. O. Asem
Deputy Chairman and Director General
Public Authority for Assessment of
Compensation for Damages Resulting
from Iraqi Aggression

Jay E. Austin
Senior Attorney
Environmental Law Institute

Asit K. Biswas
President
Third World Centre for Water
Management

Lieutenant Commander
Michael J. Boock
International Environmental Law
Advisor
US Department of Defense

Ernest Briskey
Kuwait Institute for Scientific Research

Carl E. Bruch
Staff Attorney
Environmental Law Institute

David D. Caron
C. William Maxeiner Distinguished
Professor of Law
University of California at Berkeley

Mark Dickie
Professor of Economics
University of Southern Mississippi

Mark A. Drumbl
Assistant Professor of Law
University of Arkansas–Little Rock

Captain Richard T. Evans
Senior Environmental Law Advisor
Chief of Naval Operations, US Navy

Richard Falk
Albert G. Milbank Professor of
International Law and Practice
Woodrow Wilson School, Princeton
University

Eric Feldman
Senior Research Associate
Environmental Law Institute

List of contributors

David P. Fidler
Associate Professor of Law
Indiana University School of
Law–Bloomington

Shelby Gerking
Professor of Economics
University of Wyoming

Alastair W. M. Hay
Reader in Chemical Pathology
Division of Clinical Sciences
School of Medicine, University of Leeds

Jean-Marie Henckaerts
Legal Advisor
International Committee of the Red Cross

Jessica D. Jacoby
Senior Research Associate
Environmental Law Institute

Carol A. Jones
Associate Director for Research
Resource Economics Division
US Department of Agriculture

Barry Kellman
Professor of Law
Director, International Criminal Justice
and Weapons Control Center
DePaul University College of Law

Jennifer Leaning
Senior Research Fellow, Harvard Center
for Population Development Studies
Director, Program on Human Security
and Complex Humanitarian Emergencies
Assistant Professor of Medicine, Harvard
Medical School

Jeffrey A. McNeely
Chief Scientist
IUCN – The World Conservation Union

Thomas A. Mensah
Past President
International Tribunal for the Law of the
Sea

Jeffrey G. Miller
Professor of Law
Pace University School of Law

Raafat Misak
Kuwait Institute for Scientific Research

Samira A. S. Omar
Kuwait Institute for Scientific Research

Captain John P. Quinn
Executive Assistant and Special Counsel
Office of General Counsel
US Navy

Adam Roberts
Montague Burton Professor of
International Relations
Oxford University

Michael N. Schmitt
Professor of International Law
George C. Marshall European Center for
Security Studies

Victor W. Sidel
Distinguished University Professor of
Social Medicine, Montefiore Medical
Center, Albert Einstein College of
Medicine
Co-President, International Physicians for
the Prevention of Nuclear War

Christopher D. Stone
Roy P. Crocker Professor of Law
University of Southern California

Richard G. Tarasofsky
Barrister and Solicitor
Senior Associate
Ecologic – Centre for International and
European Environmental Research

Silja Vöneky
Ph.D. (Law)
University of Heidelberg and the Max-
Planck-Institute of Public International
Law and Comparative Law

W. Kip Viscusi
Cogan Professor of Law and Economics
Director of the Program on Empirical
Legal Studies
Harvard Law School

Arthur H. Westing
Westing Associates in Environment,
Security, & Education

ACKNOWLEDGEMENTS

This volume is the result of a two-year research project spearheaded by the Environmental Law Institute (ELI), in cooperation with the Smithsonian Institution and the Kuwait Foundation for the Advancement of Sciences. This effort culminated in the "First International Conference on Addressing Environmental Consequences of War: Legal, Economic, and Scientific Perspectives," held at the Smithsonian grounds in Washington, D.C. in June 1998. Most of the essays published here originally were presented at that Conference; following the Conference, the contributors continued to research and update their material, in particular to take account of developments such as the NATO action in Kosovo. The editors' gratitude goes first to these authors, who endured weeks of our editorial badgering and in response produced a number of truly outstanding, original contributions.

The editors also would like to acknowledge the assistance of the Conference's Advisory Committee, which included honorary members Dr. Mostafa Tolba, Justice Christopher Weeramantry, and the late Admiral Elmo Russell Zumwalt, Jr.; working group members Dan Bodansky, Laurence Boisson de Chazournes, Michael Bothe, Richard Falk, Philippe Sands, Richard Tarasofsky, and Arthur Westing (Law and Policy); Asit Biswas, Joseph Brain, Sylvia Earle, Ruth Etzel, and Samira Omar (Science); and Carol Jones, Paul Portney, V. Kerry Smith, and Robert Stavins (Economics). Many of these scholars contributed to the present volume, and all were generous with their time and candid advice on how to think about and refine such an inherently broad and unruly topic.

Thanks also are due to the Conference Executive Committee, in particular Adel Asem, Hadi Abdal, Mahmood Abdulraheem, Karen Kerr, Irene Pereira, and Scott Schang, for their input and steady support; to I. Michael

Heyman, Secretary of the Smithsonian Institution, and his efficient and patient staff; and to Conference keynote speakers President Oscar Arias, President Mikhail Gorbachev, and Bobby Muller for lending their considerable reputations to inspire and publicize new work in this field. Finally, we would like to acknowledge our colleagues at ELI, especially Bill Futrell, Elissa Parker, Eric Feldman, Jessica Jacoby, and Steve Dujack, for their contributions and their willingness to devote substantial institutional resources to an atypical, but highly rewarding, project.

FOREWORD

In the last three decades of the twentieth century, the world community started focusing on global environmental challenges and the ways in which such challenges could be effectively addressed. The 1972 United Nations Conference on the Human Environment, which resulted in the establishment of the United Nations Environment Programme, and the 1992 United Nations Conference on Environment and Development were landmarks in setting the global agenda to protect the environment and pursue sustainable development. States and people have joined forces to tackle common environmental challenges such as: global climate change; loss of biological diversity; destruction of the ozone layer; desertification; and transboundary impacts of persistent toxic substances. Further globalization in the new century will accelerate trans-border cooperation in environmental and sustainable development issues, which, in any case, do not respect any boundaries.

These decades also witnessed devastating damage to people and the environment as a result of inter-state wars and armed civil conflicts. Defoliants were used in Southeast Asia as a means of war, causing long-term hazards to human health and the environment. In the Gulf, deliberate oil burning and discharge were used in hostilities, which seriously damaged the marine and coastal environment, caused transboundary air pollution and contaminated soil and groundwater. The human environment, people's livelihoods, was the target of aggression during conflicts in Kosovo. Armed conflicts in Afghanistan and West and Central Africa forced millions of people to become refugees, posing significant stress to the environment. Weapons of mass destruction – nuclear, chemical or biological – could cause devastating environmental consequences and such weapons have continued to be in the arsenals of a number of states.

If we are to take the path towards sustainable development in the years to come, we must address the root causes that prevent us from achieving it. The ambivalence between increasing global environmental cooperation and intensified environmental damage associated with armed conflicts is one of the major points in that regard. In a wider context, the inter-linkages between environmental degradation and security require more attention. Environmental damage caused by war or by maintaining pre-paredness for war could be a factor for further instability and insecurity. From the environmental perspective, unsustainable patterns of consumption of raw materials, land or energy, unsustainable forms of development, or competition for the use of shared natural resources could threaten international peace and security. Consideration of such inter-linkages would require an holistic approach to target a range of key issues such as poverty, inadequate economic or development policies, injustice, and inequalities in multi-racial and multi-ethnic societies.

It is our responsibility to protect and enhance the environment, which enables people to enjoy a healthy and productive life in harmony with nature. As part of the process towards sustainable development, we need to consider issues associated with the environmental consequences of war, and identify realistic, innovative policy responses. A solution to this challenge will provide us with a key to the gate leading to a peaceful and sustainable world that we owe to future generations. The collection of articles in this book should enhance our understanding of the issues at stake, and are a valuable contribution to the discussion on the environ-mental consequences of war.

Klaus Toepfer
Executive Director
United Nations Environment Programme

INTRODUCTION

JAY E. AUSTIN AND CARL E. BRUCH

For centuries, military commanders have deliberately targeted the environment, seeking to obtain any possible advantage over their adversaries. In the Third Punic War, Roman legions salted the ground around Carthage to prevent the Carthaginians from recovering and challenging Rome; in the US Civil War, General Sherman cut a wide swath of destruction across the South in an attempt to break the morale of the Confederacy; in World War I, the British set afire Romanian oilfields to prevent the Central Powers from capturing them; in World War II, Germany and the Soviet Union engaged in "scorched earth" tactics; and in the Korean War, the United States bombed North Korean dams.[1]

The Vietnam War showcased the increasingly devastating environmental effects of modern military technology, with entire ecosystems targeted. The United States engaged in a massive defoliation campaign to preclude the growth of groundcover,[2] and even attempted to change

---

[1] See Adam Roberts, "Environmental Issues in International Armed Conflict: The Experience of the 1991 Gulf War," in Richard J. Grunawalt et al. (eds.), *Protection of the Environment during Armed Conflict* (Newport, R.I.: Naval War College, 1996), p. 225 (describing the destruction of Romanian oilfields by Colonel Norton Griffiths); Harry G. Summers, "Desolation and War: Necessity and Choice," paper delivered at the First International Conference on Addressing Environmental Consequences of War: Legal, Economic, and Scientific Perspectives, Washington, D.C. (June 1998) (manuscript on file with editors) (describing environmental impacts of Sherman's march to the sea, World War II, and the Korean War); see also Michael D. Diederich, Jr., " 'Law of War' and Ecology – A Proposal for a Workable Approach to Protecting the Environment through the Law of War," *Mil. L. Rev.* 136 (1992), 137 (discussing Persian commander Cyrus II diverting the Euphrates River during a siege of Babylon, Boers burning grasslands to deny forage to the British in the Second Anglo-Boer War, and Chinese dynamiting a dike to prevent Japanese troops from advancing in World War II).

[2] E.g., Arthur H. Westing, *Ecological Consequences of the Second Indochina War* (Stockholm: Almqvist & Wiksell Int'l, 1976), pp. 28, 47.

weather patterns via cloud seeding over North Vietnam to hamper enemy troop movements and provide protection for US bombing missions.[3] Since then, the public health implications of environmental warfare in Vietnam – primarily birth defects, diseases, and premature death associated with exposure to Agent Orange – have become apparent.[4] The scale, severity, and longevity of these environmental impacts sparked the first international legal provisions specifically prohibiting environmental warfare: the 1976 Environmental Modification Convention (ENMOD) and the 1977 Additional Protocol I to the 1949 Geneva Conventions (Protocol I). Notwithstanding international condemnation of such tactics, Central American internal conflicts of the 1980s saw further use of defoliation campaigns, albeit to a lesser degree than in the Vietnam War.[5]

The 1990–91 Gulf War may have seen the most concerted effort to destroy an enemy's environment, as Iraqi troops detonated more than 700 Kuwaiti oil wells, igniting over 600 of them. Smoke from the fires created black rain in Iran and Turkey, and possibly extended as far east as India.[6] Oil lakes created by damaged oil wells have seeped through the desert soils, contaminating the water table.[7] In an attempt to clog Kuwaiti desalinization plants and hinder an amphibious landing, Iraq also discharged an estimated 6 to 11 million barrels of crude oil directly into the Gulf, devastating

[3] E.g., Arthur H. Westing, *Weapons of Mass Destruction and the Environment* (London: Taylor & Francis, 1977), pp. 55–60; Seymour M. Hersh, "Rainmaking is Used as Weapon by US," *N.Y. Times* (July 3, 1972), A1; "Senator C. Pell Says He Believes US Military Forces Use Rain-Making to Cause Flooding and Death in Vietnam," *N.Y. Times* (June 27, 1972), A12.
[4] E.g., Arnold Schecter et al., "Agent Orange and the Vietnamese: The Persistence of Elevated Dioxin Levels in Human Tissues," *Am. J. Pub. Health* 85 (1995), 516; D. A. Savitz et al., "Vietnamese Infant and Childhood Mortality in Relation to the Vietnam War," *Am. J. Pub. Health* 83 (1993), 1134. But see Alastair Hay, "Defoliants: The Long-Term Health Implications," chapter 16 in this volume (questioning whether the public health data show these effects).
[5] E.g., *Guatemala: A Political Ecology*, EPOCA Green Paper No. 5 (1990), p. 13 (reporting the use of 2,4–D and 2,4,5–T, the herbicidal ingredients of Agent Orange, as well as paraquat in defoliation campaigns in regions of guerrilla activity); Bill Hall and Daniel Faber, *El Salvador: Ecology of Conflict*, EPOCA Green Paper No. 4 (1989), pp. 1, 7, 8–9 (describing scorched earth strategies, as well as the defoliation associated with heavy bombing and white phosphorus); Bill Weinberg, *War on the Land: Ecology and Politics in Central America* (1991), pp. 63–64 (detailing incendiary bombs, napalm, and white phosphorus used in El Salvador).
[6] Hunay Evliya, "Black Rain in Turkey: Possible Environmental Effects of the Gulf War," *Envtl. Sci. & Tech.* 26 (1992), 873; "Black Rain on Bushehr Province of Iran," *L.A. Times* (Jan. 24, 1991), A7.
[7] Thomas Canby, "After the Storm," *Nat'l Geographic* 180 (Aug. 1991), 2, 7; see also Samira A. S. Omar et al., "The Gulf War Impact on the Terrestrial Environment of Kuwait: An Overview," chapter 12 in this volume.

the marine environment.[8] The releases of oil also had tragic effects on migratory birds that were caught in oil lakes and slicks. The public health impacts from exposure to the oil smoke and particulates have started to manifest themselves in the form of respiratory ailments.[9]

While the Vietnam War was the first to isolate the environmental consequences of war as a separate legal issue, the 1990–91 Gulf War created such severe environmental devastation that the international community was compelled to create an institution to enforce legal norms. After the war, the UN Security Council declared Iraq liable for all damages arising as a result of its illegal invasion and occupation of Kuwait, explicitly including environmental damages and depletion of natural resources, and established the United Nations Compensation Commission to review claims and make compensation awards. While the UNCC's mandate is limited to the 1990–91 Gulf War, it is notable as the first international body charged with evaluating and compensating for wartime environmental damages, and its decisions will necessarily carry significant weight in future endeavors.

As in most conflicts, the environmental damage in the 1990–91 Gulf War was not unilateral. The region is now littered with as much as 300 tons of armor-piercing depleted uranium (DU) ammunition used by Coalition (largely US) forces.[10] The Coalition forces dropped a total of 88,500 tons of ordnance during the forty-three days of the Gulf War, much of which targeted environmental infrastructure, such as sewage treatment plants,[11] and some of which remained on the ground unexploded. No objective study of the ecological, health, or economic effects of these actions is available.[12]

More recently, Colombian rebels have detonated petroleum pipelines, spilling millions of barrels of crude oil into rivers, contaminating drinking and irrigation water, killing fish and other wildlife, contributing to

---

[8] E.g., "Millions of Gallons of Crude Oil Flow into Persian Gulf from Kuwaiti Tanks," *Int'l Env't Rep.* 14(2) (Jan. 30, 1991), 37; see also Mahmood Y. Abdulraheem, "War-Related Damage to the Marine Environment in the ROPME Sea Area," chapter 13 in this volume.

[9] E.g., K. T. Kelsey et al., "Genotoxicity to Human Cells Induced by Air Particulates Isolated during the Kuwait Oil Fires," *Envtl. Res.* 64 (1994), 8; Basem R. Saab and Salim M. Adib, "Acute Asthmatic Attacks in Bahrain in the Wake of the Gulf War: A Follow-up," *J. Envtl. Health* 58(9) (1996), 23.

[10] Saul Bloom et al. (eds.), *Hidden Casualties II: The Environmental, Health and Political Consequences of the Persian Gulf War* (1994), p. 135.

[11] *Ibid.*, pp. 146–48.

[12] For one reason, see John Horgan, "US Gags Discussion of War's Environmental Effects," *Sci. Am.* (May 1991), 24.

forest fires and oil pollution, sterilizing soil, and harming riverside communities.[13] The aquatic impacts extended beyond national borders to Venezuela, placing the Venezuelan government in the delicate position of trying to recover damages from the Colombian government for impacts to its rivers caused by Colombian rebels. Kurdish rebels in Turkey have adopted a similar tactic of detonating Turkish petroleum pipelines, although to a lesser degree.[14]

The 1999 Kosovo conflict raised further environmental issues. Serbian forces and militias poisoned wells and allegedly engaged in scorched earth tactics to spur Kosovar Albanians to leave their homes.[15] NATO's 78-day bombing campaign caused severe damage to certain areas, particularly around the oil refinery, petrochemical, and fertilizer plant complex at Pancevo and at the industrial facilities of Novi Sad.[16] Again, the issue of depleted uranium came to the fore, and targeting of civilian infrastructure such as sewage treatment facilities has reportedly caused environmental damage not only in Yugoslavia, but also downstream in Romania and Bulgaria.[17]

The Kosovo conflict also marked the broadest public participation to date in assessing and reporting on wartime environmental damage. During the conflict, nongovernmental organizations and concerned citizens monitored and documented the environmental effects of the bombing on Yugoslavia and neighboring countries, generating a steady stream of reports on the Internet and in the media.[18] Immediately following the cessation of hostilities, the United Nations Environment Program established an expert task force (including NGO representatives) to assess environmental damage, as it had done after the 1990–91 Gulf War. These experiences suggest an emerging role for the environmental NGO com-

---

[13] E.g., "Colombia Urges UN to Designate Bombing of Pipelines as Environment Treaty Violation," *Int'l Env't Rep.* 21 (1998), 175.

[14] "Turkey: Kurds Blow up Oil Pipeline," *N.Y. Times* (Mar. 24, 1999), A15.

[15] E.g., R. Jeffrey Smith, "Refugees Scavenge for Shelter in Scorched Earth of Kosovo," *Wash. Post* (Aug. 5, 1999), A14; R. Jeffrey Smith, "Poisoned Wells Plague Towns All Over Kosovo," *Wash. Post* (Dec. 9, 1998), A30 (citing an estimate of thousands of poisoned wells).

[16] E.g., Regional Environmental Center for Central and Eastern Europe, *Assessment of the Environmental Impact of Military Activities during the Yugoslavia Conflict: Preliminary Findings* (June 1999), available at http://www.rec.org/REC/Announcements/yugo/contents.html.

[17] *Ibid.*

[18] E.g., *ibid.*; "Hungary Finds Air Contaminated in Wake of NATO Strikes," ITAR-TASS (June 7, 1999).

4

munity: monitoring and publicizing the environmental consequences of war in order to assist ongoing efforts to hold militaries accountable for their wartime actions. They also suggest that wartime environmental damage will continue to be a legitimate area of inquiry and assistance, alongside concerns about human rights, refugee populations, and civilian infrastructure.

Ironically, war occasionally can benefit the environment. During the Nicaraguan civil war of the 1980s, timber felling ceased; conversion of forests to agricultural land slowed and stopped; animal trafficking largely halted; and fishing harvests fell as fishermen, fearing naval mines, stayed ashore, which allowed depleted stocks to recover.[19] Many of the remaining intact ecosystems in Central America continue to be threatened by conversion by agrarian peasants, except for those seeded with landmines during the civil wars. Similarly, perhaps the most biologically diverse area on the Korean Peninsula is the heavily mined Demilitarized Zone, a 4-km-wide no-man's land where there is no development or hunting.[20]

Of course, in all of these conflicts, the human toll has been enormous. Given the broader context of wartime calamity, emphasis on the environment may seem inappropriate or misguided. Yet even here, the primary concern is humanitarian and anthropocentric: at some point, incidental or intentional environmental harm can become so severe that it harms human health, especially that of innocent civilians. Inhalation of excessive smoke and airborne toxics can lead to respiratory ailments and cancers, ingestion of persistent toxics and radionuclides can cause both short- and long-term health impacts, and many of the substances mobilized during environmental warfare are mutagenic or teratogenic, affecting not just the present population but also future generations. Environmental damage also impairs the long-term ability of the civilian population to support itself, destabilizing society and sowing the seeds for further conflict. And

---

[19] Bernard Q. Nietschmann, "The Effects of War and Peace on Nicaragua's Environments," paper delivered at the First International Conference on Addressing Environmental Consequences of War: Legal, Economic, and Scientific Perspectives, Washington, D.C. (June 1998) (manuscript on file with editors); Pascal O. Girot and Bernard Q. Nietschmann, "The Río San Juan," *Nat'l Geographic Res. & Exploration* 8(1) (1992), 52, 58–59.

[20] Ke Chung Kim, "Preserving Biodiversity in Korea's Demilitarized Zone," *Sci.* 278 (1997), 242; see also William K. Stevens, "Unlikely Tool for Species Preservation: Warfare," *N.Y. Times* (Mar. 30, 1999), D1 (describing how American bison survived primarily in "buffer zones between warring tribes").

beyond these human concerns, enhanced public awareness of environmental issues over the past three decades and the increasing globalization of environmental issues has led some commentators to advocate wartime constraints on purely ecological, non-anthropocentric grounds.[21]

Perhaps the most candid response to critics who question the importance of addressing and legislating against wartime environmental damage is to acknowledge that it, like most of international humanitarian law, is an incrementalist enterprise. The history of the law of war has been one of a gradual narrowing of what the community of nations considers to be acceptable, indeed civilized, methods of combat. This is true whether one considers the laws restricting weapons, which have steadily progressed from banning gas and explosive bullets to condemning weapons of mass destruction to the recent focus on landmines, which are both a humanitarian and an environmental problem; or whether one considers the laws restricting wartime actions and targets, which have expanded to protect not only combatants, but also prisoners of war, the civilian population, property, and historical and cultural monuments. Now that the law of war recognizes not only humanitarian concerns, but also our material, cultural, and aesthetic legacy, it is a small leap to propose an "environmental law of war." To the extent that this effort derives from the law-of-war tradition, it may seem inadequate to skeptics who question the efficacy of any attempts to place restrictions on warfare, or who believe that such restrictions are only enforced against nations that, like Iraq, are thoroughly defeated in combat. Yet even the most ardent critics of the existing norms generally admit that gradualist reforms can exist side by side with more radical proposals – including those that seek to curtail the waging of war altogether.

This book draws upon papers presented at and research connected to the "First International Conference on Addressing Environmental Consequences of War: Legal, Economic, and Scientific Perspectives," which was co-sponsored by the Environmental Law Institute, the Smithsonian Institution, and the Kuwait Foundation for the Advancement of Sciences in June 1998 in Washington, D.C. Numerous other conferences, articles, and books have considered the legal regime for preventing or redressing

[21] See the discussion in Christopher D. Stone, "The Environment in Wartime: An Overview," chapter 1 in this volume.

wartime environmental damage, and similar efforts have attempted scientifically to assess and value environmental impacts of particular conflicts.[22] The Washington conference and this resulting volume are unique in bringing together lawyers, scientists, economists, military officers, and ethicists to consider how to address environmental consequences of war in a multidisciplinary manner. By considering the issue from a variety of perspectives, we have sought to improve communication among the different disciplines, and to ask what they need from each other, what are their current limitations, and what are the opportunities for collaborating to develop necessary methodologies in the future.

The book begins with basic cultural principles, examines the existing legal norms and institutions for preventing and redressing wartime environmental damage, considers the scientific and economic methodologies for assessing and valuing the damage within a legal framework, and then looks forward to a variety of proposed and emerging institutions for preventing, assessing, valuing, and redressing the environmental consequences of war. It takes as its starting point the existence of a relevant framework of international law that defines the scope of the issues, creates and empowers institutions to address these issues, and devises appropriate remedies. Science and economics are explored insofar as they operate in the service of this legal regime, by providing the necessary factual elements of proof, defining the extent of damage and causation, and placing an economic value on the damages to be awarded.

At the same time, science and economics necessarily interact with and help shape the legal regime. For instance, the ability of ecological and public health sciences to predict long-term damage currently is quite limited. As a result, it is difficult, if not impossible, to discern the full extent of damage immediately after it occurs. In the peacetime context, this has occasionally required long-term environmental monitoring and remediation programs, although the legal profession generally favors closure and prefers to adjudicate all issues, including the amount of damages, as early

---

[22] For a review of the relevant legal, economic, and scientific literature, see Environmental Law Institute, *Annotated Bibliography* (June 1998) (prepared for the First International Conference on Addressing Environmental Consequences of War: Legal, Economic, and Scientific Perspectives), available at http://www.eli.org/pdf/annotated.pdf; for a review of some of the major legal initiatives to address wartime environmental damage after the 1990–91 Gulf War, see Michael N. Schmitt, "War and the Environment: Fault Lines in the Prescriptive Landscape," chapter 3 in this volume.

as possible. Similarly, the lack of economic valuation techniques that apply reliably to wartime environmental damages may have contributed heavily to the decision to focus on environmental assessment, remediation/ restoration, and monitoring costs following recent conflicts in Colombia and the 1990–91 Gulf War.

Part I of the book surveys the ethical, moral, and religious bases for constraining the environmental consequences of war. While many of the predominant religious and ethical traditions mandate respect for the environment, and some specifically impose limits on militaries when it comes to environmental harm, it is worth considering (and this book does not seek to answer) to what extent these tenets are universally held. Part I also frames a series of overarching threshold questions that subsequent parts seek to address.

Building on these basic principles, Part II examines the legal framework for preventing, assessing, remediating, and assigning liability for wartime environmental damage. Section A focuses on the international law-of-war and humanitarian law provisions constraining wartime environmental damage and allowing redress for that damage. This section highlights various inadequacies in the existing legal framework and suggests different ways of resolving these issues within the law-of-war context. One particular gap – the dearth of norms governing internal armed conflicts – proves particularly problematic. Section B canvasses legal regimes other than the law of war to highlight relevant legal principles, experiences, and mechanisms that could help clarify the existing law of war and fill in gaps. For instance, in considering the various international and national experiences with environmental damage, different authors converge on recommending a remediation fund that would supplement the emerging civil and criminal norms.

Part III examines a range of techniques and issues relating to the scientific assessment of ecological impacts (Section A) and public health impacts (Section B). Experience with major peacetime environmental catastrophes such as oil spills, deforestation, and wildlife destruction provides some basis for assessing wartime environmental damage. Moreover, some of the tools for assessing damage have been developed specifically to weigh the impacts of military preparation, highlighting the link between the preparations for and the actual conduct of war. However, in wartime as in peacetime, long-term environmental impacts are notoriously difficult to predict with any accuracy; in fact, experience has shown that even short-term impacts can be seriously under- or over-estimated.

Part IV presents a range of economic methodologies for valuing ecological and natural resource damages and public health damages. In economics, the exceptional nature of war becomes particularly acute. Although there are a wealth of well-developed methodologies for valuing peacetime damages, the contributors raise a host of difficulties in applying these methodologies to a wartime context, where damage is on a larger scale and more severe than typically considered, the infrastructure for redressing the damage is taxed beyond normal, and the cultural assumptions relied upon by these mostly Western methodologies may not extend to other cultures.

Such methodological difficulties highlight a need for more research on the subject, but they also suggest that the legal regime may need modifications to account for the limitations of the existing scientific assessment and economic valuation techniques. For instance, difficulties in long-term assessment suggest the need for immediate mitigation and restoration action coupled with long-term monitoring and remediation in order to restore fully the injured party to its prewar state. On the other hand, a lack of internationally agreed-upon economic valuation techniques for wartime environmental damage suggests that the legal system may need to reconsider the relevance to war of the range of compensable environmental damages normally awarded in peacetime.

Looking forward, Part V examines a range of underutilized and proposed international mechanisms for preventing, assessing, and punishing wartime environmental damage. These include a proposed convention on special protected areas, akin to the Cultural Property Convention; the inspection mechanism of the Chemical Weapons Convention, which provides a comprehensive tool for investigating claimed violations of that convention, and whose experience could provide for an analogous mechanism for investigating claims of wartime environmental wrongs; the Article 90 inspection mechanism of Protocol I; and the nascent International Criminal Court, which includes environmental war crimes in its purview.

Not explicitly addressed in this volume are a number of other important relationships between war and environmental protection, in particular the various strands of thought that are loosely grouped under the heading of "environmental security."[23] Rather simply put, this inquiry concerns itself with how shortages of natural resources and other environmental stresses lead to disputes that can escalate to armed conflict – the environmental *causes* of war rather than the environmental effects of war. Still, there is no doubt that the two topics are related: Excessive wartime damage to civilian resources or the needs of displaced refugee populations can destabilize the transition to peace, leading to a vicious cycle of further conflict and environmental damage. Conversely, an increased emphasis on peacetime environmental cooperation can both bring former combatants closer together – as with the Central American "Peace Parks"[24] – or prevent conflict from occurring in the first place.[25] Clearly, these possibilities also warrant further investigation.

Finally, the Epilogue considers in detail the 1999 Kosovo conflict, which serves as a case study of many of the unresolved legal and methodological issues in preventing, assessing, valuing, and assigning responsibility and liability for wartime environmental damage. Sadly, the Kosovo conflict also highlights the fact that wartime environmental damage is likely to remain an issue for some time to come, particularly until the relevant legal norms are clarified and strengthened and the necessary institutions established and empowered to enforce these norms.

[23] E.g., Arthur H. Westing, "The Environmental Component of Comprehensive Security," *Bull. Peace Proposals* 20 (1989), 129–34; Thomas F. Homer-Dixon, "On the Threshold: Environmental Changes as Causes of Acute Conflict," *Int'l Security* 16 (1991), 76; Robert D. Kaplan, "The Coming Anarchy," *Atlantic Monthly* 273(2) (Feb. 1994), 44.

[24] E.g., Jeffrey A. McNeely, "War and Biodiversity: An Assessment of Impacts," chapter 14 in this volume; Lothar Brock, "Peace Through Parks: The Environment on the Peace Research Agenda," *J. Peace Res.* 28 (1991), 407–23; see also Ricardo A. Navarro, "The Environmental Consequences of War: The Case of El Salvador," paper delivered at the First International Conference on Addressing Environmental Consequences of War: Legal, Economic, and Scientific Perspectives, Washington, D.C. (June 1998) (manuscript on file with editors) (describing "Forests of Reconciliation").

[25] E.g., Deborah Sandler et al. (eds.), *Protecting the Gulf of Aqaba: A Regional Environmental Challenge* (Washington: Environmental Law Institute, 1993); Moshe Hirsch, "Environmental Cooperation between Former Belligerents in the Middle East: Some Structural Factors" (May 1998) (manuscript on file with editors).

PART I

GENERAL PRINCIPLES

INTRODUCTION

CARL E. BRUCH

For as long as war has devastated the environment, moral and religious codes have sought to prevent or minimize the environmental impacts of wartime actions. Even in biblical times, Deuteronomy commanded:

> When you are at war, and lay siege to a city for a long time in order to take it, do not destroy its trees by taking the axe to them, for they provide you with food; you shall not cut them down. The trees of the field are not men that you should besiege them. But you may destroy or cut down any trees that you know do not yield food, and use them in siege-works against the city that is at war with you, until it falls.[1]

Although this is an anthropocentric perspective, applying only to the extent that environmental damage clearly harms society, it has been the basis for much of the Judeo-Christian scholarship in the area, including the development of the principle of *bal tashchit*, a rabbinical interpretation enjoining environmental waste and destruction.[2]

Similarly, the Qur'an enjoins Muslims from harming trees in a jihad, a Muslim holy war.[3] In fact, some Muslim armies included an officer who had the specific duty to ensure that "trees are not burnt, nor unjustifiably pulled out and that women, children, the elderly and unoffending priests or monks should not be harmed. He also ascertains that water and

---

[1] *The New English Bible with the Apocrypha* (1971), Deuteronomy 20:19–20.

[2] E.g., Jewish Theological Seminary, "Bal Tashchit: The Development of a Jewish Environmental Principle," http://www.jtsa.edu/org/coejl/source/tashchit.htm.

[3] M. I. H. Farooqi, *Plants of the Quran* (Lucknow: Sidrah Publishers, 1992), p. 25; Al-Hafiz B. A. Masri, "Islam and Ecology," in Fazlun Khalid and Joanne O'Brien (eds.), *Islam and Ecology* (New York: Cassell, 1992), pp. 1, 13 (quoting Tabari, *Exegesis of the Qur'an*; also noting that the Qur'an contains about 500 verses on the relationship between humanity and the environment).

medicine are given to the prisoners of war."[4] Although generally prohibiting destruction of any plant in wartime, the Qur'an permits such destruction under grave military necessity.[5] The Buddhist and Hindu principle of *ahimsa* mandates avoiding unnecessary harm, and cultivating a respect for the environment, which may apply in both peace and war.[6]

Many of these religious norms have been incorporated into current international law. Most prominent among these is the Just War tradition, which maintains that people may take up arms to combat egregious wrongs but imposes limitations to ensure that the conflict remains "just." With roots in Catholic theology, the Just War tradition has heavily influenced the development of the international law of war, addressing both the reasons for going to war (*ius ad bellum*) and how adversaries conduct war (*ius in bello*).[7] In fact, Gregory Reichberg and Henrik Syse[8] have argued that the Just War tradition provides not only a possible philosophical framework for addressing wartime environmental damage, but also an ethical and legal vocabulary. Their work has highlighted how particular environmental wartime damage may implicate various elements of the tradition, with the *ius in bello* factors of discrimination and proportionality being the two most relevant. Significantly, these two principles pervade the modern body of law of war, from custom, through the 1977 Additional Protocol I to the 1949 Geneva Conventions, to the 1998 Rome Statute of the International Criminal Court.

In the following chapter, Christopher Stone reviews the moral, ethical, and religious underpinnings for legal constraints on wartime environmental damage. Asking a series of nine overarching questions, Stone explores the current norms, and questions where future developments should occur. In the process, Stone presents some threshold issues that

[4] Khalid and O'Brien, *Islam and Ecology*, p. 34 (quoting Al-Taratib al-Idariyya).
[5] *Sura Hashr*, verse 5.
[6] See generally Ranchar Prime, *Hinduism and Ecology: Seeds of Truth* (New York: Cassell, 1992); see also Michael D. Diederich, Jr., "'Law of War' and Ecology – A Proposal for a Workable Approach to Protecting the Environment through the Law of War," *Mil. L. Rev.* 136 (1992), 137, 153.
[7] See Michael Walzer, *Just and Unjust Wars: A Moral Argument with Historical Illustrations* (New York: Basic Books, 1977); William O'Brien, *Conduct of Just and Limited War* (New York: Praeger, 1981).
[8] Gregory Reichberg and Henrik Syse, "Protecting the Natural Environment in Wartime: Ethical Considerations from the Just War Tradition," *J. Peace Research* 37 (2000), 449–68 (originally presented at First International Conference on Addressing Environmental Consequences of War: Legal, Economic, and Scientific Perspectives, Washington, D.C. (June 1998).

should be kept in mind throughout this volume: What are the realistic scenarios of wartime environmental damage that need to be addressed? Where are new norms necessary to prevent and redress wartime environmental damage? How should damages be measured and collected?

In considering the different ethical, moral, legal, scientific, and economic issues in this volume, the cultural dynamic must be considered. Notwithstanding the Judeo-Christian, Islamic, Buddhist, and Hindu norms described above, Western nations have driven much of the development of international law, including the law of war, humanitarian law, and international environmental law. Additionally, scientific methods for evaluating the impacts of war might be incapable of assessing wartime impacts on some cultures, such as the claim that environmental damage has "driven the gods away" or otherwise destroyed the spiritual meaning of a place. Similarly, economic tools for assessing natural resource and public health damages were developed in the West, and include assumptions that do not translate easily across cultures. For instance, the lost wages metric for valuing morbidity and mortality implies that a person from a developed country is "worth" more than a person from a developing country – a result that is unpalatable to most. In order for the norms constraining and redressing environmental consequences of war to have universal applicability, it will be necessary to consider how to broaden the values reflected in these norms.

1

THE ENVIRONMENT IN WARTIME:
AN OVERVIEW

CHRISTOPHER D. STONE

Introduction

Concern over the fate of the environment in war has a long history. Deuteronomy forbade the destruction of fruit trees during siege of an enemy's city.[1] In *On the Law of War and Peace*, Grotius (in a chapter on "Moderation in Devastating a Country, and Similar Matters") did his best to marshal some other early authority for sheltering the environment from hostile action. He summons Philo, the first-century Jewish philosopher, who chided: "Why vent anger on inanimate things, which are themselves kindly, and bring forth fruit? Do trees, like the men who are your enemies, display signs of hostility, so that for the things they do or threaten to do, they must be uprooted?"[2]

Nonetheless, Grotius was well aware that such expressions of concern were exceptional and probably influenced conduct little. Indeed, at one point Grotius, anticipating von Clausewitz, appears to acknowledge that

---

[1]   When thou shalt besiege a city a long time, in making war against it to take it, thou shalt not destroy the trees thereof by forcing an axe against them: for thou mayest eat of them, and thou shalt not cut them down *for the tree of the field is man's life* to employ them in the siege; Only the trees which thou knowest that they be not trees for meat, thou shalt destroy and cut them down: and thou shalt build bulwarks against the city that maketh war against thee, until it be subdued.
    Deuteronomy 20:19–20 (Holy Bible, King James version (1611)
    (italics added).
[2] Hugo Grotius, *On the Law of War and Peace* (L. S. Loomis trans., 1949), p. 325 (quoting Philo, *On the Constitution*, p. 13).

realpolitik rendered devastation acceptable "if by it the enemy is reduced quickly to suing for peace."[3] In the last analysis, the demands of military and political necessity were hard to resist, then as now.

In fact, while Grotius did not suppress his sympathy with farmers and beasts and fields,[4] he rested his appeal for moderation less on environmental consciousness than on prudent self-interest: the kings of Macedon, he reminded his readers, "were lenient so the realm might be the richer."[5] Deuteronomy's injunction against cutting trees extended only to fruit trees, and on the distinctly homocentric ground that "the tree of the field is man's life."

Two developments have forced us to reconsider our posture towards the environment in wartime. The first is the rise of environmentalism. The second half of the twentieth century witnessed heightened alarm over damage to the environment from all causes. The course of human development, even in peace, is taxing our biosphere. Species are disappearing; forests are shrinking; the oceans are sullied and overfished; the atmosphere and ozone layer are subject to stresses whose implications are, if uncertain, certainly worrisome. These concerns have spurred a growth in environmental laws and activities at local, regional, and international levels.

The second development involves advances in military technology. New weaponry threatens to amplify the environmental hazards bred by economic development and population growth. The most dramatic specter is the "nuclear winter" that many scientists maintain would follow an extensive nuclear exchange.[6] But even hostilities on a more limited scale threaten to add the environment to the casualty lists of modern warfare. The Second Indochina War demonstrated that, already by the 1970s, the arsenals of advanced nations included such environmental modification

---

[3] *Ibid.*, p. 360 (quoting Proclus). Compare *ibid.* (quoting Onesander to the effect that the commander should "remember to wreck the enemy's country, burn it and leave it desolate") with Carl von Clausewitz, *On War*, book I (1832), p. 76 (Michael Howard and Peter Paret eds. and trans., 1984) ("to introduce into the philosophy of war itself a principle of moderation would be an absurdity").

[4] See Grotius, *On the Law of War and Peace*, pp. 362–63.   [5] *Ibid.*, p. 362.

[6] See P. R. Ehrlich et al., "Long-term Biological Consequences of Nuclear War," *Sci.* 222 (1983), 1293; see also Carl Sagan, "Nuclear War and Climactic Catastrophe: Some Policy Implications," *Foreign Aff.* 62 (1983), 257. But see Stanley L. Thomson and Stephen H. Schneider, "Nuclear Winter Reappraised," *Foreign Aff.* 64 (1987), 981 (suggesting exaggerations in earlier estimates).

techniques as defoliation, rainmaking, and massive plowing.[7] Far more disruptive weaponry may have been developed since, and certainly has been envisioned. And, indeed, the Gulf War of 1990–91 underscores the fact that a belligerent need not have access to particularly high technology to scar the environment.

The convergence of these two trends – heightening environmental consciousness and advancing weaponry – has inspired a spate of environment-shielding conventions. The list includes, certainly, the Convention on the Prohibition of Environmental Modification Techniques (ENMOD),[8] and the 1977 Additional Protocol I to the Geneva Conventions of 1949 (Protocol I).[9] The various treaties that limit the testing of weapons in the atmosphere and outer space, while not strictly speaking "environmental warfare" agreements, have to be grouped with the general movement. Similarly included are the 1959 Antarctic Treaty[10] and the 1967 Convention on the Uses of Outer Space,[11] which aim to "zone" specific affected areas out of warfare. Arthur Westing, who has written in this area extensively, has surveyed many others that might be included in this class.[12]

Where does the international community stand legally, ethically, and technically? Where should the international community be heading? This chapter raises several overarching questions, many of which other authors investigate and seek to answer through in-depth analysis in specific, targeted cases.

---

[7] Arthur H. Westing, *Ecological Consequences of the Second Indochina War* (Stockholm: Almqvist & Wiksell Int'l, 1976), p. 82.

[8] Convention on the Prohibition of Military or Any Other Hostile Use of Environmental Modification Techniques (ENMOD) (done at New York, Dec. 10, 1976; entered into force, Oct. 5, 1978), 31 U.S.T. 333, T.I.A.S. No. 9614, reprinted in *I.L.M.* 16 (1977), 88.

[9] Protocol Additional to the Geneva Conventions of August 12, 1949, and Relating to the Protection of Victims of International Armed Conflicts (Protocol I) (done at Geneva, June 8, 1977; entered into force, Dec. 7, 1978), reprinted in *I.L.M.* 16 (1977), 1391; see also Protocol Additional to the Geneva Conventions of August 12, 1949, and Relating to the Protection of Victims of Non-international Armed Conflicts (done at Geneva, June 8, 1977; entered into force, Dec. 7, 1978), reprinted in *I.L.M.* 16 (1977), 1442.

[10] The Antarctic Treaty (done at Washington, Dec. 1, 1959; entered into force, June 23, 1961), 12 U.S.T. 794, 402 U.N.T.S. 71.

[11] Treaty on Principles Governing the Activities of States in the Exploration and Use of Outer Space, Including the Moon and other Celestial Bodies (done at Washington, London, and Moscow, Jan. 27, 1967; entered into force, Oct. 10, 1967), 18 U.S.T. 2410, 610 U.N.T.S. 205, reprinted in *I.L.M.* 6 (1967), 386.

[12] Arthur H. Westing, "Environmental Warfare: An Overview," in Arthur H. Westing (ed.), *Environmental Warfare: A Technical, Policy and Legal Appraisal* (London and Philadelphia: Taylor & Francis, 1984), pp. 3–10.

A question of ethics

The first question is one of ethics: How *ought* the environment to be treated in wartime? This is an issue prior to the questions of practicality that follow from it – questions of how to create a bureaucratic atmosphere that will facilitate execution of the "right" decisions in the fracas of war. It is too easy to jump into the discussion supposing we know what is morally right – protection of the environment – and are faced only with designing institutions that will insulate commanders and politicians from some overriding, morally indifferent, principle of "military and political necessity." The truth is not so simple.

Imagine that a military engagement is shifting towards a jungle area of a sort that environmentalists call a "hot spot," that is, a region unusually abundant in biological diversity. An attacking commander who has his enemy on the run knows this. Assume that pursuant to his army's manual, the commander has an environmental ethicist on his staff. His military intelligence, however, tells him that the enemy is using the area to stage a major counter-attack. He can drive the enemy out, but only by recourse to an environment-disturbing bombardment. How does the environmental ethicist respond, then? Suppose the commander refuses to accept military advantage as the last word. He is open to moral arguments. He wants to do the right thing. But what moral principles does the ethicist advance, when he asks how he is to trade off people – his own troops – for biodiversity? What *ought* he to do?

The question is hard because the whole area of ethics and warfare – not just the environmental dimensions – is riddled with conundrums. The bombing of cities, sieges, partisans, blockades, and hostages all open moral Pandora's boxes for those who have the nerve to raise the lids.[13] But in each of those areas, hard as they are, the issue is at least one of weighing the fate of human against human. There is therefore available, at least in theory, a common metric of utility: 10,000 lives extinguished versus a million saved. Or, if we are uneasy about the verdicts of utility, we can advance on the dilemma with some variant of the Golden Rule (or of Kantianism): "How would you, as the bombardier, evaluate the action you are about to take if you were in the shoes of those down on the ground below?"

---

[13] See Theodore J. Koontz, "Noncombatant Immunity in Michael Walzer's *Just and Unjust Wars*," *Ethics & Int'l Aff.* 11 (1997), 55.

The point is this: If the problems of targeting populated areas, blockades, sieges, and the various other interpersonal conflicts are hard to resolve even with aid of traditional ethical guidelines, how much harder is it to weigh humans, on one pan of the scale, against some quality of the environment, on the other? We can put ourselves in the shoes of a hostage, perhaps, but we cannot put ourselves in the hooves of a horse – or ask, how would we feel if we were a species or a mountain top?

So, the first issue is: If we are committed to taking nature into account, by what accounting do we do so? What is right *for the environment*?

Have we undertaken – should we and could we undertake – to protect nature?

The second question, which follows closely from the first, is one of intellectual history. We commonly speak as though the world community were on the brink of accounting for nature as such, and not merely as one more element of human-serving property such as coal or iron. The relatively recent diplomatic activity over environmental warfare agreements provides scant evidence that the world community is on the verge of any real revolution in morals and attitude.

To illustrate what a truly revolutionary treaty would look like, imagine a convention that, at nontrivial cost, sheltered an endangered species of plant or insect of no prospective benefit to humankind, now or in the future. More precisely, imagine a decision to safeguard a species even when the cost of doing so exceeds the option value, that is, a figure that captures the theoretical value based on the probability that the species will turn out to have some use value, presently unknown, in the future. Domestically, the Endangered Species Act[14] and, internationally, CITES[15] may serve as examples of agreements that at least in some cases are prepared to subordinate human utility to survival of some element of nature; these can be called environmental in a revolutionarily strong or deep sense. But when surveying existing environment-affecting agreements, it is not clear which of them can be labeled "environmental" even in more moderate senses.

[14] Endangered Species Act, 16 U.S.C. §§ 1531–1543 (1973).
[15] Convention on International Trade in Endangered Species of Wild Fauna and Flora (done at Washington, Mar. 13, 1973; entered into force, July 1, 1975), 27 U.S.T. 1087, 993 U.N.T.S. 243.

Consider the 1980 Land Mine Protocol.[16] Of course, it affects the environment – it is hard to imagine an arms treaty that does not – but the effect is entirely incidental to the safeguarding of humans. Indeed, the environmental impact is not even certain. It has been suggested that the mining of delicate landscapes, such as in the Sinai and the Korean Demilitarized Zone, is, however much a threat to humans, a benefit to the environment by providing the natural terrain with a macabre reprieve from human incursion.

In the main, even those military treaties that aim to protect the environment do so, like Deuteronomy,[17] only incidentally, as part of an effort to safeguard human health and welfare. For example, Protocol I prohibits bombing dams not (as environmentalists might propose) absolutely on the grounds of preserving rivers, but only to the extent that the destruction "may cause the release of dangerous forces . . . and consequent severe losses among the civilian populations."[18] The same homocentrism motivates agreements that limit radioactivity and the use of chemical and bacteriological agents: because many substances that imperil humans can also disrupt the nonhuman environment, the protection of persons from these things benefits nature indirectly. But protecting nature is, at most, only a contributing rationale.

There is at least one noteworthy exception. Article 35(3) of Protocol I prohibits methods of warfare "expected . . . to cause widespread, long-term and severe damage to the natural environment" – independently, it can be argued, of demonstrable impact on humans.[19] But given the vagueness of the terms – how "severe"? how "widespread"? – the import of this article is unclear. To illustrate, had Article 35(3) been applicable in the Gulf War of 1990–91, it is not clear whether it would have been violated by Iraq (as by the maritime consequences of oil releases) or by the United States (as by the airborne consequences of destroying weapons depots).[20]

In sum, the second question is this: How strong a sentiment is there for treaties that go beyond the prudence of the kings of Macedonia, and beyond concern for non-combatants, to require belligerents to leave

---

[16] Convention on Prohibitions or Restrictions on the Use of Certain Conventional Weapons which may be Deemed to be Excessively Injurious or to Have Indiscriminate Effects and Protocols (done Oct. 10, 1980; entered into force, Dec. 2, 1983), reprinted in *I.L.M.* 19 (1981), 1524.   [17] See Deuteronomy, note 1 above.

[18] Protocol I, Art. 56(1).   [19] *Ibid.*, Art. 35(3); see also *ibid.*, Art. 55(1).

[20] As explained below, the long-term damage from these actions is anything but certain.

certain ecosystems intact for their intrinsic, non-instrumental worth, or for the sake of future generations?[21]

What are the real threats to the environment in wartime?

Almost everyone will agree that, whatever the rationale for environmental warfare restrictions (whether placed on a homocentric or "intrinsic worth" foundation), the fate of the environment in wartime merits concern. But what are the fates, the scenarios, that drive the concern? The list of threats is easy to embroider. In an effort to be inclusive, the environmental warfare literature appears to include a number of specters that are farfetched and fanciful.

ENMOD, for example, holds itself out as guardian against the following list of illustrative perils: "earthquakes, tsunamis, an upset in the ecological balance of a region, changes in weather patterns (clouds, precipitation, cyclones of various types) . . . changes in climate patterns, . . . ocean currents . . . the state of the ozone layer . . . the ionosphere."[22]

Granted, a belligerent might, by setting off nuclear explosions along geological fault lines within its enemy's territory, trigger a devastating earthquake.[23] But surely any nation with the nuclear technology (and delivery capability) to pull off such a stunt, and the willingness to use it, would think of a less roundabout way to hector an enemy. (There is the additional issue – which is put aside here – of whether it is wise to discourage a nation committed to using nuclear weapons to drop them along a fault zone rather than on a city.) One wonders, too, about the much-discussed threat of weather control as weaponry. Even if a belligerent should develop the capacity to control micro-climate, it is unclear how a

[21] The 1972 World Heritage Convention takes such an approach for cultural monuments, as well as for some features of the landscape. Convention Concerning the Protection of the World Cultural and Natural Heritage (done at Paris, Nov. 16, 1972), 27 U.S.T. 37, Arts. 6(1) and 6(3) (recognizing that the cultural and natural heritage "constitutes a world heritage for whose protection it is the duty of the international community as a whole to co-operate" and obliging parties "not to take any deliberate measures which might damage directly or indirectly the . . . natural heritage . . . situated on the territory of other States Parties to this Convention." As of June 1, 1999, 156 countries had signed; the United States has signed but has yet to ratify.).

[22] See Committee of the Conference on Disarmament (CCD), No. CCD/520, *Report of the Working Group of the Plenary of the CCD* (1976), pp. 6–7.

[23] Hallan C. Noltimier, "Techniques for Manipulating the Geosphere," in Westing, *Environmental Warfare*, pp. 25–26 (but noting that energy is actually lost in the translation from nuclear to seismic, i.e., less seismic energy comes out than the nuclear energy that went in).

command could put the technology to military advantage, particularly in a manner that did not backfire against its own troops.[24]

Others have suggested that a belligerent might activate a quiescent volcano,[25] melt the polar ice,[26] or create drought conditions.[27] Adventure movies aside, is anyone seriously worried that some fiendish belligerent (presumably a safely landlocked nation) is going to melt the polar ice caps in order to erode his enemy's (and everyone else's) coastline?

Of course, evaluating the strategic merits of the various techniques that have been discussed lies beyond my own expertise. But surely an expert in military affairs should review the proposed perils, discard those that are utterly farfetched, and help focus the dialog on the third question: Which scenarios impel the most seriously concentrated attention?

For what threats is additional law needed?

Even when the realistic threats have been ferreted out, there will remain to be considered: Which of the threats are presently unaddressed (or inadequately addressed) by other conventions, or even general principles of international law, so that additional treaty law is demanded?

As a start, consider the applicability and reach of ordinary, peacetime environmental treaties and principles. Certainly, in times of peace, if Nation *A* should interfere with Nation *B*'s climate or river flow (whether incidentally or with deliberate hostile intent), *A* would bear state responsibility. There are many widely accepted declarations and principles that prohibit a nation from allowing activities within its jurisdiction or control to cause significant injury to the environment of another state (or for that matter to commons areas beyond *A*'s frontiers).[28]

Is Nation *A* immune from these existing obligations if it initiates its environmental modification in the pursuit of war? To illustrate, assaulting an enemy with drought would appear to be a bizarre, lethargic, and

---

[24] Jozef Goldblat, "The Environmental Modification Convention of 1977: An Analysis," in Westing, *Environmental Warfare*, pp. 53, 56.

[25] E.g., Noltimier, "Techniques for Manipulating the Geosphere," p. 28.   [26] *Ibid.*, p. 29.

[27] E.g., Ernö Mészáros, "Techniques for Manipulating the Atmosphere," in Westing, *Environmental Warfare*, pp. 13, 19.

[28] Restatement (Third) of the Foreign Relations Law of the United States (1986), § 601; see also Principle 21, Stockholm Declaration of the United Nations Conference on the Human Environment (1972), reprinted in *I.L.M.* 11 (1972), 1416; see also Principle 21, UNGA World Charter for Nature, reprinted in *I.L.M.* 22 (1983), 455.

improbable way to wage war. But even if some country should attempt it, it is not clear that the general, peacetime environmental laws do not cover the claims that would arise. In fact, from the complainant's point of view, proof is easier under the nonmilitary law. State responsibility does not require proof of hostile intent, and the harm, to be cognizable, needs only to be appreciable; there is no requirement, as in Protocol I, that the action complained of "prejudice the health or survival of the population."[29]

Why, then, new laws? Arthur Westing has suggested that the force of normal environmental – and presumably other peacetime – treaties may be suspended during hostilities, displaced by the laws and necessities of war.[30] Others who have examined the issue conclude otherwise.[31] Certainly the question of suspension-in-wartime is worth pursuing.[32]

But even if the ordinary laws are so suspended – an issue by no means clear – it does not follow that the environment would be left unprotected barring further law. The environment would receive the protection of specific rules of warfare, such as those of the Hague Conventions which restrain occupying states from overexploiting resources such as the occupied state's forests.[33] Other features of the environment would receive some safeguarding from the general law-of-war restraints of "necessity" and "proportionality."[34] Indeed, regardless of whether the combatants

---

[29] Protocol I, Art. 55(1).

[30] Arthur H. Westing, "Environmental Protection from Wartime Damage: The Role of International Law," in N. P. Gleditsch (ed.), *Conflict and the Environment* (Dordrecht and Boston: Kluwer Academic Pub., 1997), pp. 535, 538.

[31] See Michael N. Schmitt, "Green War: An Assessment of the Environmental Law of International Armed Conflict," *Yale J. Int'l L.* 22 (1997), 1, 36 n. 184. Both the International Committee of the Red Cross (ICRC) and the Munich Conference Reports concluded that environmental laws were largely applicable during hostilities. *Ibid.*

[32] See Westing, "Environmental Protection from Wartime Damage," p. 538 (considering the issue to be left open by the 1969 Vienna Convention on the Law of Treaties); Silja Vöneky, "Peacetime Environmental Law as a Basis of State Responsibility for Environmental Damage Caused by War," chapter 7 in this volume; cf. Vienna Convention on the Law of Treaties (done at Vienna, May 23, 1969; entered into force, Jan. 27, 1980), Art. 73, reprinted in *I.L.M.* 8 (1969), 679 (referring to application after hostilities).

[33] Convention (No. IV) Respecting the Laws and Customs of War on Land, with Annex of Regulations (done at The Hague, Oct. 18, 1907; entered into force, Jan. 26, 1910), Art. 55, 36 Stat. 2277 (1911).

[34] See Richard A. Falk, "Methods and Means of Warfare: Counterinsurgency, Tactics, and the Law," in Peter D. Trooboff (ed.), *Law and Responsibility in Warfare: The Vietnam Experience* (Chapel Hill: Univ. of North Carolina Press, 1975), pp. 37, 40. What is often referred to as the Martens Clause, enshrined in Hague Convention No. II, provides: "Until a more complete code of the laws of war has been issued, the high contracting Parties deem it expedient to

have signed a particular environmental accord, such as ENMOD or
Protocol I, the Hague Conventions probably represent, at this point, generally accepted principles of international law in proscribing destruction
of property not justified by military necessity, operations not directed
against legitimate military targets, and operations that produce incidental
environmental damage clearly disproportionate to the military advantage
they achieve.[35]

In like vein, the prospect that an upriver riparian state might disrupt the
flow of a major river – the Tigris, the Euphrates, or the Nile – is one that
certainly deserves our attention. But it is worth remembering that this is a
prospect that could arise either within or outside the context of warfare. If
the situation merits addressing (as it well may), it is not clear why amendments of the laws of war are required, or preferable to other tactics such
as strengthening the international watercourse laws and making them
specifically applicable in times of war and peace alike, to eliminate any
ambiguity.

The thrust of these points is not to undermine efforts to shield the environment, but to exhort focus on those scenarios that, in view of existing
gaps and realities, warrant most urgent attention. The issue can be summarized in the form of a non-rhetorical fourth question: Are new norms
really needed, and, if so, for what circumstances?

What procedural reforms should be on our agenda?

Ideally, procedures should be considered in addition to only substantive
rules. Perhaps the main impediment to a detailed discussion of procedures
is that it remains unclear, as noted above, what exactly are the scenarios

---

declare that, in cases not included in the Regulations adopted by them, the inhabitants and the
belligerents remain under the protection and the rule of the principles of the law of nations, as
they result for the usages established among civilized peoples, from the laws of humanity, and
the dictates of the public conscience." Hague Convention No. II with Respect to the Laws and
Customs of War on Land (done at The Hague, July 29, 1899; entered into force, Sept. 4, 1900),
32 Stat. 1803 (1907); see also Protocol I, Art. 2.

[35] See Conrad Harper, "Opening Address," in Richard Grunawalt et al. (eds.), *Protection of the
Environment During Armed Conflict* (Newport, R.I.: Naval War College, 1996), pp. 8, 10–11.
Admiral Carlson M. LeGrand (J.A.G.) reflects the position that the basic restraints on "excessive" and misdirected force of the Hague and Geneva Conventions are accepted principles of
customary international law. See Carlson M. LeGrand, "Framing the Issues," in Grunawalt
et al., *Protection of the Environment*, p. 26.

of primary concern. Presumably, the procedures appropriate for dealing with sudden lethal tsunamis are not the same as those required by the prospect of gradual and hostile climate shifts.

Even if restricted to general observations, therefore, it might be appropriate to identify and assess some general procedural options. To illustrate, ENMOD suggestively provides that a party believing that another party is in violation may lodge its complaint with the UN Security Council.[36] That avenue may provide advantages over the procedures otherwise available to a complainant – or at least constitute a worthwhile supplement; for example, review initiated in the Security Council may be more difficult for a wrongdoer to frustrate than other alternatives, such as a complaint filed in the International Court of Justice.[37]

Other general procedural issues can be raised. Even if the environment-regarding norms already in place are adequate, how can they be made effective? As a start, to achieve compliance, norms have to make sense to those responsible for implementing them. This does not mean merely that those in command ought ideally to accept the rationale of the law as sensible ("make sense" in a motivational way – a "cultural" issue discussed below). Earnest willingness aside, the laws must "make sense" in that those subject to the law understand what it means for them to do.[38]

For the laws to "make sense" in this second sense, certain clarifying procedures may be required. To illustrate, ENMOD prohibits weapons that have an effect on the environment that will be "widespread," "long-lasting," and "severe."[39] In what circumstances can a commander be

---

[36] ENMOD, Art. 5(3).

[37] For example, because of jurisdictional uncertainties it may be easier for an ICJ complaint to be effectively ignored; see *Nuclear Tests (Austl. v. Fr.)*, 1973 I.C.J. 99 (June 22); see also Stephen Boyd et al., "Current Developments Concerning the Settlement of Disputes Involving States by Arbitration and the World Court," *Am. Soc'y Int'l Law Proc.* 83 (1989), 568, 584 (discussing the decision by the United States not to appear to answer the merits of Nicaragua's suit before the International Court of Justice when Nicaragua brought suit); see also *Legality of Use of Force (Yugosl. v. US)*, 1999 I.C.J. (June 2) (in a case alleging, *inter alia*, excessive environmental damage from US bombing, the Court held that the ICJ does not have compulsory jurisdiction over the United States).

[38] See Abram Chayes and Antonia Chayes, *The New Sovereignty: Compliance with International Regulatory Agreements* (Cambridge, Mass.: Harvard Univ. Press, 1995), pp. 10–13 (non-compliance often a result of ambiguity).

[39] ENMOD, Art. 1. The CCD has tried to elaborate in the Understanding relating to Article 1. For example, "severe" is suggested to mean "involving serious or significant disruption or harm to human life, natural and economic resources, or other assets." CCD, *Report of the Working Group*, p. 6.

expected accurately to forecast those effects in advance, with any degree of confidence? Experience with environmental impact assessments, which require an actor to make the same sort of prediction before a housing development is approved or a dam is built, have shown how time-consuming and controversial these procedures can be. It is necessary to consider, then, how much harder it must be for commanders in the field to make such judgments under battle pressures, without an environmental agency's assets, expertise, or leisure. The issue then becomes: Are there training and command procedures that, in view of the circumstances, might make legal requirements to account for environmental damage more realistically attainable?

What is the role of ex post remedies?

This chapter has thus far addressed the role of norms that aim to head off environmental damage by restricting the conduct of belligerents during the course of hostilities. As indicated, no one imagines that it will be easy to tilt the attention of commanders away from their own assets in favor of the environment; nor even is it clear, morally, in what circumstances they ought to be so distracted. Indeed, is it realistic to expect the military to be more constrained on behalf of the environment than on behalf of other innocent victims of war, such as civilians? Even if there are practical restrictions in sensitizing belligerents during the course of hostilities, there remains the option of ex post remedies in the form of compensation or (less likely) punishment after the battlefields have been cleared.

Ex post remedies may appear inferior to strategies – such as prohibitions on specific weapons and tactics – that seek to head off damage directly, before it occurs. Nonetheless, the prospect of future damages or punishment casts a shadow over the present which may exercise an indirect constraint on how operations unfold. Moreover, even if the prospect of ex post remedies fails to avert some environmental damage collectively deemed unlawful, the remedy itself, if in the form of a damage award, can nourish a special fund earmarked for the restoration of the environment. It may not be possible to protect the environment from all injury; but we can take steps, after the war is over, to mend the damage.

This was, of course, the path pursued in closing the Gulf War of 1990–91. The terms of United Nations Security Council Resolution 687, which are the heart of the terms for armistice, provide in paragraph 16 that the

United Nations "reaffirms that Iraq is liable under international law for any . . . damage, including environmental damage and the depletion of natural resources . . . as a result of Iraq's unlawful invasion and occupation of Kuwait."[40] Paragraph 18 creates a fund to provide compensation for claims that come under paragraph 16, and establishes a United Nations Compensation Commission (UNCC) to administer it.

The Resolution raises several important questions. First, the Security Council "reaffirms" Iraq's liability "under international law." One may well wonder, upon which specific law or laws the United Nations rested Iraq's accountability. If a court had disposed of the matter, the court would be expected to elaborate specifically what acts of Iraq violated which principles or treaties. One possibility is that the Security Council, judging the invasion and occupancy to be illegal, believed that all consequential damages were justly assessable, without more. This appears to be the construction of the UNCC.

There are other possibilities that came up in the United Nations debates. The Security Council might have deemed specific Iraqi actions independently wrongful (wrong, even if they had been done by a victim of aggression). Presumably – for we are left to surmise – the massive pumping of oil into the Gulf[41] and the systematic destruction of the oilfields with attendant atmospheric pollution[42] could have been the critical violations. But if these were the unlawful acts, exactly which laws or principles did they violate? The United States maintained that these Iraqi actions were militarily unnecessary and disproportionate, and therefore violated customary international norms and the Fourth Geneva Convention. Other nations apparently rested their judgment on other theories, including the carrying forward of peacetime environmental laws.[43]

Interpretation of the Gulf War precedent is doubly cloudy, because even assuming that lack of military necessity was the legal basis for holding Iraq accountable, it is far from clear that Iraq was in violation of those norms on the facts. Several commentators, including members of the US military, have pointed out that the acts ordinarily cited above did result in military advantage. For example, the smoke from the burning fields "covered"

---

[40] S.C. Res. 687, UN SCOR, 46th Sess., 2981st mtg., para. 16, UN Doc. S/RES/687 (1991), reprinted in *I.L.M.* 30 (1991), 847, 852.
[41] See Schmitt, "Green War," 17–18. [42] *Ibid.*, 18. [43] *Ibid.*, 27.

Iraqi operations from the Allied Force's aerial attacks, and the oil hampered its naval actions.[44]

It is regrettable that the UN Security Council, by providing so little in the way of justification, failed to advance the world community's understanding of belligerents' legal obligations. But in the last analysis, it is not clear that paragraph 16 needs to rest on Iraq's having violated any legal norm at all. Reparations are, after all, remedial;[45] and while, arguably, unconscionable terms may not be exacted as the price of peace,[46] certainly the imposition of "damages" on an aggressor (should we say "loser"?) is not an unconscionable term of armistice. This would seem to be true whether or not the acts that caused the damage (perhaps not even the initial use of force) violated international law. To illustrate, there seems to be no reason why Iraq might not be held to reparations for acts that violate Hague IV, even if Iraq, not being signatory to Hague IV, is not liable for violations of Hague IV directly. May this not be one of the most significant precedents to come out of the 1990–91 Gulf War: that environmental damages may come to be imposed as a matter of course, in the context of exacting reparations?[47]

In fact, while we are considering ex post relief, it is worth observing that the victors are not limited to money damages (which are hard to exact

---

[44] Col. Charles Dunlap, USAF, in Grunawalt et al., *Protection of the Environment*, pp. 14–15 (questioning Conrad Harper following his "Opening Address"); see also Schmitt, "Green War," 20–21.

[45] It may be an open question whether sums demanded by a victor as condition of armistice need to be remedial. Could a victor exact more than its damages as the price of peace? See note following.

[46] Query what limits the law may impose on the conditions the victors may impose on the side facing defeat (short of the requirement that, in battering the losers into further disarray, the winning side must continue to observe the laws of war). In other words, is there, as well as a "just war," a "just peace"? See Vaughn A. Ary, "Concluding Hostilities: Humanitarian Provisions in Cease-Fire Agreements," *Mil. L. Rev.* 148 (1995), 186, 189 (concluding that "the negotiation of peace is no longer a private matter left to the discretion of the adversaries" and implying a role for the United Nations and international standards). The question originates at least no later than the Melian Dialogue that Thucydides reports (with some liberties) in his *History of the Peloponnesian War*. See Thucydides, *History of the Peloponnesian War*, book V (Rex Warner trans., 975), pp. 400–08.

[47] See William M. Arkin et al., *On Impact: Modern Warfare and the Environment. A Case Study of the Gulf War* (1991), p. 65 (indicating that oil spilled into the Gulf has likely caused long-term damage both to subsistence fishing and to the 1,000-boat, multi-million dollar fishing industry). There is nothing like this in either Germany's or Japan's terms of surrender at the end of World War II.

from the typical vanquished). The victors can compel the vanquished to ratify international agreements as a price of peace. At Versailles, Germany was compelled to accept the application of certain multilateral conventions in the fields of radio, telegraph, the posts, fisheries, and more.[48] No one is advancing the Treaty of Versailles as a paragon of peace accords, but this precedent, too, is intriguing: might the terms of peace not include forcing the vanquished to ratify ENMOD or the Basel Convention or some other environmental accord?

How are damages to be measured?

Suppose that the victors do pursue the monetary route, choosing to exact reparations for environmental damage. Two serious issues arise. First, how are damages to the environment to be calculated? And then, how, as a practical matter, can they be made collectible?

Using UN Security Council Resolution 687 to illustrate the problem of calculating environmental damages, the starting point is to note that the recovery of most commercial damages, for example, those arising from "injury to foreign governments, nationals and corporations," is independently provided for in paragraph 16. From this, it may be inferred that damage to the environment in the same paragraph refers to losses beyond those that would show up in lost profits or property damage. In other words, environmental damage from setting wells afire must mean something beyond the cost of ruined equipment and lost sales. Similarly, environmental damage to coastal waters and tidepools must mean something beyond what is required to compensate the commercial fishermen, who would have independent bases of relief. But how is that "beyond" calculated? Note that insofar as fishing grounds are managed as public goods (quotas in the harvest not being privatized), payment into an environmental fund for the repair of the fishing grounds could be a reasonable way to compensate the fishermen. Nonetheless, a fund authorized to restore the environment might well require more resources than one aimed only at restoring an equivalent level of commercial productivity.

---

[48] See Stuart Hull McIntyre, *Legal Effect of World War II on Treaties of the United States* (The Hague: M. Nijhoff, 1958), p. 307 (referring to Articles 282 through 287: "Germany bitterly complained about Article 284 in which she agreed in advance to accept any new radiotelegraphic conventions which might be formulated within the next five years.")

The first problem is predicting the physical impacts over time. For example, no one is certain how much oil spilled into the Gulf during the 1990–91 hostilities; estimates have been given of 2.5 to 3 or 4 million barrels,[49] or even (from the US Department of Defense) 7 to 9 million.[50] Whatever is the right figure for the total spill, there is the further question, how much of it can be attributed to deliberate action of the Iraqi forces?[51] Or, indeed, how much resulted (as apparently did the first spill) from Allied bombing of Iraqi targets?[52] Moreover, whatever the quantity attributable to the aggressor's wrongful actions, for a number of reasons, including nature's ability to heal itself to some extent, it is very difficult to forecast the long-term consequences on environmental variables, such as durability of affected ecosystems. During the 1983 Iran–Iraq War, the rupturing of three wells in the Nowruz field off the coast of Iran spilled some 1.9 million barrels into the Gulf. Most of 1983's resulting slick is assumed to have wound up in the deep Gulf, but its environmental impact is still unknown.[53]

The second difficulty is this: even if, in face of all the uncertainties, we estimate the amount of (wrongfully) spilled oil and biologists reckon the consequential physical damage, how do economists put a dollar value on the damage? To illustrate, take the physical near-term consequence: the fact that by February 1991 the oil slick had killed an estimated 20,000 birds, including cormorants, flamingos, and herons.[54] In the case of ordinary assets, such as the destroyed platforms, the damage is the market cost of rebuilding the facilities: but what is the "value" of the birds – or the sea turtles, marine mammals, and flora that perished with them?

The question is not rhetorical. Assessing such damages is not qualitatively harder than issues of natural resource damage assessment that US and other courts grapple with as a matter of course, as when they assess environmental damages against corporate polluters. But domestic experience has shown that there are competing methodologies, and that choice among them is controversial. One approach is to regard Kuwaiti people

---

[49] Arkin et al., *On Impact*, p. 63.   [50] See Schmitt, "Green War," 18.

[51] The DOD figure is reportedly an estimate of deliberate Iraqi action. See *ibid.*

[52] See *ibid.* (reporting various US and French bombardments that likely resulted in some of the oil spill. The United Nations Compensation Commission, Decision No. 7, appears to hold Iraq liable for damages resulting from actions "by either side.")

[53] See Arkin et al., *On Impact*, p. 18 (suggesting that assessment of oil damage to the Gulf ecosystem should account for decades of intense prewar oil exploration and transport).

[54] *Ibid.*, p. 65.

and the territory of Kuwait as the sole victims, confining compensation for losses in Kuwait, as Kuwaitis might measure them according to some contingent valuation technique. To illustrate, environmental damage to the sea coasts might be measured, theoretically, either by (1) what it costs to restore the environment to its original condition, or (particularly if total restoration is infeasible) (2) the amount of money that the people of Kuwait would be willing to pay (or need to receive) to restore them to the same welfare level they enjoyed on account of the environment being the way it was in its original, pre-damaged state.[55]

On the other hand, this approach may be too narrow. First, we might want to recognize the interests that people outside Kuwait have in the Kuwaiti environment. Even Americans who had no present plans to travel to the Kuwaiti coast to see the marine life might have been willing to pay some premium for the option to go should they change their minds; that lost *option value* might be considered part of the damage. Similarly, non-Kuwaitis might have lost the *bequest value* the area had to them: the amount they would have paid to preserve the area's environment as a global heirloom for their descendants.[56]

Second, we might want to recognize claims for extraterritorial damages: acts that occurred in Kuwait undoubtedly had effects on the environments of other nations and on the global commons. Their inclusion appears particularly appropriate if aggressive war is regarded as a wrong not only to the nation invaded, but a wrong *erga omnes*: to the entire world community. In other words, viewing A's aggression towards B not only as a wrong to B, but to the whole community of nations, would support holding A liable for damages incurred by the entire community. Whether these effects were, in the circumstances of the 1990–91 Gulf War, de minimis is something addressed by others.[57]

---

[55] See generally W. Michael Hanemann, "Valuing the Environment Through Contingent Valuation," *J. Econ. Persp.* 8 (1994), 19 (discussing contingent valuation and its limitations; the issue also contains a valuable symposium on the subject).

[56] But see Richard W. Dunford et al., "Whose Losses Count in Natural Resource Damages?" *Contemp. Econ. Pol'y* 15 (1997), 77 (advocating exclusion of alleged losses of persons having no knowledge of the damaged resource, on view that absence of such knowledge precludes welfare, as well as comparable critique of lost uses of natural resources by foreigners).

[57] See generally Luan Low and David Hodgkinson, "Compensation for Wartime Environmental Damage: Challenges to International Law After the Gulf War," *Va. J. Int'l L.* 35 (1995), 405, 408–12 (reviewing some of the impacts of the Gulf War on the environment).

Can damages be collected?

Assessing the damages the violator must pay is one thing, albeit complex; it is quite another thing, and probably even harder, to collect them. Here, too, the "lesson" of the 1990–91 Gulf War is not assuring. Iraq has never paid, and payment does not appear imminent. True, there are special circumstances: the fund was to have been financed from Iraqi oil sales, which an embargo has restricted. Moreover, the UNCC has yet to issue any decisions on the environmental dimensions of its task. But the delay we have seen in settling the Gulf War bill is probably not anomalous.[58] It is typical, one imagines, that by the end of the war the loser will be economically depleted, even more so than Iraq. (The worldwide pool of frozen Iraqi assets reportedly amounts to $8 billion, as against early estimated claims of $100 billion in war damage and $180 billion overall).[59] Typically, too, reparations items that are politically more urgent than environmental repair will take precedence – most notably, assurances that the loser is disarmed and that infrastructure damage is compensated. Indeed, had Iraq been allowed to reenter the oil market, it would have had a higher prospect of regaining short-term solvency than almost any vanquished nation of this century. This only highlights the question: How, and in what circumstances, can compensatory damages be made effective? This also suggests that to the extent that collection of damages is infeasible, the case for punishing individuals intensifies.

How can we create conditions favorable to compliance?

Even if favorable legal norms and procedures can be put in place, securing compliance with them is a separate challenge. This is particularly so during during hostilities. Lives are on the line, even national survival. These

---

[58] One of the most celebrated cases in international environmental law involves a judgment that the UK won against Albania for mining the Corfu Channel, with resulting loss of forty-four sailors and two British vessels in 1946. A judgment for £12.5 million was entered in 1951 after the ICJ held Albania liable. See *Corfu Channel (UK v. Alb.)*, 1949 I.C.J. 4 (Apr. 9). In 1996, it appeared that the UK would finally receive 10 percent of the judgment, and even receipt of that fraction turned upon fortuities – the torturous route of returning gold seized by the Nazis. See "Nazi Gold Dispute Settled After 50 Years," Press Association Newsfile, Oct. 29, 1996.

[59] See Elyse J. Garmise, "The Iraqi Claims Process and the Ghost of Versailles," *N.Y.U. L. Rev.* 67 (1992), 840 ($80 billion relates to outstanding prewar debts).

are not circumstances that foster ethical or even legal reflection. Grotius supported many acts that would now be rejected by principles almost universally observed – for example, the victor's right to kill after surrender not only the vanquished soldiers and their leaders, but all who resided in enemy territory.[60] St. Aquinas threw up his hands with the judgment, "necessity knows no law."[61] It is hard to read the literature on warfare and not find some signs of moral improvement. Overall, however, Richard Falk judges the laws of warfare to have had at most a meager influence.[62] Other critics even suggest that the law of war has actually operated to legitimate, rather than limit, military violence against civilians.[63] Others may find more hopeful signs of progress. But however effective law-of-war restraints have been in shielding their traditional subjects (such as prisoners and noncombatants), the law clearly has a harder task injecting concern for nature into the military command's calculus. Moreover, regard for the law will certainly be harder to achieve, the more it takes as its aim protection of the environment in what is called a strong or deep sense – that is, when the law asks the commander to sacrifice military advantage in the interests of nature itself or of future generations, rather than the interests of present dependent populations. And the concern is not only for the environment in wartime: unless there is strong cultural support for environmental preservation, even the postwar remedies discussed in the text above are likely to go unenforced or compromised.

This is not to say that we should abandon any hope of injecting concern for the environment, even in a deep sense, into the military context. Rather, it focuses attention on a question that extends beyond the law and into culture: How does one change cultural norms – that is, the prevailing, largely unconscious sense of what are the legitimate motives of human action?

The question is not specific to the environment. In general, what keeps most people from committing serious offenses in most well-functioning societies is not the fear of formal sanctions; it is the force of attitudes and principles about fairness, moral misgivings about the infliction of pain, and respect for possessions. Indeed, and obviously, any survey of civiliza-

[60] See Donald A. Wells, *War Crimes and Laws of War* (Lanham, Md.: University Press of America, 1984), p. 30.
[61] St. Thomas Aquinas, *Summa Theologica*, vol. I–II (1946), Q. 96, Art. 6, p. 75.
[62] Falk, "Methods and Means of Warfare," 35–55.
[63] Chris af Jochnick and Roger Normand, "The Legitimation of Violence: A Critical Analysis of the Gulf War," *Harv. Int'l L.J.* 35 (1994), 387.

tion will reveal a host of cultural norms respecting labor, marriage, and feeding, the sorts of activities that govern everyday people in their everyday lives. And one can certainly find kernels of sympathy for the environment widespread throughout cultures. The task here, however, is more specific and profound: how to nourish those kernels into something that can stand firm even in the face of "military necessity".

In the late 1980s, Arthur Westing, with the support of Stockholm International Peace Research Institute and the United Nations Environment Program, organized a conference on "Cultural Norms, War and the Environment" to provide different perspectives on this very issue.[64] What are the contributions, respectively, of the law, formal education, and national leaders to the formation of the relevant cultural norms? I must admit I have no better answers today than I provided then. But I view recent attention to the subject of environmental consequences of war as a positive sign that whatever it is that moves ideas along, this idea – that the environment should have the protection of an innocent noncombatant – is thankfully not going to go away. We are just renewing, if not beginning, that dedication.

---

[64] See Arthur H. Westing (ed.), *Cultural Norms, War and the Environment* (Oxford and New York: Oxford Univ. Press, 1988).

PART II

THE LEGAL FRAMEWORK

INTRODUCTION

CARL E. BRUCH

The body of treaties, customs, and practices governing the environmental consequences of armed conflict is a dynamic and rapidly growing area of international law. Until relatively recently, relevant legal provisions were vague, not directly mentioning the environment. In response to US actions in the Vietnam War, however, the international community adopted the 1976 Convention on the Prohibition of Military or Any Other Hostile Use of Environmental Modification Techniques (ENMOD) and the 1977 Additional Protocols I and II to the Geneva Conventions of 1949.

In addition to the environment-specific provisions of these treaties, authors in this section highlight legal constraints found in a variety of other treaties and international custom protecting property, civilian objects, and cultural heritage, which can provide protection without even mentioning the word "environment." The different provisions can be divided generally into those that govern targeting choices and those that govern weapons choices; both kinds of regimes can be useful for addressing different aspects of wartime environmental protection. In addition, human rights treaties, arms control agreements, customary international law, and domestic and international peacetime environmental norms also prove useful when considering how to prevent and redress wartime environmental harm.

While this section emphasizes those norms applicable to international armed conflict, there also is a need to consider military operations other than war, which include peacetime training operations, as well as police actions or other activities that do not rise to the level of formally declared war. US Navy Captain John P. Quinn et al. analyze environmental constraints imposed on the continuum of military actions ranging from peace to full-scale armed conflict. They discuss the durability of peacetime environmental norms in the context of a sliding scale theory "under which the force and effect of peacetime environmental norms, both international and domestic, gradually diminish as military necessity increases." Although Quinn et al. find reality to be more complex than the sliding scale model, the simplicity of their model provides an interesting (if perhaps too general) way to conceptualize the continued applicability of peacetime environmental norms to military activities.

The norms embodied in law-of-war and humanitarian treaties, as well as the body of customary international law, generally apply universally. And to the extent that these norms address wartime environmental damage in specified narrow circumstances (for example, "long-term, widespread and severe" damage to the environment), commentators generally hold that these provisions also apply universally, even though less than one-half of the world's nations have ratified the treaties specifically addressing wartime environmental damage. Thus, most of the provisions in ENMOD and Protocol I appear to have become norms of customary international law, although questions about their status may have been one of the reasons why the UN Security Council did not rely on them to hold Iraq liable in 1991. Arthur Westing cites incorporation of these provisions into military handbooks as evidence of their customary nature. Similarly, Adam Roberts observes that notwithstanding the US non-accession to Protocol I, many of the US military manuals have incorporated its provisions in practice, as have those of other countries.

As countries incorporate relevant environmental and law-of-war norms into their military handbooks and training regimens, the often vague international law provisions constraining wartime environmental damage are given form and force. In particular, Quinn et al. observe that military manuals both reflect and portend developments in customary international law through advancing state practice and *opinio iuris*. In the wartime context, handbooks include environmental considerations for determining lawful targets and weapons. Military commanders thus become familiar with the norms constraining environmental damage during wartime, and the military will, paraphrasing Quinn et al., "fight like it trains." For example, the US military stations lawyers conversant in the law of war – including those provisions that constrain environmental damage – alongside military commanders during armed conflict. These lawyers review decisions regarding targeting and weapons choice to ascertain whether the decisions comport with the international law of war and the military's own procedures, often in real time. The Kosovo conflict added a new wrinkle: "virtual" military lawyers offering real-time advice on the legitimacy of targets from a computer console in Germany.[1]

During peacetime, Westing points out, most nations exempt the military from civilian rules, but an increasing number (now at least nineteen countries, as well as NATO) hold their militaries to civilian laws, including environmental ones. Westing's chapter highlights the development of permanent environmental divisions and programs in the defense ministries of at least eleven nations. Additionally, Quinn et al. describe how military operational law handbooks – governing actions in military operations other than war – increasingly incorporate domestic environmental law, international environmental law, and the host nation's domestic law. While military handbooks do not resolve all issues, Roberts, Michael Schmitt, and Richard Falk all recognize the contribution they can make in implementing the existing norms constraining wartime environmental damage.

Responsibility for wartime environmental damage

To date, there has been a dearth of cases establishing responsibility – national or individual, civil or criminal – for wartime actions causing environmental damage. Following World War II, the Nuremberg Tribunal acquitted German General Lothar Rendulic of charges arising from his "scorched earth" tactics, finding that he reasonably, but mistakenly, believed they were necessary.[2] Following the environmental damage in the Vietnam War, the international community adopted ENMOD and Protocol I, but there was no attempt to establish responsibility, let alone liability.

The 1990–91 Gulf War presented the first real test of the post-Vietnam norms. While holding Iraq liable for environmental damage, the UN Security Council premised liability on Iraq's aggression rather than on any specific violation of substantive environmental norms. In addition, Schmitt observes, the initial investigations into individual liability for

---

[1] Michael Ignatieff, "The Virtual Commander," *The New Yorker* (Aug. 2, 1999), 33–34.

[2] *Trials of War Criminals before the Nuernberg Military Tribunals under Control Council Law No. 10*, pt. XI (1949), p. 1297; but see *The Trial of German Major War Criminals: Proceedings of the International Military Tribunal Sitting at Nuremberg Germany*, pt. 22 (1950), p. 517 (holding General Alfred Jodl guilty of war crimes associated with scorched earth destruction in Northern Norway, Leningrad, and Moscow).

environmental war crimes in the Gulf War terminated when political leaders decided that "we have not yet arrived at the point where the international community is willing to put its credibility, commitment, and the full force of its conscience behind environmental crimes prosecutions in . . . the same way that it has demanded accountability in the context of Rwanda and Bosnia."

In the midst of NATO's 1999 bombing campaign in Kosovo and Serbia, Yugoslavia filed suit against ten NATO countries before the International Court of Justice, a suit that included claims of environmental war crimes under Protocol I. While the merit of the claims remains uncertain, the ICJ's procedural disposition of the case highlighted its limited power to address environmental consequences of war. The Court held that it manifestly lacked jurisdiction against the United States and Spain because these countries had not consented to ICJ jurisdiction in the case at hand, and that it lacked prima facie jurisdiction against the other eight countries.[3]

Indeed, one of the primary problems with the existing norms addressing environmental consequences of war is the lack of standing bodies charged with enforcing the norms. The 1998 Rome Statute establishing the International Criminal Court is an important step towards giving force to the provisions by declaring certain wartime actions that are damaging the environment to be war crimes. While the substantive norms and enforcing institution embodied in the Rome Statute offer great potential for determining individual responsibility, it remains to be seen whether the ICC will come into being and what role it will have (see the analysis by Roberts and Schmitt in this section, as well as that of Mark Drumbl and Jean-Marie Henckaerts in Part V).

Adequacy of existing norms

Even if institutions were created to apply existing norms constraining wartime environmental damage, they would find these norms lacking – a widely held view in the international community. Schmitt finds the norms "substantially flawed" for many reasons: vagueness in their terms and provisions; cultural, temporal, conceptual, and contextual differences in placing values on the competing interests; gaps in the normative

[3] E.g., *Legality of Use of Force (Yugoslavia v. United States)* (1999), available at http://www.icj-cij.org/icjwww/idocket/iyus/iyusframe.htm.

structure; competing anthropocentric and environmental interests; and a lack of knowledge about environmental effects in making normative, targeting, or valuation decisions. Falk further faults the existing norms for not allowing reasonable implementation during wartime; for their arbitrary enforcement, which leads to perceptions of "victor's justice"; and for being "of a manifestly incidental character" in conventions that focus on protecting people rather than the environment. Even Roberts, who advocates merely clarifying existing norms and strengthening their implementation, agrees that the norms in ENMOD and Protocol I are of limited value because they apply only to the most severe damage. At the same time, Roberts asserts that the older, general humanitarian rules (such as those found in the Martens Clause) provide the strongest protection for the environment during wartime.

In addition to problems of vagueness, many believe that existing norms are "quite modest" (Westing) and "have little or no application" (Roberts) when it comes to addressing the environmental consequences of non-international conflicts, which constitute the vast majority of current conflicts. For example, the only treaty that specifically addresses non-international armed conflicts is the 1977 Additional Protocol II to the 1949 Geneva Conventions, which, unlike Protocol I, has no environmental provisions; Articles 13–15 protecting the civilian population (including objects indispensable to its survival) and installations containing dangerous forces provide nominal environmental protection. During negotiation of the treaty establishing the International Criminal Court, nations considered the possibility of defining environmental war crimes for internal conflicts, but specifically rejected the proposal. These lapses perhaps stem from similar gaps in the UN Charter and norms of collective security, which traditionally emphasize maintaining peace among nations,[4] while paying little direct attention to internal conflicts. Recent efforts by commentators to broaden collective security to include social, economic, and environmental concerns may signal a shift that would lay the groundwork for addressing internal conflicts,[5] but the ICC negotiations show that such a shift is still in its infancy.

[4] E.g., UN Charter, ch. VII (prescribing the UN Security Council duties and powers in protecting international security); see also Art. 2(4) (stating that Members "shall refrain in their international relations from the threat or use of force").

[5] E.g., Rosemary Righter, *Utopia Lost: The United Nations and World Order* (New York: 20th Century Fund Press, 1995), ch. 11 (discussing President Mikhail Gorbachev's 1987 article that sought to broaden the concept of collective security).

Roberts observes that while belligerents in internal conflicts can adopt various environmental protocols, much remains to be done in strengthening the norms governing internal conflicts. Considering the traditional presumption against nations intervening in "domestic" matters of other nations, as exhibited by the international reluctance to become involved in conflicts in the former Yugoslavia (first Bosnia, then Kosovo), the desperate lack of formal, universal norms governing internal conflicts is likely to continue.

Further, to the extent that the existing norms address the use of inhumane weapons with environmental impacts, there is serious international disagreement over certain weapons, including depleted uranium, antipersonnel mines, and nuclear weapons. The United States uses DU for armor-piercing ammunition, and in some cases as ballast in missiles. DU is radioactive, persists in the environment for a long time due to its long half-life, and readily forms dust that is easily mobilized. Coalition forces used DU widely in the 1990–91 Gulf War, and some assert that DU is to blame for Gulf War Syndrome,[6] although causal proof remains elusive. The United States' use of DU in the 1999 Kosovo conflict again caused some in the international community to question DU as an inhumane weapon. Voluntary retirement of such weapons is not unprecedented; indeed, the US military is considering exchanging its lead ammunition, relied upon by militaries around the world for hundreds of years, for plastic polymer ammunition, given lead's toxicity and long-term threat to public health and the environment.[7]

Finally, aside from their vast potential for immediate human death and suffering, nuclear weapons could cause a nuclear winter that could threaten all life on this planet – the ultimate environmental consequence of war – but most law-of-war conventions (including Protocol I) do not address, or specifically exempt, nuclear weapons. While the recent International Court of Justice advisory opinion on the *Legality of the Threat or Use of Nuclear Weapons* could have clarified the relevant norms, Roberts terms the opinion "Delphic," and he calls for strengthened arms control initiatives to reduce the impacts from the manufacture, testing, use, and disposal of nuclear weapons. Less than two years after the ICJ decision, India and Pakistan dramatically joined the "nuclear club," and other nations appear eager to follow suit.

[6] E.g., "New International Campaign against Depleted Uranium Weapons Launched," Campaign Against Depleted Uranium press release (May 17, 1999).
[7] Colin Nickerson, "Army Testing a Safer Ammo for Environment," *Boston Globe* (July 25, 1999), A1.

Next steps

Considering the lack of agreement on the status of relevant norms, various commentators advocate focusing on the existing legal provisions, seeking new agreements on specific issues, and improving adherence to existing law. For example, Westing advocates that a first step is to lobby non-parties to ratify five key international agreements. Taking a broad view, Westing also sees environmental education of the public and military, as well as increased support for sustainable development and democracy building, as integral steps in limiting environmental damage from military actions.

In addition to clarifying and strengthening existing norms, Roberts suggests a variety of steps to implement the current norms (many of which are explored in detail in the next section): developing capacity to conduct wartime and postwar environmental clean-up efforts, establishing international peacekeeping forces, and incorporating environmental norms into international military enforcement operations. Additionally, Roberts favors further discussion on the wartime application of peacetime environmental law, a topic that Silja Vöneky explores in depth in chapter 7.

Another option to clarify, crystallize, and advance environmental norms preventing and redressing wartime environmental damage is a new convention focused on the topic. This is sometimes termed a "Fifth Geneva Convention," an environmental law-of-war treaty in the tradition of the four Geneva Conventions of 1949, or an "Ecocide Convention," similar to the Genocide Convention.

While Schmitt ultimately looks forward to such a broad environmental convention, in the meantime he advocates providing unequivocal notice of what constitutes illegal and unacceptable behavior under existing norms (for instance, by incorporating norms into military manuals), as well as strengthening enforcement of existing norms. To accomplish this, Schmitt recommends creation of (1) a committee of experts to improve understanding of the science involved and to develop scientific indicators for evaluating the environmental consequences of military actions during armed conflict, and (2) a group of legal experts to clarify the vagueness in the existing body of law.

Falk unabashedly advances the boldest approach. Seeing an important role for the non-governmental community, he proposes a global conference at which governments and non-governmental organizations could work together to develop an "ecocide" convention. In the meantime, Falk poses the possibility that the UN General Assembly could adopt a resolution generalizing the principles under which Iraq was held liable for its actions in Kuwait (particularly those causing environmental damage), thus removing the taint of victor's justice.

Reflecting his long-standing criticism over the usefulness of such an initiative, Roberts articulates many problems with the call for a broad new convention, among them that existing law is not as lacking as many commentators assert and that such a convention could distract attention and resources from the need to address specific issues. Still, Falk maintains that members of the international community should consider "that which seems necessary rather than content themselves with what they deem possible, especially if the possible shows little sign of adequacy."

Taking the chapters in this section together, a picture emerges of a patchwork of law-of-war, humanitarian, and environmental norms that have developed in response to particular crises: the transition to modern warfare that shocked the public conscience, poison gas in World War I, indiscriminate targeting of civilian areas in World War II, and defoliation and alleged weather manipulation in the Vietnam War. Although the 1990–91 Gulf War has yet to yield new norms, the wholesale environmental destruction in Kuwait has caused the international community to reconsider the old norms, forced national militaries to take the topic seriously, and may yet lead to practical norms through the remediation and compensation mechanism of the United Nations Compensation Commission.

In most cases, environmental protection has been incidental to humanitarian concerns, and the present attempts to elicit environmental norms from general principles of humanity rest on uncertain ground. Those who contend that the existing norms are sufficient focus their attention on implementation, such as the ongoing incorporation of environmental norms into military handbooks. On the other hand, reformers call for clarification and crystallization of the norms through initiatives to build international consensus. In the end, both informal and formal efforts face the political challenge of convincing nations to accept further limitations on the way they conduct war, as well as the increasingly important challenge of limiting how nations conduct military actions within their own borders and during peacetime.

2

THE LAW OF WAR AND ENVIRONMENTAL DAMAGE

ADAM ROBERTS

The central question addressed here is simple. Are international legal provisions that could restrict environmental damage from military operations adequate? The focus is mainly on the law of war, otherwise known as "international humanitarian law" – a body of law that is applicable in the first place to international wars between states. However, the chapter also touches briefly on: (1) international legal restraints on environmental damage in other situations, including civil wars and UN-authorized operations; and (2) some other international legal restraints on environmental damage in war, especially those embodied in arms control agreements.

This chapter argues that existing legal restraints affecting the impact of war on the environment are far more extensive than may at first appear. They encompass many provisions that – while having as their primary purpose safeguarding people from injury and property from wanton destruction – do in fact also provide a basis for preserving the environment. Extensive as such legal restraints are, there is no claim that they are complete.

In particular, this chapter is a plea to abandon the assumption, made by some lawyers and others, that those very few provisions in the law of war that actually use the word "environment" can be viewed as the centerpiece of legal protection of the environment in war. As will become apparent, such an approach is deficient, because the provisions in question only apply in very exceptional circumstances, and in any case they are in treaties by which fewer states are bound than are bound by certain other relevant treaties, especially the 1949 Geneva Conventions.

Every cause needs to be protected against its own zealots. It may be a mistake to try to prioritize protection of the environment over other issues

47

relating to the conduct of military operations. In war, even more than in peace, environmental considerations often have to take their place along-side other factors, including the saving of the lives of both soldiers and civilians. The important thing is to develop a legal and institutional framework in which environmental factors are properly represented and considered; and to recognize that environmental considerations often work with, rather than against, more general considerations of prudence and professionalism.

The present chapter is not a study of implementation. It does not describe in any detail how rules and norms relating to the environment are or are not reflected in state policy and military action. However, it recognizes the centrality of this issue, and it does refer briefly to a few episodes of implementation. Effective implementation is not a matter of law alone, but also of political and military culture. Furthermore, there have been instances in which the actual policies of states and military commanders have been, if anything, in advance of their formal legal obligations. Implementation involves moral ambiguity: not least because, as indicated below, it still occasionally depends on threats of reprisals.

There is no systematic coverage of the largely separate subjects of environmental issues as one central purpose of defense policy ("environmental security"); as a possible cause or justification for military action (for example, in response to massive environmental despoliation by a state); as a problem that can arise in processes of disarmament, in particular through the destruction of stockpiles; or as a basis for national legislation imposing environmental standards on a state's armed forces in peace or in war. Nor is human rights law covered, though it can be a basis for claims regarding environmental protection. Nor is there any consideration here of how to determine the scope and cost of environmental damage, and how to manage the question of compensation. As in the case of Iraq after the 1990–91 Gulf War, the duty to pay compensation may be based more on a state's culpability for starting a war than on its violations of the *ius in bello* addressed in this chapter, though the actual amount of compensation may be determined by a wider range of factors, including the extent of the environmental outrages it committed.

The 1990–91 Gulf War was the main event that provoked the recent and contemporary interest in the environmental effects of war.[1] The various

---

[1] Surveys in 1991–92 reflected the growing interest: Antoine Bouvier, "Protection of the Natural Environment in Time of Armed Conflict," *Int'l Rev. Red Cross* 285 (1991); articles by Michael Bothe, Arne Willy Dahl, and Paul C. Szasz in *Disarmament* 15(2) (1992), 101–61; Glen Plant

Iraqi "oil crimes" in that war, being by general agreement violative of already existing rules, highlighted the salience, and difficulty, of questions of implementation; and led to the UN Security Council's strong emphasis on compensation for environmental as well as other forms of damage. Other actions in the 1990–91 Gulf War – including the dumping of mines and war material in the desert, the bombing of nuclear installations, and the damage to the water supply in Iraq – also caused environmental concern, but the question of whether they constituted violations of existing law did not admit of such a clear answer. Finally, the war involved a risk of use of atomic, biological, and chemical weapons, and serious attempts by the US-led Coalition to discourage such use by Iraq.

Since the 1990–91 Gulf War, there have been many major international conferences on war and the environment that looked at international legal issues: including those in London (June 1991), Ottawa (July 1991), Munich (December 1991), and Newport, R.I. (September 1995). There were also several studies and investigations by expert groups, including one under the auspices of the International Committee of the Red Cross (ICRC) in 1992–93. These meetings resulted in many summaries and proposals, of which this chapter takes account. Since 1991 there have also been important new developments in law and practice, including two new treaties on landmines, all of which suggests that limiting the effects (including the environmental ones) of war remains an important issue in international politics and diplomacy.

There have been many proposals for negotiation for a new overarching convention on war and the environment. A different approach is suggested here. Further action is indeed needed, but in different directions. The conclusions outline ways in which the law might be developed and implementation improved.

Provisions of the law of war

What, if anything, does the law of war say about protection of the natural and man-made environment? This is one of the many areas in which the law of war consists of a disparate body of principles, treaties, customary rules, and practices, which have developed over the centuries in response

(ed.), *Environmental Protection and the Law of War: A "Fifth Geneva" Convention on the Protection of the Environment in Time of Armed Conflict?* (1992) (based on a June 3, 1991 London Conference on the Protection of the Environment in Time of Armed Conflict).

to a wide variety of practical problems and moral concerns. The main emphasis in what follows is on law-of-war treaties. With the one exception of the 1998 Rome Statute of the International Criminal Court, all the treaties mentioned had entered into force by March 1, 1999.[2]

The word "environment" did not occur in any treaty on the law of war until 1976 and 1977, when it was mentioned in two. This does not mean that before 1976 there was no protection of the environment, but rather that different words were used; and that such protection is found in a variety of forms and contexts. The pre-1976 treaties on the law of war relate to protection of the environment obliquely rather than directly, both through general statements of principle and through detailed regulations.

UNDERLYING LAW-OF-WAR PRINCIPLES

In considering what the law of war has to say about environmental damage, it is useful to start with the underlying principles. Most of these principles have a bearing on the question of environmental destruction. The principles, though ancient in origin, are reflected in many modern texts and military manuals.[3] They include the principle of proportionality, particularly in its meaning of proportionality in relation to the adversary's military actions or to the anticipated military value of one's own actions; the principle of discrimination, which is about care in the selection of methods, of weaponry, and of targets; the principle of necessity, under which belligerents may only use that degree and kind of force, not otherwise prohibited by the law of armed conflict, which is required for the par-

---

[2] The texts of laws of war agreements cited in this chapter can be found in Dietrich Schindler and Jiří Toman (eds.), *The Laws of Armed Conflicts*, 3rd edn. (Dordrecht: M. Nijhoff, 1988); and Adam Roberts and Richard Guelff, *Documents on the Laws of War*, 2nd edn. (Oxford: Oxford Univ. Press, 1989) (3rd edition appearing 2000). These books also contain lists of states signing and adhering. This chapter ascribes treaties to the year in which the text was adopted: in several cases this is one year before the first signatures by states.

[3] Modern military manuals referring to some or all of these principles include US Dep't of the Army, *The Law of Land Warfare*, FM 27–10 (Washington, D.C., July 1956), pp. 3–4; United Kingdom, *Manual of Military Law* (London, 1958), pt. III, pp. 1–2; US Dep't of the Navy, Office of the Chief of Naval Operations and Headquarters, US Marine Corps and Dep't of Transportation, US Coast Guard, *The Commander's Handbook on the Law of Naval Operations*, NWP 1–14M/MWCP 5–2.1/COMDTPUB P5800.7 (Formerly NWP 9 (Rev. A)) (3rd edn., Norfolk, Va., Oct. 1995), p. 5–1. (An *Annotated Supplement* to this handbook, providing extensive reference to sources, was issued by the Oceans Law and Policy Department, US Naval War College, November 1997 and appeared as vol. 73 of its International Law Studies series in 1999.)

tial or complete submission of the enemy with a minimum expenditure of time, life, and physical resources; and the closely related principle of humanity, which prohibits the employment of any kind or degree of force not required for the purpose of the partial or complete submission of the enemy with a minimum expenditure of time, life, and physical resources.[4]

Each of these four principles strongly points to the conclusion that actions resulting in massive environmental destruction, especially where they do not serve a clear and important military purpose, would be questionable, even in the absence of specific rules of war addressing environmental matters in detail.[5] When the four principles are taken together, such a conclusion seems inescapable.

Richard Falk has suggested that there are, in addition, two "subsidiary principles" that "seem to be well-grounded in authoritative custom and to have relevance to the array of special problems posed by deliberate and incidental environmental harm." These are the principles of neutrality and of inter-generational equity.[6] The proposition that these are in fact key principles of the law of war, though it may be unorthodox, is serious.

1868 ST. PETERSBURG DECLARATION

The St. Petersburg Declaration on explosive projectiles, in ringing words which were to prove terribly problematic in subsequent practice, declared that "[t]he only legitimate object which States should endeavour to accomplish during war is to weaken the military forces of the enemy."[7] While this principle does not rule out all environmental despoliation, it does indicate the illegality of such kinds of action as lack a clear military purpose.

---

[4] On the history of principles of the laws of war, see particularly James Turner Johnson, *Just War Tradition and the Restraint of War: A Moral and Historical Inquiry* (Princeton, N.J.: Princeton Univ. Press, 1981), pp. 196–228. For an excellent critique of the principle of necessity's somewhat outdated emphasis on "complete submission of the enemy," see Tony Rogers, *Law on the Battlefield* (Manchester: Manchester Univ. Press, 1996), pp. 5–6.

[5] A particularly useful survey, which includes a discussion of the customary principles of necessity, proportionality, and humanity, is Michael N. Schmitt, "Green War: An Assessment of the Environmental Law of International Armed Conflict," *Yale J. Int'l L.* 22 (1997), 1, 52–62.

[6] Richard Falk, "The Environmental Law of War: An Introduction," in Plant, *Environmental Protection and the Law of War*, p. 85.

[7] Declaration Renouncing the Use, in Time of War, of Explosive Projectiles under 400 Grammes in Weight (done at St. Petersburg, Nov. 29, 1868), reprinted in *Am. J. Int'l L.* 1 (Supp.), 95.

1899 AND 1907 HAGUE CONVENTIONS AND DECLARATIONS

Several of the Hague Conventions and Declarations of 1899 and 1907 contain provisions with a bearing on the environment. For example, in the 1907 Hague Convention IV on land war, the preamble refers to the need "to diminish the evils of war, as far as military requirements permit," and goes on to state in the famous Martens Clause:

> Until a more complete code of the laws of war has been issued, the high contracting Parties deem it expedient to declare that, in cases not included in the Regulations adopted by them, the inhabitants and the belligerents remain under the protection and the rule of the principles of the law of nations, as they result from the usages established among civilized peoples, from the laws of humanity, and the dictates of the public conscience.[8]

The Martens Clause was adopted at the 1899 and 1907 Hague conferences principally because the powers had not been able to agree on detailed rules on certain problems relating to occupied territories and the treatment of resistance: but the clause was written in general terms, and has been widely seen as having a broader application. Its wording is reflected in articles and preambles in a number of subsequent treaties, including the four 1949 Geneva Conventions, the 1977 Geneva Protocols I and II, and the 1980 UN Convention on Certain Conventional Weapons. The relevance of this clause to environmental protection has been widely accepted.[9]

In the regulations annexed to the 1907 Hague Convention IV, Article 22 states: "The right of belligerents to adopt means of injuring the enemy is not unlimited." Geoffrey Best has commented: "Post-1945 extensions of that principle from its traditional application to enemy persons and properties to the natural environment are no more than logical, given the novel and awful circumstances that have suggested them."[10] Several other

---

[8] Convention (No. IV) Respecting the Laws and Customs of War on Land, with Annex of Regulations (done at The Hague, Oct. 18, 1907; entered into force, Jan. 26, 1910), 36 Stat. 2277 (1911), T.S. No. 539.

[9] The relevance of the Martens Clause to environmental protection is asserted in paragraph 7 of the 1994 ICRC/UNGA Guidelines on Protection of the Environment in Times of Armed Conflict. See also Theodor Meron, "Comment: Protection of the Environment During Non-international Armed Conflicts," in Richard J. Grunawalt et al. (eds.), *Protection of the Environment During Armed Conflict* (Newport, R.I.: Naval War College, 1996), pp. 356, 371–72.

[10] Geoffrey Best, "Historical Evolution of Cultural Norms Relating to War and the Environment," in Arthur H. Westing (ed.), *Cultural Norms, War and the Environment* (Oxford: Oxford Univ. Press, 1988), p. 20.

provisions of the Hague Regulations are relevant to certain instances of environmental damage. Article 23(g) states that it is especially forbidden "to destroy or seize the enemy's property, unless such destruction or seizure be imperatively demanded by the necessities of war." (This raises the question, discussed further below, of whether "property" encompasses, say, the atmosphere.) Articles 28 and 47 prohibit pillage – which is more or less synonymous with "plundering," and can be defined as the robbery of property of various types.[11] Section III, which consists of Articles 42–56 and deals with military occupations, contains many provisions having a potential bearing on environmental protection. Article 55 is the most obvious, but not the only, example: "The occupying State shall be regarded only as administrator and usufructuary of public buildings, real estate, forests, and agricultural estates belonging to the hostile State, and situated in the occupied country. It must safeguard the capital of these properties, and administer them in accordance with the rules of usufruct."

It could be further argued that the rules in 1907 Hague Conventions V and XIII, relating to neutrality in land and naval war respectively, by requiring belligerents to respect the sovereign rights of neutral powers, prohibit environmental damage seriously affecting a neutral state. This is a typical case in which protection of the environment, even where it is not mentioned in existing law, may nonetheless be a logical implication of such law.

1925 GENEVA PROTOCOL

The 1925 Geneva Protocol on gas and bacteriological warfare provides one basis for asserting the illegality of forms of chemical warfare having a harmful effect on the environment.[12] The scope of the Protocol has been the subject of a number of controversies, some of which have included matters relating to the environment. In 1969, during the Second Indochina War, and following reports of US use of chemicals in Vietnam, a UN General Assembly Resolution (which unsurprisingly did not receive

---

[11] Rudolf Bernhardt (ed.), *Encyclopaedia of Public International Law* (Amsterdam: North-Holland Publishing Co., 1982), vol. IV, p. 139 (defining "pillage" as involving the obtaining of property against the owner's will, and with the intention of unjustified gain).

[12] Protocol for the Prohibition of the Use in War of Asphyxiating, Poisonous or other Gases, and of Bacteriological Methods of Warfare (done at Geneva, June 17, 1925; entered into force, Feb. 8, 1928), 26 U.S.T. 571, T.I.A.S. No. 8061, reprinted in *I.L.M.* 14 (1975), 49.

unanimous support) addressed the issue, declaring that the 1925 Geneva Protocol prohibits the use in armed conflicts of:

(a) Any chemical agents of warfare – chemical substances, whether gaseous, liquid or solid – which might be employed because of their direct toxic effects on man, animals or plants;

(b) Any biological agents of warfare – living organisms, whatever their nature, or infective material derived from them – which are intended to cause disease and death in man, animals or plants, and which depend for their effects on their ability to multiply in the person, animal or plant attacked.[13]

The history of the 1925 Geneva Protocol has been marked by one complexity that bears on environmental protection. There is evidence that fear of reprisals played some part in the non-use of chemical weapons by various belligerents in World War II,[14] and by Iraq in the 1990–91 Gulf War.[15] In several such episodes, the threat of retaliation, whether or not in kind, has helped to buttress the 1925 Geneva Protocol regime. It has only been where that threat was absent, for example because the victim state lacked a capacity to threaten effective retaliation, that chemical weapons have been employed.

A reprisal may be defined as a coercive retaliatory measure, normally contrary to international law, taken in retaliation by one party to a conflict with the specific purpose of making an adversary desist from particular actions violating international law. It may be intended, for example, to make the adversary abandon an unlawful practice of warfare.[16] A reprisal may sometimes be similar in character to the act complained of, but it does not have to be so.

A threat of reprisals was implicit in the reservations made by many states when they originally acceded to the 1925 Geneva Protocol. At least

---

[13] UN General Assembly Resolution (hereinafter GA Res.) 2603A (XXIV) of December 16, 1969 (80 in favor, 3 against, 36 abstentions).

[14] A useful and judicious discussion of the many factors involved in non-use of gas in World War II is Edward M. Spiers, *Chemical Warfare* (London: Macmillan, 1986), pp. 62–88. He also stresses the attitudes of political leaders and the non-assimilation of gas weapons by military commanders.

[15] Explored further in Adam Roberts, "The Laws of War in the 1990–91 Gulf Conflict," *Int'l Security* 18(3) (1993/94), 163–64.

[16] For a skeptical survey see Frits Kalshoven, *Belligerent Reprisals* (Leiden: Sijthoff, 1971). For the definition of reprisals, this chapter also draws on (German) Federal Ministry of Defence, *Humanitarian Law in Armed Conflicts: Manual* (Bonn: Federal Ministry of Defence, August 1992), para. 476; and on the slightly revised version of the same paragraph in Dieter Fleck (ed.), *The Handbook of Humanitarian Law in Armed Conflicts* (Oxford: Oxford Univ. Press, 1995), p. 204 (this book is the English version of the German manual, with extensive commentary).

thirty states parties (including many major powers, and all five that became permanent members of the UN Security Council) specified in reservations that the Protocol would cease to be binding in regard to any enemy state whose armed forces or whose allies fail to respect the Protocol's prohibitions.[17]

This more or less explicit reliance on reprisals as one basis of the 1925 Geneva Protocol regime is under challenge. This is partly because of doubts about the utility of reprisals generally. It is also because the adoption in 1972 of the Biological Weapons Convention, prohibiting possession (not just use) of biological weapons, undermined the credibility of threats of retaliation in kind. The adoption in 1993 of the Chemical Weapons Convention may have a similar effect in undermining the credibility of threats of reprisal by chemical weapons. Since 1972, eleven of the thirty-plus states that had made reservations safeguarding this right of reprisal have withdrawn these reservations.[18] In 1991, two other states, Canada and the United Kingdom, made more qualified and limited withdrawals of their reservations: they only retracted them insofar as they relate to recourse to bacteriological methods of warfare.[19] On January 29, 1992, President Yeltsin declared a Russian withdrawal of the USSR's "reservations concerning the possibility of using biological weapons as a response." However, Russia has not informed the Depositary of this.[20]

---

[17] However, in 1975 the United States, the last of the "Permanent Five" to become a party, used a form of words in its reservation to the 1925 Additional Protocol implying that biological weapons would not be used in any reprisal. (The United States became a party to the Biological Weapons Convention in the same year, so had committed itself to abolishing its stocks of such weapons.)

[18] Between 1972 and 1997, eleven states withdrew their reservations to the 1925 Geneva Protocol, presumably because of their apparent inconsistency with the 1972 Biological Weapons Convention or the 1993 Chemical Weapons Convention: Ireland (1972); Australia (1986); New Zealand (1989); Czechoslovakia (1990); Romania, Chile, Bulgaria (1991); The Netherlands (1995); South Africa, France (1996); and Belgium (1997). Source: communication to the author from French Foreign Ministry, acting as Depositary (Sept. 1997).

[19] Original English texts of the partial withdrawals of reservations to the 1925 Geneva Protocol by Canada (August 1991) and United Kingdom (November 1991) supplied by the Department of Foreign Affairs and Trade in Ottawa, and the Foreign and Commonwealth Office in London (Sept. and Dec. 1997).

[20] Letter dated January 30, 1992 from the Representative of the Russian Federation addressed to the President of the Conference on Disarmament transmitting the text of the statement made on January 29, 1992 by B. N. Yeltsin, the President of the Russian Federation, on Russia's policy in the field of arms limitation and reduction, UN Doc. CD/1123 (Jan. 31, 1992), p. 7. The failure to notify the Depositary was confirmed in a communication to the author from French Foreign Ministry (June 23, 1998).

In general, it is not yet possible to conclude that the world has moved beyond threats of retaliation as one basis for ensuring observance of the law of war, including in respect of the environment.

The four 1949 Geneva Conventions are concerned above all with the task of protection of victims of war. However, one of these agreements, 1949 Geneva Convention IV (the Civilians Convention) contains a large number of provisions bearing on protection of the environment. It builds on the similar provisions of the 1907 Hague Regulations in such matters as its general prohibition of pillage (Article 33), and in several provisions of the section on occupied territories, especially Article 53: "Any destruction by the Occupying Power of real or personal property belonging individually or collectively to private persons, or to the State, or to other public authorities, or to social or co-operative organizations, is prohibited, except where such destruction is rendered absolutely necessary by military operations."

The ICRC commentary on this article contains the following assessment on the question of "scorched earth" policies:

> A word should be said here about operations in which military considerations require recourse to a "scorched earth" policy, i.e. the systematic destruction of whole areas by occupying forces withdrawing before the enemy. Various rulings of the courts after the Second World War held that such tactics were in practice admissible in certain cases, when carried out in exceptional circumstances purely for legitimate military reasons. On the other hand the same rulings severely condemned recourse to measures of general devastation whenever they were wanton, excessive or not warranted by military operations.[21]

Article 147 of 1949 Geneva Convention IV, and similar articles in Conventions I and II, confirm that grave breaches of the Convention include "extensive destruction and appropriation of property, not justified by military necessity and carried out unlawfully and wantonly." This provision has some application in armed conflict generally, as well as in occupied territory.[22] Such prohibited destruction could include much that has serious environmental effects. The fact that this prohibition is contained

---

[21] Jean S. Pictet (ed.), *Commentary on Geneva Convention IV* (Geneva: ICRC, 1958), p. 302.

[22] *Ibid.*, pp. 597–602 (explaining that Article 147 covers a wide range of provisions of the convention, including pillage, but then apparently viewing its application as mainly being in occupied territory).

in a treaty that has virtually universal acceptance by states, and is indisputably in force in international wars, adds to its significance.

A critical question that arises from the cited provisions of the 1907 Hague Regulations and of the 1949 Geneva Convention IV concerns the extent to which the term "property" can be interpreted to encompass public goods (not necessarily under specific ownership) such as common land, forests, the atmosphere, water resources, and the open seas. Assuming that "property" can be interpreted in a broad manner, the cited provisions may constitute the strongest ground for asserting the illegality of a great deal of wanton environmental destruction in war.

1954 HAGUE CULTURAL PROPERTY CONVENTION

The Hague Cultural Property Convention and First Protocol seek to protect a broad range of objects, including groups of historic buildings, archaeological sites, and centers containing a large amount of cultural property. [23] All such property is to be protected from exposure to destruction, damage, and pillage. In many cases, action that was wantonly destructive of the environment would also risk violating the provisions of this convention. A main problem with this convention, exposed by the war in the former Yugoslavia, has been the familiar one: lack of effective mechanisms for responding to violations. The Second Hague Protocol, opened for signature at The Hague on May 17, 1999, supplements the 1954 Convention in a number of ways, which include elaborating the principles of individual criminal responsibility and universal jurisdiction, and establishing regular procedures for implementation. [24]

1976 ENMOD CONVENTION

Environmental aspects of warfare were addressed by name and directly in two agreements concluded in 1976 and 1977. In both cases, one important stimulus to new lawmaking was the Second Indochina War, and in particular the United States' use of forest and crop destruction, and rainmaking techniques.

---

[23] Convention for the Protection of Cultural Property in the Event of Armed Conflict (done at The Hague, May 14, 1954; entered into force, Aug. 7, 1956), U.N.T.S. No. 3511.

[24] Copy of the Protocol supplied by the International Standards Section, UNESCO, Paris, May 28, 1999.

The first of these two agreements is the 1976 UN Convention on the Prohibition of Military or Any Other Hostile Use of Environmental Modification Techniques.[25] This accord (otherwise known as the ENMOD Convention) deals essentially, not with damage to the environment, but with the use of the forces of the environment as weapons.[26] Article I prohibits all "hostile use of environmental modification techniques having widespread, long-lasting or severe effects as the means of destruction, damage or injury" to the adversary. Article II then defines "environmental modification techniques" as "any technique for changing – through the deliberate manipulation of natural processes – the dynamics, composition or structure of the Earth, including its biota, lithosphere, hydrosphere and atmosphere, or of outer space." An authoritative UN understanding which was attached to the text of the Convention already in 1976 provides a non-exhaustive list of phenomena which could be caused by environmental modification techniques: these include, among other things, "an upset in the ecological balance of a region."[27]

A critical factor limiting the value of the provisions of the ENMOD Convention concerns the meaning to be attached to the phrase in Article I: "widespread, long-lasting or severe effects." This was the subject of a 1976 understanding of the Conference of the Committee on Disarmament at Geneva:

> It is the understanding of the Committee that, for the purposes of this Convention, the terms "widespread," "long-lasting" and "severe" shall be interpreted as follows:
>
> (a) "widespread": encompassing an area on the scale of several hundred square kilometres;

---

[25] Convention on the Prohibition of Military or Any Other Hostile Use of Environmental Modification Techniques (done at New York, Dec. 10, 1976; entered into force, Oct. 5, 1978; for the United States, Jan. 17, 1980), 31 U.S.T. 333, T.I.A.S. No. 9614, reprinted in *I.L.M.* 16 (1977), 88.

[26] For an analysis of the 1976 Convention on Environmental Modification Techniques, and of the general issue of environmental warfare in the sense of using the forces of the environment as weapons, see Arthur H. Westing (ed.), *Environmental Warfare: A Technical, Legal and Policy Appraisal* (London and Philadelphia: Taylor & Francis, 1984).

[27] The texts of the Understandings in connection with the ENMOD Convention were transmitted by the Committee of the Conference on Disarmament (CCD) in Geneva to the UN General Assembly on September 2, 1976, and are reprinted in Hearing Before the Committee on Foreign Relations, US Senate, 95th Congress, Second Session, on the Convention on the Prohibition of Military or Any Other Hostile Use of Environmental Modification Techniques, 3 October 1978 (Washington, D.C.: US Gov't Printing Office, 1978), pp. 11–12.

(b) "long-lasting": lasting for a period of months, or approximately a season;

(c) "severe": involving serious or significant disruption or harm to human life, natural and economic resources or other assets.

It is further understood that the interpretation set forth above is intended exclusively for this Convention and is not intended to prejudice the interpretation of the same or similar terms if used in connexion with any other international agreement.[28]

In summary, the ENMOD Convention covers only the special case of major uses of the forces of the environment as weapons, and is of no relevance to most instances of damage to the environment in war.

1977 ADDITIONAL PROTOCOL I

The second law-of-war agreement directly referring to the environment is the 1977 Protocol I Additional to the Geneva Conventions of 1949.[29] Since there is controversy about the content, status, and utility of its environmental provisions, this must be covered in some detail.

Articles 35 and 55 deal specifically with the question of damage to the natural environment. (This is distinct from the manipulation of the forces of the environment as weapons, which had been addressed in the ENMOD Convention.) Article 35, which is in a section on "Methods and Means of Warfare," states in full (the third paragraph being the most explicit on the environment):

1. In any armed conflict, the right of the Parties to the conflict to choose methods and means of warfare is not unlimited.
2. It is prohibited to employ weapons, projectiles and material and methods of warfare of a nature to cause superfluous injury or unnecessary suffering.
3. It is prohibited to employ methods or means of warfare which are intended, or may be expected, to cause widespread, long-term and severe damage to the natural environment.

Note the conjunction "and" in "widespread, long-term and severe", which is distinct from "or" in the ENMOD Convention. Similarly, Article 55,

---

[28] *Ibid.*

[29] Protocol Additional to the Geneva Conventions of August 12, 1949, and Relating to the Protection of Victims of International Armed Conflicts (Protocol I) (done at Geneva, June 8, 1977; entered into force, Dec. 7, 1978), reprinted in *I.L.M.* 16 (1977), 1391.

the second article referring specifically to damage to the environment, states in full:

1. Care shall be taken in warfare to protect the natural environment against widespread, long-term and severe damage. This protection includes a prohibition of the use of methods or means of warfare which are intended or may be expected to cause such damage to the natural environment and thereby to prejudice the health or survival of the population.
2. Attacks against the natural environment by way of reprisals are prohibited.

In addition to addressing specifically damage to the natural environment, this accord contains extensive provisions protecting the civilian population and civilian objects. Many of them, while not mentioning the environment by name, do in fact prohibit certain forms of military action destructive of the environment. Article 48, entitled "Basic Rule," states, "the Parties to the conflict shall at all times distinguish between the civilian population and combatants and between civilian objects and military objectives and accordingly shall direct their operations only against military objectives."

Article 52, on "General Protection of Civilian Objects," similarly provides a framework for protecting civilian objects. Subject to certain important provisos in paragraphs 3 and 5, Article 54, paragraph 2, states:

It is prohibited to attack, destroy, remove or render useless objects indispensable to the survival of the civilian population, such as foodstuffs, agricultural areas for the production of foodstuffs, crops, livestock, drinking water installations and supplies and irrigation works, for the specific purpose of denying them for their sustenance value to the civilian population or to the adverse Party, whatever the motive, whether in order to starve out civilians, to cause them to move away, or for any other motive.

Thus, Protocol I's protection of the environment is not at all restricted to the two articles that actually mention the environment. Similarly, in Article 56, dealing with "Protection of Works and Installations Containing Dangerous Forces," paragraph 1 states:

Works or installations containing dangerous forces, namely dams, dykes and nuclear electrical generating stations, shall not be made the object of attack, even where these objects are military objectives, if such attack may cause the release of dangerous forces and consequent severe losses among the civilian population. Other military objectives located at or in the vicinity of these works or installations shall not be made the object of attack if such attack may cause the release of dangerous forces from the works or installations and consequent severe losses among the civilian population.

This article is qualified by the second paragraph, which in effect says that the protection it offers ceases if the military objective in question is used in regular, significant, and direct support of military operations. Thus, the article does not give total immunity from attack. Where hydro-electric generating stations or nuclear power plants are contributing to a grid in regular, significant, and direct support of military operations, militarily necessary attacks against them are not prohibited.[30] Despite this qualification, during the 1980s the US government argued that the article gave too great a degree of immunity to dams, dikes, and nuclear electrical generating stations.[31] A further US criticism was that the provisions of Article 56 could be construed as preserving "the right of a defender to release dangerous forces to repel an attacker."[32]

Much else in Protocol I has a bearing on the environment. For instance, in the chapter on Civil Defense, which seeks to give protection to various measures intended to alleviate the effects of hostilities or disasters, Article 61 defines the tasks of civil defense forces to include, *inter alia*: decontamination and similar protective measures; emergency repair of indispensable public utilities; and assistance in the preservation of objects essential for survival.[33]

The US Army's *Operational Law Handbook* succinctly identifies a key innovative element in Protocol I:

> The primary difference between GP I [Protocol I] and the protections found with the Hague Regulations or the Geneva Conventions is that once the degree of damage to the environment reaches a certain level, GP I does not employ the traditional balancing of military necessity against the quantum of expected destruction. Instead, it establishes this level as an absolute ceiling of permissible destruction.[34]

---

[30] On this point, see especially George H. Aldrich, "Prospects for United States Ratification of Additional Protocol I to the 1949 Geneva Conventions," *Am. J. Int'l L.* 85 (1991), 12–13. Aldrich had been the head of the US delegation to the conference that adopted the two 1977 Additional Protocols.

[31] For a detailed and impressive critique of Article 56, see the discussion in the book-length article by W. Hays Parks, "Air War and the Law of War," *Air Force L. Rev.* 32 (1990), 212–18. Dr. Parks became Chief of the International Law Team, International Affairs Division, Office of the Judge Advocate General of the Army; he was also (see note on p. 222 of the article) author of the revised US Army Field Manual 27–10, entitled *The Law of War*.

[32] Parks, "Air War and the Law of War," 212.

[33] Protocol I, Art. 61, para. (a), items ix, xii, and xiv.

[34] Judge Advocate General's School, US Army, *Operational Law Handbook*, 1st rev. edn., JA 422 (1997), p. 5–18.

A familiar difficulty regarding the environmental provisions of Protocol I is that the definitions of the terms "widespread, long-term and severe" are different from, and more severe than, those in the ENMOD Convention.[35] They exclude a great deal of minor and short-term environmental damage. There is an extensive body of legal writing on the issue, the very existence of which is a warning against relying strongly on the particular provisions containing this phrase. Bothe, Partsch, and Solf went so far as to say: "Arts. 35(3) and 55 will not impose any significant limitation on combatants waging conventional warfare. It seems primarily directed to high level policy decision makers and would affect such unconventional means of warfare as the massive use of herbicides or chemical agents which could produce widespread, long-term and severe damage to the natural environment."[36]

Can Protocol I's key rules on the environment be said to reflect customary law, and thus be generally binding anyway? A number of the general rules that have implications for the environment, including Article 48 and much of Article 52, are widely accepted as customary law. However, Articles 35(3) and 55 are not pre-existing rules of customary law. Greenwood acknowledges that the United States (whose position is explored further below) and Germany view these articles as representing a new rule. He then states, "Nevertheless, while there is likely to be continuing controversy about the extent of the principle contained in Article 35(3), the core of that principle may well reflect an emerging norm of international law."[37] While there may still be scope for disagreement on this point, one positive indicator is that the numerous declarations and reservations to Protocol I do not relate to Articles 35(3) and 55, with the solitary exception of an

[35] On the distinction between the terms "widespread," "long-term," and "severe" as used in the ENMOD Convention and Protocol I, see especially Yves Sandoz et al. (eds.), *International Committee of the Red Cross, Commentary on the Additional Protocols of 8 June 1977 to the Geneva Conventions of 12 August 1949* (Geneva: M. Nijhoff for ICRC, 1987), pp. 410–20 and 662–64.

[36] Michael Bothe et al., *New Rules for Victims of Armed Conflicts: Commentary on the Two 1977 Protocols Additional to the Geneva Conventions of 1949* (The Hague: M. Nijhoff, 1982), p. 348.

[37] Christopher Greenwood, "Customary Law Status of the 1977 Geneva Protocols," in Astrid J. M. Delissen and Gerard J. Tanja (eds.), *Humanitarian Law of Armed Conflict: Challenges Ahead* (Dordrecht: Nijhoff, 1991), pp. 102–3, 105, 108, and 110. As to Article 56, Greenwood suggests (p. 110) that there are grounds for doubting whether the special additional protection it affords to dams, dikes, and nuclear power stations has the status of customary law. See also Christopher Greenwood, "Customary International Law and the First Protocol of 1977 in the Gulf Conflict," in Peter Rowe (ed.), *The Gulf War 1990–91 in International and English Law* (London: Routledge, 1993), pp. 63–88.

anodyne UK statement at ratification in 1998: "*Re* Article 35, paragraph 3 and Article 55. The United Kingdom understands both of these provisions to cover the employment of methods and means of warfare and that the risk of environmental damage falling within the scope of these provisions arising from such methods and means of warfare is to be assessed objectively on the basis of the information available at the time."[38]

Treaties on environmental issues can reinforce and give specificity to law-of-war agreements, and can also call for their general application. A case in point is the 1997 UN Convention on International Watercourses, whose drafters no doubt had provisions of Protocol I as well as other treaties in mind when they included the following provision: "International watercourses and related installations, facilities and other works shall enjoy the protection accorded by the principles and rules of international law applicable in international and non-international armed conflict and shall not be used in violation of those principles and rules."[39]

Many of the provisions of Protocol I prohibit certain types of reprisal.[40] In particular, attacks in the form of reprisals against the natural environment, and against civilians, are prohibited. However, this does not necessarily mean that absolutely all acts of reprisal are prohibited. At ratification of this agreement, a number of states made declarations which, in interpreting some of its provisions, appeared to keep open the possibility of reprisals. The clearest such cases are Italy's in 1986, Germany's in 1991, and the United Kingdom's in 1998. Italy's long statement of interpretation included the following: "Italy will react to serious and systematic violations by an enemy of the obligations imposed by Protocol I and in particular its Articles 51 and 52 with all means admissible under international law in order to prevent any further violation." Germany's declaration on this point was virtually identical. The United Kingdom's statement regarding Articles 51–55 asserted in considerable detail a qualified right of reprisal.[41]

---

[38] UK statement (f) (January 28, 1998).

[39] Article 29, "International watercourses and installations in time of armed conflict", of the 1997 UN Convention on the Law of the Non-Navigational Uses of International Watercourses, (adopted by the UN General Assembly on May 21, 1997 in GA Res. 51/229), text in UN Doc. A/RES/51/229 (July 8, 1997), p. 12, reprinted in *I.L.M.* 36 (1997), 700.

[40] Explicit prohibitions on reprisals are contained in Protocol I, Arts. 51(6), 52(1), 53(c), 54(4), 55(2), and 56(4). For a succinct discussion of the background, see Frits Kalshoven, *Constraints on the Waging of War* (Geneva: ICRC, 1987), pp. 102–4.

[41] Text of Italy's statements of interpretation (made in 1986) and of Germany's declarations (1991) supplied to the author by the Swiss Federal Department for Foreign Affairs, July–September 1988 and July 1997. The Italian statement can also be found in Schindler and Toman,

Thus the institution of the reprisal, although by no means generally accepted in international society, is not yet dead. If it were to fall completely into disuse, the question would inevitably be raised as to what the sanction underlying the law of war is to be, if it is not reprisals by belligerent states.

In conclusion, of all the law-of-war sources which have been cited, Protocol I has the strongest provisions limiting damage to the environment. As has been seen, these provisions are not limited to one or two articles, but permeate many parts of the agreement. They supplement in a variety of ways the earlier rules bearing on the environment. However, because some important states are not yet parties, and because of doubts about the customary law status of some of its provisions, there is a need for caution about the manner and extent to which it should be relied on as a basis for proclaiming the illegality of certain acts of environmental despoliation. The fact that Articles 35 and 55 only really prohibit the most extreme forms of environmental destruction reinforces the need to look to other articles (as well as other treaties) to provide guidance in more normal situations. Paradoxically, the Protocol's provisions that do not specifically mention the environment are more useful as a basis for assessing the legality or otherwise of particular practices than are those that do make such mention.

1980 CERTAIN CONVENTIONAL WEAPONS CONVENTION AND PROTOCOLS

The preamble of the UN Convention on Certain Conventional Weapons repeats the exact words of Protocol I, Article 35(3), which were quoted in full above; and also recalls a number of other general principles which could have a bearing on environmental damage. Protocol III annexed to the Convention deals with incendiary weapons. Article 2, paragraph 4 of Protocol III states, in a notably weak formulation: "It is prohibited to make forests or other kinds of plant cover the object of attack by incendiary weapons except when such natural elements are used to cover, conceal or

The Laws of Armed Conflicts, pp. 712–13; and Roberts and Guelff, Documents on the Laws of War, p. 465. Text of UK statement at ratification in 1998 supplied by Foreign and Commonwealth Office, London (Feb. 1998).

camouflage combatants or other military objectives, or are themselves military objectives."

The 1996 Amended Protocol II annexed to the CCW Convention deals with weapons such as mines, replacing as between parties the original Protocol II on the same subject.[42] Amended Protocol II has relevance to environmental protection in that its Article 3(8) prohibits the indiscriminate use of mines; and Article 10 provides for removal of minefields. Its Article 1, as noted below, provides for its application to internal as well as international conflicts.

Amended Protocol II, which entered into force in December 1998, is a more modest measure than the 1997 Ottawa Convention (see below). Amended Protocol II, which is concerned with limitations on use rather than on possession, will retain its relevance because it imposes limits on more types of mine than the Ottawa Convention, and because it will continue in force as between parties who are not bound by the Ottawa Convention. The Ottawa Convention's preamble, in calling for early ratification of this Protocol, implies a degree of compatibility between the two instruments.

1997 OTTAWA ANTI-PERSONNEL MINE CONVENTION

The Convention on the Prohibition of the Use, Stockpiling, Production and Transfer of Anti-Personnel Mines and on their Destruction, concluded at Oslo on September 18, 1997 and opened for signature in Ottawa in December 1997, goes further, prohibiting all use, development, production, stockpiling, and transfer of anti-personnel mines. Its Article 5 provides for clearance of mined areas. Since the treaty provides for a total ban of anti-personnel mines by participating states, it prohibits the use of such weapons in civil as well as international wars.[43] However, it does not limit all types of landmines, and many major countries (China, India, Pakistan, Russia, and the United States) are not parties.

---

[42] Amended Protocol II on Anti-Personnel Land-Mines to the 1980 UN Convention on Certain Conventional Weapons (concluded, May 3, 1996; entered into force, Dec. 3, 1998), reprinted in *I.L.M.* 35 (1996), 1209.

[43] 1997 Convention on the Prohibition of the Use, Stockpiling, Production and Transfer of Anti-Personnel Mines and on Their Destruction (opened for signature in Ottawa, Dec. 3–4 , 1997; entered into force, Mar. 1, 1999), reprinted in *I.L.M.* 36 (1997), 1507.

The Statute of the International Criminal Court (ICC), adopted in Rome on July 17, 1998, is of course not primarily concerned with defining new crimes, but rather with seeing to implementation of existing law. Its useful summary of war crimes (Article 8) is essentially based on existing treaty law. It refers to several prohibitions that have relevance to environmental protection. These include, in the exact words of the 1949 Geneva Convention IV: "extensive destruction and appropriation of property, not justified by military necessity and carried out unlawfully and wantonly." The Statute's summary of provisions of Protocol I includes "intentionally directing attacks against civilian objects, that is, objects which are not military objectives," and also "[i]ntentionally launching an attack in the knowledge that such attack will cause incidental loss of life or injury to civilians or damage to civilian objects or widespread, long-term and severe damage to the natural environment which would be clearly excessive in relation to the concrete and direct overall military advantage anticipated."[44]

These words appear to introduce a proportionality test into environmental despoliation. This was not evident in the actual wording of Protocol I as cited earlier, but could provide one means of getting over the hurdle of interpreting "widespread, long-term and severe." There will be many difficulties in bringing the ICC into existence, not least because sixty states parties are required before the Statute can enter into force. Its existence, or the prospect thereof, may make states take war crimes issues seriously, and the Statute's enumeration of offenses is valuable.

SOME POSSIBLE GROUNDS FOR CRITICISM OF LAW-OF-WAR RULES

There are many possible grounds for criticism of the law-of-war rules briefly outlined above. They are dispersed in too many types of sources and in too many different agreements; they lack specificity; they rely heavily on the always hazardous process whereby commanders balance

[44] 1998 Statute of the International Criminal Court (not yet in force), UN Doc. A/CONF.183/9 (July 17, 1998), Art. 8, paras. 2(a)(iv), 2(b)(ii), and 2(b)(iv), reprinted in *I.L.M.* 37 (1998), 999–1069. (These sources contain the uncorrected text: over fifty corrections were subsequently notified to states by the Depositary. The passages referred to here are not affected by the corrections.)

military necessity against other considerations; they have not caught up with the growing concern in many countries about environmental issues; and the means of investigating complaints and punishing violations are not always clear. Above all, there is no effective means of ensuring that an admittedly disparate set of principles and rules is actually accepted, understood, and implemented; and there is much scope for disagreement about what are acceptable targets and methods where risks to the environment are involved. Finally, as discussed further below, their application to civil wars is limited; and law-of-war treaties do not directly address the problem of nuclear use.

Because pre-1976 treaties on the law of war contain no mention of the word "environment," and focus mainly on prohibitions of wanton destruction, they suffer from some inherent limitations. As noted above, their use of the term "property" leaves room for ambiguity as to whether it encompasses some environmental goods such as the air we breathe. Despite such weaknesses, these older rules constitute the strongest legal basis for asserting the illegality of much environmental destruction in war.

Finally, some of the newer law-of-war rules which attempt to deal directly with protection of the environment – especially those in the 1976 ENMOD Convention and in Protocol I – have serious limitations. The particular provisions of these two agreements that specifically mention the environment appear to apply only in the case of very extreme damage. As a result, other provisions of Protocol I may be less contentious, and of more practical use in environmental protection. Also, these treaties have failed to secure universal assent: as of January 1, 1999, there were 64 states parties to ENMOD, and 152 to Protocol I. These figures compare with 188 for the four 1949 Geneva Conventions. During the 1990–91 Gulf War there was a tendency in public statements about environmental damage to refer mainly to these newer rules, because they do mention the word "environment" as such. However, since Iraq was not a party to either ENMOD or Protocol I, and several other states involved were not a party to one or the other, reference to these agreements was of limited value. Reference to provisions from earlier treaties would have been legally sounder and more directly relevant to the circumstances that were faced. This is not to suggest that such an approach would have stopped Saddam Hussein in his tracks, but rather that the key problem was not lack of law, but lack of effective implementation.

US attitudes to environmental provisions of 1977 Additional Protocol I

The fact that the United States is not a party to Protocol I raises two questions here. First, is US non-participation in the Protocol due in part to rejection of any of its environmental provisions? Second, can any risks of misunderstanding or lack of coordination between the United States and actual or potential allies (the great majority of whom are parties) be minimized, at least so far as the provisions with a bearing on the environment are concerned?

US official thinking on Protocol I is more public than that in other states, and involves a wide range of issues. Historically, a central problem has been US unease at the expansion of the category of lawful belligerents to encompass certain guerrilla combatants, an issue that is not pursued here.

Despite its non-accession to Protocol I, the US government explicitly recognized, long before Iraq's invasion of Kuwait, that many of this agreement's provisions either reflect customary law or merit support on other grounds. The key question here, therefore, is whether the US government views the provisions that have a bearing on protection of the environment as meriting support.

When, on January 29, 1987, President Reagan transmitted the 1977 Additional Protocol II to the US Senate for its advice and consent to ratification, he said in his letter of transmittal:

> we can reject Protocol I as a reference for humanitarian law, and at the same time devise an alternative reference for the positive provisions of Protocol I that could be of real humanitarian benefit if generally observed by parties to international armed conflicts. We are therefore in the process of consulting with our allies to develop appropriate methods for incorporating these positive provisions into the rules that govern our military operations, and as customary international law. I will advise the Senate of the results of this initiative as soon as it is possible to do so.[45]

Earlier in January 1987, Michael J. Matheson, Deputy Legal Advisor, US State Department, had given a fuller account of US government thinking about Protocol I. He acknowledged that US non-ratification left a gap, and gave some indication as to how it might be filled:

---

[45] President Reagan's letter of transmittal of 1977 Additional Protocol II to the US Senate, S. Treaty Doc. No. 2, 100th Cong., 1st Sess., at III (1987), reprinted in *Am. J. Int'l L.* 81 (1987), 910–12.

Protocol I cannot be now looked to by actual or potential adversaries of the United States or its allies as a definitive indication of the rules that US forces will observe in the event of armed conflict and will expect its adversaries to observe. To fill this gap, the United States and its friends would have to give some alternative clear indication of which rules they consider binding or otherwise propose to observe.

. . . in our discussions with our allies to date we have not attempted to reach an agreement on which rules are presently customary law, but instead have focused on which principles are in our common interests and therefore should be observed and in due course recognized as customary law, whether they are presently part of that law or not.[46]

Mr. Matheson went on to list "the principles that we believe should be observed and in due course recognized as customary law, even if they have not already achieved that status." His partial listing of these principles did not include those that explicitly address the protection of the natural environment. Indeed, he indicated that the US administration was opposed to the principle in Article 35 regarding the natural environment, saying that it was "too broad and ambiguous and is not a part of customary law."[47] He was also reported as expressing US opposition to the rule on protection of the environment in Article 55 on the ground that it was "too broad and too ambiguous for effective use in military operations. He concluded that the means and methods of warfare that have such a severe effect on the natural environment so as to endanger the civilian population may be inconsistent with other general principles, such as the rule of proportionality."[48] Matheson and Judge Abraham Sofaer, Legal Advisor, at the US State Department, also criticized in detail the provisions of Article 56, concerning works and installations containing dangerous forces; as have some subsequent official US writings.[49]

---

[46] "Sixth Annual American Red Cross–Washington College of Law Conference on International Humanitarian Law," *Am. U. J. Int'l L. & Pol'y* 2 (1987), 420 and 422. For Judge Sofaer's similar remarks on consultations with allies, see *ibid.*, 471. For subsequent similar statements by Matheson, see American Society of International Law, *Proceedings of the 81st Annual Meeting, Boston, Massachusetts, April 8–11, 1987* (Washington, D.C., 1990), pp. 28 and 29. For a subsequent authoritative account of the state of US-led discussions to fill the gap left by US non-ratification of Protocol I, see the major critique of the Protocol by Parks, "Air War and the Law of War," 222–23.

[47] "ARC–WCL Conference on International Humanitarian Law," 424.

[48] *Ibid.*, 436; see also ASIL, *Proceedings of the 81st Annual Meeting*, pp. 29–31.

[49] "ARC–WCL Conference on International Humanitarian Law," 427 and 434 (Matheson); and 468–69 (Sofaer). For US criticisms of Article 56, see also Parks, "Air War and the Law of War."

In the public polemics about whether or not the United States should ratify Protocol I, there had not been a systematic and sustained debate about these particular provisions bearing on the environment. George Aldrich did go so far as to assert that these provisions may be verging on the status of customary law: "While these provisions of Articles 35 and 55 are clearly new law – 'rules established by the Protocol' – I would not be surprised to see them quickly accepted as part of customary international law insofar as non-nuclear warfare is concerned."[50] This is optimistic, at least in the sense that the US government does not seem to share this view. The awkward truth is that the United States has a history of skepticism about those provisions of Protocol I that explicitly mention the environment.

However, it does not appear that the United States has been so opposed to some other provisions of Protocol I that, as noted earlier, may actually have greater practical utility in limiting environmental damage in war. The critically important Article 54(2), prohibiting attacks on objects indispensable to the life of the civilian population, has not proven controversial.[51]

US non-participation in Protocol I may be regretted by many US allies and cause some complications in joint operations. However, it need not be a barrier to practical cooperation in devising guidelines and policies to limit much of the environmental damage of war. This is both because the United States, along with its allies, is bound by many provisions in other international agreements; and because the United States does accept at least some of the relevant provisions of Protocol I even if it has not ratified this agreement and has expressed concern about Articles 35, 55, and 56. Further, some US military manuals (as mentioned below) have taken the avoidance of environmental damage seriously, and in so doing have drawn on some provisions of Protocol I.

The United States is a non-participant in several other law-of-war treaties, in particular: the 1954 Hague Cultural Property Convention, the Amended Protocol II to the 1980 CCW Convention, the 1997 Ottawa

---

[50] Aldrich, "Prospects for United States Ratification of Additional Protocol I," 14. This article, a response to the critiques of the Protocol, is in some respects incomplete. Referring to Matheson's remarks in January 1987, Aldrich says simply: "With respect to the articles concerning the environment, no explanation was offered" (p. 12). This does slightly less than justice to Matheson's remarks as cited above. Curiously, Aldrich does not refer at all to one major US critique of Protocol I. Parks, "Air War and the Law of War."
[51] Schmitt, "Green War," 77–78.

Convention on Anti-Personnel Mines, and the 1998 Rome Statute of the International Criminal Court. All, it so happens, have some bearing on the environment. This pattern of US non-participation reflects a series of US concerns about the development of the law of war that are not essentially about environmental issues and cannot be explored here.

Arms control treaties

Several other bodies of international law could have a bearing on environmental protection in war, including human rights law and "peacetime" international environmental law. Arms control and disarmament agreements are among the more significant, yet they have been mentioned very little in writing on the subject.[52] Their application in wartime is not automatic in every case, but nonetheless they merit consideration as one important complement to law-of-war agreements. The following four treaties, all of which are in force, have particular relevance to environmental protection.

1959 ANTARCTIC TREATY

The Antarctic Treaty was partly motivated by the desire to preserve the fragile ecology of the Antarctic. It prohibits military activities and nuclear tests in the region.

1963 PARTIAL NUCLEAR TEST BAN TREATY

The pressures that led to the Partial Nuclear Test Ban Treaty included widespread concern about the effects of nuclear testing on the atmosphere and thereby on the food chain. Perhaps the main effect of its prohibition of nuclear tests in the atmosphere, in outer space, and under water was to limit pollution of the land, air, and sea environments. This treaty has been supplemented by the 1996 Comprehensive Test Ban Treaty.

---

[52] There is no reference to arms control accords in chapter 5, "Environmental Law in Operations," of the US Army's *Operational Law Handbook*; but there is reference to US legislation under the Antarctic Treaty, as well as under other international treaties to which the US is a party, at p. 5–21.

1972 BIOLOGICAL WEAPONS CONVENTION

The Biological Weapons Convention completely prohibits developing, producing, stockpiling, or otherwise acquiring or retaining all bacteriological (biological) and toxin weapons, and associated weapons, equipment, or means of delivery. Such weapons are of a type that could have a serious impact on the environment, not least by rendering large areas uninhabitable. The mechanisms for monitoring the implementation are minimal, apart from the explicit provision in Articles VI and VII for UN Security Council involvement in receiving and acting upon complaints of violations.

1993 CHEMICAL WEAPONS CONVENTION

The Chemical Weapons Convention similarly prohibits all development, production, stockpiling, etc., of a wide range of weapons of a type that could have a serious impact on the environment. As with the Biological Weapons Convention, monitoring the implementation of its provisions, even in peacetime, presents many difficult problems. Article XII provides for the application of collective measures by states parties, including, in cases of particular gravity, bringing the issue to the attention of the UN General Assembly and Security Council. Under the terms of the Chemical Weapons Convention (and in sharp contrast to the Biological Weapons Convention), a significant new organization for the sole purpose of monitoring its provisions – the Organization for the Prohibition of Chemical Weapons – was established in The Hague in 1997.[53]

Summary of existing rules: the ICRC/UN approach

While many rules, drawn from a wide variety of sources, have a bearing on the environmental consequences of war, there has been a shortage of clear and succinct summaries of their provisions. This lack has been widely noted in the 1990s. The majority of international lawyers who looked at the matter, and most governments, favored the course that was adopted: not negotiating a new convention, but rather securing authoritative reports,

---

[53] See Barry Kellman, "The Chemical Weapons Convention: A Verification and Enforcement Model for Determining Legal Responsibility for Environmental Harm Caused by War," chapter 23 in this volume.

General Assembly resolutions, draft military manuals, and so on, drawing together existing principles and provisions in a simple and intelligible way.

This has been the trend of developments at the United Nations. In December 1991, the UN General Assembly suggested further consideration of environmental protection in wartime, in conjunction with the ICRC.[54] The ICRC then convened a meeting of experts on the protection of the environment in time of armed conflict, held in Geneva in April 1992, and on June 30 submitted an eighteen-page report to the UN General Assembly. This emphasized the need to observe existing law in this area, and the ICRC's continued willingness to address the matter. It also identified a number of issues for further research and action.[55] This was one input into ongoing discussions in the Sixth Committee, resulting in a November 1992 resolution which was the General Assembly's most important pronouncement on the subject. It recognized the importance of the 1907 Hague Convention IV and the 1949 Geneva Convention IV, as well as later agreements. The resolution stated unambiguously in its preamble "that destruction of the environment, not justified by military necessity and carried out wantonly, is clearly contrary to existing international law," and then in its operational part said that the General Assembly:

1. *Urges* States to take all measures to ensure compliance with the existing international law applicable to the protection of the environment in times of armed conflict;
2. *Appeals* to all States that have not yet done so to consider becoming parties to the relevant international conventions;
3. *Urges* States to take steps to incorporate the provisions of international law applicable to the protection of the environment into their military manuals and to ensure that they are effectively disseminated.[56]

---

[54] UN General Assembly Decision 46/417 of Dec. 9, 1991, requesting the Secretary-General to report on activities undertaken in the framework of the ICRC regarding protection of the environment in time of armed conflict. See also GA Res. 46/54 of the same date, which referred to the Draft Code of Crimes against the Peace and Security of Mankind, adopted by the International Law Commission, Article 26 of which sought to declare criminal "an individual who wilfully causes or orders the causing of widespread, long-term and severe damage to the natural environment." *I.L.M.* 30 (1991), 1584; *Y.B. United Nations* 45 (1991), 823 and 848–49.

[55] This ICRC paper was published as "Protection of the Environment in Times of Armed Conflict: Report of the Secretary-General," UN Doc. A/47/328 (July 31, 1992). The present writer took part in the three Meetings of Experts in Geneva in April 1992, January 1993, and June 1993, that assisted in drawing up the various ICRC documents on the matter in 1992–94.

[56] "Protection of the Environment in Times of Armed Conflict," GA Res. 47/37 (Nov. 25, 1992) (adopted without a vote). For a summary of UN discussions up to and including that resolution, see Virginia Morris, "Protection of the Environment in Wartime: The United Nations General Assembly Considers the Need for a New Convention," *Int'l Law.* 27 (1993), 775–82.

After 1992, the UN General Assembly put the issue on a back-burner called "United Nations Decade of International Law," and remained content to express support for work done under ICRC auspices. The ICRC, following two further meetings of experts in January and June 1993, produced a new report defining the content of existing law, identifying problems of implementation, suggesting what action needed to be taken, and drawing up model guidelines for military manuals.[57] These ICRC/UNGA guidelines, as revised in 1994 in the light of comments from governments, are a useful summation of existing law.[58] In resolutions in 1993 and 1994, the General Assembly particularly supported the emphasis on guidelines for such manuals; and in 1994 it in effect endorsed the guidelines.[59] The General Assembly has not subsequently taken the issue any further. This is sensible, as a reasonably good job had been done, and it was not obvious that there was new ground needing to be covered in this particular forum or, if so, a consensus on how to cover it.

Unfortunately, the German military manual, originally published in 1992, makes the fundamental, and distressingly common, mistake of apparently equating environmental protection in war with the specific environmental provisions of the 1976 ENMOD Convention and Protocol I. All three entries on "environment" impale themselves on the words "widespread," "long-term," and "severe."[60] However, two major US manuals issued later draw on a wider range of legal provisions, including those mentioned in the ICRC/UNGA guidelines document.[61]

---

[57] "Protection of the Environment in Time of Armed Conflict," submitted by the UN Secretary-General to the 48th session of the General Assembly, UN Doc. A/48/269 (July 29, 1993). This 27-page document took up the main elements of, and essentially superseded, the ICRC's July 1992 report (A/47/328) mentioned above, note 55. The new document included a 4-page appendix of "Guidelines for Military Manuals and Instructions on the Protection of the Environment in Time of Armed Conflict."

[58] The revised ICRC/UNGA text, "Guidelines for Military Manuals and Instructions on the Protection of the Environment in Times of Armed Conflict," was issued as an Annex to UN Doc. A/49/323 (Aug. 19, 1994). The text also appears in an appendix to Hans-Peter Gasser, "For Better Protection of the Natural Environment in Armed Conflict: A Proposal for Action," *Am. J. Int'l L.* 89 (1995), 641–44.

[59] See "United Nations Decade of International Law," UNGA Res. 48/30 (Dec. 9, 1993) (adopted without vote), paras. 11–14; see also UNGA Res. 49/50 (Dec. 9, 1994), para. 11 (without formally approving the guidelines, inviting states to disseminate them widely).

[60] Fleck, *Handbook of Humanitarian Law*, secs. 401, 403, and 1020.

[61] The first is US Dep't of the Navy, *The Commander's Handbook on the Law of Naval Operations*, p. 8–2. The second is US Army, *Operational Law Handbook*, ch. 5, "Environmental Law in

Application of rules in hard cases

CIVIL WARS

Since 1945 at least, civil wars have been much more common than inter-state wars. In some cases, they have had serious environmental consequences. They have contributed, for example, to severe famine and to rendering land unusable through the wholesale distribution of anti-personnel mines. Many counter-insurgency campaigns have involved use of defoliants and other measures to make land inhospitable to guerrillas.

Many of the civil wars in the post-1945 period have started as, or eventually become, internationalized civil wars. There is some support for the view that foreign forces involved in such wars, whether in support of insurgents or of incumbent governments, should be bound by the full range of laws applicable in international armed conflicts.[62] However, this principle is not yet universally agreed, nor is it always easy to apply. In particular, if an incumbent government agrees to an act that might otherwise be illegal (say the use of defoliants, or certain forms of gas), then the external force may regard international rules as of diminished application in the particular case.

The implementation of rules of restraint is often difficult in civil wars, for three reasons. First, such wars are often conducted by forces with minimal training and weak command structures. Second, the aim of parties in such wars is often to drive people from their homes and land, an aim which in itself is likely to involve violations of the law of war. Finally, governments and their foreign allies may feel free to engage in actions that would be more open to question if carried out beyond their national borders, and in an undeniably international war. Further, governments may consider their internal adversaries to be criminals, not lawful belligerents.

Operations," pp. 5–1 to 5–22 (containing a notably full and nuanced treatment of environmental protection). For further discussion of military manuals and guidelines, see Arthur H. Westing, "In Furtherance of Environmental Guidelines for Armed Forces during Peace and War," chapter 6 in this volume.

[62] See especially Theodor Meron, *Human Rights in Internal Strife: Their International Protection* (Cambridge: Grotius Publications, 1987); Hans-Peter Gasser, "Internationalized Non-International Armed Conflicts: Case Studies of Afghanistan, Kampuchea, and Lebanon," *Am. U. L. Rev.* 33 (1983), 145–61.

In formal legal terms, most law-of-war treaties have little or no application to purely internal conflicts. Before the mid-twentieth century, the principal international agreements governing the law of war applied only to armed conflict between states and had no formal bearing on non-international armed conflicts. However, the Lieber Code, issued to the Union Army on April 24, 1863, was applied by the forces of the United States during the American Civil War. Certain regional agreements (such as the 1928 Havana Convention on Civil Strife) related to internal conflicts. Also, customary international law provided that the law of war might become applicable to a non-international conflict through the doctrine of "recognition of belligerency." The doctrine of recognition of belligerency appears to have fallen into decline, though there are some modern near-equivalents.

Certain international agreements have established a basic written regime, not dependent upon recognition of belligerency, which provides that fundamental humanitarian principles may be applicable in non-international armed conflicts. Common Article 3 of the four 1949 Geneva Conventions states that in the case of an armed conflict not of an international character occurring in the territory of one of the parties to the Conventions, each party to the conflict shall be bound to apply, as a minimum, certain fundamental humanitarian provisions; but these provisions do not include any that protect property or the environment. Article 3 does offer towards the end the following small consolation: "The Parties to the conflict should further endeavour to bring into force, by means of special agreements, all or part of the other provisions of the present Convention."

The 1977 Additional Protocol II relating to non-international armed conflicts is intended to develop and supplement common Article 3 of the 1949 Geneva Conventions without modifying its existing conditions of application. The provisions of Protocol II with most relevance to environmental protection are Article 14 (protection of objects indispensable to the survival of the civilian population) and Article 15 (protection of works and installations containing dangerous forces). These legal provisions are minimal.

Evidence of the difference between the regimes for international and internal armed conflict can be found in the statutes of the international criminal tribunals for Yugoslavia and Rwanda. The 1993 Statute of the International Criminal Tribunal for the Former Yugoslavia, which draws mainly on the law governing international armed conflict, contains provision for prosecuting for wanton destruction in Articles 2(d) and

3(b).[63] In sharp contrast, the 1994 Statute of the International Criminal Tribunal for Rwanda, apparently basing itself on the assumption (essentially correct) that the events in Rwanda were a civil war, follows the very limited provisions of common Article 3 and the 1977 Additional Protocol II, and contains virtually nothing on the protection of property and things: there is just a brief reference to pillage in Article 4(f).[64]

The 1996 Amended Protocol II on Mines, annexed to the 1980 Convention on Certain Conventional Weapons, states in Article 1 that it applies not only to international armed conflicts, but also "to situations referred to in Article 3 common to the Geneva Conventions of 12 August 1949" – that is, to civil wars. This constitutes a remarkable extension of the scope of application of the CCW Convention, reflecting the huge international concern about the indiscriminate after-effects of mine-laying.

The 1997 Ottawa Anti-Personnel Mine Convention, by committing the states parties not to use, develop, stockpile, or transfer such weapons "under any circumstances," applies equally to civil and international wars.

The 1998 Statute of the International Criminal Court contains within Article 8 a succinct outline of war crimes in non-international armed conflicts. A few bear on the environment, including a prohibition of pillaging and a qualified prohibition of destruction of property: "Destroying or seizing the property of an adversary unless such destruction or seizure be imperatively demanded by the necessities of the conflict."[65]

Quite apart from the specific provisions mentioned above, insurgent or government authorities involved in civil wars may unilaterally or by agreement declare their acceptance of at least certain aspects of the law of war, such as the 1949 Geneva Conventions, and the law of war may thereby be relevant to non-international armed conflicts. Thus, although the range of international rules binding in non-international conflicts is undeniably limited, there remain considerable possibilities for states and insurgent movements, as a matter of policy, to adopt practices or accept national or international legal standards that go beyond their rather narrow formal legal obligations.[66]

---

[63] Statute of the International Criminal Tribunal for the Former Yugoslavia, contained in UN Doc. S/25704 (May 3, 1993), approved in UN Security Council Res. 827 (May 25, 1993), reprinted in *I.L.M.* 32 (1993), 1192.

[64] Statute of the International Criminal Tribunal for Rwanda, approved in and annexed to UN Security Council Res. 955 (Nov. 8, 1994), reprinted in *I.L.M.* 33 (1994), 1602.

[65] 1998 Statute of the International Criminal Court, Art. 8, paras. 2(e)(v) and 2(e)(xii).

[66] A matter pursued in more detail in Westing, "In Furtherance of Environmental Guidelines."

NUCLEAR WEAPONS

Any massive exchange of nuclear weapons would utterly destroy the environment, as well as a great deal else. That would seem to constitute an argument for their complete prohibition. However, there has not been anything approaching complete abolition. Apart from problems about reliable verification of complete nuclear disarmament, this has been partly because these weapons have been valued for their general deterrent functions, and partly because of their more specific value in deterring use of nuclear or other weapons of mass destruction by an adversary. For example, as indicated earlier, it is possible that during the 1990–91 Gulf War, Iraq was deterred from using weapons of mass destruction by various threats of retaliation made by the United States. If this is the case, then a very extreme threat (including one that would involve environmental destruction) was one means of discouraging a slightly less extreme threat (which would also have involved major environmental damage). This is an unsatisfactory basis for maintaining restraint in international conflicts, but there is no point in denying its existence altogether.

The position adopted by nuclear weapons states has generally been to accept a wide range of limitations on their testing and deployment, but to be more cautious as regards restrictions on use. Thus, it was established during the negotiations that led to the 1977 Additional Protocols that nuclear weapons were not under discussion. To reinforce the point, at signature of Protocol I the United States stated that "the rules established by this protocol were not intended to have any effect on and do not regulate or prohibit the use of nuclear weapons"; and the UK made an almost identical statement, which it repeated at ratification in January 1998.

In the course of the hearings leading to its Advisory Opinion on the *Legality of the Threat or Use of Nuclear Weapons*, the International Court of Justice was presented by some states with arguments "that any use of nuclear weapons would be unlawful by reference to existing norms relating to the safeguarding and protection of the environment." The Court's judicious consideration of this subsidiary question concludes:

> The Court thus finds that while the existing international law relating to the protection and safeguarding of the environment does not specifically prohibit the use of nuclear weapons, it indicates important environmental factors that are properly to be taken into account in the context of the

implementation of the principles and rules of the law applicable in armed conflict.[67]

The central question that the UN General Assembly had asked the Court was: "Is the threat or use of nuclear weapons in any circumstance permitted under international law?" The Court's answer to this question was:

> It follows from the above-mentioned requirements that the threat or use of nuclear weapons would generally be contrary to the rules of international law applicable in armed conflict, and in particular the principles and rules of humanitarian law;
>
> However, in view of the current state of international law, and of the elements of fact at its disposal, the Court cannot conclude definitively whether the threat or use of nuclear weapons would be lawful or unlawful in an extreme circumstance of self-defence, in which the very survival of a State would be at stake.[68]

Following this Advisory Opinion, the Rome conference of June–July 1998, which adopted the ICC Statute, did not include use of nuclear weapons as such in the Statute's enumeration of war crimes and crimes against humanity.

Whatever the views on the adequacy or otherwise of the ICJ's Delphic opinion, the manufacture, testing, use, and disposal of nuclear weapons all pose severe environmental problems. These merely reinforce the case, the main strength of which derives from other considerations, for serious efforts at arms control between the existing nuclear powers, and for maintenance of an effective regime of non-use and non-proliferation.

Should a new convention be sought?

The question of restraints on environmental despoliation in war will remain important. Any wars in future decades and centuries are likely to be in areas where there are high chances of the environment being affected. This is mainly because economic development results in the availability of substances (oil, chemicals, and nuclear materials being the most obvious examples) that can very easily be let loose, whether by accident or by

---

[67] This was in a part of the Advisory Opinion that appears to have been agreed upon unanimously. International Court of Justice, Advisory Opinion on *Legality of the Threat or Use of Nuclear Weapons* (July 8, 1996), *I.C.J. Reports* (1996), 243, para. 33.

[68] *Ibid.*, 266, part E. (Voting: seven votes to seven, with the President's casting vote in favor.)

design, on the all-too-vulnerable land, air, and water on which we depend; because some parts of the natural environment are becoming more constricted and fragile due to peacetime trends; because much of the environment in which we live (especially water supplies) depends on the smooth running of an infrastructure easily disrupted by war; because some weapons (nuclear weapons being only the most extreme case) may themselves have terrible effects on the environment; and because environmental goods (including land, clear air and water, and pollution prevention) may well actually be causes of future conflicts.

Is the negotiation of an overarching new convention on war and the environment the best way to address the numerous issues that will arise? The events of the 1990–91 Gulf War drew attention to the apparent absence of a simple, formally binding, set of rules about the impact of war on the environment. In the war's immediate aftermath there were, therefore, many serious arguments for some new attempt at codification. Yet the demand for a grand new codification had several defects:

1. It was sometimes based on incomplete evaluations of existing law, in which the contents and utility of key provisions were ignored or underestimated. In fact, as indicated above, the existing law of war does say a lot that bears on damage to the environment: clear and authoritative exposition of this was needed just as much as new legislation.
2. It risked distracting attention from specific issues (including those with an environmental dimension, such as anti-personnel mines) that needed to be tackled in treaty form.
3. It involved an underestimation of the potential risks in negotiating a major new treaty on this subject, not least that there might be significant retreats from positions already attained in Protocol I and other agreements.
4. It paid too little attention to the fact that the real problem exposed by the Iraqi acts of despoliation in the 1990–91 Gulf War was not the lack of law, but the lack of adequate means to ensure its implementation.

In the years following the 1990–91 Gulf War, the majority of experts involved in international discussions clearly took the view that negotiation for a major new agreement covering the general subject of war and the environment might secure little if any advance. Indeed, many considered that such an attempt could run into fundamentally intractable problems (of which there had already been foretastes in other negotiations) about defining the natural environment; about defining damage to it; about working out exactly which environmentally damaging acts are forbidden; about distinguishing between intentional, collateral, and completely unexpected damage to the environment; about whether certain kinds of destruction, including even scorched earth, are permissible in certain circumstances, including to a defending state within its own national territory; about establishing exactly what military-related activities could be permitted in any specially protected environmentally important areas; and about the applicability of existing international norms in non-international armed conflicts. The question of nuclear weapons would inevitably be raised, and it would probably be as hard as ever to bring such weapons within the framework of specific rules of the law of war. Other questions would be hardly less awkward. The powers that took part in the coalition in the 1990–91 Gulf War, for example, were not about to assert that absolutely all destruction of oil targets was impermissible. They may also have feared that other sensitive issues would be raised in such negotiations.[69]

These concerns about negotiating a major new convention raise a general issue. In the law of war, especially as it affects the environment, detailed provisions have many advantages, but also weaknesses. First, they are vulnerable to the passage of time. Second, there is always a need for interpretation of rules and principles in the light of circumstances and new technical developments. In particular, there is often a need to balance environmental considerations against such factors as the importance of particular military objectives and the need to save soldiers' lives.

Conclusions: some legal and practical proposals

If negotiating a grand new convention is considered inappropriate, does this mean passively accepting existing law as the best that can be achieved? This is a false choice. This concluding section suggests some courses of action that could usefully be pursued.

There is a built-in danger, in considering law-of-war aspects of environmental damage, of excessive preoccupation with what can be done to protect the environment during actual armed combat. As Paul Szasz has wisely

[69] James P. Terry, "The Environment and the Laws of War: The Impact of Desert Storm," *Naval War C. Rev.* 45(1) (1992), 65 ("The US concern regarding more restrictive environmental provisions is that they could be implemented only at the expense of otherwise lawful military operations – such as attacking targets which require fuel-air explosives (FAE) for their destruction.")

said, "the measures that can be taken before a particular conflict arises, and in any event before an actual combat operation has begun, and especially those that can be taken after the end of the conflict, appear to have been somewhat neglected even though they may well be less controversial and more effective."[70] Some of the following proposals reflect this view.

FOCUS ON EXISTING LEGAL PROVISIONS

There remains a need to draw attention to the wide range of existing provisions (extending well beyond those that explicitly mention the environment), and their actual or potential relevance to environmental protection in military operations. At the same time, there is a need to ensure effective implementation of existing law. The law's purposes, principles, and content need to be properly incorporated into the teaching of international law and relations; into military manuals and training; and into the minds and practices of political leaders, diplomats, and international civil servants.

NEW AGREEMENTS ON SPECIFIC ISSUES

Within the law-of-war framework, there is a strong case for concentrating any negotiations, not on a grand overall convention, but on agreements on specific issues. This was done in the case of the two agreements of 1996 and 1997 on landmines. Future possible topics for such negotiations could include the use and disposal of environmentally harmful substances in weapons and other military equipment, that is, weapons that happen to contain hazardous substances, as distinct from weapons which use the harmful qualities of such substances for their effect. A possible example is depleted uranium in munitions.

WIDER ADHERENCE TO EXISTING TREATIES

While some agreements that bear on environmental protection in war have achieved near-universal formal adherence from states, others have not. Encouraging non-party states to become parties is not a simple matter. It is often merely code language for encouraging the United States to become a party to Protocol I. Advocacy of US participation in this and

[70] Paul Szasz, "Comment: The Existing Legal Framework, Protecting the Environment During Armed Conflict," in Grunawalt et al., *Protection of the Environment*, p. 284.

certain other treaties on the law of war is likely to fail if it is not based on an understanding of the reasons why the United States has chosen not to ratify these treaties. However, many considerations, not limited to environmental issues, point to the conclusion that the United States should reconsider its refusal to ratify Protocol I. In particular, the United States risks becoming isolated in NATO on this matter. Apart from the United States and France (which is likely to ratify before long), the only NATO member that is not a party to Protocol I is Turkey. Since in practice the US armed forces take the Protocol seriously, ratifying the agreement with reservations, as many NATO allies have done, would be the sensible course.

WARTIME APPLICATION OF PEACETIME ENVIRONMENTAL LAW

To what extent are peacetime environmental agreements and national environmental laws formally applicable, or at least in practice applied, to the activities of armed forces, including during armed conflicts and military operations? The question has two main aspects: to what extent do peacetime environmental obligations persist during wartime between (1) opposing belligerents, and (2) belligerents and neutrals? There is already an extensive if disparate body of writing on this question;[71] and, as noted, the International Court of Justice touched on it in the 1996 Advisory Opinion on the *Legality of the Threat or Use of Nuclear Weapons*. More examination is required, especially of actual practice on the continued application of treaties during armed conflicts.

INVESTIGATION AND ASSISTANCE

There is a need for systematic investigation of environmental damage in war, especially where such damage is associated with serious effects on people, whether the war concerned was international or largely internal. For example, more than a decade after the end of the Iran–Iraq War of 1980–88, there is a need for fuller investigation and assistance to victims in the affected areas of both countries. There has been a notable lack of follow-up of Iraq's March 1988 use of chemical weapons inside Iraq

---

[71] An admirable and judicious summary of various views on the role of peacetime environmental prescriptions during armed conflict is in Schmitt, "Green War," at 36–41; see also Silja Vöneky, "Peacetime Environmental Law as a Basis of State Responsibility for Environmental Damage Caused by War," chapter 7 in this volume.

against the Kurdish-inhabited town of Halabja and nearby settlements, an attack which took place in the context of the Iran–Iraq war. There continues to be a hideous health problem there, with evidence of high rates of stillbirths and deformities. Very little international assistance is reaching the inhabitants; the extent to which the area itself is or is not contaminated is not known; and important evidence of the effects of chemical weapons is being lost. All this has not been on the agenda of any major international body – not the UN Security Council, nor UNSCOM, nor the World Health Organization (WHO). Developing a culture of investigation and assistance will require care to avoid, to the maximum extent possible, perceptions of political bias. Since Iraq has made strong complaints about the environmental effects of depleted uranium in weapons used by Coalition forces in the 1990–91 Gulf War, and whatever the skepticism may be among Western military experts, it would be right to provide for investigation and assistance regarding this issue.

WARTIME AND POSTWAR ENVIRONMENTAL CLEAN-UP EFFORTS

There has been little exploration of the extent to which wartime as well as postwar environmental clean-up efforts can have legal and physical protection. Such efforts, which face obvious difficulties, may involve a wide variety of highly specialized personnel drawn from different professions, agencies, and nationalities. A legal basis for protection of postwar and (to a lesser extent) wartime clean-up efforts can be found in some provisions on humanitarian relief efforts in the 1949 Geneva Conventions; in Protocol I, including its provisions on civil defense workers; and in the Protocols on Mines annexed to the 1980 UN Convention on Certain Conventional Weapons. The 1994 UN Convention on the Safety of United Nations and Associated Personnel[72] provides one further legal basis for protection of such efforts.

INTERNATIONAL PEACEKEEPING FORCES

Should international peacekeeping forces have particular responsibilities for preventing and minimizing environmental damage? There are some

---

[72] Convention on the Safety of United Nations and Associated Personnel, reprinted in *I.L.M.* 34 (1995), 482–93; *U.K. Misc.* 23 (1996), Cm. 3363.

precedents for UN peacekeeping forces exercising such a role. In 1992, fighting in the former Yugoslavia involved a risk of the Peruca dam being breached, which could have led to major loss of life downstream. The local UN Protection Force (UNPROFOR) commander took action. Subsequently, in Resolution 779 of October 6, 1992, the UN Security Council stated that it "approves the report of the Secretary-General including the steps taken to ensure the control of the Peruca dam by the UN Protection Force." This ex post facto mandate illustrates the way in which environmental issues have entered into the work of peacekeeping forces in practice, in advance of formal legal provision for them.

INTERNATIONAL MILITARY ENFORCEMENT OPERATIONS

Similarly, should international military enforcement operations – whether under UN, alliance, or national control – have specific instructions or rules of engagement to minimize environmental damage? During the naval enforcement operations in the Adriatic during the war in the former Yugoslavia, the NATO/WEU forces were successful in finding means of stopping sanctions-busting oil tankers without threatening to sink them and thereby create a maritime oil hazard. Such experiences, which probably owe more to common sense than to law, need to become more widely known as examples of international good practice.[73]

In summary, this chapter has argued that the existing international legal basis for environmental protection in armed conflicts is a stronger starting point than is sometimes supposed. Its limitations, which concern deficiencies in their content and difficulties in securing implementation, could not easily be eliminated by trying to draw up a new overall treaty on the subject. On this basis, the chapter suggests instead the following approaches: drawing attention to the wide range of existing legal provisions; negotiating agreements on specific issues, rather than on the environment as a grand abstraction; encouraging states to become parties to certain treaties to which they are not yet parties, which means raising the touchy subject of US ratification of Protocol I and several other treaties; exploring

---

[73] For a useful survey of environmental issues in both peacekeeping and enforcement operations, see James A. Burger, "Environmental Aspects of Non-international Conflicts: The Experience in Former Yugoslavia," in Grunawalt et al., *Protection of the Environment*, pp. 333–45; see also the ensuing comments and discussion at pp. 346–80.

further the application of peacetime environmental law in war; developing a stronger international culture of investigation and action following environmental destruction in war; extending protection to wartime environmental clean-up efforts; and considering whether international peacekeeping forces and international military enforcement efforts should have specific authority to limit environmental damage arising from hostilities.

3

WAR AND THE ENVIRONMENT: FAULT LINES IN THE PRESCRIPTIVE LANDSCAPE

MICHAEL N. SCHMITT

> [W]e must face the fact that war and its forms result from the ideas, emotions and conditions prevailing at the time.
>
> CARL VON CLAUSEWITZ[1]

The rise of normative consciousness

Throughout history, man has caused tremendous damage to the environment during armed conflict. In the seventeenth century, for instance, the Dutch flooded their own lands by destroying dikes to arrest the onslaught of foreign invaders.[2] More recently, Allied attacks on Romanian oilfields and facilities during World Wars I and II – in particular those at Ploesti – seriously damaged the surrounding terrain.[3] Despite these and the countless other incidents that could be cited to illustrate war's oft-devastating environmental impact, only with the Vietnam conflict did the international community begin to focus seriously on this reality.[4] Von Clausewitz's

---

[1] Carl von Clausewitz, *On War*, book VIII, Michael Howard and Peter Paret (eds.), indexed edn. (Princeton, N.J.: Princeton Univ. Press, 1984), p. 580.

[2] On these and other environmentally destructive events, see Yves Sandoz et al. (eds.), *International Committee of the Red Cross, Commentary on the Additional Protocols of 8 June 1977 to the Geneva Conventions of 12 August 1949* (Geneva: M. Nijhoff, 1987), pp. 666–67.

[3] On the World War I destruction of the Romanian oilfields to keep them from the invading Central Powers forces, see Charles R. M. F. Cruttwell, *A History of the Great War, 1914–1918* (Oxford: Clarendon Press, 1934), pp. 297–98. On the World War II raids, see generally James Dugan and Carroll Stewart, *Ploesti: The Great Ground–Air Battle of 1 August 1943* (Washington, D.C.: Brassey's, 1998).

[4] For a comprehensive account of environmental damage during the Vietnam conflict, see Arthur H. Westing, *Ecological Consequences of the Second Indochina War* (Stockholm: Almqvist & Wiksell Int'l, 1976); see also Richard Carruthers, "International Controls on the Impact on the Environment of Wartime Operations," *Envtl. & Plan. L.J.* 10 (1993), 38, 40.

classic maxim about the context of war was soon to be validated vis-à-vis the environment and the normative architecture that would emerge to protect it.

It was not the scale of environmental destruction caused during that struggle which attracted attention; indeed, far greater devastation had been wrought in earlier conflicts. Instead, general anti-war fervor, growing environmental awareness, and the vivid images of what was occurring made possible by televised mass media operated synergistically to awaken much of the collective conscience.[5] The normative result was twofold: (1) the conclusion of the Environmental Modification Convention (ENMOD), a treaty limiting use of environmental modification as a method of warfare;[6] and (2) inclusion in the 1977 Additional Protocol I to the Geneva Conventions of 1949 of two provisions that limit the environmental damage permitted during international armed conflict.[7]

In the years following these tentative first steps, the issue faded into relative obscurity – until Iraqi leaders began threatening environmentally catastrophic actions if Coalition forces attempted to expel them from Kuwait after their 1990 invasion of that country.[8] In January 1991, the

---

[5] Cf. George H. Aldrich, "Prospects for the United States Ratification of Additional Protocol I to the 1949 Geneva Conventions," *Am. J. Int'l L.* 85 (1991), 1, 14 (noting concerns in official Washington circles, such as when the State Department's Office of the Legal Advisor argued against use of defoliants beyond South Vietnamese and Laotian territory – their use in South Vietnam was consensual – in order to avoid creating any arguable precedent for their use by others).

[6] Convention on the Prohibition of Military or Any Other Hostile Use of Environmental Modification Techniques (done at New York, Dec. 10, 1976; entered into force, Oct. 5, 1978; for the United States, Jan. 17, 1980), 31 U.S.T. 333, T.I.A.S. No. 9614, reprinted in *I.L.M.* 16 (1977), 88. That ENMOD was a reaction to the experiences of the Vietnam conflict is clear from the Congressional hearings on the Convention. See Hearings to Hear Testimony on the Convention on the Prohibition of Military or Any Other Hostile Use of Environmental Modification Techniques Before the Senate Comm. on Foreign Relations, 96th Cong. (1979); Environmental Modification Treaty: Hearings on the Convention on the Prohibition of Military or Any Other Use of Environmental Modification Techniques Before the Senate Comm. on Foreign Relations, 95th Cong. (1978).

[7] Protocol Additional to the Geneva Conventions of August 12, 1949, and Relating to the Protection of Victims of International Armed Conflicts (Protocol I) (done at Geneva, June 8, 1977; entered into force, Dec. 7, 1978), Arts. 35(3) and 55, reprinted in *I.L.M.* 16 (1977), 1391.

[8] "Partial Text of Statement by Iraq's Revolution Command Council," Reuters, Sept. 23, 1990, available in LEXIS, News Library, Allnws File (quoting Saddam Hussein as announcing that "[t]he oil areas in Saudi Arabia and in other parts of the States of the region and all the oil installations will be rendered incapable of responding to the needs of those who came to us as occupiers in order to usurp our sovereignty, dignity and wealth"); Gayle Young, "Cheney: 'Clock is Ticking' for War," UPI, Dec. 23, 1990, available in LEXIS, News Library, Allnws File (quoting Iraqi Defense Minister, Said Tuma Abbas, as threatening: "Cheney will see how land burns under the feet of his troops and stooges").

Iraqis made good their threat when they began pumping oil into the Persian Gulf and setting Kuwaiti oil wells ablaze.[9] The Iraqi actions generated near universal condemnation, but very little tangible normative progress in addressing environmental damage during hostilities. To date, no one has been held culpable for the environmentally deleterious Iraqi actions, though the United Nations has endeavored to impose state responsibility to some extent through the mechanism of a Compensation Commission (UNCC).[10] Interestingly, the basis for Iraqi liability under that program was the wrongful occupation of Kuwait – a violation of the *ius ad bellum*, specifically UN Charter Article 2(4) – and damage ensuing therefrom, rather than any violation of an environmental

---

[9] For an analysis of the Iraqi releases of oil, see US Dep't of Defense, *Conduct of the Persian Gulf War: Final Report to Congress* (Washington, D.C.: US Gov't Printing Office, 1992), p. 624 (estimating that Iraq dumped 7–9 million barrels of oil – about forty-two times the size of the *Exxon Valdez* spill – into the Gulf); see also Kuwait Environmental Protection Council, *State of the Environment Report: A Case Study of Iraqi Regime Crimes Against the Environment* (1991), pp. 29–33; William M. Arkin, "The Environmental Threat of Military Actions," in Richard J. Grunawalt et al. (eds.), *Protection of the Environment During Armed Conflict* (Newport, R.I.: Naval War College, 1996), pp. 116, 119 (noting that Iraq practiced its destructive acts in December 1990 by detonating six oil wells and igniting oil basins in occupied Kuwait). For an analysis of Iraq's destruction and ignition of Kuwaiti oil wells, see US Dep't of Defense, *Conduct of the Persian Gulf War*, p. 624 (Iraq damaged or destroyed 590 oil well heads; of these, 508 were set ablaze, while the 82 others were damaged so as to allow oil to flow freely from them); Sylvia A. Earle, "Persian Gulf Pollution: Assessing the Damage One Year Later," *Nat'l Geo.* (Feb. 1992), 122 (estimating that the fires generated a level of heat equal to 500 forest fires and produced daily soot equivalent to 10 percent of that produced worldwide through biomass burning).

[10] SC Res. 674, UN SCOR, 45th Sess., 2951st mtg., para. 8, UN Doc. S/RES/674 (1990), reprinted in *I.L.M.* 29 (1990), 1561, 1563 (stating that "under international law [Iraq] is liable for any loss, damage or injury arising in regard to Kuwait and third States, and their nationals and corporations, as a result of the invasion and illegal occupation of Kuwait"); SC Res. 686, UN SCOR, 46th Sess., 2978th mtg., UN Doc. S/RES/686 (1991), para. 2(b), reprinted in *I.L.M.* 30 (1991), 568, 569 (demanding that Iraq "accept in principle its liability under international law for any loss, damage, or injury" resulting from the Kuwait occupation); SC Res. 687, UN SCOR, 46th Sess., 2981st mtg., UN Doc. S/RES/687 (1991), paras. 16–19, reprinted in *I.L.M.* 30 (1991), 847, 852 (reaffirming Iraq's liability in the ceasefire Resolution, which also urged creation of an organization to handle claims deriving from the occupation, with payment coming from a fund capitalized by an Iraqi oil export levy); SC Res. 692, UN SCOR, 46th Sess., 2987th mtg., UN Doc. S/RES/692 (1991), reprinted in *I.L.M.* 30 (1991), 864 (establishing the UNCC). For discussions on the UNCC, see Ronald J. Bettauer, "The United Nations Compensation Commission – Developments Since October 1992," *Am. J. Int'l L.* 89 (1995), 416; John R. Crook, "The United Nations Compensation Commission – A New Structure to Enforce State Responsibility," *Am. J. Int'l L.* 87 (1993), 144. As of April 30, 1997, the Commission had received 2,640,503 claims for a total of over $20 billion. The filing period for most claims expired in February 1997. For current information on the activities of the Commission, see its home page at http://193.135.136.30/uncc/start.htm.

prescription.[11] Not surprisingly, the environmental trauma suffered during the short war led to no new "hard law" on the subject.

Nevertheless, the events did ignite a firestorm of international debate over the legal regime's efficacy. As early as June 1991 a conference sponsored by Greenpeace, the London School of Economics, and the British Centre for Defence Studies convened and considered a notional "Fifth Geneva Convention on the Environment."[12] Soon thereafter, the Canadian government sponsored a similar conference,[13] as did the International Council of Environmental Law in cooperation with the Commission on Environmental Law of the International Union for the Conservation of Nature and Natural Resources.[14] In the years that followed, additional environmental conferences were held under the auspices of the United Nations[15] and the US Naval War College.[16] Contemporaneously, the Sixth Committee (Legal) of the UN General Assembly and the International Committee of the Red Cross were studying the topic and both issued reports thereon.[17]

[11] See SC Res. 687, para. 16 ("Iraq . . . is liable under international law for any direct loss, damage, including environmental damage and the depletion of natural resources, or injury to foreign Governments, nationals and corporations, as a result of Iraq's unlawful invasion and occupation of Kuwait"); see also Compensation Commission, Governing Council Decision No. 7, UN Doc. S/AC.26/1991/7/REV. 1, para. 34, reprinted in United Nations, *The United Nations and the Iraq–Kuwait Conflict, 1990–1996* (1996), p. 429 (holding that Iraq would also be responsible for damage caused by Coalition forces because, but for the initial Iraqi wrongfulness, such damage would not have occurred).

[12] Glen Plant (ed.), *Environmental Protection and the Law of War* (1992) (including Conference proceedings and the Draft Convention). For an earlier proposal, see "Proposed International Convention on the Crime of Ecocide," reprinted in Richard A. Falk, "Environmental Warfare and Ecocide – Facts, Appraisal, and Proposals," *Bull. Peace Proposals* 4 (1973), 80, 93–95 (1973) (the Emergency Conference Against Environmental Warfare in Indochina, held in 1972 in Stockholm, adopted this Convention on Ecocide).

[13] See Michael N. Schmitt, "Green War: An Assessment of the Environmental Law of International Armed Conflict," *Yale J. Int'l L.* 22 (1997), 1, 23–24.

[14] International Council of Environmental Law, *Law Concerning the Protection of the Environment in Times of Armed Conflict, Final Report of Consultation of Dec. 13–15, 1991* (the Munich Conference).

[15] See Rio Declaration on Environment and Development, UN Doc. A/CONF.151/REV. 1 (1992), prin. 24, reprinted in *I.L.M.* 31 (1992), 874. ("Warfare is inherently destructive of sustainable development. States shall therefore respect international law providing protection for the environment in times of armed conflict and cooperate in its further development, as necessary.")

[16] Grunawalt et al., *Protection of the Environment* (conference proceedings).

[17] On the activities of the Sixth Committee, see "United Nations Decade of International Law: Report of the Secretary-General on the Protection of the Environment in Times of Armed Conflict," UN GAOR, 48th Sess., Provisional Agenda Item 144, UN Doc. A/48/269 (1993); see also the various Summary Records of Meeting, UN Docs. A/C.6/47/SR. (1992); cf. "Protection

At the risk of oversimplification, the sum of this debate appears to be a preponderant assessment of prescriptive adequacy; therefore, so the prevailing view holds, political capital is best spent by ensuring greater accession to and enforcement of the existing law of armed conflict as it applies to both traditional humanitarian interests and the environment.[18] In the aftermath of the Iraqi actions, this is unsurprising. Appalled by Iraqi excesses, the international community, for both visceral and political reasons, *wanted* Saddam Hussein and his cohorts to be guilty of offenses against the environment. Operating within an essentially positivist legal culture, this required a search for "rules that had been broken." Of course, the international community looked where it had in the past: Hague law (relating to protected persons, such as civilians and prisoners of war), Geneva law (governing methods and means of combat, occupation, and neutrality),[19] customary law, and, to a more limited extent, Protocol I. Given this cognitive predilection towards finding violations, violations were found. But, of course, the individual culprits have thus far escaped personal punishment. This was explained away by alleging a failure of that classic scapegoat of international law – enforcement.

It is the purpose of this chapter to challenge this characterization by highlighting existing fault lines in the prescriptive landscape. To do so, the core content of the relevant law of armed conflict will first be briefly set forth.[20] The chapter then identifies four fault lines in that corpus of law

of the Environment in Times of Armed Conflict," Letter from the Permanent Minister of the Hashemite Kingdom of Jordan and of the United States of America to the Chairman of the Sixth Committee (Sept. 28, 1992), UN GAOR 6th Comm., 47th Sess., Agenda Item 136, UN Doc. A/C.6/47/3 (1992) (providing a useful catalogue of relevant customary and conventional law). The ICRC "Guidelines" are printed in UN GAOR, 49th Sess., Annex, Agenda Item 139, 49–53; see also Hans-Peter Gasser, "For a Better Protection of the Natural Environment in Armed Conflict: A Proposal for Action," *Am. J. Int'l L.* 89 (1995), 637, 641–43.

[18] "United Nations Decade of International Law: Report of the Secretary-General," para. 40; e.g., John H. McNeill, "Protection of the Environment in Time of Armed Conflict: Environmental Protection in Military Practice," in Grunawalt et al., *Protection of the Environment*, p. 542 ("the existing legal regime is adequate in concept, and adequate in terms of its infrastructure. What is lacking is, of course, enforcement") (see also comments by John Norton Moore and Dieter Fleck in the same volume); see generally Adam Roberts, "The Law of War and Environmental Damage," chapter 2 in this volume.

[19] For a discussion of the international instruments that fall into the categories of Hague and Geneva law, and of those that display elements of both, see Frederic DeMulinen, *Handbook on the Law of War for Armed Forces* (1987), pp. 3–4.

[20] This chapter does not address the separate issue of the applicability of peacetime prescriptions during international armed conflict. On their survivability, see Silja Vöneky, "Peacetime Environmental Law as a Basis of State Responsibility for Environmental Damage Caused by

that render it, despite mainstream assertions to the contrary, less than adequate, perhaps even somewhat quixotic. Finally, a few tentative thoughts on possible curative approaches are offered.[21]

The prescriptive landscape

ENVIRONMENT-SPECIFIC TREATY LAW

The catalogue of conventional law drafted with the specific intent of protecting the environment during hostilities is slim, consisting entirely of the two treaties cited above: Protocol I and ENMOD. Within the former instrument, there are but two relevant provisions, Articles 35(3) and 55(1). At first reading, each appears to provide substantial protections for the environment.

> **Article 35(3).** Basic rules
> It is prohibited to employ methods or means of warfare which are intended, or may be expected, to cause widespread, long-term and severe damage to the natural environment.

> **Article 55.** Protection of the natural environment
> 1. Care shall be taken in warfare to protect the natural environment against widespread, long-term and severe damage. This protection includes a prohibition of the use of methods or means of warfare which are intended or may be expected to cause such damage to the natural environment and thereby to prejudice the health or survival of the population.
> 2. Attacks against the natural environment by way of reprisals are prohibited.

The distinction between the two is subtle. Article 35(3) operates along a continuum. At a certain point, damage to the environment during an armed conflict may rise to the level of being "widespread, long-term and severe." When that happens, the method or means of warfare causing it becomes prohibited. There are no other factors, such as the military

---

War," chapter 7 in this volume; Michael Bothe, "The Protection of the Environment in Times of Armed Conflict: Legal Rules, Uncertainty, Deficiencies and Possible Developments," *Germ. Y.B. Int'l L.* 34 (1991), 54, 59; see also *Techt v. Hughes*, 128 N.E. 185, 191 (N.Y.), cert. denied, 254 U.S. 643 (1920) (Cardozo, J.) ("[i]nternational law to-day does not preserve treaties or annul them, regardless of the effects produced. It deals with such problems pragmatically, preserving or annulling as the necessities of war exact. It establishes standards, but it does not fetter itself with rules").

[21] This assessment develops ideas originally presented in Schmitt, "Green War."

necessity of the operation or the amount of harm sustained by civilians and civilian property, that come into play. By contrast, Article 55, which also acts on a continuum, adds the further requirement that the environmental damage prejudice the health or survival of the population; if it does not, Article 55(1) is of no effect, regardless of how much the environment suffers. By January 18, 2000, there were 156 parties to Protocol I, including most potential coalition partners of the United States such as the United Kingdom (January 1998). The United States, Iraq, and Iran are among notable non-parties.[22] The fact that key military powers remain outside the treaty regime is particularly important, because its environmental provisions are not considered declaratory of customary international law.[23]

Whereas the Protocol I provisions limit effect on the environment, ENMOD disallows certain modifications of it as a means of warfare. The operative provision is Article I:

Article I.
1. Each State Party to this Convention undertakes not to engage in military or any other hostile use of environmental modification techniques having widespread, long-lasting or severe effects as the means of destruction, damage or injury to any other State Party.
2. Each State Party to this Convention undertakes not to assist, encourage or induce any State, group of States or international organization to engage in activities contrary to the provisions of paragraph 1 of this article.

The narrow scope of the prohibition is apparent. It is limited to situations in which the requisite level of harm results from the use of the environment as a "weapon." Specifically, by the terms of the convention the prohibitory effect only extends to a "technique for changing – through the deliberate manipulation of natural processes – the dynamics, composition

---

[22] ICRC documents web site, http://www.icrc.org/unicc/ihl_eng.nsf/web?OpenNavigator (accessed April 5, 2000); see also Abraham D. Sofaer in "Agora: The US Decision Not to Ratify Protocol I to the Geneva Conventions on the Protection of War Victims," *Am. J. Int'l L.* 82 (1988), 784.

[23] "United Nations Decade of International Law: Report of the Secretary-General," p. 5. For a non-official, but generally considered authoritative catalogue of the Protocol I provisions considered declaratory of customary international law, see Michael J. Matheson, "Session One: The United States Position on the Relation of Customary International Law to the 1977 Protocols Additional to the 1949 Geneva Conventions," *Am. U. J. Int'l L. & Pol'y* 2 (1987), 419; see also International and Operational Law Division, Office of the Judge Advocate General, Dep't of the Air Force, *Operations Law Deployment Deskbook*, tab 12 (summarizing Protocol I and the US position thereon).

or structure of the earth, including its biota, lithosphere, hydrosphere, and atmosphere, or of outer space."[24] The lack of a requirement that the environment be the object of damage or destruction mitigates ENMOD's narrowness to a degree: so long as the environmental modification causes widespread, long-lasting, or severe effects, the convention has been breached. As of April 5, 2000, sixty-eight states have ratified ENMOD, including the United States, Russia, and the United Kingdom. France and China are not parties.[25] Note that Iraq, Iran, and Syria are signatories, but have not ratified ENMOD. As signatories, such states are obligated to do nothing inconsistent with the terms of the convention until they have expressed an intent not to ratify it.[26]

GENERAL TREATY LAW

The paucity of environment-specific treaty law is partially mitigated by more generally applicable provisions scattered throughout the law of armed conflict. While less specific, such provisions preserve the environment through broad protections of civilians and civilian property and restrictions on the methods and means of warfare. The 1907 Hague and 1949 Geneva Conventions, Protocol I, and the Chemical and Conventional Weapons Conventions contain the core prescriptions in this category. Lest they be dismissed as peripheral, it must be emphasized that this second tier of treaty law fills consequential voids left by the environment-specific rules of Protocol I and ENMOD.

The Fourth Hague Convention[27] contains a number of provisions with substantive (albeit in the case of some, peripheral) impact on military

---

[24] ENMOD, Art. II; see also "Understanding Relating to Article II, Report of the Conference of the Committee on Disarmament," UN GAOR, 31st Sess., Supp. No. 27, UN Doc. A/31/27 (1976), pp. 91–92, reprinted in Dietrich Schindler and Jiří Toman (eds.), *The Laws of Armed Conflicts*, 3rd edn. (Dordrecht: M. Nijhoff/Geneva: H. Dunant Institute, 1988), p. 168 (non-exclusive examples include earthquakes, tsunamis, an upset in a region's ecological balance, changes in weather patterns, changes in climate patterns, changes in the state of the ozone layer, and changes in the state of the ionosphere).

[25] ICRC Treaty Database, http://www.icrc.org/ihl (accessed April 5, 2000).

[26] Vienna Convention on the Law of Treaties (done at Vienna, May 23, 1969; entered into force, Jan. 27, 1980), 1155 U.N.T.S. 331, Art. 18, reprinted in *I.L.M.* 8 (1969), 679.

[27] Convention (No. IV) Respecting the Laws and Customs of War on Land, with Annex of Regulations (done at The Hague, Oct. 18, 1907; entered into force, Jan. 26, 1910), 36 Stat. 2277, 205 Consol. T.S. 277.

operations affecting the environment.[28] Three are commonly cited as being normatively meaningful in the environmental context. Article 23(g) has the widest application: "[I]t is especially forbidden . . . To destroy or seize the enemy's property, unless such destruction or seizure be imperatively demanded by the necessities of war."[29] Many have charged that Iraq's actions in the Gulf War violated this article, a codification of the customary international law principle of military necessity.[30]

The second provision of Hague IV providing consequential environmental protection is Article 55, which requires a belligerent occupying enemy territory to safeguard public buildings, real estate, forests, and agricultural estates in accordance with the rules of usufruct. This principle allows use of the property by the occupying power, but no permanent alteration or destruction of it. Thus, an occupier may reasonably exploit natural resources in occupied territory, but may not act irresponsibly or maliciously in doing so. Applying the provision to the occupation of Kuwait, for example, damage to government-owned lands caused by the oil releases would violate the usufructory obligations of the Iraqi occupiers.[31]

A third provision of Hague IV that could prove useful in protecting the environment is the Martens Clause contained in the preamble, which is generally considered to be customary international law:

[28] See *ibid.*, Art. 22 ("the right of belligerents to adopt means of injuring the enemy is not unlimited"); Geoffrey Best, "The Historical Evolution of Cultural Norms Relating to War and the Environment," in Arthur H. Westing (ed.), *Cultural Norms, War and Environment* (Oxford and New York: Oxford Univ. Press, 1988), p. 18 (asserting, before the Gulf War, that the provision is environmentally relevant); see also Hague IV, Art. 23(e) (forbidding the employment of "arms, projectiles or material calculated to cause unnecessary suffering"); Leslie C. Green, "'Unnecessary Suffering,' Weapons Control and the Law," in Leslie C. Green, *Essays on the Modern Law of War*, 2nd edn. (Ardsley, N.Y.: Transnational Pub., 1998), p. 329.

[29] For analysis rejecting the contention that this provision is applicable only to state property, see US Dep't of the Army, *International Law*, vol. II, Pamphlet No. 27-161-2 (1962), p. 174; Jean S. Pictet (ed.), *International Committee of the Red Cross, Commentary: Geneva Convention Relative to the Protection of Civilian Persons in Time of War* (Geneva: ICRC, 1958), p. 301.

[30] E.g., Michael Bothe, "Environmental Destruction as a Method of Warfare: Do We Need More Law?" *Disarmament* 15 (1992), 101, 104 (arguing that the Iraqi actions violated this provision of Hague IV); US Dep't of Defense, *Conduct of the Persian Gulf War*, pp. 623–24; James P. Terry, "The Environment and the Laws of War: The Impact of Desert Storm," *Naval War C. Rev.* (1992), 61, 63 (commenting that if Iraq had observed Hague IV there would not have been any significant environmental harm done to Kuwait); but see Leslie C. Green, "The Environment and the Law of Conventional Warfare," *Can. Y.B. Int'l L.* 29 (1991), 222 (noting that Iraqi actions may well have had military reasons).

[31] See US Dep't of Defense, *Conduct of the Persian Gulf War*, pp. 623–24.

Until a more complete code of laws has been issued, the high Contracting Parties deem it expedient to declare that, in cases not included in the Regulations adopted by them, the inhabitants and the belligerents remain under the protection and the rule of the principles of the laws of nations, as they result from the usages established among civilized peoples, from the laws of humanity, and from the dictates of public conscience.[32]

This clause, which is also found in Protocol I,[33] operates in the absence, or during the development, of more specific prescriptive norms. Thus, to the extent that customary or conventional law falls short in terms of environmental protection, resort may be made to the "laws of humanity" and "dictates of public conscience" to provide some marginal degree of protection.

The provision found in the 1949 Geneva Conventions considered most applicable to the environment is Article 53 of the Fourth Convention:[34]

Article 53.
Any destruction by the Occupying Power of real or personal property belonging individually or collectively to private persons, or to the State, or to other public authorities, or to social or cooperative organizations, is prohibited, except where such destruction is rendered absolutely necessary by military operations.

Like Article 23(g) of Hague IV, it codifies the principle of military necessity; it is also – as with Hague IV Article 55 – limited to actions of an occupier in occupied territory. Iraqi acts in occupied Kuwait during the Gulf War are widely alleged to have violated this provision.[35] Of particular importance is the fact that pursuant to Article 147 of Geneva IV, violations of Article 53 constitute "grave breaches" whenever the destruction caused is extensive, unjustified by military necessity, and carried out wantonly.[36] Characterization as a grave breach requires all parties to the convention to

---

[32] Hague IV, preamble, Art. 22.   [33] Protocol I, Art. 1, para. 2.

[34] Geneva Convention Relative to the Protection of Civilian Persons in Time of War (Geneva IV) (done at Geneva, Aug. 12, 1949; entered into force, Oct. 21, 1950), Art. 53, 6 U.S.T. 3516, 75 U.N.T.S. 287.

[35] E.g., Luis Kutner and Ved P. Nanda, "Draft Indictment of Saddam Hussein," *Denv. J. Int'l L. & Pol'y* 20 (1991), 91, 93 (draft indictment of Saddam Hussein prepared for the UN Secretary-General by the Commission for International Due Process of Law); Adam Roberts, "Environmental Issues in International Armed Conflict: The Experience of the 1991 Gulf War," in Grunawalt et al., *Protection of the Environment*, pp. 222, 250 (Iraqi actions violated Article 53).

[36] Geneva IV, Art. 147; see also US Dep't of Defense, *Conduct of the Persian Gulf War*, p. 624 (Iraqi actions constituted grave breaches); Roberts, "Environmental Issues in International Armed Conflict," p. 250 (same); Bothe, "Environmental Destruction," 104 (same).

search for offenders (or those who have ordered the offenses) and either initiate enforcement proceedings themselves (regardless of the accused's nationality) or transfer the prisoner for trial to another party.[37]

Like its progenitors of 1949, Protocol I contains numerous provisions that provide indirect, though substantial, safeguards for the environment. For instance, Article 35(1), expressing the customary law limitation on the right of belligerents to choose methods or means of warfare, Article 35(2), proscribing actions causing unnecessary suffering, and Article 51, forbidding indiscriminate attacks,[38] all furnish environmental protection in specific contexts. However, the seminal environmentally relevant provisions in general treaty law are Articles 52, 51(5)(b), and 57(2)(a)(iii) of Protocol I.

Article 52 both forbids making civilian objects the "object of attack or of reprisals" and restricts attacks "strictly to military objectives."[39] The term "civilian objects" is defined broadly as "all objects which are not military objectives";[40] military objectives are "those objects which by their nature, location, purpose or use make an effective contribution to military action and whose total or partial destruction, capture or neutralization, in the circumstances ruling at the time, offers a definite military advantage."[41] The term "civilian object" can reasonably be interpreted as including all components of the environment – land, air, flora, fauna, atmosphere, high seas, etc. – that do not present an advantage (such as cover) to a military operation. For example, to justify the "attacks" on the Kuwaiti oil wells convincingly, Iraq would have had to articulate the definite military advantages yielded thereby; those advantages could be neither speculative, nor non-military in nature.

Assuming that an opponent is not directly attacking the environment, Articles 51(5)(b) and 57(2)(a)(iii) – the first codifications of the customary law principle of proportionality – are at the heart of environmental protection.[42] They provide:

---

[37] Geneva IV, Art. 146.

[38] For a definition of "indiscriminate attacks," see Protocol I, Art. 51, para. 4 ("Indiscriminate attacks are: (a) those which are not directed at a specific military objective; (b) those which employ a method or means of combat which cannot be directed at a specific military objective; or (c) those which employ a method or means of combat the effects of which cannot be limited as required by this Protocol . . .").

[39] *Ibid.*, Art. 52, paras. 1–2. [40] *Ibid.*, Art. 52, para. 1. [41] *Ibid.*, Art. 52, para. 2.

[42] For an excellent analysis of proportionality in the context of Protocol I, see William J. Fenrick, "The Rule of Proportionality and Protocol I in Conventional Warfare," *Mil. L. Rev.* 98 (1982), 91; see also Stefan Oeter, "Methods and Means of Combat," in Dieter Fleck (ed.), *The Handbook of Humanitarian Law in Armed Conflicts* (New York: Oxford Univ. Press, 1995), pp. 105, 177–86.

Article 51. Protection of the civilian population

. . .

5. Among others, the following types of attacks are to be considered as indiscriminate:

. . .

(b) an attack which may be expected to cause incidental loss of civilian life, injury to civilians, damage to civilian objects, or a combination thereof, which would be excessive in relation to the concrete and direct military advantage anticipated.

Article 57. Precautions in attack

. . .

2. With respect to attacks, the following precautions shall be taken:
(a) those who plan or decide upon an attack shall:

. . .

(iii) refrain from deciding to launch any attack which may be expected to cause incidental loss of civilian life, injury to civilians, damage to civilian objects, or a combination thereof, which would be excessive to the concrete and direct military advantage anticipated . . .

Restated, collateral damage to civilian objects resulting from an attack must be outweighed by the concrete and direct military advantage that accrues to the attacker before an attack is allowed. Therefore, both mission planners and those executing a mission are obligated to conduct a balancing test in which the quantum and nature of any environmental damage likely to ensue from the military operation is factored in.

Two articles of Protocol I provide substantial indirect environmental protections not found in customary law. The first is Article 54(2):

Article 54. Protection of objects indispensable to the survival of the civilian population

. . .

2. It is prohibited to attack, destroy, remove or render useless objects indispensable to the survival of the civilian population, such as foodstuffs, agricultural areas for the production of foodstuffs, crops, livestock, drinking water installations and supplies and irrigation works, for the specific purpose of denying them for their sustenance value to the civilian population or to the adverse Party, whatever the motive, whether in order to starve out civilians, to cause them to move away, or for any other motive.

Food-producing agricultural areas, crops, livestock, drinking water, irrigation works, and other objects within the coverage of the article are obvious components of the environment, and benefit from the provision's protection if a belligerent's goal is to deny them to the civilian population.[43] Article 54 effectively outlaws scorched earth operations, such as those which occurred during World War II, at least insofar as the actor had the requisite wrongful intent. In one well-known case (related primarily to the customary international law principle of necessity), German General Rendulic was acquitted for destruction he ordered to be committed during the German withdrawal from Norway during World War II. The basis for the acquittal was his reasonable, but mistaken, belief that the destruction was necessary because Soviet forces were chasing him. In fact, they were not.[44] Also note that a state may conduct scorched earth operations on its own territory to deny an invading force sustenance, as the Soviets did in World War II.

The second significant protection unique to Protocol I that provides substantial indirect environmental protections not found in customary law is Article 56:

> **Article 56.** Protection of works and installations containing dangerous forces
> 1. Works or installations containing dangerous forces, namely dams, dykes and nuclear electrical generating stations, shall not be made the object of attack, even where these objects are military objectives, if such attack may cause the release of dangerous forces and consequent severe losses among the civilian population. Other military objectives located at or in the vicinity of these works or installations shall not be made the object of attack if such attack may cause the release of dangerous forces from the works or installations and consequent severe losses among the civilian population.

Obviously, release of the contemplated dangerous forces (e.g., radioactivity or floodwaters) could have dire consequences for the environment. Article 56 does provide an exception to the general prohibition if dams or dikes are used for other than their normal function in regular, significant, and direct support of military operations and attack is the only feasible way of terminating support.[45] When the proposed target is a nuclear electrical generating station, attack is only permissible if the station supplies "electric power in regular, significant and direct support

---

[43] But see Protocol I, Art. 54, para. 3 (exception to the prohibition if the covered objects are used as sustenance solely for the members of the armed forces or in direct support of military actions).

[44] *Hostage Case (US v. List)*, 11 T.W.C. 759 (1950). For a case involving destruction in the Soviet Union, see *High Command Case (US v. Von Leeb)*, 11 T.W.C. 462 (1950).

[45] Protocol I, Art. 56, para. 2(a).

of military operations and if such attack is the only feasible way to terminate such support."[46] Other military objectives in the vicinity of these works and installations can be attacked only when attack is the sole feasible way to arrest their "regular, significant and direct support of military operations."[47] It should be noted that despite assertions to the contrary, the dangerous forces contemplated by the provision do not extend to the release of oil.[48]

Finally, numerous other conventions limit methods and means of warfare that could potentially harm the environment. Among the most important are the Gas Protocol, Biological Weapons Convention, Chemical Weapons Convention, and Certain Conventional Weapons Convention.[49] To different degrees, these treaties limit the use of environmentally harmful weaponry such as chemicals (including herbicides), biologicals, mines, booby traps, and incendiaries. While the prohibitory provisions in each instrument provide the environment with de facto protection, the sole prescription bearing directly on the environment is Article 2(4) of Protocol III of the Certain Conventional Weapons Convention.[50] It disallows making "forests or other kinds of plant cover

---

[46] *Ibid.*, Art. 56, para. 2(b).   [47] *Ibid.*, Art. 56, para. 2(c).

[48] *Official Records of the Diplomatic Conference on the Reaffirmation and Development of International Humanitarian Law Applicable in Armed Conflicts*, vol. 15, para. 326; see also Michael Bothe et al., *New Rules for Victims of Armed Conflicts* (The Hague and Boston: M. Nijhoff, 1982), p. 352; but see William M. Arkin et al., *On Impact: Modern Warfare and the Environment: A Case Study of the Gulf War* (1991), p. 140 ("It is unclear whether oil wells constitute installations containing 'dangerous forces.' The examples given in Protocol I . . . are not meant to be exhaustive, and a liberal construction could say that the release of the force of the oil fires and spills is covered.").

[49] Protocol for the Prohibition of the Use in War of Asphyxiating, Poisonous or other Gases, and of Bacteriological Methods of Warfare (done at Geneva, June 17, 1925; entered into force, Feb. 8, 1928), 26 U.S.T. 571, T.I.A.S. No. 8061, reprinted in *I.L.M.* 14 (1975), 49; Convention on the Prohibition of the Development, Production and Stockpiling of Bacteriological (Biological) and Toxin Weapons and on Their Destruction (done at London, Moscow, and Washington, Apr. 10, 1972; entered into force, Mar. 26, 1975), 26 U.S.T. 583, reprinted in *I.L.M.* 11 (1972), 310; Convention on the Prohibition of the Development, Production, Stockpiling and Use of Chemical Weapons and on Their Destruction (done Jan. 13, 1993), reprinted in *I.L.M.* 32 (1993), 800; Convention on the Prohibition or Restrictions on the Use of Certain Conventional Weapons which may be Deemed to be Excessively Injurious or to Have Indiscriminate Effects (done Oct. 10, 1980), reprinted in *I.L.M.* 19 (1980), 1524 (including a preambular provision stating that "it is prohibited to employ methods or means of warfare which are intended, or may be expected, to cause widespread, long-term and severe damage to the natural environment," which has received little attention in the environmental context).

[50] Protocol (III) on Prohibitions or Restrictions on the Use of Incendiary Weapons, reprinted in *I.L.M.* 19 (1980), 1523.

the object of attack by incendiary weapons except when such natural elements are used to cover, conceal or camouflage combatants or other military objectives, or are themselves military objectives." Other conventions that have some environmental effect include the Cultural Property Convention and the World Heritage Convention.[51]

The most recent progress in safeguarding the environment during armed conflict is the prohibition on "widespread, long term and severe damage to the natural environment which would be clearly excessive in relation to the concrete and direct military advantage anticipated" found in Article 8 of the International Criminal Court Statute, adopted in Rome in July 1998.[52] This Statute was not signed by the United States, albeit for reasons unrelated to its environmental provision, and it will not come into effect until sixty states have ratified it. Yet, its importance with regard to environmental damage during armed conflict cannot be overstated, for it articulates both a substantive norm (based in great part on that articulated in Protocol I) and sets forth an enforcement methodology.

CUSTOMARY INTERNATIONAL LAW

Arguably, customary international law, especially the principles of military necessity and proportionality, fills much of the prescriptive lacunae in the conventional law mélange.[53] Customary international law is particularly important in the law of armed conflict because of the non-party status of certain pivotal global players, most notably the United States, in the relevant treaty regimes.

Military necessity is the principle that forbids destructive acts unnecessary to secure a military advantage, in other words, acts of wanton destruction.[54] The classic formulation is that expressed by the US Military

---

[51] Convention for the Protection of Cultural Property in the Event of Armed Conflict (done at The Hague, May 14, 1954; entered into force, Aug. 7, 1956), 249 U.N.T.S. 240; Convention for the Protection of the World Cultural and Natural Heritage (done Nov. 16, 1972), 1037 U.N.T.S. 151, reprinted in *I.L.M.* 11 (1972), 1358.
[52] Statute of the International Criminal Court (done at Rome, July 17, 1998), Art. 8.2(b)(iv), UN Doc. A/CONF.183/9*, www.un.org/icc, reprinted in *I.L.M.* 37 (1998), 999.
[53] For a discussion of how the principle of humanity – prohibiting inhumane methods and means of warfare, and usually applied to human suffering – may conceptually offer an avenue for expanding protection of the environment, see Schmitt, "Green War," 62.
[54] E.g., Agreement for the Prosecution and Punishment of the Major War Criminals of the European Axis Powers and Charter of the International Military Tribunal (done Aug. 8, 1945), Art. 6(b), 59 Stat. 1544, 82 U.N.T.S. 279 (making "the wanton destruction of cities, towns or

Tribunal in the *Hostage Case*: "The destruction of property must be imper-atively demanded by the necessities of war. Destruction as an end in itself is a violation of international law. There must be some reasonable connec-tion between the destruction of property and the overcoming of the enemy forces."[55]

In its official Gulf War Report, the US Department of Defense dismissed the possibility that Iraq's destruction of Kuwaiti oil wells and release of oil into the Gulf had any but negligible military utility, concluding that Iraq violated the principle of necessity.[56] The report suggested that the Iraqis may have hoped to impede amphibious operations or disrupt Coalition operations by fouling desalination plants. However, it labeled the effect as negligible. As to the ignition of oil, the report was more condemnatory:

> As the first Kuwaiti oil wells were ignited by Iraqi forces, there was public speculation the fires and smoke were intended to impair Coalition forces' ability to conduct both air and ground operations, primarily by obscuring visual and electro optical sensing devices. Review of the Iraqi actions makes it clear the oil well destruction had no military purpose, but was simply punitive destruction at its worst. For example, oil well fires to create obscur-ants could have been accomplished simply through the opening of valves; instead, Iraqi forces set explosive charges on many wells to ensure the great-est possible destruction and maximum difficulty in stopping each fire.

The report went on to assert that the fact that the wells were only set ablaze in Kuwait is further evidence of malevolent intent. Of course, the point made about opening the valves on the oil wells bears on whether the destruction of the oil wells was necessary, not on whether the technique of setting the oil afire was militarily necessary. Moreover, an assertion that a state did not destroy its own resources proves little: that state may simply have made a different cost-benefit analysis when considering destruction in the homeland as opposed to elsewhere. In fact, there is some evidence that the smoke was effective as an obscurant.[57] That said, the DOD conclu-sion is most likely correct, even though the evidence cited is less than fully persuasive.

villages or devastation not justified by military necessity" a war crime); for an excellent survey of the principle, see Burrus M. Carnahan, "Lincoln, Lieber and the Laws of War: The Origins and Limits of the Principle of Military Necessity," *Am. J. Int'l L.* 92 (1998), 213.
[55] *Hostage Case*, 1253–54.
[56] US Dep't of Defense, *Conduct of the Persian Gulf War*, pp. 625–26.
[57] See Arkin et al., *On Impact*, p. 141.

The customary international law principle of proportionality requires that military actions not cause injury to civilians (incidental injury) or damage to civilian objects (collateral damage) disproportionate to the anticipated military advantage likely to result.[58] Calculated in terms of the operation as a whole rather than short-term, immediate benefits,[59] proportionality is essentially a balancing test between military and humanitarian values. Note that by the Protocol I Articles 51 and 57 standard, the advantage weighed against collateral damage and incidental injury is that which is "definite and concrete." The Protocol introduced this construction, but the standard arguably delineates a customary international law threshold since most states view the articles as declaratory of customary international law. In fact, neither Michael Matheson (the Deputy Legal Advisor at the US State Department) nor the Air Force expressed any opposition to the Protocol I proportionality articles, other than the provisions on reprisal.[60] Therefore, by negative implication, it may be reasonably concluded that the United States does not oppose the articles.

Finally, a customary principle that pervades both proportionality and military necessity – and which enjoys a degree of autonomous normative valence – is that of "military objective."[61] This principle, which Protocol I purports to codify in its Article 52 restriction of attacks to military objectives, has proven somewhat controversial. Recall that Article 52 requires an attack to result in some definite military advantage. The requisite nexus between actual military operations and the object to be attacked remains unsettled.[62] The ICRC takes a restrictive approach, ruling out any advantage that is arguably "potential or indeterminate."[63] By contrast, the United States supports a relatively liberal interpretation of military objective. For

---

[58] See generally Judith G. Gardam, "Proportionality and Force in International Law," *Am. J. Int'l L.* 87 (1993), 391.   [59] See Oeter, "Methods and Means of Combat," p. 179.

[60] US Dep't of the Air Force, *Operations Law Deployment Deskbook*, tab 12, pp. 15–17; Matheson, "The United States Position," 426–27 (while not using the term "definite and concrete," stating that the United States supports the principle "that attacks not be carried out that would clearly result in collateral civilian casualties disproportionate to the expected military advantage").

[61] See Horace B. Robertson, Jr., "The Principle of Military Objective in the Law of Armed Conflict," in Michael N. Schmitt (ed.), *The Law of Military Operations* (Newport, R.I.: Naval War College, 1998).

[62] Compare Sandoz et al., *Commentary on the Additional Protocols*, p. 619 (defining "direct" as "acts of war which by their nature or purpose are likely to cause actual harm to the personnel and equipment of the enemy armed forces") with W. Hays Parks, "Air War and the Law of War," *Air Force L. Rev.* 32 (1990), 1, 113–45.

[63] Sandoz et al., *Commentary on the Additional Protocols*, p. 636.

instance, the authoritative *Commander's Handbook on the Law of Naval Operations* states that "[e]conomic targets that indirectly but effectively support and sustain the enemy's war-fighting capability may . . . be attacked."[64]

The debate is relevant in the environmental context because the destruction of some potential targets over which the pundits might disagree would cause significant environmental damage. The obvious example is oil. Certain states rely heavily on oil exports to finance their military. In such cases, oil indirectly but effectively supports war-fighting capability; yet the direct nexus between oil profits and actual military operations is somewhat attenuated. By a restrictive interpretation, the oil is a civilian (economic) target, and may not be attacked, period. By the liberal interpretation, it is a valid target which may be attacked so long as the resulting collateral environmental damage is proportionate to the military advantage that accrues. As a non-party to Protocol I, the United States can attempt to avoid the dispute by simply arguing that directness ("definite military advantage") is not an element of the customary international law principle of military objective, and thus not relevant to US operations. Obversely, states that view the article as declaratory of customary law would characterize the debate as bearing on the operations of all states, Protocol I parties or not.

Fault lines

Difficulties in developing and implementing norms constraining environmental damage during armed conflict fall into four categories: (1) prescriptive and definitional vagueness; (2) discordant valuation paradigms (including problems arising from the contextual, cultural, conceptual, and temporal aspects of determining value); (3) normative lacunae; and (4) goal dissonance.

---

[64] US Navy/Marine Corps/Coast Guard, *The Commander's Handbook on the Law of Naval Operations*, NWP 1-14M, MCWP 5-2.1, COMDTPUB P5800.7 (1995), para. 8.1.1 (labeling this a "statement of customary law," citing General Counsel, Dep't of Defense, Letter of Sept. 22, 1972, reprinted in *Am J. Int'l L.* 67 (1973), 123–24); see also NWP 1-14M, Annotated Version (1997), p. 8-3, n. 11 (specifically deferring on "whether this rule permits attacks on war-sustaining cargo carried in neutral bottoms at sea, such as by Iraq on Iranian tankers carrying oil exported by Iran during the Iran–Iraq war").

PRESCRIPTIVE AND DEFINITIONAL VAGUENESS

The most egregious definitional conundrum present in the environmental law of armed conflict is that surrounding the terms "widespread," "long-term," and "severe." Recall that both of the instruments specifically addressing the topic – Protocol I and ENMOD – use them to set forth standards of unacceptable harm. Although this approach would appear as sagacious draftsmanship, in fact the commonality only foments confusion.

To begin with, the terminology is generally undefined in Protocol I and ill-defined in ENMOD. With regard to the former, the ICRC Commentary and other sources of negotiating history provide no indication of what the verbiage was intended to mean beyond the Rapporteur's rather laconic comment that "long-term" was generally understood as measured in decades. The adjectives "severe" and "widespread" were left unexplained and undefined. In fact, the sole suggestion of what the standard envisages *en complet* appears in the Rapporteur's account of some delegates referring to "battlefield destruction in France in the First World War as being outside the scope of the prohibition." According to the Rapporteur, "it appeared to be a widely shared assumption that battlefield damage incidental to conventional warfare would not normally be proscribed."[65]

As the Diplomatic Conference putting the Additional Protocol together was underway, so too was the drafting of the United Nations-sponsored Environmental Modification Convention. When the paradoxical dynamic of two international conventions relating to wartime environmental damage proceeding apace was raised during the Protocol I negotiations, the United States representative quickly opined that the comparison was one of apples and oranges – of complementary, not identical, fruit. In his mind, Protocol I extended to the use of virtually any weapon causing the cited level of harm, but was restricted to periods of actual armed conflict. By contrast, ENMOD was restricted to intentional manipulation of the earth's processes, but applied beyond situations involving armed conflict in the classic sense. Characterized in Hague and Geneva law terms, Protocol I was of Geneva pedigree, for it protected the environment regardless of the weapon of destruction; ENMOD was classic Hague law in that it restricted a particular means of warfare.[66] The Commentary does

---

[65] *Official Records*, vol. 15, p. 268, reprinted in Sandoz et al., *Commentary on the Additional Protocols*, p. 417.   [66] See Sandoz et al., *Commentary on the Additional Protocols*, pp. 414–15.

not indicate the existence of any measurable dissent to this characterization of complementariness in diversity.

This dismissal of concern proved ill-advised. What resulted was normatively determinative terminology that varies in meaning depending on the prescriptive context in which it applies. Confusion was inevitable. As noted, aside from the brief comment regarding "long-term" by the Rapporteur, Protocol I is definitionally silent. On its face, so too is ENMOD. However, the Committee on Disarmament appended a number of understandings to ENMOD when forwarding it to the General Assembly in September 1976. One understanding sought to clarify the meaning of the terms in question:

> **Understanding relating to article 1**
> It is the understanding of the Committee that for the purposes of this Convention, the terms "widespread", "long-lasting" and "severe" shall be interpreted as follows:
>
> (a) "widespread": encompassing an area on the scale of several hundred square kilometres;
> (b) "long-lasting": lasting for a period of months, or approximately a season;
> (c) "severe": involving serious or significant disruption or harm to human life, natural and economic resources or other assets.[67]

Whereas the definitions of "widespread" and "long-lasting" are capable of some degree of quantifiable application, it is debatable whether the qualifiers "serious or significant" add much to cure the manifest vagueness of "severe." Since the standard is stated in the disjunctive, for instance, when would disruption or harm be serious but not significant, or significant but not serious? Moreover, note inclusion of the word "disruption": would mere disruption suffice, or must there be some physical damage?

What is possibly more troubling is the extent to which the definition of "long-lasting" in ENMOD (months) differs from the sole indication of the meaning in Protocol I (decades). This difference not only demonstrates the degree to which the ENMOD–Protocol I terminology is subject to widely dissimilar (albeit reasonable) interpretations, it also illustrates the fallacy of resort to ENMOD's text, negotiating history, subsequent explication, and application in state practice when attempting to discern the

[67] "Understanding Relating to Article I, Report of the Conference of the Committee on Disarmament," UN GAOR, 31st Sess., Supp. No. 27, UN Doc. A/31/27 (1976), pp. 91–92, reprinted in Schindler and Toman, *The Laws of Armed Conflicts*, p. 168.

normative content of widespread, long-term, and severe in Protocol I – and vice versa. Lest one be tempted to employ this otherwise hermeneutically sensible methodology, the ENMOD understanding itself cautions that "the interpretation set forth above is intended exclusively for this Convention and is not intended to prejudice the interpretation of the same or similar terms if used in connexion with any other international agreement."[68]

Further compounding comprehension of this seemingly transparent common terminology is the incongruency of conjunctive presentation in Protocol I and disjunctive construction in ENMOD. Before the threshold of permissible environmental harm is breached in the Protocol, the damage incurred must be widespread and long-term and severe. This appears to set a much higher standard of injury than ENMOD, which proscribes modification of the environment in such a way as to cause widespread or long-term or severe destruction, damage, or injury.

A potential red herring issue is that of whether the standards refer to an individual act of environmental damage or to a grouping of such acts. Some have asserted that when the "consequences of an individual mission would probably fall below these thresholds, such missions would not be prohibited, despite the fact that overall damage would clearly fall well outside allowed limits."[69] Indeed, one commentator reported the United States as having stated that using herbicides to modify the environment would not be prohibited unless an individual use breached the standard.[70] Surely these contentions are incorrect. For instance, US criticism of Iraq's actions during the Gulf War were made as to the actions considered in their entirety. No commentator argued that temporal or spatial separation of incidents excused them. To assert otherwise would eviscerate the normative valence of the prescriptive system for safeguarding the environment. Instead, all reasonably related acts (a single operation with multiple phases or acts with a common purpose) should be grouped for the purpose of evaluation.

Reduced to basics, there are but two prescriptive instruments that specifically address the environment during armed conflict, and both use

---

[68] "Understanding Relating to Article I."

[69] Richard Carruthers, "International Controls on the Impact on the Environment of Wartime Operations," *Envtl. & Plan. L.J.* 10 (1993), 38, 47.

[70] Jozef Goldblat, "The Environmental Modification Convention of 1977: An Analysis," in Arthur Westing (ed.), *Environmental Warfare: A Technical, Legal and Policy Appraisal* (London and Philadelphia: Taylor & Francis, 1984), pp. 53, 55.

identical terms to set forth their normative standards. However, that terminology is used in different contexts (harm to the environment v. harm generally), ill-defined, interpreted variously depending on the instrument at hand, and applied in differing ways (conjunctively v. disjunctively).

In this confusing prescriptive milieu, policymakers and military commanders will be hard-pressed to foresee accurately when the potential environmental destruction of proposed operations is likely to be judged a breach of either the environment-specific Protocol I or ENMOD proscriptions.[71] While some states have explicitly recognized the problem of prescriptive vagueness,[72] there is a risk that state practice will likely develop such that either: (1) commanders intent on securing the maximum operational and tactical flexibility will make conclusory decisions that the attack in question will not cause the degree of harm envisioned by the treaties; or (2) states likely to generate such harm through their operations will engage in auto-interpretation leading to environmental harm thresholds so high that violations rarely, if ever, occur.

Even assuming an environmentally benevolent intent on the part of a state crafting its own definitions, achieving viable equipoise among Protocol I's conjunctively expressed terms would prove elusive. Most notably, environmental harm which clearly exceeds two of the standards may not meet the third. For example, the destruction of all members of a species which occupies a limited region may be "long-term" and "severe" since it is irreversible. But, if the range of the species is spatially restricted, the definition of "widespread" might not be satisfied. While the article's conjunctivity was clearly intended to deter pertinacious environmental concerns from interfering with achieving desired military objectives, a definition of one of these autonomously valent terms which sets the bar too high risks rendering them vacuous *in toto*. The challenge is to articulate balanced interpretations encompassing the harm that the global community would want to proscribe without hindering military operations

---

[71] Cf. Wil D. Verwey, "Protection of the Environment in Times of Armed Conflict – Do We Need Additional Rules?" in Grunawalt et al., *Protection of the Environment*, pp. 559–60.

[72] E.g., Turkish Interpretive Statement Filed at Time of Signature (May 18, 1977), reprinted in *Multilateral Treaties Deposited with the Secretary General*, http://www.un.org/Depts/Treaty (visited April 30, 1998) (at the time of signing ENMOD, declaring that the "terms 'widespread,' 'long-lasting' and 'severe effects' . . . need to be clarified" and that "[s]o long as this clarification is not made the Government of Turkey will be compelled to interpret itself the terms in question and consequently it reserves the right to do so as and when required").

that foster community values.[73] Although goal dissonance will be revisited more fully later, it is telling to recognize its definitional component.[74]

In fact, the environmental destruction caused by Iraq during the Gulf War would suggest that both of these standards are of de minimis import in any but the most extreme circumstances. To begin with, none of the Iraqi actions implicated ENMOD because there was no attempt to modify natural processes. Further, in spite of the significant environmental damage caused by release of between 7 and 9 million barrels of oil in the Gulf and setting fire to over 600 oil wells, even the United States has questioned whether the requirements of long-term and severe were satisfied; indeed, it has suggested that Articles 35(3) and 55(1) "were not intended to prohibit battlefield damage caused by conventional operations and, in all likelihood, do not apply to Iraq's actions in the Persian Gulf War."[75] Curiously, the DOD report charges that the oil well fires "had no military purpose" and were "simply punitive," but then labels them "battlefield damage." Perhaps the better approach would have been simply to limit its analysis to its point that the damage did not rise to the long-term (measured in decades) threshold. Assuming the Gulf War environmental violence does not meet the definitional requisites of the Protocol I proscriptions, then, a fortiori, the terms must be applied in an extraordinarily circumscribed manner.

If the definitional quagmire of ENMOD and Protocol I hinders effective environmental protection during armed conflict, might other prescriptive norms prove curative? Unfortunately, many suffer from definitional imprecision as well. Among this group, the most significant is the customary international law principle of military necessity, as codified in Article 23(g) of Hague IV and Article 53 of Geneva IV. When, for instance, is destruction of the environment, either directly or indirectly, imperatively demanded, the standard of Hague IV and that propounded in the *Hostage Case*? Use of the adjective "imperatively" would suggest a relatively high

---

[73] Glen Plant, "Government Proposals and Future Prospects," in Plant, *Environmental Protection and the Law of War*, pp. 170, 194 ("spatial criteria are not always relevant to the seriousness of an impact in overall environmental terms").

[74] Cf. Federal Ministry of Defence of the Federal Republic of Germany, *Humanitarian Law in Armed Conflicts: Manual* (1992), para. 403, reprinted and commented on in Fleck, *Handbook of Humanitarian Law* (defining widespread, long-term, and severe as single concept: " 'widespread' 'long-term' and 'severe' damage to the environment is a major interference with human life or natural resources which considerably exceeds the battlefield damage to be regularly expected in war"). [75] See US Dep't of Defense, *Conduct of the Persian Gulf War*, p. 625.

degree of necessity; after all, imperative is defined as "absolutely necessary, urgent, compelling."[76] Yet, recall that the *Hostage Case* clarified the phrase by requiring "some reasonable connection between the destruction of the property and the overcoming of the enemy forces."[77] This would appear to be a much lower standard of necessity than that of "imperatively demanded" standing alone.

Taking the "reasonable connection" clarification at face value, the obvious predicaments lie in determining how direct the advantage that accrues to the military actor has to be, and, if direct enough, how likely the advantage sought is to occur. Consider an example from the Gulf War. Assume arguendo that Iraq released oil into the Persian Gulf to hinder possible US Marine Corps amphibious operations by fouling the engines of landing craft and disrupting Marine activities along the shore. The advantage sought is quite direct – the target of the spill is the enemy force itself. On the other hand, if the intent was simply to demoralize the Kuwaiti population through the specter of millions of dollars of their natural resources being poured aimlessly into the Gulf, then the relationship between the act and the anticipated advantage would likely be judged overly attenuated. Exacerbating the problems of determining directness is the fact that very different motivations may potentially underlie acts causing environmental damage. Absent express statements regarding the purpose of the actions, the subjective intent behind an act is difficult to pinpoint; for instance, malevolent intent was ascribed to the Iraqis during the Gulf War, but the evidence thereof was largely circumstantial. Finally, whenever appraising possible military necessity, one needs to calculate both the likelihood of the tactic proving successful and the chances of the presumed scenario unfolding. Therefore, an analysis of dumping of oil to counter amphibious landing is bifurcated: (1) how likely was the oil spill to hinder amphibious operations?; and (2) how likely were the amphibious operations to occur?

Along the same lines as the ambiguity of the "imperatively demanded" standard, when is an action rendered so absolutely necessary by military operations that the limits placed on occupying forces in Article 53 of Geneva IV become inoperative? Absolute necessity logically suggests a conditional threat of sorts: if a force does not take a particular action likely to cause otherwise forbidden harm to occupied territory, X will happen.

[76] *Webster's New World Dictionary*, 2nd Coll. edn. (New York: Simon & Schuster, 1986).
[77] *Hostage Case*, pp. 1253–54.

But what is the X to which the exception applies? In other words, what condition of absolute necessity in occupied territory would release an occupier from its duty to refrain from destroying real or personal property? No ready answer presents itself.

Admittedly, military necessity can be difficult to apply regardless of whether the environment is the object upon which the act of necessity operates. In a number of contexts, environmental factors can render application of the principle more difficult than would otherwise be the case. First, Article 23(g) prohibits unnecessary destruction or seizure of the enemy's property; similarly, Article 53 extends by its own terms to the real or personal property of the occupied state or its citizens.[78] Components of the environment such as land, water, flora, and fauna should readily be considered protected property. By a restrictive interpretation, the same might not hold for the atmosphere, ozone layer, climate, or perhaps even some species of migratory fauna.[79] Though legal concepts of property evolve over time, the meaning of treaty provisions such as Articles 23(g) and 53 is far less subject to interpretive evolution than customary law.

More troubling is a relative lack of understanding about the nature of effects on the environment. Today, it is possible to predict the direct effects of a conventional weapon system attack with impressive exactitude. Consider an attack on a building, the destruction of which has been determined to be reasonably connected with the overcoming of the enemy (the *Hostage Case* standard). Mission planners can reliably determine the type and number of weapons to use against the building based on known accuracy and destructive force. However, as demonstrated with the oil spills and fires during the Gulf War, environmentally based attacks may involve unleashing untried, untested, or directionally random forces. As a result, military necessity calculations are frustrated due to difficulties in assessing the extent to which the tactic employed will yield militarily useful outcomes.

---

[78] Regarding the principle of necessity codified in Article 53 of Geneva IV, see Pictet, *ICRC Commentary*, p. 320 (noting "[i]t is therefore to be feared that bad faith in the application of the reservation may render the proposed safeguards valueless; for unscrupulous recourse to the clause concerning military necessity would allow the Occupying Power to circumvent the prohibition set forth in the Convention," and urging occupying powers to interpret the provision reasonably and "with a sense of proportion in comparing the military advantages to be gained with the damage done").

[79] On this issue, see Anthony Leibler, "Deliberate Wartime Environmental Damage: New Challenges for International Law," *Cal. W. Int'l L.J.* 23 (1992), 67, 105–6.

This latter point bears on the Protocol I derivation of the principle of military necessity, the concept of military objective as expressed in Article 52(2). By that provision, attacks are limited to military objectives, that is objectives the destruction, capture, or neutralization of which offer a "definite military advantage." The debate over the term "definite" has already been mentioned. Exploitation of environmental features could yield a military advantage. For example, if an avenue of attack is down a narrow valley, the valley is a military objective. Similarly, if the enemy is using a river as a line of communication, the river is a military objective. An attacker may have to factor specific prohibitions, such as Protocol I Articles 35(3) and 55, and customary international law, such as proportionality, into operational planning, but, *sans plus*, the valley and river are military objectives. But what of the Kuwaiti oil wells that were set ablaze during the Gulf War? Characterizing them as military objectives would require an understanding of both the attacker's subjective intent and the likely objective result of the attack. If the wells were attacked wantonly, then in that particular context they were not military objectives and, thus, immune. By contrast, if they were destroyed, for example, to create smoke to obscure the vision of Coalition aircraft attacking Iraqi targets, as some have suggested, then they may well have been military objectives. It is important to emphasize "may" because a fair assessment of any failed tactic (the bombing campaign against Iraq was devastating despite all Iraqi counter-measures) depends on whether a reasonable warfighter would expect it to bear its intended fruit. If not, the wells could not be objectively labeled military objectives. In other words, the status of military objective is both subjectively and objectively determined, and this determination is always contextual when the environment is involved. Although military necessity's contextuality is a truism that applies to all objects that are not inherently military in nature, the uncertainty surrounding the effects on and uses of the environment during military operations make asseverations of necessity especially suspect.

Finally, the entire issue of prescriptive vagueness is driven by the cognitive perspective of the policymaker or warfighter. This subject will be explored more fully later, but in the instant context it is critical to understand that vagueness inevitably revolves around the circumstances in which the actor finds him or herself; actual assessments of any definitionally vague norms are inevitably contextual and individualized. During armed conflict, these determinations tend to be especially self-serving. A commander whose forces are at risk may use the vagueness to rationalize environmentally destructive actions. Given the nature of war and human motivations, legitimate doubt will often be resolved in favor of destroying the environment to further the mission; to believe otherwise is to misunderstand the brutality of war. This being so, vagueness is an invitation to rationalization in trying times. Alternatively, those who need not resort to such measures to survive, as well as those who fall victim to them, are bound to take an expansive view of the prescriptions. Allegations of victor's justice are most likely to ring true when the normative boundaries are unclear.

To summarize, existing law simply does not provide military commanders with adequate notice of what degree of environmental destruction is prohibited. With the guarded exception of ENMOD and, to a certain degree, the provisions regarding works and installations containing dangerous forces,[80] objects indispensable to the survival of the civilian population,[81] and the use of incendiaries,[82] the textual law exhibits insufficient environmental specificity, an indispensable requirement for predictability. Though careful legal analysis and the development of appropriate military doctrine can help clarify these norms, the confusion caused by usage of common terminology with disparate meanings and broadly stated prescriptive formulae is self-evident.

DISCORDANT VALUATION PARADIGMS

Prescriptive vagueness frustrates attempts to ascertain where along the continuum of damage or injury a particular prescription activates. While performing such analytical tasks is challenging, much more cognitively complex are balancing tests that weigh one community value against another. In the law of armed conflict, the seminal balancing test is the principle of proportionality, the customary international law principle codified in Protocol I Articles 51 and 57. Like other prescriptive standards, proportionality calculations are ultimately placed along a continuum: at some point, a proportionate act becomes disproportionate. But before this linear function may be accomplished, the proportionality value must be calculated. To do so, a balancing test is performed in which the "concrete and direct military advantage anticipated" from an attack is weighed

---

[80] Protocol I, Art. 56.   [81] *Ibid.*, Art. 54.   [82] See generally Protocol III.

against the collateral damage to civilian objects or incidental injury to civilians likely to result. There is near-universal agreement that unintended ("not the object of the attack") damage to the environment should be factored in when calculating collateral damage. The difference between advantage and harm is then assessed by placement on the proportionality continuum.

Optimally, normative balancing tests should balance like values. Unfortunately, proportionality calculations are heterogeneous, balancing military against humanitarian values. When expected unavoidable harm to civilians and civilian property outweighs the extent to which the target's damage, destruction, or neutralization fosters overall military aims, the mission planner (or those tasked with executing the mission) must either cancel the attack or employ a less destructive weapon system or tactic. In the abstract, this cognitive task appears easy. In practice, the dissimilarity of the military and humanitarian value categories confounds the determination. What, for example, is the value of an aircraft, command and control facility, communications node, or tank in terms of human lives? The crippling of how many children is justified by the destruction of a motor pool in the vicinity of a school? To what extent does denial of petroleum, oil, and lubricants (POL) to the enemy outweigh damage to a fragile marine ecosystem? Absent a common currency against which to measure dissimilar values, any hope of definitively resolving such intellectual and moral enigmas is phantasmagoric at best.[83]

Paradoxically, then, this most protective of normative principles proves difficult to apply. The inherent valuation dissimilarity is compounded by four discordant valuation paradigms that are particularly obfuscatory in the environmental context. Complicating matters even further is the increased complexity that environmental valuation adds to some important intellectual tasks in proportionality analysis.

Contextually determined valuation paradigms

The value dissimilarity quandary is exacerbated by the context of valuation. The term "context" as used here refers to the attendant circumstances: what is, or will be, happening at the time and place of the act being

---

[83] See Howard S. Levie, "The 1977 Protocol and the United States," *St. Louis L.J.* 38 (1993–94), 469, 482, reprinted in Michael N. Schmitt and Leslie C. Green (eds.), *Levie on the Law of War* (Newport, R.I.: Naval War College, 1998).

evaluated. As an example, destruction of naval vessels is unlikely to be particularly significant in a land campaign, but would be of great value in the face of an amphibious landing. Similarly, cratering an airfield is less vital once air supremacy has been attained than it is in the initial days of a conflict. Dumping oil into the Gulf during the Gulf War was arguably of greater military advantage in advance of the possible amphibious assault than in the waning days of the conflict, when the fight was all but over.

Analogous contextuality presents itself when assessing the other side of the coin, harm to protected objects and persons. Diminished electrical generating capacity, for instance, is of far greater import in an urban, industrialized area than a remote, rural village. Destruction of land used for agricultural production is more devastating to a nation that produces its own food than one that relies on food imports. If a coastal area is fouled by oil, the collateral damage is likely to be more severe if the site is a poor country's fishing ground, than if it is used for recreation by a wealthy state.

Dissimilarity and contextuality issues pervade any proportionality analysis, regardless of whether damage to the environment is involved. However, the relative uncertainty surrounding environmental damage aggravates analytical complexity. For example, after Iraq had threatened to use the oil weapon but before it had done so, portents of environmental doom were heard from many quarters.[84] In fact though, the international scientific community determined over time that the initial environmental prognosis was exaggerated.[85] The problem is that a decisionmaker (whether policymaker or operational commander) cannot benefit from post-factum assessments of collateral damage. They must act, and be judged, on the evidence in hand at the moment the decision is made. With respect to environmental harm, the Gulf War taught that proportionality

---

[84] "Scientists Warn of Environmental Disaster from a Gulf War," Reuters, Jan. 2, 1991, available in LEXIS, News Library, Allnws File (warning by an experienced engineer that igniting oil installations could result in the generation of smoke equal to that of a nuclear explosion, thereby blocking out sunlight and causing temperatures to drop by as much as 68 degrees); see also "Experts Warn of Global Fallout from Warfare: Scientists Say that Smoke from Blazing Kuwait Oil Fields Could Affect the Climate," *L.A. Times* (Jan. 3, 1991), A8.

[85] "State of the Environment: Updated Scientific Report on the Environmental Effects of the Conflict Between Iraq and Kuwait," Governing Council of the UN Environment Program, 17th Sess., UN Doc. UNEP/GC.17/Inf.9 (1993), pp. 12–13 (asserting that global climate was unaffected, and no serious human health problems occurred); see also "Report on the UN Inter-Agency Plan of Action for the ROPME Region," UN Environment Program, Oct. 12, 1991, reprinted in Mark Weller (ed.), *Iraq and Kuwait: The Hostilities and Their Aftermath* (Cambridge: Grotius Publications, 1991), p. 339 (effect of the oil spills).

conclusions are often scientifically speculative, and thus proportionality calculations involving environmental harm are qualitatively more difficult than would otherwise be the case.

Culturally determined valuation paradigms

Although military advantage assessments are contextually determined, they are generally consistent across cultures. An aircraft, for instance, is no more or less militarily valuable in and of itself to an Iraqi than to a Canadian. Its inherent value is a constant. What changes is its contextual value. In other words, value is determined by the context in which it is used: enemy defensive and offensive assets, relative geographical advantages and disadvantages, tactics, industrial capability, nature of the campaign, weather, etc. The catalogue of variables that contribute to or detract from contextual value is nearly infinite. In the end, however, an aircraft is an aircraft is an aircraft to the warfighter, irrespective of nationality.

By contrast, humanitarian values are computed contextually (the immediately surrounding attendant circumstances) and culturally (who is acting or being acted on). Take human life itself. In a culture replete with misery and suffering, the subjective (certainly not objective) value of a life to that culture's inhabitants may well be less than that which a socially, or economically, advanced society's inhabitants would attribute to it. Such cross-cultural valuation paradigms trouble responsible human beings, who abhor the thought of gradations in the "value" of human life. Nevertheless, far too much empirical evidence of the granularity of humanitarian values exists to ignore this reality. For example, compare the treatment of the interned Japanese-Americans with Hitler's treatment of German Jews. Both are tragic examples of state mistreatment of its own citizens, but it would be hard to deny that the official German policy placed a lesser value on Jewish lives than American policy did on those of the Nisei. Thus, to the extent that different societies value certain civilians and civilian objects differently, proportionality equations will yield conflicting results.

The existence of cross-cultural valuation paradigms extends to collateral environmental damage. Different countries value their environments differently. The issue here is not context (beyond cultural context). For example, a field of corn is of greater value in a starving society than a well-fed one. The difference is contextual: it is not the society that drives the distinction, but rather the relative degree of hunger. Culturally disparate valuations of the environment, on the other hand, are driven by cultural perspectives. One group of people may simply be more sensitive to the environment than another, whether due to uniform education, common upbringing, reliance on the environment for well-being, dominant religious affiliation, shared experiences and needs, etc. To illustrate, consider distressed states. They are less likely to value environmental health than developed countries, not because the environment offers them less, but because they have more pressing concerns.

As a result, different cultures (often defined in terms of a state) assign different values for a particular quantum and quality of environmental collateral damage in the proportionality equation, and thereby arrive at disparate conclusions as to the normative boundaries within which belligerents must operate. While this dynamic is not unique to environmental damage, it is certainly more pernicious when the environment is involved. After all, if the global community cannot agree on the value of the one thing all humans have in common, life itself, how is it to ever reach consensus on the value of a habitat, species, or water or air quality?

Conceptually determined valuation paradigms

While cross-cultural valuation paradigms complicate environmental proportionality calculations by leading to conflicting results as between particular groups of people, the effect of conceptually determined valuation paradigms is much more subtle. A conceptual valuation paradigm may pervade a culture, but need not. Instead, disparate conceptual paradigms can be present in a single society.

Conceptually, there are two distinct ways to value the environment. Most common is valuation based on utilitarian principles. This anthropocentric approach considers the degree to which the environment contributes to human well-being through provision of food, shelter, clothing, fuel, and even quality of life. The greater the contribution, the greater the weight accorded environmental collateral damage in performing proportionality calculations.

At the other end of the spectrum lie those who would factor in the environment's intrinsic value, that is the value that exists independently of any contribution to humankind. For instance, a species of birds should be protected because they "are," not just because they constitute an important link in the food chain or provide humans with aesthetic enjoyment. Lest advocates of this approach be dismissed as wild-eyed radicals, remember that humans make many intrinsically based valuations. Indeed, one would hope that the core humanitarian value – life – is valued not because of what it offers others, but rather in and of itself. Religious and moral values are also archetypal. Many people would argue that faith and morality should be pursued even when human suffering results, not because doing so benefits the actor, but rather because it is the "right" thing to do. In light of such mainstream assertions, cognitive perspectives embracing intrinsic valuation are hardly beyond the pale.

Intrinsic valuation characterizes human understanding; whether it has a place in proportionality calculations regarding environmental damage is a different matter altogether. This issue will be discussed more fully in the following section, but at this juncture it is useful to highlight three approaches.

The first approach is to include only anthropocentric valuation in proportionality calculations. Doing so is not to deny the value of the environment, but instead simply represents acceptance of exclusively derivative environmental protection. While this approach may fail to capture the true value of the environment being damaged, it does offer the benefit of applicative ease (relative to the other approaches). Applied to a hypothetical situation based on the Gulf War oil dumping incidents, purely anthropocentric valuation would consider the human cost of denying people the benefits of the area that the oil was spilled into, including exploitation of its resources.

A moderate intrinsic value approach acknowledges both anthropocentric and intrinsic value, but would defer to the former should they conflict. Returning to the dumping example, assume that by dumping oil into waters off its shores a state could significantly impede an amphibious landing. Assume further that the amphibious assault, because of the proximity of civilian population centers, would cause significant civilian injuries and damage to civilian property. In this case, a moderate intrinsic value approach would discount (but not ignore) the intrinsic value factored into the proportionality calculation in an effort to reflect anthropocentric concerns fully. Lesser weight would be attributed to the environmental harm in an effort to minimize the human suffering (incidental injury and collateral damage) likely to be caused by an enemy's action.

Finally, a radical intrinsic value approach would likewise acknowledge both anthropocentric and intrinsic value, but would not discount the former if it operated at cross purposes with the latter. By this approach, if the definite and concrete military advantage expected to accrue from an attack was outweighed by either a combination of anthropocentric and intrinsic value *or* by one of the two values alone, then the operation would be forbidden as disproportionate. Using the hypothetical dumping scenario, so long as the environmental damage caused to the Gulf exceeded the anticipated military gain, the dumping would be disallowed regardless of the human suffering that might result therefrom. In a sense, this is what happens whenever there is an absolute prohibition on a weapon system or tactic. As an example, consider the absolute prohibition on permanently blinding lasers. There is little question that their use could be militarily necessary and proportional. For instance, such lasers could be used for perimeter defense of a remote installation away from any significant civilian population. The victims would be combatants (enemy troops) and the incidental injury would be de minimis. Nevertheless, their use is forbidden.[86]

Cognitive perspectives intrude on orderly and predictable proportionality determinations in yet another way. In many situations, regard for environmental concerns may place military personnel at greater risk. For example, assume placement of surface-to-air missile systems at an oilfield. To attack the missile sites risks spilling oil or igniting it. Also assume that diverting around the fields is not tactically sound because of air defenses elsewhere, and because doing so will measurably decrease the fuel available to conduct the attack and engage in defensive maneuvering. Does the analysis set forth above for conflicting humanitarian values (measured in terms of collateral damage and incidental injury) apply here? Unlike that situation, the human value (the pilot's life) being weighed against the environmental damage is not one that would otherwise be protected by inclusion in the humanitarian value side of the proportionality scale. After all, the pilot is a combatant and, as such, a legitimate target. Instead, aircrew risk is normally accounted for in proportionality determinations by adjusting the military advantage valuation downward – the greater the risk, the less the collateral damage and incidental injury necessary to outweigh it because less military advantage accrues to the attacker.

---

[86] Convention on the Prohibitions or Restrictions on the Use of Certain Conventional Weapons which may be Deemed to be Excessively Injurious or to Have Indiscriminate Effects, Protocol on Blinding Laser Weapons (Protocol IV) (done Oct. 13, 1995), reprinted in *I.L.M.* 35 (1996), 1218; see also Michael N. Schmitt, *"Bellum Americanum:* The US View of Twenty-First Century War and its Possible Implications for the Law of Armed Conflict," *Mich. J. Int'l L.* 19 (1998), 1051 (discussion of this issue in the context of the principle of humanity).

This turns the conflicting values analysis on its head. Even though aircrew risk falls on the other side of the proportionality equation, the aircrew's life is nevertheless an anthropocentric value. From an anthropocentric cognitive perspective, purely intrinsic environmental value is not recognized, so the proportionality calculation remains unaltered. However, by both the moderate and radical cognitive perspectives, the valence of the intrinsic humanitarian (the environment in this case) value is effectively enhanced because of the negative effect of aircrew risk on military advantage.

Thus, from whatever direction proportionality is approached, and as with the other valuation paradigms, the play of proportionality calculations is very much dependent on one's conceptual perspective. The proportionality principle is well settled, but its consistent application is frustrated by diverse perspectives on what should be included in the balancing process. As has been demonstrated, the cognitive approach adopted can prove normatively dispositive.

Temporally determined valuation paradigms

The final valuation paradigms that render application of the proportionality principle so troublesome in the environmental context are those that are temporally determined. Temporal valuation is essentially contextual valuation, but exhibits sufficient independent valence to merit separate mention.[87] It is a recognition that value systems evolve and that, therefore, the value factored into the humanitarian side of the proportionality balancing test will fluctuate over time even if the objective harm caused does not. In 1938, for example, the Chinese destroyed the Huayuankow Dam on the Yellow River in order to stem the tide of Japanese invaders by flooding the land in their path.[88] The flood tragically destroyed millions of acres of farmland and killed thousands of Chinese civilians. Yet, nary a whimper was heard over this devastating environmental impact. (Also consider the lack of attention given to the floods caused by Allied "dam-busting" during World War II.) Were this incident to occur sixty years later, the volume of environmental protest would be deafening. Similarly, compare the bombing of the Ploesti oil facilities with the Iraqi actions of 1991. No

[87] See Bothe, "Protection of the Environment," 56.
[88] Sandoz et al., *Commentary on the Additional Protocols*, p. 667.

expressions of concern over the consequent environmental damage followed the former missions, whereas in the latter environmental damage was the almost exclusive focus of attention.

Myriad factors explain this trend towards attributing increasingly greater value to the environment over the past decades. Of course, Iraq's Gulf War environmental operations focused global attention on the subject. But even beyond that there are numerous contributory factors. Advances in science have highlighted the importance to human well-being of many heretofore misunderstood environmental dynamics. Environmental education has improved, as has the effectiveness of environmentally focused non-governmental organizations such as Greenpeace and the Sierra Club. Precision weaponry has driven down the acceptability of collateral damage generally.[89] This latter phenomenon is particularly relevant to environmental damage because such damage most often results from rather crude applications of force for which advanced precision weaponry offers viable alternatives. To illustrate, if one side wishes to deny POL to an opponent today, it can effectively shut down the electricity to the POL storage facility; it is seldom necessary to attack storage facilities themselves.

In fairness, the reality of temporal valuation variability is universal; the value of all objects considered when assessing proportionality evolves over time. However, variability arguably constitutes a greater obstacle to the principle's consistent application in the environmental context because the evolutive process therein is more marked than with regard to other civilian objects. To illustrate, one need only consider how much attention has been devoted to warfare's methods and means of late (blinding lasers, anti-personnel mines, etc.); the same phenomenon has not been apparent vis-à-vis protected objects or individuals. The sole exception in the field of "Geneva law," as evidenced by the recurring international conferences on the subject since the Gulf War, is the environment. This being so, it is in assessing the environment that the proportionality principle suffers its greatest temporal vagaries.

Intellectual tasks

In addition to the effect that discordant valuation *bouleversement* has upon the working of the proportionality principle, consideration of the

---

[89] See generally Schmitt, "*Bellum Americanum.*"

environment when making such calculations complicates two fundamental intellectual tasks. The first is that of determining precisely what
collateral damage to include in the calculation. Recall that likelihood
of occurrence and of success affects military necessity assessments. So too
it does with proportionality. Both the likelihood that the anticipated military advantage and that the expected harm will occur should be factored
into the assessment. But how much deference, if any, should be paid to
likelihood in readjusting proportionality calculations? For instance, if
the military advantage of the anticipated gain just slightly outweighs the
expected collateral damage and incidental injury, should the attack be permissible if the likelihood of the foreseeable military advantage is low and
that of the unintended harm to civilians and civilian objects high?

While this is not the place to resolve such matters, incorporation of
environmental damage into the equation clearly exacerbates the process.
Over time, mission planners and warfighters have compiled considerable
data and experience on collateral effects during attacks. Reliability and
accuracy data is readily available for all weapon systems, sophisticated
intelligence collection can identify civilians and civilian objects in the target area, and training is regularly conducted on avoiding collateral damage
and incidental injury. Unfortunately, environmental damage is such a
nascent concern that the knowledge, experiential, and training bases are
limited. Despite concerted efforts to improve this situation, performance
of this particular intellectual task remains – for the moment – somewhat
haphazard and speculative.

A second intellectual task complicated by environmental concerns is
assessing reverberating effects by following the chain of causation from
the initial use of force to subsequent consequences. The reverberating
effects issue came to the fore as a result of the Gulf War air campaign
against Iraqi command-and-control assets.[90] Recall that the bombing
effort focused in significant part on bringing down the Iraqi electrical
grid. This resulted in hospitals and other critical humanitarian functions
in Iraq being denied electricity, which in turn hindered their ability to
deliver essential services. Human suffering resulted, suffering which

---

[90] For an excellent analysis of the issue of reverberating effects in the context of air attacks on
Iraq's electrical grid, see James W. Crawford, "The Law of Noncombatant Immunity and the
Targeting of National Electrical Power Systems," *Fletcher Forum of World Aff.* (Summer/Fall
1997), 101.

allegedly was not adequately considered when making the initial proportionality calculations.[91]

As discussed elsewhere in this chapter, imperfect knowledge about the impact of warfare on the environment makes it difficult to arrive at reliable estimates of potential reverberating effects.[92] The surface has yet to be scratched in understanding the scale or nature of environmental interrelatedness and interdependence. A mere decade ago, reputable scientists were reporting that if Iraq ignited Kuwaiti oil wells, as eventually occurred, the smoke produced would likely shield parts of the earth from sunlight and thereby cause temperatures to drop drastically.[93] This would, in turn, dramatically affect flora and fauna. In fact, nothing of the sort happened. If scientists struggle to predict environmental reverberating effects accurately, the efforts of those tasked with folding them into their decision-making processes – policymakers and warfighters – are unlikely to fare much better, no matter how sincere.

NORMATIVE LACUNAE

The aforementioned fault lines centered on challenges in understanding what the applicable law means. It is equally important to grasp the limited scope of the prescriptive landscape. While recognition of the somewhat narrow situations addressed by the law hardly represents a jurisprudential epiphany, the point does bear on the adequacy of the law in furnishing the desired environmental safeguards.

Turning first to specific prescriptions, note how high the thresholds for applicability have been set. Before the Protocol I prohibitions of Articles 35(3) and 55 provide any protection, the damage must be widespread, long-term, and severe. No one criterion alone will suffice. Even if it did, the quantum of damage necessary to implicate the prohibition would be grave nevertheless, for if long-term is viewed as being measured in decades, widespread and severe must also, for reasons of internal consistency, be interpreted as setting high levels of damage.

---

[91] Chris af Jochnick and Roger Normand, "The Legitimation of Violence: A Critical Analysis of the Gulf War," *Harv. Int'l L. J.* 35 (1994), 387, 399–402 (criticizing the air campaign's effect on the civilian population).

[92] See generally James Gleick, *Chaos: Making a New Science* (New York: Viking, 1987), pp. 9–13 (in the context of explaining chaos theory, discussing the "Lorenz Effect," in which a butterfly beating its wings in Tokyo purportedly can cause a thunderstorm in New York).

[93] See "Scientists Warn of Environmental Disaster."

For its part, ENMOD enjoys a lower applicability threshold; its terms have been defined much more liberally, the most notable example being the characterization of long-term as measured in terms of seasons. More-over, ENMOD applies to any form of damage, not simply environmental damage, and satisfaction of any of the three criteria suffices to activate the prohibition. While this appears promising from an environmental protection point of view, ENMOD only enjoins techniques that involve manipulating environmental processes. Such efforts in warfare are rare; instead, environmental damage most often results from standard military methods and means of combat. A point in fact is the relative consensus that the deliberate spilling of oil and the setting on fire of oil wells by Iraq in the Gulf War did not violate ENMOD.[94]

Most of the non-environmentally specific prescriptions that could be interpreted as extending to the environment suffer similar limitations. The customary international law principles of necessity and proportionality, like the codified iterations in Protocol I, are widely applicable but suffer from the debilitating maladies posited earlier. Article 23(g) of Hague IV exclusively applies to damage of enemy property. It would not cover damage occurring on either neutral territory or in the global commons (such as the exclusive economic zone, high seas, international airspace, and space). Unfortunately, environmental harm is especially liable to have transboundary effects, whether due to winds, currents, presence of species on the territory of multiple states or in international waters, or through reverberating effects such as the impact of a species' demise on an extended food chain. Article 55 of the same instrument is also of restrained application, coming into effect only during periods of occupation and only for acts committed by an occupier against state property. Geneva IV's Article 53 similarly addresses only damage occurring at the hands of an occupying force, although it does apply to all property, not simply that belonging to the state. Despite the example of Iraqi environmental misdeeds in occupied Kuwait, it is much more likely that environmental damage will occur during ongoing hostilities, well before a formal state of occupation comes into being.

Although the non-environmentally specific prohibitions in Protocol I possess greater protective promise, the non-participation of the United

---

[94] US Dep't of Defense, *Conduct of the Persian Gulf War*, p. 625.

States – the world's sole remaining superpower – diminishes the convention's direct efficacy. Furthermore, those articles setting forth the normatively capacious principles of military necessity and proportionality (52, 51, and 57) are difficult to apply for reasons outlined earlier. Much more precise are Articles 54 and 56. By limiting attacks on objects indispensable to the survival of the civilian population, the former extends protection explicitly to such components of the environment as agricultural areas, livestock, and water supplies, and implicitly to objects (the destruction of which would place the environment at risk) such as fuel, electricity, and lines of communication essential to providing sustenance to the civilian population.[95] Though Article 54's standard is relatively unambiguous, it does not apply in a number of situations. For instance, objects may be destroyed if the survival of the civilian population is not at stake, as would be the case if there were large food reserves available. Nor would the prohibition apply if the purpose of the destruction was not to deny sustenance value. In other words, denial of sustenance value may be the effect of an action; it may simply not be the action's purpose. As an example, if fields are burned to create barriers to an advancing force or to clear a field of fire around a camp, Article 54 would not apply despite any ensuing civilian hardship. Of course, if the action would create excessive civilian suffering, the rule of proportionality and the limitation on starvation would intervene to forbid it. Inclusion of this *mens rea* element significantly degrades the article's reach; conflicting claims as to intent would certainly rear their head in the event of an enforcement effort.

Article 56's protection of dams, dikes, and nuclear electrical generating stations which might release dangerous forces if attacked (with consequent severe losses among the civilian population) likewise offers the environment significant protection. Attacks on any of these targets could have severe environmental consequences. That said, the provision's caveats bind its reach.

---

[95] Compare Leibler, "Deliberate Wartime Environmental Damage," p. 107 (overstating the limitations of the article by suggesting that since it is restricted to destruction intended to deny sustenance to the civilian population, "at least from the perspective of environmental protection Article 54 is of negligible utility") with Protocol I, Art. 54, para. 3(b) (objects not used solely as sustenance for enemy forces may not be destroyed if the effect is to leave the civilian population with so little food or water that starvation results).

In the first place, and despite assertions to the contrary, Article 56 extends only to dams, dikes, and nuclear electrical generating stations. The list is exhaustive, not illustrative.[96] Moreover, if an opponent uses dams or dikes for other than their normal function "in regular, significant, and direct support of military operations and . . . attack is the only feasible way to terminate such support," they may be attacked.[97] Examples would include emplacement of radar or surface-to-air missiles (other than strictly for defense of the facility) at the location.[98] Because of the greater risk that attack of a nuclear facility poses, attacks thereon are more restricted. Before it may be struck, the station must be providing electricity "in regular, significant, and direct support of military operations," and the only way to arrest that support is through its attack.[99] Thus, while the protective effect of Article 56 is relatively robust when it applies, it applies in somewhat narrow circumstances. To compound matters, the restrictions are not generally considered declaratory of customary international law.

One might also note in passing the definitional vagueness of the terminology used to set the prescriptive threshold: regular, significant, and direct. The ICRC Commentary dismisses this point quickly by urging that "these terms merely express common sense, i.e., their meaning is fairly clear to everyone."[100] This is a conclusory statement without empirical or experiential foundation. The Commentary then goes on to define the terms through use of further vagueness. "Regular" is "some continuity in use"; "significant" is "sizable having a real and effective impact"; "direct" is a "relation between the act and its effect [that is] close and immediate."

Might the Martens Clauses of Hague IV and Protocol I fill the lacunae in the prescriptive landscape? The clauses do appear promising, for they apply during periods of prescriptive evolution caused by discordant valuation paradigms or prescriptive vagueness. But the Martens Clauses fall victim to the very flaws they would purport to remedy. Who are the "civilized peoples" and how might the "dictates of public conscience" be discerned? The terms are both vague and ambiguous. In fact, history has

---

[96] *Official Records*, vol. 15, para. 326; Bothe et al., *New Rules*, p. 352.
[97] Protocol I, Art. 56, para. 2(a).
[98] Sandoz et al., *Commentary on the Additional Protocols*, p. 671 (citing the examples of a dike that forms part of a system of fortifications and a road across a dam that is used as an essential route for the movement of armed forces, but cautioning that the usage still must be tested against the "regular, significant, and direct" criteria).   [99] Protocol I, Art. 56, para. 2(b).
[100] Sandoz et al., *Commentary on the Additional Protocols*, p. 671.

demonstrated that exhortatory calls on the conscience of mankind all too often fall on deaf ears.

The final fault line posited is goal dissonance. Until the Vietnam War, the environment was viewed in entirely anthropocentric terms, a fact evident in the absence of any mention of it in instruments governing the conduct of hostilities. Whatever degree of protection the environment received derived wholly from existing protections of civilians and civilian objects. However, in the aftermath of the environmental destruction of that war, the environment *qua* environment became a cognitive reality. Once this occurred, a shift in cognitive perspectives was unavoidable, hence the emergence of intrinsic value notions.

The most notable example was and remains Article 35(3) of Protocol I. Its verbiage is completely devoid of any mention of effect on human beings. Therefore, so long as an act causes the requisite degree of widespread, long-term, and severe damage, a proposed operation is forbidden, even if the net result is greater human suffering. For example, imagine attack on a nuclear facility in a remote region of a belligerent's country following credible announcements by the belligerent that it intends to use nuclear weapons against military targets near civilian population centers. Applying proportionality principles, the military advantage to be gained by such an attack is so high that it would probably outweigh the resulting nuclear contamination even if the environmental damage caused by that contamination rose to the widespread, long-term, and severe level. This is particularly true given the unlikelihood of civilian casualties. Under Article 35(3), the attack would be forbidden regardless of how many civilian lives might be saved. Therein lies the goal dissonance. Under this intrinsic value provision, environmental values are so dominant that they are considered in a vacuum.

It is essential not to confuse this conundrum with that expressed earlier vis-à-vis cognitively determined valuation paradigms. The concern there was one of how much *weight* to accord the environment when conducting balancing tests such as proportionality. Even by the radical intrinsic value cognitive perspective, anthropocentric values are given some due; they simply are not permitted to diminish the play of environmental damage in the proportionality equation. The goal dissonance problem is more insidious because human values risk not being factored in at all.[101]

What is interesting is that Article 35(3) is the sole provision that operates in isolation of anthropocentric values. For instance, Article 56 requires that attacks on dams, dikes, and nuclear electrical generating stations result in "severe" losses among the civilian population before they are disallowed (unless, of course, they are otherwise forbidden by necessity or proportionality). Similarly, Article 54(2) is purely anthropocentric in that its prescriptive scheme is based on survival of the civilian population.

ENMOD is a tougher case. Although the intrinsic value–anthropocentric dichotomy is not raised by its terms, the requisite degree of damage necessary to activate its provisions is not expressed in environmental terms; any damage suffices. In this sense, it is anthropocentric. Yet, at the same time, ENMOD resembles Article 35(3) of Protocol I by imposing an absolute prohibition which does not factor in the principles of military necessity or proportionality. This is an intrinsic value formulation that accepts the possibility that human values might suffer for environmental ends.

More to the point is Article 35(3)'s counterpart – Article 55 of Protocol I – which is anthropocentric in nature as evident in the provision's reference to acts which "prejudice the health or survival of the population." The incongruity of two articles in the same instrument bearing on the same genre of harm, but responsive to different ends, can be explained by the dynamics of negotiation. At the Diplomatic Conference, a number of intrinsic value advocates argued for per se restrictions on environmental damage. To pacify this group, Article 35(3) was included.[102]

But more than political appeasement was involved. Article 35(3) represented a recognition by anthropocentrics of a competing camp. Indeed, lest the provision be dismissed as politicized surplus, it must be remembered that today it binds 150 states, including many with which the United States is likely to conduct combined operations. Additionally, the approach retains its influence. In the aftermath of the Gulf War, a number of proposals for normative revision evidenced intrinsic value undertones.

---

[101] *Ibid.*, p. 410 ("this is a matter not only of protecting the natural environment against the use of weapons or techniques deliberately directed against it, nor merely of protecting the population and the combatants of the countries at war against any of these effects, but also one of protecting the natural environment itself").

[102] *Official Records*, vol. 15, para. 359; see also Bothe et al., *New Rules*, p. 345.

At the 1991 London Conference sponsored by Greenpeace and others, for example, multiple options were proposed for limiting environmentally destructive means and methods of warfare. None were crafted in terms of human values. Thus, the relevant section of the proposed new convention provided:

Section I: Methods and means of warfare
A. A provision establishing the threshold at which methods and means of warfare are prohibited because of their intended or expected impact upon the environment. There appear to be approximately four options for change:

Option (a): prohibiting the employment of methods or means of warfare which are intended, or may be expected, to cause *any* (except *de minimis*, or "insignificant", or "unappreciable") damage to the environment;

Option (b): prohibiting it at least where the damage is widespread, long-lasting *or* severe;

Option (c): prohibiting it as under alternative (b), but adding a fourth alternative criterion, "significant (or 'appreciable') and irreversible".

Option (d): choosing some mid-way position between alternative (b) and the existing high threshold as it appears in Article 35(3) of Protocol I.[103]

Later, the final conference report at the 1991 Munich Conference suggested that future prescriptive schemes be based on protection of the environment per se.[104] Although the Munich Conference did not recommend a new convention, it did suggest the compilation of two lists. The first would delineate those activities that could harm the environment, with some subject to absolute prohibition and others to be addressed through conditional prescriptive schemes. The second list would be a registry of protected areas. Countervailing trends have been equally apparent. For instance, the whole idea of intrinsic valuation received scant attention at the Naval War College conference in 1995. Thus, the challenge for those seeking a coherent strategy for crafting a normative architecture to protect the environment is a shared prioritization of goals. Presently, this remains merely an aspiration.

---

[103] Plant, "Government Proposals," p. 192.
[104] International Council of Environmental Law, *Final Report of Consultation*, paras. 10, 13.

Thoughts on possible curative approaches

The sky is not falling. To argue that the law is not perfect, even to assert that it is seriously flawed, is not to contend that it serves no useful purpose. Quite the contrary, today warfighters (at least those in advanced militaries) are highly sensitized to their obligation to consider potential environmental damage during operational planning. The international legal community deserves much of the credit for this positive enculturation.

Nevertheless, the prescriptive landscape does evidence certain fault lines that weaken its normative effect. Four have been identified: vagueness, discordant valuation paradigms, prescriptive lacunae, and goal dissonance. While it is not the purpose of this chapter to bridge the gap between *lex lata* and *lex ferenda*, perhaps a few tentative thoughts on possible curative approaches to the fault lines might prove beneficial.

In any structured endeavor, a necessary first step is to identify the desired end. To be effective, normative architectures governing environmental harm during armed conflict must exhibit two core attributes: enforceability and notice.

If law is to deter wrongful conduct, it must be enforceable. This requires that the enforcing entity, generally the international community, be perceived as possessing the will and capacity to enforce. Additionally, when deterrence breaks down, that will and capacity must become manifest; the enforcer has to take on the violator, lest a precedent be set encouraging future miscreants to ignore the law.

Considerable effort has been devoted of late to the creation of effective international enforcement regimes. In sharp contrast to the global community's relative listlessness in the face of Iraqi war crimes,[105] the ad hoc

---

[105] For initial steps taken to hold Iraqi war criminals accountable, see War Crimes Documentation Center, Office of the Judge Advocate General, US Army, *Report on Iraqi War Crimes (Desert Shield/Desert Storm)* (1992), esp. pp. 45–48 (unclassified version on file at the Naval War College Library, Newport, R.I.) (finding that the environmental damage was unlawful even though it could not definitively ascertain the rationale behind the Iraqi actions); Letter from the Deputy Permanent Representative of the United States of America to the United Nations, Addressed to the President of the Security Council, UN Doc. S/25441 (1993); Conrad Harper, "Opening Address," in Grunawalt et al., *Protection of the Environment*, p. 13 (arguing that "we have not yet arrived at the point where the international community is willing to put its credibility, commitment, and the full force of its conscience behind environmental crimes prosecutions in . . . the same way that it has demanded accountability in the context of Rwanda and Bosnia").

tribunals for the former Yugoslavia and for Rwanda are proving capable of bringing war criminals and human rights abusers to justice.[106] Efforts to establish an International Criminal Court, despite concerns by certain states regarding possible overreaching,[107] are also promising in this regard.[108] That the Court's Statute includes a provision characterizing certain environmental harm as a war crime is especially noteworthy, although it remains premature to speculate on the likely effectiveness of the Court or the manner in which it is likely to apply its environmental prescription.

Also promising is inclusion – so far limited – of environmental provisions in the law-of-war manuals of several countries. Military manuals are critical components of the lawmaking process. Michael Reisman and William Lietzau have quite accurately pointed out that military manuals are "often the litmus test of whether a putative prescriptive exercise has produced effective law. Without adequate dissemination, this putative international lawmaking is an exercise in the elaboration of myth through *lex stimulata* rather than the installation of an effective operational code."[109] Germany has one of the most progressive manuals.[110] In the United States,

---

[106] On the work of the Tribunals, see William Fenrick, "The Development of the Law of Armed Conflict through the Jurisprudence of the International Criminal Tribunal for the Former Yugoslavia," in Michael N. Schmitt and Leslie C. Green (eds.), *The Law of Armed Conflict: Into the Next Millennium* (Newport, R.I.: Naval War College, 1998); see also M. Cherif Bassiouni, *The Law of the International Criminal Tribunal for the Former Yugoslavia* (Irvington-on-Hudson, N.Y.: Transnational Publishers, 1996).

[107] E.g., US Dep't of Defense, *DOD Briefing Paper, International Criminal Court* (Mar. 27, 1998) ("We are concerned that an ICC lacking appropriate limits and checks and balances could be used by some governments and organizations for politically motivated purposes. Since war crimes make up the majority of the offenses subject to the jurisdiction of the court, actions of the armed forces are the most likely target of frivolous referrals or politically-targeted or otherwise inappropriate prosecutions. We are concerned about proposals that could subject military personnel of countries that abide by the laws of armed conflict and have national mechanisms to enforce compliance with them by their service members to ICC criminal investigation for actual or threatened military action. We must preclude the creation of a so-called "proprio motu" (independent) prosecutor with unbridled discretion to start investigations. We are also concerned that some countries have supported overly broad and vague definitions of war crimes.").

[108] On the ICC, see Bengt Broms, "The Establishment of an International Criminal Court," in Yoram Dinstein and Mala Tabory (eds.), *War Crimes and International Law* (The Hague and Boston: M. Nijhoff, 1996), p. 183; International Law Commission, "Draft Statute for an International Criminal Court," in *Report of the International Law Commission on the Work of its Forty-Sixth Session*, U.N. Doc. A/49/355 (Sept. 1, 1994), p. 3.

[109] W. Michael Riesman and William K. Lietzau, "Moving International Law from Theory to Practice: The Role of Military Manuals in Effectuating the Law of Armed Conflict," in Horace B. Robertson, Jr. (ed.), *The Law of Naval Operations* (Newport, R.I.: Naval War College, 1991), p. 1.

[110] See Fleck (ed.), *Handbook of Humanitarian Law*.

only the Naval law-of-war manual addresses the subject employing a "due regard" formulation familiar in maritime and aerial navigation, but innovative in the law of war.[111] Interestingly, the "San Remo Manual," which was drafted under the auspices of the International Institute of Humanitarian Law by a group of international experts as a "restatement" of the law of naval operations also adopts the due regard approach.[112] It will be telling to see how the new multiservice US law-of-armed-conflict manual currently being drafted will treat the topic of environmental damage during warfare. Currently, the most comprehensive treatment of the subject available to US forces is the Army's *Operational Law Handbook* (devoting an entire chapter to the subject), which is not a formally author-ized law-of-armed-conflict manual.[113] All told, these provisions greatly facilitate domestic prosecution of those who would ignore the environ-mental prescriptions during hostilities.

Effective enforcement is only a part of the recipe for potency.[114] Deter-rence requires unequivocal notice of what conduct is prohibited because normative clarity permits states that voluntarily subject themselves to the rule of law to make their conduct conform accordingly. It also permits those who do not conform to understand when they are risking sanction.

A convention on protecting the environment during armed conflict, assuming it were carefully drafted to avoid the pitfalls identified through-out this chapter, would be responsive to deficiencies in placing parties on notice of what is expected of them (and provide a tangible basis for enforcement). After all, when widely adopted and expressive of meaning-ful norms, treaty law is the cleanest way to generate a fresh normative

---

[111] US Navy/Marine Corps/Coast Guard, *The Commander's Handbook*, NWP 1–14M, para. 8.13 ("It is not unlawful to cause collateral damage to the natural environment during an attack upon a legitimate military objective. However, the commander has an affirmative obligation to avoid unnecessary damage to the environment to the extent that it is practicable to do so consistent with mission accomplishment. To that end, and as far as military requirements per-mit, methods or means of warfare should be employed with due regard to the protection and preservation of the natural environment. Destruction of the natural environment not neces-sitated by mission accomplishment and carried out wantonly is prohibited. Therefore, a commander should consider the environmental damage which will result from an attack on a legitimate objective as one of the factors during targeting analysis.").

[112] Louise Doswald-Beck (ed.), *San Remo Manual on International Law Applicable to Armed Conflicts at Sea* (Cambridge and New York: Cambridge Univ. Press, 1995), para. 44.

[113] International and Operational Law Dep't, US Army, *Operational Law Handbook* (2000), ch. 15.

[114] For a superb analysis of the implementation of the law of armed conflict, see Adam Roberts, "Implementation of the Laws of War in Late-Twentieth-Century Conflicts," in Schmitt and Green, *The Law of Armed Conflict*.

architecture. Unfortunately, the time is not ripe for such an effort. Before the international community can move towards new law it must perform two preparatory tasks, both of which would constitute effort well expended even if calls for new law prove stillborn: (1) developing scientific indicators for evaluating environmental consequences of war; and (2) clarifying vague provisions in the existing law.

First, a deeper and more robust understanding of the danger that warfare poses to the environment is required. The absence of reliable data on the effect of military operations cripples commanders and policymakers tasked with applying core prescriptions such as necessity or proportionality, let alone the specific prohibitions regarding environmental damage. Even assuming a prescriptively omniscient commander who knows what "widespread, long-term, and/or severe" means in normative terms, without scientific information as to the effects of a proposed operation, performance of the relevant intellectual tasks will unavoidably smack of "guesstimation."

The requisite understanding must take the form of measurable scientific data. Only the scientific community can analyze the scientific phenomenon that is environmental damage; and only that community can provide reliable and usable "indicators" of environmental harm to military commanders and political decisionmakers. There are few, if any, scientific protocols or standards in place to meet this need. The result, as evidenced during the Gulf War, is inevitably a battle of the experts over probable effects and appropriate criteria. Rather than waiting for the next conflagration, internationally agreed-upon scientific indicators should be developed now, before the passions and politics of ongoing armed conflict once again complicate their development.

There are many viable options for forging agreement on appropriate indicators. Perhaps the best immediate approach would be the creation of a Committee of Experts, possibly under the auspices of the United Nations, World Health Organization, or International Committee of the Red Cross, with a broad base of state representation. The desired output would be twofold: (1) an analysis of the type and extent of environmental damage likely to be caused by military operations; and (2) development of a methodology for temporally, spatially, and substantively assessing its severity, including any reverberating effects. For instance, these could include agreed-upon criteria and protocols for measures of toxicity and concentration, identification of particularly damaging substances, water and air quality criteria, and criteria related to specific environments, environmental processes, or species. Examples of measurable criteria might include degree of flora or fauna destruction; concentrations of pollutants in the air, land, or water; concentrations of pollutants in biomass (bodies of humans or animals); effects on endangered species; and effects on reproductive capabilities.

Due to the infinite variety of scientific measures and subjective valuations that contribute to any net assessment of environmental injury, and the variety of environments that may be injured, it is impossible to arrive at absolute criteria for impermissible harm. Legal standards regarding the environment must be somewhat abstract and general in nature to account for evolution and advances in our knowledge of environmental harm and the causes thereof. Thus, the criteria must be in the form of indicators of harm, rather than normative trip-wires. In sum, the goal would be to identify criteria that could be universally accepted as indicative of environmental harm, and thereby allow consideration of the environmental law of armed conflict to focus on application of the law to the facts, rather than on the evidence itself.

Once the science has been clarified, the second foundational step would be to attack vagueness in the law constraining environmental consequences of war. Over the past decade, the plethora of international conferences have tended to be broad-brush in focus. What the international legal, policy, and scientific communities need to focus on is resolving, or at least clarifying, what it is the law actually intends to prohibit. A highly inclusive Committee of Experts formed under the sponsorship of such organizations as the International Law Commission, International Law Association, or ICRC – not unlike that suggested above in the purely scientific context – could be charged with directly addressing the prescriptive vagueness. In fact, the ICRC took on just such a task at the behest of the United Nations soon after the Gulf War, and the resulting ICRC Guidelines were completed in 1994. The General Assembly has urged all states to consider their inclusion in law-of-armed-conflict manuals. The Guidelines, benefiting from the work of the scientific Committee of Experts suggested above, would serve as an excellent point of departure for the effort suggested in this essay. However, greater state participation would enhance the acceptability of the result.

While any endeavor along these lines might seem daunting (and so it certainly would be to some extent), agreed-upon "understandings" of obfuscatory terminology such as Protocol I's "widespread, long-term and severe" standard would be invaluable. So too would analysis of indeterminate terms found elsewhere (e.g., "imperative," "absolutely necessary," and "property"). The Committee of Experts could also provide authoritative commentary on the methodology for calculating proportionality, the relevant factors that should be considered in the process, and the weight to be accorded those factors. Lastly, the Committee could tie together the underlying goals of all relevant norms in order to provide a common point of departure for the future development of responsive normative architecture.

For practical reasons, the work would not be "lawmaking" in character. At this point in time, any effort to fashion binding interpretations would likely fall victim to politicization and infighting, such as has occurred in the context of developing an International Criminal Court. The very fact that the result would constitute persuasive – *vice* controlling – authority would be an opportunity, for its non-binding nature would allow states to tolerate specificity in articulated standards and relatively unfettered and objective commentary. As a result, its normative force would be subtle, yet, as a strawman generated through an inclusive and credible process, powerful. Such interpretations could easily become the point of departure in understanding the application and prescriptive valence of this body of law.

Combined, the two notional efforts described would alleviate a great deal of the normative turbulence generated by the prescriptive fault lines. Enhanced understanding of the science would facilitate efforts to fashion greater prescriptive specificity. It would also ease efforts to find common ground between discordant valuation paradigms by allowing informed evaluation of alternative approaches instead of the viscerally based discourse that all too often pervades contemporary discussion. In particular, the committee focusing on prescriptive coherence could prove an apposite forum in which to work through much of the cognitive dissonance that pervades the subject area. As an honest broker, this committee could highlight the potential dangers to humankind of intrinsic valuation run amuck, while also making evident the need to adopt a perspective more sophisticated and more responsive to actual community values than pure anthropocentrism. Thus, it would serve the critical task of clarifying shared goals. In the process, actual (*vice* possible) prescriptive voids would be identified, and future efforts to fill them would benefit from enjoying a distinct vector in which to proceed.

Ultimately, the point being made in this chapter is simple. Despite claims to the contrary, the international environmental law of armed conflict is substantively flawed – not fatally, but flawed nonetheless. The time is propitious to turn the attention of the international community to fault lines in that corpus of law and mount efforts to address them. This process need not, and should not, include convening a conference to craft new law – yet. Instead, curative efforts should focus on first things first: understanding the science involved and clarifying what has been done to date. Only once that has been done can true progress be made.

4

THE INADEQUACY OF THE EXISTING LEGAL
APPROACH TO ENVIRONMENTAL
PROTECTION IN WARTIME

RICHARD FALK

An introductory perspective on the environmental law of war

This chapter takes issue with the prevailing consensus among international law experts that existing legal norms and standards provide an adequate foundation for environmental protection and assessment of liability
arising from wartime damage.[1] This conviction of adequacy appears to be
based on several distinct, and complementary, lines of reasoning: first of
all, that these existing norms and standards establish a reasonably workable and practical balance in combat settings between environmental
protection and the pursuit of military necessity; second, that any further
weighting of this legal balance in favor of environmental protection would
be politically futile and legally demoralizing, as it would not elicit necessary support from important governments, especially that of the United
States; third, that the attempt to produce a more coherent and comprehensive legal framework would result in an unwieldy and time-consuming
process, possibly encompassing as much as several decades from start
to finish;[2] and fourth, that by far the most constructive available means
to strengthen environmental protection in wartime would be to devote
greater energy to the implementation of existing standards, and thereby
to forget chasing after the rainbow of a more ambitiously coherent and
restrictive approach.

---

[1] For a convenient standard summary of this consensus see J. Ashley Roach, "The Laws of War
and the Protection of the Environment," *Env't & Security* 1(2) (1997), 53–67.
[2] Yves Sandoz, respected specialist of the International Committee of the Red Cross, suggested a
thirty-year cycle as the time required to make operative a major modification in the law of war.
Remarks at First International Conference on Addressing Environmental Consequences of
War, Washington, D.C. (June 10, 1998).

There is much that is appealing about adopting such a modest demeanor. It is certainly correct that significant additional work could be done by way of implementing existing environmental standards in both preventive and reactive modes. Such activity might well demonstrate that restrictions on environmentally harmful tactics in wartime are to be taken more seriously by political leaders and military commanders than in the past. In my view, however, such an outcome seems at least as unattainable on the basis of the existing framework of vague and scattered legal norms as would the adoption of a special new convention dedicated exclusively to the subject of environmental protection in wartime. The present legal framework does not provide a realistic basis for acceptable levels of implementation under wartime conditions. At most, it leads to an arbitrary and ad hoc pattern of enforcement that often tends to be punitive in character.

At present, environmental accountability is invoked, if at all, in relation to a state that has been defeated and devastated in a war to the point of surrender. Such a state may well find itself diplomatically isolated in the postwar political atmosphere. In contrast, a victorious state or a state with geopolitical clout tends to be exempted from any accountability for its environmentally destructive wartime policies. In this regard, it is important to compare the response of the international community to the environmentally destructive tactics relied upon by the United States during the Vietnam War with its response to those of Iraq during the Gulf War. It is also necessary to assess fully the environmental consequences of the NATO bombing campaign against the former Yugoslavia.

Admittedly, this problem of unevenness of application is wider than its bearing on environmental protection, pertaining to the law of war as a whole. I would maintain, however, that a clear and forceful articulation of relevant legal standards pertaining to environmental protection in wartime would likely have a beneficial effect, generating debate as to their feasibility and leading to an adjustment in tactical thinking by military planners and commanders. In this regard, it is fruitful to compare the debates relating to prohibition of biological and chemical weaponry, calls for general nuclear disarmament, and the campaign leading up to the treaty banning anti-personnel landmines.

At the same time, it is certainly useful to point out the potential contributions that could be made by more energetic and genuine efforts at self-enforcement of environmental restraints. These efforts can assume various forms, and complement efforts to strengthen the relevant sections of the law of war. Sensitizing the military by way of revised, environmentally sensitive field manuals issued to armed forces by their own governments definitely could have a beneficial impact on the design and execution of combat activities, especially if emphasized in connection with tactical adjustments in war-fighting. According a greater role to environmental protection in the setting of combat, if so reinforced, is likely to be reflected in military maneuvers, field exercises, and training programs, and then presumably in war plans and war itself. Although I think it is worth exploring such alternatives for policymakers, it strikes me as naïve to hold out any great expectations that dramatic results will be achieved without the pressure of a grassroots campaign leading to a more focused outlawing of environmental warfare.

Overwhelmingly, the military ethos in wartime continues to be dominated by considerations of patriotism and the drive to prevail. This stress on doing what is necessary to win a given battle in the course of a war almost inevitably produces a climate of opinion that confers virtually unlimited discretion on military commanders in the field. Such leaders continue to be judged and guided back home mainly by calculations related to achieving victory or avoiding defeat in combat. In addition, more recently, heavy pressure is placed on commanders in the field from Western countries to take whatever steps are required, including giving up on a totally satisfactory military and political outcome, to ensure that losses of life among troops are kept to a minimum. These non-military priorities relating to casualties have been particularly evident in the setting of peacekeeping operations and undertakings that can be described under the heading of humanitarian intervention.[3] In these settings, the insurgent side is usually treated as falling altogether outside the protection of the law of war, and has only a limited incentive to abide by its constraints.[4] The experiences of

---

[3] For general background see Sean D. Murphy, *Humanitarian Intervention* (Philadelphia: Univ. of Pennsylvania Press, 1996); on the impact of "costs" (human and financial) on the conduct of military operations, see Richard Falk, "The Complexities of Humanitarian Intervention," *Mich. J. Int'l L.* 17 (1996), 491–513.

[4] To some extent the two 1977 Additional Protocols to the Geneva Conventions of 1949 respond to this gap. Protocol I pertaining to "international armed conflicts" does have a provision, Article 35(3), that explicitly prohibits either side from "methods or means of warfare which are intended, or may be expected, to cause widespread, long-term and severe damage to the natural environment." Protocol II, devoted to "non-international armed conflicts," is more rudimentary, and makes no reference to any prohibitions concerning modes of warfare. For relevant texts, see Burns H. Weston, Richard A. Falk, and Hilary Charlesworth (eds.), *Supplement of Basic Documents to International Law and World Order*, 3rd edn. (St Paul: West Publishing Co., 1997), pp. 237–60.

the 1990s lend support to this assessment, especially the shallow interventions in Somalia and Bosnia, and most dramatically the NATO air war in Kosovo. It should also be noted that such contexts of international and non-international civil warfare seem more and more to comprise the main phenomena of war.

In the face of such tendencies and pressures, the likelihood during wars of this character is that protection of the environment as a goal of public policy will be ineffective. It seems unlikely that the combat options of commanders in the field will be restricted without a much more concerted effort at both intergovernmental and grassroots levels. I do not see how this effort can be organized except by pushing for the adoption of a special agreement that imposes restraints explicitly and self-consciously for the sake of environmental protection, thereby challenging the sacred cow of military necessity to some extent.

There is another threshold issue present here. It centers on the fact that the evolution of the law of war has been preoccupied with providing protection for the civilian population, and in this respect exhibits a highly anthropocentric orientation. Indeed, the Geneva Conventions of 1949 and the two 1977 Protocols were crafted in direct response to a preoccupation with the wartime victimization of various categories of vulnerable persons (civilians, prisoners of war, wounded and sick soldiers, shipwrecked soldiers), as even the formal titles of the various treaty documents disclose. The great contributions of the International Committee of the Red Cross are also measured exclusively by reference to humanitarian criteria.[5] In this regard, the inclusion of environmental protection in the law of war is of a manifestly incidental character, and may even cut against the grain of humanitarian concerns. If environmental protection results in exposing people, whether armed forces or civilians, to additional risks of war-related injuries, then it seems to be inconsistent with the basic humanitarian spirit of the undertaking. To sort out this relationship between insulating society from some of the worst effects of warfare and upholding the long-term social interest in environmental quality is one of the justifications for undertaking to address the environment as an autonomous category within the framework of the law of war.

---

[5] See, e.g., International Committee of the Red Cross, "Fundamental Rules of International Humanitarian Law Applicable in Armed Conflicts," reprinted in Weston, Falk, and Charlesworth, *Basic Documents*, p. 261, n. 4, in which no reference is made to environmental protection.

Thus, it seems valuable to explore the argument for a more satisfactory approach, while viewing the existing framework of weak legal norms embodied in international humanitarian law as a holding pattern with immediate applicability in relation to the aftermath of recent conflicts. For example, it is quite possible that valuable results might be achieved in a variety of special situations in the continuing UN/US effort to enforce norms against Iraq. There is also a small risk that discrediting the sanctions policy against Iraq may spill over to undermine the authority of any efforts to impose liability for environmental harm. Post-ceasefire attempts to hold Iraq accountable for various categories of damage done to Kuwait have been widely criticized as a punitive peace of the sort that was imposed on Germany by the Versailles Treaty after World War I. This line of criticism will gain further weight if the substantial environmental harm caused by the NATO war over Kosovo is not similarly subjected to legal scrutiny. In this regard, it is noteworthy that the Council of Europe's Congress of Local and Regional Authorities passed a motion that at least acknowledged the evidence of environmental harm.[6] However, the motion expressed only a vague willingness to lend "assistance," but revealed no impulse even to consider imposition of possible liability, restoration costs, or reparations for the NATO-caused environmental damage.[7] An impression of double standards is unavoidable.

Nevertheless, on balance, this process of implementation against Iraq to date can be provisionally endorsed, although it should not be interpreted as an overall endorsement of the retention of sanctions so many years after the ceasefire, or of a "punitive peace." The treatment of Iraq's responsibility for environmental harm would gain credibility if the United Nations, as an integral part of its formal action, were explicitly to generalize from any specific imposition of liability on Iraq for environmental harm. Only in this way can the taint of victor's justice and a punitive peace be removed. It also remains important to ensure that the imposition of additional financial obligations on Iraq is not allowed to become the occasion for further suffering by the Iraqi people, who have been continuously and severely victimized for years after the 1991 ceasefire. Sanctions have been maintained in such a way as to amount to a form of warfare waged *exclusively* against the civilian population of an already war-torn country.

---

[6] See Green Cross International, Press Release, June 24, 1999.   [7] *Ibid.*

Regardless of how one views the adequacy of international law covering environmental harm from warfare, it is important to craft a response to Iraqi behavior that sends proper signals to the rest of the international community. But beyond this, the motivation to hold Iraq liable for environmental harm arising from its tactics in the Gulf War should not be confused with the larger task of assessing whether the law of war as it now stands adequately addresses the issue of environmental protection in wartime.

The legal challenge

As already noted, the adequacy of existing standards of international humanitarian law relative to the environment needs to be considered within the broader context of bringing law to bear on the conduct of war. To what extent, and in what respects, is it a viable undertaking? Or should this effort be viewed largely as hypocritical, without the intention or expectation of being able to alter belligerent behavior to any appreciable extent?

It is important to acknowledge the fragility of the humanitarian law of war in general, and how this bears on the more focused inquiry into preventing environmental harm and assessing liability. Admiral Elmo Russell "Bud" Zumwalt, Jr., a renowned and ethically sensitive military leader, argues that there is a definite disposition for battlefield commanders to rely on any tactic or weapon that is "militarily helpful" within a given combat setting, without deference to legal or moral obstacles that stand in the way.[8] He adds that something tends to be understood as militarily helpful if it enables one side to prevail on the battlefield or if it appears to save the lives of its soldiers. In the heat of battle, according to Admiral Zumwalt, military commanders will cast legal considerations aside if they appear to impair the pursuit of their assigned mission. Admiral Zumwalt concludes that these priorities and practices on the battlefield have been consistently endorsed by political leaders, who tend to defer to the military on their choice of both tactics and weaponry, so long as they remain within the parameters set as war goals.

Admiral Zumwalt's view of the wartime ethos is accurate in most regards, yet overstated, and seemingly phrased with the United States

---

[8] Remarks at First International Conference on Addressing Environmental Consequences of War, Washington, D.C. (June 10, 1998).

chiefly in mind. The inhibitions on use of weapons of mass destruction, while not inviolate, seem significant even when a military justification based on winning quickly or saving lives could be put forward. Since World War I, there has been a reluctance to use chemical or biological weapons in war, which made Iraq's recourse to such weaponry in the Iran–Iraq War and against Kurdish villages appear particularly shocking. Atomic bombs were used in 1945, but on grounds that remain controversial and in a setting where no prior inhibition existed. The legal challenges directed against the status of nuclear weapons are undoubtedly a factor inducing continued restraint, although the degree of the restraint has not yet been strongly tested.[9]

During the Cold War, there was a reluctance on the part of American and Soviet political leaders to employ tactics that seemed likely to produce an escalation or deepening of an ongoing conflict, even in the face of contrary recommendations by field commanders. For many years during the Vietnam War, military commanders urged attacks on North Vietnamese sanctuaries in Cambodia and on the Laotian portions of the "Ho Chi Minh Trail," but, until Nixon, political leaders rejected the idea, primarily because they feared a wider war.

But the effectiveness of these norms of restraint is a contextual matter. It arises because the military ethos has been seriously challenged for some prudential reason, quite likely involving acute concerns of morality, prospects of retaliation, and it is linked even to ultimate matters of human survival. As such, the challenge is reinforced, most of all, by considerations of political costs, including the perception that such a use of weaponry will be denounced as illegal and immoral.

With respect to environmental constraints on warfare, such clarity does not exist. Existing standards embodied in the law of war are easily and consistently subordinated to ideas of "mission accomplishment," and impose

---

[9] The most authoritative effort to confront the issue of legality of nuclear weaponry was made by the International Court of Justice in its Advisory Opinion of 1996. The majority decision expressed the strong view that a threat or use of nuclear weapons might possibly be legal in the setting of a state confronting an extreme threat to its own survival, but that all states have a legal duty to pursue disarmament in good faith. See *Legality of the Threat or Use of Nuclear Weapons* (July 8, 1996), *I.C.J. Reports* (1996), p. 226; see also Richard Falk, "Nuclear Weapons, International Law and the World Court: A Historic Encounter," *Am. J. Int'l L.* 91 (1996), 235–48; Jonathan Schell, *The Gift of Time: The Case for Abolishing Nuclear Weapons Now* (New York: H. Holt & Co., 1998); Arundhati Roy, "The End of Imagination," *The Nation* (Sept. 28, 1998), 11–19.

almost no discernible restraints. The operational logic is again that set forth by Admiral Zumwalt, which in effect means that anything goes so long as it has a military rationale in relation to either the mission objective or saving lives. Indeed, from the perspective of a military actor, almost any environmentally harmful initiative can be given a subjectively acceptable legal rationale, and this includes the massive oil spills and disastrous well fires caused by Iraq during the Gulf War. For example, there is credible testimony by experts that the smoke caused by the fires and oil slicks caused by the spills complicated the Coalition's tasks of bombing and pursuing the retreating Iraqi troops.

It also needs to be appreciated that most policymakers conceive of themselves as "realists" with respect to the relevance of the law to war. Realism implies that the material pursuit of national interests prevails over contrary considerations, and that in ultimate matters of war and peace, law and morality are to be ignored if adherence interferes with the attainment of military objectives. In a sense, realism as a policy orientation is only another way of expressing the view that in any specific combat context, the commander will be guided mainly by considerations relating to the assigned mission and the safety of troops under his or her command.

There is a further complication in applying existing legal standards to assess responsibility for environmental harm. If legal standards are consistently ignored by prevailing patterns of practice, then there is influential support for the view that the norms themselves need to be reshaped to reflect the actual outlook and behavior of governments and individuals acting on their behalf. Such an argument has been made with respect to disregarding the prohibitions on the use of non-defensive force that were written into the United Nations Charter as core elements.[10] Of course, the experience of law with environmental destruction as a deliberate tactic is extremely limited, especially if measured by reference to specific standards embodied in international treaty instruments.

The two main steps taken to establish constraints in international law were the 1976 Environmental Modification Convention (ENMOD)[11] and

---

[10] Anthony C. Arend and Robert J. Beck, *International Law and the Use of Force: Beyond the U.N. Charter Paradigm* (London and New York: Routledge, 1993); A. Mark Weisbrud, *Use of Force: The Practice of States Since World War II* (University Park, Pa.: Pennsylvania State Univ. Press, 1997).

[11] Convention on the Prohibition of Military or Any Other Hostile Use of Environmental Modification Techniques (Dec. 10, 1976; entered into force, Oct. 5, 1978), 31 U.S.T. 333.

the 1977 Additional Protocol I to the Geneva Conventions of 1949.[12] Neither Iraq nor the United States has fully ratified either of these treaties, and so their obligatory status would depend on one of two lines of legal reasoning: either the treaties were declaratory of already existing customary international law, or the treaties have been so generally accepted as to have become binding custom for all states. But even if this hurdle could be cleared, the Zumwalt perspective would still seem to apply. True, the US government went along with the negotiation of some constraints on environmental methods of warfare in light of its experience in the Vietnam War, but the formulations agreed upon were such as to authorize in future wars most of what was done in Vietnam. It remains quite easy to reconcile military destruction of the environment with a rationale either for victory in the war or for saving lives.

Also, it must be conceded that many of the customary ideas about wartime constraints are rooted in medieval ideas of "just war" that are Eurocentric in character. As a result, they are without real significance for the non-Western world, which tends to treat war as an unconditional test of wills to be settled on the battlefield. It should be further realized that the practice and the lawmaking process of international law were coexistent with the maintenance of colonial empires. Not only were the norms Eurocentric, but so too were the processes of law creation – which as a result lacked authority outside of Europe. In a sense, whatever claims to compliance can be associated with the law of war are tainted by this historical identification of the law of war with the still-remembered realities of colonial domination and exploitation.

Finally, a focus on "environmental consequences of war" does not specify the legal goals being pursued. In particular, the prevention of harm is not sharply distinguished from a concern about liability and legal responsibility for compensation. Of course, there is a presumed connection between imposing legal responsibility and deterring behavior that inflicts the illegal environmental consequences; the prospect of liability should be designed to deter the harm-producing tactics. In my view, the emphasis on liability for harm should be subordinated to prevention of the harm in the first instance, although the two concerns are interwoven.

---

[12] Additional Protocol I to the Geneva Conventions of August 12, 1949, and Relating to the Protection of Victims of International Armed Conflicts (June 8, 1977; entered into force, Dec. 7, 1978), *I.L.M.* 16 (1977), 1391.

It is from this perspective that existing standards seem so feeble, being very general, abstract, and vague, subject to loopholes, dispersed, and engulfed by the surrounding preoccupation with international humanitarian law. Norms relating to environmental protection are in a sense misclassified by being situated within Protocol I. At a minimum, these norms never came into being in an atmosphere in which the participating states concentrated their attention on the specifics of environmental protection. That is, the effort to discourage adverse environmental consequences in war has never been undertaken in an atmosphere likely to generate an appropriate legal, moral, and political consciousness on the part of the participants.

Indeed, lawmaking for wartime environmental protection has in all instances, with the partial and largely irrelevant exception of the ENMOD Convention, been very much of a sideshow, without a serious impact. ENMOD was focused on environmental protection, but its scope is directed at manipulating basic environmental processes in a manner that causes "widespread, long-lasting, or severe damage or injury to any other party."[13] In any event, it is not a widely ratified treaty, leaving advocates of applicability only with the argument that its norms have been sufficiently widely endorsed on an intergovernmental basis to become universally applicable as rules of customary international law.

Let us consider the application of these standards to the most prominent instances of adverse environmental consequences arising from deliberate combat tactics of belligerents – namely, the Vietnam War and the Gulf War. First, there is the question of double standards. In Vietnam, the US government had the clout to keep concerns about its extensive defoliation and crop and forest destruction off the global environmental agenda even at the 1972 Stockholm Conference on the Human Environment. True, these concerns resurfaced in a muted fashion during the negotiations that resulted in the 1977 Additional Protocols, and produced the most relevant positivistic statements of prohibition in Articles 35(3) and 55 of Protocol I. But even here, the results are extremely suspect. Besides the failure of many important states to ratify this agreement, the scope of the norms seems to keep even the most environmentally pernicious Vietnam practices outside the domain of prohibition. This is so because the prohibition of Protocol I requires that the environmental damage be

[13] ENMOD, Art. I, para. 1.

146

"widespread," "long-term," *and* "severe." Additionally, the United States delegation insisted on making a formal declaration to the effect that environmental damage resulting from use of nuclear weapons "would, of course, be excluded" from the scope of Articles 35(3) and 55.[14]

It is debatable whether such an "understanding" really circumscribes the more general textual language or expresses a view accepted at the time by other parties to the treaty-making process. However, the mere assertion of the claim that nuclear weaponry has a legal exemption from liability for environmental consequences of wartime actions is suggestive of how trivial the enterprise was regarded at the time by the leading state in the world. The implication here is that not only are nuclear states given a generally privileged position in international society, but that in addition, and quite astoundingly, even the "normal" laws of war do not apply to instances of nuclear mass destruction. Such a one-sided spin to the law of war bears quite directly on the acrimonious debate that followed the Indian and Pakistani nuclear tests of Spring 1998.

The UN response to the Vietnam War was in radical variance with its response to the tactics of environmental destruction relied upon by Iraq in the Gulf War. Here, with strong geopolitical backing, the UN Security Council in Resolution 687 condemned Iraq's actions and imposed liability, including a legal obligation to compensate for the damage caused by deliberately dumping millions of barrels of oil into the Gulf and by setting fire to some 600 oil wells.[15] The point is not that such a judgment is on its face unreasonable under the circumstances, but rather that it contrasts with the earlier pattern in Vietnam. Part of this difference can be explained by changes in the global setting, which had made recourse to the Security Council unavailable in Cold War confrontations. Despite this, the differing responses to allegations of environmental harm resulting from the two wars makes it difficult to avoid the impression of "victor's justice" and "punitive peace" after the Gulf War, compared to turning a blind eye after the Vietnam War.

There exists an important argument against the approach I advocate that arises directly out of the present historical situation: namely, that by criticizing the existing law of wartime environmental protection and its

---

[14] For the text of this reservation, as submitted at the time of signature, see Adam Roberts and Richard Guelff (eds.), *Documents on the Laws of War*, 1st edn. (Oxford: Clarendon Press/New York: Oxford Univ. Press, 1982), p. 462.

[15] SC Res. 687, UN SCOR, 46th Sess., 2981st mtg., p. 7, UN Doc. S/RES/687 (1991).

uneven application, one is unwittingly helping Iraq to avoid liability for its acts of wanton environmental destruction committed during the Gulf War. The further point here is that even if such an effort can be criticized as "victor's justice," it would concretely vindicate Kuwait's claims of harm and provide some relief to the country and its people for enduring a traumatic and criminal war of aggression waged by Iraq. Holding Iraq legally responsible for the environmental harm inflicted by its deliberate tactics would also have the effect of establishing a legal precedent that supports the view that flagrant forms of environmental destruction are illegal, a precedent to be taken seriously in relation to damage claims arising out of future wars.

In this respect, the imposition of legal responsibility on Iraq would bear some resemblance to earlier undertakings at Nuremberg and Tokyo that held surviving German and Japanese leaders individually responsible for crimes of state committed in World War II. Here, too, scholars and journalists leveled the charge of "victor's justice,"[16] but despite a flawed beginning, the Nuremberg legacy has endured to exert an influence. The movement to create a foundation for the further evolution of international criminal law has been most recently evident in the creation and subsequent operations of the ad hoc criminal tribunals for former Yugoslavia and Rwanda, established by the Security Council under Chapter VII of the UN Charter.[17] It was again evident in the 1998 Rome Conference of governments working towards the establishment of a permanent International Criminal Court. The efforts to prosecute Augusto Pinochet and Slobodan Milošević for crimes against humanity are important additional international moves to impose legal and criminal accountability. The argument in favor of regarding present international law as sufficient attempts to encourage us to overlook the arbitrariness of these precedents, but to be opportunistic about taking advantage of occasions for implementation when and if they arise. Thus, Iraq's conduct in the Gulf War, and its subsequent international pariah status, provides an almost ideal occasion for the imposition

[16] See especially the principled criticisms of Richard H. Minear, *Victors' Justice: The Tokyo War Crimes Trial* (1971).
[17] See generally Theodor Meron, "War Crimes Come of Age," *Am. J. Int'l L.* 92 (1998), 462; see also Meron, "The Case for War Crimes Trials in Yugoslavia," *Foreign Aff.* 72 (1993), 122; Roger S. Clark and Madeleine Sann (eds.), *The Prosecution of International Crimes: A Critical Study of the International Tribunal for the Former Yugoslavia* (New Brunswick: Transaction Publishers, 1996).

of liability in circumstances where the accused state resorted to tactics that deliberately caused spectacular and massive harm.

In response, I would argue that it is important to do as much as possible to put the actions taken against Iraq on a principled basis, precisely to avoid the impression of a vindictive peace. One way of generating somewhat greater respect for the law of war in general, and of legal standards protective of the environment in particular, would be for the UN General Assembly to adopt a resolution that generalized the principles of responsibility imposed on Iraq in Security Council Resolution 687. These principles could be made applicable in the future to all belligerent participants in warfare. Such an initiative could clarify the agreed normative basis for imposing responsibility for environmental harm. It would be comparable to what the General Assembly's resolution on the Nuremberg Principles achieved with respect to the contested matter of individual criminal accountability for violations of the law of war or commission of crimes against the peace and crimes against humanity.[18] Yet even this measure would only be a first step towards a more thorough re-evaluation of the existing norms.

The present legal regime has seemingly been eroded by NATO's bombing tactics during its Kosovo campaign. These tactics involved more than unavoidable environmental side-effects of heavy bombing directed against an industrialized country. Instead, it is clear that NATO deliberately attacked environmentally sensitive targets despite the obvious prospect of serious pollution of regionally important international waterways and other forms of environmental harm.[19] Here, the inadequacy of international

---

[18] See "Affirmation of the Principles of International Law Recognized by the Charter of the Nuremberg Tribunal," UN General Assembly Res. 95(I) (Dec. 11, 1946); "Principles of International Law Recognized in the Charter of the Nuremberg Tribunal and in the Judgment of the Tribunal," adopted by the UN International Law Commission (Aug. 2, 1950), reprinted in Weston, Falk, and Charlesworth, *Basic Documents*, pp. 149, 193–99.

[19] The preliminary reports of environmental harm arising from the NATO war include the following major concerns: systematic bombing of oil refineries, petrochemical plants, chemical and fertilizer factories, and pharmaceutical plants, which posed pollution threats, including to the Danube River and Black Sea, as well as to the entire natural and human habitat of the Balkan region; and use of depleted uranium weapons, which spread radioactive materials dangerous to health. Apparently there were also 60 kilograms of highly enriched uranium stored at the Vincha Institute of Nuclear Sciences near Belgrade, which if destroyed would likely have spread radioactive contamination in the area. At present, there exists no direct prohibition in international law against striking such a target. E-mail communication with arms control expert Jozef Goldblat (June 21, 1999). In light of renewed concern about the environmental

149

environmental law during wartime is evident in two overlapping ways: either the tactics relied upon were not prohibited, and existing legal standards thus are woefully insufficient to protect the environment; or the tactics were violations of international law, but the political atmosphere is such that no effort is likely to be made to impose legal accountability in some meaningful form. Either way, the case for legal reform seems strengthened.

The political challenge

It is tempting to criticize the position taken here by a dismissive contention that "the best is the enemy of the good." But such a dismissal seems unwarranted. What is being questioned is more basic – whether it is in any fair sense appropriate to regard the existing law and practice of war pertaining to environmental harm as "good." Further, what I am urging as necessary is still very far from the "best," and is really itself a moderate variant of the "good." The recommended line of reform intends only to establish clear and unconditional boundaries of prohibition on tactics of warfare deliberately designed to inflict serious environmental harm.

It would also be significant if such clarity came about as a result of a widely attended international conference of governments representing as many of the world's peoples as possible, as well as providing an ample opportunity for participation by environmental NGOs and other interested groups in civil society. International law to a large extent depends for its effectiveness on the internalization and voluntary acceptance of international rules and standards, as well as on their reinforcement by public opinion, and thus it is of great relevance that the substantive provisions be adopted by way of a participatory process. With respect to the development of both international human rights law and international environmental law, this interplay between governmental lawmaking and grassroots pressure is evident.

There is a further caveat of a political nature. Even if appropriate legal standards could be agreed upon by way of intergovernmental negotiations, there likely would ensue a struggle of a high order to obtain ratification by leading states and – even more difficult – to ensure their

damage caused by modern air war, especially when conducted in a sustained way against an industrialized country, there may be increased support for clarifying the relationship between the law of war and environmental protection.

subsequent compliance. Yet without such a struggle, we would be resigning ourselves to the illusion that international law as it is currently formulated addresses the environmental consequences of warfare in a satisfactory manner. The advocacy of a distinct legal effort, despite the political obstacles, stems from a strong conviction that the existing norms are not clear and definite enough, and that we lack a political and moral climate that exerts compliance pressures. It also reflects the view that the current approach to wartime environmental protection rests primarily on regarding it as a lesser-included topic under the general heading of "international humanitarian law."

It is important to realize that the elaborate effort that would be needed to produce a single coherent protocol or treaty instrument would itself be valuable for the participants; it would serve to educate government representatives and it would heighten media interest and public awareness. The existence of such a lawmaking process would also undoubtedly generate in due course a combination of grassroots activism and bureaucratic understanding that could easily induce a spiral of self-enforcement in most prewar settings. Against this background, a stronger regime of environmental protection could be put in place to deter harm during wars, and provide the grounds for compensation claims and individual criminal responsibility if a belligerent state should in the future adopt tactics that intentionally or negligently produce major environmental harm.

It has seemed increasingly important for civil society to be mobilized around concerns involving the laws of war if meaningful substantive reforms are to be achieved. Governments left on their own seem to lack the political will at this time to strengthen the law of war across a wide spectrum of concerns. The contribution of civil society is partly to exert pressure on governments to be more receptive with respect to lawmaking initiatives that are needed for human well-being, and thereby to neutralize bureaucratic obstacles to reformist steps, especially those erected by military establishments and their industrial counterparts.

The experience with anti-personnel landmines[20] bolsters both sides of the argument as to how to assess existing international law relative to the

---

[20] Convention on the Prohibition of the Use, Stockpiling, Production and Transfer of Anti-Personnel Mines and on Their Destruction (Sept. 18, 1997), reprinted in *Int'l Rev. Red Cross* 320 (1997), 563–78. The treaty was signed by more than 120 countries at the conclusion of negotiations in Ottawa, Canada, and came into force in September 1998 after the deposition at the UN of the fortieth instrument of ratification.

environment during wartime. On the one hand, it supports the view that the lawmaking cycle can be dramatically shortened if well-organized transnational civic groups working together on a common campaign of planetary scope can mount sufficient political pressure. It illustrates also the new political possibilities of coalitions in which governments join forces with a movement that has taken shape in transnational civil society. Such a process of political mobilization can also benefit from media exposure and the visible commitment of global celebrities; the role of Princess Diana in the anti-landmines campaign is illustrative. And finally, the legitimating role of the Nobel Peace Prize given to Jody Williams and the International Campaign to Ban Landmines was a further addition to a "soft power" assault on militarist thinking in several key countries that continued to insist that such weaponry was needed to handle certain battlefield challenges, or that at the very least it possessed cost/benefit advantages as compared to substitutes.[21]

On the other hand, it is important to acknowledge the refusal of the United States and several other major states to go along with the treaty of prohibition as drafted and signed by more than 100 governments in Ottawa in 1997. Such a refusal can be invoked to show that it is futile to push law beyond the limits of geopolitics. That is, if purported legal obligations exceed the limits of what the most powerful states are prepared to do at a given time, then the insistence on going forward may produce an empty legalistic gesture. Such a gesture is unlikely to alter the behavior of objecting states, and may induce a cynical backlash with regard to the wider role of international law. From such a perspective, the wisdom of working hard with what exists, even if insufficient, commends itself to those who deem politics to be the art of the possible.

The comparison between banishing landmines and avoiding wartime environmental harm seems quite illuminating. In both instances, there already exists a skeletal legal framework that seems on its face to be inadequate for the substantive challenge posed. Yet in both settings, strong political arguments are mounted to contend that it is impractical to work for the establishment of a more effective legal regime. Of course, the comparison is far from perfect. Prohibition of anti-personnel landmines imposes relatively minor economic costs in carrying out particular military missions without reliance on such weaponry. The prohibition

---

[21] See Jody Williams, "Land Mines: Dealing with the Environmental Impact," *Env't & Security* 1 (1997), 107–23.

could be accepted without altering in any substantive way the primacy of military necessity. The same cannot be said about a more comprehensive ban on environmentally harmful tactics where, to be effective, the prohibition would in some situations have to override assessments of military necessity, and thus almost inevitably raise questions about upholding goals in war that may be inconsistent with victory.

Ultimately, the question is what it is reasonable to expect by way of legal reform at a given time. The flow of history can either speed up or slow down our calculations of feasibility, and our sense of what it is possible to achieve within a given time frame is exceedingly modest. Such uncertainty reinforces the argument that jurists should recommend that which seems necessary rather than content themselves with what they deem possible, especially if the possible shows little sign of adequacy. As already observed, the existing norms and standards have only a limited and ambiguous scope for legal applicability, and, as a result, are subject to arbitrary patterns of implementation that involve "double standards" and "victor's justice." Beyond this, the absence of any concerted effort to create a coherent legal approach has produced a very low level of awareness and concern about the environmental consequences of warfare. To resign ourselves to such a questionable legal regime, simply because a better one seems not to be currently negotiable, is to accept an unwarranted counsel of despair that overlooks the potential role of transnational civic activism in changing perceptions of political feasibility.

The remarkable results achieved by the grassroots campaign to ban anti-personnel landmines in the face of a similar set of discouraging factors should offer some encouragement. A comparable transnational coalition of NGOs has put the question of the legality of nuclear weaponry on the global political agenda despite strong geopolitical resistance. I am not suggesting that these campaigns have been entirely successful or are completely analogous to concerns related to environmental harm caused by war. I do contend that they support the view that perceptions of what governments seem likely to agree upon within a present climate of opinion should not be used to determine the outer limits of feasible reform.

Conclusion

In summary, then, existing standards of international law seem arbitrary and inconsistent in application. In addition, to the extent they are embodied in treaties, these standards have not been ratified by several key states, and their status in customary international law is quite uncertain. Further, the ENMOD norms are too remote from battlefield practices to have much current relevance, while the Protocol I norms are too closely tied to humanitarian law to function adequately for purposes of environmental protection. As a result, existing international law does not presently provide the moral or political foundations for a credible legal regime to prevent severe environmental harm as a side effect of high-intensity warfare or to impose liability upon governments that resort to environmental warfare as a deliberate tactic. Beyond this, there has been no consciousness-raising process at an international level that would lead the governments of the world to adjust their training programs and instruction manuals in such a way as to minimize adverse environmental consequences arising from warfare.

Such a legal regime is needed to protect the general well-being of the peoples of the world, to safeguard the global commons, and to set "reasonable" limits on legally acceptable modes of warfare. It is crucially important that these limits are not allowed to be set aside by contextual appeals to military necessity or by an exemption from coverage of strategic bombing and nuclear weaponry, potentially the most environmentally destructive weaponry. To shape an adequate legal regime for environmental protection requires a separate dedicated effort of major proportions. It cannot be achieved as an incidental aspect of international humanitarian law, with its focus on human vulnerability in the course of war.

Such a viewpoint, then, favors an international campaign to push for an effective regime of standards and procedures dedicated to prevention and punishment of deliberate, incidental, and negligent environmental harm in war. This campaign can build on the experience currently being accumulated with Iraq, using this as a precedent for a more systematic legal foundation that is not as dependent on the vagaries of political context to achieve its applicability. This experience should be supplemented by an assessment of the environmental damage done in the NATO war over Kosovo. The goal of such a campaign would be to establish a climate of opinion that would lead enough governments to believe that it is worthwhile to initiate a lawmaking process to generate adequate legal standards. This campaign would have two distinct elements: (1) a global conference to draft a convention dedicated to the prevention and punishment of deliberate, incidental, and negligent environmental harm, specifying the main types of harm, degrees of liability by governments and individuals, and institutional mechanisms for verifying violations and assessing responsibility; and (2) a related undertaking to establish "ecocide" as a crime complementing the crime of "genocide."

It should be understood that this outlook takes a somewhat long-range view of the challenges posed by the environmental consequences of war. It also proceeds from a political and moral assumption that movement in this direction will depend in its initial phases on a major grassroots effort, combined to the extent possible with proposals put forward by states within the UN system and on an intergovernmental basis. This process will succeed only to the extent that an international climate of opinion supportive of such a regime of prohibition and punishment can be established. Even in this event, it will be necessary to proceed through a long negotiating process to achieve a meaningful consensus among governments on the character of adequate standards that can effectively supplant the current "comfort level" that is insulating this subject matter from scrutiny and reformist initiatives.

5

UNITED STATES NAVY DEVELOPMENT OF OPERATIONAL–ENVIRONMENTAL DOCTRINE

CAPTAIN JOHN P. QUINN, CAPTAIN RICHARD T. EVANS, AND
LIEUTENANT COMMANDER MICHAEL J. BOOCK

Introduction

Protection of the environment during training and operations is an important priority of the United States Navy. Maintaining the appropriate balance between environmental protection and mission achievement is a complex proposition, as the focus of operations shifts along the continuum from peacetime training, to military operations other than war, to warfare itself. This chapter describes the United States Navy's efforts – in concert with other military services, the Joint Staff, and international military organizations – to develop environmental protection doctrine and policy that provides appropriate guidance for operational staff and leaders in this critically important area. This chapter gives substantial treatment to military operations other than war (MOOTW).

First, this chapter helps to identify the essential linkages through which legal principles pertaining to the protection of environment in military operations are given real-world effect. Clear international consensus on appropriate norms for environmental protection during war, even if achievable, would be considerably less effective without meaningful translation of those norms into military doctrine and policy governing battlespace practice. Environmental protection can be much more efficiently achieved through prevention of environmental injury in the first place (a result of enlightened operational decisionmaking) than through post-conflict damage assessment, recovery from and/or prosecution of responsible parties, and efforts to remedy the damage.

The views expressed in this chapter are those of the authors alone, and do not necessarily reflect the official policy or position of the US Department of Defense or the US government.

Second, for the foreseeable future the prospect of all-out world war – full-scale multinational conflict on several continents – is thankfully minimal. By contrast, it is virtually certain that most nations will continue to conduct military training and exercises, and that many states will periodically engage in large-scale military operations other than war. Environmentally sound peacetime and MOOTW practices by the world's military forces would thus have an immediate, widespread, and positive environmental effect.

Closely related to the second reason, peacetime military training and exercises – and to a certain extent MOOTW operations as well – are rehearsals for war. The maxim "train like you fight" dictates that peacetime training and exercises be as realistic as possible, in order to maximize the probability of quick success with minimal casualties during war. The corollary, "fight like you train," establishes the relevance of peacetime and MOOTW practices to the objective of constraining wartime environmental damage: units accustomed to environmentally sound peacetime and MOOTW operations are predisposed to carry those perspectives into battle.[1]

Finally, a review of evolving military environmental protection guidance is important for present purposes because this doctrine may portend developments in the law itself. The environmental initiatives of the world's military forces, undertaken with their governments' sanction and encouragement, even if not by specific legislative direction, reflect emerging state practice.[2] In many instances environmental protection requirements adopted by the US Navy for peacetime operations exceed the minimum requirements imposed by US domestic legislation or international norms. For example, although not required under the MARPOL Convention[3] or by

---

[1] Hans-Peter Gasser, "The Debate to Assess the Need for New International Accords," in Richard J. Grunawalt et al. (eds.), *Protection of the Environment During Armed Conflict* (Newport, R.I.: Naval War College, 1996), pp. 521, 522 ("It may well be hoped that a growing awareness of ecological considerations in normal times will strengthen the resolve to respect such standards in armed conflict as well.").

[2] See W. Michael Reisman and William K. Lietzau, "Moving International Law from Theory to Practice: The Role of Military Manuals in Effectuating the Law of Armed Conflict," in H. G. Robertson, Jr. (ed.), *The Law of Naval Operations* (Newport, R.I.: Naval War College, 1991), pp. 1–18.

[3] MARPOL is the combination of the International Convention for the Prevention of Pollution from Ships, done at London, Nov. 2, 1973, IMCO Doc. MP/Conf/WP.35 (1973), and the Protocol of 1978 Relating to the International Convention for the Prevention of Pollution from Ships, 1973, done at London, Feb. 17, 1978, entered into force, Oct. 2, 1983, IMCO Doc. TSPP/CONF/11 (1978), reprinted in *I.L.M.* 17 (1978), 546. The 1973 Convention is not intended to enter into force and be applied on its own.

domestic law, in 1990 the Navy required its warships to retain waste plastic on board for shore disposal, to the extent that limited storage space would permit. The Navy has since developed and nearly completed installation in surface warships of a plastic waste processor, which will melt, compress, and sanitize all shipboard plastic waste, for recycling or disposal in port.

Over time, particularly when these policymaking efforts are undertaken multilaterally, these practices may influence emerging norms of customary international law. Additionally, to the extent that an environmental protection ethic is an integral part of military culture and is perceived to be consistent with military requirements, military organizations are less likely to resist international agreement proposals that seek to enhance environmental protection in military operations.

This chapter begins with an examination of the purpose and need for operational–environmental guidance to military commanders. Next is a discussion of the factors that led the Navy to select the "Naval Warfare Publication" (NWP) format as the vehicle through which to promulgate operational–environmental doctrine. The significant challenges involved in drafting clear and useful guidance in this area are then addressed. Finally, the chapter reviews the efforts of the US Navy and other military services to prepare operational–environmental doctrine, and looks ahead to future developments in this area.

The impetus for operational–environmental doctrine

In the waning years of the twentieth century, few observers disputed that environmental protection in military operations worldwide is an increasingly important priority. As discussed in this section, a number of factors have spurred the US Navy and other military services to develop environmental protection guidance that spans the continuum from peace to war.

Compliance with domestic and international law is a substantial impetus for the Navy's development of operational–environmental doctrine. US law imposes a host of significant environmental requirements affecting naval training and exercises. Most major US pollution control statutes include a provision requiring federal entities, including the armed forces, to comply with federal, state, and local environmental requirements to the same extent as any other person.[4] Other federal statutes

---

[4] See, e.g., Clean Water Act § 313, 33 U.S.C. § 1323; Clean Air Act § 118, 42 U.S.C. § 7418; Solid Waste Disposal Act § 6001, 42 U.S.C. § 6961.

create environmental obligations directed solely towards federal entities.[5] Acknowledging these requirements years ago, the US Navy adopted a proactive policy regarding the development of sound and workable domestic requirements for US Navy activities.

The results of this successful approach are today enshrined in Navy policy guidance and even in the domestic environmental law of the United States itself. The Navy and Marine Corps have extensive environmental instructions addressing virtually all aspects of naval activity, both ashore and afloat.[6] Thus, recognizing that the pollutant discharge requirements of the Clean Water Act[7] could significantly affect warship operations, the Navy sponsored a 1996 amendment to the Clean Water Act that designated the Navy and the US Environmental Protection Agency (EPA) as coregulators for purposes of warship discharges to US waters. The amendment specifies a sensible and workable set of criteria for regulating such discharges, in an effort to harmonize important national priorities of environmental protection and national defense.[8] Under this "Uniform National Discharge Standards" provision of the Clean Water Act, the following criteria govern the development of warship discharge standards: the nature of the discharge; the environmental effects of the discharge; the practicability of using a marine pollution control device to control the discharge; the effect that installation or use of a marine pollution control device would have on the operation or operational capability of the vessel; applicable United States law; applicable international standards; and the economic costs of installation or use of a marine pollution control device. In this context, the term "marine pollution control device" means both pollution control hardware and pollution prevention practices.

The broad geographic reach of certain US environmental requirements significantly magnifies their importance to operational commanders. Several environmental statutes that can directly affect operations at

---

[5] E.g., National Environmental Policy Act, 42 U.S.C. § 4332(2)(C) (environmental impact assessment); Endangered Species Act, 16 U.S.C. § 1536(a)(2) (consultation to ensure that federal actions are not likely to jeopardize the continued existence of protected species); Coastal Zone Management Act, 16 U.S.C. § 1456(c)(1)(A) (to ensure that federal activities carried out within or outside the coastal zone are consistent to the maximum extent practicable with the enforceable policies of approved management programs developed by states of the United States).

[6] E.g., Chief of Naval Operations Instruction 5090.1B (Nov. 1, 1994) (a book-length, 25-chapter document prescribing, among other things, requirements pertinent to environmental planning, ship discharges, oil spills, marine sanctuaries, and species protection).

[7] 33 U.S.C. §§ 1251ff.   [8] 33 U.S.C. § 1322(n).

sea – such as the Endangered Species Act, the Marine Mammal Protection Act, the Act to Prevent Pollution from Ships, and the Ocean Dumping Act – expressly apply in whole or in part beyond US territory.[9] Although devoid of language establishing extraterritorial application, the National Environmental Policy Act's (NEPA)[10] environmental planning requirements were in one case found to be applicable to a proposed National Science Foundation action in Antarctica.[11] As an extraterritorial complement to NEPA, in Executive Order 12114 the President mandated NEPA-like environmental analysis in connection with federal agency actions undertaken beyond US territory.[12] Thus, Department of the Navy practice is to evaluate, under NEPA, the environmental impacts that occur within the continental United States and in the territorial sea.

In addition to applicable domestic law, operational commanders must also comply with applicable environmental requirements emanating from international environmental law, host nation law, and the law of armed conflict.[13] For example, the Basel Convention on the Control of Transboundary Movements of Hazardous Wastes and their Disposal affects the movement and disposition of hazardous waste generated during military operations. Similarly, host nation law may impose environmental requirements applicable to naval operations conducted within the territory, territorial sea, or exclusive economic zone of foreign countries. Officers who ascend to positions of leadership at sea or on operational staffs must be made aware of these requirements. For them, naval doctrine and policy bridges the gap between existing legal requirements and operational decisionmaking.

Important policy concerns also impel the development of operational–environmental guidance for military commanders. Military force is increasingly employed in MOOTW and in combat operations designed to

---

[9] See, e.g., Endangered Species Act, 16 U.S.C. § 1538(a); Marine Mammal Protection Act, 16 U.S.C. § 1372(a); Act to Prevent Pollution from Ships, 33 U.S.C. § 1902(a); Ocean Dumping Act, 33 U.S.C. § 1401(c). [10] 40 U.S.C. §§ 4321ff.

[11] *National Science Foundation v. Massey*, 986 F.2d 528 (D.C. Cir. 1993).

[12] Executive Order 12114, 3 C.F.R. 356 (1980), para. 1-1 (stating that this Executive Order "represents the United States government's exclusive and complete determination of the procedural and other actions to be taken by Federal agencies to further the purpose of the National Environmental Policy Act, with respect to the environment outside the United States").

[13] For a brief compendium of suggested international guidelines – based in part on the law of war – concerning protection of the environment in times of armed conflict, see International Committee of the Red Cross, *Guidelines for Military Manuals and Instructions on the Protection of the Environment in Times of Armed Conflict*, UN Doc. A/49/323, Annex (1994).

be swift and decisive. Worldwide television media may broadcast coverage of such operations in virtually real time. In many cases the political objectives for which military force is employed contemplate near-term constructive interaction with the nation against which military force is employed, once the crisis has passed. Environmentally irresponsible operations in these situations could undermine the objectives for which military force is being employed, and could be self-defeating. On the other hand, careful and visible attention to environmental considerations in the conduct of MOOTW and war, consistent with operational requirements, can assist in maintaining public support both internationally and domestically. This may be particularly important where coalition maintenance is necessary, or where specific legislative branch approval of the operation is required.

Development of operational–environmental guidance

Having established that operational–environmental guidance for military commanders is necessary, and that the guidance must afford adequate latitude for operational commanders, the next question is the format such guidance should take. Within the military services there exists an abundance of directives, instructions, manuals, handbooks, policy statements, and other guidance covering virtually every aspect of military activity. All echelons of the Navy chain of command issue written directives, from the Secretary of the Navy and the Chief of Naval Operations levels down through individual ships and shore stations. The selection of an appropriate format and issuing authority is the key to maximizing the effectiveness of the guidance.

Among the many guidance documents issued within the Department of the Navy are publications issued by the Navy Warfare Development Command, and directed to operational planners and implementers. Denoted "Naval Warfare Publications" (NWP), these book-length documents are intended for use by operational commanders and supporting staff elements. NWPs outline Navy policy in such broad areas as command and control, intelligence, operations, logistics, and planning.

In October 1995, the Navy issued NWP 1-14M, *The Commander's Handbook on the Law of Naval Operations.*[14] NWP 1-14M essentially

---

[14] NWP 1-14M, developed by the Naval War College, replaced NWP 9A, an earlier iteration bearing the same name. NWP 1-14M has also been promulgated by the United States Marine Corps and the United States Coast Guard as guidance for their operational commanders.

restates, in straightforward terms, the international law requirements of immediate concern to operational commanders at sea. NWP 1-14M consists of two parts. The Law of Peacetime Operations (Part I) addresses such topics as the Law of the Sea, sovereign immunity, and the protection of persons and property at sea. The Law of Naval Warfare (Part II) addresses such topics as the principles of the law of armed conflict, the law of neutrality, and the law of targeting. Within the law of targeting discussion, paragraph 8.1.3 specifically addresses environmental protection:

> It is not unlawful to cause collateral damage to the natural environment during an attack on a legitimate military objective. However, the commander has an affirmative obligation to avoid unnecessary damage to the environment to the extent that it is practical to do so consistent with mission accomplishment. To that end, and so far as military requirements permit, methods or means of warfare should be employed with due regard to the protection and preservation of the natural environment. Destruction of the natural environment not necessitated by mission accomplishment and carried out wantonly is prohibited. Therefore, a commander should consider the environmental damage which will result from an attack on a legitimate military objective as one of the factors during targeting analysis.

Recognizing the increasing importance of environmental protection in naval operations, in 1996 the Navy decided that this topic warranted coverage in a separate Naval Warfare Publication. NWP 4-11, *Environmental Protection*, will be devoted entirely to environmental protection across the operational continuum, from peace to war. The publication is currently being developed.

The use of the Naval Warfare Publication format is significant for a number of reasons. Because the format will be familiar to operators, they will more easily assimilate the guidance provided. When issued by the Navy Warfare Development Command, the new operational–environmental guidance will stand on an equal footing with doctrine issued on core mission functions. This will underscore the document's importance to persons charged with carrying out its direction. The Naval Warfare Publication format will thus encourage assimilation of an environmental protection ethic into the Navy's operational culture, which will result in the maximum environmental protection consistent with mission accomplishment.

Peace	MOOTW	War

5.1 The operational continuum

Challenges in preparing operational–environmental guidance

Today's naval forces can be said to operate at all times at some point along a continuum that ranges from peace through MOOTW to war, as illustrated in Figure 5.1. MOOTW operations, though conducted to promote peace, often entail some application of force. Recent examples of MOOTW include the oil tanker escort operation undertaken during the "Tanker War" in the Persian Gulf beginning in 1987; the enforcement of United Nations sanctions against Iraq between 1990 and the present; and the peacekeeping operations undertaken in Somalia in 1992, and in the former Yugoslavia from 1992 through the present. The international community's response to the 1990 Iraqi invasion of Kuwait is an excellent example of how the activities of an international military coalition can shift from peace, to MOOTW, to war, and back to MOOTW.

As previously discussed, at each point on the operational continuum modern naval forces are subject to a host of environmental constraints of domestic and international origin. One of the most significant challenges to providing clear, useful, and legally correct operational–environmental guidance to operational commanders is that the limits of peace, MOOTW, and war are often not clearly defined. The threshold question, then, is often a determination of the applicable operational category.

Even where the operational category can be identified with reasonable certainty, however, determining the full panoply of applicable environmental requirements during MOOTW and war may still be difficult. To be sure, certain law of armed conflict[15] limitations on the means and methods of warfare protect the environment. Few people, if any, would dispute that the principles and spirit of the law of armed conflict also apply during MOOTW.[16] The more difficult challenge is to ascertain the extent to which

---

[15] See *ICRC Guidelines.*
[16] See, e.g., US Department of Defense Directive 5100.77, "Department of Defense Law of War Program" (July 10, 1979) ("the Armed Forces of the United States shall comply with the law of war in the conduct of military operations and related activities in armed conflict, however such conflicts are characterized").

5.2 The sliding scale theory

domestic and international environmental law continues to apply in the context of MOOTW and war.

One common perception on this issue is that there exists a sort of "sliding scale" (illustrated in Figure 5.2) under which the force and effect of peacetime environmental norms, both international and domestic, gradually diminish as military necessity increases.

The sliding scale theory may be a useful representation of the durability of peacetime international environmental norms. Such norms may be regarded as continuing in force during MOOTW and war to the extent consistent with the law of armed conflict.[17] The law of armed conflict in this context is thus not only a set of limitations on the use of military force, but also an implied authorization to take certain actions – not otherwise prohibited under the law of armed conflict – that peacetime international environmental norms would forbid.

Although appealing for its simplicity, the sliding scale theory does not accurately reflect the letter of domestic US environmental law as applied to MOOTW and war scenarios. With one exception, no US environmental statute expressly provides for its suspension during periods of armed conflict.[18] Furthermore, no US statute expressly affords an operational commander the discretion to balance the statute's mandates against military necessity. For the most part, US environmental statutes allow only very limited exemptions due to exigent circumstances, and only after Presidential or Cabinet-level involvement.[19] As noted above, most such

---

[17] See *ICRC Guidelines.*
[18] Act to Prevent Pollution from Ships, 33 U.S.C. § 1902(b)(2)(B) (expressly suspending certain requirements during time of war or declared national emergency).
[19] See, e.g., Clean Water Act, 33 U.S.C. § 1323(a) (empowering the President to temporarily exempt designated federal activities from environmental requirements if "in the paramount interests of the United States"); Clean Air Act, 42 U.S.C. § 7418(b) (same); Solid Waste Disposal Act, 42 U.S.C. § 6961(a) (same); Endangered Species Act, 16 U.S.C. § 1536(j) (empowering the Secretary of Defense to obtain an exemption from ESA requirements upon the Secretary's determination that "such exemption is necessary for reasons of national security," but only after a lengthy interagency consultation process); but cf. Marine Mammal Protection Act, 16 U.S.C. §§ 1361–1421h (no national interest or national security "safety valve").

statutes do not apply outside the United States, but a few statutes important to naval operations do have extensive extraterritorial reach. In addition to imposing environmental requirements that may persist during MOOTW and war, domestic US law also requires that operational commanders carry out their military duties zealously and effectively. Failure to obey a lawful order, or dereliction in the performance of duty, are punishable offenses.[20] The willful failure of a member of the armed forces to do his or her utmost to "encounter, engage, capture or destroy . . . enemy . . . vessels . . . which it his duty to so encounter, engage, capture or destroy" is punishable by death.[21] Under some circumstances, a tension can arise between a commander's domestic legal obligation to carry out the mission effectively and his or her obligation to protect the environment. For example, an attack on an enemy vessel surrounded by endangered whales may kill or injure some of the whales, and possibly violate both the Endangered Species Act and the Marine Mammal Protection Act. On the other hand, refraining from such an attack could violate the commander's orders, or be in derogation of his or her duties to defend his or her command and to carry the fight zealously to the enemy.

Should the conduct of an individual military commander in these circumstances be called into question through court-martial or civilian judicial process, the sliding scale theory may well predict the likely outcome. In deciding whether to prosecute individual defendants, both military and civilian authorities would consider many factors, including whether the prospective defendant's conduct was reasonable under the circumstances. The exercise of appropriate prosecutorial discretion should ensure that military commanders faced with an unavoidable "Hobson's choice" between mission accomplishment and environmental protection would not be prosecuted. It remains to be seen, however, whether a US District Court would apply the sliding scale in a citizen suit action brought against a military department to enforce extraterritorial environmental requirements during MOOTW or combat operations.

In view of the complexities outlined above, it is extremely difficult to articulate operational–environmental doctrine that reconciles the commander's potentially competing operational and environmental obligations.

---

[20] 10 U.S.C. § 892. [21] 10 U.S.C. § 899.

Navy operational–environmental doctrine

The Navy Warfare Development Command, assisted by Navy and Marine Corps operational planners and environmental officials, is drafting Naval Warfare Publication 4–11, entitled *Environmental Protection*. Given the complexities discussed above, and the myriad ways in which naval ships, aircraft, vehicles, sensors, and weaponry can potentially affect the environment, preparation of a comprehensive guide to the environmental law applicable in every operating scenario would be virtually impossible. Instead, the Publication will attempt to provide operational commanders with a thumbnail sketch of the legal mandates applicable in each category of naval operations, and a firm sense of the appropriate relationship of environmental protection to other priorities.

When completed, NWP 4-11 will lead operational planners through the drafting of a tailored environmental annex (denoted "Annex L") to operations orders for specific events. Annex L will establish a framework for assessing the environmental effects of the mission as a whole, as well as for incorporating protective measures into every phase of the operation. Throughout the assessment process, the planners will be required to identify alternative means of accomplishing the objectives in order to provide the operational commander with options for minimizing any adverse environmental effects. Planners will also identify the environmental consequences of various contingencies that could occur. Having completed this process, the planners will then recommend appropriate mitigation measures that can be implemented consistent with mission accomplishment.

Other military efforts to prepare operational–environmental guidance

In addition to the Navy efforts described above, each of the US military services has or is developing some form of operational–environmental guidance for field commanders. In 1997, the Air Force issued its *Environmental Guide for Contingency Operations*, which summarizes environmental responsibilities of engineer forces during peacetime, MOOTW, and wartime deployment of Air Force units. The Army and the Marine Corps are jointly developing a field manual entitled *Military Environmental Protection*. The manual will include a handy pocket-size guide that can be issued to individual soldiers.

The Chairman of the Joint Chiefs of Staff is reviewing existing Joint Staff doctrine and will incorporate environmental considerations where necessary. Joint (multiservice) doctrine publications in the operations, planning, and engineering series have been identified for environmental updates. Concurrently, the Office of the Secretary of Defense (OSD) is drafting an overarching instruction on "Environmental Security for Military Operations Overseas." When completed, it is anticipated that the OSD instruction will provide broad policy guidance mandating adherence to the highest environmental standards achievable consistent with the operational circumstances.

Although not operational in focus, the highly successful OSD initiative to improve the environmental performance of US military installations in foreign countries is a further indicator of Departmental commitment to sound environmental practices. In 1991, OSD directed the military services to develop baseline environmental standards for US installations worldwide.[22] Designed to protect human health and the environment, the standards were prepared in consideration of generally accepted environmental standards applicable to Department of Defense facilities in the United States. Standards were developed to address a wide range of environmental concerns, such as air pollution, water pollution, hazardous and medical waste management, oil spills, asbestos, underground storage tanks, natural resources conservation, endangered species protection, and the preservation of historic and cultural resources. These baseline standards comprise the Overseas Environmental Baseline Guidance Document (OEBGD).

OSD further directed designated military commands to prepare "final governing standards" for each nation in which the US maintains a substantial installation. These final governing standards incorporate the OEBGD standard for each environmental area of concern, unless applicable host nation law establishes a standard more protective of human health and the environment. In such cases, the final governing standards incorporate the host nation requirement. United States military installations overseas then comply with the final governance standard, pursuant to Executive Order 12088.[23] The Department of Defense Overseas

---

22 Department of Defense Directive 6050.16, "Department of Defense Policy for Establishing and Implementing Environmental Standards at Overseas Installations."
23 Executive Order 12088, 3 C.F.R. 243 (1979) (requiring federal agencies to ensure that the construction or operation of US facilities in foreign countries complies with the environmental "pollution control standards of general applicability" in the host nation).

Environmental Compliance initiative goes well beyond the Executive Order's mandate by addressing environmental protection concerns other than pollution control (such as species preservation), as well as by requiring compliance with OEBGD standards that frequently are more stringent than host nation standards of general applicability.

The OSD Overseas Environmental Compliance initiative is expressly inapplicable to off-installation operational and training deployments of US forces. The initiative does apply, however, to logistics support functions provided to those deployments from US military installations overseas, such as hazardous waste management. The real significance of this effort for present purposes is its demonstration of long-term Department of Defense commitment to environmental responsibility outside the United States, even in the absence of detailed statutory direction. This same commitment is evident in the various military service initiatives described above to develop pragmatic environmental guidance for their operational forces.

Federal law provides only very general guidance regarding the development of an environmental protection regime for US military installations worldwide: "The Secretary of Defense shall *develop a policy for determining applicable environmental requirements* for military installations located outside the United States. In developing the policy, the Secretary shall ensure that the policy gives consideration to adequately protecting the health and safety of military and civilian personnel assigned to such installations."[24] Construed narrowly, the specific mandate could have been satisfied merely by identifying and complying with environmental requirements applicable at US military installations in foreign countries. These would include any applicable requirements of international law, host nation law, and US law having extraterritorial effect. Instead, OSD went much further by developing, as a matter of policy, a comprehensive and detailed set of environmental controls. The Navy monitors compliance with overseas environmental requirements through regularly scheduled environmental compliance evaluations conducted by senior echelons of command, and through environmental inspections conducted by the Navy Inspector General.

A final initiative worthy of mention here is the North Atlantic Treaty Organization (NATO) development of a Standardization Agreement

---

[24] Pub. L. No. 101-510, § 342 (1990) (emphasis added).

(STANAG) for environmental protection. Undertaken by NATO's Military Agency for Standardization Joint Service Board, the agreement will address procedures for environmental protection in multinational operations such as MOOTW. The Standardization Agreement seeks to standardize environmental planning and training among NATO armed forces, and to establish an environmental protection policy that is consistent with mission accomplishment.

The future course of operational–environmental doctrine

The numerous initiatives currently in progress in the United States and elsewhere to develop operational–environmental guidance are indicative of a widely held commitment to accord environmental considerations their proper place in military operational decisionmaking. Based on developments subsequent to the 1990–91 Gulf War, several predictions can be ventured concerning the future course of these efforts.

First, military operational–environmental guidelines will continue to mature and evolve as they are tested empirically in future MOOTW and military conflicts. Given the intense interest in this area among legal scholars and the world's militaries, the experience of any military force in applying operational–environmental principles under fire will likely be closely scrutinized for lessons learned.

Second, the operational–environmental guidance currently being issued by individual military services will, over time, become homogenized. This desirable trend will be due in part to the military services' preference for standardization in the name of interoperability, and also in part to the shared and limited database of experience upon which future refinements in the guidance will be based. This common perspective on the role of environmental considerations in operational–environmental decisionmaking will reinforce these values within military forces, and increase the likelihood of appropriate conduct during MOOTW and war.

Finally, the development of operational–environmental guidance by the military services on their own initiative will almost certainly outpace the development of new law on this subject by the international legal community. This too is a desirable phenomenon. The world community and the military services themselves need environmentally sound military operations now. Both interests are best served by early and positive action to incorporate firmly an environmental dimension into operational–environmental decisionmaking. In the coming years, new or refined norms within the law of armed conflict may emerge from the environmentally responsible course being charted today by the US Navy and other world military organizations.

6

IN FURTHERANCE OF ENVIRONMENTAL GUIDELINES FOR ARMED FORCES DURING PEACE AND WAR

ARTHUR H. WESTING

Background

Unsustainable discharges of waste gases into the atmosphere and large numbers of species extinctions throughout the world are but two of many indications of the increasingly deleterious impact of humankind on the global biosphere. With the civil sector of society responsible for most of this abuse, it is only natural that attempts at ameliorative action are directed almost exclusively towards that sector. However, a number of arguments readily suggest the importance of not overlooking the military sector of society in conserving the environment.

First, although military activities now contribute only about 3 percent to total human activities worldwide (as measured in terms of gross national products),[1] every bit of ameliorative action is valuable in the increasingly dire environmental circumstances prevailing today. Second, some military activities have the potential for being environmentally disruptive at levels disproportionately high in relation to their contribution to overall human activities, thus requiring particular attention. Such examples include, among others: the Yellow River Valley (1938), Gruinard Island (1942), northern Norway (1944), Hiroshima and Nagasaki (1945), Enewetak (Eniwetok) Atoll (1952), Vietnam and Laos (1970), Kuwait

The author is pleased to acknowledge information from Carl Bruch (Washington), Jean-Marie Henckaerts (Geneva), and Masa Nagai (Nairobi); as well as suggestions from Richard G. Tarasofsky (Bonn) and Carol E. Westing (Putney).
[1] US Arms Control and Disarmament Agency, *World Military Expenditures and Arms Transfers 1996*, 25th edn. (Washington, D.C., 1997), p. 49.

and the Persian Gulf (1991), Eritrea (1991), abandoned military bases in Estonia and Latvia (1991), and Cambodia (1992).[2] Third, there is a tendency for the military sector to consider itself immune from applicable restraints on environmental abuse, especially during wartime, but also during peacetime. Fourth – some would add – the military sector to some extent does not contribute to human welfare and thus becomes a prime candidate for curtailment.

Since many people are unaware of – or perhaps unwilling to accept – the pervasiveness of military activities in the world, it will be useful to remember that some 163 of the 192 current sovereign states maintain regular armed forces.[3] Indeed, about 10 percent of all government expenditures in the world today are devoted directly to maintaining those regular forces.[4] Additionally, there consistently exist thirty or more insurgent forces, although any one of them on a somewhat less permanent basis. Moreover, although many states are at peace much of the time – with their armed forces engaged primarily in training, garrison duty, patrolling, weapon testing, and serving as a threat – from time to time they also engage in combat, both beyond and (now more frequently) within their own borders. Indeed, well over 100 governments have made hostile use of their armed forces merely since the end of World War II in support of their multifarious foreign and domestic policy agendas.[5]

The extent to which societal concerns over the deteriorating global environment have extended into military sectors is described below, primarily as a means of supporting them and facilitating their spread. The peacetime situation is noted first, followed by that of wartime. Touched upon finally are some thoughts of where we must go from here, primarily at this stage in order to reveal means for achieving a wider acceptance of the existing military guidelines.

[2] E.g., Arthur H. Westing, *Warfare in a Fragile World: Military Impact on the Human Environment* (London: Taylor & Francis, 1980).
[3] US Arms Control and Disarmament Agency, *World Military Expenditures*, p. 36.
[4] *Ibid.*, p. 49.
[5] R. L. Sivard, *World Military and Social Expenditures*, 16th edn. (Washington, D.C.: World Priorities, 1996), pp. 18–19; Dan Smith, *State of War and Peace Atlas*, 3rd edn. (London: Penguin Books, 1997), pp. 90–95; H. K. Tillema, "Foreign Overt Military Interventions in the Nuclear Age," *J. Peace Res.* 26 (1989), 179–96, 419–20; Arthur H. Westing, "War as a Human Endeavor: The High-Fatality Wars of the Twentieth Century," *J. Peace Res.* 19 (1982), 261–70.

Peacetime guidelines

With the military sector of a state widely accepted to be concerned with supreme national interests, it is equally widely taken for granted that the military sector is beyond the reach of a state's civil sector, in both democratic and totalitarian states. Indeed, in at least four states – Germany, Serbia/Montenegro, Switzerland, and the United Kingdom – the armed forces are explicitly exempted in whole or in part from domestic environmental protection legislation.[6] Moreover, numerous multilateral environmental protection treaties dealing with the marine environment specifically exempt naval ships from their constraints.[7] And, at US insistence, the 1997 Kyoto Protocol to the 1992 Framework Convention on Climate Change[8] also includes a military exemption provision.[9]

It is thus gratifying to point out that in at least nineteen states – Bangladesh, Croatia, Denmark, Finland, India, Indonesia, Iran, Malaysia, Maldives, the Netherlands, Norway, Pakistan, Poland, South Africa, Sri Lanka, Sweden, Thailand, the United States, and Vietnam – national environmental protection legislation applies equally to the military and civil sectors, at least domestically during peacetime.[10] Moreover, the North Atlantic Treaty Organization (NATO) recently developed a set of detailed environmental guidelines for armed forces during peacetime, and

---

[6] United Nations Environment Program, "Application of Environmental Norms by Military Establishments: Report of the Executive Director," Doc. UNEP/GC.18/6 & Add.1 (Nairobi: UNEP, Feb. 27 and May 14, 1995); United Nations Environment Program, "Meeting on Military Activities and the Environment, Linköping, 27–30 June 1995: Background Paper," Doc. UNEP/MIL/2 (June 13, 1995); United Nations Environment Program, "Meeting on Military Activities and the Environment, Linköping, 27–30 June 1995: Report of the Meeting," Doc. UNEP/MIL/3 (July 7, 1995).

[7] Arthur H. Westing, "Environmental Dimensions of Maritime Security," in Jozef Goldblat (ed.), *Maritime Security: The Building of Confidence*, Document No. UNIDIR/92/89 (Geneva: UN Institute for Disarmament Research, 1992), pp. 91–102.   [8] U.N.T.S. 30822.

[9] J. Warrick, "Pentagon Green Light: It Secured Exemption in Warming Treaty," *Int'l Herald Trib.* (Paris, Jan. 10, 1998), 10.

[10] UNEP, "Application of Environmental Norms"; UNEP, "Meeting on Military Activities: Report"; United Nations Environment Program, "Sub-regional Meeting on Military Activities and the Environment, Bangkok, 26–28 June 1996: Report of the Meeting," Doc. UNEP/MIL/SEA/1 (Nairobi: UNEP, June 28, 1996); United Nations Environment Program, "Sub-regional Meeting on Military Activities and the Environment, Bangkok, 29–31 October 1996: Report of the Meeting," Doc. UNEP/MIL/SA/1 (Nairobi: UNEP, Nov. 15, 1996).

suggested that these would be appropriate for any state to adopt.[11] The NATO guidelines promote environmental responsibility and in essence urge that, within limits, the military sector of a state should comply with the environmental rules established for its civil sector. Indeed, NATO would suggest that the military sector should serve as an example to the rest of society through the military's own sound environmental practices.

Even in the absence of military–civil parity before domestic law, it is clear that environmental concerns are beginning to pervade the armed forces of the world. In recent years, the defense ministries of at least eleven states have established permanent environmental divisions and programs, including those in Bulgaria, Croatia, the Czech Republic, Denmark, Germany, Hungary, Pakistan, Sweden, the United Kingdom, the United States, and Vietnam.[12] The United States appears to have done this more thoroughly and elaborately than any other state, with one senior Pentagon official proudly referring to the US armed forces as now being "lean, mean, and green."[13] Moreover, for better or worse, thirteen or more states assign to their armed forces the enforcement of environmental protection laws, including: Bangladesh, Bhutan, Cambodia, India, Indonesia, Laos, Malaysia, Maldives, Myanmar, Nepal, Philippines, Sri Lanka, and Thailand.[14]

Finally, it is useful to note the role of the United Nations in sensitizing the world to issues relating to peacetime environmental guidelines for the military sector. Prompted in part by the Programme of Action for Sustainable Development ("Agenda 21") adopted by the 1992 United Nations Conference on Environment and Development,[15] the United Nations

[11] North Atlantic Treaty Organization, *Environmental Guidelines for the Military Sector* (Brussels: North Atlantic Treaty Organization, Committee on the Challenges of Modern Society, 1996).
[12] UNEP, "Application of Environmental Norms"; UNEP, "Meeting on Military Activities: Background Paper"; UNEP, "Meeting on Military Activities: Report"; UNEP, "Sub-regional Meeting on Military Activities: 26–28 June 1996"; UNEP, "Sub-regional Meeting on Military Activities: 29–31 October 1996."
[13] Sherri W. Goodman, "DoD's [US Department of Defense's] Vision for Environmental Security," *Defense Issues* 9(24) (1994), 1–8; Sherri W. Goodman, "United States Action in the Field of Security and the Environment," in Institut de Relations Internationales et Stratégiques (ed.), *Deuxièmes Conférences Stratégiques Annuelles de l'IRIS* (Paris, 1997), pp. 223–32; Renew America (ed.), *Today America's Forces Protect the Environment* (Washington, D.C., 1995); US Department of Defense, Environmental Security (Directive No. 4715.1) (Feb. 24, 1996).
[14] UNEP, "Sub-regional Meeting on Military Activities: 26–28 June 1996"; UNEP, "Sub-regional Meeting on Military Activities: 29–31 October 1996."
[15] United Nations, *Agenda 21: Programme of Action for Sustainable Development; Rio Declaration on Environment and Development; Statement of Forest Principles* (New York: United Nations, 1993) (Publication No. DPI/1344), p. 201, para. 20.22(h).

Environment Program (UNEP) in 1993 sent a questionnaire to all states regarding military application of environmental norms.[16] In 1995 and 1996, on the advice of the United Nations Commission on Sustainable Development,[17] the United Nations followed up its questionnaire with a series of three regional intergovernmental conferences on military activities and the environment.[18] Recently, the United Nations General Assembly repeatedly has urged that all states observe environmental norms in the drafting and implementation of additions to international arms control and disarmament law.[19]

Wartime guidelines

Any consideration of constraints on environmental disruption during wartime must perforce distinguish between *international* armed conflicts and the now far more common *non-international* armed conflicts. This distinction is important because the law of war (international humanitarian law) is applicable primarily to international armed conflicts. Thus, the law of war is of formal concern primarily to states parties to the relevant law-of-war treaties while engaged in international armed conflict among themselves, at least to the extent that the relevant instruments (or portions of them) have not become customary international law and thus unavoidably binding on all states. The treaty-imposed environmental constraints associated with non-international armed conflicts are quite modest. However, this present study does not analyze either the law of war or the associated

[16] Application of Environmental Norms by Military Establishments, UNEP Governing Council Decision No. 17/5 (May 21, 1993); UNEP, "Application of Environmental Norms."

[17] United Nations Commission on Sustainable Development: Report on the Second Session (UN Economic and Social Council, Official Records, May 16–27, 1994), UN Doc. E/1994/33/Rev.1–E/CN.17/1994/20/Rev.1, ch. 1, paras. 186–87.

[18] Application of Environmental Norms by Military Establishments, UNEP Governing Council Decision No. 18/29 (May 25, 1995); UNEP, "Meeting on Military Activities: Background Paper"; UNEP, "Sub-regional Meeting on Military Activities: 26–28 June 1996"; UNEP, "Sub-regional Meeting on Military Activities: 29–31 October 1996."

[19] General and Complete Disarmament: Observance of Environmental Norms in the Drafting and Implementation of Agreements on Disarmament and Arms Control, GA Res. 50/70 M, UN GAOR (Dec. 12, 1995) (157 [85 percent] in favor, 2 abstentions, 4 against, 22 absent = 185); General and Complete Disarmament: Observance of Environmental Norms in the Drafting and Implementation of Agreements on Disarmament and Arms Control, GA Res. 51/45 E, UN GAOR (Dec. 10, 1996) (138 [75 percent] in favor, 27 abstentions, 4 against, 16 absent = 185); General and Complete Disarmament: Observance of Environmental Norms in the Drafting and Implementation of Agreements on Disarmament and Arms Control, GA Res. 52/38 E, UN GAOR (Dec. 9, 1997) (160 [86 percent] in favor, 6 abstentions, 0 against, 19 absent = 185).

law of arms control, including their fundamental principles, their strengths and weaknesses, their ambiguities, and their applicability to environmental constraints.[20]

Of more immediate concern in this study than the law of war are the self-imposed environmental constraints on a state's military sector that the state itself might adopt irrespective of its treaty commitments. To the extent that such national constraints exist, they are to be found incorporated in the rules of engagement in the military manuals of a state. For example, the United States has done just that, based in part on its treaty commitments and in part on constraints to which it is not internationally obligated.[21] Thus, even though the United States has not ratified 1977 Additional Protocol I on international armed conflicts,[22] operational instructions for the US Army legal branch nonetheless spell out the key environmental provisions of that instrument, suggesting that these largely repeat constraints to which the United States is already committed in one way or another.[23] In fact, the actual rules of engagement for the US Navy and Marine Corps simply incorporate some of the environmental constraints established by that instrument.[24] Moreover, the US Navy and

[20] See, e.g., Richard Falk, "The Inadequacy of the Existing Legal Approach to Environmental Protection in Wartime," chapter 4 in this volume; Jozef Goldblat, *Arms Control: A Guide to Negotiations and Agreements* (London: Sage Publications, 1994); Rymn J. Parsons, "The Fight to Save the Planet: US Armed Forces, 'Greenkeeping,' and Enforcement of the Law Pertaining to Environmental Protection During Armed Conflict," 10 *Geo. Int'l Envtl. L. Rev.* 10 (1998), 441–500; Adam Roberts, "The Law of War and Environmental Damage," chapter 2 in this volume; Michael N. Schmitt, "Green War: An Assessment of the Environmental Law of International Armed Conflict," *Yale J. Int'l L.* 22 (1997), 1–109; Richard G. Tarasofsky, "Legal Protection of the Environment During International Armed Conflict," *Netherlands Y.B. Int'l L.* 24 (1993), 17–79; Arthur H. Westing, "Environmental Protection from Wartime Damage: The Role of International Law," in Nils Petter Gleditsch (ed.), *Conflict and the Environment* (Dordrecht: Kluwer Academic Publishers, 1997), pp. 535–53.
[21] John P. Quinn et al., "United States Navy Development of Operational–Environmental Doctrine," chapter 5 in this volume; Judge Advocate General's School, US Army, *Operational Law Handbook*, JA 422(94) (Charlottesville, Va., 1993), ch. 5; US Dep't of the Navy, Office of the Chief of Naval Operations and Headquarters, US Marine Corps and Dep't of Transportation, US Coast Guard, *The Commander's Handbook on the Law of Naval Operations*, NWP 1-14M/MWCP 5-2.1/COMDTPUB P5800.7 (formerly NWP 9 [Rev. A]) (3rd edn., Washington, D.C., Oct. 1995). For background, see Richard J. Grunawalt, "The JCS [Joint Chiefs of Staff] Standing Rules of Engagement: A Judge Advocate's Primer," *Air Force L. Rev.* 42 (1997), 245–58.
[22] Protocol Additional to the Geneva Conventions of August 12, 1949, and Relating to the Protection of Victims of International Armed Conflicts (done at Geneva, June 8, 1977; entered into force, Dec. 7, 1978), *I.L.M.* 16 (1977), 1391; *Am. J. Int'l L.* 72 (1977), 457; U.N.T.S. 17512.
[23] US Army, *Operational Law Handbook*, pp. 18–19.
[24] US Navy, *The Commander's Handbook on the Law of Naval Operations.*

Marine Corps rules of engagement include the following important paragraph – believed to be the first in the military manual of any state that specifically requires protection of the environment during armed conflict[25] – under the heading "Environmental Considerations":

> It is not unlawful to cause collateral damage to the natural environment during an attack upon a legitimate military objective. However, the commander has an affirmative obligation to avoid unnecessary damage to the environment to the extent that it is practicable to do so consistent with mission accomplishment. To that end, and as far as military requirements permit, methods or means of warfare should be employed with due regard to the protection and preservation of the natural environment. Destruction of the natural environment not necessitated by mission accomplishment and carried out wantonly is prohibited. Therefore, a commander should consider the environmental damage which will result from an attack on a legitimate objective as one of the factors during targeting analysis.[26]

The International Committee of the Red Cross (ICRC) has long taken it upon itself to be the custodian of the law of war.[27] As part of this humanitarian task, the ICRC recently singled out environmental constraints and produced a set of model guidelines extracted primarily from all relevant portions of the law of war (to some considerable extent, of course, from 1977 Protocol I).[28] The ICRC offered these guidelines to all states through the United Nations, as well as through its own subsequent efforts, for incorporation into their respective military manuals. Currently, the ICRC is seeking to determine the extent to which states may have revised their military manuals on the basis of its environmental guidelines. At the same time, it is developing a full-blown model military manual that is to incorporate those environmental guidelines.

National military manuals are of utmost value, even if they have not as yet incorporated environmental constraints. Consequently, appropriate development and adoption of military manuals by armed forces everywhere is a high priority. The potential efficacy of military manuals takes

---

[25] J. Ashley Roach, "The Laws of War and the Protection of the Environment," *Env't & Security* 1(2) (1997), 53–67; see also Quinn et al., "United States Navy Development of Operational–Environmental Doctrine."

[26] US Navy, *The Commander's Handbook on the Law of Naval Operations.*

[27] International Committee of the Red Cross, *Law of War: Prepared for Action. A Guide for Professional Soldiers* (Geneva, 1995).

[28] International Committee of the Red Cross, *Guidelines for Military Manuals and Instructions on the Protection of the Environment in Times of Armed Conflict* (Geneva, 1993) (reprinted in UN Doc. A/49/323, 49–53 (1994); *Am. J. Int'l L.* 89 (1994), 641–44).

several forms:[29] (1) military manuals translate the abstractions that comprise the law of war into practical rules for application by armed forces; (2) by exposing armed forces to a military manual in peacetime, the manual's contents are already ingrained in times of armed conflict; (3) a military manual converts a largely unenforceable body of international legal norms into a more readily enforceable body of national regulations; and (4) through its open publication, a military manual permits – and even invites – a military adversary to conform to reciprocal humanitarian constraints.

What next?

In considering environmental military priorities for the future, this chapter focuses less on peacetime shortcomings than on wartime shortcomings; and as to the wartime shortcomings, it is less concerned with international armed conflicts than with non-international armed conflicts.

It is of course important that the states presently not parties to the several existing key multilateral treaties that establish wartime constraints of special environmental value be urged to rectify that dereliction. There are five treaties that are especially important: (1) the *1925 Geneva Protocol* on chemical and biological warfare[30] (with 59 non-parties out of 192, as of May 26, 1999), with the states acceding without any second-use reservation;[31] (2) the *1977 Additional Protocol I* (with 38 non-parties out of 192, as of May 31, 1999) together especially with its optional *Article 90* fact-finding commission (with 137 non-parties out of 192);[32] (3) the *1977 Additional Protocol II* on Non-international Armed Conflicts (with 46 non-parties out of 192, as of May 31, 1999);[33] (4) the *1980 Certain Conventional*

---

[29] W. Michael Reisman and William K. Lietzau, "Moving International Law from Theory to Practice: The Role of Military Manuals in Effectuating the Law of Armed Conflict," in H. G. Robertson, Jr. (ed.), *The Law of Naval Operations* (Newport, R.I.: Naval War College, 1991), pp. 1–18.

[30] Protocol for the Prohibition of the Use in War of Asphyxiating, Poisonous, or other Gases, and of Bacteriological Methods of Warfare (done at Geneva, June 17, 1925; entered into force, Feb. 8, 1928), L.N.T.S. 2138, 26 U.S.T. 571, T.I.A.S. No. 8061, reprinted in *I.L.M.* 14 (1975), 49.

[31] Arthur H. Westing, "Towards Eliminating the Scourge of Chemical War: Reflections on the Occasion of the Sixtieth Anniversary of the Geneva Protocol," *Bull. Peace Proposals* [now *Security Dialogue*] 16 (1985), 117–20.

[32] See generally Jean-Marie Henckaerts, "International Legal Mechanisms for Determining Liability for Environmental Damage under International Humanitarian Law," chapter 24 in this volume.

[33] Protocol Additional to the Geneva Conventions of August 12, 1949, and Relating to the Protection of Victims of Non-International Armed Conflicts (done at Geneva, June 8, 1977; entered into force, Dec. 7, 1978), U.N.T.S. 17513, *I.L.M.* 16 (1977), 1442.

Weapons Convention (with 119 non-parties out of 192, as of May 26, 1999), necessarily with its optional *Protocol II* on the use of landmines (with 124 non-parties out of 192; and with 156 non-parties out of 192 of its amended version of 1996);[34] and (5) the *1997 Anti-Personnel Mine Convention* (with 112 non-parties, as of May 26, 1999).[35] Among other institutions and individuals, both socially oriented and environmentally oriented NGOs might take on this lobbying task. On the other hand – with the exceptions of a proscription against nuclear weapons[36] and the demilitarization of protected areas (nature reserves) of outstanding universal value[37] – seeking to augment existing restraints through newly devised and more stringent treaty obligations[38] should be primarily a normative exercise and long-term objective, especially with respect to non-international armed conflicts.

Arguably, raising the awareness in both the general public and the armed forces throughout the world of the rapid deterioration of the global biosphere would be of even greater immediate value than campaigning for increased treaty adoption. Indeed, there has in recent decades been a progressive development of environmental norms in the world community.[39] In some instances, it may suffice merely to publicize the specific importance for a state to incorporate some environmental constraints into its rules of engagement regardless of whether it is a party to the relevant multilateral instruments. Nonetheless, it is difficult to over-emphasize the importance of pervasive environmental education.[40] For the states parties to law-of-war instruments, it is useful to remember that, among others, the four 1949 Geneva Conventions, their two 1977 Additional Protocols, and the

---

[34] Convention on Prohibitions or Restrictions on the Use of Certain Conventional Weapons which may be Deemed to be Excessively Injurious or to Have Indiscriminate Effects (and Protocols) (done at Geneva, Oct. 10, 1980; entered into force, Dec. 2, 1983), U.N.T.S. 22495.

[35] Convention on the Prohibition of the Use, Stockpiling, Production and Transfer of Anti-Personnel Mines and on their Destruction (done in Oslo, Sept. 18, 1997; entered into force, Mar. 1, 1999), U.N.T.S. 35597.

[36] Arthur H. Westing, "Proposal for an International Treaty for Protection against Nuclear Devastation," *Bull. Peace Proposals* [now *Security Dialogue*] 20 (1989), 435–36.

[37] Arthur H. Westing, "Protected Natural Areas and the Military," *Envtl. Conservation* 19 (1992), 343–48.

[38] E.g., Richard A. Falk, "Proposed Convention on the Crime of Ecocide," in Arthur H. Westing (ed.), *Environmental Warfare: A Technical, Policy and Legal Appraisal* (London: Taylor & Francis, 1984), 45–49; World Conservation Union (IUCN) and International Council on Environmental Law, Draft Convention on the Prohibition of Hostile Military Activities in Protected Areas (1995); see also Falk, "The Inadequacy of the Existing Legal Approach."

[39] Arthur H. Westing, "Core Values for Sustainable Development," *Envtl. Conservation* 23 (1996), 218–25.

[40] Arthur H. Westing, "Global Need for Environmental Education," *Env't* 35(7) (1993), 4–5, 45.

1980 Certain Conventional Weapons Convention all require that their contents be incorporated into school curricula or otherwise disseminated.[41]

Widespread educational efforts, both formal and informal, throughout
all levels and age groups of society are especially important in the long
term if insurgent forces of the world are to adopt environmental constraints. Environmental constraints on insurgent forces will have to be
self-imposed, deriving from some combination of at least four factors: (1)
previously inculcated environmental values; (2) the need not to alienate
the civilian population; (3) an attempt to minimize environmental damage to a domain over which the insurgents hope to gain control; and (4) a
desire to facilitate acceptance of their legitimacy by the outside world. This
is the case because, on the one hand, insurgent forces are beyond the reach
of domestic law, and, on the other hand, existing treaty constraints dealing
with non-international conflicts are purposely weak so as not to undermine the national sovereignty of the states parties and also so as not to
legitimize and encourage insurgencies.

A comparison of states parties with states non-parties to certain key
law-of-war provisions suggests an approach to achieving suitable environmental norms that is more sweeping and long-term than education. Such
a comparison shows a clear correlation between acceptance of the law of
war and the level of democratization (including human rights and governmental integrity) on the one hand and the overall stage of social and economic development on the other hand.[42] Thus, successful efforts to spread
democracy and support sustainable development would have the further
benefit of reducing the frequency of non-international armed conflicts,
which are so inherently intractable in terms of the law of war.

To reiterate, with non-international armed conflicts having become so
prevalent in recent times, the key hope for greater wartime environmental
constraints will hinge not only upon the success of pervasive educational
efforts at all levels, but (somewhat more indirectly) also upon the spread of
democracy and the achievement of sustainable development.

Conclusion

This contribution rests on two basic premises: (1) that society has by no
means rejected the use of force with deadly, destructive, and disruptive

---

[41] The four Geneva Conventions of August 12, 1949 (entered into force, Oct. 21, 1950), T.I.A.S.
Nos. 3362–65. [42] Westing, "Environmental Protection from Wartime Damage," 548–50.

intent for the ultimate resolution of conflicts, whether international or non-international; and (2) that the global biosphere is increasingly beleaguered, inter alia, with its natural resources and natural sinks now being utilized unsustainably. It then follows that efforts to protect the environment cannot be restricted to the civil sector of society, but must as well embrace the military sector, during both peacetime and wartime.

Current efforts by various agencies – such as the United Nations and NATO – to have domestic environmental protection legislation equally applicable to the civil and military sectors at least during peacetime should be supported. In fact, at least nineteen states already do so.

As to wartime, it is gratifying to recognize that the great majority of states (now 80 percent or more) have adopted 1949 Geneva Convention IV as well as its 1977 Additional Protocol I, which together add direct and indirect environmental constraints on the pursuit of international armed conflict. It is thus incumbent on everyone to support the efforts of the United Nations, the International Committee of the Red Cross, and other agencies (1) to make adoption of these two key components of international humanitarian law more nearly universal; (2) to have more governments incorporate the included environmental constraints into their military manuals and rules of engagement; and (3) to encourage the education mandated by those instruments.

Non-international armed conflict is as yet poorly served by international humanitarian law, a dilemma difficult to address owing in large part to issues of national sovereignty. Beyond working towards the more nearly universal adoption of 1977 Additional Protocol II and the 1997 Anti-Personnel Mine Convention, it is of overriding importance that widespread efforts be made to foster environmental education. It is crucial that this be done at all age levels, in both the formal and informal educational spheres, and in both the civil and military sectors. This is suggested so that the environmental norms thereby instilled will serve here regardless of the existence or acceptance of appropriate treaty obligations. Finally, democratization, the rule of law, and the achievement of sustainable development must be fostered worldwide as potent means of reducing the number of non-international wars.

B · LESSONS FROM OTHER LEGAL REGIMES

INTRODUCTION

JAY E. AUSTIN

In view of the heated debate about the status and effectiveness of international law-of-war treaties for protecting the environment during armed conflict, it is prudent also to examine norms, rules, and enforcement mechanisms derived from other legal regimes. The environmental protection systems that have had the luxury of evolving under peacetime conditions generally are more nuanced and tailored to their subject matter than the sporadic attempts to incorporate environmental concerns into the law of war. While they of course do not address the extreme circumstances encountered in full-scale armed conflict, many peacetime environmental treaties and domestic statutes have state-of-the-art provisions for deterring and remedying the same kinds of impacts – for example, catastrophic oil spills or deforestation – commonly found during wartime. Thus, at least where it is possible to consider these impacts in isolation, environmental and other peacetime laws may prove useful for wartime environmental protection, either through their direct application or through analogizing and adapting them into the law-of-war regime.[1]

One large question, alluded to in the previous section, is whether global and international environmental treaties such as the Framework Convention on Climate Change or the Convention on Biological Diversity remain in effect during armed conflict. If it could be shown, for example, that oil well fires had led to excessive emissions of greenhouse gases, that could

---

[1] See United Nations Environment Program, "Report of the Working Group of Experts on Liability and Compensation for Environmental Damage arising from Military Activities" (May 17, 1996), para. 15 ("Where [applicable international law] rules do not yield a clear result for a specific question . . . other rules are relevant because they may provide an appropriate pattern for resolving a concrete problem in accordance with equitable principles. These other rules are, thus, applied by analogy or serve as a source of inspiration for the decision of a particular case.").

serve as an additional basis for holding the state that caused the fires responsible and liable. In her chapter, Silja Vöneky argues that whether a peacetime environmental treaty will be applicable and binding during wartime depends on the character of the treaty, and whether it is sufficiently similar to other categories of treaties that are considered applicable in wartime under general international law. According to Vöneky, peacetime environmental treaties (and customary international law) would remain applicable during wartime to the extent that they purport to protect "the interests of the state community as a whole." Applying this analysis, major area-based treaties such as the United Nations Convention on the Law of the Sea (UNCLOS) and the Antarctic Convention could serve as a source of norms governing military activities within their respective areas of jurisdiction. In addition, treaties regulating the global commons, such as the stratosphere or the biosphere, also could remain binding on belligerent states.

The potential advantages of integrating peacetime environmental law with the law of war can be illustrated by examining a relevant peacetime treaty in detail. The chapter by Thomas Mensah analyzes the provisions found in UNCLOS and its associated liability conventions. Taken together, these instruments spell out a comprehensive international and national regime for establishing liability and assessing and recovering monetary compensation for marine pollution. They provide for strict, albeit limited, liability for spills of oil and other hazardous substances, and permit recovery from responsible parties for clean-up costs, personal injury, property damage, economic loss, and "impairment of the environment." The conventions deal with liability of individual actors, not state responsibility per se, and they may have limited applicability to military and government vessels. However, Mensah notes that UNCLOS and the other conventions "may . . . be applicable to warships and other government vessels engaged in war activities if they cause environmental damage," and that military activities are not absolutely excluded from the UNCLOS dispute settlement procedures. This conclusion suggests that states parties, especially coastal states, should explore the potential use of UNCLOS to deter and sanction wartime pollution of the marine environment.

In any case, the structure of the UNCLOS regime remains a powerful model that could be incorporated into future measures to address wartime environmental damage. Of particular interest are the 1971 International Convention on the Establishment of an International Fund for

Compensation for Oil Pollution Damage and the 1996 Convention on Liability and Compensation for Damage in Connection with the Carriage of Hazardous and Noxious Substances by Sea. These conventions each created an international fund – sustained by fees on the shipment of oil and hazardous substances, respectively – to compensate for damage above and beyond the limited liability of shipowners, as well as in cases where recovery from the responsible party is impossible or inadequate. The existence of these funds has led observers to suggest that a comparable fund be created to remediate wartime environmental damage (see, for example, Mahmood Abdulraheem's chapter in Part III). The problem of finding solvent defendants is particularly acute in the aftermath of war, given the large scale of wartime damages, the ravaged state of most postwar economies, and the enormous number of competing claims.

David Caron, who has studied this problem in the context of the United Nations Compensation Commission, argues that "without the provision of dedicated funds, one realistically must acknowledge that it will be a rare instance where the necessary funds are made available for environmental restoration." He further emphasizes the importance of setting priorities within the environmental sphere, suggesting as a first step "the creation of a fund for the restoration of designated areas of special environmental importance, such as World Heritage Sites, damaged by armed conflict." In Caron's view, such a fund initially could be financed either by the international community as a whole, or by those states that have been most responsible for past wartime environmental damage. But Caron also acknowledges that at present there is little support for an international fund that would depend on infusions of money from the coffers of national governments, describing this phenomenon as "donor fatigue."

An alternative proposal is made by Jeffrey Miller, who arrives at similar conclusions from a very different starting point. Focusing on experience with US environmental law, Miller canvasses both common law tort doctrines and pollution control statutes, highlighting the policy goals that underlie each. Drawing analogies from Superfund, the Oil Pollution Act, and the Surface Mining Control and Reclamation Act, he outlines a proposed international regime of strict liability for wartime environmental damage, supplemented by a remediation fund. While Miller concedes that most states are unlikely to agree to be strictly liable for the consequences even of their justified military actions, he argues that the fund could stand alone as a no-fault solution, and address severe damages regardless of the responsible party's culpability or ability to pay. Miller offers two alternative means of generating revenue for the fund: by imposing assessments directly on states, with "the heaviest burden on states most likely to cause environmental damage in war . . . calculated on the basis of the size of the army, the size of the arsenal, the types of weapons in the arsenal, etc."; or by "making assessments not on the use by states of weapons, munitions, and other war material, but on the manufacturers or sellers of such products." Either alternative likely would require a major international negotiation on a par with the negotiations that yielded the UNCLOS liability conventions.

Experience from peacetime environmental remediation funds can provide guidance not only for creation of a fund for wartime damages, but also for its implementation. In peacetime as in wartime, the monies available usually are much less than those needed to remediate the damage fully, so a fund's guidelines typically set priorities for its use – for instance, the National Priorities List created by the US Superfund legislation. Similarly, as Caron notes, wartime environmental damage is often so pervasive and severe that it would be helpful to have an institutional framework in place to assess the various impacts quickly, to rank the affected areas and environmental functions, and to undertake remediation efforts accordingly. Peacetime experience suggests that priority should be placed on rapid mitigation, which can reduce the overall remediation costs; on areas, perhaps designated during peacetime, that are of particular environmental importance due to their uniqueness or the significance of the environmental functions they perform;[2] and on areas suffering particularly severe damage. Prescribed criteria can help to ensure that, in administering an environmental trust fund, the directors or trustees fulfill their fiduciary duty to ensure that funds are spent appropriately.

One logical outgrowth of the fund proposals has been calls for a standing emergency response task force, which have come from former Soviet President Mikhail Gorbachev, among others.[3] Such a task force would be particularly effective because it would be able to undertake mitigation efforts more rapidly than larger national bureaucracies, which must allocate the

---

[2] For description and analysis of an area-based proposal that focuses on prevention of wartime environmental damage, see Richard G. Tarasofsky, "Protecting Specially Important Areas During International Armed Conflict: A Critique of the IUCN Draft Convention on the Prohibition of Hostile Military Activities in Protected Areas," chapter 22 in this volume.

[3] Mikhail Gorbachev, Keynote Address at the First International Conference on Addressing Environmental Consequences of War, Washington, D.C. (June 10, 1998).

necessary funds and detail personnel. A standing task force could be financed by the wartime environmental damage fund, although the task force also could, where possible, seek subrogation for its efforts from the party that caused the damage. To limit expenses, this task force could be composed of a small coordinating staff that maintains a large roster of environmental experts who could be made available at short notice. Governments and international organizations also could detail skilled personnel to the task force as necessary. For example, many relief workers and military personnel have gained valuable experience in assessing, monitoring, mitigating, and remediating environmental damage after the Gulf War and the Kosovo conflict; the international community could capitalize on this expertise in addressing the environmental consequences of future armed conflicts.

While these proposals are promising, much valuable experience with wartime environmental damage has already been gained through the United Nations Compensation Commission's resolution of claims from the 1990–91 Gulf War. The Commission's authority to address environmental claims derives from Security Council Resolution 687, which held Iraq "liable under international law for any direct loss, damage, *including environmental damage and the depletion of natural resources*, or injury to foreign Governments, nationals and corporations, as a result of Iraq's unlawful invasion and occupation of Kuwait."[4] With liability presumed, the UNCC focuses primarily on assessing the amount of damages. In his report to the Security Council, the UN Secretary-General described the UNCC's mandate narrowly: "The Commission is not a court or an arbitral tribunal before which the parties appear; it is a political organ that performs an essentially fact-finding function of examining claims, verifying their validity, evaluating losses, assessing payments and resolving disputed claims; it is only in this last respect that a quasi-judicial function may be involved."[5]

Nevertheless, as the first international body expressly charged with assessing wartime environmental damages, the UNCC's every decision in this area will have great precedential value. Beyond the initial Security Council Resolutions, the Commission did not receive much substantive guidance. Its operating rules permit it to base decisions on Resolution 687 and other relevant Security Council Resolutions; on criteria established

---

[4] UN Security Council Res. 687 (Apr. 8, 1991), reprinted in *I.L.M.* 30 (1991), 847 (emphasis added).
[5] Report of the Secretary-General on the compensation provisions of Security Council Resolution 687 (May 2, 1991), quoted at http://193.135.136.30/uncc/introduc.htm.

and decisions issued by the UNCC Governing Council; and, "where necessary, other relevant rules of international law."[6] The Governing Council
quickly defined the categories of environmental claims that the UNCC
would consider: abatement and prevention of environmental damage;
"reasonable measures" already taken and future measures that are
"reasonably necessary" to clean and restore the environment; reasonable
monitoring and assessment of environmental damage and public health
impacts; and depletion of or damage to natural resources.[7]

Given the focus on damages, the law of war's incomplete coverage of
environmental damages, and the reliance on the lawyer's old standby of
"reasonableness," it was inevitable that the Commission would need to
consider peacetime laws and valuation methods for applicable principles.
As a result, attorneys practicing before the UNCC, not content to rely
solely on Resolution 687's near-absolute presumption of liability, also
cited international environmental treaties, customary international law of
civil liability, and precedent from the Iran–US Claims Tribunal to establish
the fact and the scope of Iraq's liability, as well as proper procedures for
handling claims. Moreover, in actually evaluating the claims, the UNCC
faces a wide range of issues that are most familiar to practitioners of
domestic environmental law: establishing baseline conditions, determining causation, assessing the impacts, and placing an economic value on
environmental damage.[8] Applied to the grim facts of groundwater pollution, formation of oil lakes, desert soil compaction, marine oil spills, and
public health impacts, these peacetime international and domestic legal
principles provide a framework for compensating for wartime environmental damage – albeit damage on an unprecedented scale.

In this same vein, Professor Caron's chapter also derives useful lessons
from agency law. Caron, a UNCC Commissioner and former staff member
on the Iran–US Claims Tribunal, observes a gradual procedural shift from
claims made by a state acting as principal (for example, the *Trail Smelter
Arbitration*) to claims made by a state acting as an agent on behalf of its

---

[6] UNCC Provisional Rules for Claims Procedure, Art. 31.

[7] UNCC Governing Council Decision 7, S/AC.26/1991/7/Rev.1 (Mar. 17, 1992).

[8] See UNEP Report, para. 15 ("Rules of national law . . . may also provide appropriate solutions
for questions deriving from the Iraqi invasion of Kuwait and therefore be relevant.") For a dis-
cussion of some relevant principles from US environmental liability law, see Jay Austin and Carl
Bruch, *The Greening of Warfare: Developing International Law and Institutions to Limit
Environmental Damage During Armed Conflict*, Environmental Law Institute Research Brief
No. 7 (June 1999), pp. 5–12.

injured nationals. As applied to environmental claims, he argues, the difference is important: a state that is not merely pursuing its own interests, but representing a damaged ecosystem, might well be required to adhere to international environmental law norms and to take a regional or global perspective when devising remediation strategies. Clearly, such a conclusion has far-reaching implications for UNCC practice and the design of future institutions devoted to addressing wartime environmental damage. Thus, Caron calls for "institutional attention and scholarly research" devoted to this and similar issues arising from his analogy to agency law precepts.

Ultimately, such creative analysis will be increasingly necessary, as the law of war and the law of reparations continue to evolve in their attempts to deter, compensate for, and remedy wartime environmental destruction. Even the most comprehensive treaty regime must rely on international custom and domestic law to fill gaps left by the drafters, to aid interpretation of ambiguous terms, and to serve as a source of innovative ideas and solutions. In the same way as international criminal tribunals have improvised and borrowed from national-level experience to give substance to concepts such as fairness, due process, and criminal intent, so too the law of war should remain receptive to the hard-won lessons from three decades of peacetime environmental protection.

7

PEACETIME ENVIRONMENTAL LAW AS A BASIS OF STATE RESPONSIBILITY FOR ENVIRONMENTAL DAMAGE CAUSED BY WAR

SILJA VÖNEKY

Perhaps the most destructive among man's many activities that threaten the environment is that of war.[1]

Introduction

Environment has always been one of the main victims of war. The experiences of the 1990–91 Gulf War brought this fact into the public consciousness more than ever before. Plants and animals were destroyed and damaged, and air and water were polluted by the burning oil wells and oil slicks to such a degree that it seemed urgently necessary to examine the question of the extent to which belligerents are responsible under international law for damages caused by them to the environment.

State responsibility for environmental damage caused by war[2] is commonly addressed in the traditional context of *ius in bello* and *ius ad bellum*. It is generally agreed that every violation of the laws of armed conflict that is attributable to a state entails the international responsibility of that

---

For more details on ideas advanced in this chapter, see Silja Vöneky, *Die Fortgeltung des Friedensumweltvölkerrechts in internationalen bewaffneten Konflikten* (The Applicability of Peacetime Environmental Law in International Armed Conflicts) (forthcoming dissertation, with English summary).

[1] Christopher C. Joyner and James T. Kirkhope, "The Persian Gulf War Oil Spill: Reassessing the Law of Environmental Protection and the Law of Armed Conflict," *Case W. Res. J. Int'l L.* 24 (1992), 29.

[2] For purposes of this analysis, the terms "war" and "international armed conflict" are used interchangeably. Both mean an international conflict involving armed operations regardless of a formal declaration of war.

state. Furthermore, a state incurs responsibility when it violates those rules of international law that prohibit recourse to force against another state, in particular Article 2(4) of the UN Charter. However, neither of these two bases of state responsibility is free from shortcomings, and even taken together they constitute only a rudimentary system of legal liability for environmental damage caused by war.

Without going into depth, it should be recalled that although there are several rules of the law of armed conflict that directly or indirectly protect the environment[3] and whose violation will lead to international responsibility, these provisions include so many gaps that even the devastation of the 1990–91 Gulf War arguably was not covered by them all.[4] For instance, the provisions of *ius in bello* protect only the environment in the territory of the belligerent states. Furthermore, the law of armed conflict does not protect the environment of areas beyond national jurisdiction and those parts of the environment that cannot be related to a single state, such as the ozone layer, the atmosphere, or climate.[5]

These loopholes of the *ius in bello* cannot be filled with reference to responsibility for the breach of the *ius ad bellum*. Although state responsibility for acts of aggression is much broader in scope than state responsibility for the breach of the *ius in bello*, there is no liability for a state acting in self-defense, whatever the ecological consequence of its warfare might be. This problem is particularly relevant, since in practice there are few

[3] E.g., Protocol Additional to the Geneva Conventions of August 12, 1949, and Relating to the Protection of Victims of International Armed Conflicts (Protocol I) (done at Geneva, June 8, 1977; entered into force, Dec. 7, 1978), Arts. 35(3), 55, reprinted in *I.L.M.* 16 (1977), 1391; Convention on the Prohibition of Military or Any Other Hostile Use of Environmental Modification Techniques (done at New York, Dec. 10, 1976; entered into force, Oct. 5, 1978), 31 U.S.T. 333, T.I.A.S. No. 9614, Art. 1(1), reprinted in *I.L.M.* 16 (1977), 88; Convention (No. IV) Respecting the Laws and Customs of War on Land, with Annex of Regulations (done at The Hague, Oct. 18, 1907; entered into force, Jan. 26, 1910), 36 Stat. 2277, T.S. No. 539, Arts. 23(g), 55.

[4] See Michael Bothe, "The Protection of the Environment in Times of Armed Conflict: Legal Rules, Uncertainty, Deficiencies and Possible Developments," *Germ. Y.B. Int'l L.* 34 (1991), 54 ff.; Michael N. Schmitt, "Green War: An Assessment of the Environmental Law of International Armed Conflict," *Yale. J. Int'l L.* 22 (1997), 1, 51ff.; Stephanie N. Simonds, "Conventional Warfare and Environmental Protection: A Proposal for International Legal Reform," *Stan. J. Int'l L.* 29 (1992), 165, 168ff.; Richard G. Tarasofsky, "Legal Protection of the Environment During International Armed Conflict," *Netherlands Y.B. Int'l L.* 24 (1993), 17, 22ff.

[5] See Simonds, "Conventional Warfare," 185; Bothe, "Protection of the Environment," 61ff. For further problems of environmental protection by the *ius in bello*, see Glen Plant and Richard G. Tarasofsky, "Armed Conflict and the Environment: The UN General Assembly Sixth Committee's Task," in H. Spieker (ed.), *Naturwissenschaftliche und völkerrechtliche Perspektiven für den Schutz der Umwelt im bewaffneten Konflikt* (1997), pp. 185, 196ff.

violations of Article 2(4) of the UN Charter as clear as those resulting from Iraq's invasion of Kuwait.

Considering the vast number of peacetime rules protecting the environment today, it seems promising to examine more closely whether and to what extent peacetime rules relating to environmental protection continue to apply during armed conflicts.[6] The potential relevance of peacetime environmental law for limiting the methods and means of warfare is often underestimated. For example, if the Convention on Biological Diversity applies to belligerent states, the use of chemicals that irrevocably damage plant life would be prohibited. Whereas it is generally held that the commencement of war does not directly affect the legal relations between a belligerent and a third, non-belligerent state,[7] the application of peacetime treaties and customs during war between belligerent states is unclear. The need to study the latter problem in more detail is often postulated.[8]

The first step for systematically analyzing the application of peacetime environmental law between belligerent states is to differentiate between the main sources of environmental law: environmental treaties and rules of customary environmental law. This chapter focuses mainly on whether peacetime environmental treaties remain in force for warring states. For the purposes of this chapter, "peacetime environmental law" refers to all norms and provisions that lead directly or indirectly to the protection of the environment and whose application is not limited to the existence of an international armed conflict.[9]

It is shown below that no special rule of international law has developed regarding the question of whether and to what extent peacetime environmental treaties bind belligerent states. Even if the general rules concerning

---

[6] For an examination of the impact of major peacetime environmental treaties on the methods and means of warfare, see Vöneky, *Fortgeltung*, ch. 3.

[7] E.g., A. D. McNair, *The Law of Treaties* (Oxford: Clarendon Press, 1961), p. 728; J. Delbrück, "War, Effect on Treaties," in R. Bernhardt (ed.), *Encyclopaedia of Public International Law* (Amsterdam: North-Holland Publishing Co., 1982), vol. IV, p. 313; Bothe, "Protection of the Environment," 54, 59; Patricia W. Birnie and Alan E. Boyle, *International Law and the Environment* (Oxford: Clarendon Press/New York: Oxford Univ. Press, 1992), p. 129.

[8] See, e.g., ICEL/IUCN, "Law Concerning the Protection of the Environment in Times of Armed Conflict," *Envtl. Pol'y & L.* 22 (1991), 63; "Protection of the Environment in Times of Armed Conflict: Report of the Secretary-General," UN Doc. A/47/328 (July 31, 1992), p. 12, para. 56; see also UN Doc. A/48/269 (July 29, 1993), p. 15, para. 76.

[9] For a general discussion of the question "what is international environmental law?" and of the problems of defining the term "environment," see Birnie and Boyle, *International Law*, pp. 1ff.

the effects of war on peacetime treaties apply only to a very limited extent to environmental treaties, it is shown that their analogous application is possible, and the argument that the law of war prevails over peacetime law as *lex specialis* is generally rejected. Thus, environmental treaties that seek to serve the interests of the state community as a whole – such as treaties protecting areas beyond national jurisdiction and "common goods" – remain in force for belligerent states.

After advocating the application of some environmental treaties, it is necessary to examine to what extent these environmental treaties bind belligerent states. In a short overview, it is argued that there are different ways to modify the obligations to protect the environment due to the extraordinary circumstances of armed conflict. One proposal, presented in this chapter, is that the doctrine of state necessity offers a particularly useful way of balancing the interests of the belligerents with the need to protect the environment during war.

Finally, the question of which rules of customary environmental law apply between belligerents is examined briefly. This analysis employs the criteria and rules identified earlier regarding the applicability of environmental treaties during war.

The applicability of peacetime environmental treaties between belligerent states

INTRODUCTION: PUTTING THE PROBLEM IN FOCUS

In legal doctrine, there is no common view on the question whether peacetime environmental treaties are applicable to belligerent states during an international armed conflict. Although the problem has been discussed in several articles in the aftermath of the Gulf War, there is far from uniform agreement. A few commentators argue against the applicability of peacetime environmental treaties during armed conflict,[10] some seem to hold

---

[10] E.g., Richard Falk, "The Environmental Law of War: An Introduction," in Glen Plant (ed.), *Environmental Protection and the Law of War* (1992), p. 87; B. Ken Schafer, "The Relationship between the International Laws of Armed Conflict and Environmental Protection: The Need to Re-evaluate What Types of Conduct are Permissible During Hostilities," *Cal. W. Int'l L.J.* 19 (1989), 287, 319; Luan Low and David Hodgkinson, "Compensation for Wartime Environmental Damage: Challenges to International Law After the Gulf War," *Va. J. Int'l L.* 35 (1995), 405, 445.

that it is unlikely that this kind of treaty can bind belligerent states,[11] and others cannot come to a definite solution to the problem.[12] In the end, however, the prevailing view in legal doctrine seems to approve the general applicability of peacetime environmental law during war.[13] Nevertheless, even commentators who share this view disagree about the extent to which the provisions bind belligerent states.[14]

The uncertainty of legal doctrine regarding these questions is not surprising. Examining the issue of persistence of peacetime environmental treaties without reference to the general rules of international law, there does not seem to be much legal basis for a sound solution. Even after the wars in Vietnam and Kuwait, with their devastating effects on the environment, no specific rule of customary international law addressing the problem has developed.

A relevant rule of customary international law would exist only if (1) states demonstrate by "general practice" that peacetime environmental treaties either are binding or may be suspended or terminated between belligerent states during an international armed conflict, and (2) states recognize this general practice as obligatory.[15] But so far there is neither

---

[11] E.g., Leslie C. Green, "The Environment and the Law of Conventional Warfare," *Canadian Y.B. Int'l L.* 29 (1991), 222, 225; Arthur H. Westing, "Environmental Protection from Wartime Damage: The Role of International Law," in Nils Petter Gleditsch (ed.), *Conflict and the Environment* (Dordrecht and Boston: Kluwer Academic Publishers, 1997), p. 538 ("Although these treaties are in principle applicable during both peacetime and wartime – being for the most part silent on that distinction – regrettably, it seems to be widely accepted implicitly among the States parties that this body of law is operative only in times and places of peace.").

[12] E.g., Richard Carruthers, "International Controls on the Impact on the Environment of Wartime Operations," *Envtl. & Plan. L.J.* 10 (1993), 38, 41; Marc A. Ross, "Environmental Warfare and the Persian Gulf War: Possible Remedies to Combat Intentional Destruction of the Environment," *Dick. J. Int'l L.* 10 (1992), 515, 535; Liesbeth Lijnzaad and Gerard J. Tanja, "Protection of Environment in Times of Armed Conflict: The Iraq–Kuwait War," *Netherlands Int'l L. Rev.* 40 (1993), 169, 172.

[13] E.g., Bothe, "Protection of the Environment," 59, 61; Birnie and Boyle, *International Law*, p. 129; Philippe Sands, *Principles of International Environmental Law* (1994), pp. 231ff.; Simonds, "Conventional Warfare," 188ff., 193ff., 215ff.; Schmitt, "Green War," 37–41; Wolff Heintschel von Heinegg and Michael Donner, "New Developments in the Protection of the Natural Environment in Naval Armed Conflicts," *Germ. Y.B. Int'l L.* 37 (1994), 281, 295, 309ff.; Margaret T. Okorodudu-Fubara, "Oil in the Persian Gulf War: Legal Appraisals of an Environmental Warfare," *St. Mary's L.J.* 23 (1991), 123, 191ff.

[14] Compare Bothe, "Protection of the Environment," 59 with Tarasofsky, "Legal Protection," 62–67; Schmitt, "Green War," 36–41.

[15] On the elements of customary international law, see generally Ian Brownlie, *Principles of Public International Law*, 4th edn. (Oxford: Clarendon Press/New York: Oxford Univ. Press, 1990), pp. 4ff.

sufficient state practice nor *opinio iuris.* There are only a few examples of state practice that could indicate that at least some provisions of peace-time environmental treaties remain in force during war. One is that the Regional Organization for the Protection of the Marine Environment (ROPME), an organ of the 1978 Kuwait Regional Convention for Co-operation on the Protection of the Marine Environment from Pollution,[16] continued its work with the participation of the belligerent states during the Iran–Iraq and 1990–91 Gulf Wars.[17] While military manuals are import-ant evidence of customary international law in armed conflicts,[18] only one of them (the US Army's *Operational Law Handbook*) contains a rule regarding the application of peacetime environmental treaties:

> Peacetime Environmental Law (PEL). In cases not covered by the specific provisions of the LOW [Law of War], civilians and combatants remain under the protection and authority of principles of international law derived from established principles of humanity and from the dictates of public conscience. This includes protections established by treaties and customary law that protect the environment during periods of peace (if not abrogated by a condition of armed conflict).[19]

Other military manuals, such as those of the US Navy, Germany, and Canada, base their environmental provisions on the rules of *ius in bello* without taking into account the applicability of peacetime environmental treaties.[20] This does not mean, however, that these states reject the applica-bility of peacetime environmental law treaties, since there are no signs that the omission means that such application is ruled out.

Even more relevant than the lack of state practice, there is no common attitude in the expressions of states after the 1990–91 Gulf War. This was evident in the discussions before the Sixth (Legal) Committee of the UN General Assembly, where the more general problem of "Protection of the Environment in Times of Armed Conflict" was discussed. Although a few

---

[16] Kuwait Regional Convention for Cooperation on the Protection of the Marine Environment from Pollution, reprinted in *I.L.M.* 17 (1978), 511.

[17] See Tarasofsky, "Legal Protection," 64, 71; Schmitt, "Green War," 39 n. 198.

[18] See Brownlie, *Public International Law*, p. 5; H. Spieker, *Völkergewohnheitsrechtlicher Schutz der natürlichen Umwelt im internationalen bewaffneten Konflikt* (1992), pp. 114ff., 123.

[19] Judge Advocate General's School, US Dep't of the Army, *Operational Law Handbook* (Charlottesville, Va., 1993), p. 5–19.

[20] US Dep't of the Navy, *The Commander's Handbook on the Law of Naval Operations* (1995), NWP 1–14M, para. 8.13; (Germany's) *Humanitarian Law in Armed Conflicts* (Aug. 1992), Arts. 401, 403, and 1020; *Canadian Forces Law of Armed Conflict*, Arts. 505, 614, and 620; see also Schmitt, "Green War," 33ff.

states argued against the application of peacetime environmental law,[21] others held that the application was possible.[22] Most states, however, took the view that further examination of this question is required.[23] The same divergence of states' opinions is manifested in the statements regarding the advisory opinion of the International Court of Justice on the *Legality of the Threat or Use of Nuclear Weapons:*[24] while some states argued in favor of the application of peacetime environmental law during armed conflict,[25] others ruled out this kind of application as a matter of principle.[26]

Bearing this in mind, it is not surprising that even in so-called "soft law" documents there cannot be found any clear provision for or against the application of peacetime environmental law during international armed conflicts. Neither the Stockholm Declaration, nor the World Charter for Nature, nor the Rio Declaration, nor Resolutions of the General Assembly that address environmental protection, contain definite rules in this regard.[27]

---

[21] E.g., Brazil, UN Doc. A/C.6/47/SR.9, para. 13, Netherlands (on behalf of the European Community), UN Doc. A/C.6/46/SR.20, para. 3.

[22] E.g., Iran, UN Doc. A/C.6/46/SR.18, para. 33; Sweden, UN Doc. A/C.6/47/SR.8, para. 33. For further details, see V. Morris, "Protection of the Environment in Wartime: The United Nations General Assembly Considers the Need for a New Convention," *Int'l Law.* 27 (1993), 775, 776ff.

[23] E.g., Argentina, UN Doc. A/C.6/46/SR.18, para. 23; Canada, UN Doc. A/C.6/47/SR.8, para. 21; Japan, UN Doc. A/C.6/47/SR.9, para. 68.

[24] International Court of Justice, Advisory Opinion on *Legality of the Threat or Use of Nuclear Weapons* (July 8, 1996), *I.C.J. Reports* (1996), 243, reprinted in *Hum. Rts. L.J.* 17 (1996), 253.

[25] E.g., Solomon Islands, Written Comments in the General Assembly Request (GA1), 94ff. and Verbatim Record 95/32, 71ff., reprinted in R. S. Clark and M. Sann, *The Case against the Bomb* (Camden, N.J.: Rutgers Univ. School of Law at Camden, 1996), pp. 160ff.; India, Further Written Comments in the WHO Request (WHO2), 12; International Court of Justice, Advisory Opinion, para. 27.

[26] United States, Written Comments in the General Assembly Request (GA1), 34ff. ("No international environmental instrument is expressly applicable in armed conflict. No such instrument expressly prohibits or regulates the use of nuclear weapons. Consequently, such an international environmental instrument could be applicable only by inference. Such an inference is not warranted because none of these instruments was negotiated with the intention that it would be applicable in armed conflict or to any use of nuclear weapons. Further, such an implication is not warranted by the textual interpretation of these instruments"); Great Britain, *ibid.*, 64, para. 3.98 (emphasizing that even if peacetime environmental law would be applicable for belligerents, it cannot be construed as prohibiting the use of nuclear weapons carried out by way of legitimate self-defense). For further details, see J. Burroughs, *The Legality of Threat or Use of Nuclear Weapons – A Guide to the Historic Opinion of the International Court of Justice* (Münster: LIT/Piscataway, N.J.: Transaction Publishers, 1997), pp. 105ff.

[27] For prescriptions against war-related activities that harm the environment, see Stockholm Declaration of the UN Conference on the Human Environment, prin. 26, UN Doc. A/CONF.48/14 (1972), reprinted in *I.L.M.* 11 (1972), 1416; World Charter for Nature, prins. 5 and 20, UN Doc. A/37/51 (1982); Rio Declaration on Environment and Development, prin. 24, UN Doc. A/CONF.151/Rev.1 (1992), reprinted in *I.L.M.* 31 (1992), 874.

The only exception is General Assembly Resolution 49/50,[28] which invites all states to disseminate widely the Guidelines for Military Manuals and Instructions on the Protection of the Environment in Times of Armed Conflict, which state that "[i]nternational environmental agreements and relevant rules of customary law may continue to be applicable in times of armed conflict to the extent that they are not inconsistent with the applicable law of armed conflict."[29] But this provision would only be a relevant element of state practice if it is implemented in the states' military manuals. Considering these examples, it seems clear that there do not exist any accepted rules of customary international law on the applicability of peacetime environmental treaties between belligerent states.

Nevertheless, it would not be correct to assume that this leaves no way to make any statements *de lege lata* regarding the problem. As the question of the application of peacetime environmental treaties during war forms part of the more general problem of the effect of war on treaties, a promising approach is to examine the general rules for applying peacetime treaties during war in international law and to analyze what conclusions may be drawn in respect to the specific problem of the effect of war on environmental treaties.

GENERAL APPLICABILITY OF PEACETIME TREATIES UNDER GENERAL INTERNATIONAL LAW

Traditionally, legal doctrine held that all treaties between belligerents terminated *ipso facto* at the outbreak of war.[30] Today, however, the dominant view is that whether a treaty continues to be in force in wartime depends on the type of treaty in question.[31] This approach can be based

---

[28] ICRC, *Guidelines for Military Manuals and Instructions on the Protection of the Environment in Times of Armed Conflict*, UN Doc. A/RES/49/50 (1995).

[29] Annex to UN Doc. A/49/323 (1994), 49, Art. 5; see also M. Kuhn, "Aktuelle Entwicklungen zum Schutz der Umwelt in bewaffneten Konflikten" (Guidelines for Military Manuals and Instructions on the Protection of the Environment in Times of Armed Conflict), *Humanitäres Völkerrecht (Informationsschriften)* (1996), 42, 47ff.; Schmitt, "Green War," 30ff.

[30] See McNair, *Law of Treaties*, p. 698; R. Ränk, *Einwirkungen des Krieges auf die nichtpolitischen Staatsverträge* (Uppsala, 1949), p. 16; M. K. Prescott, "How War Affects Treaties between Belligerents: A Case Study of the Gulf War," *Emory Int'l L. Rev.* 7 (1993), 197, 201.

[31] See McNair, *Law of Treaties*, pp. 702ff.; L. Oppenheim and H. Lauterpacht (eds.), *International Law*, 7th edn. (London: Longmans, 1952), vol. II (*Disputes, War and Neutrality*), p. 303; Schmitt, "Green War," 37ff.

on sufficient state practice: even if the practice of states seems to vary over time, for certain kinds of treaties clear rules have been established regarding their applicability between belligerent states.[32] This seems particularly true for five categories of treaties, where legal doctrine and state practice commonly hold that these treaties bind state parties even during international armed conflict: (1) treaties expressly providing for continuance during war; (2) treaties that are compatible with the maintenance of war; (3) treaties creating an international regime or status; (4) human rights treaties; and (5) *ius cogens* rules and obligations *erga omnes*.

Treaties that expressly provide for continuance during war

First of all, it is not disputed that treaties that expressly provide for continuance during war cannot be suspended or terminated, and that, vice versa, treaties may be suspended or terminated during war when expressly provided.[33] Most environmental treaties, however, fail to address this issue directly.[34] One exception is the 1954 Convention for the Prevention of Pollution of the Sea by Oil (OILPOL), which permitted state parties "[i]n case of war or other hostilities . . . [to] suspend the operation of the whole or any part of the present Convention."[35] Besides this, international conventions establishing civil liability regimes exempt damage caused by measures and means of warfare.[36] Nevertheless, this does not mean that the applicability of these conventions during armed conflicts is per se excluded, as their application is not limited to peacetime but to non-military conduct only.

---

[32] Delbrück, "War, Effect on Treaties," pp. 311ff.

[33] E.g., *ibid.*, pp. 312ff.; Oppenheim and Lauterpacht, *International Law*, p. 304; Schmitt, "Green War," 38ff.; see also Institut de Droit International, "The Effects of Armed Conflicts on Treaties" (Resolution of Aug. 28, 1985), *Annuaire de l'Institut de Droit Internationale* 61 II (1986), 278, Art. 3.

[34] Tarasofsky, "Legal Protection," 61ff.

[35] International Convention for the Prevention of Pollution of the Sea by Oil (done at London, May 12, 1954; entered into force, July 26, 1958), 12 U.S.T. 2989, T.I.A.S. No. 4900, 327 U.N.T.S. 3, Art. XIX(1). This convention was replaced by the 1973 Convention for the Prevention of Pollution by Ships, reprinted in *I.L.M.* 12 (1973), 1085, which does not contain a similar provision.

[36] See Tarasofsky, "Legal Protection," 62 n. 234; Sands, *Principles of International Environmental Law*, p. 231, n. 327; Christopher York, "International Law and the Collateral Effects of War on the Environment: The Persian Gulf," *S. Afr. J. Hum. Rts.* 7 (1991), 269, 283.

Treaties that are compatible with the maintenance of war

Even without an explicit provision, it is generally agreed that belligerents are not allowed to suspend or terminate peacetime multilateral treaties whose execution is compatible with the maintenance of war.[37] Thus, peacetime environmental treaties whose application does not limit methods and means of warfare – such as, for example, obligations to protect the marine environment during land warfare – continue to apply during war even between belligerent states.[38]

Treaties creating an international regime or status

Even more important than the applicability of compatible environmental treaties is the question of the continuing validity of treaties that impose upon belligerents additional and higher standards to protect the environment than the traditional laws of armed conflict. The first type of treaties that generally bind belligerent states, even though they can interfere with military interests, are the so-called "treaties creating an international regime or status."[39] These treaties establish a territorial order in the general interest of the international community, such as treaties providing for the demilitarization or neutralization of zones or the internationalization of waterways.[40]

Whether any peacetime environmental treaties create "objective regimes" in precisely this sense is questionable. Although treaties for the use and protection of areas beyond national jurisdiction – such as the high seas, the deep sea-bed, outer space, and Antarctica – are similar to treaties that provide objective regimes since the former also regulate state conduct in a certain territory, only some commentators support the view that the Antarctic Treaty and its supplementing conventions fall into this

---

[37] E.g., *Techt v. Hughes*, 128 N.E. 185 (N.Y. 1920); R. Ränk, "Modern War and the Validity of Treaties," *Cornell L.Q.* 38 (1953), 511, 520; Christopher M. Chinkin, "Crisis and the Performance of International Agreements: The Outbreak of War in Perspective," *Yale J. World Pub. Ord.* 7 (1981), 177, 185; Prescott, "How War Affects Treaties," 208ff., 214 (quoting at 208, *Techt v. Hughes*: "provisions compatible with a state of hostilities, unless expressly terminated, will be enforced").

[38] See Tarasofsky, "Legal Protection," 64; Simonds, "Conventional Warfare," 195, 215; *ICRC Guidelines*, Art. 5.

[39] E.g., McNair, *Law of Treaties*, p. 720; E. Klein, *Statusverträge im Völkerrecht* (Berlin, Heidelberg and New York: Springer, 1980), pp. 295ff.; Oppenheim and Lauterpacht, *International Law*, p. 304.   [40] For details, see Klein, *Statusverträge*, pp. 1ff., 349ff.

category.[41] Others deny this with the convincing arguments that it was not the intention of the parties of the Antarctic Treaty to establish an order with effect *erga omnes*, and that the Antarctic Treaty does not provide a territorial order.[42] It is therefore disputed whether environmental treaties directly fall within the ambit of the rule of general international law that treaties providing objective regimes bind belligerents.[43]

Human rights treaties

Human rights treaties are another type of treaty commonly regarded as applicable during war, even though they impose additional restraints on the methods and means of warfare.[44] This view was shared by the drafters of the Institut de Droit International (IDI) Resolution, which asserts: "The existence of an armed conflict does not entitle a party unilaterally to terminate or to suspend the operation of treaty provisions relating to the protection of the human person, unless the treaty otherwise provides."[45]

Applied to the protection of the environment during war, this position means that to the extent that human rights treaties include provisions protecting the environment, these provisions continue to apply during war. Generally, it has been acknowledged that traditional human rights entitling individuals to the protection of private goods – such as life, well-being, or property – give indirect protection against certain environmental damage.[46] This, however, requires a parallel infringement upon one of these private goods. While the question of which kinds of environmental damage infringe individual human rights is under dispute, it seems

---

[41] E.g., *ibid.*, pp. 18, 62ff., 116ff.; A. Verdross and B. Simma, *Universelles Völkerrecht*, 3rd edn. (Berlin: Duncker & Humblot, 1984), pp. 488ff., 745; Tarasofsky, "Legal Protection," 63.

[42] See R. Wolfrum, *Die Internationalisierung staatsfreier Räume* (Berlin and New York: Springer, 1984), p. 96, n. 253.

[43] For reasons why treaties concerning the high seas and outer space do not create objective regimes, see Klein, *Statusverträge*, pp. 111ff., 122ff.

[44] See, e.g., J. C. Bluntschli, *Das moderne Völkerrecht der civilisirten Staten als Rechtsbuch dargestellt* (Nördlingen: C. H. Beck, 1878), p. 296 (cited by Ränk, *Einwirkungen des Krieges*, P. 17); Advisory Opinion of the Secretary General of the United Nations concerning the Effects of World War I on Minority Rights (July 4, 1950), UN Doc. E/CN.4/367, 12ff.; D. Fronhöfer, *Der internationale Menschenrechtsschutz bei inneren Konflikten* (1994), p. 59; W. Kälin and L. Gabriel, "Human Rights in Times of Occupation: An Introduction," in W. Kälin (ed.), *Human Rights in Times of Occupation: The Case of Kuwait* (1994), 1, 26, 79.

[45] Institut de Droit International, "The Effects of Armed Conflicts," Art. 4.

[46] E.g., Dinah Shelton, "Human Rights, Environmental Rights, and the Right to Environment," *Stan. J. Int'l L.* 28 (1991), 103, 112; Birnie and Boyle, *International Law*, p. 192.

that only massive and severe damage to the environment constitutes a violation of human rights.

Besides the protection of individual rights, a few human rights treaties recognize a right to a healthy environment. For instance, Article 12 of the 1966 Covenant on Economic, Social, and Cultural Rights[47] refers to the right to improvement of environmental hygiene. Although this – as with other rights to a healthy environment[48] – is only a so-called collective right, to be guaranteed by government action but with no possibility for individual enforcement,[49] it can be infringed by military measures during an international armed conflict. Most recently this has been confirmed by Kälin, who states in his "Report on the Situation of Human Rights in Kuwait under Iraqi Occupation" as special rapporteur of the Commission on Human Rights that:

> Warfare often affects the natural environment; such consequences do not, *per se*, constitute human rights violations. However, . . . it can be concluded that not only in peacetime but also in times of armed conflict, the deliberate causing of large-scale environmental damage which severely affects the health of a considerable proportion of the population concerned, or creates risks for the health of future generations, amounts to a serious violation of the right to the enjoyment of the highest attainable standard of health as embodied in art. 12 of the International Covenant on Economic, Social and Cultural Rights.[50]

Apart from this, it is commonly held that no independent right to a decent environment has yet become part of international law[51] and that no human rights are embodied in environmental law treaties, although some environmental treaties contain provisions that expressly aim to protect the environment in order "to safeguard human health" or to secure "the health of the coastal population."[52]

---

[47] International Covenant on Economic, Social and Cultural Rights (done at New York, Dec. 16, 1966; entered into force, Jan. 3, 1976), UN Doc. A/6316 (1967), reprinted in *I.L.M.* 6 (1967), 360.

[48] E.g., African Charter on Human and Peoples' Rights, *I.L.M.* 21 (1982), 59, Art. 24; Additional Protocol to the American Convention on Human Rights in the Area of Economic, Social and Cultural Rights, *I.L.M.* 28 (1989), 156, Art. 11, para. 1.

[49] See Birnie and Boyle, *International Law*, p. 193.   [50] Kälin, *Human Rights*, p. 119, para. 208.

[51] E.g., Birnie and Boyle, *International Law*, p. 192; Shelton, "Human Rights," 104; J. P. Eaton, "The Nigerian Tragedy, Environmental Regulation of Transnational Corporations, and the Human Right to a Healthy Environment," *B.U. Int'l L.J.* 15 (1997), 261, 298.

[52] But see *Annuaire de l'Institut de Droit Internationale* 61 II (1986), 199, 222 (asserting that the term "treaty provisions relating to the protection of the human person" must be interpreted to cover provisions for the protection of the environment).

Ius cogens *rules and obligations* erga omnes

The final group of treaty provisions that are generally accepted as remaining in force during war are rules that form part of the *ius cogens* of international law or are obligations *erga omnes*.[53] If environmental treaties contain peremptory norms of international law or provisions that have an effect *erga omnes*, they are without doubt also binding upon belligerent states. It is far from clear, however, whether any provisions of peacetime environmental law are *ius cogens* or *erga omnes* obligations, or which provisions they are. When the International Court of Justice provided examples of obligations *erga omnes* in its *Barcelona Traction* decision, it did not mention duties for the protection of the environment.[54] Nevertheless, some commentators argue that certain environmental obligations belong to the *ius cogens* or have an effect *erga omnes*. Thus, for example, Brunnée wrote that "pollution reaching such a degree that it would represent a threat to the entire international community (e.g. critical ozone depletion or climate change) would be in conflict with a peremptory norm of international law."[55] Similarly, it is argued that the prohibition of massive damage to the environment has an effect *erga omnes*.[56] Others assert that obligations for the protection of an environmental good of common concern[57] and for the protection of common spaces[58] are norms that have *ius cogens* or *erga omnes* character.[59]

[53] Chinkin, "Crisis and the Performance," 188; Tarasofsky, "Legal Protection," 65. On the different concepts of *ius cogens* and *erga omnes*, see G. Gaja, "Obligations *Erga Omnes*, International Crimes and *Jus Cogens*: A Tentative Analysis of Three Related Concepts," in J. Weiler et al. (eds.), *International Crimes of States* (Berlin and New York: De Gruyter, 1984), pp. 151ff.

[54] *Barcelona Traction Case* (Second Phase), *I.C.J. Reports* (1970), 3, 32.

[55] J. Brunnée, " 'Common Interest' – Echoes from an Empty Shell," *Zeitschrift für ausländisches öffentliches Recht* 49 (1989), 791, 804ff.; see also S. Kadelbach, *Zwingendes Völkerrecht* (Berlin: Duncker & Humblot, 1992), p. 320; contra U. Beyerlin, "Staatliche Souveränität und internationale Umweltschutzkooperation," in U. Beyerlin et al. (eds.), *Recht zwischen Umbruch und Bewahrung, Festschrift für Rudolf Bernhardt* (Berlin and New York: Springer, 1995), pp. 937, 952; K. Ipsen, *Völkerrecht*, 3rd edn. (1990), p. 171.

[56] P. Patronos, *Der konzeptionelle Ansatz im Umweltvölkerrecht* (Frankfurt-on-Main and New York: P. Lang, 1997), pp. 140, 326.

[57] H. Hohmann, *Präventive Rechtspflichten und Prinzipien des modernen Umweltvölkerrechts* (Berlin: Duncher & Humblot, 1992), pp. 215ff.; F. L. Kirgis, "Standing to Challenge Human Endeavors that Could Change the Climate," *Am. J. Int'l L.* 84 (1990), 525, 527.

[58] See Birnie and Boyle, *International Law*, p. 85; R. Wolfrum, "Purposes and Principles of International Environmental Law," *Germ. Y.B. Int'l L.* 33 (1990), 308, 325ff.

[59] See Brunnée, " 'Common Interest'," 805ff. (viewing the principles of good neighborliness, equitable utilization of shared resources, and the duty to provide timely and adequate information about serious pollution incidents as *ius cogens*).

A sound basis for the premise that obligations for the protection of the environment are peremptory norms or have effects *erga omnes* can be seen in the ILC's Draft Principles on State Responsibility. Article 19 paragraph 3(d) lists as one example of an international crime, "a serious breach of an international obligation of essential importance for the safeguarding and preservation of the human environment, such as those prohibiting massive pollution of the atmosphere or the seas."[60]

If one looks at the material criteria that characterize peremptory norms of international law and obligations *erga omnes*, there cannot be much doubt that the prohibition of massive damage to the environment fulfills these criteria. So it is a widely shared view that peremptory norms protect "overriding interests of the international community of states"[61] and that states can be held to have a legal interest in protecting obligations *erga omnes* "in view of the importance of the rights involved"[62] and because of their "fundamental character."[63] It can hardly be disputed today that, from an objective point of view, the state community as a whole has a fundamental interest in protecting the environment against massive pollution.[64]

Nevertheless, fulfillment of this material criterion is not sufficient for the existence of either peremptory norms or obligations *erga omnes*. Instead, it is primarily decisive if states generally acknowledge that certain obligations for environmental protection are peremptory or *erga omnes* norms of international law. In contrast to the period when the ILC Articles on State Responsibility were drafted, today there seem to be good reasons to hold the view that at least the prohibition of massive pollution of the environment is a peremptory norm of international law and an obligation with effect *erga omnes*. Since then, however, peacetime environmental law has developed dynamically, states have submitted to a great number of specific obligations for environmental protection, and these obligations go far beyond that of protecting the environment against massive damage.

---

[60] *Y.B. Int'l L. Commission* (1980), vol. II/2, p. 32.

[61] Lauri Hannikainen, *Peremptory Norms (Jus Cogens) in International Law* (Helsinki: Finnish Lawyers' Pub. Co., 1988), pp. 207ff.; Brunnée, "'Common Interest'," 801ff.; A. Verdross, "*Jus Dispositivum* and *Jus Cogens* in International Law," *Am. J. Int'l L.* 60 (1966), 55, 58 ("these rules . . . do not exist to satisfy the needs of the individual states but the higher interest of the whole international community").

[62] *Barcelona Traction Case*, 32.

[63] Theodor Meron, *Human Rights and Humanitarian Norms as Customary Law* (1989), p. 192.

[64] Brunnée, "'Common Interest'," 805 ("There are no interests more fundamental and vital to the existence of the international community than the prevention of life-threatening environmental degradation.").

Interim conclusion

As an interim conclusion, it seems that only those treaties for environmental protection that provide for their continuance during war or are compatible with the maintenance of war, provisions for the protection of the environment of *ius cogens* or *erga omnes* character, and human rights provisions that require the preservation of a certain condition of the environment will continue to be in effect for belligerent states. According to the preceding analysis, the huge number of environmental treaties that restrict the methods and means of warfare and that entail no provisions with *ius cogens/erga omnes* character can be suspended or terminated by the state parties that take part in an international armed conflict. This finding would not correspond with the international legal order, however, if the question of the applicability of peacetime environmental treaties could be answered by an analogous application of the general rules of the effect of war on treaties. This problem will be further examined in the next section.

Solving the new problem with old rules: the question of the applicability of peacetime environmental treaties answered by analogy

While it appears that few, if any, peacetime environmental treaties clearly fall within the five categories of peacetime treaties that continue to apply during wartime, some environmental treaty provisions may be sufficiently similar to one or more of the categories that they could be said to have force during wartime.[65] This section examines whether any environmental treaties are sufficiently similar to one of the enumerated categories of peacetime treaties commonly held applicable between belligerent states during an armed conflict, and thus continue to apply during wartime.

THE EFFECT OF WAR ON TREATIES FOR THE USE AND PROTECTION OF AREAS BEYOND NATIONAL JURISDICTION

As previously mentioned, international agreements regulating the protection and use of areas beyond national jurisdiction – such as the high seas,

---

[65] For more about the use of analogy in international law, see G. Dahm et al., *Völkerrecht* (Berlin and New York: W. de Gruyter, 1989), vol. I/1, p. 81; A. Bleckmann, *Grundprobleme und Methoden des Völkerrechts* (Freiburg: Alber, 1982), pp. 221ff.; U. Fastenrath, *Lücken im Völkerrecht* (Berlin: Duncker & Humblot, 1991), p. 138; regarding the use of analogy for peacetime environmental law to the wartime context, see generally Vöneky, *Fortgeltung*.

the deep sea-bed, outer space, and Antarctica – have certain similarities with treaties establishing objective regimes. In order for these treaties governing areas beyond national jurisdiction to be unaffected by the outbreak of armed conflict, they must be similar to treaties creating objective regimes at least insofar as it is relevant for the continued application of the latter. It is therefore necessary to have a closer look at why treaties creating an objective regime are applicable during armed conflict.

Some argue that these treaties remain valid for all state parties during armed conflicts because state parties intended to create a permanent order.[66] However, it is highly questionable what the "real" intentions of state parties were in any particular treaty, as they did not expressly address the effects of the outbreak of war on the treaty.[67] More convincing, therefore, is the view that treaties creating an objective regime continue to have force during wartime because they seek to serve the interests of the state community as a whole.[68] In this vein, the UN Secretary-General stated, in a 1950 advisory opinion on the effects of World War I on minority rights treaties, that the outbreak of an armed conflict did not terminate those treaties "qui concernent des situations permanentes d'intérêt général."[69] Thus, peacetime treaties regulating the protection of areas beyond national jurisdiction that seek to serve the interests of the state community as a whole would be sufficiently similar to treaties creating an objective regime that they continue to apply between belligerents.

While international law traditionally provided that all states have an equal right to the uninterrupted use of areas beyond national jurisdiction,[70] and thereby served only the national interest of the single states, today treaties protecting areas beyond national jurisdiction appear to protect these areas in the common interest of the state community as a whole.[71] Three extraterritorial areas (covered in two treaties) readily come to mind in the environmental context: the deep sea-bed and the sea itself

---

[66] A. D. McNair, "Les Effets de la Guerre sur les Traités," *RdC* 59 (1937 I), 527, 575.

[67] See, e.g., Chinkin, "Crisis and the Performance," 191.

[68] Klein, *Statusverträge*, pp. 297ff.; M. Sibert, *Traité de Droit International Public* (Paris: Dalloz, 1951), vol. II, p. 355; K. Doehring, "Das Gutachten des Generalsekretärs der Vereinten Nationen über die Fortgeltung der nach dem ersten Weltkrieg eingegangenen Minderheitenschutzverpflichtungen," *Zeitschrift für ausländisches öffentliches Recht* 15 (1954), 521, 525ff.   [69] Advisory Opinion of the Secretary General on World War I, 13.

[70] Wolfrum, "Purposes and Principles," 322.

[71] See *ibid.*; Alexandre C. Kiss, "The International Protection of the Environment," in R. MacDonald and D. Johnston (eds.), *The Structure and Process of International Law* (The Hague and Boston: M. Nijhoff, 1983), pp. 1067, 1084ff.

under the UN Convention on the Law of the Sea (UNCLOS),[72] and the Antarctic Treaty System.

UNCLOS

According to UNCLOS Article 136, the deep sea "area" (the sea-bed, ocean floor, and subsoil beyond the limits of national jurisdiction)[73] and its resources are the "common heritage of mankind." By their plain language, the provisions of Part XI of UNCLOS aim to conserve this area in the interest of present and future generations, and not to serve national interests of the state parties. The subsequent provisions confirm this: states may not "claim or exercise sovereignty or sovereign rights over any part of the area or its resources," and "[a]ll rights in the resources of the area are vested in mankind as a whole."[74] Additionally, all activities in the area shall be carried out for "the benefit of mankind as a whole."[75] Thus, the overall aim of the UNCLOS provisions regarding the deep sea-bed is to benefit the whole community of states. The treaty's institutional management reflects the same values, as the "International Sea-bed Authority" acts expressly on behalf of mankind as a whole in organizing and controlling all activities in the area.[76]

That this conclusion is valid even with respect to military activities in the area is demonstrated by Article 141 of UNCLOS, which asserts that the deep sea-bed and the ocean floor shall be used "for peaceful purposes" only. The common view is that this peaceful-use clause must be interpreted as a prohibition of aggressive activities (in the sense of Article 2(4) of the UN Charter), and not as a prohibition on all military activity.[77] Even with this limited meaning, this express peaceful-use clause in Part XI shows that the principle of the common heritage of mankind (to serve the general interest of the state community as a whole) also includes military activities in the area, and that at a minimum an act of aggression is deemed contrary to the interest of the state community as a whole.

---

[72] United Nations Convention on the Law of the Sea (done at Montego Bay, Dec. 10, 1982), UN Doc. A/CONF62/122, reprinted in *I.L.M.* 21 (1982), 1261.   [73] *Ibid.*, Art. 1(1)(1).

[74] *Ibid.*, Arts. 137(1), 137(2).

[75] *Ibid.*, Art. 140(1); see also Art. 143 (marine scientific research).

[76] *Ibid.*, Arts. 137(2), 156 et seq.; Art. 1(1)(2).

[77] R. Wolfrum, "The Principle of the Common Heritage of Mankind," *Zeitschrift für ausländisches öffentliches Recht* 43 (1983), 312, 319ff.

Even more important for the protection of the environment during armed conflict, the provisions of Part XII of UNCLOS address the protection and preservation of the marine environment. These provisions seek to serve the interest of the state community as a whole, as illustrated by Article 192: "States have the obligation to protect and preserve the marine environment." Without reference to the national interests or rights of the state parties, this provision obliges all states to protect the marine environment per se and is therefore an obligation in the general interest of the state community as a whole.[78] Therefore, Article 192 shows that the overall purpose of Part XII of UNCLOS is to protect the environment in the common interest. Even in cases where an obligation protecting the environment seems to serve primarily national interests, as in Article 194(2),[79] it has to be interpreted in light of the general rule, articulated in Article 192, of protecting the marine environment in the common interest. Thus, as with treaties that provide objective regimes, the UNCLOS provisions protecting the environment seek to serve the interests of the state community as a whole. Consequently, just as belligerents are bound to treaties establishing objective regimes, belligerents are bound by these environmental provisions in UNCLOS during wartime.

It bears mentioning, however, that there is a practical limitation in applying UNCLOS during an armed conflict. Article 236 states that the UNCLOS provisions regarding the protection and preservation of the marine environment do not apply to "any warship, naval auxiliary, other vessels or aircraft owned or operated by the State and used, for the time being, only on government non-commercial service." Nevertheless, according to this article, each state is still obliged at least to "ensure . . . that such vessels and aircraft act in a manner consistent, so far as reasonable and practicable, with this Convention." Moreover, there is no exemption for war-related damage to the environment that is caused by means other than the aircraft and vessels mentioned in Article 236. This means that, for instance, environmental damage caused by introducing oil into the sea from land-based oil pipelines or offshore facilities during war is covered by the UNCLOS provisions as normal peacetime conduct.

---

[78] Birnie and Boyle, *International Law*, pp. 85 n. 17, 253, 255, 257; Alexandre C. Kiss and Dinah Shelton, "Systems Analysis of International Law: A Methodological Inquiry," *Netherlands Y.B. Int'l L.* 68 (1986), 45, 64; Kiss, "International Protection," 1084ff.

[79] "States shall take all measures necessary to ensure that activities under their jurisdiction or control are so conducted as not to cause damage by pollution to other states and their environment."

It is unclear, however, whether Article 87(2) of UNCLOS, which requires states to exercise their freedom of the high seas "with due regard for the interests of other states," applies during wartime. While not part of the environmental protections of Part XII, it has an impact on the environmental protection of the high seas. If this provision binds belligerent states, they will be forbidden from damaging the high seas environment to such an extent as to render other legitimate uses of the high seas, such as fishing, impossible. Unlike the provisions of Part XII, the wording of the article seems to secure national interests in the use of the high seas. It is plausible, however, that the aim of protecting the marine environment in the general interest established in Article 192 applies to the interpretation of all UNCLOS provisions that lead – even indirectly – to environmental protection. According to this line of reasoning, the obligation of Article 87(2) would bind belligerent states during an armed conflict in the same way that treaties providing objective regimes bind belligerents.

The Antarctic Treaty System

The aim of serving the interest of the state community as a whole also underlies the Antarctic Treaty System. In the preamble of the Antarctic Treaty, the state parties confirm that "it is in the interest of *all mankind* that Antarctica shall continue forever to be used exclusively for peaceful purposes and shall not become the scene or object of international discord"[80] and its primary objective is to ensure that only activities for peaceful purposes take place in the Antarctic, thus prohibiting any military activities.[81] Consider also the provision that territorial claims can be neither supported nor denied by actions while the Antarctic Treaty is in force.[82] Although this provision seems to benefit those states that claimed territory before the Antarctic Treaty was ratified, the Treaty serves the interest of the community of states as a whole because it resolves disputes about territorial rights while the Antarctic Treaty is in force.[83] The same is true for the other material provisions of the convention, such as the general freedom of scientific investigation (Article II) and the agreement of state parties to cooperate to that end (Article III).

---

[80] The Antarctic Treaty (done at Washington, D.C., Dec. 1, 1959; entered into force, June 23, 1961), 12 U.S.T. 794, T.I.A.S. No. 4780, 402 U.N.T.S. 71, preamble, para. 2 (emphasis added).
[81] For interpretation of the peaceful purpose clause, see Wolfrum, *Internationalisierung*, pp. 62ff.
[82] Antarctic Treaty, Art. IV, para. 1; see also Wolfrum, *Internationalisierung*, p. 62.
[83] See Klein, *Statusverträge*, p. 65, n. 58.

While some might argue that the treaty does not serve the common interest of the state community as a whole since the freedom of scientific investigation is limited to the state parties, this position is erroneous since the Antarctic Treaty is open for accession by any member of the United Nations,[84] and some treaties providing objective regimes likewise restrict the use of the territory to contracting parties.[85] Similarly, the fact that only the limited number of state parties that are consultative parties may participate in the formulation of measures furthering the principles and objectives of the treaty does not prevent characterizing the Antarctic Treaty as promoting the interests of the state community as a whole, since the material provisions of the treaty serve the common interest.[86] In addition, the consultative parties have emphasized on several occasions their responsibility towards the world community.[87] In the end, it can be stated that the Antarctic Treaty seeks to protect the interests of the community of states[88] to the same extent as treaties providing for objective regimes.

If one shares this view, the aim of serving the community of states as a whole cannot be denied to the other treaties of the Antarctic Treaty System, including the Convention for the Conservation of Antarctic Seals, the Convention on the Conservation of Antarctic Marine Living Resources, the Convention on the Regulation of the Antarctic Mineral Resource Activities, and the Protocol on Environmental Protection to the Antarctic Treaty.[89] Thus, the Convention on the Conservation of Antarctic Marine

---

[84] Antarctic Treaty, Art. XIII, para. 1.   [85] See Klein, *Statusverträge*, pp. 61ff.

[86] Antarctic Treaty, Art. IX; see Wolfrum, *Internationalisierung*, pp. 69ff.; but see C. Tomuschat, "Obligations Arising for States Without or Against Their Will," *Recueil des Cours* IV (1993), 198, 245ff. (doubting this thesis); R. Lagoni, "Convention on the Conservation of Antarctic Living Resources: A Model for the Use of a Common Good?," in R. Wolfrum (ed.), *Antarctic Challenge III: Conflicting Interests, Cooperation, Environmental Protection, Economic Development* (Berlin: Duncker & Humblot, 1983), pp. 93, 106ff. (asserting that "from a legal point of view, the Contracting Parties of the Convention do not represent all mankind, for they simply do not have the mandate to do so. Neither do they act as a trustee for mankind as a whole, because there exists no settlor for this trust . . . the Contracting Parties are primarily and mainly acting on behalf of their own and for their own benefit").

[87] See, e.g., Catherine Redgwell, "The Protection of the Antarctic Environment and the Ecosystem Approach," in Michael Bowman and Catherine Redgwell (eds.), *International Law and the Conservation of Biological Diversity* (London and Boston: Kluwer Law Int'l, 1996), pp. 109, 113; Patronos, *Der konzeptionelle Ansatz*, pp. 332ff.

[88] See Wolfrum, *Internationalisierung*, pp. 92, 96; J. A. Frowein, "Die Staatengemeinschaft als Rechtsbegriff im Völkerrecht," *Liechtensteinische Juristen Zeitung* 12 (1991), 141, 143; see also note 41 above (commentators arguing that the Antarctic Treaty provides an objective regime).

[89] Convention for the Conservation of Antarctic Seals, reprinted in *I.L.M.* 11 (1972), 251, preamble, paras. 2, 3 (protecting seals from commercial exploitation); Convention on the

Living Resources recognizes the "importance of safeguarding the environment and protecting the integrity of the ecosystem of the seas surrounding Antarctica."[90] Also, the Convention on the Regulation of the Antarctic Mineral Resource Activities and the Protocol on Environmental Protection to the Antarctic Treaty seek to protect the environment per se.[91] For example, the Protocol on Environmental Protection expressly designates Antarctica "as a natural reserve, devoted to peace and science,"[92] and the Protocol's provisions for environmental protection – especially in Annexes II to V – do not refer to national interests in any way.

THE EFFECT OF WAR ON TREATIES PROTECTING COMMON GOODS AND GLOBAL ENVIRONMENTAL RESOURCES

Certain environmental treaties, especially those protecting common goods and global environmental resources, may be sufficiently similar to human rights conventions that they may be said to bind belligerents during armed conflict just as the human rights conventions bind belligerents. The main characteristic of human rights treaties is – similar to treaties establishing objective regimes – that they seek to protect a common good in the interest of the state community as a whole.[93] The International Court of Justice confirmed this in its *Advisory Opinion Concerning Reservations to the Genocide Convention*: "[I]n such a convention the contracting States do not have any interest of their own; they merely have, one and all, a common interest."[94] Likewise, the European Commission of Human Rights

Conservation of Antarctic Marine Living Resources, reprinted in *I.L.M.* 19 (1980), 841; Convention on the Regulation of the Antarctic Mineral Resource Activities, reprinted in *I.L.M.* 27 (1988), 868; Protocol on Environmental Protection to the Antarctic Treaty, reprinted in *I.L.M.* 30 (1991), 678.

[90] Preamble, para. 1; see also preamble, para. 9; Birnie and Boyle, *International Law*, pp. 450ff.

[91] To the former, see Wolfrum, "Purposes and Principles," 317; Hohmann, *Präventive Rechtspflichten*, p. 340; A. Watts, *International Law and the Antarctic Treaty System* (Cambridge: Grotius Publications, 1992), p. 264.

[92] Art. 2; see also Art. 3 and preamble, para. 7 ("Convinced that the development of a comprehensive regime for the protection of the Antarctic environment and dependent and associated ecosystems is in the interest of mankind as a whole"); Redgwell, "Protection of the Antarctic," 123; Birnie and Boyle, *International Law*, p. 193; Watts, *Antarctic Treaty System*, pp. 282ff.

[93] W. Kälin, "Menschenrechtsverträge als Gewährleistungen einer objektiven Ordnung," in W. Kälin et al. (eds.), *Aktuelle Probleme des Menschenrechtsschutzes, Berichte der Deutschen Gesellschaft für Völkerrecht* 33 (Heidelberg: C. F. Müller, 1993), pp. 9ff.; D. Schindler, "Kriegsrecht und Menschenrechte," in U. Häfelin et al. (eds.), *Menschenrechte, Föderalismus, Demokratie – Festschrift zum 70. Geburtstag von Werner Kägi* (Zürich: Schulthis, 1979), pp. 327, 341.

[94] *Advisory Opinion Concerning Reservations to the Genocide Convention, I.C.J. Reports* (1951), 23, 69.

decided that the aim of the European Convention on Human Rights is not for the state parties "to concede to each other reciprocal rights and obligations in pursuance of their individual interest but to realize the aims and ideals of the Council of Europe."[95] This feature of treaties protecting human rights is the main reason why state parties cannot suspend or terminate human rights treaties during an armed conflict.[96] The next step then is to examine the extent to which environmental treaties entail similar elements.

International agreements protecting common goods (such as climate, the ozone layer, or biodiversity)[97] and those protecting global environmental resources[98] are generally thought to protect elements of the environment that are considered essential for the whole state community.[99] According to Wolfrum, "[t]he essential criterion of the respective treaties is that they oblige the State parties to prohibit or to control certain activities within their territories while the measures to be enacted by the states are of essential importance not only for themselves but rather for the state community as a whole as well."[100]

Nevertheless, it needs to be kept in mind that the aim of protecting the environment can never be separated as easily from national interests as can the aim of protecting human rights. Since environmental protection always has some impact on states' territorial integrity or their right to utilize certain elements of the environment, it will always relate to national interests. Thus, in determining whether a treaty that governs common goods or global environmental resources is sufficiently similar to human rights treaties so that it continues to apply during armed conflict, the question becomes whether the main purpose of an environmental treaty is to protect environmental goods per se, with the protection of territorial integrity or other national interests being only a side effect.

---

[95] *Pfunders Case* of 1961 (No. 788/60), *Y.B. Eur. Convention Hum. Rts.* 4 (1961), 116, 139; see also B. Simma, *Das Reziprozitätselement im Zustandekommen völkerrechtlicher Verträge* (Berlin: Duncker & Humblot, 1973), pp. 176ff.; Bleckmann, *Grundprobleme*, pp. 229ff.

[96] See Advisory Opinion of the Secretary General on World War I, 12ff.

[97] See Wolfrum, "Purposes and Principles," 327; Kiss, "International Protection," 1083ff.; Birnie and Boyle, *International Law*, pp. 154, 390ff.

[98] Hohmann, *Präventive Rechtspflichten*, pp. 388, 349; Michael J. Glennon, "Has International Law Failed the Elephant?" *Am. J. Int'l L.* 84 (1990), 34 (defining a global environmental resource as "a natural resource located within the territory of one country but broadly enjoyed, and arguably needed, by the world community as a whole").

[99] Kiss, "International Protection," 1084ff.   [100] Wolfrum, "Purposes and Principles," 327.

The Framework Convention on Climate Change

The Framework Convention on Climate Change is a classic example of an environmental treaty protecting a common good.[101] The first paragraph of the preamble confirms that "the change in the Earth's climate and its adverse effects are a common concern of humankind." By this, the state parties recognize that the purpose of the convention is not to protect national interests, but to serve the common interest of the state community as a whole. Other paragraphs of the preamble reinforce this approach, for instance where the state parties are determined "to protect the climate system for present and future generations."[102] The aim to protect a part of the environment in the common interest cannot be addressed more precisely.

Even more relevant, the operative part of the convention emphasizes protection of the environment in the common interest. For example, Article 3 echoes the preamble in recognizing that protecting the climate system benefits present and future generations of humankind.[103] Further, states have common responsibilities to achieve this goal, even if the responsibilities differ according to the states' capabilities.[104] Even development policies are subject to the common aim, as states have only the right to "sustainable" development,[105] commonly characterized as a "development that meets the needs of the present without compromising the ability of future generations to meet their own needs."[106]

In addition to the content of its provisions, the structural similarities between the Convention on Climate Change and human rights treaties show that the convention seeks to protect a common good in the interest of the state community as a whole. Like human rights treaties, the Convention on Climate Change entails no *do-ut-des* obligations and no reciprocal rights, but only unilateral duties whose fulfillment does not lead to any direct advantage to the state parties.[107] Thus, it can be concluded that the convention seeks to protect a common good in the interest of the state community as a whole, as do human rights treaties, and so the Convention on Climate Change continues to apply during armed conflict.

---

[101] Framework Convention on Climate Change, reprinted in *I.L.M.* 31 (1992), 849.
[102] Preamble, last para.; see also preamble, paras. 2, 6.   [103] Art. 3, para. 1.
[104] Art. 3, para. 1; Art. 4.   [105] Art. 3, para. 4.
[106] UNEP Governing Council Doc. UNEP/GC.15/L.37 (1989), annex II; Birnie and Boyle, *International Law*, pp. 122ff.
[107] See generally Kiss, "International Protection," 1085; Wolfrum, "Purposes and Principles," 327.

The Convention on Biological Diversity and other universal treaties protecting common goods

The same structure and aim can be found in other global treaties commonly categorized as environmental treaties protecting common goods or global environmental resources. These include the Convention on Biological Diversity,[108] the Vienna Convention for the Protection of the Ozone Layer,[109] the UNESCO World Heritage Convention,[110] the Convention on Wetlands of International Importance,[111] the Convention on the Conservation of Migratory Species of Wild Animals,[112] and the Convention on International Trade in Endangered Species of Wild Fauna and Flora.[113] All of these environmental treaties oblige state parties to protect an environmental good per se, and without an immediate advantage resulting from the fulfillment of the obligations for the contracting states.[114] In addition, the preambles to these conventions often expressly advance the purpose of serving the interest of the community of states as a whole.[115] Therefore, these environmental treaties are sufficiently similar to human right treaties that one can argue that they continue to apply to belligerent states, as do the human rights treaties.

---

[108] Convention on Biological Diversity, reprinted in *I.L.M.* 31 (1992), 822.

[109] Vienna Convention for the Protection of the Ozone Layer (done at Vienna, Mar. 22, 1985; entered into force, Sept. 22, 1988), reprinted in *I.L.M.* 26 (1987), 1529; see also Birnie and Boyle, *International Law*, p. 391; Wolfrum, "Purposes and Principles," 327, 329.

[110] Convention for the Protection of the World Cultural and Natural Heritage (done at Paris, Nov. 16, 1972; entered into force, Dec. 17, 1975), 1037 U.N.T.S. 151, reprinted in *I.L.M.* 11 (1972), 1358; see Birnie and Boyle, *International Law*, pp. 449ff.; Wolfrum, "Purposes and Principles," 327; Dahm et al., *Völkerrecht*, pp. 451ff.; Kiss, "International Protection," 1084ff.

[111] Convention on Wetlands of International Importance, reprinted in *I.L.M.* 11 (1972), 963; see also Kiss, "International Protection," 1084ff.; Wolfrum, "Purposes and Principles," 328.

[112] Convention on the Conservation of Migratory Species of Wild Animals, reprinted in *I.L.M.* 19 (1980), 15; see also Kiss, "International Protection," 1084; Hohmann, *Präventive Rechtspflichten*, pp. 349, 392.

[113] Convention on International Trade in Endangered Species of Wild Fauna and Flora (CITES) (done at Washington, D.C., Mar. 3, 1973; entered into force, July 1, 1975), 27 U.S.T. 1087, T.I.A.S. No. 8249, reprinted in *I.L.M.* 12 (1973), 1085; see also Kiss, "International Protection," 1084ff.; Wolfrum, "Purposes and Principles," 328; Hohmann, *Präventive Rechtspflichten*, pp. 349, 392.

[114] For further analysis, see Vöneky, *Fortgeltung*, ch. 8.

[115] E.g., CITES, preamble, para. 1; Convention on the Conservation of Migratory Species of Wild Animals, preamble, paras. 1, 2; World Heritage Convention, preamble, paras. 3, 7; Convention on Biological Diversity, preamble, para. 3.

Regional treaties: the European Wildlife Convention and the African Convention on the Conservation of Nature

In addition to global and universal environmental treaties that have similarities with human rights treaties, some regional environmental treaties aim to protect an environmental good in the interest not only of the state parties but in the interest of the community of states as a whole. Examples include, for instance, the 1979 Convention on the Conservation of European Wildlife and Natural Habitats[116] and the 1968 African Convention on the Conservation of Nature and Natural Resources.[117] Thus, the preamble of the former states that "wild fauna and flora constitute a natural heritage of aesthetic, scientific, cultural, recreational, economic and intrinsic value that needs to be preserved and handed on to future generations."[118] Similarly, the preamble of the latter provides that the state parties are "[f]ully conscious that soil, water, flora and fauna resources constitute a capital of vital importance to mankind, . . . Desirous of undertaking individual and joint action for the conservation, utilization and development of these assets by establishing and maintaining their rational utilization for the present and future welfare of mankind."[119]

Regional human rights treaties – such as the 1981 African Charter on Human and Peoples' Rights and the 1969 American Convention on Human Rights[120] – show that there is no general or systematic principle that prevents regional treaties from aiming to protect a common good in the interest of the whole community of states. Therefore, it is not the global application of a treaty that is decisive in characterizing it as protecting a good in the general interest. The critical element is that the state parties seek to serve the interest of the state community as a whole, which is reflected in the absence of reciprocal rights and obligations.

---

[116] E.g., Birnie and Boyle, *International Law*, p. 193; Dahm et al., *Völkerrecht*, p. 451, n. 62; Kiss, "International Protection," 1084.

[117] African Convention on the Conservation of Nature and Natural Resources (1968), 1001 U.N.T.S. 4; see also Kiss, "International Protection," 1084.

[118] Preamble, para. 4.

[119] Preamble, paras. 1, 6.

[120] African Charter on Human and Peoples' Rights, reprinted in *I.L.M.* 21 (1982), 59; American Convention on Human Rights, reprinted in *I.L.M.* 9 (1970), 673.

The third category of environmental treaties that could bind belligerents during armed conflict includes treaties governing the use and protection of shared natural resources. Following the previous analysis, these treaties will continue to apply only if they seek to protect an environmental good in the common interest of the state community as a whole.

The term "shared natural resource" relates to environmental components that are situated so as to affect territories of more than one state, without being a *res communis*.[121] Shared natural resources include, for example, international watercourses, rivers, and lakes. Generally, commentators hold that the main purpose for regulating the use and conservation of a shared resource is to ensure a balance of interests between the concerned parties.[122] In this sense, Kiss asserts that the foundation of the concept of shared natural resources "is the common concern which a limited number of states . . . have in a given resource, so that they should share the benefit."[123] Wolfrum confirms this analysis: "Looking at the objective of the agreements on the utilization of shared natural resources, one realizes that they tend to secure the economic utilization of the commonly shared resources by the participating States, and that the protection of the environment ranks only in second place."[124] Thus, to the extent that treaties governing the use and protection of shared resources oblige state parties not primarily in the interest of the international community of states as a whole but rather in the interest of the state parties concerned, they do not bind belligerent states.

The Rhine Conventions

A typical example of treaties protecting shared natural resources in the interests of the state parties concerned is the pair of Conventions for the

[121] Birnie and Boyle, *International Law*, pp. 114ff.; P. T. Stoll, "The International Environmental Law of Cooperation," in R. Wolfrum (ed.), *Enforcing Environmental Standards: Economic Mechanisms as Viable Means* (Berlin and New York: Springer, 1996), pp. 39, 59ff.
[122] Birnie and Boyle, *International Law*, p. 117; Wolfrum, "Purposes and Principles," 321.
[123] Kiss, "International Protection," 1080; see also Birnie and Boyle, *International Law*, p. 115; Stoll, "Law of Cooperation," 59.
[124] Wolfrum, "Purposes and Principles," 321; see also Stoll, "Law of Cooperation," 60 n. 60 ("Aspects of protection were considered later and only to that extent, that a direct necessity was felt to protect in substance what was supposed to be used.").

Protection of the Rhine against Chemical Pollution and for the Protection against Pollution by Chlorides.[125] According to paragraph 3 of its preamble, the primary aim of the former convention is to improve the quality of the water of the Rhine not for its own sake but in order to improve the utilization of its water.[126] Since France is the main source of chloride pollution to the Rhine, the latter convention obliges France to reduce discharges of these chemicals, but the costs for doing so are divided between all of the contracting states, so that France and Germany carry 30 percent of the costs each, the Netherlands 34 percent, and Switzerland 6 percent.[127] The reciprocity of France's duty to reduce pollution and other state parties' duty to pay compensation is obvious. In contrast to treaties protecting human rights or common environmental goods, the fulfillment of the obligations results in immediate advantages for the state parties concerned.

The Danube River Convention

It is debatable whether the conclusion that treaties governing shared resources primarily seek to serve national interests of the contracting states is true for all treaties regulating the use and protection of a natural resource shared by two or more states. As the regional environmental treaties mentioned above show, states sharing a natural resource can agree to protect the resource in the interest of the state community as a whole.[128]

In comparison to the Rhine Conventions, the Convention on Cooperation for the Protection and Sustainable Use of the Danube River[129] seems to serve to a lesser extent the national interest of the state parties and more the protection of the Danube environment for its own sake. Accordingly, the last paragraph of the preamble states that the state parties

[125] Convention for the Protection of the Rhine against Chemical Pollution, BGBl. (1978), vol. II, 1054; Convention for the Protection of the Rhine against Pollution by Chlorides, BGBl. (1978), vol. II, 1065; see also Wolfrum, "Purposes and Principles," 321.
[126] Preamble, para. 3 ("désireux d'améliorer la qualité des eaux du Rhin en vue de ces utilisations"); for the aim of protecting Rhine water usage, see preamble, paras. 2, 4; see also Art. 1.
[127] See Art. 7.
[128] E.g., Convention on the Conservation of European Wildlife and Natural Habitats (done at Berne, Sept. 17, 1979; entered into force, June 1, 1982), E.T.S. No. 104; African Convention on the Conservation of Nature and Natural Resources.
[129] Convention on Cooperation for the Protection and Sustainable Use of the Danube River, BGBl. (1996), vol. II, 875.

are "[s]triving at a lasting improvement and protection of the Danube River and of the waters within its catchment area", and, according to Article 2 paragraph 1, "[t]he Contracting Parties shall strive at achieving the goals of a sustainable and equitable water management, including the conservation, improvement, and the rational use of surface waters and ground water in the catchment area as far as possible." Finally, Article 2 paragraph 5 provides that water management cooperation between the state parties shall be directed to "protect ecosystems." Ultimately, it remains questionable whether the main aim of this treaty is to protect the environment only for the national interests of the utilization of the water of the Danube River, or whether there exists some sort of environmental protection of a more general interest.

THE PROBLEM OF *LEX SPECIALIS*

To summarize the previous examination, environmental treaties that seek to protect certain components in the interest of the community of states as a whole remain in force during an international armed conflict, even for belligerent states, just as treaties providing objective regimes and those protecting human rights continue to bind belligerents. Therefore, the provisions of UNCLOS relating to the deep sea-bed and the protection of the environment, the Antarctic Treaty, as well as treaties protecting environmental common goods and global environmental resources will bind warring state parties during an international armed conflict.

Yet, this line of argument faces a particular difficulty: *lex specialis derogat lege generali* (specific laws govern over general laws). Commentators have often advanced this argument generally to deny the applicability of peacetime environmental treaties between belligerent parties during an armed conflict: since the law of armed conflict is a specialized set of laws, to the extent that its provisions are contrary to those of general peacetime law for environmental protection, the law of armed conflict prevails.[130] Today, however, the traditional dichotomy between the international law of war on the one hand and the law of peace on the other hand is

---

[130] See, e.g., Green, "Environment and the Law of Conventional Warfare," 226 (regarding applicability of UNCLOS to belligerent states); Heintschel von Heinegg and Donner, "New Developments," 295; Glen Plant, "Environmental Damage and the Laws of War: Points Addressed to Military Lawyers," in Hazel Fox and Michael A. Meyer (eds.), *Armed Conflict and the New Law: Effecting Compliance* (1993), vol. II, pp. 159, 162.

dissolving.[131] Thus, as previously noted, human rights treaties and treaties providing objective regimes are commonly held to apply during armed conflicts. Still, it could be argued that even if some peacetime treaties undermine this general rule, the obligation of belligerents to protect the environment during armed conflict is exclusively laid down in the law-of-war treaties, where state parties agreed only to prohibit certain strictly limited damages to the environment.

Several objections can be raised against the argument that the law of armed conflict is meant to be the only regulation for environmental protection during wartime. For instance, the so-called Martens Clause,[132] which is part of the customary law of armed conflict, provides the possibility of supplementing the law of war in accordance with the "dictates of the public conscience." Today, the dictates of public conscience would include considerations of humanity as well as environmental protection.[133] More important, the *lex specialis* thesis runs the danger of begging the question if it cannot be proved that the states commonly hold that protecting the environment during war shall be determined only by the law of war. As shown above, there is no common view precluding the application of peacetime environmental treaties during armed conflict. The claim that the law of armed conflict as *lex specialis* supersedes peacetime environmental law in general is therefore not convincing.[134]

Exceptions, derogations, and the non-derogable core of obligations protecting the environment

Having stated that several types of peacetime environmental treaties continue to apply between belligerent states, it is necessary to consider at least briefly the extent to which these treaties bind belligerent states. It cannot be doubted that if environmental standards bound parties during an armed conflict in the same way as during peacetime, the duty to fulfill

---

[131] See Lijnzaad and Tanja, "Protection of Environment," 172; Tarasofsky, "Legal Protection," 21, 62.

[132] Convention (No. IV) Respecting the Laws and Customs of War on Land, with Annex of Regulations (done at The Hague, Oct. 18, 1907; entered into force, Jan. 26, 1910), preamble, 36 Stat. 2277, U.N.T.S. No. 539; for further references, see also Tarasofsky, "Legal Protection," 32ff.; Betsy Baker, "Legal Protections for the Environment in Times of Armed Conflict," *Va. J. Int'l L.* 33 (1993), 351, 352 n. 3.

[133] Simonds, "Conventional Warfare," 188; Tarasofsky, "Legal Protection," 35; Bothe, "Protection of the Environment," 56.

[134] For this result, see Simonds, "Conventional Warfare," 188.

these treaties would hardly be realistic. Although it is beyond the scope of this chapter to examine this problem in depth, some general comments may be made in respect to the possibilities for modifying the duties of peacetime environmental treaties generally applying to belligerents due to the extraordinary circumstances of international armed conflict.

In legal doctrine, there are four dominant approaches regarding the limitation of peacetime treaty obligations in cases of armed conflict. These are: (1) express derogation clauses; (2) inherent limitations of the treaty concerned; (3) justifications recognized in the law of state responsibility, particularly the state of necessity; and (4) general principles of international law relating to the suspension and termination of treaties.

EXPRESS DEROGATION CLAUSES

First of all, it is clear that if a peacetime treaty entails special derogation clauses for emergency situations or war – as do the major human right treaties[135] – these clauses must be applied.

Peacetime environmental treaties entail such express derogation clauses very rarely. One example is Article XIX of OILPOL (quoted above); another one is Article XVII of the African Convention on the Conservation of Nature and Natural Resources, which provides that "[t]he provisions of this Convention shall not affect the responsibilities of Contracting States concerning: (i) the paramount interest of the State" and that "[t]he provisions of this Convention shall not prevent Contracting States: (i) in time of famine, (ii) for the protection of public health, (iii) in defence of property, to enact measures contrary to the provisions of the Convention, provided their application is precisely defined in respect of aim, time and place." Some environmental treaties do not entail general derogation clauses, but have clauses allowing variances for particular obligations.[136] Other provisions permit state parties not to fulfill certain information duties, if the transfer of information could affect national security.[137]

---

[135] E.g., International Covenant on Civil and Political Rights (done at New York, Dec. 16, 1966; entered into force, Mar. 23, 1976), UNGA Res. 2200 (XXI), 21 UN GAOR, Supp. (No. 16) 52, UN Doc. A/6316 (1967), Art. 4, reprinted in *I.L.M.* 6 (1967), 368; European Convention on Human Rights, Art. 15; American Convention on Human Rights, Art. 27.

[136] E.g., Convention on Wetlands of International Importance, Art. 2, para. 5 (any Contracting Party has the right "because of its urgent national interests, to delete or restrict the boundaries of wetlands" already included in the List of Wetlands of International Importance); see also Art. 4.   [137] See, e.g., UNCLOS, Art. 302.

INHERENT TREATY LIMITATIONS

The second approach applies to treaties where express derogation clauses are missing but the obligations can be modified by reference to inherent limitations. For example, some commentators assert that Articles 2(1) and 4 of the Covenant on Economic, Social, and Cultural Rights recognize that the extraordinary circumstances of an armed conflict can modify the standards and obligations for protecting human rights.[138]

This technique for modifying the peacetime standards can be applied to environmental treaties where the fulfillment of an obligation is linked to the "particular conditions and capabilities" of the states or where the duties are only to be fulfilled "as far as possible and appropriate."[139] But this approach is of limited use for environmental treaties, since many provisions of environmental treaties, especially in the supplementing protocols, lay down absolute obligations.

JUSTIFICATIONS RECOGNIZED IN THE LAW OF STATE RESPONSIBILITY

The third and most important approach to modifying peacetime environmental standards is to rely on the justifications recognized under the general international law of state responsibility. If the conditions of one of the justifications are met by the circumstances of an international armed conflict, a state cannot be responsible for the injury of a peacetime treaty obligation.

While the justifications of *force majeure*, fortuitous event, distress, and consent do not have any special significance in armed conflict in comparison with peacetime, justifications on grounds of self-defense, countermeasures in respect of an internationally wrongful act, and necessity are especially useful during international armed conflicts. However, with the justifications of self-defense and lawful countermeasures, only a state that is a victim of an act of aggression or another unlawful act can claim these justifications, and in practice this can be proven very rarely. At the same time, non-compliance with an international obligation can be justified by these reasons only insofar as this duty was directed against the unlawful

[138] See Kälin and Gabriel, "Human Rights in Times of Occupation," 23ff., 83.
[139] E.g., UNCLOS, Art. 194, para. 1; Convention on Biological Diversity, Arts. 7–11, 14.

act.[140] As shown above, environmental protection treaties that aim to serve the interest of the state community as a whole do not contain reciprocal rights and obligations but oblige a state vis-à-vis all the other state parties. A violation of these environmental treaties can therefore only be justified against those contracting states that have taken part in the previous unlawful act.

These difficulties do not arise in regard to the justification because of a state of necessity, as this justification does not depend on a previous unlawful act.[141] Although the doctrine of necessity has been considered by the ILC as "deeply rooted in the general theory of law," necessity is accepted only under very limited conditions due to the danger of abuses. According to the ILC, it is at least required that an act whose wrongfulness shall be precluded was the "only means of safeguarding an essential interest of the State against a grave and imminent peril" and the act did not seriously impair essential interests of other states.[142] Additionally, the action must be strictly necessary for that purpose.[143]

An obviously "essential" state interest is protecting the nation against an enemy. Non-compliance with peacetime environmental standards is justified if it is the only means to secure the safety of the nation, so long as no interest of greater importance is violated. In the end, the interest in fulfilling a certain obligation to protect the environment must be considered in relation to the interest of the derogating state in safeguarding its security. Thus, the more that an international armed conflict threatens state security interests, the more that peacetime environmental standards may not be fulfilled. But if an "essential" obligation to protect the environment is seriously violated or is a *ius cogens* obligation,[144] a state of necessity provides no justification.

---

[140] International Law Commission, Draft Articles on State Responsibility, Part I, *Y.B. Int'l L. Commission* (1980), vol. II/2, Art. 30 ("The wrongfulness of an act of a State not in conformity with an obligation of that State towards another State is precluded if the act constitutes a measure legitimate under international law against that other State"); ILC Draft Articles on State Responsibility, Part II, Art. 11 ("The injured State is *not* entitled to suspend the performance of its obligations towards the State which has committed the internationally wrongful act to the extent that such obligations are stipulated in a multilateral treaty to which both States are parties and it is established that: . . . such obligations are stipulated for *the protection of collective interests* of the States parties to the multilateral treaty . . .") (emphasis added). On the justification of self-defense, see J. Oraá, *Human Rights in States of Emergency in International Law* (Oxford: Clarendon Press/New York: Oxford Univ. Press, 1992), p. 221.

[141] See Oraá, *Human Rights*, pp. 221 ff.   [142] ILC Draft Articles on State Responsibility, Art. 33.

[143] See Oraá, *Human Rights*, p. 222 (further references).

[144] See ILC Draft Articles on State Responsibility, Art. 33, para. 2.

GENERAL PRINCIPLES RELATING TO THE SUSPENSION AND TERMINATION OF TREATIES

A fourth approach considers the general principles of international law relating to suspension and termination of treaties on grounds of a material breach, supervening impossibility of performance, and fundamental change of circumstances.[145] These principles will apply at least to the same extent during international armed conflict as during peacetime, since belligerent states shall not be given fewer possibilities to suspend their treaty obligations than contracting parties in peacetime.

These general principles also entail several limitations. For instance, it is generally acknowledged that a material breach cannot be invoked to suspend or terminate peremptory norms of international law.[146] An impossibility of performance and a fundamental change of circumstances may not be invoked when it is the result of a breach of an international obligation by the party invoking the ground.[147] If a breach of the *ius ad bellum* is such a "breach of an international obligation," an aggressor state cannot terminate or suspend environmental treaty obligations by claiming impossibility of performance or fundamental change of circumstances.

THE NON-DEROGABLE CORE

Having shown that warring states can modify peacetime environmental standards that are applicable during war, the question of which obligations remain in force for belligerents – that is, what are the "core obligations" for protecting the environment during war – has to be answered. First, it is undisputed that *erga omnes* and *ius cogens* obligations must be fulfilled without exception. Additionally, as was shown above, all possibilities for modifying, suspending, or derogating from certain provisions protecting the environment are subject to very strict conditions. For instance, the most important justification – a state of necessity – is limited to cases where non-compliance is necessary and proportional. The absolute standard of peremptory norms and the limitations of necessity and proportionality

---

[145] See Tarasofsky, "Legal Protection," 65ff.; Ipsen, *Völkerrecht*, pp. 1050ff.; A. Gioia, "The Projected Convention on Chemical Weapons and its Application in Time of Armed Conflict," *The International Spectator* 27 (1992), 25, 32.

[146] See Vienna Convention on the Law of Treaties, Art. 60, para. 5.

[147] See *ibid.*, Arts. 61(2), 62(2).

provide a fruitful approach for determining the core of environmental standards applicable during an armed conflict on a case-by-case basis.

The applicability of peacetime customary environmental law between belligerent states

Until now, the question has remained open regarding which rules of *customary* international environmental law apply between belligerent states. The short answer is that the solution to this question follows the same approach as that developed for the application of peacetime environmental treaties during war. As a result, customary rules protecting the environment that entail *ius cogens* or *erga omnes* obligations bind warring states. The same is true for customary rules that oblige states to protect the environment in the interest of the state community as a whole. In addition, those customary environmental rules that are compatible with the maintenance of war continue to apply between belligerents.

It is open to question how the transfer of rules for the application of peacetime environmental treaties to customary environmental provisions can be justified. The rules identified in this chapter only treat the question of the applicability of peacetime treaties. On the other hand, the conditions of emergence of international rules (custom or treaty) are unimportant in regard to their precedence when the rules collide. The decisive element for solving the conflict of customary rules protecting the environment with rules of the *ius in bello* is whether these customary rules entail the same or similar material obligations as rules of environmental treaties. It would be inconsistent to argue on the one hand that treaty rules protecting the environment bind belligerent states in addition to the law of war in an armed conflict, and on the other hand that the corresponding customary rules protecting the environment are superseded by the *ius in bello*.

This solution is contrary to the argument of some commentators that all rules of customary environmental law bind states during war. The argument relies on the wording of the rules of customary environmental law that does not preclude application during armed conflicts. Neither the customary rule not to cause serious transfrontier damage to components of the environment[148] nor the customary duties of information,

---

[148] Kiss and Shelton, "Systems Analysis," 121ff.; Wolfrum, "Purposes and Principles," 309ff.

consultation, or cooperation regarding environmental matters[149] explicitly states that it binds states only during peacetime conduct. Nevertheless, this does not mean that these customary obligations are per se applicable during war. As mentioned above, a "general practice" and *opinio iuris* is constitutive for a rule of customary international law. This applies to the whole normative content of these rules, as well as to their applicability. The application of rules of customary environmental law during war therefore requires that there is sufficient state practice and *opinio iuris* regarding such application. But as for the case of environmental treaties, the necessary state practice cannot be proved for customary rules of environmental law.[150]

Conclusion

The protection of the environment during armed conflicts today rests upon two pillars: on the one side the classical rules of the laws of war and on the other side the peacetime rules for environmental protection. The latter have the great advantage that numerous treaties together protect nearly all components of the environment and bind a huge number of states. In addition, environmental treaties develop dynamically. By applying peacetime environmental rules during armed conflict, the environment benefits from mechanisms for its protection that are continually developing during peacetime.

Although not all kinds of peacetime rules protecting the environment bind belligerents, at least four groups of peacetime treaties and customary rules protecting the environment remain applicable even if the obligated states take part in armed attacks:

(1) treaties and customary rules protecting the environment that expressly provide for continuance during war;
(2) treaties and customary rules protecting the environment that are compatible with the maintenance of war;
(3) *ius cogens* rules and obligations *erga omnes* protecting the environment;

and, in analogy to human rights treaties and treaties providing objective regimes:

---

[149] Brunnée, " 'Common Interest'," 795.   [150] See Vöneky, *Fortgeltung*, chs. 4, 11.

(4) treaties and customary rules that oblige the states to protect the environment in the interest of the state community as a whole.

In particular, the last criterion includes many peacetime environmental treaties and provisions, such as provisions in UNCLOS governing the use and protection of the deep sea-bed and the protection of the marine environment, the Antarctic treaties, the Convention on Climate Change, the Convention on Biological Diversity, and the Vienna Convention for the Protection of the Ozone Layer. On the other hand, it is doubtful whether treaties governing the use and protection of shared resources oblige state parties in the interest of the whole state community and not only in their own national interest. In such cases, treaties governing shared resources probably do not bind belligerents. However, this question needs to be answered on a case-by-case basis.

In the end, the more the states oblige themselves to protect the environment in the interest of the whole international community, the more this protection will apply during wartime and the more the environment will be secured against wartime destruction. Each treaty concluded with the aim of protecting the environment in the common interest is a further step towards broadening the basis of state responsibility for environmental damage caused during war. It fills the "normative lacunae"[151] that characterize the protection of the environment by the traditional laws of war.

---

[151] Michael N. Schmitt, "War and the Environment: Fault Lines in the Prescriptive Landscape," chapter 3 in this volume; see also *Archiv des Völkerrechts* 37 (1999), 25, 57.

8

ENVIRONMENTAL DAMAGES UNDER THE
LAW OF THE SEA CONVENTION

THOMAS A. MENSAH

Introduction

The principle that a state is responsible for environmental damage attributable to it is well established in international law. Both the Stockholm Declaration of the 1972 UN Conference on the Human Environment and the Rio Declaration of the 1992 Conference on Environment and Development contain clear statements on the obligation of states to ensure that activities undertaken by them or under their jurisdiction do not cause damage outside their areas of jurisdiction.[1] There is ample case law in the jurisprudence of international judicial bodies and arbitral tribunals to support the proposition that a state can be held responsible for, and be liable to pay compensation or make other appropriate reparation for, damage that results from its failure to fulfill its obligations in respect of activities undertaken by it or on its behalf or within its jurisdiction. A state that suffers damage as the result of an act or omission of another state contrary to international or national law may bring a claim for compensation against the offending state.[2]

A court or arbitral tribunal that is seised of a claim from one state for compensation for environmental damage against another state will

---

The views expressed herein are those of the author. They are not to be attributed in any way to the International Tribunal for the Law of the Sea.

[1] Declaration of the United Nations Conference on the Human Environment, UN Doc. A/CONF.48/14 (1972), Principle 21; Declaration of the United Nations Conference on Environment and Development, UN Doc. A/CONF.151/26 (1992), Principle 2.

[2] See *Lake Lanoux Arbitration (France v. Spain)*, I.L.R. 24 (1957), 101 (Arb. Trib. 1957); *Trail Smelter Arbitration (US v. Canada)*, I.L.R. 9 (1941), 315; *Case Concerning the Gabcíkovo-Nagymaros Project (Hungary v. Slovak Republic)*, I.L.M. 32 (1993), 1293.

normally be competent to deal with all aspects thereof, including the existence or otherwise of liability, the basis of such liability (including any
exonerations), the extent of the damage attributable to the state alleged to
be liable, and the quantum of compensation to be paid, having regard to
the circumstances of the case. In the absence of criteria or procedures
developed for the assessment of damage or the determination of the levels
of appropriate compensation in the specific case, the court or tribunal will
be expected to apply general principles of international law in dealing with
these questions.

Similarly, a natural or juridical person may be held responsible for environmental damage caused by the act or omission of that person where such
act or omission constitutes non-compliance with applicable national or
international law. Claims for compensation in such cases may be covered
by national or international law, and may be brought before the competent
court or tribunal, either by the person who actually suffered damage or by
a state on behalf of that person.[3]

The 1982 United Nations Convention on the Law of the Sea[4] establishes
a legal regime for protection and preservation of the marine environment
from pollution and other forms of degradation arising from all possible sources. The convention identifies the principal sources of pollution
as land-based sources, the atmosphere, vessels, exploration of sea-bed
resources, and other equipment operating in the marine environment.[5]

The convention declares general principles regarding the rights and obligations of states, international organizations, and other non-state operators
with regard to measures to be taken to prevent, reduce, and control pollution of the marine environment from the various sources. For this purpose, states and international organizations are urged to take appropriate
steps to establish suitable rules, regulations, recommended practices and
procedures for dealing with the problem at the national, regional, and
global levels. The convention also calls upon states to cooperate for "the
implementation of existing international law and the further development
of international law relating to responsibility and liability for the assessment of and compensation for damage and the settlement of disputes, as
well as, where appropriate, development of criteria and procedures for the

[3] E.g., the *Trail Smelter Arbitration*, where most of the claims were brought by the United States
on behalf of US nationals and business enterprises that had suffered damage.
[4] United Nations Convention on the Law of the Sea, UN Doc. A/CONF.62/122 (Dec. 10, 1982),
I.L.M. 21 (1982), 1261.   [5] *Ibid.*, Art. 194, para. 3.

payment of adequate compensation, such as compulsory insurance or compensation funds."[6]

The laws and procedures to be developed are expected to specify the responsibility and liability of states and other entities for damage that may be caused as a result of failure to comply with the rules of the convention or other applicable international instruments. The objective of the liability and compensation schemes envisaged under the convention is to assure "prompt and adequate compensation or other relief in respect of all damage caused by pollution of the marine environment by natural or juridical persons."[7] Thus, under the convention, both states and non-state entities may be responsible for environmental damage and may, accordingly, be liable to pay compensation or make other appropriate reparation for damage to the marine environment when such damage is rightly attributable to them.

With regard to states, the convention sets out the general principle that they "are responsible for the fulfilment of their international obligations concerning the protection and preservation of the marine environment." They "shall be liable in accordance with international law" for failure to fulfill their obligations.[8] As far as non-state entities are concerned, the convention enjoins states to ensure that "recourse is available in accordance with their legal systems for prompt and adequate compensation or other relief in respect of damage caused by pollution of the marine environment by natural or juridical persons under their jurisdiction."[9]

The convention and the assessment and recovery of compensation

The Convention on the Law of the Sea does not establish precise legal rules for assessment and recovery of compensation for damage resulting from pollution of the marine environment. As envisaged in the convention, procedures and relevant criteria for the assessment and recovery of compensation for marine environmental damage have been developed in a number of international civil liability conventions. Among these, the following are noteworthy: the 1969 International Convention on Civil Liability for Oil Pollution Damage, as revised by its 1992 Protocol;[10] the 1971 Convention on the Establishment of an International Fund for

---

[6] *Ibid.*, Art. 235, para. 3. [7] *Ibid.*, para. 2. [8] *Ibid.*, para. 1. [9] *Ibid.*, para. 2.
[10] International Convention on Civil Liability for Oil Pollution Damage (Nov. 29, 1969), 973 U.N.T.S. 3, *I.L.M.* 9 (1970), 45; 1992 Protocol to the International Convention on Civil Liability for Oil Pollution Damage, IMO Doc. LEG/CONF.9/15 (Dec. 2, 1992).

Compensation for Oil Pollution Damage, as revised by its 1992 Protocol;[11] the 1977 Convention on Civil Liability for Pollution Resulting from Exploration for and Exploitation of Seabed Mineral Resources;[12] and the 1996 Convention on Liability and Compensation for Damage in Connection with the Carriage of Hazardous and Noxious Substances by Sea.[13] Also relevant, though not directly, is the 1988 Convention on the Regulation of Antarctic Mineral Resource Activities.[14]

The procedures for assessment and recovery of environmental damage established in these conventions are based on more or less the same assumptions as those postulated in Article 235 of the Convention on the Law of the Sea, in that they seek to ensure the availability of "prompt and adequate" compensation for damage to all victims, including states, public authorities, and juridical and natural persons. They establish mechanisms and procedures for the recovery of compensation and also criteria for assessing damage to be paid.

MECHANISMS FOR THE RECOVERY OF COMPENSATION

Recovery of compensation for environmental damage may be sought through the dispute-settlement mechanism established under the Convention on the Law of the Sea. This system of dispute settlement is intended to supplement the procedures available to states and other entities under national and international law. States and entities that suffer pollution damage may seek compensation for such damage through any of the mechanisms and procedures that are applicable or that may be convenient to them for one reason or another. In each case, it is the mechanism selected that will determine whether the claimant is entitled to compensation for the damage complained of. Where compensation is deemed to be

---

[11] Convention on the Establishment of an International Fund for Compensation for Oil Pollution Damage (Dec. 18, 1971), *I.L.M.* 11 (1972), 284 (Fund Convention); 1992 Protocol to the Convention on the Establishment of an International Fund for Compensation for Oil Pollution Damage, IMO Doc. LEG/CONF.9/16 (Dec. 2, 1992).

[12] Convention on Civil Liability for Pollution Resulting from Exploration for and Exploitation of Seabed Mineral Resources (May 1, 1977), reprinted in United Nations Environment Program, *Selected Multilateral Treaties in the Field of the Environment* (1983), p. 474.

[13] Convention on Liability and Compensation for Damage in Connection with the Carriage of Hazardous and Noxious Substances by Sea (HNS Convention) (May 3, 1996), *I.L.M.* 35 (1996), 1415.

[14] Convention on the Regulation of Antarctic Mineral Resource Activities (June 2, 1988), *I.L.M.* 27 (1988), 868.

appropriate, the court or tribunal will establish the form and extent of the compensation or other relief deemed to be suitable in the particular case. The procedures and mechanisms for the recovery of compensation established or envisaged under the convention include those enumerated in the United Nations Charter: negotiation, mediation, conciliation, and so on.[15] But they also include procedures leading to some form of "binding decision," as provided for in the convention or in the relevant provisions of other conventions or agreements. These latter procedures include domestic or international judicial procedures, insurance or other financial securities, and compensation funds.

Recovery of compensation through judicial procedures

Where the parties in the dispute are not able to resolve it through non-judicial procedures, the claim may be brought before a court or other judicial body with competence to deal with the issues raised. Such a body may be either a national court or an international tribunal that has automatic jurisdiction in the matter or to which the parties to the case have agreed to submit it. Jurisdiction in particular cases may be conferred on one court or another by an applicable international agreement or national law.

Claims for compensation by states or non-state entities may be brought before a domestic court. A domestic court may have competence to determine the right of the claimant to receive compensation and, where appropriate, to assess the compensation due. In most cases claims for compensation are to be submitted to the courts of the state in which the damage is caused.[16] Claims may also be submitted to the courts of the state in which the activity that caused the damage was undertaken.[17] Additionally claims may be brought before the courts of other states, for example, before the court of the state of nationality, residence, or location of registered offices of the person from whom compensation is being claimed.[18] The convention recognizes the suitability of national courts for this purpose. Accordingly, it provides that states shall "ensure that recourse is available in accordance with their legal systems for prompt and adequate

---

[15] UN Charter, Art. 33, para. 1.
[16] 1969 Civil Liability Convention, Art. IX; 1996 HNS Convention, Art. 38.
[17] Convention on Civil Liability for Damage Caused During Carriage of Dangerous Goods by Road, Rail and Inland Navigation (Oct. 10, 1989), Art. 19.
[18] 1996 HNS Convention, Art. 38, para. 3.

compensation or other relief in respect of damage caused by pollution of the marine environment by natural or juridical persons under their jurisdiction."[19]

States also may claim compensation for environmental damage from other states through international procedures. Compensation may be claimed by a state against another state for damage caused to the nationals of the claimant state. Procedures for such claims are available under general international law. They include recourse to international courts or tribunals or arbitral tribunals, as may be agreed between the claimant state and the state from which compensation is claimed.

Finally, compensation may be sought through the special procedures established for dispute settlement under the convention.[20] These include the International Tribunal for the Law of the Sea (ITLOS), the International Court of Justice (ICJ), and arbitral tribunals and special arbitral tribunals established under Annexes VII and VIII to the convention, respectively. Article 288 of the convention gives competence to the ITLOS and the ICJ to deal with disputes regarding the interpretation or application of provisions of the convention if the states parties to the dispute have selected either of them as their preferred mechanism for settlement of disputes, in accordance with Article 287 of the convention.[21] Such a dispute may arise in connection with a claim for compensation for environmental damage suffered as a result of alleged non-compliance with some provisions of the convention.[22] A similar competence is available to arbitral tribunals constituted in accordance with Annex VII to the convention, if the parties to the dispute are obliged to submit the dispute to such a tribunal or if they agree to do so.

All the tribunals referred to in Article 287 of the convention may also have jurisdiction to deal with claims under any other agreement which relates to the law of the sea, if the agreement confers jurisdiction on any one of them.[23] Annex VIII to the convention provides a special mechanism for dealing with disputes involving, inter alia, pollution of the marine environment, including pollution from vessels or by dumping. Depending on the choice of the parties involved, a claim for compensation for damage

---

[19] Law of the Sea Convention, Art. 235, para. 2.   [20] *Ibid.*, Art. 287.   [21] *Ibid.*, paras. 1 and 2.

[22] See *ibid.*, Art. 297, para. 1(c). Other provisions of the convention dealing with possible claims for compensation for damage to the marine environment include Articles 31, 235(1), and 263.

[23] See *ibid.*, Art. 288, para. 2; see also *ibid.*, Annex VI (Statute of the International Tribunal on the Law of the Sea), Arts. 20 and 21.

to the marine environment may be submitted to a special arbitral tribunal constituted under Annex VIII.[24]

Recovery of compensation from insurance or other financial security

One of the mechanisms for the recovery of compensation envisaged under Article 235 of the convention is "compulsory insurance." Compulsory insurance as a means of guaranteeing compensation for victims of marine pollution damage is one of the features of civil liability conventions. This makes it possible for persons who suffer damage to obtain compensation from insurance or other financial security maintained by the party who would otherwise have been obliged to pay compensation for the damage.

Compulsory insurance is required for activities that are deemed to pose a high risk of damage. The civil liability conventions require persons who engage in such activities to maintain compulsory insurance or to have other appropriate financial security to cover their potential liability for damage.[25] Persons who suffer damage are able to seek compensation directly from the persons providing the insurance or other financial security, without having to make an approach to the person actually liable for the damage.[26] Such an arrangement significantly simplifies the claims process, since all that a claimant for compensation needs to do is to demonstrate that the damage suffered is covered by the insurance. Where the person providing the insurance or other security is satisfied that the claim is covered by the insurance and also that the compensation being claimed is reasonable under the circumstances, the claim will in most cases be settled without the matter being submitted to a court or tribunal.

Recovery of compensation through compensation funds

The other mechanism mentioned in Article 235 for recovery of compensation for environmental damage is the "compensation fund." Compensation funds make it possible for compensation for damage to be paid, not necessarily by the person actually liable for the damage, but from a fund established to make compensation available to victims of damage under certain conditions. Such compensation funds have been established under

---

[24] *Ibid.*, Annex VIII, Art. 1.   [25] 1969 Civil Liability Convention, Art. VII, para. 1.
[26] *Ibid.*, para. 8.

international conventions to cover damage resulting from specified activities. The first was established in 1971 to provide compensation for pollution damage resulting from accidents involving oil tankers.[27] A similar fund was established in 1996 in the corresponding convention for damage arising from the carriage by sea of hazardous and noxious substances.[28] The compensation funds provide additional (or alternative) compensation for those who suffer damage where the compensation from the liable party is not adequate to cover the damage suffered, or where no compensation at all can be recovered from the liable party.[29] Like the compulsory insurance schemes, compensation funds simplify the claims process and make it easier for those who suffer damage to receive "adequate" compensation as "promptly" as possible.

CRITERIA FOR THE ASSESSMENT OF DAMAGE AND COMPENSATION FOR DAMAGE

The Law of the Sea Convention does not set out conditions and criteria for the assessment of and recovery of compensation for damage caused by states or natural and juridical persons. But it does provide that states shall "co-operate to develop appropriate criteria and procedures for payment of prompt and adequate compensation."[30] The 1969 Civil Liability Convention and the 1996 Hazardous and Noxious Substances Convention (HNS Convention) have developed some criteria for this purpose in connection with damage arising from maritime carriage of polluting cargoes. With minor exceptions, the regimes in the two conventions are basically the same. They have the following common features:

(1) They are not based on, and do not involve, state responsibility as such. The party liable to pay compensation in every case is the entity responsible for the activity that was the cause of the damage. Where a state is held liable, it is solely on the ground either that it is itself responsible for the damage concerned, or that it has agreed to accept liability on behalf of an entity within its jurisdiction or control.[31]

---

[27] 1971 Fund Convention.   [28] 1996 HNS Convention.
[29] See 1971 Fund Convention, Art. 4, para. 1; 1996 HNS Convention, Art. 14, para. 1.
[30] Law of the Sea Convention, Art. 235, para. 3.
[31] 1971 Fund Convention, Art. 14, para. 2, provides that a state party may voluntarily assume an obligation incumbent on a person in its territory in respect of the payment of contributions to the compensation fund. A similar provision is found in the 1996 HNS Convention, Art. 21.

(2) The obligation to pay compensation for damage is not necessarily based on fault or a wrongful act on the part of the person liable. Rather, liability to compensate arises solely on the basis that the damage resulted from an activity undertaken by or on behalf of that person. Liability may be avoided only where it is proved that one or more of the limited exceptions expressly provided for in the conventions apply.

(3) To ensure that compensation will in fact be available, the schemes require the person who would be liable for damage to maintain compulsory insurance or other financial security to cover liability in the event of damage. Insurance or other security required is to cover the maximum level of compensation that the person concerned can be required to pay under the relevant conventions. Persons who suffer damage are permitted to seek compensation directly from the person providing insurance or other form of financial guarantee, and they need not address themselves to the person liable.

(4) In order to facilitate insurance, the conventions set limits on the level of compensation to be paid by the party liable in respect of any single incident. Where the regime provides for compulsory insurance or other appropriate financial guarantees, the insurance or guarantee required must cover liability up to the limit set for the party concerned.[32] However, there is no limit to the compensation payable if the damage resulted from the "personal act or omission" of the person liable, and the act was "committed with the intent to cause such damage, or recklessly and with knowledge that such damage would probably occur."[33] In that case, that person will be liable to pay compensation for the entire damage suffered.

(5) The conventions recognize that limitation of liability can lead to situations in which some damage might not be fully compensated for by the person liable. It is to deal with this eventuality that supplemental means of compensation, in the form of compensation funds, are established.

---

[32] The owner of a ship is required to maintain insurance or other financial security "in the sum fixed by applying the limits of liability prescribed [in the Convention] to cover his liability for pollution damage under this Convention." 1969 Civil Liability Convention, Art. VII, para. 1.
[33] 1969 Civil Liability Convention, Art. V, para. 1, as amended by its 1992 Protocol, Art. 4, para. 4; see also 1996 HNS Convention, Art. 9, para. 2.

(6) Except in a few cases, the decision whether compensation is payable for damage and the assessment of the amount of compensation due is made by national courts and other competent bodies in the states parties to the relevant conventions. Thus, the 1969 Civil Liability Convention provides that "where an incident has caused pollution damage in the territory . . . of one or more Contracting States, or preventive measures have been taken to prevent or minimize pollution damage in such territory . . . actions for compensation may only be brought in the courts of any of such Contracting State or States."[34] To implement this provision, each contracting state is required to "ensure that its Courts possess the necessary jurisdiction to entertain such actions for compensation."[35] Further, except for the cases expressly provided for in the relevant conventions, any decision given by a national court with jurisdiction as provided under the convention is to be "recognized" and "enforceable" in all other contracting states.[36]

ISSUES IN CONNECTION WITH ASSESSMENT
AND RECOVERY OF COMPENSATION

The party liable for damage

The civil liability conventions operate on the basis of the "polluter pays" principle. This means that the person whose activity causes the pollution damage is the person held responsible, and is obliged to pay compensation for the damage. The first layer of liability is imposed on the carrier of the substances that cause damage. Thus, both the 1969 Civil Liability Convention and the 1996 HNS Convention place liability for damage primarily on the owner of the ship in which the substances were being carried at the time of the incident that resulted in the damage.[37] The shipowner is liable

---

[34] 1969 Civil Liability Convention, Art. IX, as amended by its 1992 Protocol, Art. 8; see also 1996 HNS Convention, Art. 38, para. 1. But the 1996 HNS Convention, Art. 38, para. 2, also permits actions to be brought before other courts, e.g. the ship's state of registry or flag state, or the state party where the shipowner has habitual residence or principal place of business, if the damage is caused outside the territorial sea of a state.

[35] 1969 Civil Liability Convention, Art. X, para. 2; see also 1996 HNS Convention, Art. 38, para. 3.

[36] 1969 Civil Liability Convention, Art. X; 1996 HNS Convention, Art. 40.

[37] 1969 Civil Liability Convention, Art. V, para. 1; see also 1996 HNS Convention, Art. 7, para. 1.

even if the ship was being operated at the time by another person. And it is also the owner who is obliged to maintain compulsory insurance or other appropriate financial guarantee to cover compensation for any potential damage.

Liability under the conventions is "channelled" exclusively to the shipowner. This means that other persons who may be involved in the incident, such as the operator of the ship, agents, employees, or servants of the owner, cannot be held liable for damage under the conventions. There are two exceptions to this, however. The first is that a person who is otherwise exempted from liability for damage may be held liable if the damage resulted from the personal act or omission of that person, "committed with the intent to cause such damage, or recklessly and with knowledge that such damage would probably result."[38] In addition, the channeling of liability to the shipowner does not affect the right of the owner to seek reimbursement from a third party if he is obliged to pay compensation for damage caused by the negligence or other wrongful act of the third party. Such "right of recourse" is reserved to the shipowner by the conventions, and may be exercised in accordance with applicable domestic or other law.[39]

However, both the 1969 Civil Liability Convention and the 1996 HNS Convention provide for significant involvement of cargo interests in making adequate compensation available for environmental damage. The conventions recognize, first, that damage results largely from the nature of the substances being carried on board the ship and, second, that the compensation which may be required of the shipowner may not suffice in all cases fully to compensate the damage caused by an incident. Therefore, to take due account of the role of the cargo in producing the damage, and also to ensure that victims of damage are able to obtain adequate compensation in cases where compensation from the shipowner is inadequate, the conventions impose an obligation on the cargo interests to provide part of the compensation. As noted above, this is done through compensation funds that supplement the compensation from the shipowner.[40] These funds are constituted by levies raised on shipments of the substances that come within the scope of the respective conventions – oil in the case of the 1969

---

[38] 1969 Civil Liability Convention, Art. III, para. 4, as amended by its 1992 Protocol, Art. 4, para. 2.

[39] *Ibid.*, Art. III, para. 5; 1996 HNS Convention, Art. 7, para. 6.

[40] See 1971 Fund Convention, Art. 4, para. 1, and 1996 HNS Convention, Art. 14, para. 1, for a description of the purposes and functions of the compensation funds they establish.

Civil Liability Convention, and hazardous and noxious substances in the case of the 1996 HNS Convention.[41] All persons who engage in transport by sea of the substances concerned are required to contribute to the fund, and the fund is obliged to pay compensation to those who suffer damage, pursuant to the terms of the relevant convention.

Limitation of liability

Both the shipowners and the compensation funds have a maximum limit fixed for the compensation they are obliged to pay for any single incident.[42] This means that where the total damage resulting from one incident exceeds the total quantum of compensation required from the shipowner, the victims can claim additional compensation from the compensation fund. However, after the maximum additional compensation required from the fund has been paid, no further compensation will be available under the regime.

There is still some controversy on this issue of limitation of liability. On the one hand, it has been claimed that it is not justifiable to deny full compensation to a victim of environmental damage on the basis of limited liability. The argument is that if anybody needs to be protected, it is the innocent victim rather than the person who chooses to engage in the business of transporting hazardous substances for profit.[43] On the other hand, it has been contended that limitation of liability is necessary if the regime is to involve compulsory insurance, since it might not be possible for the shipowner to obtain insurance or other financial guarantees to cover liability if liability under the regime were to be unlimited.[44]

---

[41] For details of the contributions system in those conventions, see 1971 Fund Convention, Arts. 10–15; 1996 HNS Convention, Arts. 16–20.

[42] 1971 Fund Convention, Art. 4, para. 4, as amended by its 1992 Protocol, Art. 6, paras. 2 and 3. The maximum limit of compensation payable for any single incident is 350 million SDRs (approximately US $182 million). The corresponding limit for the HNS Fund is 250 million SDRs (approximately US $130 million). 1996 HNS Convention, Art. 14, paras. 5 and 6.

[43] Statement of the Delegation of Canada at the 1969 International Conference on Marine Pollution Damage, in IMO Publication of the Official Record (1973), p. 510 ("the notion of limited liability . . . is detrimental to a victim's rights . . . and implied that any one who had suffered damage as a result of pollution was not entitled to adequate compensation but only to limited compensation").

[44] Statement of the Delegation of the United Kingdom at the 1969 International Conference on Marine Pollution Damage, in *ibid.*, p. 487. ("The United Kingdom considers that, in order to enable the shipowner to obtain insurance cover, the principle of limitation of liability should be accepted, except in the case of an incident arising from the fault or privity of the owner.")

Accordingly, it has been suggested that the alternative to a system of limitation of liability (which guarantees that at least some compensation will be payable regardless of the financial capacity of the shipowner) is to impose unlimited liability on the shipowner, with the possibility that no insurance will be obtained to cover the liability. Such a solution could lead to situations in which the victims of damage will not obtain any compensation at all, for example where an uninsured shipowner is financially incapable of paying any compensation.[45] Whatever the merits of the respective positions, the general tendency in international conventions, as in many national legal systems, is to provide for some form of maximum ceiling for compensation for environmental damage. In most cases the issue will be not whether limitation of liability is acceptable but, rather, what the appropriate limit of liability should be.

Basis of liability

The civil liability conventions operate on the basis that the transportation by sea of oil and other substances that have a known potential to cause environmental damage is an inherently hazardous activity. For that reason, those who engage in that activity should be subject to a stricter legal regime, especially as regards their responsibility for damage that may result from their activities. In particular, it is agreed that their responsibility for damage, and consequential liability to pay compensation, should not necessarily depend on proof of any wrongdoing on their part. On that basis, it has been suggested that liability for damage caused by such activity should be without any exonerations whatsoever, in other words "absolute." But while there is general agreement that liability in these cases should not be based on fault, the suggestion to impose absolute liability on the shipowner has not found sufficient support.

The solution that has met with general acceptance is to make liability of the shipowner "strict." This means that a claimant does not have to prove any intentional or negligent act or omission on the part of the shipowner in order to be entitled to compensation for damage. All that needs to be demonstrated is the fact that damage has been caused and that the damage resulted from an incident involving a ship of the person from whom

---

[45] On the issue of limitation of liability in maritime law, see generally Gotthard Gauci, "Limitation of Liability in Maritime Law: An Anachronism?", *Marine Pol'y* 19 (1995), 65.

compensation is claimed. Nevertheless, there are certain situations in which no liability will attach to the owner of a ship for damage that is proved to have resulted from an incident involving the ship. This happens in the few clearly defined situations where the conventions specify that the shipowner should be relieved of liability. In the 1969 Civil Liability Convention and 1996 HNS Convention, these are situations where the damage: (1) resulted from an act of war, hostilities, civil war, insurrection, or a natural phenomenon of an exceptional, inevitable, and irresistible character; (2) was wholly caused by an act or omission done with the intent to cause damage by a third party; or (3) was wholly caused by the negligence or other wrongful act of any government or other authority for the maintenance of lights or other navigational aids in the exercise of that function.[46] The owner may also be wholly or partially exonerated from liability to a person who suffers damage if the damage resulted wholly or partially from an act or omission of that person done with the intention to cause damage, or negligently.[47]

It is to be noted that in each case, the burden of proving that a particular exoneration applies to any damage rests on the shipowner. Article III of the 1969 Civil Liability Convention states that "no liability shall attach to the owner *if he proves that*" any of the enumerated exceptions applies.[48]

Similarly, the obligation of a compensation fund to pay compensation is not based on any fault or negligence. However, the fund also may be exonerated from the obligation to pay compensation in certain clearly defined circumstances. For example, and most relevant to the question of wartime environmental damage, the funds are not obliged to pay compensation for damage caused as a result of acts of war, or damage caused by a warship or other government non-commercial vessels.[49] However, the exonerations applicable to the funds are more restricted than those available to the person primarily liable. Thus, as already noted, shipowners are exonerated if the damage results from a "natural phenomenon of an exceptional, inevitable and irresistible character"; or "an act or omission done with the

---

[46] 1969 Civil Liability Convention, Art. III, para. 2; 1996 HNS Convention, Art. 7, para. 2. The HNS Convention also relieves the shipowner of liability for damage if it was due to the "failure of the shipper or any other person to furnish information concerning the hazardous and noxious nature of the substance shipped." *Ibid.*, Art. 7, para. 2(d).

[47] 1969 Civil Liability Convention, Art. III, para. 3.

[48] *Ibid.*, para. 2 (emphasis supplied). Paragraph 3 of the same article states that the exoneration will apply "if the owner proves . . ."

[49] 1971 Fund Convention, Art. 4, para. 2; 1996 HNS Convention, Art. 14, para. 3.

intent to cause damage by a third party"; or "the negligence or other wrongful act of any Government or other authority responsible for the maintenance of lights or other navigational aids in the exercise of that function."[50] However, these exonerations are not available to either the International Oil Pollution Compensation (IOPC) Fund or the International Hazardous and Noxious Substances Fund.

Nature of damage to be compensated

The Law of the Sea Convention envisages the development of law regarding liability and compensation in respect of "damage caused by pollution of the marine environment."[51] The civil liability conventions so far developed provide compensation specifically for pollution damage. As defined in the relevant provisions, "pollution damage" includes damage to persons (personal injury, including loss of life), property damage (loss of or damage to property), and environmental damage ("impairment of the environment"). In the 1969 Civil Liability Convention, "pollution damage" is defined as "damage by contamination." This means that damage covered by the convention, whether to persons or to property, has to be the result of "physical contamination" by oil. Hence where damage does not involve such physical contamination, as for example where damage is caused by fire or explosion resulting from the spillage of oil from a tanker, persons who suffer damage or injury from the fire or explosion will not be entitled to recover compensation from the shipowner under the 1969 Civil Liability Convention, since the damage will not qualify as "pollution damage," as defined in the convention.

The 1996 HNS Convention adopts a different approach, dealing both with pollution damage in the sense of the 1969 Civil Liability Convention, and with damage from hazardous and noxious substances, even where there is no "contamination" by those substances.[52] This means that damage by fire and explosion from oil, which is excluded from the scope of the 1969 Civil Liability Convention, will be entitled to compensation under the 1996 HNS Convention. Thus, with the adoption of the HNS Convention, the regime of the civil liability conventions dealing with shipborne

---

[50] 1969 Civil Liability Convention, Art. III, para. 2; see also 1996 HNS Convention, Art. 7, para. 2.
[51] Law of the Sea Convention, Art. 235, para. 2.
[52] 1996 HNS Convention, Art. 1, para. 6(a) and (b). The same approach has been adopted in the 1992 Civil Liability Protocol.

substances extends to nearly all the possible types of environmental damage resulting from the operation of ships.

Persons entitled to compensation

The civil liability conventions apply to damage caused to natural or juridical persons as well as to states, national governments, and other public bodies. As the Convention on the Law of the Sea stipulates, the objective of the law on responsibility and liability is to assure "prompt and adequate compensation" in respect of "all damage caused by pollution of the marine environment" as a result of the acts of "natural or juridical persons under their jurisdiction." To achieve that objective, the civil liability conventions cover all types of damage resulting from pollution of the marine environment, and they provide the possibility of compensation to all persons who suffer damage from pollution.[53] In particular, they give appropriate recognition to the independent role of non-state entities, whether as parties who may be responsible and liable for damage or as persons who may suffer damage and seek to claim compensation.

MEASURES OF DAMAGES

The civil liability conventions contain generally similar criteria and conditions for the assessment and recovery of damages. They also categorize the various heads of damages to be compensated. These include clean-up costs, costs of preventive measures, personal injury, property damage, economic loss or loss of income, and "impairment of the environment."

Clean-up costs. Clean-up costs include the expenses incurred in cleaning an ecosystem that has been polluted or otherwise degraded by an incident. Costs may arise in connection with the removal of spilled oil from beaches and coastal waters; the cleaning of soot coating from trees, houses, and equipment; the neutralization of chemical contamination of property, flora, or fauna; and so on. Clean-up costs may be incurred by governments and other public authorities as well as by private entities (individuals and companies). The costs of such measures, to the extent that they are deemed to be "reasonable" in the circumstances of the particular case, will be

---

[53] "Claimants may be individuals or partnerships or public or private bodies, including a state itself, municipalities and other local authorities." IOPC Fund Claims Manual, para. 3.

recoverable from the person liable or the party providing insurance or other financial guarantee on behalf of that person or, where applicable, the relevant compensation fund.

Costs of preventive measures. Costs incurred in taking measures reasonably necessary to prevent or limit damage following an incident are recoverable as "compensation for pollution damage." Both the 1969 and 1996 Conventions contain provisions that permit the "costs of preventive measures" to be compensated, no matter who takes the measures or where the measures are taken.[54] Thus, if the owner of a ship takes measures or causes measures to be taken to prevent or minimize damage from an incident involving the ship, the owner will be entitled to claim compensation for the costs incurred, so long as the court or authority concerned is satisfied that the measures were reasonable in the circumstances. The rationale is that it is in the interest of environmental protection (and also of potential damage victims) that all persons in a position to prevent or reduce damage from an incident should be given suitable incentives to do so.

In the 1969 Civil Liability Convention, preventive measures were defined as "any reasonable measures taken after an incident has occurred to prevent or minimize pollution damage,"[55] and "incident" was defined as "an occurrence . . . which causes pollution damage."[56] The implication of these provisions, read together, was that measures taken in respect of an incident would only be considered as "preventive measures" under the convention if pollution damage actually resulted from the incident. If, for example, following the stranding of a laden tanker, the shipowner managed successfully to prevent any escape of oil, the measures taken to achieve this would not be deemed to be "preventive measures," since the occurrence did not "cause pollution damage." The shipowner would, therefore, not be entitled to claim reimbursement for the expenses incurred in taking what were useful and necessary measures.

This approach was considered to be both unduly restrictive and incompatible with the principle that all concerned should be encouraged to take necessary and reasonable measures to prevent pollution damage in the first place. For that reason, the provisions were revised in the 1992 Protocol, which defines "incident" as "any occurrence . . . which causes pollution damage or creates a grave and imminent threat of causing such

---

[54] 1969 Civil Liability Convention, Art. I, para. 7; 1996 HNS Convention, Art. 1, para. 7.
[55] 1969 Civil Liability Convention, Art. I, para. 8.   [56] *Ibid.*

damage."[57] This revised provision makes it clear that measures reasonably taken to prevent pollution, if they succeed in preventing damage altogether, will still qualify as preventive measures and will, accordingly, be entitled to compensation under the convention.

Personal injury. Damage, to the person resulting from pollution, is compensable. Compensation includes expenses resulting from impairment of health arising from such causes as fouling of the air by oil, escape of chemicals, or an explosion or a fire resulting from a maritime incident. Compensation may also be due for direct personal injury and loss of life. In considering certain claims for personal damage, the Executive Committee of the IOPC Fund took the view that, "in the light of discussions at the 1969 International Conference on Oil Pollution Damage which adopted the 1969 Civil Liability Convention, the Convention in principle covered personal injury caused by contamination, whereas personal injury resulting from other causes was not admissible."[58]

Property damage. Compensation is payable for damage to property, such as loss of or damage to property resulting from pollution damage or other damage covered by the civil liability conventions. The conventions do not give a detailed description of the types of property damage that will be covered. However, the IOPC Fund, which has been largely responsible for responding to claims for compensation under both the 1969 Civil Liability Convention and the 1971 Fund Convention, has developed a comprehensive set of guidelines giving a fairly clear indication of the scope of coverage of the 1969/1971 liability and compensation regime. The main outlines of the IOPC guidelines are equally applicable to the 1996 HNS Convention. The categories of property damage for which the IOPC Fund has accepted the obligation to pay compensation include contamination and consequential damage to: property such as fishing boats and gear, recreational boats (yachts), piers, and harbour works; fisheries resources, such as oyster beds, fish farms, aquaculture facilities; and property on land, such as houses, beach huts, commercial and industrial installations.[59]

Economic loss or loss of income. An example of economic loss covered by the civil liability conventions would be loss of income resulting from stoppage of or reduction in business activity as the result of a pollution

---

[57] 1992 Protocol to the 1969 Civil Liability Convention, Art. 2, para. 4.
[58] Annual Report of the IOPC Fund (1996), p. 64.
[59] See, for example, the claims against the *Sea Empress* (1996), reported in Annual Report of the IOPC Fund (1997), pp. 86–95.

incident. Thus, where hotels and other persons providing tourist services are prevented from doing business, the persons suffering the damage will be entitled to claim compensation for the loss of income attributable to the stoppage or reduction of activity. As the IOPC Fund Claims Manual puts it, "economic loss can include . . . loss of income resulting from restriction of fishing activity or from closure of coastal industrial installations, as well as loss of income by resort operators (hoteliers and restauranteurs)."[60]

Impairment of the environment. In addition to damage to persons and property and the costs of preventive measures, the civil liability conventions provide for compensation for "impairment of the environment" – damage to the environment itself, not necessarily involving damage to any person or item of property or other loss incurred by any specific individual. But this head of damages is given a very restricted scope in the conventions.

The 1969 Civil Liability Convention had defined "pollution damage" as "loss or damage . . . by contamination."[61] On this basis, the Assembly of the IOPC Fund, which first had occasion to consider the provision's implementation, concluded that "pollution damage" as used in the convention was to be understood as damage by contamination that results in "quantifiable loss." In particular, the Assembly rejected "the assessment of compensation for damage to the marine environment on the basis of an abstract quantification of damage calculated in accordance with theoretical models."[62] The same approach was taken by the Director of the Fund. In an opinion to the Assembly, the Director stated that the 1969 and 1971 Conventions were "designed to provide compensation to victims of pollution damage," and that "claims which did not relate to compensation to a specific victim fell outside the scope of the Convention."[63]

While there was general agreement in the IOPC Assembly on this interpretation, some doubt was expressed about it. For example, in a statement to the IOPC Assembly, the Italian delegation stated that the 1969 and 1971 Conventions "did not exclude compensation for environmental damage which was not quantifiable." In the delegation's view, a state "had the legal right to compensation for damage to the environment which had irrevers-

---

[60] IOPC Fund Claims Manual, para. 7.4. The same paragraph also states that the IOPC pays compensation only for "quantifiable economic loss actually sustained."
[61] 1969 Civil Liability Convention, Art. I, para. 6.
[62] Assembly of the IOPC Fund, Res. No. 3 (Oct. 1980).
[63] Study by the Director of the IOPC Fund, Doc. FUND/EXC.30/2, summarized in Annual Report of the IOPC Fund (1991), pp. 68–69.

ible consequences or where the environment could not be re-instated."[64] This position was endorsed by the Court of Appeal of Italy, which concluded that the definition of pollution damage was wide enough to include damage to the environment "which prejudices immaterial values and which cannot be assessed in monetary terms according to market prices." According to the Court, compensation to be paid in such cases consists of "the reduced possibility of using the environment." In support of this position, the Court stated that "the environment must be considered as a unitary asset, separate from those of which the environment is composed (territory, territorial waters, beaches, fish, etc.) and it includes natural resources, health and landscape. The right to the environment belongs to the State, in its capacity as representative of the collectivities."[65]

To resolve the controversy arising from the different interpretations of the convention, the states parties took the opportunity of the 1992 Revision Conference to modify the definition of "pollution damage," and thus put the matter fully to rest. In the 1992 Protocol to the 1969 Civil Liability Convention, the definition of "pollution damage" was revised to state expressly that "compensation for impairment of the environment other than losses of profit from such impairment shall be limited to costs of reasonable measures of reinstatement actually undertaken or to be undertaken."[66] The amendment makes it clear that compensation will be payable for measures designed to restore the damaged environment to the condition it would have been in but for the pollution – or as near to that conclusion as is feasible in the circumstances. However, compensation will not be payable for damage to the environment where such damage cannot be "quantified," as for damage alleged to result, for example, from "the reduced possibility of using the environment."

The approach in the 1992 Protocol has been adopted in most of the civil liability regimes, including those outside the purview of the Law of the Sea Convention. Examples include the 1989 Geneva Convention on Civil Liability for Damage Caused During Carriage of Dangerous Goods by Road, Rail and Inland Navigation,[67] and the 1993 Council of Europe Convention on Civil Liability for Damage Resulting from Activities

---

[64] *Ibid.*   [65] *Ibid.*; see also Annual Report of the IOPC Fund (1996), pp. 39ff.

[66] 1992 Protocol to the 1969 Civil Liability Convention, Art. 2, para. 3.

[67] Convention on Civil Liability for Damage Caused During Carriage of Dangerous Goods by Road, Rail and Inland Navigation (1989), Art. 5.

Dangerous to the Environment (Lugano Convention).[68] The latter convention provides that "compensation for impairment of the environment other than for loss of profit from such impairment, shall be limited to the costs of reasonable measures of re-instatement actually undertaken or to be undertaken."[69]

WHAT ARE REASONABLE MEASURES OF RESTORATION OF IMPAIRED ENVIRONMENT?

Although it is now generally agreed that "reasonable costs" of restoring impaired environment are to be compensated, there is no such agreement on the nature and extent of the measures that may be considered as "reasonable." The 1969 and 1996 civil liability conventions do not provide precise guidelines on the issue, and such guidelines as may be gleaned from general international law are not sufficiently precise or definitive. For example, the International Law Commission's Draft Articles on Liability of States for Acts Not Prohibited by International Law propose that the liable state will be required to bear the costs of any reasonable operation to restore, as far as possible, the conditions that existed prior to the occurrence of harm, "or if that proves impossible, to reach agreement on monetary or other compensation for the deterioration suffered."[70] In like vein, the Lugano Convention defines measures of restoration as "any reasonable measures to reinstate or restore damaged or destroyed components of the environment, or to introduce, where reasonable, the equivalent of these components into the environment."[71]

The issue is addressed extensively in the 1993 European Commission Green Paper on Liability for Environmental Damage, which recognizes that "an identical reconstruction may not be possible . . . however, there should be a goal to clean-up and restore the environment to the state which, if not identical to that which existed before the damage occurred, at least maintains its necessary permanent functions."[72] A similar approach is

---

[68] Lugano Convention on Civil Liability for Damage Resulting from Activities Dangerous to the Environment, *I.L.M.* 32 (1993), 1228.   [69] *Ibid.*, Art. 2, para. 7(c).
[70] International Law Commission, Draft Articles on Liability of States for Acts Not Prohibited by International Law, Sixth Report of the Special Rapporteur, UN Doc. A/CAN.4/428 (1990), Art. 24(a).   [71] Lugano Convention, Art. 2, para. 8.
[72] "Green Paper on Remedying Environmental Damage," Communication from the European Commission to the European Council and Parliament and the Economic and Social Committee, Comm. 47 (1993).

adopted in the legislation of the United States, which permits certain public authorities to bring action for damage to natural resources caused by the release of hazardous substances or by oil spills. Compensation recovered is to be devoted to the restoration of the damaged resources or the acquisition of their equivalent.[73]

For this purpose, a number of economic methods and criteria have been suggested. These include: (1) the price that the environmental resource might command in the market; (2) the economic value attached to the use of the environmental resource, such as travel costs for recreational use and so on; (3) the "contingent valuation" methods to measure the willingness of individuals to pay for environmental goods such as clean water, clean air, or the preservation of endangered species, usually taken from public opinion surveys.[74]

While these approaches have attracted considerable support from governments and commentators, doubts have been expressed about their acceptability, especially with respect to feasibility and cost-effectiveness. Thus, the European Commission Green Paper, in suggesting that restoration should aim at ensuring that the restored environment can "maintain its necessary permanent functions," also cautioned that there are limits to what should be attempted, stating: "Even if restoration or clean-up is physically possible, it may not be economically feasible . . . restoration of an environment to the state it was in before the damage occurred could involve expenditure disproportionate to the desired results. In such a case it might be argued that restoration should only be carried out to the point where it is still cost-effective."[75] The Green Paper also notes that "such determinations involve difficult balancing as well as of economic and environmental values."[76] The same approach was adopted by the US Court of Appeals, First Circuit, in the case of *Commonwealth of Puerto Rico v. S.S. Zoe Colocotroni.*[77] In that case, the Court recognized that there may be circumstances where direct restoration of the affected area would be

---

[73] See the Comprehensive Environmental Response, Compensation, and Liability Act (1980) and the Oil Pollution Act (1990), 42 U.S.C. §§ 9601ff. (1997).

[74] On the issue of valuing environmental damage, see Carol A. Jones, "Restoration-Based Approaches for Compensation for Natural Resource Damage: Moving Towards Convergence in US and International Law," chapter 19 in this volume; Catherine Redgwell, "Compensation for Oil Pollution Damage: Quantifying Environmental Harm," *Marine Pol'y* 16 (1992), 90; N. D. Koroleva, "Ecological Damage: Responsibility for Pollution of the Marine Environment," *Marine Pol'y* 16 (1992), 86.   [75] "Green Paper," para. 5.2.

[76] *Ibid.*   [77] 628 F.2d 652 (1st Cir. 1980).

either physically impossible or so disproportionately expensive that it would not be reasonable to undertake such a remedy.

Whatever the merits of the respective positions on the issue, the fact is that the prevailing rule in the existing international civil liability regimes is that compensation is payable for the expenses of restoring the impaired environment, if this can be done. The issue of whether any measures of restoration undertaken or contemplated are reasonable will depend on the circumstances of each particular case, as determined by the court or tribunal dealing with the claim.

Conclusion: relevance of the conventions to environmental damage during war

The Convention on the Law of the Sea specifically states that its provisions regarding the protection and preservation of the marine environment do not apply to "any warship, naval auxiliary, other vessels or aircraft owned or operated by the State and used, for the time being, only on government non-commercial service."[78] However, each state is obliged "to ensure . . . that such vessels and aircraft act in a manner consistent, as far as reasonable and practicable, with this Convention."[79] The 1969 Civil Liability Convention and the 1996 HNS Convention include similar provisions excluding warships from their scope of application.[80] However, a state party may decide to apply the HNS Convention to its warships.[81]

It is also worth recalling that Article 30 of the Convention on the Law of the Sea specifically obliges warships to "comply with the laws and regulations of the coastal State concerning passage through the territorial sea."[82] Even more pertinently, the convention declares that the flag state "shall bear international responsibility for any loss or damage to the coastal State resulting from the non-compliance by a warship or other governmental ship operated for non-commercial purposes with the laws and regulations of the coastal State concerning passage through the territorial sea or with the provisions of this Convention or other rules of international law."[83] This would appear to suggest that, in spite of the exclusion of the application of the "environmental provisions" of the Law of the Sea Convention

---

[78] Law of the Sea Convention, Art. 236.   [79] *Ibid.*
[80] 1969 Civil Liability Convention, Art. IX; 1996 HNS Convention, Art. 4, para. 4.
[81] *Ibid.*, Art. 4, para. 5.   [82] Law of the Sea Convention, Art. 30.   [83] *Ibid.*, Art. 31.

to warships, the regime for the assessment and recovery of compensation for environmental damage may nevertheless be applicable to warships and other government vessels engaged in war activities if they cause environmental damage to a state in violation of the provisions of the convention or other rules of international law. Where this is the case, a court or tribunal seised of a claim against the flag state of the warship may well feel obliged to have reference to the rules, procedures, and criteria in the convention, or those adopted pursuant to it, when considering the nature and extent of compensation to be paid for the damage in any particular situation.

Reference may also be made to the provision of the convention that gives to states parties discretion to exclude from the dispute settlement procedures "disputes concerning military activities by government vessels and aircraft engaged in non-commercial service."[84] In this regard, it is important to note that this provision does not altogether exclude such disputes from the procedures in Section 2 of Part XV. Indeed, the fact that the convention gives discretion to states parties to exclude military activities from the dispute settlement regime would seem to argue in favor of the view that such disputes do come within the scope of Section 2 of Part XV, in cases where the state party concerned has not excluded them in the manner provided for that purpose in the convention. This view is further reinforced by the fact that the convention has a specific provision which absolutely excludes certain other categories of disputes from the dispute settlement procedures of Section 2.[85] The fact that disputes concerning military activities are not excluded under that provision, but are to be excluded at the discretion of the state party, appears to indicate that those disputes must be deemed to fall within the scope of the Section 2 procedures, unless and until they have been specifically excluded by the state party or parties concerned.

On this basis, the provisions of the Law of the Sea Convention, and the regimes for the assessment and recovery of environmental damage developed pursuant to it or compatible with it, may be of some relevance in discussing issues of liability and compensation for environmental damage arising from the consequences of war.

---

[84] *Ibid.*, Art. 298, para. 1(b).   [85] *Ibid.*, Art. 297, paras. 2 and 3.

9

THE PLACE OF THE ENVIRONMENT IN
INTERNATIONAL TRIBUNALS

DAVID D. CARON

Introduction

War can be destructive not only to lives and property, but also to the more fundamental structure of our world, the environment.[1] In attempting to address the consequences of war for the environment, one may try to prevent war from starting or to prevent an ongoing war from extending to particularly sensitive environments. This chapter assumes that the prevention effort has failed at least in part and that one therefore must also consider (1) the mitigation of the consequences that flow from the harm to the environment, (2) the possible restoration of the environment harmed, and (3) legal and financial responsibility for such mitigation and restoration as a possible deterrent. In all three of these areas, international adjudication can play a role.

In the twentieth century, there have been numerous international adjudicatory institutions created to address international wrongs. These include ad hoc arbitrations, claims commissions, and permanent tribunals. Sometimes these mechanisms were employed to resolve a specific question, such as a boundary dispute. Often these mechanisms followed particularly earth-shattering events, such as revolution and war. This essay

The author has served as a Commissioner with the second "E" Panel of the United Nations Compensation Commission. The views expressed herein are those of the author and do not necessarily reflect the views of the Commission.

[1] For a recent significant statement of this view, see the Rio Declaration on Environment and Development (1992), Principle 24. For relatively early and explicit international statements of this view, see the preamble of the Convention on the Prohibition of Military or Any Other Hostile Use of Environmental Modification Techniques, recommended for adoption by UN General Assembly Res. 31/72 (Dec. 10, 1976), entered into force, Oct. 5, 1978, 1108 U.N.T.S. 151; UN General Assembly Res. 35/8 (Oct. 30, 1980), entitled "Historical Responsibility of States for the Preservation of Nature for Present and Future Generations."

considers the place of the environment in international institutions created to address the latter situation.

In considering this topic, I address two fundamental questions that have substantial implications for how an international mechanism should be structured so as to address an environmental claim. First, precisely what is an environmental claim? What is the relationship between the claimant and the environment it claims to represent? Second, from where are the monies for mitigation and restoration to come? These two questions provide a basis for assessing international mechanisms, and, in that light, the present design of mechanisms appears inadequate. Simultaneously, I emphasize my doubt that the issue is with the tribunals per se – institutions usually find ways to perform the tasks entrusted to them. Rather, the issue generally is antecedent to the institution and embedded in the political decisions to entrust or not to entrust certain matters to it.

The nature of an environmental claim

The literature of the history of international environmental law identifies several milestones. One is the Stockholm Conference of 1972. Another is the Rio Conference of 1992. A more curious one, but central to the question posed by this essay, is the *Trail Smelter Arbitration* in which awards were made in 1938 and 1941.[2] The *Trail Smelter Arbitration* is relevant because it is often referred to as the first arbitration about the environment – even though the word "ecology," and certainly the phrase "environmental movement," did not enter common speech for several more decades.

In that case, a smelter in the town of Trail in the eastern part of the Canadian province of British Columbia had been releasing atmospheric pollutants that allegedly damaged orchards, timber, and crops in eastern Washington State. The arbitral tribunal found some of the alleged damage to have occurred and to be compensable, and awarded the US monies for those portions.

The significance of the *Trail Smelter Arbitration* lies in the recognition that there is nothing new about international claims regarding property, including real property. Consequently, we are drawn to ask what is new about an "environmental" claim? The example of the *Trail Smelter Arbitration* indicates that there are at least two possible meanings to "environmental

---

[2] *Trail Smelter Arbitration* (*US v. Canada*), 3 R.I.A.A. 1911 (1938); 3 R.I.A.A. 1938 (1941).

claim" and "environmental consequences of war." On the one hand, there is the question, as Professor Stone phrases it,[3] of what the consequences of war are for nature. On the other hand, there is the question of the consequences for a society, collectively or individually, when war affects that society through disruption of the environment. If one is thinking in terms of the second aspect, there is no question in my view that international tribunals have addressed and can address environmental claims when what is meant is resultant property damage (i.e., damage to real property, damage to crops or other parts of the environment with a commercial value) or health effects. In an installment of claims recently concluded at the United Nations Compensation Commission (UNCC), for example, monies were awarded for a claim by a corporation for the costs of repainting a small facility in Saudi Arabia, near the Kuwaiti border, that had been covered with oily smoke from the Gulf War oil fires.[4]

The challenge is to identify those aspects of an environmental claim that are fundamentally different from a property claim. Is it merely that different valuation methods need to be devised for resources not already given a value by the market? If that is all that is different, then I find the difference not great. I believe there is more of a difference, however, and that difference goes fundamentally to the nature of a claim regarding the environment. It is this difference that international adjudication mechanisms do not take into account adequately at present, and it is this failure that not only leaves the environmental issue perhaps unaddressed, but also makes the task of adjudicating the claim more difficult.

Therefore, at its root, the question that must be addressed is how a claims process may be said to be about the environment, or, in a more conventional sense, about the representation of a community's interest in the environment. In answering this question, one will go a substantial distance in also addressing the relationship between the claimant and the environment.

This chapter approaches the question posed as a problem of agency.[5] An agent acts on behalf of a principal. What does this mean in terms of claims

---

[3] See Christopher Stone, "The Environment in Wartime: An Overview," chapter 1 in this volume.
[4] See Paragraph 251 of the Report and Recommendations Made by the UNCC Panel of Commissioners Concerning the First Installment of "E2" Claims (July 3, 1998) and approved by Decision 53 of the UNCC Governing Council.
[5] For a valuable introduction to agency as an analytical approach, see John W. Pratt and Richard J. Zeckhauser (eds.), *Principals and Agents: The Structure of Business* (Boston: Harvard Business School Press, 1991).

regarding the environment? What does it mean to act as an agent for the environment, or for a community's interest in that environment? And, most importantly, how may institutions be structured to monitor the performance of the agent?

An assessment of current institutions in light of these questions reveals a quite weak position accorded to the environment. This position reflects the deeply embedded notion that it is the consequences of war for the claimant, rather than the environment, that are to be addressed by such mechanisms. In other words, is the claimant a *principal* in possession of an asset called the environment that has been damaged, or is the claimant instead an *agent* executing the directions and will of a community (the principal) regarding the environment? The significance of thinking in terms of agency becomes evident if one contrasts other areas of international life where the role of the state has shifted from solely that of principal to include that of agent. A striking example is the place of the individual in international tribunals.

THE SHIFT TO AGENCY IN THE CASE OF INDIVIDUALS BEFORE INTERNATIONAL TRIBUNALS

At the beginning of the twentieth century, if one state injured the national of another state, then the state of the injured national was said also to be wronged and could espouse the claim against the state that had wronged its national. This process, termed "diplomatic protection," is, in the words of the Permanent Court of International Justice, a situation in public international law whereby "in taking up the case of one of its nationals, by resorting to diplomatic action or international judicial proceedings on his behalf, a State is in reality asserting its own right, the right to ensure in the person of its nationals respect for the rules of international law."[6]

The idea that a diplomatic protection claim is in reality the claim of the state was made strikingly clear in the American–Turkish Claims Settlement of 1937, where numerous claims were rejected almost immediately because they were filed directly with the Commission by private counsel representing the nationals. The Agreement of December 24, 1923, between the United States and Turkey establishing the Commission had provided

---

[6] *Panevezys-Saldutiskis Railway Case* (*Estonia v. Lithuania*), 1939 P.C.I.J. (ser. A/B) No. 76 (Judgment of Feb. 28), p. 16.

for governmental espousal of claims. The Commission took the position that the direct presentation of claims by nationals was incompatible with the idea of diplomatic protection: "It would, of course, be monstrous to suggest that a government would through some subterfuge pretend to support a claim without having any knowledge of what, if anything, had in some way come before the Commission."[7]

Likewise, in the *Trail Smelter Arbitration* previously mentioned, the individual farmers in eastern Washington State themselves were, at least in theory, not the claimants. Therefore, the place of not only the environment, but the individual farmers in eastern Washington State themselves, was distant from the tribunal. If the US government had chosen to do so, it could have simply refused to espouse the claim of the nationals. It likewise could have settled the claim without the agreement of the nationals. Indeed, in theory, under international law it need not even have turned the monies awarded over to the nationals, since the injury was to it – although payments in that instance indeed were made by the US to the individuals who had been injured.[8]

In more recent times, the individual's place before the institution in many instances is stronger, and correspondingly the state's involvement increasingly is that of an agent acting on behalf of its nationals. This tendency follows the growth of human rights law over the same period and the recent resurgence of claims institutions. The trend can be seen in the Iran–United States Claims Tribunal and is quite explicit in the case of the United Nations Compensation Commission.

For example, Article II(1) of the Claims Settlement Declaration establishing the Iran–United States Claims Tribunal did not provide, as would be expected in the case of diplomatic protection, that the Tribunal might decide claims of the United States or Iran brought "on behalf of the interests of its nationals" or "on the basis of injury to its nationals." Rather, the language of this provision provided jurisdiction over the "claims of nationals of the United States and of Iran." Indeed, the Claims Settlement Declaration provided that the nationals themselves would present their claims to the Tribunal; a supplemental clause provided that when the claim was less than $250,000, the claim *might also* be presented by the

<hr>

[7] Neilsen and Maktos, *American–Turkish Claims Settlement* (Washington, D.C.: Government Printing Office, 1938), p. 6. See also J. Moore, *International Law Digest*, vol. VI (1906), p. 616.
[8] See, e.g., "Fume Damage Claimants are Receiving Certificates on Last of $78,000 Award," *The Colville Examiner* (June 24, 1939), 1.

government of that national.[9] Claims of US nationals in fact were filed and argued by the nationals asserting the claims. Likewise, it was the national that decided whether to withdraw or to accept settlement of a claim. Also significant was the fact that the Tribunal's Security Account satisfied awards *directly* to the benefit of the national who presented the claim and was the named party, and not to the benefit of the government of that national. Likewise, it was against the national, and not the government of that national, that the Tribunal Rules required entry of counterclaims and awards of costs.[10]

In the case of the UNCC, the claims of more than 2 million individuals have been filed with the Commission, primarily by governments. Two examples make clear, however, that the governments file such claims not as principal, but rather as agent. First, in the UNCC it does not appear that a government has the capacity to prevent the presentation of the claim of a person residing in its territory. Under Decision 1 of the Governing Council, "the Council may request an appropriate person, authority or body to submit claims on behalf of persons who are not in a position to have their claim submitted by a Government."[11] The focus is thus on the individual rather than the state within which the individual resides. Indeed, numerous claims have been filed with the Commission by the UNDP or the UNHCR, although it was not necessary to rely upon the authority quoted above as the basis for such representation.

Second, and more significant, the government as agent is monitored by the UNCC in the performance of its role. Decision 18 of the Governing Council of the UNCC offers important insights in this regard.[12] To reiterate, under diplomatic protection, it is the state that receives the award. The state in such cases does not have any duty to inform the tribunal of what it ultimately does with the funds received. The UNCC process is quite different. Decision 18 requires that all governments receiving awards must: (1) prior to or immediately following receipt of payment, inform the UNCC in writing on arrangements made for distribution of the funds to claimants; (2) within six months of receipt, distribute the specified

---

[9] Iran–US Claims Settlement Declaration, Art. III(3).
[10] See Iran–US Claims Tribunal Rules, Introduction and Definitions, para. 3c; *ibid.*, Arts. 32 and 40.
[11] "Criteria for Expedited Processing of Urgent Claims," UNCC Decision No. 1, UN Doc. S/AC.26/1991/1 (1991), para. 19.
[12] "Distribution of Payments and Transparency," UNCC Decision No. 18, UN Doc. S/AC.26/Dec. 18 (1994).

funds to named claimants; (3) not later than three months after the deadline for distribution, inform the UNCC on the amounts distributed and the reasons for any non-payment; and (4) after distribution of all payments received, provide a final summary account of all distributions made.[13] If a government fails to distribute the funds received, fails to submit adequate reports, or does not in the view of the Governing Council provide satisfactory reasons for non-payment, the Governing Council "may decide not to distribute further funds to that particular government."[14] Funds received which have not been distributed to claimants owing to inability to locate such claimants "shall be reimbursed to the Compensation Fund."[15] In establishing their arrangements for distribution, governments may deduct processing costs from payments made to claimants, but such fees (1) shall not be imposed until the government involved provides "explanations satisfactory to the Governing Council"; (2) shall be commensurate with the actual expenditure of governments; and (3) should not exceed 1.5 percent of amounts payable in categories A, B, and C (individual claims for forced departure from Kuwait, for serious personal injury or death, or for damages up to US $100,000), or 3 percent of amounts payable in categories D, E, and F (individual claims for damages above US $100,000, claims of corporations and other entities, and claims of governments and international organizations, including environmental damage claims).[16] Moreover, if the governments intend to convert the United States dollar payments into other currencies for distribution, they shall notify the Council on the method of conversion and exchange rate to be used.[17]

Taken together, the provisions of Decision 18 reflect an astounding shift. I do not mean to imply that the practice of diplomatic protection is wholly gone, but rather that in certain institutional contexts we have witnessed the development of a view of the state as agent rather than principal. The crucial point to note is that there has not been a similar development for environmental claims.

THE SHIFT TO AGENCY IN THE CASE OF ENVIRONMENTAL CLAIMS

How would the agency perspective be extended to claims regarding the environment? This question leads once again to an examination of the

[13] *Ibid.*, paras. I(2), I(3), I(4), and I(6).   [14] *Ibid.*, para. I(5).   [15] *Ibid.*, para. I(6).
[16] *Ibid.*, para. I(1).   [17] *Ibid.*, para. I(7).

fundamental nature of a claim regarding the environment. To begin this examination, assume that an armed conflict has caused substantial harm to a marsh area. The marsh is owned in part by an individual who harvested oysters, in part by a corporation that ran a duck-shooting establishment, and in part by the government, which had hoped to create a resort there. All three of these entities have claims as principals – the injury to their property and the surrounding property has diminished the value of their assets. At the same time, it does not necessarily appear to be the case that paying the claims of these three entities will address the environmental consequences of the war. More subtle foundational aspects of the environment seem possibly unaddressed. The health of the marsh, for example, is likely to be essential to fisheries in the region. It may have been an important waystation for migratory and endangered species of birds. Who may be said to own these aspects? Who may be said to have the duty to pursue the interests of a broader community in these aspects?

We tend to think that the individual or the corporation does not "own" such aspects and does not have a duty to represent such aspects. In contrast, the state as sovereign often is viewed as owning such aspects of the environment as *parens patriae* of the people. It is the state that holds such aspects of the environment in trust as an agent of its nation and increasingly as the logical agent of the international community. The state is the natural candidate to be the agent because the land, the territory, is so fundamentally a part of the state.

If the state is viewed only as a principal rather than an agent, then the "environmental claim" is no more than the state defines it to be. If the state is the principal, then it is the state's choice as to whether it wishes to bring a claim at all. It could decline to bring a claim, preferring to spend its investigatory resources on assisting individuals, corporations, and ministries in the preparation of their claims. If the state is the principal, it could also simply not spend the money to restore the environment. Recall how individual claims before the UNCC are very different in this regard.

THE TERMS OF THE AGENCY

A shift to greater use of the idea of agency requires that the terms of that agency be described. This is a substantial question and a detailed answer is beyond the scope of this essay. The following, however, sketches the outline of a response.

First, the employment of an agency perspective on the claim of a state will require a test to distinguish when a state claimant acts as principal or as agent. Broadly, the line between agent and principal can be phrased in quite straightforward terms: when the state asserts an interest comparable to what a participant in the market would have asserted, the state claims as a principal, but the interest asserted cannot be one requiring a use of the environment contrary to the minimal requirements of applicable international environmental law. For example, assume there was a war in Central Africa that destroyed many of the last rhinoceroses. On the one hand, the state as principal potentially could have a claim for loss of tourism at a government resort in the park; on the other hand, the state as principal could not claim for the export value of the rhino horns if either the harvesting or export of the horns is prohibited under applicable international law. In contrast, those state interests not comparable to what a private participant might assert – for example, ecosystem damage – would place the state in the position of an agent. Thus a state could assert claims as both principal and agent – principal for its loss of legitimate use, agent for what it holds in trust for a broader community.

Second, the employment of an agency perspective on the claim of a state will require a clear definition of the principal. An agent acts to protect the interests of the principal. In the case of the environment, the principal may be said to be the environment itself, but any examination of that choice leaves one without guidance as to what is to be valued more or less in an environment altered by war. In terms of sovereignty, the principal is the people of that nation. In terms of international law and international governance, it is the people of the nation with that minimal respect for the environment required by applicable international customary and treaty law. In this sense, the international community has a minimal interest in the environment that the state should represent as agent, and the people of the nation involved may have an interest above and beyond the international community's interest that the state also should represent as agent.

A related question asks whether there are agents other than the state that may present environmental claims. International agencies such as UNEP would perhaps more naturally have an ecosystemic perspective encompassing several states. In contrast, a state's preoccupation with borders may result in the state confining its claim and restoration efforts to its territories. A purely territorial view of an environmental claim leads to potential redundancies in investigation of the harm. In this sense, state agents would have a duty to cooperate with other agents of a shared environment in pursuing their nations' interests in that environment.

Third, the employment of an agency perspective on the claim of a state will require articulation of the minimal expectations of the international community and the possibly greater expectations of the nation involved. In terms of the international community, for example, the state should seek to mitigate the damage that has occurred, prepare contingency plans, and protect specially sensitive habitats and species. These minimal interests in the environment in all likelihood also will be required by the nation itself.

Another implication of thinking in terms of agency is that some issues surrounding valuation, for example, are clarified. Claims presented by principals tend to be those market interests ascertainable by accepted methods. It is the claims presented as agent for more foundational, long-term, and often unknown damage to the environment that are more problematic. Simultaneously, the terms of the agency give more guidance than merely restoration of the *status quo ante*, e.g., the removal of oil from rocks on a polluted shore. It may cost the same amount to clean oil from hard sandy areas as it does from a marsh – yet in terms of the health of the environment involved, it may be more important to restore the marsh. The terms of agency thus can provide priorities leading the agent to focus, for example, on critical habitats and the range of biodiversity. The duties of the agent to consider mitigation and restoration lead to the need for scientific assessment of the environmental impact that occurred. The knowledge gained through such efforts will in turn have a feedback effect on the suggested methods to be employed for valuation. It often seems that many of the natural resource valuation methods utilized in litigation seek to compensate for the lack of such knowledge. In other words, the cost of restoring the previous situation, even if other measures ultimately are to be taken, serves as a proxy for a value that cannot otherwise be calculated. However, if available funds are limited, as in the case of the Gulf War and the UNCC, then it seems wasteful indeed to spend substantial amounts calculating the proxy when direct restoration and mitigation efforts are clearly needed.

The challenge of conflicting demands on limited funds

Other chapters in this volume address the ethical difficulty and likely result of a military commander choosing between increased casualties to troops

DAVID D. CARON

under his or her command and the environmental damage likely to result from protective measures such as defoliation. Likewise, there can be a conflict for relief workers between humanitarian relief and environmental relief, though this is not meant to imply that international humanitarian law does not both directly and indirectly lead to protection of the environment.[18] One anecdotal example from the end of the Gulf War concerns a relief worker who saw injured animals roaming Kuwait City, apparently released from the zoo by Iraqi troops, but who felt ethically obligated to continue searching for injured persons instead.

A related tension, more political than ethical, can arise later with regard to compensation. Simply put, there often are no funds for compensation after an armed conflict. When there are funds, there almost always will be fewer funds available than those likely to be awarded for the consequences of the war. And thus there will be a tension between the amount of funds that should be allocated to research, planning, and restoration of the environment and those allocated for the payment of the immediate tangible claims of individuals, corporations, and states.

The UNCC is an example of how uncertainty as to the amount of funds available actually helped all concerned avoid this choice for the time being. No one knows how much money ultimately will be placed in the Compensation Fund to pay awards of the Commission. At present, the Fund is to receive 30 percent of Iraq's future oil revenues for an indefinite period. The claims before the UNCC total approximately US $200 billion. In contrast with this uncertain situation, let us assume that the Fund had been established with a set amount of US $80 billion. In that case, I believe there would be a very difficult discussion as to the priority to be given to the substantial amounts necessary to restore the environment. In essence, the state would have a conflict of interest and need to mediate between its roles as agent for interests in the environment and agent for the claims of its nationals and corporations. Indeed, it may well have a conflict of interest between its own claims as principal and as agent.

A solution to the ethical tension for the relief worker is for there to be two different types of relief workers. The ethical dilemma is partly a personal one, but it is also a professional one. If one relief worker is given a humanitarian mandate while another is given an environmental mandate,

---

[18] See "Protecting the Environment During Armed Conflict Is Part of International Humanitarian Law," *Bull. Int'l Red Cross*, No. 198 (July 1992).

then in the professional sense the ethical dilemma is resolved. One is the agent of humanity seeking to ameliorate human suffering. The other is an agent seeking to ameliorate the suffering of animals and damage to the environment.

Similarly, to resolve the conflict of interests that will arise whenever there exist limited funds for addressing environmental consequences of war, it is preferable that there be separate sources of funds for compensation, restoration, and mitigation efforts. Proposals for "Funds" abound, and thus one realistically must acknowledge the limited resources of donor states. At the same time, without the provision of dedicated funds, one realistically must also acknowledge that it will be a rare instance where necessary funds are made available for environmental restoration. One possibility would be the creation of a fund for the restoration of designated areas of special environmental importance, such as World Heritage Sites, damaged by armed conflict. This Fund would be established by the international community generally, or perhaps initially by those states who in the past have most harmed the environment during war, with a right of subrogation for the Fund against the state that caused the damage. Such an approach would focus funds first on those areas most critical to the long-term health of the planet, make funds available rapidly while mitigation is still possible, and incidentally encourage priority listing under such arrangements.

Conclusion: directions for reform and an agenda for research

The preceding discussion has identified a number of areas that would benefit from both institutional attention and scholarly research: the role of various possible agents (i.e., states, intergovernmental organizations, and non-governmental organizations); the terms of the agent's charge, a scholarly effort that could draw effectively on scholarly literature concerning international environmental law specifically and trusteeship and stewardship concepts generally; the means by which funds might be dedicated to environmental claims; and the mechanisms by which the performance of agents may be monitored. As to this last area, mechanisms deserving study include the transparency and reporting requirements employed by the UNCC for claims by individuals. In this sense, I also would recommend that the UNCC consider adopting mechanisms along the lines of those in Decision 18 for certain of the claims regarding the environment. A different monitoring approach employed by the Marshall Islands Nuclear Claims Tribunal is the creation of an institutional actor who speaks on behalf of unrepresented principals. In the case of that Tribunal, there exists a "Defender of the Fund" who represents the interests of all claimants in the integrity of the Fund by commenting on claims presented to the Tribunal.[19] Finally, I would note that some monitoring can be directly incorporated into the substantive standards used for compensation – e.g., "reasonable" costs of restoration.

At the outset of this essay, I asserted that adjudication of environmental claims can be important not only to restoration, but also to the mitigation of harm. However, mitigation must be addressed in a timely manner. In this regard, as I have written elsewhere,[20] I believe that the UNCC, extraordinarily innovative in so many respects, has not been as successful as regards the environmental claims. In hindsight, for example, at the very beginning of the UNCC's work, the Governing Council simultaneously with its consideration of urgent humanitarian claims could have addressed the possibility of ongoing environmental damage by a relatively modest grant of funds to UNEP, the World Health Organization, or the various Gulf State national research institutions. These funds could have been used for proposals aimed at various research or direct mitigation actions – or, as phrased in Decision 7, "reasonable monitoring and assessment of the environmental damage for the purposes of evaluating and abating the harm."[21]

More modestly, the UNCC could have established "approval and monitoring" processes that would give some measure of assurance that approved restoration efforts ultimately would be regarded as compensable under the criteria set forth in Decision 7. Such assurances of even partial recovery might have influenced budgetary decisions internal to claimant states as to their own efforts to monitor, assess, and abate harm.[22] Simultaneously, a

---

[19] For information concerning the Marshall Islands Nuclear Claims Tribunal, one may write to the Tribunal at Post Office Box 702, Majuro, Marshall Islands, 96960.

[20] See David D. Caron, "The UNCC and the Search for Practical Justice," in R. Lillich (ed.), *The United Nations Compensation Commission* (Irvington, N.Y.: Transnational Publishers, 1995), pp. 367, 375–77.

[21] "Criteria for Additional Categories of Claims," UNCC Decision No. 7, UN Doc. S/AC.26/1991/7/Rev.1 (1992), para. 35(c).

[22] For a report of the complex state of affairs shortly after the conclusion of the war, see John H. Cushman, Jr., "Environmental Claims for Damage by Iraq Go Begging for Data," *N.Y. Times* (Nov. 12, 1991), B7.

process to approve and monitor abatement efforts could have been struc-
tured so as to coordinate research and abatement efforts of the various
Gulf States.[23] This is not to say that efforts were not made by the United
Nations family of organizations as a whole.[24] Nor is it to say that only the
UNCC had a role to play immediately after the conclusion of the war.
Rather, it is to say that the UNCC, along with others, had a part to play in
promoting the abatement of further harm.

The good news is that the ever-innovative UNCC has continued to pursue
a proactive role. The states that suffered the environmental consequences
of the invasion and occupation of Kuwait by Iraq are coordinating their
efforts with the assistance of the Secretariat in new and encouraging ways.

---

[23] For other discussions of the UNCC process, particularly the substantive law to be applied to
the environmental claims, see "Report of the Working Group of Experts on Liability and
Compensation for Environmental Damage Arising from Military Activities," U.N. Doc.
UNEP/Env.Law/3/inf.1 (Oct. 15, 1996); Sonja Boelaert-Suominen, "Iraqi War Reparations
and the Laws of War: A Discussion of the Current Work of the United Nations Compensation
Commission with Specific Reference to Environmental Damage During Warfare," *Zeitschrift
für öffentliches Recht* 50 (1996), 225–316; Ruth Mackenzie and Ruth Khalastchi, "Liability and
Compensation for Environmental Damage in the Context of the Work of the United Nations
Compensation Commission," *Rev. Eur. Comm. & Int'l Envtl. L.* 5 (1996), 281–89.

[24] As to the efforts within the UN generally, see, e.g., "Introductory Report of the Executive
Director: Environmental Consequences of the Armed Conflict between Iraq and Kuwait," UN
Doc. UNEP/GC.16/4/Add.1 (May 10, 1991) (indicating, *inter alia*, efforts to create a fund for
research on the damage).

10

CIVIL LIABILITY FOR WAR-CAUSED ENVIRONMENTAL DAMAGE: MODELS FROM UNITED STATES LAW

JEFFREY G. MILLER

Introduction

This chapter explores civil liability doctrines in United States law relevant to an international liability regime for war-caused environmental damage. Those doctrines come from two separate but related fields: the common law of torts and the statutory law of environmental protection. To varying degrees they both shift the burden of environmental damage from innocent or random victims to those engaging in or benefiting from the damage-causing activity. In environmental law circles, this is often called the "polluter pays" principle. Clearly, neither set of doctrines was designed to provide compensation for war-caused environmental damages. Moreover, their use for that purpose would have to contend with countervailing doctrines of sovereign immunity and justification. Nevertheless, the principles behind the doctrines – deterrence of damage-causing conduct, provision of fairness between those damaged and those damaging, and maximization of public wealth – may be appropriate as a starting point from which to devise such an international regime. A treaty establishing an international regime could deal with the sovereign immunity and justification defenses.

While principles behind tort and pollution control legal doctrines may be relevant underpinnings for an international compensation regime for war-caused injury, this chapter concludes that another concept developed in United States environmental statutes provides the most practical alternative: a remediation fund derived from assessments on weapons, ammunition, and other war material. Such assessments could be on a sliding scale, with proportionately higher charges on weapons with the greatest

264

potential to damage the environment. Such a mechanism would avoid much of the fact-finding inherent in most tort law, the regulatory rigidity of pollution control law, and the high transaction costs of both regimes. To a large extent, it would avoid subjecting sovereign states to fault-finding processes or to assessments made directly against them. Yet it would deter war-caused environmental damage and perhaps, to some extent, even war itself by raising the cost of weapons whose use most damages the environment. Such a scheme would provide a fund that could be used to remedy environmental damage shortly after it occurs, rather than after years of litigation over who was at fault or whether the damage was justified.

This chapter contains detailed and documented examinations of both the common law of torts and the statutory law of environmental protection in the United States insofar as they may be pertinent to the international liability regime under consideration. In examining the degree to which these doctrines of United States law would be useful in devising an international liability regime for war-caused damage, three inquiries are relevant. To what extent do these doctrines serve their own stated goals of providing deterrence, fairness, and economic efficiency? How easily are they administered, and at what cost? And finally, how intrusive would they be on national sovereignty?

First, however, the purpose of establishing such an international regime should be considered. Is it to compensate for environmental damage? To remediate environmental damage? To deter environmental damage? Or to deter war itself? Compensation alone does not necessarily remedy environmental damage or restore environmental integrity. Indeed, if environmental damage is diffuse and long-range, there is no logical party to receive compensation. Compensation protects the environment only if it is directed towards restoring the environment or providing offsetting alternative environmental improvements. But this really points to the second possible purpose, remediating environmental damage, a purpose that such a regime can serve. It can also serve the purpose of deterring war-caused environmental damage, by making the cost of warfare that causes environmental damage more expensive than the cost of warfare that does not cause such damage. However, such a regime would not appear to be an effective means of deterring warfare generally. While it would raise the cost of conducting war, it probably would not make the cost prohibitive. And it would not ameliorate any of the many non-economic considerations leading to war.

This leaves remediating environmental damage and deterring environmental damage as the dominant reasons for establishing an international liability regime. The principles underlying United States tort and environmental law serve both of these purposes. But the legal approaches involved serve those purposes with varying effectiveness and at different costs. As stated above, neither United States tort law nor environmental protection law provide remediation or compensation for war-caused environmental damage. For the most part, however, they easily could be adapted to do so. The following discussion assumes that such adaptations have been made.

Common law of torts

There is not a single common law of torts in the United States, but rather a separate set of tort law from each of its fifty states. Because state common-law tort doctrines are more similar than different, however, it is possible to discuss them as general concepts. Two causes of action in tort designed to protect land interests – nuisance and trespass – seem particularly suited to remedying environmental injury. Other tort causes of action designed more to compensate for personal injury – negligence and strict liability – also may be used to address environmental injury. Indeed, the use of tort law to redress environmental damage is developed enough to be a recognized field of study.[1]

Trespass and private nuisance are closely related to environmental damage because they provide remedies for many kinds of damage to land. But the ultimate rationale behind them is to protect property interests, not environmental interests. Thus, their relevance to compensation for environmental damage is limited. Negligence, strict liability, and public nuisance, on the other hand, are not as closely associated with environmental damages, because they usually provide remedies for damages to personal integrity and public rights to peace and safety. But the rationales behind them – deterrence, fairness, and economic efficiency – are well conceived to protect environmental interests.

Tort law deters damage-causing conduct by making the damage-causing party compensate for the damage and by perhaps requiring him to cease his damaging conduct. The deterrence rationale of tort law is inherent in its twinned origin with criminal law as a means of keeping the public

---

[1] E.g., Gerald W. Boston and M. Stuart Madden, *Law of Environmental and Toxic Torts* (St. Paul, Minn.: West Publishing Co., 1994).

peace. Tort law and criminal law developed primarily to deter damage to public and private rights that, if left unchecked, could lead to a breach of the peace. Much environmental damage is not of this nature, although perhaps equally harmful to society. Criminal law recently has been adapted to deter damage to the environment. Tort law also deters damage to many environmental interests and easily could be adapted to protect a broad array of environmental interests.

Tort law provides fairness between damaged and damaging parties by making the latter compensate the former for their damage. This rationale too is inherent in tort's twinned origin with criminal law, providing a peaceful means of redress for damage instead of violence and vengeance. This aspect of tort law is touted as its primary purpose by those who see it as an instrument of corrective justice. Corrective justice takes many guises, for example promoting moral conduct, returning injured parties to the *status quo ante*, discouraging the creation of non-reciprocal risks, and preventing the unjust enrichment of the damaging party. But, in the end, all of these guises are but different aspects of promoting fundamental fairness. Once it is recognized that damage to the environment ultimately damages society, fundamental fairness demands that those who damage the environment remediate societal damage, just as it demands that they compensate for damage to individuals.

Tort law promotes economic efficiency by deterring conduct that causes inefficient results. This rationale is of relatively recent origin, resulting from the application of economic theory to jurisprudence. It too takes many guises, for example reduction of accident costs, maximizing societal productivity and wealth, deterring involuntary transfers of wealth, and preventing market avoidance. But in the end, all of these guises are but different aspects of promoting economically efficient and beneficial behavior. Conduct that causes damage to individuals is economically inefficient because it reduces rather than increases societal resources. Once it is recognized that the environment is a societal resource of paramount importance, the relevance of economic efficiency for deterring environmental damage is as clear as its relevance for deterring damage to individuals.

As relevant as these rationales for tort law are to providing compensation for war-caused environmental damage, it must be recognized that other legal doctrines, both within and beyond tort law, stand in the way of such application. In one guise or another, some variety of justification defense applies to tort causes of action. For instance, the Restatement

(Second) of Torts lists twenty-one separate justification defenses to trespass, including self-defense, defense of others, and public necessity.[2] The
Restatement version of the public necessity justification includes invasions
for the purpose of averting an imminent public disaster, including protection against or repulsion of a "public enemy."[3] Indeed, the Restatement's
commentary notes the recognition of a similar privilege arising under war
or martial law power for military forces occupying, removing, or destroying property for protection against a public enemy.[4] And it recognizes a
privilege for members of the armed forces acting pursuant to lawful orders
to inflict harmful contact on persons and personality interests.[5] The application of these doctrines in a wartime context is self-evident.

Sovereign immunity bars suits against the government in the absence
of a waiver of immunity. While immunity can be traced back to the old
English maxim that "the King can do no wrong," it is strongly rooted in the
practical concept that "there can be no legal right as against the authority
that makes the law on which the right depends."[6] The US Congress has
enacted a broad waiver of sovereign immunity for torts.[7] Because of the
fundamental nature of sovereign immunity, however, courts interpret
waivers of it narrowly.[8] In any event, there is a specific exception to the
waiver for "any claim arising out of the combatant activities of the military
or naval forces . . . during time of war."[9] Because waivers of sovereign
immunity are interpreted narrowly, exceptions to those waivers are interpreted broadly, particularly when the damage complained of was caused
by military activity.[10] In addition to preserving its own sovereign immunity, the United States recognizes the sovereign immunity of other nations
against suits in United States courts.[11] While there are several significant exceptions to its recognition of the sovereign immunity of other
nations,[12] they are not relevant here. The strength of sovereign immunity
in domestic law is a direct reflection of the reluctance of states to subject
themselves to international regimes that limit their own sovereignty.

---

[2] Restatement (Second) of Torts (1965), §§ 191–211.   [3] *Ibid.*, § 196 cmt. a.
[4] *Ibid.*, § 196 cmt. i.   [5] *Ibid.*, § 146.
[6] *Kawananakoa v. Polybank*, 205 U.S. 349, 353 (1907).   [7] 28 U.S.C. §§ 1346, 2674–80 (1997).
[8] See *United States Dep't of Energy v. Ohio*, 503 U.S. 607 (1992).   [9] 28 U.S.C. § 2680(j) (1997).
[10] See *Koohi v. United States*, 976 F.2d 1328 (9th Cir. 1992), in which suit against the United States
was barred when its warship mistakenly shot down an Iranian airliner near an active military
zone, killing 290 civilian passengers. The court stated that as long as the plane was downed for military purposes or to protect lives, property, or other interests, sovereign immunity barred suit.
[11] 28 U.S.C. § 1604 (1997).   [12] 28 U.S.C. § 1605 (1997).

With this in mind, we will begin our survey of tort law with the two causes of action most often associated with environmental damage: trespass and nuisance. Nuisance is actually two distinct causes of action, one for injuries to public rights and one for injuries to the use and enjoyment of private property. We will then survey causes of action less often associated with environmental damage, but well suited to addressing it: negligence and strict liability. Strict liability is also two distinct causes of action, one for injuries caused by abnormally dangerous activities and one for injuries caused by defective products.

TRESPASS

Traditionally, trespass was unauthorized interference with the plaintiff's right of exclusive possession of property, caused by the defendant's invasion of the plaintiff's property or by another physical invasion resulting directly from the defendant's action. Trespass was actionable even if it caused no tangible damage, and even if it was unintentional and without negligence.[13] The severe and absolute liability of trespass reflected the ancient importance of real property in Anglo-American law. As real property has lost its economic primacy and private property rights have become less absolute, trespass too has become less absolute. While intentional trespass without damage still may be actionable, it now supports only nominal damages.[14] While unintentional or non-negligent invasions were traditionally recognized as trespass, they now are not always so recognized.[15] On the other hand, invasions that are indirect rather than direct may be actionable in trespass, while formerly they were not.[16]

When a hunter walks across the land of another, without permission of the landowner, he is trespassing because he has physically invaded the other's land. If he stands on his own land and fires a bullet that falls onto

---

[13] W. Page Keeton et al., *Prosser and Keeton on Torts* (St. Paul, Minn.: West Publishing Co., 1984), § 13, pp. 67–88.

[14] Restatement § 163 provides that intentional trespass is actionable in the absence of damage, and § 165 provides that negligent trespass is actionable only if it causes damage.

[15] Restatement § 166 provides that accidental trespass is actionable only if it results from willful or reckless conduct or from an abnormally hazardous activity.

[16] While courts traditionally held that the entry of solid matter, such as rocks from blasting, was a direct trespassory invasion of property, and that the entry of gas from other operations was an indirect non-trespassory invasion – see *Waschak v. Moffatt*, 379 Pa. 441 (1954) – that distinction is rejected by many more recent decisions, e.g., *Martin v. Reynolds Metals Co.*, 221 Or. 86 (1959).

the land of another, again he is trespassing, for he has caused a physical invasion of the other's land. Even if he stands on his own land and fires a bullet all the way across another's land to the other side, he is trespassing, for a trespass may occur above the surface of the land as well as on the surface.[17] Similarly, if a blaster comes onto the land of another without permission, and detonates an explosive charge resulting in a crater, he is trespassing. Even if he detonates the explosive charge on his own land and it throws rocks onto the land of another, he is trespassing.[18] These invasions, of course, are lesser versions of physical invasions by armies, arms, and armament that cause environmental damage during war.

But trespass provides a remedy only for the person with the exclusive right to possession of the property, while environmental damage is of concern because it affects those far beyond the immediate possessor of land. While unauthorized deforestation of real estate damages the possessor's interest to the extent of the value of the stolen timber, massive deforestation may damage people halfway around the world by its contribution to global warming effects, and future generations may by damaged by the unavailability of pharmaceutical and other scientific knowledge lost with the forest. Only if the protected interest in land is legally recognized to transcend current possessory interests and to encompass present and future ecological interests, is the destructive invasion of land a wrong to present and future society as a whole. This is more than an issue of measuring damages, but also an issue of standing; it would be a windfall to the property owner to be compensated for these societal trespassory damages to the environment. Recognizing a broader interest in land for purposes of trespass would mean that the government or persons other than the landowner could bring a trespass action for environmental damages to private land – a fundamental change in the tort.

Nonetheless, the nearly strict-liability nature of trespass for damaging invasions of land is a relevant factor to keep in mind in devising a legal regime for war-caused environmental damage. It also should be remembered that the twenty-one justification defenses discussed above were developed for application in trespass causes of action. They include self-defense, defense of others, and public necessity. Most parties to a war

---

[17] *Whittaker v. Stangvick*, 100 Minn. 386 (1907); Restatement § 158 cmt. i, illus. 6; Restatement § 159 cmt. f, illus. 4.

[18] Such damage by blasting has long been held actionable under trespass. See Smith, "Liability for Substantial Physical Damage to Land by Blasting," *Harv. L. Rev.* 33 (1920), 442.

would believe that any trespasses resulting from their activities would be justified by one or another of these defenses. Similarly, the United States has not waived its sovereign immunity for trespass for military purposes during time of war.

NUISANCE

Public and private nuisance encompass two distinct and very different causes of action, which have different origins and serve different purposes. Both, however, are more apt to be used to secure injunctive relief against future damage than are the other causes of action discussed here. Thus, they are the closest tort-law antecedents to statutory approaches for preventing present or future environmental damage.[19]

Public nuisance had its origin in criminal nuisance.[20] It was originally an action brought by the government, on behalf of the public, to prevent or seek compensation for a public injury. A public nuisance is "an unreasonable interference with a right common to the general public."[21] Thus the government might sue a gun club in public nuisance to abate the firing of lead shot at skeet over a river, interfering with the river's use for transportation and recreation, with its use as a source of water for domestic purposes, and its use as a source of fish and ducks.[22] The issues in the case would be whether: (1) these uses of the river were public rights, a legal issue; (2) the rights were interfered with by the skeet shooting, a factual issue; and (3) the interference was unreasonable, a balancing of both factual and legal aspects. Such a balancing is normally encountered when a court considers whether to provide injunctive relief, and, if so, what relief to provide. But with nuisance, it is also an element of the cause of action. It seeks to weigh the value and extent of the public rights injured by the complained-of private actions against the value and extent of the private actions.[23] Thus nuisance cases, like the negligence cases discussed below, are extremely fact-dependent.

While public nuisance was developed as a governmental cause of action, it may be brought by private individuals who suffer damage different from

---

[19] William H. Rogers, Jr., *Environmental Law: Air and Water* (1986), vol. I, § 1.1, p. 1.
[20] Keeton et al., *Prosser and Keeton on Torts*, § 86, p. 617.   [21] Restatement § 821B(1).
[22] See *Connecticut Coastal Fishermen's Ass'n v. Remington Arms*, 989 F.2d 1305 (2nd Cir. 1993).
[23] Restatement § 821B(2).

that suffered by the general public.[24] The difference, however, must be a difference in kind, not just in degree. Thus in the above example, a local resident who can no longer drink water or take and eat fish from the river because it is polluted with lead cannot maintain a public nuisance suit, because her injury is the same as the public's injury. But commercial fishermen whose livelihood is harmed suffer damage that differs from that suffered by the general public, and may maintain suit to enjoin the pollution and receive damages for pollution that has already occurred.[25]

Public nuisance includes such actions as interference with public safety by shooting off fireworks in the street,[26] interference with public peace from loud noises,[27] and interference with public comfort from bad odors.[28] Surely the much greater interferences with public rights occasioned by armed invasion, aerial bombing, and other acts of war are the sorts of interferences that constitute public nuisances. But the same justification defenses that could defeat trespass come back in another guise in nuisance: they are the very sorts of factors that are weighed in favor of the defendant in determining whether its invasion was unreasonable.[29] Moreover, the United States has not waived its sovereign immunity for public nuisance caused by military activity in time of war.

Private nuisance, on the other hand, has nothing to do with the vindication of public rights. It is an unreasonable "nontrespassory invasion of another's interest in the private use and enjoyment of land."[30] While public nuisance protects public rights, private nuisance protects private rights in land. Private nuisance is similar to trespass, but it protects use and enjoyment of land while trespass protects exclusive possession of land. Private nuisance protects against indirect and non-physical invasions of lands,

---

[24] *Ibid.*, § 821C.
[25] See *Union Oil Co. v. Oppen*, 501 F.2d 558 (9th Cir. 1974); *Burgess v. M/V Tamano*, 370 F. Supp. 247 (D. Me. 1973). [26] *Landau v. City of New York*, 180 N.Y. 48 (1904).
[27] *Town of Preble v. Song Mountain, Inc.*, 308 N.Y.2d 1001 (1970).
[28] *Transcontinental Gas Pipe Line Corp. v. Gault*, 198 F.2d 196 (4th Cir. 1952).
[29] See *Weinberger v. Romero-Barcello*, 456 U.S. 305 (1982), in which the court held that a trial court was justified in refusing to enjoin the Navy from dropping practice bombs in the ocean without a Clean Water Act permit, in apparent violation of that Act, because it "would cause grievous, and perhaps irreparable harm, not only to Defendant Navy, but to the general welfare of this Nation." This was not a nuisance case, but the importance of military activities, even in peacetime, in the balance of whether to enjoin an action for a statutory violation only underlines their importance in the balance required by a common law tort.
[30] Restatement § 821D.

while trespass protects only against direct and physical invasions. Thus private nuisance may be more easily invoked than trespass against odors, noise, vibrations, and low-level pollution.[31] But the same sort of balancing applied in public nuisance is also applied in private nuisance,[32] for not all interferences with the use and enjoyment of land are private nuisances, just unreasonable interferences.[33]

The same difficulties arise in applying private nuisance to war-caused environmental damages that arise when applying trespass – the private nature of the interests protected or, when applying public nuisance to such damages, the importance of national defense. And here again, the United States has not waived its sovereign immunity to suits of this nature. Further, private nuisance appears to offer no principles that may be appropriate in devising an international liability regime for war-caused environmental damages that are not already offered by trespass and public nuisance.

NEGLIGENCE

Although negligence is not commonly associated with environmental damage, it is the most commonly used cause of action in tort, and may be used to seek compensation for environmental as well as other types of damages. When a person's actions cause damage, he is liable in negligence if his actions foreseeably can cause damage and he fails to take reasonable care to avoid damage. The reasonableness of care is determined under the circumstances of the particular case, weighing the burden of taking care against the likelihood that the damage will occur in the absence of care and the severity of the damage that could occur.[34] The justification considerations discussed earlier come to bear here as part of the burden of taking care and of the circumstances of the particular case. Negligence seeks to avoid damage by deterring careless actions and to place the liability for damage on the parties best able to prevent the damage. Thus, while the transportation of oil by tanker is a function of great social utility, when the oil tanker owner fails to provide competent command through dangerous waters,

---

[31] Keeton et al., *Prosser and Keeton on Torts*, § 87, pp. 619–26.
[32] Indeed, the balancing to determine whether a private nuisance exists is far more elaborate than the balancing to determine whether a public nuisance exists. Compare Restatement § 821(2) with §§ 826–28.   [33] *Waschak*, 379 Pa. 441.
[34] *United States v. Carroll Towing Co.*, 159 F.2d 169 (1947). See also Restatement §§ 282 and 283.

where care is known to be required, and incompetent command results in a collision and an oil spill, the failure is negligence.[35]

The deterrence of unnecessary damage by negligence has much to recommend it in the context of war-caused environmental damage. Much war-caused damage could be avoided by exercising reasonable care to avoid unnecessary damage when choosing targets, choosing weapons for the targets, and delivering weapons to those targets. And it seems just to place the liability for environmental damage caused by war on those in the best position to avoid it. On the other hand, the intensity of the factual determination in deciding whether reasonable care was taken under all the circumstances makes negligence an unrealistic vehicle on the field of battle. The factual surroundings of individual instances of damage and the difficulty of recreating them after the fact would defeat many, if not most, attempts to use the doctrine. Indeed, the application of the doctrine to the multiplicity of individual damage-causing actions in war could overwhelm any system created to adjudicate them. In addition, negligence-based liability means finding fault with sovereign nations, not a process to which nations happily subject themselves.

Finally, negligence would only deter or compensate for damage caused when reasonable care was not taken to avoid damage. In the context of war, considerable damage will result even when reasonable care is taken to avoid damage. Negligence would not deter this conduct or compensate for damage caused by it. Ultimately, it does not seem a satisfactory tool to address the compensation issue in the context of war. But its deterrence and liability-shifting functions should be kept in mind as worthy of consideration in addressing the issue in that context.

STRICT LIABILITY

Strict liability is a characteristic of two distinct causes of action, strict liability for abnormally dangerous activities and strict liability for defective consumer products. While the nature of the liability is similar for each tort, one arises from an activity, even if flawlessly conducted, while the other arises from a product, but only if it is defective. Despite their

---

[35] In *Hazelwood v. State of Alaska*, 946 P.2d 875 (1997), the Supreme Court of Alaska upheld the conviction of the captain of the *Exxon Valdez* for criminally negligent discharge of oil in such circumstances, using a civil negligence standard in a criminal negligence prosecution.

differences, the purposes and policies behind the two causes of action are very similar.

Strict liability for abnormally hazardous activities picks up where negligence leaves off. Under this cause of action, when a person engages in an abnormally dangerous activity not commonly engaged in, he is liable for damage resulting from that activity regardless of how much care he has taken to avoid the damage. As elaborated in Sections 519 and 520 of the Restatement, the determination to apply strict liability is a question of balancing the abnormally dangerous nature of the activity against the social utility of the activity. This is very like the balance applied to determine whether an activity is negligently conducted. There are two new factors in the balance, however; the inability to eliminate the dangers posed by the activity even with utmost care, and the uncommonness of the activity. But both of these factors are reflections of the fairness and utilitarian rationales underlying negligence doctrine. Because of strict liability's resemblance to negligence, it is not surprising that it serves purposes similar to those served by negligence. It shifts liability for damage from those suffering the damage to those best able to avoid or bear the cost of the damage, either by taking utmost care in the activity, by not engaging in the activity, or by internalizing all the costs of the activity (including the damage caused by it). By internalizing the costs, the actor will pass the costs of damage caused by the activity to all those who benefit from it,[36] serving both fairness and economic or social utilitarian goals.[37]

Strict liability for abnormally dangerous activities appears at first to be ideally designed to address environmental damage from war. Warfare is an extremely dangerous activity. The likelihood that it will cause damage is high. The nature and extent of the damage that it may cause is extreme. Even with the utmost care, damage cannot be eliminated. Indeed, in one sense damage (although not necessarily environmental damage) is the very purpose of war. In this regard it mirrors the activity addressed by the

---

[36] *Indiana Harbor Belt R.R. Co. v. American Cyanamid Co.*, 916 F.2d 1174, 1177 (7th Cir. 1990); *Atlas Chem. Indus., Inc. v. Anderson*, 514 S.W.2d 309, 315–16 (Tex. Civ. App. 1974), aff'd in part, rev'd in part, 524 S.W.2d 681 (Tex. 1975).

[37] *Atlas Chem. Indus.*, 514 S.W.2d 309; Guido Calabresi and Jon T. Hirschoff, "Toward a Test for Strict Liability in Tort," *Yale L.J.* 81 (1972), 1055. Restatement § 519, cmt. d, states that the reasons for strict liability are that one who for his own purpose creates an abnormal risk of danger to his neighbors should bear responsibility for harm if it occurs, and that abnormally dangerous activities should pay their own way. This in effect blends corrective justice and economic efficiency rationales.

earliest strict liability cases: civilian blasting.[38] Fortunately, warfare also is an uncommon activity. To be sure, there is warfare somewhere in the world at all times but, like blasting, it is still not a common activity in society. But is there great social utility in warfare? The winners will almost always believe there was great social utility for their resistance to the aggression or expected aggression of others. Indeed, the world may judge warfare justified in order to oppose genocide and tyranny. This does not entirely eliminate use of strict liability, however, as the social utility of the activity is often ignored when the other factors are strong enough. Even if the social utility of the damage-causing activity is great, it still meets the goals of fairness and utilitarianism to shift the burden of damage from those innocently suffering it to those benefiting from the activity.[39]

Strict liability for unreasonably dangerous defective products is one of the three traditional causes of action in the field of products liability (the other two are negligence and breach of warranty). Its application beyond the sale of food unfit for human consumption is of comparatively recent origin.[40] As embodied in Section 402A of the Restatement,[41] the seller of a product is strictly liable for defective conditions in the product that are unreasonably dangerous to the consumer. The unreasonably dangerous condition may result from a defect in design, a defect in manufacture, or a failure to warn of a danger inherent in the product. Liability applies even though the seller has exercised the utmost care with regard to the product. Because no privity is necessary between the seller and the consumer, strict liability extends from the store that sells the product to the ultimate consumer all the way up to the manufacturer of the product, and runs not only to the consumer but to unrelated third parties. Indeed, through various means, usually the onus for defective products is ultimately placed on the manufacturer.

Strict liability for defective products serves the same purposes and goals as strict liability for abnormally dangerous activities. It places liability on the person best able to prevent the damage. And it internalizes the cost of damage inevitably occurring from use of a product, in essence shifting the loss from randomly damaged consumers to all those who benefit from use of the product. This serves goals of both fairness and utilitarianism.

[38] E.g., *Bradford Glycerine Co. v. St. Mary's Woolen Mfg. Co.*, 60 Ohio St. 560 (1899).
[39] *Siegler v. Huhlman*, 81 Wash.2d 448 (1972).
[40] *Greenman v. Yuba Power Prod., Inc.*, 59 Cal.2d 697 (1963).
[41] A new Restatement (Third) includes a revision of strict liability. The present discussion examines strict products liability as it is restated in § 402A of the Restatement (Second).

Nonetheless, strict liability for abnormally dangerous activities remains a separate and distinct cause of action from strict liability for unreasonably dangerous defective products. An activity is not abnormally dangerous just because it involves a dangerous product.[42] And if an activity is abnormally dangerous, and involves a dangerous product, it is the person conducting the activity, not the manufacturer of the product, who is liable.[43] Further, a product may be subject to strict liability only if a defect creates the danger. Thus there is no strict liability for guns, alcohol, tobacco, and other products causing damage because of their very nature, rather than because of a defect.[44]

Why do the fairness and utilitarian rationales for liability shifting not apply to products that are inherently dangerous as well as to products that are dangerous because they are defective? One answer might be that the consumer has chosen to undertake a risk that is obviously inherent in the product when he buys it, while he has not chosen to undertake an unknown risk from a hidden defect in the product. But the non-consumer injured by the product has undertaken neither risk, and strict liability does not depend on whether the injured party is the consumer or an unrelated third party.[45] Another answer might be that the purpose of strict product liability is to deter unsafe design and manufacture of products, not to deter the design and manufacture of defect-free products. But why not adopt the rationale of strict liability for abnormally hazardous activities and spread the cost of damage caused by such products among all that use and benefit from them? The answer might be that such a legal regime would raise the price of such products to the point at which only the rich could afford them, an unacceptable result in a society with egalitarian aspirations.

The application of strict products liability to environmental damage caused by war would impose liability on the manufacturers of arms and armaments. As currently conceived under American law, however, it would be of only incidental value in providing compensation for damage to the environment, because it applies only if the damage is caused by defects in the products rather than by the very nature of the product. Arms and armaments, however, cause damage because they are designed to do so.

---

[42] See *Indiana Harbor Belt R. R. Co.*, 916 F.2d 1174.

[43] See *City of Bloomington v. Westinghouse Elec. Corp.*, 891 F.2d. 611 (7th Cir. 1988), in which it was held that a manufacturer of PCBs, dangerous compounds, was not liable for the abnormally dangerous activity of burning them. [44] Restatement § 402A, cmt. i.

[45] Keeton et al., *Prosser and Keeton on Torts*, § 100.

Statutory law of environmental protection

Statutory environmental law falls into two broad categories: the management of natural resources and the control of pollution and waste disposal. Although the two obviously overlap, they involve different sets of legal doctrines, come from different origins, and have different characteristics. Because damage caused by war is more analogous to damage caused by pollution and waste disposal, this chapter focuses on that category of environmental law.

For some, environmental law is premised on the proposition that nature is a paramount value, to be protected for its own sake. But for most, it is premised on the proposition that a healthy environment is good for human society. After all, law is a human institution, developed to protect society and social values. By recognizing that damage to the environment is damage to society, environmental law makes the environment a legally cognizable societal interest. When injury to the environment is seen as a legally cognizable interest, it is a small step to develop tort law as a means of redressing environmental damages.[46] It is also a small step to recognize that the rationales underlying tort law – deterrence, fairness, and economic efficiency – apply equally to environmental law.

The relationship between environmental law and deterrence of environmental damage is obvious. Environmental law seeks fairness too. It is at its most comfortable when it seeks to redress the unfairness of one member of society exposing non-consenting members of society on a non-reciprocal basis to unhealthy or life-threatening conditions in the environment. Environmental law seeks economic efficiency as well by requiring environmentally damaging activities to internalize the cost of the environmental damage they cause, in essence spreading the cost of the damage to all those who benefit from the activities. Economic efficiency has another role in environmental law: seeking to assure that environmental regulation does not itself become economically and socially wasteful by imposing greater burdens protecting the environment from damage than the value of the damage avoided.

---

[46] Most of the pollution control statutes create what is effectively an environmental public nuisance cause of action. While these nuisance actions may only be brought by the government, one statute allows similar actions to be brought by private citizens, 42 U.S.C. § 6972(a)(1)(B) (1997).

When environmental law adopted strict liability as much of the basis for control of pollution and waste disposal, it effectively adopted many of the doctrinal underpinnings of tort law, especially those associated with strict liability for abnormally hazardous activity. The reasons for imposing strict liability in environmental law are similar to those for imposing it in tort: deterrence, fairness, and economic efficiency. It is fair that those who profit from spewing toxic fumes over a community bear the burden of the damage caused rather than innocently and randomly affected victims. Moreover, the factory owner is in the best position to bear the burden, by making a different product, making the product differently, or internalizing the burden in the price of the product sold so that all benefiting from the product pay for those hurt by it. While this is commonly called the "polluter-pays" principle in environmental circles, its rationale is no different from the deterrence, fairness, and economic efficiency rationales underlying tort law. But it does extend the fairness and utilitarian principles from personal integrity and personal property rights recognized and protected by tort law to the environmental integrity and societal rights recognized and protected by environmental law.

Even sovereign immunity and justification apply in a similar manner in environmental and tort law. The United States has not waived its sovereign immunity broadly for environmental requirements as it has for torts. Rather, it has waived its immunity on somewhat different terms in each statute[47] and often has allowed exemptions for national security reasons. Although no justification defenses apply as such to environmental causes of action, equitable justifications can be taken into account by courts in determining whether to impose a remedy and, if so, what remedy to apply. National security interests have been recognized as reasons not to enjoin military activities that apparently violated environmental requirements.[48]

REGULATION OF PRESENT AND FUTURE POLLUTION AND WASTE DISPOSAL

Pollution and waste control is primarily forward-looking; it seeks to prevent future damage to the environment by proper management of pollution and waste disposal today and tomorrow. It generally follows the

---

[47] Compare the Clean Water Act, which has broad waivers, 33 U.S.C. §§ 1323(a) and 1365(a) (1997), with the Marine Protection, Research, and Sanctuaries Act, which has only a limited one, 33 U.S.C. § 1415(g) (1997).   [48] *Weinberger*, 456 U.S. 305.

polluter-pays model; the person producing pollution or waste must properly manage its disposal and/or pay for that management or disposal. Thus a factory producing water pollution must install, maintain, and operate the required pollution control equipment and pay the cost thereof.[49] If the factory discharges into a publicly operated sewage system instead of directly into surface water, it must pay a user charge to the treatment works to defray its cost of treating the industry's waste, and may also have to partially treat its wastes before discharging them to the public system.[50] Even individuals discharging their household waste to a publicly operated sewage system normally pay user charges on a similar basis. When pollution or waste comes from a publicly operated activity, this pattern still prevails. When the Department of Defense discharges water pollution to surface water or to a publicly owned sewage treatment facility, it is responsible for pollution control to the same degree as a private party is responsible.[51]

There are exceptions to this general pattern. When pollution or waste from the general public is being controlled or managed by a publicly operated facility, the cost of the facility may be split among several governmental entities with progressively larger tax bases.[52] A more important exception for the purpose of the present discussion is for ubiquitous pollution sources, e.g., consumer products such as automobiles, wood stoves, or home furnaces. While an individual polluting consumer product may be a negligible pollution source in itself, the universe of similar products may be a very significant pollution source in the aggregate. Nevertheless, owners and operators of these sources may be underregulated or not regulated at all because they are too numerous to deal with effectively or would be politically difficult to regulate.

Indeed, air pollution from automobiles is primarily addressed by regulation prior to the time that automobiles or the gasoline that powers them reaches consumers. Because emissions are a function of the volume of gasoline burned, the automobile manufacturer is required to produce an

---

[49] 33 U.S.C. §§ 1311(a) and (b), 1342(k) (1997).

[50] 33 U.S.C. § 1317(b) (1997); 40 C.F.R pt. 403 (1997).   [51] 33 U.S.C. § 1323 (1997).

[52] The primary example of this is that part of the cost of municipal sewage treatment plants traditionally has been paid by federal and state funds, as well as local funds. Some sort of a federal grant program was in place for this purpose from the late 1940s through the late 1980s. See 33 U.S.C. §§ 1281–99 (1997). This grant program was replaced in the late 1980s by a revolving loan fund administered by the states, 33 U.S.C. §§ 1381–87 (1997).

automobile fleet that meets standards for fuel economy.[53] The manufacturer is also required to design and manufacture vehicles that burn fuel efficiently, resulting in as few emissions as possible, and to capture emissions that do occur.[54] The gasoline producer is required to produce and sell fuel that is both compatible with the resulting automobiles and is itself relatively free of pollutants in its emissions when burned.[55] Although conceptually simple, this regulatory system is in fact complex and difficult to manage.

As difficult as this regulatory system may be, dealing primarily with a few hundred automobile and gasoline production facilities is relatively efficient compared to dealing with tens of millions of individual automobile owners. To be sure, the full benefit of emissions controls on automobiles cannot be realized without some sort of program to require the maintenance of the controls by automobile owners, but that can be targeted to areas of greatest need[56] and is greatly simplified by regulation at the manufacturing end of the consumer chain.

Environmental damage from many consumer products is addressed by other management and regulatory controls. Materials such as asbestos, PCBs, and chlorofluorocarbons are banned altogether from use in most consumer goods.[57] Pesticides may be sold only for uses that are determined, among other things, by their potential to cause environmental damage.[58] Manufacturers of airplanes, railroad engines, air compressors, and similar devices must design them to meet noise pollution standards.[59] Beverage bottlers in many states must distribute their products in recyclable bottles and collect and return deposits on returned bottles to promote recycling, thus preventing waste and litter.

Two dominant models guide the determination of how much pollution control to require of individual pollution sources. The first employed was the environmental standards model. This model establishes standards for the level of environmental purity necessary to sustain human health or other desired uses. The environment is then analyzed to determine

[53] 49 U.S.C. §§ 32901ff. (1997).   [54] 42 U.S.C. §§ 7521–44 (1997).

[55] 42 U.S.C. § 7545 (1997).

[56] In the US, motor vehicle emissions control inspections are required only in areas not meeting ambient standards for the air pollutants most notably produced by such emissions. 42 U.S.C. §§ 7511a(a)(2)(B), (b)(4), (c), and (d) (1997).

[57] 15 U.S.C. §§ 2605(e), 2641–56 (1997); 42 U.S.C. §§ 7671a and 7671c (1997).

[58] 7 U.S.C. §§ 136–136y (1997). Pesticide regulation, like automobile emissions regulation, does impose liability on the end user of the product. But both place their primary emphasis on regulating the manufacturer.   [59] 40 C.F.R. pts. 201–11 (1997).

whether pollution abatement is necessary to achieve the standards and, if so, how much pollution must be abated to achieve them. Finally, the pollution reduction necessary is apportioned among individual pollution sources contributing to the degradation to be rectified. This model prevents wasteful expenditure on pollution reduction that is not needed to achieve the desired level of environmental purity. Although economically pleasing, it has been criticized for having unintended anti-environmental consequences, and for being difficult and expensive for regulators to implement.

As a result of the latter criticism, this model has given way in varying degrees to the second model, technology-based standards.[60] The second model establishes standards for categories of pollution sources based on the pollution control they can achieve using available and affordable technology and management practices. Progressively greater pollution control can be required over time by using progressively more stringent definitions of what is affordable. This model has been criticized as resulting in wasteful expenditures, to the extent that it requires pollution source controls even when they are not needed to achieve health or ambient environmental standards.

Both of the models are implemented by elaborate regulatory and enforcement programs that are criticized for requiring the support of large bureaucracies and for entangling the regulated public in inflexible procedures, reporting requirements, and "red tape." As a result, there are constant attempts to make the resulting programs more flexible and friendly towards the regulated community. For example, some pollution control programs offer incentives to provide greater pollution control than is required by existing standards. Some of the programs provide flexibility to encourage achieving standards by more efficient or cheaper means. Similarly, a pollution source for which pollution control is especially expensive may be allowed to substitute control of pollution by another

---

[60] The original technology-based standards were adopted as the primary means of securing pollution abatement in the Federal Water Pollution Control Amendments of 1972, Pub. L. 92–500, 2, 86 Stat. 844, codified at 33 U.S.C. § 1311(b) (1997); and 86 Stat. 850, codified at 33 U.S.C. § 1314(b) (1997). They have subsequently been adopted as the primary approach for controlling contamination from the disposal of hazardous and solid waste in the Resource Conservation and Recovery Act, 42 U.S.C. § 6924 (1997), and the primary approach for controlling emissions of hazardous air pollutants under the Clean Air Act Amendments of 1990, Pub. L. 101–549, Title III, § 301, 104 Stat. 2531, codified at 42 U.S.C. § 7412(d).

source that is cheaper but not otherwise required.[61] Although these economic options to traditional regulation have been much touted, their use is limited and there is some suspicion that their use may be manipulated to defeat the intended environmental improvement.

A final environmental control model is that of study and disclosure. Environmental impact and alternatives assessments may be required to be developed in an open, public process before major government actions or private actions that are undertaken with government approval.[62] New chemical products may be marketed only after their environmental effects have been studied and disclosed to the government.[63] The types and amounts of hazardous chemicals used at a facility and the amounts of them that enter the environment may be required to be disclosed to the surrounding community, creating pressure to curtail unnecessary uses of such material.[64] While these measures are not free from criticism for causing delay and burden, they escape all of the criticisms of heavy-handed and needlessly expensive governmental requirements leveled at the programs explicitly requiring pollution control and management.

It is difficult to imagine the dominant pollution control models applied to wartime activity. Any sort of prior public process in which it is determined how much environmental damage may be caused, where it may be caused, and how it may be caused, would completely eliminate any tactical advantages of surprise. Limiting any of these by a bureaucratic process would strangle the ability of commanders to react to developments in the war field. On the other hand, establishing technology-based standards for weaponry used in war based on their environmental destructiveness appears practicable and has some precedent. Some technologies may be prohibited altogether, e.g., mustard gas, biological weapons, or landmines. Others may require controls, e.g., sophisticated guidance systems for bombs.

In a larger sense, however, these programs establish that the deterrence, fairness, and economic efficiency principles underlying tort law are just as relevant to protecting public environmental rights as they are to protecting personal integrity and property rights.

---

[61] Such "pollution trading" was embraced in the 1990 Clean Air Act Amendments as part of a new control strategy for requiring then largely unregulated coal-fired power plants in the Midwest to achieve sulfur oxide emissions reductions, 42 U.S.C. § 7651b (1997).

[62] National Environmental Policy Act, 42 U.S.C. §§ 4321–70d (1997).

[63] Toxic Substances Control Act, 15 U.S.C. §§ 2601–92 (1997).

[64] Emergency Planning and Community Right-to-Know Act, 42 U.S.C. §§ 11001–50 (1997).

REMEDIATION OF ENVIRONMENTAL DAMAGE FROM
POLLUTION AND WASTE DISPOSAL

All of the environmental programs described above are forward-looking; they do not deal with environmental damage that has already occurred. Indeed, only a few programs deal with remediation of or compensation for environmental damage. The earliest program developed for that purpose addressed the environmental damage from oil spills. A more recent program addressing environmental damage from the past disposal of hazardous substances was modeled largely on the oil spill regime. A program was also developed to remediate environmental damage from coal mining.

As with the other environmental programs, sovereign immunity applies to these liabilities, but it has been waived to varying degrees. On the other hand, the remedial programs expressly exclude liability for damage that is caused solely by acts of war. To the extent that war-caused damage is addressed by the programs, remedial or compensatory costs are borne by the government or by a fund made up of assessments on those causing similar damage.

Like the pollution control programs, these measures are based on strict liability, placing it on the person best able to prevent the damage to be remediated. But they carry that doctrine farther, not only requiring such persons to remediate and compensate for damage resulting from their activities, but also requiring them to contribute to funds to pay for the remediation of and compensation for similar damage resulting from the activities of others who for whatever reason cannot provide remediation and compensation.

Oil spills. The goals of the oil spill program are to deter spills, to see that spills that do occur are remediated, and to shift the cost of spill damage and clean-up from the government to those responsible for the spills. The oil spill program began around 1970, in the wake of major oil spills off the coasts of England and California. It put the onus on owners and operators of ships and other facilities spilling oil to report the spills immediately to the responding government authorities, to contain the spill, and to clean the oil from the environment.[65] A ship's liability for the costs of containment and clean-up was strict, but it was limited to an amount that was

---

[65] Water Quality Improvement Act of 1970, Pub. L. 91–224, §§ 101–12, 84 Stat. 91, originally codified at 33 U.S.C. § 1161 (1972), now codified at 33 U.S.C. § 1321 (1997). The program is described generally in Sheldon M. Novick et al., *Law of Environmental Protection* (Deerfield,

thought to be insurable at a reasonable premium price.[66] Strict liability was also qualified by a limited number of causation defenses, including sole causation by war.[67] A small fund was created from general governmental revenues to pay for the clean-up of abandoned spills and clean-up costs that exceeded the limits of the spilling ships' strict liability.[68]

Over time, but particularly in reaction to the *Exxon Valdez* spill, the oil spill program has been augmented[69] by making the owner or operator of the spilling vessel liable not only for containment and remediation costs, but also for natural resource and other damages.[70] The small government clean-up fund drawn from general revenues has been replaced by a substantial fund based on a tax of crude oil received at refineries or oil product imports.[71] For some spills, this fund is augmented by an assessment on the owners of the oil, as opposed to the owners of vessels.[72] Finally, shipowners are required to use technology to minimize the potential for oil spills[73] and to develop plans for responding to spills that do occur.[74]

From the beginning of the oil spill program, there has been a synergy between United States law and international law.[75] Oil pollution can implicate international law in a number of ways; for example, it can occur on the high seas, far from any national dominion, or emanate from a ship registered in one nation and damage the environment of another nation. Indeed, the first US oil spill legislation, the Oil Pollution Act of 1961,[76]

Ill.: Clark Boardman Callaghan, 1997), § 13.05; Donald W. Stever et al., *Law of Chemical Regulation and Hazardous Waste* (New York: C. Boardman Co., 1997), § 6.02.

[66] 33 U.S.C. § 1321(f)(1) (1997).

[67] It is a defense to liability if the shipowner can prove that the spill was caused *solely* by an act of God, an act of war, negligence by the United States government, or the act or omission of a third party not in privity with the owner. 33 U.S.C. § 1321(f)(1) (1997).

[68] The size of the original fund was $35 million, 33 U.S.C. § 1321(k) (1972). Compare this to the over $3.3 billion in costs for clean-up and damages in the *Exxon Valdez* spill.

[69] The primary revision of the program is the Oil Pollution Act of 1990, Pub. L. 101–380, 100 Stat. 559, codified at 33 U.S.C. §§ 2701ff. (1997).   [70] 33 U.S.C. § 2702 (1997).

[71] 26 U.S.C. § 4611 (1997).

[72] Under the Trans-Alaska Pipeline Authorization Act, the shipowner and the TAPAA fund are both strictly liable for damages and clean-up costs from a spill. The fund is collected from the owner of every barrel of oil as it is loaded onto a vessel from the pipeline. 43 U.S.C. §§ 1651–65 (1997).

[73] For instance, double hulls are required for tanker vessels, 49 U.S.C. 3707a (1997).

[74] 33 U.S.C. § 1321(j)(5) (1997); 46 U.S.C. § 2101(39) (1997).

[75] The evolving relationship between international oil spill conventions and United States law on the subject is discussed in Antonia J. Rodriguez (ed.), *Benedict on Admiralty* (New York: M. Bender, 1997), vol. III, §§ 115–19, which also reproduces texts of many of the relevant international documents.   [76] 33 U.S.C. §§ 1001ff. (1997).

was enacted to implement the earlier International Convention for the Prevention of Pollution of the Sea by Oil.[77] Both forbid, with exceptions,[78] the discharge of oil from ships within 50 miles of the seacoast.

While both the convention and the legislation were expanded from time to time,[79] neither dealt with liability for spills beyond a penalty provision. Following the *Torrey Canyon* spill in 1967, however, the International Convention on Civil Liability for Oil Pollution Damage of 1969[80] did just that. This convention established strict liability for the ship from which a spill occurred, but limited the liability, setting the pattern for the 1970 US legislation discussed above. Significantly, the convention did not cover spills from warships.[81] The relatively low liability limitations contained in the 1969 Convention were increased significantly in a 1992 Protocol,[82] following the *Exxon Valdez* spill.

The 1969 Convention was augmented by the International Convention on the Establishment of an International Fund for Compensation for Oil Pollution Damage,[83] which entered into force in 1978. This convention set up a compensation fund from a charge levied on persons in signatory countries receiving oil that had been shipped on the high seas. It was supplemented by private agreements among both tanker owners[84] and oil producers, refiners and marketers,[85] although these agreements have expired.[86] These private funds were available only for government clean-up costs, whereas the funds established by the conventions also could be claimed by private parties damaged by spills. Thus, international law provided a model for compensation funds derived from charges on damage-

---

[77] 2 U.S.T. 2989, T.I.A.S. No. 4900 (1954).

[78] Notably, when necessary to secure the safety of a ship, to prevent damage to a ship or its cargo, to save life at sea, or when caused by damage to the ship or unavoidable leakage. See 33 U.S.C. § 1003(a) and (b) (1997).

[79] The evolution of the Convention is chronicled in Rodriguez, *Benedict on Admiralty*, vol. III, § 115.

[80] International Convention on Civil Liability for Oil Pollution Damage (Nov. 29, 1969), 973 U.N.T.S. 3, *I.L.M.* 9 (1970), 45. The Convention entered into force in 1975.

[81] *Ibid.*, Art. XI, para. 1.

[82] 1992 Protocol to the International Convention on Civil Liability for Oil Pollution Damage, IMO Doc. LEG/CONF.9/15 (Dec. 2, 1992).

[83] Convention on the Establishment of an International Fund for Compensation for Oil Pollution Damage (Dec. 18, 1971), *I.L.M.* 11 (1972), 284.

[84] Tanker Owners Voluntary Agreement Concerning Liability for Oil Pollution (TOVALOP) (Jan. 7, 1969), *I.L.M.* 8 (1969), 497.

[85] Contract Regarding an Interim Supplement to Tanker Liability for Oil Pollution (CRISTAL) (Jan. 14, 1971), *I.L.M.* 10 (1971), 137.   [86] Rodriguez, *Benedict on Admiralty*, vol. III, § 119.

causing materials well before similar funds were established under United States law.

Hazardous substance releases. As Love Canal and other incidents of environmental contamination from past disposal practices captured national attention, a comprehensive program was developed to remediate environmental damage caused by almost any sort of release of hazardous substances into the environment.[87] It was modeled in large part on the oil spill remediation program, and to some extent on "imminent and substantial endangerment" authorities in the pollution control statutes.[88] In a sense, Congress has done the balancing that courts do in public nuisance cases, concluding that the balance weighs in favor of having the parties responsible for the hazardous substance release clean it up and compensate for the damage it causes. The original goals of this program are to protect the environment and the public from releases of hazardous substances originating from past hazardous waste disposal and to shift the cost of remediating such contamination from the government to those responsible for the contamination. As the enormous liability imposed on industry became apparent over time, however, the value of the program in deterring careless disposal of hazardous substances was recognized.

This program places strict liability,[89] similar to that under the oil spill program, on an expanded set of responsible parties[90] for both remedial costs and natural resource damage from releases of hazardous substances. As with the oil spill program, there are exemptions to strict liability for releases caused solely by particular events, including acts of war.[91] All such

---

[87] Comprehensive Environmental Response, Compensation and Liability Act (CERCLA) of 1980, 42 U.S.C. §§ 9601ff. (1997). For descriptions of this program, see Novick et al., *Environmental Protection*, §§ 13.05[3], 13.06[2] and [3]; Stever et al., *Chemical Regulation*, §§ 6.04 to 6.09.   [88] See, e.g., 42 U.S.C. § 6972 (1977).

[89] The statute does not use the term "strict liability," but the only defenses it provides to liability are three of the sole cause defenses that are provided for oil spills. 42 U.S.C. § 9607(b) (1977). Courts have universally construed CERCLA liability as being strict. E.g., *United States v. Monsanto*, 858 F.2d 160 (4th Cir. 1989); *Tanglewood East Homeowners v. Charles-Thomas, Inc.*, 849 F.2d 1568 (5th Cir. 1988).

[90] Responsible parties include: the owner or operator of the contaminated property; the owner or operator of the property at the time the hazardous substances were placed on the property; the person who arranged for the hazardous substance to be placed on the property (usually the person producing the hazardous substance as a waste); and the person who transported the hazardous substances to the property. 42 U.S.C. § 9607(a) (1977).

[91] However, the United States has waived its sovereign immunity under this statute to a considerable extent and has developed a program to remediate contamination on federal installations, particularly on military installations. 42 U.S.C. § 9620 (1997).

parties at a contaminated site are jointly and severally liable for remediation or the cost of remediation.[92] The government may either allow or order the responsible parties to remediate the site directly, or the government may do so itself and later sue the responsible parties to recover its costs.[93] When the government performs the remedial work, it draws from a fund made up of clean-up costs it recovers from responsible parties, and a tax on corporations, specified chemicals produced or imported, and petroleum product imports and crude oil received at refineries.[94]

The program has proven costly. Remediation of a typical contaminated site costs in excess of US $30 million and has run as high as US $2 billion.[95] Criticisms of the program are varied. Industry complains that it must pay twice, once in the form of a tax to the clean-up fund and then again for the remediation of sites where it is a responsible party. It complains that liability is retroactive, making it pay for disposal practices that took place before enactment of the program and which were perfectly legal and normal at the time. It complains that the harshness of joint and several liability pressures parties with minimal connection to a contaminated site to pay far more than their proportionate share of clean-up costs in settlements to avoid the cost of litigation, which are significant. Finally, it complains that government remediation is driven to pristine levels in areas which are far from pristine.

There are, of course, counters to all these criticisms. Industry does not pay twice for the same clean-up; where responsible parties pay for a clean-up, the Fund does not pay. Liability for the present consequences of past actions, even actions that were perfectly legal at the time they occurred, is the substance of tort law in general and nuisance law in particular. And although many complain about the theoretical liability of a party responsible for 1 percent of the waste at a site for 100 percent of the clean-up cost of the site, there are no actual examples of such liability. The application of the doctrine of contribution among jointly and severally liable tortfeasors helps to assure that such results will happen rarely, if ever. To be sure, there

---

[92] The statute nowhere mentions joint and several liability, but from the beginning courts have held liability under the statute to be joint and several. *United States v. Chem-Dyne Corp.*, 572 F. Supp. 802 (S. D. Ohio 1983).   [93] 42 U.S.C. §§ 9604, 9606–7 (1997).

[94] 42 U.S.C. § 9611 (1997); 26 U.S.C. §§ 4611–12, 4661–62 (1997). The tax, however, has expired.

[95] *United States v. Shell Oil Co.*, 605 F. Supp. 1064 (D. Colo. 1985) (United States sought $1.8 billion in estimated remedial costs for the Rocky Mountain Arsenal Site near Denver); Michael Gerrard, "Demons and Angels in Hazardous Waste Regulation," *Nw. U. L. Rev.* 92 (1997), 722 (average cost of CERCLA remedial action exceeds $30 million).

are high transaction costs with this and most other liability schemes. And there is much disagreement on how much contaminated areas should be decontaminated. This last argument will carry over to any liability scheme for war-caused environmental damage.

It is worth noting that the complementary program regulating the current treatment, storage, and disposal of hazardous wastes[96] is calculated to prevent future contaminated sites of the kind requiring remediation under the above-described program. It does so not only by stringent regulation of the treatment, storage, and disposal of hazardous waste, but also by requiring owners and operators of disposal, storage, and treatment facilities to close the facilities and provide post-closure care to prevent releases of hazardous substances into the environment after cessation of operations and to accumulate trust funds sufficient to pay for the closure and post-closure care of the facilities.[97]

Coal mining. Coal mining has created extensive environmental damage, particularly the disfigurement of land from strip mining and pollution of surface water from acid mine drainage. The coal mining program requires current strip mining operations to return mined land to as close to its original contour and use, as soon as possible after the coal is removed.[98] The water pollution control program requires current mining operations to remove the acidity and other pollutants from mine water before discharging it to surface waters.[99] After cessation of mining operations, mine owners and operators also are required to close the mines to prevent further environmental damage, to provide post-closure care to prevent environmental damage, and to accumulate trust funds sufficient to pay for the closure and post-closure care of the mines.[100] A tax on every ton of coal produced is placed in a fund which the government may use to remediate damage from mining that occurred before the control program went into effect.[101] The cost of remediating damage from past mining practices, however, far outstrips the funds available for the purpose.[102]

[96] Resource Conservation and Recovery Act, 42 U.S.C. §§ 6901ff. (1997).
[97] 40 C.F.R. §§ 164.110 to .151 (1997).
[98] Surface Mining Control and Reclamation Act of 1977 (SMCRA), 30 U.S.C. §§ 1201ff. (1997). The SMCRA program and its accomplishments are described in detail in James M. McElfish, Jr. and Ann E. Beier, *Environmental Regulation of Coal Mining* (Washington, D.C.: Environmental Law Institute, 1990).
[99] 33 U.S.C. §§ 1331(a), 1342 (1997); 40 C.F.R. pt. 434 (1997).
[100] McElfish and Beier, *Coal Mining*, pp. 253–63.   [101] 30 U.S.C. §§ 1231, 1232 (1997).
[102] McElfish and Beier, *Coal Mining*, p. 253.

Application to war-caused environmental damage

Of the tort causes of action, strict liability for abnormally dangerous activities would best serve the purposes of remediation and deterrence of wartime environmental damage. Since war is an abnormally dangerous activity, application of this cause of action would provide remediation for all environmental damage caused by war and would deter conducting war by environmentally damaging means when there are less damaging means available. It would be relatively easy to apply, requiring fewer transaction costs than causes of action with more factual issues. It also is non-judgmental; its application would not depend upon determining that a state has acted in a wrongful or aggressive manner. This should make it easier for potentially belligerent states to subscribe to it. There remains, however, the political issue of whether states would willingly subscribe to a regime subjecting them to potentially enormous costs of unavoidable damage in wars that they view as necessary for their own survival, the survival of a political or economic system, the survival of a religious or ethnic group, or even the survival of the environment. Another problem is that warring nations may be too impoverished as a result of their conflicts to pay the actual costs of remediation, no matter how strict the liability. This is particularly a problem, of course, for losing parties.

Public nuisance would meet some of these concerns by weighing the social value of conducting war against the environmental costs of the war. But to the extent the balance between relevant factors justifies the conduct of the warring state in causing environmental damage, the remedial and deterrence purposes of the liability scheme would not be served. Of course, the remedial costs could be passed onto the other warring state, for whom the balance probably tips in the opposite direction. In the judgment of history and politics, this usually will be the losing party, who will often be in a poor position to provide for environmental remediation. The imposition of what may be crushing reparations would be unlikely to produce the desired environmental restoration, because reparations would not be paid or would be paid only over a protracted period of time. Even if reparations are paid, however, they may have counterproductive effects, promoting social unrest in the impoverished losing state, leading to more violence and war. Because public nuisance weighs so many factors, it is difficult to apply. It is also judgmental, labeling the state that is found to have created a public nuisance as having committed a wrong against the rest of the world. This could discourage potentially belligerent states from subscribing to such a legal regime.

While public nuisance can be applied to the conduct of war itself, negligence could be applied either to the conduct of war or to individual actions taken in a war; in either case it has all the same difficulties as public nuisance. In the latter case, those difficulties are multiplied by the number of individual actions that must be considered. The enormous number of actions that could be addressed as negligent in a war and the corresponding number of factual situations that would have to be reconstructed to do so makes this approach of dubious value.

Strict liability for defective products does not address the major cause of environmental damage from war: defect-free products (weapons) causing precisely the types of damage they were designed to cause. But it does raise the question of whether weapons or other identifiable means of warfare that cause significant environmental destruction due to their design should be singled out, individually or as a class, for special treatment. There is ample international precedent for forbidding altogether the use of weapons that have particularly pernicious effects. Weapons of an especially environmentally destructive nature could be similarly outlawed. If they were, a state using them would be liable for the resulting environmental damage under the doctrine of negligence per se. Another approach would be a legal regime making users of such weapons strictly liable for environmental damage resulting from their use, rather than outlawing their use altogether. Either of these approaches would deter the use of weapons of an especially environmentally destructive nature and provide remediation for much environmental destruction, and they would do so in a manner already used by the family of nations. Of course, they would not deter or provide remediation for environmental damage caused by routine means of warfare.

The purpose of pollution control law is to prevent environmental damage in the first place. This protects the environment better than liability schemes, which provide remediation for damage once it occurs, presumably with some deterrent effect. But the world does not seem ready to subject the conduct of war to the relatively rigid types of processes, prohibitions, and restrictions inherent in pollution control programs. The effective implementation of such a regime would impose significant restrictions on statehood, and require an international bureaucracy that is able to intrude into national conduct by unrestricted inspections and to impose sanctions on nations for non-complying activity. Experience to date with international inspections suggests such a regime is unlikely to be embraced by the most belligerent states.

It should be noted, however, that the adoption of a tort-based liability scheme could well be a step towards a more ordered regime based on the pollution control model. And while the pollution control model may be an unlikely one to consider at this stage, some of its components may be useful. For example, the idea of technology-based standards can be applied both to prohibit the use of relatively environmentally damaging weapons and to allow the use of relatively non-damaging weapons. This would reinforce traditional prohibitions on the use of particularly pernicious weapons. The pollution control model for widely used products, primarily regulating the manufacture of the products rather than their use, reinforces the utility of this approach.

An international liability regime based on the oil spill, hazardous substance release, and coal mining remedial programs would incorporate the most useful legal devices examined above and could be tailored to avoid their most problematic effects. Such a scheme would be based on strict liability, which best meets the deterrence and remedial purposes of the regime. A warring state that causes environmental damage would be strictly liable for remediating the damage. This scheme would solve the problem of strictly liable parties that are unable to pay for remedial measures by providing a backup fund collected in advance. It could encourage the use of environmentally friendly weapons and discourage the use of environmentally unfriendly weapons by adjusting the assessments on their use or sale. It could avoid the reluctance of states to accept potentially enormous liability for what may be justified wars by adopting only the remedial fund approach instead of making any attempt to seek remediation costs for particular damage from any particular state. Assessments for such a fund should place the heaviest burden on states most likely to cause environmental damage in war. Such a charge could be calculated on the basis of the size of the army, the size of the arsenal, the types of weapons in the arsenal, etc. The use of the fund could be restricted to environmental damage that arises after its creation, or it could be available for damage that occurred before.

The fund approach also could be made more politically palatable by making assessments not on the use by states of weapons, munitions, and other war material, but on the manufacturers or sellers of such products. Of course, this would not insulate states from assessments when they produce such materials themselves rather than purchasing them on the international market. But even then, intrusion on their sovereignty would be minimized by making a neutral, non-judgmental assessment. Indeed, since arms production is a business, the assessment would be on the state in a proprietary capacity rather than in a sovereign capacity.

The fund approach deters war-caused environmental damage by raising the cost of weapons that cause such damage. It provides fairness by shifting the cost of environmental damage away from the environment itself and that part of international society most directly suffering the damage. It dilutes fairness somewhat by placing the cost on weapons purchasers (to whom the cost will be passed by the manufacturers) rather than just on weapons users. But that is more fair than leaving the burden where it was imposed by the weapons users themselves. Finally, the fund approach provides for economic efficiency. It incorporates into the cost of the weapons the cost of the environmental damage they cause: they pay their own way. And it avoids most of the criticisms leveled against both tort and environmental liability systems.

Of all the liability approaches, the fund scheme is the least intrusive on the sovereignty of nations. And it requires the lowest transaction costs to implement. It does leave some hard questions for economists and environmental managers. To what extent should environmental damage be remedied? What are the costs of remediation? How should assessments be established for different types of arms and ammunition to account for the damage they can cause? All but the last question, however, are issues that are common to any liability scheme that might be adopted.

PART III

ASSESSING THE IMPACTS –
SCIENTIFIC METHODS AND ISSUES

A · ECOLOGICAL AND NATURAL RESOURCE IMPACTS

INTRODUCTION

JESSICA D. JACOBY

Scientific assessment of the environmental impacts of wrongful actions forms the evidentiary basis for any case – wartime or peacetime, civil or criminal – by establishing the nature and extent of the damages. Assessment of impacts also provides a basis for rehabilitation. The methods for evaluating damages and appropriate restoration measures are as numerous and varied as the impacts themselves. Experience has shown, however, that the reliability of most of these methods is problematic at best. The chapters in this section provide an overview of the various ecological consequences of wars, relying primarily on examples from the 1990–91 Gulf War. They also provide valuable insight into the issues surrounding scientific methods for predicting and assessing these consequences.

Most impacts of war are multi-faceted. Aerial bombardment, for example, obviously has dire effects on terrestrial ecosystems. However, it also often destroys civilian infrastructure, such as sewage treatment facilities and electrical plants, which is vital to maintaining clean water and air. Classifying such impacts can be extremely difficult. In his chapter, Asit Biswas categorizes the various impacts he addresses by media – water, land, air, and other natural resources – although he acknowledges that such boundaries are necessarily somewhat artificial. Similarly, Samira Omar et al. and Mahmood Abdulraheem focus their chapters on the impacts of the 1990–91 Gulf War on the terrestrial and marine resources of Kuwait, respectively. Finally, Jeffrey McNeely discusses how wartime impacts affect biodiversity. In the end, a very intricate overall picture emerges, one that reflects the complex nature of war itself.

Omar et al. paint a harrowing picture of the 1990–91 Gulf War's impacts on Kuwait's terrestrial environment. Certainly the most notorious incident of this war was the intentional detonation of most of Kuwait's oil wells. The fires, and the "oil lakes" that formed after the fires were extinguished, have had a number of effects on the water, soil, air, flora, and fauna of Kuwait, several of which are detailed in the chapter. Air quality was severely impaired over the short term by the plumes of smoke, which stretched at one point for over 100 kilometers. The soils in and around the oil lakes were contaminated to varying extents, and soil farther away was covered by combusted and partially combusted oil particulates spread by the smoke plumes. Leachates from these oil-contaminated soils have entered the groundwater. Numerous birds and animals were either killed in the fires, or drowned in the oil lakes. In addition to the fires, Kuwait's fragile desert ecosystems and vital urban infrastructure were adversely impacted by the movement of vehicles, digging of trenches, aerial bombardment, and placement of thousands of landmines.

Abdulraheem's chapter delineates the impacts of the same conflict on the marine environment of the Persian Gulf, Gulf of Oman, and Arabian Sea, known collectively as the ROPME Sea Area (RSA). Development, particularly that associated with the petroleum industry, had already taken its toll on the RSA's various ecosystems, but the deliberate discharge of approximately 10 million barrels of oil during the Gulf War – the biggest oil spill in history – dwarfed the pre-existing damages. Abdulraheem notes that fisheries already taxed by over-harvesting and waters already polluted by anthropogenic discharges of more than 1 million barrels of oil per year were devastated by this spill, which affected the most shallow and highly productive area of the RSA. Further, he observes that fallout from the smoke plumes might actually cause more harm over the long term than the spills themselves.

McNeely addresses the impacts of modern warfare on the planet's biodiversity. Impacts on air quality, pollution of water resources, and debris from conventional weapons or destruction of infrastructure have numerous traumatic effects on the species that depend upon those resources as critical habitat. McNeely also discusses less obvious, but just as dire, consequences for biodiversity: the use of protected areas for military purposes, destruction of seed banks, the destructive impacts of large numbers of refugees or displaced persons on habitat, and so on. In other words, he concludes, both direct and indirect impacts to the ecology of an area can be detrimental to the biodiversity contained therein.

As exemplified by the various methods discussed by these authors, many of the standard ecological monitoring tools can be useful for determining air, water, and soil pollution resulting from wartime activities. For larger-scale impacts, aerial reconnaissance and remote sensing can be useful; these methods were extremely helpful in determining the extent of the damages from the oil fires in Kuwait.[1] Biological census can help to measure the impacts on various species, although this can be an expensive method; counting casualties is a related tool. Genetic analysis might be used to roughly determine impacts to the genetic material of species expected to suffer long-term consequences from causes such as radiation.

Each of these methods has its limitations. Remote sensing provides a general view of damage over large areas, but to truly understand the implications of what is shown through sensing images, appropriate groundwork is imperative. A biological census is usually limited to particular species, which tend to be larger "indicator" species that are easier to observe rather than more basic life forms that constitute the foundations of ecosystems; species also often avoid human contact, making accurate censuses difficult. Further, it can be hard to isolate the precise cause of particular population declines, and to link them to a specific action such as a war, chronic habitat loss associated with land conversion, climatic variations, natural population fluctuations, or a host of other possible causes. Finally, genetic analysis requires high levels of expertise and sophisticated equipment, and is often extremely expensive. Lack of baseline data regarding genetic makeup of the species being studied presents further difficulties.

In addition, the unpredictable nature of ecological systems makes reliance on any single method for assessing impacts unlikely to provide a meaningful level of accuracy. Such systems exhibit site-specific fluctuations that complicate our predictive and assessment capabilities for determining the ecological consequences of war. They also often behave in a non-linear fashion, with small changes resulting in amplified reactions that are nearly (if not completely) impossible to predict, and limiting our possibilities for establishing categorical "lessons learned." To complicate the situation further, by its very nature, war has social, political, cultural,

---

[1] See, e.g., Farouk El-Baz et al., "Detection by Satellite Images of Environmental Change Due to the Gulf War," in F. El-Baz and R. M. Makharita, *The Gulf War and the Environment* (USA: Gordon and Breach Science Publishers, 1994).

and economic dimensions that all affect the ultimate character of the impacts on the ecology where it takes place.

Another difficulty involved in determining the precise origin, extent, and ramifications of the ecological impacts of wars is a general lack of baseline data for comparison. Abdulraheem points to the absence of baseline data available on conditions in the RSA – the result of a lack of regional cooperation due, at least in part, to the Iran–Iraq War. Likewise, the lack of regional cooperation in itself acts as a constraint on effective rehabilitation efforts following wars. Conversely, civil wars are unlikely to have a clearly demarcated "end," and continued conflict and the need for domestic cooperation can stand in the way of meaningful assessment efforts.

Even if these efforts are completed, attempts at rehabilitation are not only technologically complex, but also extremely expensive, and often require exorbitant funds over long periods of time in order to complete remediation. Biswas identifies an apparent lack of interest in these issues on the part of scientists and funders as a major constraint on effective action. He also elaborates on the methodological constraints inherent in standard environmental impact assessment (EIA) procedure as another constraint on predicting the impacts of wars accurately. The EIA process itself lacks essential feedback mechanisms whereby those assessing the process might determine its effectiveness. Without such feedback and analysis, Biswas argues, it is impossible to rely on our predictive capabilities for the ecological impacts of wars. One example of the current attempts to overcome these obstacles is the ongoing effort of the United Nations High Commission for Refugees to establish environmental indicators by which to monitor and evaluate aspects of its efforts in areas affected by refugees.[2]

The need for improving our predictive capabilities is apparent in the context of the legal framework addressing the environmental consequences of war, discussed in previous chapters. As Michael Schmitt points out in chapter 3, future efforts in the legal and policy arenas need to be focused on determining precisely what it is the law intends to prohibit. Without a scientific basis for understanding what wartime impacts are and may be, this is a virtually impossible task. A related issue, addressed in detail by Silja Vöneky, is whether, and to what extent, peacetime rules relating

---

[2] United Nations High Commission for Refugees, "Environment: Recent Developments," available at http://www.unhcr.ch/environ/devels.html.

to environmental protection, which rely heavily on scientific knowledge, continue to apply during armed conflicts. For example, McNeely points to the possible application of the Convention on Biological Diversity as a potential constraint during war.

Beyond the impacts themselves, the methods used for predicting and assessing them, and the legal context in which both are set, there are additional issues that complicate the picture of the relationship between natural resources and war. The entire premise of this section of the book is that violent conflict leads to adverse consequences for the environments in which it takes place. As McNeely points out, however, war also can have positive effects on natural systems, however unintentional or short-lived they may be. For example, it has been hypothesized that the big game of the American Plains were kept from extinction before Europeans arrived by the existence of "buffer zones" between warring Indian tribes; this "no man's land," kept open by constant warfare, functioned basically as a game reserve.[3] McNeely analyzes this phenomenon further and states that war can even be seen as an adaptive mechanism through which humans retain their ability to stay within the productive limits of their ecosystems.

Another issue of increasingly current relevance is that of "environmental security." Depletion of common resources frequently fosters violent conflict, both domestically and internationally. Current global trends of overpopulation, increasing development, and the resulting pressure on our resource base ostensibly will engender further environmental security issues. Conversely, preserving natural resources might also become a tool for preventing war. McNeely suggests "Parks for Peace" as one such tool, with nations working together to develop cooperative management schemes for protecting resources that cross borders.

In the end, international technological and financial cooperation will be necessary to address the issues surrounding scientific assessment of the environmental consequences of war appropriately and thoroughly. Abdulraheem calls upon the United Nations to develop a funding mechanism, similar to those discussed in Part II, whereby victims of wartime environmental damage could take advantage of monetary resources made available by the international community. A portion of those funds could be utilized for initial reconnaissance and assessment of the damage, which

---

[3] William K. Stevens, "Unlikely Tool for Species Preservation: Warfare," *N.Y. Times* (Mar. 30, 1999), D1.

in turn could help set mitigation priorities and guide further expenditures. Even more immediately, Michael Schmitt calls in chapter 3 for the creation of a multi-disciplinary committee of experts to analyze environmental damage likely to be caused by military operations and develop a methodology for determining its severity. Such proposals merit further consideration when determining a future course of action, preferably before the emergence of new conflicts leads to further environmental devastation.

11

SCIENTIFIC ASSESSMENT OF THE LONG-TERM ENVIRONMENTAL CONSEQUENCES OF WAR

ASIT K. BISWAS

Introduction

The environmental impacts of wars are almost invariably adverse, regardless of whether they are caused by direct military actions or strategic counteractions, or collateral damages, or are the result of military support activities before or after the war. The total environmental damage caused by a specific war is the result of several factors. These include: the type of war (conventional, biological, chemical, or nuclear); the types of weapons and extent to which they are used; the duration and intensity of the war; the extent and type of terrain over which the war is fought; the strategies used during the war; and the prewar environmental conditions. These factors also affect the duration of the specific environmental impacts. It has been estimated that some 200 armed conflicts have occurred since World War II, mostly in developing countries. These wars have killed more than 20 million people and displaced several millions more, causing serious environmental and economic damages.[1]

Environmental impacts of wars

The environmental impacts of wars are often multi-dimensional. They also often have repercussions in areas long distances away from those of concentrated battle and over prolonged periods of time, long after the wars have ended. Several possible environmental impacts of war are explored below.

[1] M. A. Tolba and O. A. El-Kholy, *The World Environment 1972–1992* (London and New York: Chapman and Hall on behalf of UNEP, 1992).

IMPACTS ON LAND

Land is affected both by direct war actions and by military operations (preparations for war). Bombs and missiles contribute to the formation of craters, compaction and erosion of soil, and soil contamination by toxic and hazardous residues. Land use patterns often change over prolonged periods of time due to the continued presence of landmines and other remnants of war. Use of biological, chemical, and nuclear weapons is also likely to change land use patterns significantly by precluding any productive use of land for very long periods of time – even centuries.

There are also those activities that specifically target land resources. For example, deliberate deforestation efforts can alter the prevailing land, water, and biotic regimes, with any number of resulting adverse consequences. Another example is the degradation of soil conditions that resulted from the oil well fires in Kuwait. Deducing the appropriate methods for amelioration of such damages to soil, as well as actually carrying them through, is likely to be a costly and technologically difficult endeavor, putting off further the productive use of the affected lands.

Use of land for military operations also contributes significantly to environmental damage. Globally, it is estimated that the amount of land used for these purposes ranges between 750,000 and 1,500,000 km^2, an area that is likely larger than the total surface areas of France and United Kingdom combined (797,000 km^2).[2] This prevents the land from being used for alternative purposes, such as urbanization, agricultural production, habitat preservation, or recreation. For example, up until the 1980s the US military was the largest holder of agricultural land in the Philippines, a significant portion of which was left idle. In Kazakhstan, more land is currently reserved for the use of the military than is made available for wheat production.

IMPACTS ON WATER

Water contamination (of both surface and groundwater) is also a common result of various types of warfare. Use of chemical, biological, or nuclear weapons can contribute to long-term water pollution, with attendant health

---

[2] World Bank, *World Development Report 1998–1999* (1998).

hazards for humans and the associated ecosystems. Appropriate remedial techniques for such contamination are often technologically impossible or extremely expensive, technologically complex, and require very high levels of scientific expertise. It is precisely these aspects that are not readily available in many countries in the developing world where most wars have been fought in recent decades.

Water and wastewater treatment plants and water distribution and sewer systems are often direct and/or indirect victims of war. During World War II, the British targeted German dams for destruction.[3] Similarly, the American military bombed dams in North Korea during the Korean War.[4] Immediately following World War II, productivity of the water distribution systems in Tokyo decreased by nearly 90 percent as a result of damage caused by the war and the channeling of resources (both financial and professional) away from efficient operation of the systems and into the war efforts.[5] By contrast, the current losses from the water distribution system in Tokyo are only 7 percent, the second best in the world after Singapore at 6 percent.[6] The direct costs of repairing the damages to water supply and wastewater systems caused by war are high. The indirect costs of such destruction to human health are simply unknown and mostly incalculable.

IMPACTS ON AIR QUALITY

In addition to the atmospheric emissions from the vehicles and other equipment used during routine war activities and military operations, serious air pollution often occurs as a result of the use of chemical, biological, and nuclear weapons. The aggressive act of setting fire to the Kuwaiti oilfields resulted in extensive air pollution in the region. Depending on the extent and nature of the air pollution and the prevailing topographical and atmospheric conditions around the area where it originates, airborne pollutants can travel over long distances, contribute to acid rain, and cause serious health hazards for humans and other living organisms located within the affected zone.

---

[3] Stockholm International Peace Research Institute/United Nations Environment Program, *Environmental Hazards of War* (London and Newbury Park: SAGE Publications, 1990).
[4] *Ibid.*   [5] Tolba and El-Kholy, *The World Environment.*
[6] Juha I. Uitto and Asit K. Biswas, *Water for Urban Areas in the 21st Century* (Tokyo and New York: United Nations Univ. Press, 1999).

NOISE

Conventional weapons and low-flying jets can generate high levels of noise (140 decibels or more) which could have long-term impacts on the hearing of people subjected to it.

RESOURCE DEPLETION

Resource depletion is an important environmental impact of war that has generally received inadequate attention. Even during peacetime, military use of energy and non-renewable resources is substantial. It has been estimated that global petroleum consumption for military purposes is about 6 percent of the total world consumption, or almost one-half of the total consumption of all developing countries combined.[7]

Nearly 85 percent of the total energy used by the United States government is for military purposes.[8] For example, the fuel used by an F-16 training jet in less than one hour is nearly equivalent to what an average US motorist uses over a period of two years.[9] The amount of energy used to produce weapons is also high: in the US it is almost equivalent to twice that of the energy directly used by the military.[10] Further, during wartime, when high technology and sophisticated weapons are used, total energy used by the military might increase by factors of five to twenty times over the levels used during peacetime, depending on the conditions that prevail during any specific war.[11]

Military uses of other non-renewable resources are also significant. For example, global military consumption of aluminum, copper, nickel, and platinum is higher than the total consumption of these metals by all the developing countries of the world combined. It has been estimated that the military accounts for 11 percent of global copper use, 9 percent of iron, and 8 percent of lead. Overall, on a global basis, between 2 and 11 percent of fourteen important minerals is consumed for military purposes: aluminum, chromium, copper, fluorspar, iron ore, lead, manganese, mercury, nickel, platinum, silver, tin, tungsten, and zinc.[12] Global consumption of aluminum, copper, nickel, and platinum for military purposes is greater

[7] Tolba and El-Kholy, *The World Environment.*
[8] United Nations Environment Program, *Internal Documents on Peace and Security* (1991).
[9] *Ibid.*   [10] *Ibid.*   [11] *Ibid.*   [12] S. S. Kim, *The Quest for a Just World Order* (1984).

than Latin America's consumption for all purposes.[13] The environmental impacts of the mining activities associated with such high levels of extraction of resources are certainly significant.

War efforts generate vast quantities of hazardous materials, the environmentally sound disposal of which is a difficult, time-consuming, and expensive task. The manufacture, maintenance, storage, and use of weapons alone generate great varieties and tremendous quantities of these wastes.

Undoubtedly, the military establishments of the United States and the countries of the former Soviet Union are two of the largest global producers of hazardous wastes. It has been estimated that the US Defense Department produces between 400,000 and 500,000 tons of toxic wastes annually.[14] This estimate does not include the hazardous wastes produced by defense contractors, or the Department of Energy, which produces nuclear weapons. Because of the secrecy invariably associated with military activities, the types and quantities of hazardous wastes generated, appropriateness of the practices currently used for their disposal, and the overall environmental and health impacts of hazardous waste management processes are virtually unknown.

Chemical warfare introduces hazardous materials to the environment. Despite this, use of such weapons has historically been widespread. Chemicals like chlorine, phosgene, diphosgene, and mustard gas were used by both sides during World War I. The British used herbicides for defoliation in Malaysia during the late 1940s and early 1950s. The United States used about 44 million litres of Agent Orange, 20 million litres of Agent White, and 8 million litres of Agent Blue over 1.7 million hectares in Vietnam from 1961 to 1971.[15] Some areas were sprayed several times. These practices contributed to serious environmental damage, such as large-scale devastation of crops, deforestation, soil loss due to reduction in vegetation, destruction of wildlife habitat, and decline in fish catch. They also had adverse impacts on human health, resulting in predisposition of

[13] *Ibid.* [14] UNEP, *Internal Documents.*

[15] Stockholm International Peace Research Institute/United Nations Environment Program, *Herbicides in War* (London and Philadelphia: Taylor & Francis, 1984).

the exposed populations to cancers, chromosomal damages, spontaneous abortions, and other conditions.[16]

The environmental and health problems associated with the safe disposal of radioactive materials and the wastes that are the result of the world's nuclear weapons programs are neither easy to quantify, nor possible to solve with the present level of technology. Accidents at nuclear facilities pose an additional problem. Up to 1995, 212 such accidents with nuclear-powered vessels can be documented worldwide. Further, at least seven nuclear-powered reactors and forty-eight nuclear warheads lie on the ocean floor because of accidents.[17] Their long-term environmental impacts are basically unknown.

An additional environmental concern that has recently surfaced is that of the US military's use of depleted uranium in ammunitions during the Gulf War and the Kosovo conflict. It is not known what the long-term environmental and health impacts on ecosystems and humans from this depleted uranium will be.

Assessment of long-term environmental impacts of war

Even though the reliable assessment of the environmental consequences of war is an important topic, it historically has been a largely ignored area of study and research. Considerable general information is currently available regarding the potential environmental impacts of wars. However, a detailed, comprehensive, and authoritative study on the actual short-, medium-, and long-term environmental impacts of a single war anywhere in the world is conspicuously absent. Environmental scholars, development experts, and political scientists, for whatever reasons, have shied away from carrying out such studies, even though the importance and relevance of such studies is indisputable.

Equally, international organizations like the various United Nations agencies (UNEP, UNDP, UNESCO, etc.) have basically ignored this critical issue. Further, in spite of its importance, no major, serious, multidisciplinary international conference on this complex subject has been organized until now. It is thus to be hoped that the interest and momentum generated by the First International Conference on Addressing

---

[16] *Ibid.*; see also Alastair Hay, "Defoliants: The Long-term Health Implications," chapter 16 in this volume.

[17] Stockholm International Peace Research Institute/UNEP, *Herbicides in War*.

Environmental Consequences of War, held in Washington, D.C. in June 1998, will go a long way to interest scholars and experts to initiate major studies in this area in the foreseeable future.

There are, of course, many generalized assessments of environmental impacts of war, but their reliability and usefulness leave much to be desired. There are many reasons why we are presently facing this sad situation, in spite of the fact that the environmental impacts of wars are generally accepted to be considerable. Since the main focus of this chapter is the scientific methods of assessing ecological damages from war, only the major scientific reasons for not being able to carry out realistic environmental assessment will be analyzed herein.

METHODOLOGICAL CONSTRAINTS

There are major methodological constraints on accurate forecasting of medium- and long-term environmental impacts. The first and most far-reaching of these is the environmental impact assessment (EIA) process itself, the likeliest tool to be used in forecasting the environmental impacts of war. The first country where EIA became a formal requirement was the United States, with the passage of the National Environmental Protection Act in 1970. Soon thereafter, EIA became mandatory in Canada and certain Western European and Asian countries.[18]

The techniques and the processes that are presently used to forecast environmental impacts have undergone only minor changes, both conceptually and methodologically, since they first came into practice in the early 1970s.[19] The most notable change during the past quarter of a century in this area has been our capacity to analyze increasing numbers of parameters and data more cost-effectively, which may be attributed to the fact that computers have become more powerful and economical.

In retrospect, environmental assessment techniques were acceptable, even laudable, in the early 1970s. They constituted a significant improvement over the then-prevailing practices. Unfortunately, these techniques have

---

[18] P. Modak and Asit K. Biswas, *Conducting Environmental Impact Assessments for Developing Countries* (New York: McGraw-Hill, 1999); Asit K. Biswas and S. B. C. Agarwala, *Environmental Impact Assessments for Developing Countries* (Oxford and Boston: Butterworth-Heinemann, 1992).

[19] Asit K. Biswas, *Water Resources: Environmental Planning, Management and Development* (New York: McGraw-Hill, 1997).

been used continuously for more than twenty-five years on the assumption that they are reliable and effectively improve environmental management practices. Similarly, international organizations, ranging from the United Nations Environment Program to the World Bank, now utilize the same techniques without ever analyzing the extent to which they effectively predict medium- to long-term environmental impacts with any degree of certainty. Hundreds of international and national guidelines are available on EIA, but scarcely a single objective study is available on the comparative effectiveness of these guidelines in predicting and managing environmental impacts.

In fact, there do exist several fundamental problems with the current environmental assessment techniques, which have been analyzed in detail.[20] While environmental assessment has become a real growth industry globally, nearly exclusive emphasis is placed on prediction of the various impacts that will likely arise from possible interventions in a project requiring assessment. Once the assessment is completed and reviewed by an appropriate governmental or legal entity, the process is considered complete for all practical purposes.

Unfortunately, the environmental assessment process, as it is practiced at present, is still an art rather than a science. There are numerous interacting physical, technical, economic, environmental, and social factors that need to be considered, making it very difficult to assess in advance the net results of all the interactions due to any specific intervention, especially one as multi-faceted as war. In addition, many environmental impacts are site-specific, making accurate predictions extremely difficult. Factors such as the time when specific problems may surface, the magnitude of each impact, and the spatial distribution of the impacts over any area provide examples of the sorts of issues that are extremely difficult to predict with accuracy.

A major reason for this unsatisfactory state of affairs is the near-total absence of monitoring and evaluation of the actual environmental impacts caused by actual interventions. Even for standard development projects, it is highly unlikely that even 0.1 percent of them, on a global basis, are currently monitored on a medium- to long-term basis.[21] In the absence of monitored results, the hypotheses on the basis of which environmental

---

[20] For example, see Modak and Biswas, *Conducting Environmental Impact Assessments*; Biswas, *Water Resources*.

[21] Biswas, *Water Resources*.

assessments are carried out cannot be validated or further improved. Thus, the biases and errors that have been inherent in the process from the beginning are continually being perpetuated all over the world.

If the situation is bad for "normal" development projects, on which hundreds of thousands of environmental assessments have already been carried out globally, it is significantly worse when assessment of the environmental impacts of wars are considered. This is partly because predicting the environmental impacts of wars involves even more complicating factors, and partly because no such comprehensive assessment has ever been carried out. On the basis of anecdotal evidence, it is clear that there are often extensive and significant differences between the predicted and actual impacts of development projects. In the case of wars, we scarcely have even a single case study where an attempt has been made to assess the environmental impacts comprehensively, let alone to compare the differences between the actual and predicted impacts. Even for the Gulf War, several years after its completion, we do not yet have sufficient object-ive and reliable assessments of its potential long-term environmental impacts. It is really an indictment on our present society, which can spend billions of dollars on a war, yet fails to make comparatively minor amounts readily available to monitor and evaluate the long-term environmental con-sequences of those wars.

One reason for the discrepancies between real and predicted impacts of wars is the considerable risks and uncertainties that are invariably associ-ated with any reliable analysis of non-linear complex systems. Water regimes and biological populations are notoriously variable by nature. Their normal perturbations are often so great that the collection of statistically significant data to make definitive cause-and-effect linkages is very expens-ive, and can even prove impossible due to political or national security reasons (such as when environmental impacts of wars are to be studied). Under such conditions, and at our present state of knowledge, it is simply not feasible to identify definitively which variations could be due to natural causes, and which are attributable to the direct and indirect con-sequences of a war.

Similarly, cause-and-effect relationships of the health impacts of wars are not easy to define, especially when the impacts are due to low levels of sustained exposure from biological, chemical, or radiological elements from natural, man-made, and/or war-related sources. The scientific basis for assessing such dose-response relationships, and the determination of which impact, or even which parts of impacts, are due to war as opposed to "normal" exposures, leaves much to be desired. Currently, it is very difficult, if not impossible, to assign a chronic health impact to a specific cause or causes stemming from any war.

The difficulties in assessing such impacts are apparent in the discrepancies between estimates for impacts of specific wars and their actual outcomes. For example, during the Vietnam War, Agent Orange was considered to be harmless to human health, even though no authoritative toxicological studies were carried out prior to its use that could withstand peer review. It was used extensively for defoliation purposes before the mutagenic and teratogenic impacts of the herbicide were realized, and only then after some American scientists challenged the thinking of the US Defense Department that the herbicide had no serious health impacts. Unquestionably, the extensive use of Agent Orange has caused extensive environmental and health damages on a long-term basis in Vietnam.[22]

The 1990–91 Gulf War is a prime example of the difficulties of predicting environmental impacts of wars, and the need for assessing what is predicted as compared to what actually happens. Several environmental impacts of this war were overestimated. For example, it was widely reported in the media during and after the war that the impacts would include:

- Changes in global climate;
- A significant increase in the rate of global warming;
- Changes in monsoon patterns, especially in Southeast Asia;
- Serious air quality problems in countries as far away as India and Bangladesh;
- The possibility of a global "nuclear winter";
- Large-scale acute and chronic health impacts; and
- Catastrophic changes in coastal ecosystems.

It is now generally agreed that the actual environmental impacts are most likely significantly less than what were forecasted. It is now mostly accepted that:

- The smoke did not affect global climate because of its low altitude. The base of the smoke plume was generally at heights between 0.5 to 2 km, and its top was typically in the range of 3 to 4 km. The plume was never

[22] For a more detailed discussion of the health impacts of Agent Orange use in Vietnam, see Hay, "Defoliants."

detected above 6 km, the height necessary for large quantities of soot to enter the jet stream. In addition, its short residence time ruled out any realistic possibility of a "nuclear winter";

- Carbon dioxide emissions from the war are now estimated at 300 million metric tons, only about 1.5 percent of the current global emissions from the burning of fossil fuels and biomass;
- The impact on global warming is likely to be so small that it would be immeasurable because the extent, intensity, and duration of the fires were not significant on a global scale;
- Long-distance transport of air pollutants has not been substantiated. No impacts have been noted in India or Bangladesh in terms of day-to-day weather, or changes in monsoon patterns;
- Ground-level concentrations of nitrogen oxides, carbon monoxide, hydrogen sulfide, and ozone did not even exceed the local standards of Kuwait and Saudi Arabia. However, there were times when sulfur dioxide levels exceeded local standards;
- Anecdotal evidence indicates that many parts of Kuwait's desert ecosystem are recovering faster than initially anticipated; and
- Long-term health impacts are unlikely to be significant, and even if these do prove to be significant, they cannot be scientifically attributed to the war because detailed baseline data are not available from earlier periods to make such comparisons statistically significant.

While no reliable scientific data are presently available to indicate that the Kuwaiti oil fires had many long-range and long-term effects on the global atmosphere, no one can question their local, and even regional, impacts. There were some 610 oil fires, covering seven oilfields to the north and south of Kuwait City. The fires consumed over 6 million barrels of crude oil and 70 million cubic meters of associated gases daily.[23] The smoke plumes were 15 to 150 km wide, at distances of 0 to 1,000 km from the fires. The plumes were not generally photochemically active until they had travelled approximately 200 km, which lessened their overall impacts. The ozone concentration occasionally exceeded 120 parts per billion inside the plume, around 1,000 km downwind from the source. Visibility, local and regional temperatures, and solar flux were also reduced under the plume.[24] The smoke particles coagulated as they were transported downwind, which

[23] Modak and Biswas, *Conducting Environmental Impact Assessments.*   [24] *Ibid.*

accelerated their removal potential by cloud and rain. The medium- to long-term impacts of the resulting soot and oil deposition over much of Kuwait and northeastern Saudi Arabia on soil, water, and biota are basically unknown at present. Unquestionably, the terrestrial biosphere of Kuwait was adversely impacted by the fires.

LACK OF SCIENTIFIC INTEREST

It should be noted that nearly all the wars during the past five decades have occurred in the developing world. Not surprisingly, environmental scientists from developed countries have shown very limited interest in such wars unless their own countries were involved, as was the case for the Vietnam War and the 1990–91 Gulf War. Even then, the interest was focused only on limited aspects of the environmental consequences; for example, on implications of using defoliant herbicides in Vietnam, or the climatic impacts of the Kuwaiti oil fires. No attempt was made to conduct comprehensive monitoring and assessment of the overall environmental impacts of these wars, even though such studies are vitally necessary.

Regrettably, scientists from the developing countries where most of these wars are taking place also have shown very little interest in this area. Further, until recently, no sustained effort has been made by international organizations to encourage sufficient funding and thorough investigation of this issue. This is despite the fact that many such countries have suffered, and will continue to suffer, from major adverse environmental impacts due to these wars. A good example of this lack of commitment is seen in the international reaction to the impacts of the Gulf War. After the initial flurry of activities immediately following the termination of the war, there has been insufficient visible sustained effort by the appropriate international organizations to monitor and objectively evaluate the environmental impacts of the war. Whatever limited efforts were made highlighted the problem of inadequate coordination and insufficient communication between the various organizations involved, and then disappeared fairly quickly after an initial indication of interests.[25]

[25] See, however, Green Cross International, *An Environmental Assessment of Kuwait, Seven Years After the War* (1998).

Conclusion

Assessment of the long-term environmental consequences of war is an important issue, but it has neither received nor is receiving adequate attention thus far. The scientific profession has first to realize that there is a major gap in our knowledge base in this subject that needs to be filled. Simultaneously, funding agencies need to be convinced that this is an important area of research that deserves priority financial support on a long-term basis.

Considering that reliable assessments of the environmental impacts of war are important at both the national and international levels, both for taking appropriate countermeasures and developing international policies and norms, this is an area of scientific investigation that should receive urgent attention. Without a reliable base of knowledge, it is simply not possible to develop and implement appropriate environmental mitigation measures in a timely, cost-effective manner.

On the other hand, in December 1998, Green Cross International (GCI) published the results of a multi-disciplinary study on the impacts of the 1990–91 Gulf War.[26] The study was funded by the Kuwait Foundation for the Advancement of Sciences, and provides information that is vital, as it may be compared with the initial predictions, and such a comparison could help to explain why many of the initial predictions were inaccurate. This comparison could also further improve the current state of the art in terms of methodologies available. It is of note that the Allies, who spent billions of dollars on this war, have so far shown no interest in conducting or promoting such a study, even though the benefits that would accrue from additional work are unquestionable. Utilizing the GCI case study as a mechanism for assessing the methodological constraints would benefit environmental assessments worldwide, both on a national and on an international level.

[26] *Ibid.*

12

THE GULF WAR IMPACT ON THE TERRESTRIAL ENVIRONMENT OF KUWAIT: AN OVERVIEW

SAMIRA A. S. OMAR, ERNEST BRISKEY,
RAAFAT MISAK, AND ADEL A. S. O. ASEM

Introduction

Kuwait constitutes a portion of the northwestern coastal plain of the Arabian Gulf. It covers an area of approximately 17,818 km², and is characterized by arid conditions, with an average annual precipitation of approximately 105 mm. Strong northwesterly winds prevail, particularly during spring and summer. The maximum wind speed is approximately 29 m/s and usually peaks in May. Summer is extremely hot, with temperatures peaking in July and August at an average of 45°C.

The population of Kuwait is 1.5 million (1995), with a maximum population density of 87 persons/km². Oil, natural gas, groundwater, and fisheries are the major natural resources in Kuwait. As of 1994, oil production was approximately 2.1 million barrels/day. The production of natural gas reached 7.6 billion m³ in 1995.[1]

The terrestrial ecosystem of Kuwait is comprised of a diversity of plant and animal species. Like most Arabian Gulf countries, Kuwait's land resources are used for livestock grazing, water production, oil production, and sand and gravel quarrying, as well as for agricultural production. Traditionally, the terrestrial environment has also been used during mild seasons for wildlife hunting (mainly for birds). During hot and dry periods, the soil becomes extremely vulnerable to wind erosion, particularly when it is disturbed or becomes barren.

---

[1] Organization of Petroleum Exporting Countries, *Annual Statistical Bulletin* (1994).

During the Iraqi invasion and occupation of Kuwait, there occurred one of the worst man-made environmental disasters of all time.[2] Personnel carriers moved across the desert lands destroying foliage, tearing up soil surfaces, and disrupting terrestrial habitats.[3] Hundreds of kilometers of ditches were dug and thousands of makeshift shelters were constructed.[4] Vast quantities of solid, semi-solid, and liquid wastes were merely discarded, causing severe pollution in the terrestrial environment, and millions of landmines were placed throughout the country.[5] Beginning on February 17, 1991, at ten- to fifteen-minute intervals, Iraqi troops exploded most of Kuwait's oil wells, causing vast amounts of oil to spew out onto the land surface.[6] The flow of this oil followed land surface depressions and formed hundreds of "oil lakes." These lakes varied in surface dimensions and penetrated, even saturated (10–20 percent), the soil to varying depths.[7]

---

[2] United States General Accounting Office, Efforts to Address Health Effects of the Kuwait Oil Fires, GAO/HRD 92–50 (1992); N. Al-Awadhi, A. El-Nawawy, and R. Al-Daher, "*In-Situ and On-Site Bioremediation of Oil-Contaminated Soil in Kuwait*," proceedings of the Third World Academy of Sciences (1992); D. Al-Ajmi, "Effects of Mixing Height and Wind Speed on the Dispersion of Air Pollution in Kuwait," Harvard Conference on Kuwait Oil-Fire Impact (1991).

[3] Al-Houty, M. Abdal, and S. Zaman, "Preliminary Assessment of the Gulf War on Kuwait Desert Ecosystem," *J. Envtl. Sci. Health* 8 (1993), 1705–26; M. N. Alaa El-Din, A. H. Dashti, A. S. Abdu, and H. A. Nasrallah, "Environmental Impacts of Burned Oil Wells and Military Operations on Some Desert Plants and Soils of Kuwait," in *Proceedings of the International Conference on the Effects of the Iraqi Aggression on the State of Kuwait, Vol. III: Environmental and Health Effects and Remediation* (Kuwait Univ., 1996).

[4] S. Zaman and F. Alsdirawi, *Assessment of the Gulf Environmental Crisis Impacts on Kuwait's Desert Renewable Natural Resources* (Kuwait Institute for Scientific Research, 1993); D. Al-Ajmi, R. Misak, A. Al-Dousari, and A. Al-Enezi, "Impact of the Iraqi War Machinery and Ground Fortifications on the Surface Sediments and Aeolian Processes in Kuwait," in *The International Conference on the Effects of the Iraqi Aggression on the State of Kuwait*.

[5] S. A. Nawawy and K. Puskas, *Proposal: Strategic Master Plan for the Management of Solid, Semi-Solid, Liquid, and Hazardous Wastes in Kuwait* (1993); M. Al-Sudairawi, R. Misak, and R. Al-Nifaisi, "Environmental Impact Assessment of the Iraqi Strategic Mine Fields in the Southern Portion of Kuwait," in *The International Conference on the Effects of the Iraqi Aggression on the State of Kuwait*; G. Karrar, M. A. Mian, and M. N. Alsa El-Din, *A Rapid Assessment of the Impacts of the Iraqi–Kuwait Conflict on Terrestrial Ecosystems, Part Two: The State of Kuwait* (Bahrain: UNEP/ROWA, 1991); M. H. Al-Attar, "An Integrated Approach for Overcoming the Adverse Environmental Impacts Inflicted Upon Kuwait During the Iraqi Occupation," proceedings of the International Symposium on Environment, Budapest (1994).

[6] Al-Awadhi et al., "*In-Situ* and On-Site Bioremediation"; Al-Attar, "An Integrated Approach."

[7] N. Al-Awadhi, M. T. Balba, K. Puskas, R. Al-Daher, H. Tsuji, H. Cheno, K. Tsuji, M. Iwabuchi, and S. Kumamoto, "Remediation and Rehabilitation of Oil-Contaminated Lake Beds in the Kuwait Desert," *J. Aridland Studies/Special Issue of Desert Technology III* 55 (1995), 195–98.

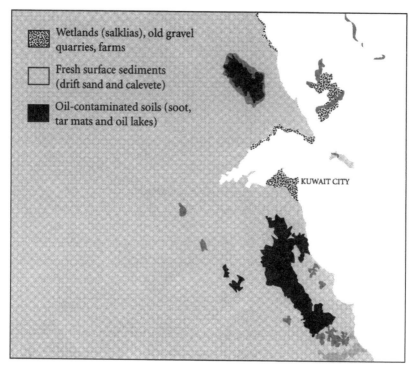

Wetlands (salklias), old gravel
quarries, farms

Fresh surface sediments
(drift sand and calevete)

Oil-contaminated soils (soot,
tar mats and oil lakes)

KUWAIT CITY

12.1 Satellite remote sensing applications in the state of Kuwait

The oil remained in the lakes in the form of sludge and non-combusted, partially combusted, and partially weathered liquid products, all of which were vulnerable to rainstorm events on the filled playa, which caused severe runoff.[8] The oil mist and soot particle fallout from the oil-fire plumes covered vast areas of downwind terrestrial surfaces. Saltwater spray used during the fire-fighting activities following the explosions further compounded the damage to the terrestrial environment. The impacts of these activities on plants, wildlife, migratory birds, sand movement, water quality, and human security were substantial.

In sum, the military activities during the occupation and liberation of Kuwait, and through the rehabilitation period of August 1990 to July 1994, included the following:

[8] M. T. Balba, "Remediation and Rehabilitation of the Jaidan Garden," proposal to the Kuwait Institute for Scientific Research (1994).

- Transport of troops, ground entrenchment, and landmine implantation (August 2, 1990 to January 16, 1991);
- Air campaigns and ground battles (January 17 to February 26, 1991);
- Oil-well fires (January to November 1991); and
- Rehabilitation and reconstruction activities (March 1991 to July 1994).

Thus, five long-term environmental consequences of the 1990–91 Gulf War were identified: soil compaction, degradation of vegetation, surface sediment disruption, soil contamination, and groundwater pollution.[9]

This chapter summarizes the immediate and long-term impacts that the 1990–91 Gulf War has had on Kuwait's terrestrial environment. It also examines the impacts of the terrestrial environment rehabilitation efforts that were undertaken during the aftermath and recovery from the war. Finally, this chapter discusses the remedial work still in progress on the terrestrial environment, as well as the tasks yet to be undertaken.

Dimensions of the impacts on Kuwait's terrestrial environment

The invasion, occupation, and liberation warfare all seriously disrupted many aspects of Kuwait's terrestrial environment.[10] The massive releases by Iraq of Kuwaiti oil made this war particularly notorious from a terrestrial environment standpoint. The United Nations Security Council resolved that Iraq was liable for all direct environmental damage to Kuwait's natural resources.[11]

OIL POLLUTION OF SOIL

The Iraqi aggression resulted in the detonation, destruction, and ignition of 1,164 oil wells (91.8 percent of the producing wells).[12] The condition of these wells was as follows: 652 blazing, 75 gushing, and 437 completely

---

[9] R. F. Misak, M. Al-Sudairawi, I. Charib, A. Al-Dousari, R. Al-Nafisi, and M. Ahmed, "Environmental Impact Assessment of the Gulf War with Emphasis on Rehabilitation Activities," prepared for the International Conference on the Long-Term Effects of the Gulf War, Kuwait (Nov. 18–20, 1996).

[10] A. H. Westing, "Environmental Protection from Wartime Damage: The Role of International Law," in Nils Petter Gleditsch (ed.), *Conflict and the Environment* (Dordrecht: Kluwer Academic Publishers, 1997).

[11] United Nations Security Council Resolution 687.

[12] A. Y. Al-Ghunaim, *Devastating Oil Wells as Revealed by Iraqi Documents* (Center for Research and Studies of Kuwait, 1997).

destroyed.[13] The intact wells that survived the explosions numbered 104.[14] The aggressive actions also included the destruction of oil refineries, storage depots, and power and water stations.

The blazing and gushing oil wells (over 700) spewed vast amounts of oil onto the land. It is estimated that over 60 million barrels were released, forming 246 oil lakes covering over 49 km^2.[15] Consequently, some 40 million tons of soil have been heavily contaminated with oil.[16] The general geographic distribution of the oil lakes and tar mats in the northern and southern areas of the country is shown in Figure 12.1.

Downwind plumes of oil particulates were carried mainly by the prevailing northwesterly winds, and resulted in the spreading of combusted and partially combusted oil components along a northwest–southeast line of land stretching from the oilfields, and covering approximately 100,000 hectares of land overall.[17] The contaminants spread across this terrestrial surface varied from layers of scattered soot, to areas hideously stained as if charred by fire, to areas covered by a measurable thickness (over 2 cm) of fallout material.[18] The extent of the deposits has been estimated by satellite imagery, aerial photography, and field screenplay. Overall, it has been estimated that more than 900 km^2 have been contaminated with oil.

Gas chromatographic/mass spectrophotometric analysis of soil taken from areas 500 and 1,500 meters from the oil fires revealed that concentrations of polycyclic aromatic hydrocarbons (PAHs) were higher in the more distant samples.[19] The concentration of benzofluoranthene/ benzopyrene increased threefold with distance.[20] While there has been no ground-confirmed mapping of these fallout areas, the projections of the movement of the aerial plumes have been calculated. It also has been estimated that the fires released upwards of half a million tons of aerial pollutants per day, much of which fell on the terrestrial environment before the plumes moved out to sea. The amount of oil lost due to both the fires and oil flows has been calculated as approximately 1.0–1.5 billion barrels. Table 12.1 summarizes these impacts on the terrestrial environment of Kuwait.

---

[13] *Ibid.*   [14] *Ibid.*

[15] N. Al-Awadhi, M. Abdal, and E. J. Briskey, "Assessment of Technologies for the Remediation of Oil-Contaminated Soil Resulting from Exploded Oil Wells and Burning Oil Fires in Kuwait," proceedings of the Third World Academy of Sciences (1997); Al-Attar, "An Integrated Approach."

[16] Al-Awadhi et al., "*In-Situ* and On-Site Bioremediation."

[17] Al-Awadhi et al., "Assessment of Technologies."   [18] *Ibid.*

[19] Al-Houty et al., "Preliminary Assessment of the Gulf War," 1705–26.   [20] *Ibid.*

Remote sensing Landsat Thematic Mapper™ data taken from 1987 to 1995 were evaluated to show the before and after terrestrial environments downwind from the damaged wells.[21] The oil from certain oil lakes has now been drained, but both heavily saturated and lightly contaminated terrestrial soils remain. In other cases, the weathering of the oil in the lakes has shrunk the circumference of the lake, with the peripheral surface areas drying and fragmenting.[22] In many cases, sand drifts have covered the visible appearance of the accumulated oil.[23] In all cases, the heavily and lightly contaminated soils remain in the terrestrial environment. Not only has the oil in the lakes penetrated the soil to varying depths (averaging 1 m), but the addition of salty water to extinguish the fires plus the rains that have followed have washed oil pollutants downward to a recorded depth of 20 m in certain areas.[24]

The composition of the oil in the lakes varied depending on the crude composition, the degree of combustion, the surface temperature of the lake, the fallout of the partially combusted oil, and the relative amount of seawater or highly brackish water used in fighting the fires surrounding a particular lake.[25] The composition of the oil and its components has also varied over time. Volatile aromatics have been lost to the atmosphere, and the overall concentration of aromatics has increased, as have resins. Thus,

[21] A. Y. Kwarteng and D. Al-Ajmi, "Using Landsat Thematic Mapper Data to Detect and Map Vegetation Changes in Kuwait," *Int'l Archives Photogrammetry and Remote Sensing* 31 (1996), 398–405; A. Y. Kwarteng and D. Al-Ajmi, "Satellite Remote Sensing Applications in the State of Kuwait," Kuwait Institute for Scientific Research report (1997); A. Y. Kwarteng, V. Singhroy, R. Saint-Jean, and D. Al-Ajmi, "RADARSAT SAR Data Assessment of the Oil Lakes in the Greater Burgan Oil Field, Kuwait," proceedings from International Symposium on the topic (1997).

[22] J. Al-Sunaimi, unpublished data for the Kuwait Institute for Scientific Research (1992); J. Saeed, H. Al-Hashash, and K. Al-Matrouk, "Assessment of the Changes in the Chemical Components of the Crude Oil Spilled in the Kuwait Desert After Weathering for Five Years," *Envt. Int'l* 24 (1998), 141–52.

[23] A. Y. Kwarteng, "Multitemporal Remote Sensing Data Analysis of the Kuwait Oil Lakes," *Envt. Int'l* 24 (1998), 121–37.

[24] Al-Attar, "An Integrated Approach"; M. N. Viswanathan, "Rainfall Induced Transport of Crude Oil Contaminants From Unsaturated Zones," Kuwait Institute for Scientific Research report WH007K (1995).

[25] J. Al-Besharah, "The Kuwait Oil Fires and Oil Lakes – Facts and Numbers," proceedings of the International Symposium on the Environmental and Health Impact of Kuwait Oil Fires, Institute of Occupational Health, University of Birmingham (1992); T. Saeed, A. Al-Bloushi, and K. Al-Matrouk, "Study of the Chemical Composition of the Oil in the Oil Lakes and Effects of Weathering on Aromatics," Kuwait Institute for Scientific Research report VR001K (1993).

Table 12.1. *Facts and figures: the consequences of war on the terrestrial environment of Kuwait*

Type of effect	Extent of damage
Number of damaged oil wells	720
Amount of oil seepage into land[a]	60 million barrels
Amount of oil in lakes[b]	24 million barrels
Number of oil lakes[c]	246
Area covered by oil lakes[d]	49 km²
Area covered by heavy oil mist fallout[e]	100,000 ha (1,000 km²)
Amount of seawater or brackish water used to extinguish oil fires[f]	5,000 million gallons
Total oil contaminated areas[g]	953 km²
Amount of heavily contaminated soil[h]	40 million tons
Aerial pollutants[i]	0.32–0.95 million m³ per day
Oil lost due to fires and oil flows	1.0–1.5 billion barrels
Amount of oil in trenches[j]	498,447 m³
Depth of oil in the oil trenches from the soil surface[k]	20–90 cm
Total number of bunkers, trenches, and weapon pits[l]	375,000
Amount of excavated loose sediments from large bunker[m]	1,700 m³
Amount of excavated loose sediments from small bunker[n]	500 m³
Number of military vehicles operating during the war[o]	About 3,500 tanks and 2,500 armored personnel carriers
Number of landmines (up to 1997)[p]	1,646,355 (1,078,705 anti-personnel and 567,650 anti-tanks)
Number of unrecovered mines in the desert[q]	33,000
Amount of recovered ordnance[r]	109,000 tons (85%)
Amount of unrecovered ordnance[s]	20,000 tons
Areas impacted from military activities[t]	about 7,500 km²
Degree of damage to terrestrial ecosystem out of total damaged area[u]	20% intensive, 42% moderate, and 38% slight
Total surface area of Kuwait affected by 1990–91 Gulf War[v]	5,458.7 km² (30.6% of Kuwait)

Notes to Table 12.1

[a] Al-Awadhi et al., "*In-Situ* and On-Site Bioremediation"; Al-Attar, "An Integrated Approach."

[b] Al-Ghunaim, *Devastating Oil Wells.*

[c] *Ibid.*

[d] *Ibid.*

[e] Al-Awadhi et al., "*In-Situ* and On-Site Bioremediation."

[f] PAAC, *Environment Damage Claims Prioritization Report* (Safat, 1997).

[g] *Ibid.*

[h] Al-Awadhi et al., "*In-Situ* and On-Site Bioremediation."

[i] A. Y. Kwarteng and T. A. Bader, "Using Satellite Data to Monitor the 1991 Kuwait Oil Fires," *Arabian J. Sci. & Eng.* 18 (1993), 95–115.

[j] Al-Ajmi et al., "Oil Trenches and Environmental Destruction."

[k] *Ibid.*

[l] Al-Ajmi *et al.*, "Impact of the Iraqi War Machinery."

[m] *Ibid.*

[n] *Ibid.*

[o] *Ibid.*

[p] Ministry of Defense of Kuwait, *Periodical Mine Clearance Report* (1997).

[q] PAAC, *Environment Damage Claims Prioritization Report.*

[r] Ministry of Defense of Kuwait, *Periodical Mine Clearance Report.*

[s] *Ibid.*

[t] Al-Ajmi et al., "Impact of the Iraqi War Machinery."

[u] Al-Ajmi and Misak, "Impact of the Gulf War on the Desert Ecosystem."

[v] F. El-Baz and R. Makharita, *The Gulf War and the Environment* (1994).

the asphaltene contents have risen over time.[26] Preliminary work has also suggested that soil particles contaminated by crude oil have been bound or aggregated together, whereas soils contaminated by aerial deposits have not exhibited such trends.[27] The heavily contaminated soils have also rendered the soils hydrophobic (unable to absorb water) and anaerobic (unable to sustain oxygen-using microbes and plant roots) and thus resulted in land unsuitable for plant growth.[28] Overall, the soot and oil mist fall-out, in addition to being washed downward, may be dried or fragmented,

[26] N. Al-Matairi and W. Eid, "Utilization of Oil-Contaminated Soil for Construction Materials," in *The International Conference on the Effects of the Iraqi Aggression on the State of Kuwait*; Saeed et al., "Assessment of the Changes in the Chemical Components."

[27] Al-Houty et al., "Preliminary Assessment of the Gulf War."

[28] S. Zaman, "Impact of the Gulf War on Kuwait's Desert Flora and Soil," in proceedings of the International Conference on Desert Development, Kuwait (March 23–26, 1998); Al-Houty et al., "Preliminary Assessment of the Gulf War"; S. Zaman, "Impact of the Gulf War on Kuwait's Desert Flora and Soil," in proceedings of the International Conference on Desert Development.

potentially adding to the threat of contamination via airborne particulates, and of uptake or deposit of these particulates into plant life.[29]

The Iraqi forces constructed huge numbers of oil trenches in the southern portion of Kuwait. The amount of oil in these trenches was estimated at 3,750 m^3/km along the length of these trenches, for a total estimated amount of approximately 498,000 m^3.[30] The oil trenches have since been refilled with soil during the rehabilitation phase, although oil still exists beneath a 20–90 cm blanket of these sediments.[31] The impact of the oil trenches on deeper soils, and ultimately on groundwater, has yet to be investigated.

DISRUPTION OF LAND SURFACE

The soils of Kuwait are highly susceptible to erosion. The ground is usually covered by several types of recent sediments, including: aeolian, residual, playa, desert plain, slope, and coastal deposits.[32] Among these, aeolian deposits are predominant and account for 50 percent of overall surface deposits.[33]

The impact of the Gulf War on some of the fragile ecosystems of this land has been assessed, including the locations, numbers, and specifications of Iraqi fortifications, such as bunkers, trenches, ammunition storage shelters, and weapon pits.[34] The series of long trenches constructed along the southern borders were filled with oil and were to have been set on fire to deter liberation. Field reconnaissance surveys of accessible areas were

[29] Al-Ajmi, "Effects of Mixing Height and Wind Speed"; A. Hussain, Z. Baroon, S. Khalafawi, T. Al-Ati, and S. Sawaya, "Heavy Metals in Fruits and Vegetables Grown in Kuwait During the Oil Well Fires," *Arab Gulf J. Sci. Res.* (1995); S. A. Omar and J. W. Bartolome, "Nutrient Variation of Plants and Soil Impacted by Oil-Well Fires Caused by Iraqi Forces During the Gulf War," in *Proceedings of the International Conference on the Effects of the Iraqi Aggression on the State of Kuwait, Vol. III*, pp. 145–65; K. Puskas, A. El-Nawawy, N. Al-Awadhi, and R. Al-Daher, "Remediation of Land Sites Suffering Hydrocarbon Contamination," proceedings of the Second Annual Conference on Hazardous Waste Management (1995); K. Puskas, N. Al-Awadhi, F. M. Abdullah, and J. C. Joseph, "Evaluation of Passive Remediation of Oil-Contaminated Soil," final report 4601, vols. I–IV (1995); Saeed et al., "Assessment of the Changes in the Chemical Components."
[30] D. Al-Ajmi, R. F. Misak, M. Al-Ghunaiem, and S. Mahfouz, "Oil Trenches and Environmental Destruction of Kuwait," Center for Research and Studies of Kuwait report (1997).
[31] Recent field survey conducted by the authors.
[32] F. I. Khalaf, "Desertification and Aeolian Processes in the Kuwait Desert," *J. Envts.* 16, 125–45.
[33] *Ibid.*
[34] D. Al-Ajmi and R. F. Misak, "Impact of the Gulf War on the Desert Ecosystem in Kuwait," in Eric Wathins (ed.), *The Middle Eastern Environment* (1995).

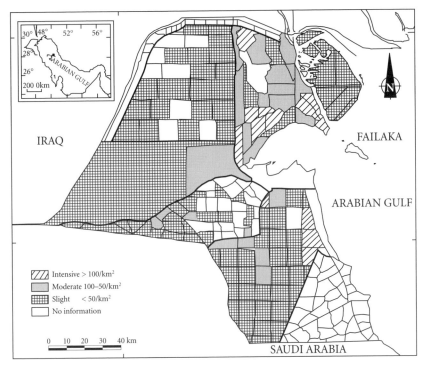

12.2 Distribution density of the total number of bunkers, trenches, and weapons pits in selected areas of Kuwait

carried out to assess the disruption of the desert surface by these military activities. Damage to the soil has accelerated erosion, as well as aeolian transportation and deposition. In sum, it was found that plant cover was destroyed, fine sediments were exposed, micro-relief was altered, soil was compacted, bedrock was fractured, vast areas of soil were contaminated, and the potential for groundwater contamination was created.

The Iraqi soldiers had established approximately 375,000 bunkers, trenches, and weapon pits. The distribution density of fortifications is presented in Figure 12.2. It has been estimated that large bunkers each yielded approximately 1,700 m^3 of excavated loose sediments, and small bunkers each yielded approximately 500 m^3.[35] Approximately 3,500 military vehicles were operating throughout Kuwait during the occupation. These vehicles were especially active in the northeastern part of the country.

[35] Al-Ajmi, "Effects of Mixing Height and Wind Speed."

Approximately 7,500 km^2 were directly impacted from this disruptive movement, which created havoc on the terrestrial ecosystems, particularly on the existence of the plant species *Haloxylon salicornicum*. Clearly, the dredging, refilling, and associated military actions have also caused major disturbances to Kuwait's soils and natural vegetation.

Al-Ajmi recently reported that the formation of sand dunes increased rapidly after the Iraqi invasion.[36] The protective layers of the soil were destroyed, exposing the underlying loose sand to the force of winds. There are now approximately 1,300 sand dunes spread throughout the Kuwaiti desert, concentrated in areas where there had been intense Gulf War activity.[37] In Wafra, for example, where disruption was extensive, moving sand has blocked irrigation canals, roads, and farm gates; destroyed produce; and covered up to 20 percent of farmland.

Taking all of the above into account, it has been estimated that the surface area of Kuwait suffered three degrees of damage: intensive (20 percent of total damaged area), moderate (42 percent of total damaged area), and slight (38 percent of total damaged area).[38]

OVERALL IMPACT ON VEGETATION, WILDLIFE, AND PROTECTED AREAS

The placement of mines, building of bunkers, fallout of oil mists, flows of oil, formation of lakes, and movement of vehicles during the war have all impacted Kuwait's vegetation. Studies have highlighted the impact of this crisis on Kuwait's desert flora, in particular. The effects are evident in vegetation structure, as well as in the chemical composition of both soil and vegetation. High levels of heavy metals were measured in plants that had been covered by oil and oil mist.

The oil lakes were also hazardous for birds and other wildlife. Upon emptying one small oil lake, the carcasses of vast numbers of birds were found, the oil having served as a trap. The desert of Kuwait harbors over 374 plant species that have enriched the habitats for both birds and

---

[36] Al-Ajmi, "Impact of the Gulf War on the Desert Ecosystem."
[37] F. El-Baz, N. Beaumont, J. Simonson, and A. Murad, "Assessment of the War Related Environmental Damage to the Desert Surface of Kuwait," prepared for the Annual Meeting of the Geological Survey of America (1993); F. El-Baz, *Kuwait Desert after Liberation* (Boston Univ. Center for Remote Sensing, 1994).
[38] Al-Ajmi, "Impact of the Gulf War on the Desert Ecosystem."

12.3 Migratory bird attracted by oil lake mistaken for water

animals.[39] These unique habitats have attracted thousands of migratory birds. Over 300 different species of birds have been reported in Kuwait, of which approximately 16 percent are endemic to the country.[40] Twenty-eight species of mammals and forty species of reptiles have also been identified within Kuwait.[41]

Alsdirawi reported on the extent of the damage to this precious bio-diversity: "The sludge killed the upper life forms by its toxicity and killed the deep life forms by suffocation. The oil lakes were mistaken for water bodies by migratory bird species as well as insects, both ended up tragically with corpses scattered in and around the black death."[42] (See Figure 12.3.) In 1998, in a single partially degraded oil lake, there were approximately seventeen fresh corpses of young Dhub (spiny-tailed lizard) found in the lake with hundreds of dead dung beetles and several bird corpses. Wildlife

---

[39] S. A. Omar, "Baseline Information on Native Plants," Kuwait Institute for Scientific Research technical report KISRI 1790 (1982); L. Boulos and M. Al-Dosari, "Checklist of the Flora of Kuwait," *J. U. Kuwait (Science)* 21, 203–18.

[40] F. Alsdirawi, "Wildlife Resources of Kuwait: Historic Trends and Conservation Potentials," PhD thesis, University of Arizona (1989).   [41] *Ibid.*

[42] F. Alsdirawi, "The Negative Impact of the Iraqi Invasion on Kuwait's Protected Areas," paper presented at the Fourth World Congress on National Parks and Protected Areas (1991).

monitoring and rehabilitation measures need to be undertaken to halt further losses of fauna.

It should be noted that seeds from annual plants are usually capable of dispersing long distances and can remain dormant for a long time, ultimately germinating with sufficient rainfall. However, perennial plants that were subjected to aerosol deposits and/or oil spills were found to contain high levels of heavy metals and need to be safeguarded from grazing by wildlife and livestock. The perennial plants that escaped from aerosol deposits dispersed seeds near the source, and thus new seedlings could not emerge due to the oil pollution. The long-term ecological consequence of this disruption on plants, both in oil-affected areas and in areas disturbed by other military actions, requires further investigation and will be influenced by mobile sand, which might cover or inhibit germination of seeds and prevent normal plant growth.[43]

At the time of the Iraqi aggression, the phenological progression of Kuwait's desert plants (that is, stages of plant growth over time) was altered by "black clouds" of oil particulates that altered temperatures and rainfall. In soot-covered sites, the survival rates of woody perennial shrubs, such as *Rhanterium epapposum* and *Haloxylon salicornicum*, were found to be almost 100 percent, but only 10 percent for the perennial euphorb *Moltkiopsis ciliata*. The survival rate for perennial grasses such as *Cyperus conglomeratus* and *Stipogrostis plumosa* was only about 50 percent. The severity of impact depended on the quantity and quality of the oil pollutants. In the oil-mist-covered sites, the only species that survived was *Haloxylon salicornicum*.[44] Oil-logged sites appeared totally devoid of vegetation.

There are several protected areas established in Kuwait. These areas, including the National Park of Kuwait, are in the Jal-Az-Zor, Jahra Pond, and Doha Reserve. The areas were established in the prewar period to protect endemic and migratory wildlife species, as well as habitats of significant value. The National Park of Kuwait, which covers approximately 330 km^2, was seriously disturbed by the land-based hostilities and bombing during the war. The external fence of the park was knocked down, trenches and fox-holes were scattered all over the area, and mines were

---

[43] Zaman, "Impact of the Gulf War on Kuwait's Desert Flora and Soil"; A. A. Dashti, "Environmental Impacts of Burned Oil Wells and Military Operations on Some Desert Plants and Soils of Kuwait," Master's thesis prepared for the Desert and Arid Zones Sciences Program, Arabian Gulf University (1993); Omar and Bartolome, "Nutrient Variation of Plants."

[44] *Ibid.*

placed intermittently from the coastal front of the park to the wadis and gullies of the Jal-Az-Zor escarpment. Research enclosures established in the prewar period, such as the Sulaibiya Field Station and various range management enclosures, were also intensively damaged by Iraqi forces. The invasion of Kuwait resulted in the complete loss of results from twenty years of efforts to protect and conserve both vegetation and wildlife in Kuwait, as well as destruction of the infrastructure of field research utilities. It took the government of Kuwait seven years to rehabilitate the park area.

IMPACT ON THE HYDROLOGICAL RESOURCES

Information on the impact of oil pollution on groundwater is scarce. Researchers have indicated that groundwater pollution may result from direct infiltration of oil from oil lakes, from leaching of combusted deposits at the ground surface by rainwater, or from subsurface leakage of oil from damaged oil-well casings.[45] Preliminary assessment of groundwater revealed that the infiltration of contaminated rainwater is likely to have a lasting effect on the groundwater. PAHs also migrate in soil during rainy periods and can possibly infiltrate the groundwater aquifer (see Figure 12.4). The most vulnerable areas are Raudhatain and Umm Al-Aish, due to the proximity of the groundwater to the surface (approximately 20 m). These two areas, the main sources of fresh groundwater in Kuwait, were contaminated with products of combustion from the oil fires. Infiltrating oil from oil lakes and contaminated water used for fire fighting affected the soil in the upper horizons of unsaturated sections of these areas. With both the surface and subsurface portions of these groundwater sources contaminated, it is likely that contaminated soils will continue to leach from infiltrating rainwater for a long period of time.

Water samples analyzed from Raudhatain and Umm Al-Aish showed fluctuations in concentrations of vanadium and nickel between 1 and 833 parts per billion (ppb) during the period from January to June, and between 1 and 73 ppb during the period from July to October 1992.[46] Hydrocarbon levels fluctuated between 1 and 190 ppb during the period from January to June 1992.[47] The relatively high levels of water contamination during the period from January to June 1992 were caused by the

---

[45] J. Al-Sulaimi, unpublished data; Saeed et al., "Assessment of the Changes in the Chemical Components."
[46] *Ibid.*   [47] *Ibid.*

12.4 Oil lakes mixed with rainwater after heavy rain showers in 1996

significant levels of contaminants in the surface and subsurface soil; the local hydrological conditions; the relatively shallow levels of intake zones of wells with respect to water table levels; and the relatively high infiltration capacities of the unsaturated zones.[48]

LANDMINES AND MILITARY DEBRIS

The Iraqi strategic minefields extended from the Arabian Gulf in the east to Wadi Al-Batin at the extreme western portion of the country.[49] It has been estimated that the mines were placed at various depths, to a linear extent of 728 km. Intensive searches had to be carried out for landmines and unexploded ordnance following the war. As an indication of the magnitude of this task, as of January 1997 the Ministry of Defense had collected a total of 1,646,355 mines.[50] The environmental effects of the ammunition left behind by the Iraqi forces, as well as of the unexploded Coalition munitions (such as cluster bombs) have not been investigated.

[48] *Ibid.*
[49] R. F. Misak, S. Mahfooz, M. Al-Ghunaim, D. Al-Ajmi, H. Malalah, and A. Muhareb, *Landmines and the Destruction of the Kuwaiti Environment* (1999).   [50] *Ibid.*

330

12.5 Some of the military damaged vehicles stacked in designated areas
in the southwest and west of Kuwait

Vast numbers of trucks, tanks, and associated damaged war machinery also had to be removed from the desert, a process that inflicted additional damage. Some of the damaged military vehicles were stacked in designated areas, particularly in the west and southwest of Kuwait. (See Figure 12.5)

Concerns also exist regarding the problem of "depleted uranium" (DU) and the risk of exposure of the population of Kuwait to radiation. The sources of DU are the anti-tank munitions used by Allied troops during the war.

FORCED NEGLECT

Significant damage to plant life resulted from "forced neglect" during the occupation, liberation, and early periods of recovery. Plants needing irrigation were not attended to during crisis periods, and many died from lack of water and nutrients. The invasion and occupation also resulted in loss of plans to enhance the visual and microclimate aspects of the country's environment, a process that had been under extensive development for almost two years.

12.6 Juaidan farm devastated by the explosion of oil wells
in the Burgan oilfield

The agricultural sector was devastated during the invasion. Before the invasion, agricultural development flourished in two areas: Abdali and Wafra. The invasion forced most of the people who worked in these areas to leave the country and these sites were subsequently occupied by Iraqi troops. Wells and sources of electricity in the two areas were destroyed. The Al-Juaidan farm was completely devastated by the sabotaged oil wells in the Burgan oilfield. (See Figure 12.6.)

Rehabilitation of Kuwait's terrestrial environment

CLEARING AND REHABILITATING THE LAND

In the post-liberation period, the government of Kuwait had to accomplish the urgent task of restoring Kuwait's damaged oil production facilities. This task was carried out in two phases, namely the *Al-Awda* project (the Return) and the *Al-Tameer* project (the Reconstruction).

The Al-Awda project commenced in March 1991. Approximately 9,000 personnel were mobilized in seven months from thirty-two different countries, with the majority coming from the Philippines, Thailand, Indonesia, the United States, the United Kingdom, and Kuwait. Twenty-seven fire-fighting teams worked ten to fourteen hours per day, seven days per week to control the burning and gushing wells. The enormous effort was accomplished in eight months, much sooner than the two to three years initially anticipated. The last well fire was extinguished on November 6, 1991.

The Al-Tameer project was managed by the Kuwait Oil Company, with assistance from Bechtel. The project involved up-streaming crude oil; drilling and repairing wells; and refurbishing gas and oil gathering centers, booster stations, storage tanks, and export facilities. The clean-up and treatment of 300 oil lakes containing approximately 20 million barrels of weathered crude oil remains a great challenge.

Some of the oil lakes were drained and the oil pumped to gathering centers or shifted to other lakes. Some of the shallow lakes were merely covered with soil brought from elsewhere. Still others dried out as a result of weathering and were covered with sand.

Extensive efforts were undertaken by teams of professionals from seven countries to clear the land of mines and military ordnance. While this process is believed to be complete (except for the oil lake-bed areas), there are occasional accidents involving remaining landmines – most often along the border between Kuwait and Saudi Arabia. Continued surveillance is required. The trenches, bunkers, ditches, and pits have been back-filled, and debris has been removed. However, the long-term impacts of these constructions and the remediation required by them still need to be assessed in order to ensure that lasting damage is minimized.

BIOREMEDIATION OF CONTAMINATED SOIL

Numerous studies have been carried out on adaptation of techniques and technologies for remediation or bioremediation of both heavily and lightly contaminated soil. The bioremediation studies were carried out with windrows and soil piles of mixed oil-lakebed contaminated soils. The data from these studies showed that controlled, irrigated, aerated solid phase biological treatment reduced oil contamination by more than 84 percent within twelve months. It was also projected that high-ring polyaromatic compounds would remain in the desert's surface soil over a long period of time and, after extensive aging, would break into small particles and be transported by mobile sand.[51]

[51] Al-Ajmi et al., "Oil Trenches and Environmental Destruction."

The results of other studies showed that passive remediation can aid in the rehabilitation of large surface areas, if those areas are not contaminated to a depth of more than 1 cm with deposited airborne soot and unburned oil droplets.[52] However, soils contaminated 2–50 cm in depth, as well as heavily contaminated oil lake beds, did not display any natural remediation. While limited studies have been conducted on plant biological system uptake, means of using plant life in biological clean-up and/or the implications of the uptakes in the plants regarding ultimate use have not been adequately studied and may be applicable to the long-term remediation of Kuwait's terrestrial environment.

Landsat Thematic Mapper™ imagery analyzed in 1995 indicated that a majority of the contaminated areas in Kuwait surrounding the oil lakes were gradually recovering in terms of vegetative growth. The surface cover of the oil lakes had decreased by 20 percent from 1992 to 1995.[53] This trend was a result of the decrease in volume and area of the beds caused by the recovery process, sand encroachment, and weathering of areas with shallow oil.

Oil lake beds covered by veneers of sand were not visible on satellite images and are still posing hazards to the environment, the extent and nature of which will require further investigation. As a result of weathering, the oil in most of the remaining oil lakes has thickened to a semi-solid mass. The chemical composition of weathered oil showed a decrease in aromatic compounds, an increase in resins, and an increase in concentration of PAHs. This indicates an increased hazard potential. Heavily contaminated soils may eventually erode, be re-suspended, and transported to populated areas during dust storms, causing potentially severe health hazards, such as short-term morbidity due to acute respiratory infection, and long-term predisposition for respiratory cancers. While remote sensing has been able to calculate the total areas of both heavily and lightly contaminated soils, the amount of soil requiring remediation has not been sufficiently quantified for action purposes. Various layers of soil and gatch (a hard calcareous layer) are also present throughout the contaminated areas. While a sample lakebed has been studied, much remains to be elucidated.

---

[52] Al-Awadhi et al., "Remediation and Rehabilitation."
[53] Kwarteng and Al-Ajmi, "Using Landsat"; Kwarteng and Al-Ajmi, "Satellite Remote Sensing Applications"; Kwarteng et al., "RADARSAT SAR Data Assessment."

REHABILITATION OF DESERT FLORA AND FAUNA

The impacted desert areas of Kuwait have not been sufficiently reseeded with native plants to support restoration of the animal life that populated those areas before the war. Although land has been leveled, microbial capabilities of the soil have been lost and not re-established. The plant species lost have also not been re-established. Therefore, the habitats for much of Kuwait's natural wildlife remain severely altered.

Reclamation of polluted areas still needs to take place, especially in the oil-logged areas where vegetation has been destroyed and rangeland productivity potentials have been reduced. Much of the landscape was severely damaged and will require a great deal of long-term restoration. The status of many species of wildlife and vegetation in protected areas also needs further assessment. Reintroduction of wildlife species needs to be investigated as a possible avenue of reinstituting populations of lost fauna. The biological diversity of the terrestrial environment also needs to be regularly monitored in order to develop practical and appropriate measures for its protection and management.

Terrestrial rehabilitation works yet to be undertaken

Much of the terrestrial rehabilitation yet to be undertaken can be summarized in outline form, as follows:

- Long-term impacts, particularly of soil compaction and heavy oil contamination, must be studied so that corrective actions and appropriate rehabilitation measures can be undertaken;
- Soil microbial research is needed to determine whether the microbial ecology of the soil has been affected by its oil-contaminated condition, by oil-well fires, by fallout from the resultant smoke, or by other military activities;
- The effect of radiation (from DU) on human health needs to be verified and investigated;
- The impact of suspended, contaminated soil particulates on human health needs to be assessed;
- Further studies are needed to establish the extent of native plant uptake of contaminants and possible resultant health hazards in the food chain;

- Pilot projects are necessary to assess the effectiveness of rehabilitation measures on specific areas damaged by military activities or oil pollution. Field demonstration trials need to be performed to assess appropriate technologies, and the results compared with treatment standards;
- Further work is needed to ferret out the total and long-term effects of the oil releases, the tarcrete, the open-burning, the detonation of mines and ordnance, and the impact of leaks from detonated mines and ordnance;
- Re-vegetation is needed with adapted plant species and ecotypes. Factors that will need to be addressed during this process include seed production potentials, germination requirements, and technologies to be applied. Flora mutations also need to be studied;
- Heavily contaminated soil must be remediated in order to restore terrestrial ecosystems. Large-scale rehabilitation needs to be considered;
- National parks need to be rehabilitated and wildlife species need to be reintroduced to the parks;
- Action plans are needed for rehabilitating and managing impacted rangelands, and for wildlife restoration at the national level;
- The long-term impact of oil wells and oil trenches on the terrestrial ecosystems and groundwater needs to be investigated; and
- Long-term potential for oil seepage into groundwater aquifers needs to be monitored and recorded on a regular basis.

Conclusion

The Iraqi occupation and the subsequent armed conflict devastated the terrestrial environment of Kuwait. The government of Kuwait adopted immediate measures after liberation to restore the oil sector and to clear ammunition from the desert. These two major achievements were completed very quickly. Likewise, intensive work was undertaken by scientists to assess the effect of military activities and oil pollution on the terrestrial environment. Quantitative and qualitative evaluations of the impacts of the war have been made, and the authors have been able to identify various hazardous components and their effects on both the ecology of Kuwait and on human health. There remains considerable work to be done in this area. With its 1992 signature of the Convention on Biological Diversity, Kuwait assumed responsibility for conserving and managing its biological resources, as well as rehabilitating damaged habitats. Work is needed to assess further the status of Kuwait's biological resources and to determine proper mitigation measures. The long-term impacts of pollutants on soil and microbial activities, as well as on groundwater, needs further assessment and evaluation.

The destruction of Kuwait's terrestrial resources requires attention from both planners and policymakers. The government of Kuwait, together with the private sector, could coordinate efforts to provide a National Action Programme to tackle land degradation and rehabilitation issues. Pilot projects investigating rehabilitation of war-damaged areas can provide valuable information on selection of proper technologies and costs of rehabilitation. It may be possible to develop a strategic plan for rehabilitating Kuwait's terrestrial environment.

13

WAR-RELATED DAMAGE TO THE
MARINE ENVIRONMENT IN THE
ROPME SEA AREA

MAHMOOD Y. ABDULRAHEEM

Introduction

BACKGROUND

The Arabian or Persian Gulf forms an arm of the Indian Ocean extending into the Arabian Peninsula, an area that constitutes the inner part of the Regional Organization for the Protection of the Marine Environment (ROPME) Sea Area – the "RSA." This new term was coined to achieve unanimity in signing the 1978 Kuwait Regional Convention for Cooperation on the Protection of the Marine Environment from Pollution. The ROPME Sea Area also includes the Gulf of Oman and the Iranian and Omani waters of the Arabian Sea. This chapter uses the terms "Gulf" and "ROPME Sea Area," or "RSA," interchangeably.

The ROPME Sea Area is a relatively small, flooded valley-estuary with a surface area of 240,000 km². It is approximately 1,000 km in length and 200–300 km in width, narrowing to only 54 km at the Strait of Hormuz. It is generally shallow, mostly less than 60 m deep, with an average depth of 35 m, but increasing to 100 m near the Strait of Hormuz. The western part of the RSA is very shallow (less than 5 m), with tidal flats extending up to 5 km.[1] The bottom topography is generally featureless with mostly soft sediments. It is muddy in the northern and northwestern parts and sandy along the southern section, reflecting the largely biogenic origin of sediments in the area (Figure 13.1).

---

[1] B. B. Habashi, A. A. H. El-Gindy, and H. Karam, "Hydro-Chemical Characteristics of the Arabian Gulf after the *Umitaka-Maru* Cruise and Other Expeditions," International Symposium on the Status of the Marine Environment in the ROPME Sea Area after the 1990–1991 Gulf War, Tokyo, Japan (1995).

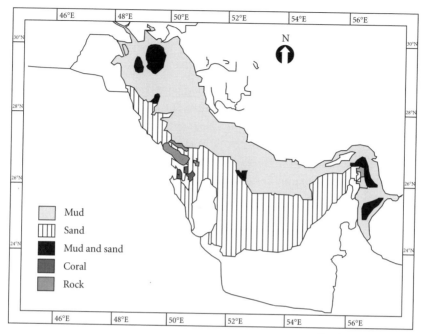

After Carpenter et al., 1997

13.1 Sediment types in the RSA

The intense sunlight and shallowness of the water makes the RSA highly productive, which has encouraged the establishment of well-developed shrimp and fin-fish fisheries in the area. The bottom sediment is dominated by carbonate sands produced by decay of microbenthic organisms, which become mixed with wind-blown dust and fluvial sediments from the rivers and settle mostly in the northwestern part of the RSA. Surrounded by the arid land masses of the Arabian Peninsula and the Iranian Zagros Mountains, the area exhibits a wider range of temperature than other sub-tropical seas. Air temperatures frequently fall to 0° C in winter and reach 50° C during summer, with water temperatures fluctuating between 10° C and 39° C. However, temperatures as low as 4° C and 7° C have been reported in shallow areas of Kuwait and Qatar, respectively.[2] The dominant northwest winds blowing across the axis of the RSA influence

[2] C. R. C. Sheppard, A. R. G. Price, and C. M. Roberts, *Marine Ecology of the Arabian Region: Patterns and Processes in Extreme Tropical Environments* (London: Academic Press, 1992).

surface circulation and often deposit large loads of desert dust on the sea surface. Surface circulation is generally counter-clockwise, which means that a large portion of marine pollution and debris generated in the area is likely to impact the Kuwaiti and Saudi Arabian coastal areas.

The arid climate also influences salinity, with dry, hot winds increasing evaporation rates, which range from 140 to 500 cm/yr, producing salinities that reach 60 parts per trillion (ppt). Near the Shatt Al-Arab delta, salinity drops to 36 ppt. However, it is not unusual to encounter salinities of over 100 ppt during summer in the shallow lagoons of the United Arab Emirates and Salwa Bay off Qatar, conditions that favor hypersaline eurythermal cyanophytes.[3] As the more dense seawater is driven eastwards by the north-west winds, it sinks under the incoming fresher seawater (36 ppt) through the Strait of Hormuz. The flushing time for the RSA is estimated at two to five years.[4]

It is to these harsh and extreme meteorological conditions that the marine life drifting from the Indian Ocean some 20,000 years ago had to adapt. The mostly calm and warm waters of the RSA also provided a major source of food, trade routes, and security for development of the sparse human settlements on its shorelines.

IMPACTS OF MAN

As oil and gas production reached commercial scale after World War II, the RSA witnessed an unprecedented influx of man and materials. The exponential rates of development and resulting demand for natural resources are demonstrated clearly by the fact that since the end of the sixties, all cities in the area (except in Iran and Iraq) have had to rely totally on desalination to produce potable water. Other resources – especially fisheries, mangroves, forests, coral reefs, oyster banks, and mudflats – have been subjected to intensive utilization and encroachment by development. Shrimp and fin-fish stocks were under severe pressure from overfishing even before the last Gulf War, and efforts to engender regional management of fisheries were progressing slowly because of the Iran–Iraq War. Releases of both treated

[3] K. E. Carpenter, F. Krupp, D. A. Jones, and U. Zajonz, FAO Species Identification Guide for Fishery Purposes: The Living Marine Resources of Kuwait, Eastern Saudi Arabia, Bahrain, Qatar, and the United Arab Emirates (Rome: FAO, 1997).
[4] P. G. Brewer and D. Dyrssen, "Chemical Oceanography of the Persian Gulf," Progressive Oceanography 14 (1985), 41–55.

and untreated sewage, as well as of industrial effluents, became a major land-based source of contamination.[5] By the end of the seventies, the oil industry in the area was producing about 60 percent of the world's crude oil exports, carried by some 10,000 tankers annually. This tanker movement, along with commercial shipping, refineries, and other heavy industry, contributes to an anthropogenic input of oil into the marine environment equivalent to more than 1 million barrels per year. It is not surprising that most monitoring programs in the area have shown that petroleum hydro-carbons are the principal marine contaminants.[6] In spite of the heavy traffic of tankers and commercial ships, the area was fortunate enough to escape major tanker collisions or groundings until the Iran–Iraq War, when the Nowruz oilfields were bombed and the Tanker War of 1980–89 took place. Unfortunately, the Iran–Iraq War was immediately followed by an even more vicious war that was especially hard on the environment.

Environmental damage from the 1990–91 Gulf War

THE OIL SPILLS

The deliberate discharge of over 10 million barrels of oil from terminals, storage tanks, oil tankers, and coastal trenches in Kuwait and Iraq has resulted in the largest oil spill yet recorded (Figure 13.2). The spill is also unique in being the only spill intentionally released as part of wartime tactics. The spill moved rather rapidly along the coastal waters of Kuwait and Saudi Arabia, traveling over 600 km before being stopped by Ras Abu Ali. It should be noted that the area most affected by the spill is the most shallow and highly productive area of the RSA.

As the oil traveled rapidly south, a significant amount was lost to evapora-tion or landed on beaches. It has been estimated that 40 percent of the oil was lost to evaporation, 10 percent to dissolution, and about 50 percent remained afloat. Out of the 5.4 million barrels that remained afloat, 22 percent was recovered, 50 percent was stranded on beaches, and about 30 percent was unaccounted for. However, there seems to be evidence that at least some of that "lost" oil had sunk to the bottom. UNEP aerial photo-graphy off the Kuwaiti southern borders showed large patches of such

[5] Regional Organization for the Protection of the Marine Environment, "Regional Report on the State of the Marine Environment of the Region," ROPME/CM–7/PREP. 2 (1990).   [6] *Ibid.*

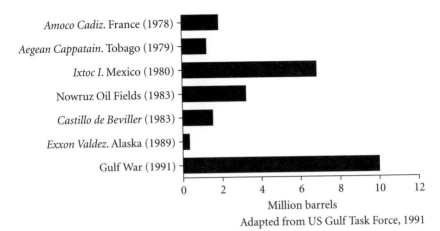

Adapted from US Gulf Task Force, 1991

13.2 World's major oil spills

sunken oil. Samples taken during the *Umitaka-Maru* cruise also indicated the presence of sunken oil in the 2,000 μg/g range.[7]

THE OIL-WELL-FIRE PLUMES

The impact on the marine environment of fallout from the plumes generated by over 600 burning oil wells in Kuwait may prove to be of greater significance than the oil spills. Estimates of the amount of oil that burned are as high as 500 million barrels, with the most dominant plume trajectories over Kuwait and the region. Here again, the plumes affected the same areas impacted by the oil spill.

The composition of the plume analyzed by a UK meteorology flight in March 1992 showed smoke levels of about 500 μg/m³. Stevens et al. also have carried out analyses of suspended matter collected from ground level and by an airborne sampling system.[8] Table 13.1 summarizes the results of their analysis; the black plumes were characterized by a large number of carbon chain agglomerates.

---

[7] N. Al-Majed, W. Rajab, and F. Al-Safar, "Levels of Pollutants in the ROPME Sea Area," International Symposium on the Status of the Marine Environment in the ROPME Sea Area after the 1990–1991 Gulf War, Tokyo, Japan (1995).

[8] R. Stevens, J. Pinto, Y. Mamane, J. Ondov, M. Abdulraheem, N. Al-Majed, M . Sadek, W. Cofer, W. Ellenson, and R. Kellogg, "Chemical and Physical Properties of Emissions from Kuwaiti Oil Fires," Fifth International Conference on Environmental Qualities and Ecosystem Stabilities, Jerusalem (1992).

Table 13.1. *Concentrations of selected compounds (g/m^3) of oil-well-fire plumes in Kuwait, 1991*

Compounds	Black plume Aug. 2, 1991	Black plume Aug. 3, 1991	Black plume Aug. 5, 1991	Mixed plume Aug. 6, 1991	White plume Aug. 7, 1991	Mixed plume Aug. 8, 1991
Na	NDB	6.0 ± 2.9	NDB	3.2 ± 0.6	905 ± 45	6.4 ± 0.6
Al	3.7 ± 3.2	3.5 ± 1.8	8.9 ± 1.3	3.7 ± 0.2	1.9 ± 1.7	3.7 ± 0.52
S	3.0 ± 1.5	18.9 ± 1.7	2.9 ± 0.5	3.9 ± 0.3	95 ± 7	3.2 ± 0.3
Cl	2.2 ± 1.1	7.1 ± 0.9	NDB	5.0 ± 0.3	1,820 ± 92	9.2 ± 0.5
SO_4	9.3	56	8.7	12	285	9.6
SO_2	133	169	12	49	319	26
Mass	755	955	493	167	4,356	22
Volatile carbon	152	183	NM	37	105	NM
Elemental carbon	142	443	NM	22	22	NM

NDB: Non-detected above filter blank.
NM: Not measured.
Adapted from Steven et al., 1992.

concentration (ng/m³)

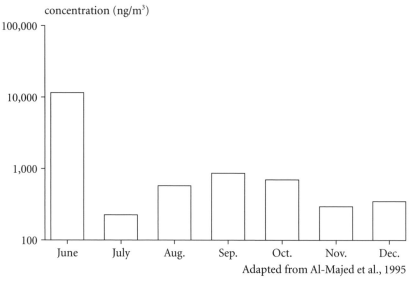

Adapted from Al-Majed et al., 1995

13.3a Levels of PHCs (ng/m³) in PM10 samples collected from Riqqa, Kuwait, 1991

concentration (ng/m³)

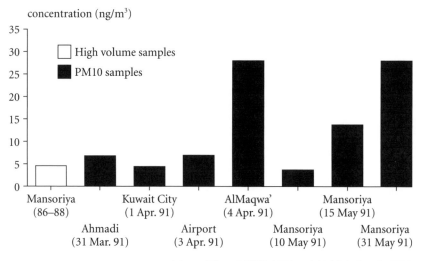

Adapted from LHVP, 1991 and Al-Majed et al., 1991

13.3b Benzo(a)pyrene levels (ng/m³) in particulate matter before and after the Gulf War

ppb (thousands)

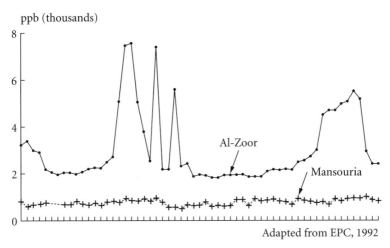

Adapted from EPC, 1992

13.4 Total hydrocarbons measured simultaneously in Mansouria and Al-Zoor, August 3–4, 1991

To develop a better understanding of what was being deposited in the marine environment, fluctuations in the levels of petroleum hydrocarbons (PHCs) in daily samples of particulate matter collected at Riqqa, south of Kuwait City, and closer to the burning oil fields, were compared with satellite images taken in the same period. High PHC levels detected on land appear to coincide with the behavior of the plume, as shown in Figure 13.3a; levels of Benzo(a)pyrene measured at ground level and associated with the plume are shown in Figure 13.3b. Consistency of the levels of PHCs with the plume behavior was also evident from the comparison of levels of PHCs monitored simultaneously at the Mansouria station with those monitored by the German Air Quality Mobile Laboratory placed at the Al-Zoor Port, as shown in Figure 13.4.

Distribution of oil and oil-burn products in the marine environment

The marine environment in the RSA has one of the world's highest rates of chronic releases of petroleum hydrocarbons from anthropogenic sources and, to a much lesser degree, from natural seepage.[9] Baseline surveys and environmental monitoring programs have not been maintained historically, so comparison between pre- and postwar levels of contaminants in the marine environment is not possible. ROPME's eighteen-month marine

[9] Regional Organization for the Protection of the Marine Environment, "Regional Report."

environment monitoring program was initiated in 1982, when almost all of the member states carried out an assessment of the natural characteristics and contaminant levels in their coastal areas. However, the program could not be maintained for all member states; the war between Iran and Iraq was a major obstacle in obtaining data from the northwest part of the RSA. The limited baseline data collected were used as an indication of the extent of the major sources of contamination. This data also provided insight into the types and magnitude of marine contaminants.[10]

Thus far, coastal surveys, national monitoring activities, and two open-sea cruises, the *Mt. Mitchell* (1992) and the *Umitaka-Maru* (1993–94), represent the extent of the efforts undertaken to assess the impacts of war on the marine environment of the RSA. Efforts to develop a sustainable follow-up program with the goal of more completely understanding the fate of oil and oil-burn products in the marine environment, as well as the subsequent rates of recovery, have had limited success.

Figure 13.5 summarizes the results of petroleum hydrocarbon analysis in marine sediments before and after the war. Baseline data from the Kuwait Environment Protection Department (EPD), now part of the Environment Protection Authority (EPA), suggests that a fivefold increase over 1986 PHC levels occurred in 1991, dropping to less than half that value by 1995.[11] Data by Fowler et al. indicate high levels of PHCs in sediments of Ras Abu Ali in Saudi Arabia, decreasing with distance towards the Strait of Hormuz.[12] Moreover, PHC levels of over 2,000 µg/g were reported off the Saudi waters, suggesting the presence of sunken oil. The breakdown of PHCs into aliphatic and aromatic compounds is shown in Figure 13.6. Maximum concentrations of PHCs were seen off Saudi Arabia, decreasing along the coast towards the Strait of Hormuz.[13]

In their study of sediment toxicity to amphipods, Randolph et al. have shown high mortality rates associated with PHC concentrations of 1,000 µg/g or higher in dry sediment.[14] Of the eleven sites sampled in Saudi

[10] *Ibid.*

[11] Environment Protection Department, Annual Report 1985; Annual Report 1991–1992; Annual Report 1995.

[12] S. Fowler, J. Readman, B. Oregioni, J. Villeneuve, and K. McKay, "Petroleum Hydrocarbons and Trace Metals in Nearshore Gulf Sediments and Biota Before and After the 1991 War: An Assessment of Temporal and Spatial Trends," *Marine Pollution Bull.* 27 (1993), 171–82.

[13] *Ibid.*

[14] R. C. Randolph, J. Hardy, S. Fowler, A. R. G. Price, and W. Pearson, "Toxicity and Persistence of Nearshore Sediment Contamination Following the 1991 Gulf War," study submitted to *Env't Int'l* (1996).

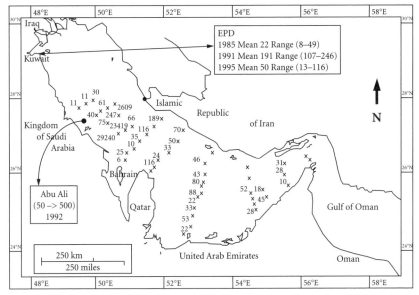

Adapted from EPD (1985, 1991, 1995), Fowler et al. (1992), and Al-Majed et al. (1995)

13.5 Distribution of PHCs in sediments before and after the Gulf War

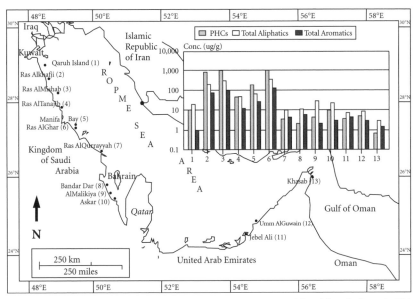

Adapted from Fowler et al., 1992

13.6 Distribution of PHCs (µg/g) in sediments after the Gulf War, showing breakdown into aliphatic and aromatic compounds

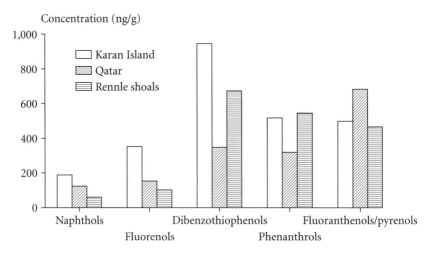

Adapted from Krahn et al., 1993

13.7 Levels of metabolites of aromatic compounds (ng/g wet wt.)
in bile samples of *Lethrinus kallopterus* species, RSA, 1992

Arabia, five proved to be toxic by this definition. The data suggest that as the soluble components of oil and the weathering products become available in the water column, toxicity increases. Being lighter than water, these products tend to accumulate in the surface microlayer. About half of the samples of the coastal surface microlayers that were done by Hardy et al. and used in bioassay tests, were shown to be toxic to echinoderm larvae.[15] Around the same time, analysis of metabolites of aromatic hydrocarbons in fish bile carried out on board the *Mt. Mitchell* identified elevated levels of naphthols, fluororentols, and phenanthrols, as well as of their parent compounds, in sediments collected in the area.[16] The same data showed that the level of dibenzothiophenols had reached over 900 μg/g.

Data on the toxicity of the surface microlayer and sediments in the RSA have led to a widespread discussion of the war's impacts on fisheries. In a preliminary assessment of the impacts, it was estimated that the shrimp populations have collapsed to about 10 percent of their prewar levels.[17]

---

[15] J. Hardy, S. Fowler, A. Price, J. Readman, B. Oregioni, E. Crecelius, and W. Gardiner, "Environmental Assessment of Sea Surface Contamination in the Gulf," UNESCO/IUCN Report (1993).

[16] M. Krahn, G. Ylitalo, J. Buzitis, J. Bolton, C. Wigren, S. Chan, and U. Varanasi, "Survey of Oil Contamination in Marine Fish and Sediments following the ROPME Sea Oil Spill," *Mt. Mitchell Workshop* (1993).

[17] International Union for the Conservation of Nature, *IUCN's Response to the 1990–91 Gulf War* (1992).

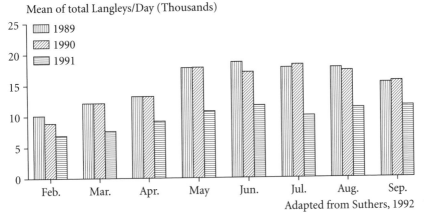

Mean of total Langleys/Day (Thousands)

Adapted from Suthers, 1992

13.8 Impacts of oil well fires on solar radiation in RSA

Support for this conclusion comes from another study, in which fieldwork showed a decrease in penaeid egg and larval abundance at Ras Tanura in 1992, compared with the years 1975–78.[18] At Safaniya, a decrease of both zooplankton and penaeid egg and larval abundance was also apparent in 1992, compared with the data available from the 1970s.[19] In Kuwait, Siddiqui and Al-Mubarak have analyzed shrimp-landing statistics before and after the war. Their results indicate a large fluctuation in the landings and catch effort over the past few years, and a declining trend in landings may be inferred.[20]

In the absence of reliable regional data, and given the stress on the stocks by overfishing and encroachment on spawning areas, it is difficult to draw a clear picture. Nevertheless, given the indicators of elevated toxicity of sediments and the sea surface microlayer, the decline in abundance, the presence of oil on beaches and at the bottom in the intertidal zone, the reduction of incidence of light (shown in Figure 13.8), and the sea temperature regime, it is not unreasonable to assume that the fisheries of the area have suffered severe impacts. Only long-term monitoring, along with intensive fishery management procedures to halt overfishing and

[18] A. R. G. Price, C. P. Mathews, R. W. Ingle, and K. Al-Rasheeid, "Abundance of Zooplankton and Penaeid Shrimp Larvae in the Western Gulf: Analysis of Pre-War (1991) and Post-War Data," *Marine Pollution Bull.* 27 (1993), 273–78.

[19] *Ibid.*

[20] M. S. Siddiqui and A. Khalid Al-Mubarak, "The Post-Gulf War Shrimp Fishery Management in the Territorial Waters of Kuwait," *Env't Int'l* 24 (1998), 105–8.

encroachment on habitats and pollution, will aid this major natural resource in recovering.

Long-term impacts of the war on the marine environment

IMPACTS ON SEAWATER QUALITY

As stated earlier, most of the countries in the region rely on desalination of seawater for the production of potable water. The Gulf Cooperation Council countries produce a total of about 2 billion m³/yr of potable water by desalination.[21] The presence of petroleum hydrocarbons and chlorine at the seawater intakes of desalination plants could produce halogenated organics, mostly as bromoform, in the volatile fraction.[22]

LONG-TERM IMPACTS OF EXPOSURE OF MARINE ORGANISMS TO AROMATIC HYDROCARBONS

Aromatic hydrocarbons represent the principal component of the soluble fraction of oil that could have detrimental long-term effects, including genetic changes, on marine organisms. This could be especially critical for larvae, which spend most of their lives in the planktonic phase, close to the sea surface where these products are likely to accumulate.[23] Thus, the rapid rates of weathering of oil in the RSA may not actually be desirable. Increased rates of weathering result in greater amounts of soluble weathering products becoming available at the surface microlayer, thus increasing the toxicity to marine organisms. The implications of such a scenario, if proven to be true, could spell a disastrous future for fisheries in the RSA if sunken oil is not removed and the chronic sources of oil pollution are not abated.

Lessons learned from the war and recommendations

The massive oil spills and deposition of oil-burn products impacted the shallowest, most highly productive, and previously stressed part of

---

[21] W. Al-Zubari, presentation at the Seventh Regional Meeting of Arab IHP Committees, Rabat, Morocco (1997).

[22] M. Y. Abdulraheem, unpublished experimental data (1994).

[23] J. Hardy et al., "Sea Surface Contamination."

the marine environment of the RSA. Recovery of the coastal lagoons and mangroves in Kuwait and Saudi Arabia can only be enhanced by greater protection efforts. Recovery of the fisheries will also require greater efforts in management, including stricter control of fishing in the area – a process that would require addressing the economic and social impacts on the fishing industry.

Recovery of the marine environment may be further enhanced by incorporating the provisions of the Kuwait Regional Convention and its Protocols into the national legislation of member states. The 1990 Protocol for the Protection of the Marine Environment against Pollution from Land-Based Sources, the 1989 Protocol Concerning Marine Pollution Resulting from Exploration and Exploitation of the Continental Shelf, and the 1998 Tehran Protocol on the Control of Marine Transboundary Movements and Disposal of Hazardous Wastes and Other Wastes all contain provisions to reduce further abuse of the marine environment. Adopting the preventive approach to oil pollution advocated by the 1978 Protocol Concerning Regional Cooperation in Combating Pollution by Oil and other Harmful Substances in Cases of Emergency, including placing a ban on substandard tankers and establishing a regional scheme of reception facilities for oily wastes and other wastes, and adopting a Memorandum of Understanding on Port State Control and Ratification of MARPOL, would enable member states to declare the area as a "Special Area" in which release of ballast waters and other wastes could be prohibited.

Important as they are, the positive impacts of the efforts outlined above may still be rendered ineffective if the land-use patterns of landfilling, dredging, and alteration of coastal morphology continues. A major activity that has devastating effects on fisheries and the ecology of the area is the drainage of the Iraqi marshes. The Iraqi regime, driven by political and military objectives, has reduced the Iraqi marshes (an estimated area of about 0.5 million hectares), to water channels that deliver river water, with all its sediment loads, agrochemicals, sewage, and industrial wastes, directly into the RSA.[24] This action has deprived the area of a giant "kidney" that previously acted as a self-sustaining waste treatment facility, and it is likely to affect the spawning grounds of shrimp and migratory fish at the Shatt Al-Arab delta and Kuwait Bay. This area has been transformed from a

---

[24] E. Maltby, *The Amar Appeal: An Environmental and Ecological Study of the Marshlands of Mesopotamia* (1994).

paradise for migratory birds of Europe and a major source of fisheries into an arid, barren land.

Finally, there is a need to transform our knowledge of the impacts of war on the marine environment of the RSA into actions that would make future generations see us in a better light. These include international support and cooperation in assessment of the long-term impacts and recovery rates, as well as in rehabilitation efforts. Such efforts would provide a better understanding of the fate and effects of petroleum hydrocarbons on the marine ecosystems and populations of arid sub-tropical seas. It is obvious that the cost and expertise of such endeavors are too heavy a burden to be borne by the ROPME region alone. The United Nations system needs to develop a mechanism by which countries that are victims of such environmental damage could utilize funds made available by the responsible party, or from a fund to be replenished by the responsible party in accordance with UN Security Council decisions. Experience gained from the establishment of oil industry funds in covering the costs of combating oil spills and compensating claims for economic and environmental damages should be used as examples by the international court systems to enhance their response to the environmental impacts of war on the marine environment.

14

WAR AND BIODIVERSITY: AN ASSESSMENT OF IMPACTS

JEFFREY A. MCNEELY

Introduction

The "peace dividend" expected by many to result from the end of the Cold War has not paid off in terms of reduced violent conflict. Indeed, the recent nuclear weapons tests by India and Pakistan demonstrate the continuing potential for highly destructive war. Some countries are facing generalized lawlessness and banditry, by marauding ex-soldiers in several African nations, drug cartels in some parts of Latin America, and organized crime in various parts of the former Soviet Union.[1] Tensions in the Middle East, parts of Africa, Central America, Ireland, Southeastern Europe, and Indonesia are further indications that war is a continuing fact of modern life.

Despite these widespread threats to national sovereignty, governments are obliged under Article 1 of the 1992 Convention on Biological Diversity to conserve their own biodiversity, and under Article 3 to ensure that activities within their jurisdiction or control do not cause damage to the biodiversity of other states.[2] Any negative impacts of war on biodiversity are clearly contrary to this international agreement, though this constraint

My thanks go to Jim Thorsell, who has provided much useful information; David Sheppard, for providing a number of articles on international peace parks; Cecile Thiery, IUCN Librarian, for helping to chase down obscure citations; and Martha Chouchena Rojas, Larry Hamilton, Calestous Juma, Richard Matthew, Jeff Sayer, Frank Vorhies, and Arthur Westing for helpful comments. Financial support for the preparation of this chapter was provided by the governments of Switzerland and Denmark. The opinions expressed in this chapter are mine alone, and are not intended to represent formal IUCN views.
[1] Michael Renner, *Fighting for Survival: Environmental Decline, Social Conflict, and the New Age of Insecurity* (New York: W. W. Norton & Co., 1996).
[2] United Nations Convention on Biological Diversity, done at Rio de Janeiro, June 5, 1992, entered into force December 29, 1993, Arts. 1 and 2.

cannot be expected to carry much weight with belligerent powers; NATO apparently did not consider biodiversity in their bombing plans over Kosovo, judging from the results.[3] But what, specifically, are the impacts of war on biodiversity? This chapter attempts to identify some of the key issues in preparing a balanced assessment of this question.

The issues are complicated, and the available evidence does not provide simple answers. However, it is hard to avoid the conclusion that modern means of transportation and communication, growing human populations and levels of resource consumption, increased vulnerabilities of inter-dependent, integrated economies, and the spread of modern instruments of war – including chemical and biological weapons – can readily make future wars extremely destructive for both people and the rest of nature.

At the same time, war is often seen as part of the way human societies adapt to changing conditions.[4] The International Commission on Peace and Food concluded that: "Historically, all landmark changes in the international political and security system have been the result of armed conflicts, wars and revolutions."[5] It appears that many, even most, societies have been defined by war, and that the organization of a society for the possibility of war has often been a principal political stabilizer. The victors who emerged from the ashes of war have sown the seeds that would produce subsequent tensions, disputes, and conflicts. It often seems that an institutional lack of capacity to adapt to change, or the inertia of vested interests in the *status quo*, means that societies inevitably become maladapted over time, eventually requiring a shock such as war to set them on a different course.[6] The role of World War II in aiding recovery from the Great Depression is one of the most familiar examples of this.

A fundamental issue is how humans stay within the productive limits of their supporting ecosystems. While most would agree that such adaptation

---

[3] Mark Fineman, "Serbia's Nightmare: The Toxic Aftermath of War," *Int'l Herald Trib.* (July 7, 1999); also, for a detailed discussion of whether peacetime conventions and treaties apply during war, see Silja Vöneky, "Peacetime Environmental Law as a Basis of State Responsibility for Environmental Damage Caused by War," chapter 7 in this volume.

[4] See, for example, Marvin Harris, *Cows, Pigs, Wars and Witches: The Riddle of Culture* (New York: Random House, 1974); Lawrence H. Keely, *War before Civilization* (New York: Oxford Univ. Press, 1996); and A. Vayda, *War in Ecological Perspective: Persistence, Change, and Adaptive Processes in Three Oceanian Studies* (New York: Plenum Press, 1976).

[5] International Commission on Peace and Food, *Uncommon Opportunities: An Agenda for Peace and Equitable Development* (London: Zed Books, 1994).

[6] Robert B. Edgerton, *Sick Societies: Challenging the Myth of Primitive Harmony* (New York: The Free Press, 1992).

should be possible through the application of knowledge and wisdom, history does not support such a rational view. In fact, war is virtually universal in human societies as a means of resolving conflicts arising from various forms of maladaptation of cultures to natural resource systems.[7] Underlying stress factors can produce or deepen rifts within and between societies, with disputes triggered by glaring social and economic disparities and exacerbated by the growing pressures of resource depletion, natural calamities, environmental degradation, and perceived excess population. Problems such as desertification, deforestation, soil erosion, and water scarcity reduce food-growing potential, worsen health effects, decrease biodiversity, and diminish life-support capacity. Any or all of these factors can lead to civil conflict and increase the likelihood of war. As Nietschmann concludes: "Degraded land and resources are as much a reason for taking up arms as are repression, invasion, and ideology."[8]

This chapter begins by briefly assessing war as one of the traditional means for human societies to adapt to changing environmental conditions, then assesses some of the positive and negative impacts of war on biodiversity. It then suggests several issues that must be addressed if modern civilization is to meet the growing security challenges of the twenty-first century. The chapter concludes by showing how conserving biodiversity can contribute to peace, building on the preamble to the Convention on Biological Diversity, which states that: "Ultimately, the conservation and sustainable use of biological diversity will strengthen friendly relations among states and contribute to peace for humankind."

The history of war and biodiversity

Today's biodiversity is, to a considerable extent, the result of the long-term interaction between people and their environments, reaching back at least as far as the origins of fire.[9] The greatest diversity of terrestrial species is

---

[7] Keely, *War before Civilization*.

[8] Bernard Nietschmann, "Battlefields of Ashes and Mud," *Nat. Hist.* 11 (1990), 35–7.

[9] See, for example, Tim Flannery, *The Future Eaters: An Ecological History of the Australian Lands and People* (New York: George Braziller, 1994); J. A. McNeely, K. R. Miller, W. V. Reid, R. A. Mittermeier, and T. B. Werner, *Conserving the World's Biological Diversity* (Gland, Switzerland: IUCN, 1994); Paul S. Martin and Richard G. Klein (eds.), *Quaternary Extinctions: A Prehistoric Revolution* (Tucson: Univ. of Arizona Press, 1984); and Clive Ponting, *A Green History of the World: The Environment and the Collapse of Great Civilizations* (New York: St. Martin's Press, 1992).

currently found in forested areas inhabited by tribal and other indigenous peoples. Within these areas exist relatively large tracts of "unoccupied" territory that serve as a sort of buffer zone between communities that may be embroiled – at least historically – in virtually constant warfare, including sneak attacks, revenge killings, kidnappings, raids on livestock, and so forth.[10] It is instructive, therefore, to examine briefly the impact on biodiversity of warfare among traditional and indigenous societies, how modern armies relate to tribal peoples, and the influence that such relations have had on biodiversity.

THE ARCHAEOLOGY AND ANTHROPOLOGY OF WAR

Archaeological evidence indicates that major fighting has a long history among human groups. In one late Paleolithic cemetery in northern Sudan, over 40 percent of those buried had stone projectile points embedded in their skeletons or intimately associated with them and many other archaeological sites contain human remains that show similar signs of violence.[11]

Several prehistoric societies moved towards fortifications during times of ecological stress. For example, the Anasazi in Arizona relocated many large tribal settlements to defensible locations in the troubled period between AD 1200 and 1300.[12] Fortifications and other signs of violent conflict greatly increased among horticultural societies in the American Great Plains when crops failed due to climate change.[13] Both archaeological evidence and traditional historical accounts indicate that the Maori of New Zealand became much more warlike as they abused their biological resources, including driving a major food source – the giant flightless birds known as moas – to extinction.[14]

One of the world's most biologically diverse areas is the upper Amazon, including parts of Venezuela, Colombia, and Brazil. It is a true "biodiversity hotspot," where borders are not well demarcated.[15] Perhaps not coincidentally, this is also an area that is occupied by a large number of different

---

[10] Keely, *War before Civilization*.

[11] *Ibid.*; see also Douglas B. Bamforth, "Indigenous Peoples, Indigenous Violence: Re-contact Warfare on the North American Great Plains," *Man* 29 (1994), 95–115.

[12] J. Haas and W. Creamer, *Stress and Warfare Among the Kayenta Anasazi of the 13th Century A.D.* (Chicago: Field Museum of Natural History, 1993).

[13] Bamforth, "Indigenous Peoples, Indigenous Violence."

[14] Flannery, *The Future Eaters*.

[15] McNeely et al., *Conserving the World's Biological Diversity*.

Indian groups who have established relationships with their environment, including elements such as warfare, infanticide, and raiding that are unacceptable in modern societies (except where they are sanctioned by the government as part of modern warfare). For example, among the Yanomamo Indians, the largest Indian group in the Amazon rainforest, 44 percent of males twenty-five or older have participated in the killing of someone, about 30 percent of adult male deaths are due to violence, and nearly 70 percent of all adults over forty have lost a close genetic relative as the result of human violence.[16]

Higher frequencies of war in traditional societies can be forecast by a history of unpredictable natural disasters and severe food shortages, as people tried to protect themselves by going to war to take resources from enemies.[17] Raids often included plundering food stores and gardens in the Americas, Polynesia, New Guinea, and Africa, leaving an enemy facing starvation and rendering large areas of territory at least temporarily uninhabitable. While this could serve to provide larger areas of habitat to various species of wildlife, it could also lead to significant increases in the pressure of human populations on the remaining wildlife populations. Losses and gains of territory were a very frequent result of warfare among pre-industrial societies, leading to dynamic tribal boundaries. These frontiers often were places supporting great diversity of species. Keeley concludes:

> Even in situations where no territory exchanges hands, active hostilities along a border can lead to development of a no-man's-land, as settlements nearest an enemy move or disperse to escape the effects of persistent raiding. Such buffer zones have been reported from Africa, North America, South America, and Oceania . . . Although such buffer zones could function ecologically as game and timber preserves, they were risky to use even for hunting and woodcutting because small isolated parties or individuals could easily be ambushed in them.[18]

These buffer zones often support a great richness of biodiversity.[19]

---

[16] Napoleon A. Chagnon, "Life Histories, Blood Revenge, and Warfare in a Tribal Population," *Sci.* 239 (1988), 985–92.

[17] Carol R. Ember and Melvin Ember, "Resource Unpredictability, Mistrust, and War," *J. Conflict Resol.* 36 (1992), 242–62.

[18] Keely, *War before Civilization.*

[19] Paul S. Martin and Christine R. Szuter, "War Zones and Game Sinks in Louis and Clark's West," *Conservation Biology* 13 (1999), 36–45.

BIODIVERSITY AND THE ANCIENT CONFLICT BETWEEN
FARMERS AND PASTORALISTS

Violent conflicts between herders and farmers go back at least to biblical times, perhaps arising from their differing ecological adaptations. Farmers are closely tied to the land, making it difficult for them to move away should they make an enemy. Pastoralists frequently move their families and herds, and doing so to avoid the consequences of a serious quarrel is no particular problem.[20] Some recent examples:

- The conflict in Somalia is the continuation of a 100-year-old movement of major Somali clans southward into agricultural areas from nomadic grazing areas that have been becoming more and more overpopulated due to mismanagement of biological resource systems;[21]
- In the Sudan, mechanized farming has been a key contributing factor to civil war between north and south that broke out in 1983 and continues today. Large-scale commercial farming and ranching projects are in conflict with peasants and pastoralists, forcing confrontation;[22]
- The bloody conflict in Rwanda, while a highly complex issue exacerbated by colonial French policy, can also be seen as yet another example of the conflict between farmer and herder. Tutsi is not exactly the name of an ethnic group: historically it meant "people who own cattle," and Hutu meant "people who farm." Note that in Rwanda, average farm size has declined from 2 hectares per family to 0.7 hectares over the past three decades, driven by population increases; land for the pastoralists has decreased as overall land for agriculture has increased .[23]

The frequent warfare between farmers and pastoralists is exacerbated by their interdependence, as each group produces something that the other needs. Farmers may also intrude on the favored habitats of nomadic peoples, leading to additional ecological pressures.[24] Thus, frontiers between

[20] Edgerton, *Sick Societies.*
[21] Robert A. Hutchison, *Fighting for Survival: Insecurity, People and Environment in the Horn of Africa* (Gland, Switzerland: IUCN, 1991).
[22] Mohamed Suliman, "Civil War in Sudan: The Impact of Ecological Degradation," in G. Bächler and K. R. Spillman (eds.), *Environmental Degradation as a Cause of War* (1996), vol. II.
[23] Günthar Bächler, "Rwanda: The Roots of Tragedy. Battle for Elimination on an Ethno-political and Ecological Basis," in Bächler and Spillman, *Environmental Degradation.*
[24] Mohamed Suliman, "War in Darfur, or the Desert vs. the Oasis Syndrome," in Bächler and Spillman, *Environmental Degradation.*

different ways of life are dynamic zones where possibilities for warfare are often the highest; this dynamism also means that such areas are often extremely rich in their biological resources because they tend to have species characteristic of the various life zones.[25]

Anthropologists argue that the age-old conflict between farmer and herder serves to maintain a balance between different forms of land use.[26] If the population of farmers increases and starts to occupy the marginal lands that can be used more sustainably for herding, this causes a violent reaction on the part of the herders that in turn may drive the agriculturalists off the marginal land. Conversely, if the herders exceed the carrying capacity of their grazing lands, they increase their raids on the farming lands, stimulating a violent reaction on the part of the farmers.

<h2 style="text-align:center">TRADITIONAL PEOPLES, BIODIVERSITY, AND THE MODERN MILITARY</h2>

Warfare between modern and traditional societies has often involved what might be termed "ecological attacks." One of the most obvious examples of this is the final destruction of the great herds of American bison, the foundation of Plains Indian life in the United States, which closely coincided with the defeat of the Sioux and Cheyenne in the 1870s. Biological warfare was also used, either accidentally or intentionally. Diseases such as smallpox, measles, and influenza had a major impact on the native populations of the Americas, Australia, and the Pacific Islands because they lacked immunity to the "new" diseases. Perhaps more important, the European colonialism – driven largely by resource depletion at home – also brought ecological transformations that disrupted traditional economies and replaced native ecosystems with new agricultural systems that produced more of the goods required by colonists, leading to fundamental – and perhaps permanent – changes in biodiversity.[27]

The relationship between indigenous peoples, colonists, the modern military, and biodiversity in the species-rich frontier region in the upper

---

[25] Peggy L. Fiedler and S. K. Jane (eds.), *Conservation Biology: The Theory and Practice of Nature Conservation, Preservation, and Management* (New York: Chapman and Hall, 1992); Michael E. Soulé (ed.), *Conservation Biology: The Science of Scarcity and Diversity* (Sunderland, Mass.: Sinauer Associates, 1986); Richard B. Primack, *Essentials of Conservation Biology* (Sunderland, Mass.: Sinauer Associates, 1993).

[26] Harris, *Cows, Pigs, Wars and Witches*; Vayda, *War in Ecological Perspective*.

[27] Alfred Crosby, *Ecological Imperialism* (New York: Cambridge Univ. Press, 1986).

Amazon occupied by the Yanomamo is a complex and fascinating one that contains several important lessons for those seeking better understanding of the relationship between biodiversity and national security. In November 1991, Brazil's President, Fernando Collor de Mello, issued a decree to give the Yanomamo partial control of their traditional lands. The decree was part of a zoning process that involved dividing the forest into protected areas, land for traditional Indian farming and hunting, and areas permitting environmentally destructive development, such as logging, building roads and dams, and mining. The decree was opposed by the Brazilian military because the Yanomamo lands extend across the borders with Venezuela and Colombia, a militarily sensitive area. The Brazilian military, which supports gold-mining interests in the region, has continued to impede full legalization of Indian land rights near its international borders, branding as subversives those scientists who are working internationally to save the Amazonian forest habitats of the indigenous peoples. A secret document was reportedly prepared by the Brazilian High War College proposing that war could be used against indigenous or environmental organizations in the Amazon.[28] Others have reported that: "The idea that the Amazon might be invaded by foreign armies aiming to stop the deforestation may appear ludicrous to foreigners, but it is taken seriously in South America and has been used to justify the Brazilian military's tight control of Amazonian policy."[29]

Conselho Indigenista Missionário (CIMI), a Brazilian human rights group, concludes that the Brazilian military sees the preservation of the rainforest and its peoples as a threat to national security, considering it necessary to "clean" the frontier strip of obstacles to more permanent investments (such as mining and dams), which spells disaster for the Indians and for the region's biodiversity.[30] This perception perpetuates the conflict between the interests of the military, indigenous peoples, and conservationists.

This military mindset is not confined to Brazil. In Venezuela, a proposal to create a Yanomamo Biosphere Reserve along the border with Brazil was rejected by the Ministry of External Relations, which was concerned that

---

[28] Damien Lewis, "Brazil's Army Loses Temper," *BBC Wildlife* (July 1990), 483.
[29] Beth A. Conklin and Laura R. Graham, "The Shifting Middle Ground: Amazonian Indians and Ecopolitics," *Am. Anth.* 97 (1995), 695–710.
[30] Conselho Indigenista Missionário, "Doctrine of National Security Threatens Brazil's Indians," *Cultural Survival Q.* 11 (1987), 63–65.

national and international public opinion would be mobilized to seek the human rights of the indigenous groups and to promote eventual self-development and self-determination. They singled out a group of Venezuelan ecologists and anthropologists as the core of an international conspiracy to undermine the ability of the government to control the Amazon territory and its native inhabitants.[31] The high-level Congress of the Armies of the Americas (CAA) used a number of distortions to reduce complex social problems into a black-and-white opposition between "national security" and "terrorist subversion," with those advocating Indian rights being linked to subversive organizations (a group that also included feminists). In essence, the CAA created a mythological history of the relationships between indigenous peoples and their land, defining the problems in terms that required military solutions, ignoring the role of indigenous ways of life in maintaining the rich biodiversity of the upper Amazon and the dependence of those peoples on the biological resources of the forest.[32]

To conclude this section, it appears that various forms of war have been part of the way traditional societies have adapted to changing conditions and – at least coincidentally – have helped contribute to the rich biodiversity found today in many areas occupied by traditional and indigenous peoples. Bringing peace to these regions will remove this means of adaptation, requiring that other ways be developed to conserve biodiversity and maintain the capacity of people to adapt to changing conditions.[33]

The impacts of war on biodiversity

NEGATIVE IMPACTS OF WAR ON BIODIVERSITY

The negative impacts of war on biodiversity often result from the collective actions of large numbers of people – both combatants and non-combatants – for whom war is a dispensation to ignore normal restraints on activities that cause environmental damage. War, and preparations for it, has negative impacts on all levels of biodiversity, from genes to species to ecosystems.

[31] Jonathan D. Hill, "Alienated Targets: Military Discourse and the Disempowerment of Indigenous Amazonian Peoples in Venezuela," *Identities* 1 (1994), 7–34.
[32] *Ibid.*
[33] See, for example, Jack Weatherford, *Savages and Civilization: Who Will Survive?* (New York: Crown, 1994); Denys Delâge, *Bitter Feast: Amerindians and Europeans in Northeastern North America* (Vancouver: UBC Press, 1993); and Robert Brain, *The Last Primitive Peoples* (New York: Crown, 1976).

These impacts can be direct, such as hunting and habitat destruction by armies, or indirect, for example through the activities of refugees.

Sometimes these impacts can be deliberate, and a new word has been added to the military vocabulary: "ecocide," the destruction of the environment for military purposes. This term clearly builds on the "scorched earth" approach of earlier times. It is possible to divide deliberate environmental manipulations during wartime into two broad categories: those involving massive and extended applications of disruptive techniques to deny to the enemy any habitats that produce food, refuge, cover, training grounds, and staging areas for attacks; and those involving relatively small disruptive actions that in turn release large amounts of "dangerous forces," or become self-generating.[34] Examples of the latter include the release of exotic micro-organisms, attempts to change rainfall patterns, and spreading of landmines (of which over 100 million now litter active and former war zones around the world).[35]

This discussion of the negative effects of war could be long and dreary, but only a few illustrative cases will be mentioned. Perhaps the most outstanding example is Vietnam, where US forces cleared 325,000 hectares of land and sprayed 72,400 cubic meters of herbicides in the name of security.[36] The impact on biodiversity was severe. Spreading herbicides on 10 percent of the country (including 50 percent of the mangroves) led to extensive low-diversity grasslands replacing high-diversity forests, mudflats instead of highly productive mangroves, major declines in both freshwater and coastal fisheries, and so forth.[37]

Africa was the setting of several recent war-related disasters for biodiversity. Like the upper Amazon, the Virunga Volcanoes region (including parts of the Central African countries of Rwanda, Democratic Republic of Congo, and Uganda) is exceptionally rich in species diversity, including the rare and endangered mountain gorilla, whose total population is only approximately 600. The civil war against the government of Rwanda was launched in 1990 from within the Virunga Volcanoes region, spreading

[34] Arthur H. Westing, *Ecological Consequences of the Second Indochina War* (Stockholm: Almqvist & Wiksell Int'l, 1976).

[35] Gino Strada, "The Horror of Landmines," *Sci. Am.* 274(5) (1996), 40–45.

[36] Arthur H. Westing, "The Environmental Aftermath of Warfare in Viet Nam," in *World Armaments and Disarmament: SIPRI Yearbook 1982* (1982), pp. 363–89.

[37] Nietschmann, "Battlefields of Ashes and Mud"; also, for a detailed discussion on the health impacts of the use of defoliants in Vietnam, see Alastair W. M. Hay, "Defoliants: The Long-term Health Implications," chapter 16 in this volume.

deeper into Rwanda until 1994 and sending large numbers of refugees fleeing to North Kivu District in what was then Zaire, which then began a civil war of its own. The headquarters of several World Heritage sites in Zaire were taken over by the military, including Garamba National Park, Virunga National Park, Kahuzi-Biega National Park, and the Okapi Wildlife Reserve. The effects of the refugees were the most damaging part of the war for biodiversity. They were felt especially heavily in the Virunga National Park, where the presence of over 700,000 refugees in five camps was a disaster for conservation because of rampant forest clearance for obtaining firewood and construction material and direct hunting of wildlife.[38]

Biodiversity exists not only in national parks, and indeed some of the most important diversity includes the domesticated plants upon which human welfare depends. War often has a devastating impact on these resources. For example, in Zaire the National Institute of Agronomic Studies and Research was overrun by 60,000 refugees, leading to the loss of forty-seven clones of cinchona and 40 hectares of coffee clones. As Biswas and Tortajada-Quiroz point out, "The cinchona clones had been developed over a period of 15 to 20 years of experimentation, to suit Zairian conditions. Since there are no storage facilities at Mulungu, no germplasms were stored. Accordingly, cinchona and coffee clones are likely to have been irretrievably lost."[39] The loss of cinchona is especially disastrous as it provides essential treatment for the local strains of malaria that have become a serious health problem, at least partly as a result of the region's wars.

A few other examples (among many that could be provided):

- The administrator and two rangers of the Saslaya National Park in Nicaragua (15,000 hectares) were kidnapped by the Contras in 1983, forcing the National Environment Agency to abandon the management of the area;[40]
- In 1996, the Kibira and Ruvubu National Parks in Burundi were used as sanctuaries and entry points for guerrillas fighting the government. As a

---

[38] Samson Werikhe, Norbert Mushenzi, and Jean Bizimana, "The Impact of War on Protected Areas in Central Africa: Case Study of Virunga Volcanoes Region," in IUCN (ed.), *Parks for Peace Conference Proceedings* (1997), pp. 155–62.

[39] Asit K. Biswas and H. Cecila Tortajada-Quiroz, "Environmental Impacts of the Rwandan Refugees on Zaire," *Ambio* 25 (1996), 403–9.

[40] Jim Thorsell (ed.), *Parks on the Borderline: Experience in Transfrontier Conservation* (Gland, Switzerland: IUCN, 1991).

result, they also became operational areas for government troops, with both sides heavily involved in poaching;[41]

- Kidepo Valley National Park, along the Sudan border in northwestern Uganda, has suffered tremendously from the strained relations between Uganda and Sudan. As Seale concludes, "wildlife populations in northern Uganda have declined greatly in the past 20 years, in large part because of civil unrest";[42]
- Under the influence of a number of historical, socio-economic, and political factors, an armed conflict in Niger has developed in recent years between the indigenous Tuareg people and the state. In Aïr Ténéré Reserve (7,736,000 hectares), also a World Heritage site, civil disturbances have led to its staff being held hostage, and to loss of life;
- India's Manas Wildlife Sanctuary, a World Heritage site, has been taken over by guerrillas from the Bodo tribe, who have burned down park buildings, looted most park facilities, killed guards, destroyed bridges, poached rhinos, elephants, tigers, and other wildlife, cleared forests, and depleted fish stocks in the Manas river;[43]
- In Sri Lanka, Wilpattu National Park was attacked by Tamil rebels in 1986, killing twenty-one staff and destroying facilities. This has caused a withdrawal of conservation staff, and a great increase in military activity in the area;[44]
- Total bird mortality resulting from the Gulf War is estimated at about 15,000–30,000, mainly seabirds, although it is estimated that large numbers of migratory birds also have died following contamination by oil during passage.[45] In addition, the basic functioning of the desert ecosystem was disrupted through the breaking up of gravel and the sand surface of the desert, creating vehicle ruts and tank tracks, and compacting desert soils (thereby hampering the growth of vegetation);[46]
- Some species are directly affected. During the Vietnam War, elephants were specifically targeted by helicopter gunships because they might be

---

[41] Philip Winter, "Wildlife and War," *Swara* (July/Aug. 1997), 6–7.

[42] Ronald G. Seale, "Parks at the Edge: The Case of Uganda," in IUCN, *Parks for Peace Conference Proceedings*, pp. 83–88.

[43] Himraj Dang, *Human Conflict in Conservation: Protected Areas, the Indian Experience* (New Delhi: Har-Anand Publications in assoc. with Vikas Pub. House, 1991).

[44] Based on discussions with Department of Wildlife Conservation staff in Sri Lanka.

[45] Robin Pellew, "Disaster in the Gulf," *IUCN Bull.* 22 (1991), 17–18.

[46] See Samira A. S. Omar et al., "The Gulf War Impact on the Terrestrial Environment of Kuwait: An Overview," chapter 12 in this volume.

used as pack animals by the Vietcong; the European bison was slaughtered nearly to extinction to supply the mess kitchens of German and Soviet troops in eastern Poland at successive stages of World War II, leaving only a score of bison by 1945; and the white rhino was exterminated from Sudan during the seventeen years of civil war from 1955 to 1972.[47]

The conclusion is not surprising: war is bad for biodiversity.

POSITIVE IMPACTS OF WAR ON BIODIVERSITY

War can also be good for biodiversity, at least under certain conditions. As Myers put it, "In some respects, indeed, wildlife benefits from warfare: combatant armies effectively designate war zones as 'off limits' to casual wanderers, thus quarantining large areas of Africa from hunters and poachers."[48] Of course, any benefits of war to biodiversity are incidental, inadvertent, and accidental rather than a planned side effect of conflict. But even so, it is useful to review some cases where war, or preparations for war, has benefited biodiversity, perhaps supporting the views of some anthropologists that war helps societies adapt to their environmental constraints. (See Table 14.1)

Demilitarized zones (DMZs) are often beneficial for biodiversity, at least temporarily. An outstanding example is the DMZ of the Korean Peninsula, which is a no-man's land 4 km wide, stretching 240 km across the peninsula; the South maintains an additional strip that averages 5.4 km in width and totals 1,529 km^2, to which access is severely restricted. This cross-section of Korean biodiversity contains habitats from the rocky east coast through the country's mountainous spine, including native pine and oak forest, the marshy interior basin of the Imjin river, and the point where the estuary of the Han River meets the intertidal flats of the muddy Yellow Sea. It provides a sanctuary for a wide diversity of Korea's species, many now rare elsewhere. About 150 red-crowned cranes from Manchuria come annually to the DMZ's central basin around Cholwon.[49] Further west, around the truce village of Panmunjom, up to 300 white-naped cranes pass through every winter. It has been found that the Korean demilitarized zone is

[47] Malcolm W. Brown, Michio Kaku, James M. Fallows, and Eric Fischer, "War and the Environment," *Audubon* 93 (1991), 88–99; Rajab Abdullah, "Protected Areas During War and Conflict. Nimule National Park: A Case Study," in IUCN, *Parks for Peace Conference Proceedings*, pp. 195–99.
[48] Norman Myers, "Wildlife and the Dogs of War," *Daily Telegraph* (Dec. 8, 1979).
[49] Colin Poole, "The Gift of No Man's Land," *BBC Wildlife* (Sept. 1991), 636–39.

Table 14.1. *Impacts of war on biodiversity*

Negative impacts	Positive impacts
Causes deforestation	Creates "no-go" zones
Increases wildlife poaching	Slows or stops developments that lead to
Destroys habitat	loss of biodiversity
Pollutes land and water	Focuses state resolve
Reduces funds for conservation	Reduces pressure on some habitats
Stops conservation projects	Disarms rural populations, thereby
Forces people onto marginal lands	reducing hunting
Creates refugees who destroy biodiversity	Can increase biodiversity-related research

an essential migratory habitat of these cranes and that they stop at some sites in the DMZ for up to 87 percent of their total migration time.[50] As Poole puts it: "Here the presence of the Cranes is especially haunting. These symbols of oriental peace and tranquillity stand sentinel between the gun-toting border guards."[51]

While the Second Indochina War was an ecological disaster, it also led to some important biological research, such as the extensive, long-term study of migratory birds in Eastern Asia carried out by the Migratory Animals Pathological Survey.[52] The pretext for this research was its relevance to the war effort, but it has yielded data that are useful for numerous civilian conservation applications; such a survey might very well not have been funded in peacetime. The watersheds through which the Ho Chi Minh trail ran (some of the most heavily bombed parts of Indo-China during the Second Indochina War) have more recently been remarkably productive in new discoveries of large mammals, including four species previously unknown to science, and the rediscovery of a species of pig that formerly was known only by a few fragmentary specimens. The new large mammal discoveries include two species of muntjak or barking deer, a unique variety of forest antelope, and a bovid ultimately related to wild cattle.[53] That such

[50] H. Higuchi et al., "Satellite Tracking of White-Naped Crane Migration and the Importance of the Korean Demilitarized Zone," *Conservation Biology* 10 (1996), 806–12.
[51] Poole, "The Gift."
[52] Elliot H. McClure, *Migration and Survival of the Birds of Asia* (Bangkok: Seato Medical Research Laboratory, 1974).
[53] Thomas C. Dillon and Eric D. Wikramanayake, "Parks, Peace and Progress: A Forum for Transboundary Conservation in Indo-China," *PARKS* 7 (1997), 36–51.

species could survive in such a heavily bombed area is testimony to the recuperative power of nature, and the ability of wildlife to withstand even the most extreme kinds of human pressure during warfare.

War sometimes stimulates governments to act more quickly than they otherwise would have. An excellent example is the United Kingdom, which going into World War II had dithered for five decades over its nature conservation program. As Sheail points out,

> Whilst the outbreak of war in September 1939 brought an immediate cessation of all official work not directly related to the war effort, the succeeding five years were of pivotal importance in re-defining the role of central and local government. In a remarkable burst of energy, ministries were restructured, legislation promoted, and fresh prescriptions for the future written, each drawing on unprecedented support for more centralized forms of planning.[54]

These efforts ensured that nature conservation and nature reserves had a place in the British program of postwar reconstruction. Nicholson found it an ironic commentary on the workings of the British system of government that it was possible, under heavy bombing and constant rocket attack, absence of key figures on military service, and petrol rationing, finally to complete a survey of the wildlife resources of the UK that had been demanded by conservationists for over fifty years.[55] This apparently was especially due to the wartime suspension of "the normal mechanisms for ensuring inaction."[56] While centralized forms of planning are now out of fashion and have been replaced by highly decentralized management and decisionmaking, it remains to be seen which is better for biodiversity; perhaps they are both part of an adaptive cycle.

Some species actually benefit from war, such as those that feed on battlefield dead. For example, Bruun says that: "During the ravages of the Hundred Years War, the wolves in Europe increased in numbers with almost explosive speed, justifying their name as 'war's brothers.' "[57] It is known that tigers were increasing in the war-torn jungles of Southeast Asia during the protracted Vietnamese War, at a time when the remaining tiger populations in more peaceful parts of the world were rapidly disappearing. During the Iran–Iraq War, sharks swam up the rivers, unusual territory for

[54] John Sheail, "War and the Development of Nature Conservation in Britain," *J. Envtl. Mgmt.* 44 (1995), 267–83.
[55] E. M. Nicholson, *The Environmental Revolution* (London: Hodder & Stoughton, 1970).
[56] *Ibid.*   [57] Bertel Bruun, "Birds, Bombs and Borders," *Explorers J.* 59 (1981), 154–59.

them, to feed on dead soldiers who had been dumped in the water.[58] And when German submarines shut down the North Atlantic fisheries during World War II, the fisheries were rejuvenated, which in turn led to bumper catches in the postwar years (subsequently followed by overfishing and steep declines, which in turn led to repeat "cod wars" between Canada and Spain over the few remaining fish).[59] These examples, among many that could be cited, indicate that biodiversity can also benefit from war, though any such benefits may be short-lived.

MIXED IMPACTS OF WAR ON BIODIVERSITY

The impact of war on biodiversity is often decidedly mixed, with a complex combination of damage and benefits. Nicaragua provides an outstanding example.[60] Engaged in civil war for over twenty years, nearly half of the country's population was relocated in one way or another, and nearly 100,000 casualties resulted. The human tragedy was immense, but biodiversity was able to recover from a long history of exploitation, as trade in timber, fish, minerals, and wildlife was sharply reduced. The domestic cattle population, which was roughly equivalent to the human population, was reduced by two-thirds, freeing pastures for re-colonization by forests, enabling the recovery of animal populations such as white-tailed deer, peccaries, monkeys, crocodiles, iguanas, large birds, and various mammalian predators. Fishing boats were destroyed and fishermen fled, leading to drastic declines in the catches of fish, shrimp, and lobsters, which in turn revitalized these fisheries. On the other hand, some hunting by soldiers had at least local negative impacts on wildlife, and new military bases and roads were established in formerly remote areas, opening them up to exploitation. Further, the country's once outstanding system of protected areas fell into neglect, and new areas planned were not established. The collapsing economy forced villagers into environmentally destructive activities, including clearing forest for firewood and harvesting wildlife for food. Nietschmann concludes that, in the end, a significant portion of this conflict was over resources and territory, not ideology.[61]

---

[58] Richard Wolkomir and Joyce Wolkomir, "Caught in the Cross-fire," *Int'l Wildlife* 22 (1992), 5–11.
[59] Mark Kurlansky, *Cod: A Biography of the Fish that Changed the World* (New York: Walher & Co., 1997).
[60] Bernard Nietschmann, "Conservation by Conflict in Nicaragua," *Nat. Hist.* 11 (1990), 42–49.
[61] *Ibid.*

In the Central and Eastern European countries occupied by Soviet troops, some 2 percent of the land was given over to military bases and the Iron Curtain functioned as a long, well-protected nature reserve.[62] In countries such as Latvia, much of the military land was in the form of undeveloped training areas that were able to maintain values for biodiversity conservation, though in many other areas the Soviet army left behind a legacy of devastation.

While war is bad for biodiversity, peace can be even worse: in the 1960s, when Indonesia and Malaysia were fighting over border claims on the island of Borneo, they did relatively little damage to its vast wilderness, but in the 1990s they were peacefully competing to cut down and sell its forests; Vietnam's forests are under greater pressure now that peace has arrived than they ever were during the country's wars; and in Nicaragua, biodiversity rejuvenated by the war is under renewed threat by people whom the war has impoverished.[63] The motivations may be nobler in times of peace, but the impacts of inappropriate development on biodiversity can be even worse than the impacts of war. Market forces are often more destructive than military forces.

Emerging issues in the study of war and biodiversity

BIOLOGICAL WARFARE AND BIODIVERSITY

One of the major driving forces behind the Convention on Biological Diversity was increasing concern about how to share more equitably the potential benefits arising from advances in biotechnology. While the revolution in biotechnology and cheap new manufacturing methods will provide obvious benefits in the biomedical and agricultural sectors, they will also open the way for development of more efficient production of biological warfare agents in much smaller facilities. Such weapons could provide countries, or even small groups, with the capacity for launching a first strike with devastating results over a wide area. One United Nations study found that a 10 ton biological weapon could kill 25 percent of the people, and make another 50 percent ill, over an area of 100,000 km^2.[64]

---

[62] Esther Wolff, "Study on Military Land in Europe: A Summary," in IUCN, *Parks for Peace Conference Proceedings*, pp. 75–78.

[63] Nietschmann, "Conservation by Conflict."

[64] British Medical Association, *Biotechnology, Weapons and Humanity* (1999).

A number of recent press reports and popular books have discussed the dangers of biological warfare. One report from the US Federal Bureau of Investigation indicates that biological weapons are being intercepted in the US at a rate of about one per month, but to date the releases have been by incompetents, so no damage has been done.[65] Leaving aside the social, economic, and health impacts of biological warfare, what are the impacts for biodiversity?[66] One of the disease organisms that is often discussed as an agent of biological warfare is anthrax. If anthrax, which is basically a disease of livestock, became endemic in a human population, it could certainly spread into domesticated and wild mammals as well, though the impact on the biodiversity of an area as a whole remains highly speculative.

The potential danger from biological weapons is likely to increase quickly, given the fairly simple procedures involved in propagating them. For example, the Japanese cult known as Aum Shinrikyo, which launched a chemical attack on the Tokyo subway system in March 1995 that killed twelve people and injured 5,000, was also working on biological weapons and had already launched at least five biological attacks (all of which failed, apparently because of low toxicity of the organisms used).[67] There are reports that terrorists are already using the Internet to spread information about biological weapons.[68] Clearly, the danger of biological warfare needs to be addressed primarily because of its impact on society, rather than because of any potential impacts on biodiversity. However, it is worth keeping in mind that any impact on human society is likely to have various impacts on biodiversity as well.

CLIMATE CHANGE, BIODIVERSITY, AND WAR

Climate historians have frequently pointed out that fundamental changes in civilizations are often associated with major climate changes, if not directly caused by them. Numerous elaborate and powerful civilizations of the past – such as the Indus, the Hittites, the Mycenaeans, and the Mali

[65] Richard Preston, "Discuss Biological Weapons," *Int'l Herald Trib.* (Apr. 22, 1998).
[66] See, for example, Laurie Garrett, *The Coming Plague: Newly Emerging Diseases in a World Out of Balance* (New York: Farvar, Straus & Giroux, 1994).
[67] Judith Miller and William J. Broad, "Secret Exercise Finds US Can't Cope with a Biological Terror Attack," *Int'l Herald Trib.* (Apr. 27, 1998).
[68] Preston, "Discuss Biological Weapons."

Empire of Africa – declined and fell because climate change made them vulnerable to invasion, another indication of the environmental linkages to war.[69] This point is increasingly relevant now because the Intergovernmental Panel on Climate Change has concluded that human-caused emissions of various greenhouse gases will change the global climate, with profound implications for both biodiversity and national security.[70]

For example, the Gulf Stream keeps Europe wet and warm rather than being as cold as Canada (Madrid is as far north as New York, while London is as far north as the Hudson Bay). In response to greenhouse warming and increased rainfall in Europe, northern Atlantic surface salinity could decrease, which would drastically decrease deep water production in the ocean just south of Iceland, deflecting the Gulf Stream and leading to a significant global cooling.[71] This could lead to famine in Europe, a significant impetus for violence on a continent with a bloody history.

With the expected rise in sea level resulting from climate change, several hundred million people living in coastal areas could be put at risk in the next several decades. Bangladesh, for example, could find some 17 percent of its territory under water, and virtually the entire country would be subject to repeated massive flooding. Some low-lying countries may become essentially uninhabitable.[72] United Nations Environment Program (UNEP) projections suggest that sea level rise, along with amplified tidal waves and storm surges, could eventually threaten some 5 million km^2 of coastal areas worldwide, an area that encompasses one-third of all crop lands, is home to more than a billion people, and supports considerable biodiversity.

Warfare is often associated with periods of severe drought or other natural calamities that exacerbate social problems. It has been found that tribal societies that had a history of expectable but unpredictable disasters, such as droughts, floods, and insect infestations, were the ones most frequently at war. In areas plagued by drought, higher numbers of raiding parties were sent out in the dry years.[73] In Ethiopia, periods of conflict and

[69] Central Intelligence Agency, *A Study of Climatological Research as it Pertains to Intelligence Problems* (Langley, Vt.: CIA, 1974).
[70] J. T. Houghton, G. J. Jenkins, and J. J. Ephraums (eds.), *Climate Change: The IPCC Scientific Assessment* (Cambridge: Cambridge Univ. Press, 1990).
[71] Wallace S. Broeker, "Thermohaline Circulation, the Achilles Heel of Our Climate System: Will Man-made CO$_2$ Upset the Current Balance?" *Sci.* 278 (1997), 1582–88.
[72] R. T. Watson, M. C. Zinyowera, and R. H. Moss (eds.), *Climate Change 1995: Impacts, Adaptations and Mitigation of Climate Change* (Cambridge: Cambridge Univ. Press, 1996).
[73] Ember and Ember, "Resource Unpredictability."

political instability invariably have reached their greatest pitch during or following major droughts, some of which have resettled up to 600,000 people, leading to even greater environmental disruption.[74] Thus, the climate change that is generally accepted to be inevitable, if not already upon us, is likely to enhance the probability and frequency of warfare through its impacts on biodiversity.

WAR, WATER, AND BIODIVERSITY

Worldwide, over 240 river basins are shared between two or more states, and five are shared among at least seven states. Relationships between the states that share these water resources are formalized in over 2,000 bilateral agreements covering various aspects of navigation, research, fishing, water quotas, and flood control. Even so, considerable tensions arise over the use of water, which (of course) is a fundamental resource for maintaining biodiversity, in addition to being essential to human welfare. The Middle East is perhaps the best example. In 1963, Egyptian President Gamal Nasser used the water issue to unite the Arab states behind him, calling for water management projects on the inflows of the River Jordan in Lebanon and Syria that could deny water to the Israelis. Very little was realized in practical terms, but it was the beginning of a political confrontation that was one of the triggers of the Arab–Israeli Six Day War of June 1967, which gave Israel an effective monopoly over the water resources of the upper Jordan valley. Access to water remains one of the major – if generally unspoken – obstacles to peace in the Middle East today.[75]

India is now pressing against the limits of its water supply. Indian politics have featured inter-state conflicts over water at least since the 1960s. Conflicts are now worsening, for example, between the states of Tamil Nadu and Karnataka in Southern India over Cauvery irrigation water, between Punjab and Haryana over Beas and Sutlej water, and between Haryana and Delhi over water from the Yamuna. Inter-sectoral conflicts are also becoming more acute due to growing urbanization and industrialization. Andra Pradesh and Karnataka are at loggerheads over the height of the Alamatti Dam on the Krishna River. And Madhya Pradesh and Gujarat are

[74] Hutchison, *Fighting for Survival.*
[75] Peter Wald, "Water as a Source of Conflict: Cross-border Water Problems in the Middle East," *Dev. & Cooperation* 2 (1997), 17–18.

in dispute over the water of the Narmada River.[76] Some experts believe that water disputes, if not attended to, will become a major domestic threat to the stability of Indian society, perhaps forcing the central government to look to its neighbors to deflect public anxiety.[77] The recent tests of nuclear weapons should be seen against this background of domestic conflict over important resources that are highly relevant to biodiversity.

BIODIVERSITY LOSS AS A CONTRIBUTOR TO WAR

Resource degradation, including loss of biodiversity, can create scarcities that push people out of the regions where they live. Insufficient supplies of firewood and timber, depleted aquifers, and soil erosion can form a feed-back loop of poverty, insecurity, and environmental degradation. As Kane points out:

> Felled trees, for example, no longer anchor soil, which washes away and clogs rivers, and the disrupted flows of water cause further soil erosion and disrupt harvests of fish. In rural areas where people directly depend on the soil and water and forests for sustenance, poverty is essentially an environmental trend. These people are usually cash poor, yet so long as they are natural resource rich, they can remain home and prosper. But when people flee poverty they are often fleeing environmental impoverishment – after the topsoil blew away or the well ran dry – in places without a rural economy that offers them alternative sources of livelihood.[78]

Resource scarcity can arise from three sources: degradation or depletion of a resource; increasing consumption of the resource (for example, due to population growth or rising per capita resource consumption); and uneven distribution that gives relatively few people disproportionate access to the resource and subjects the rest to scarcity. Resource scarcity can lead to declining agricultural production, economic hardship, migrations of people from areas of environmental stress, and tensions within and among groups – a mélange of factors that contribute to violent conflict.[79] When

[76] Peter Gleick, "Water and Conflict: Freshwater Resources and International Security," *Int'l Security* 18 (1993), 79–112.
[77] Peter Gleick, "Freshwater: A Source of Conflict or Cooperation," in Bächler and Spillman, *Environmental Degradation*, pp. 1–26.
[78] Hal Kane, "The Hour of Departure: Forces that Create Refugees and Migrants," *Worldwatch Paper* 125 (1995), 1–56.
[79] Thomas F. Homer-Dixon, "Environmental Scarcities and Violent Conflict: Evidence from Cases," *Int'l Security* 19 (1994), 5–40.

resource scarcity reduces the ability of states to meet the needs of their population, dissatisfaction can lead to declining state authority, which sooner or later nurtures collective violent action. Homer-Dixon concludes:

> Within the next 50 years, the planet's human population will probably pass 9 billion, and global economic output may quintuple. Largely as a result, scarcities of renewable resources will increase sharply. The total area of high-quality agricultural land will drop, as will the extent of forests and the number of species they contain. Coming generations will also see the widespread depletion and degradation of aquifers, rivers, and other water resources; the decline of many fisheries; and perhaps significant climate change.[80]

Resource scarcities in many parts of the developing world are already contributing to violent conflicts that are probably early signs of an upsurge of violence in the coming decades that will be induced or aggravated by even more acute scarcity. Poor societies will be particularly affected because they are less able to buffer themselves from resource scarcities and resulting social crises. These societies typically already suffer acute hardship from shortages of water, forests, and fertile land. A major problem is that fast-moving, unpredictable, and complex environmental problems can over-whelm efforts at constructive social reform. Moreover, scarcity can sharply increase demands on key institutions, such as the state, while it simultaneously reduces their capacity to meet those demands. These pressures increase the chance that the state will either disintegrate or become more authoritarian, both of which enhance the likelihood for war.

CONSERVING BIODIVERSITY AS A CONTRIBUTION TO PEACE

On a more positive note, in at least some countries, today's military sees conserving biodiversity as an important part of its mission. Throughout Europe, the peacetime military has formally recognized that it has a key role to play in conserving biodiversity on its estate, with implementation of this principle varying from voluntary undertakings by the military to legally binding guidelines and fully elaborated management plans. In the United Kingdom, the Ministry of Defence has entered into formal agreements with the statutory conservation agencies that designate part of the military estate as Sites of Special Scientific Interest. And in the US, the

[80] *Ibid.*

Department of Defense issued an Ecosystem Management Policy Directive in 1994 that articulated a biodiversity conservation policy to "maintain and improve the sustainability and native biological diversity of terrestrial and aquatic, including marine, ecosystems while supporting human needs, including the DOD mission."[81]

Some countries use biodiversity conservation efforts to help promote domestic peace. Lebanon suffered a violent and bloody civil war from 1974 to 1990, resulting in significant loss of human life, massive destruction of property, fragmentation and weakening of the central authority, and various forms of environmental degradation. Following peace, a massive building boom further accelerated the rate of environmental destruction, as contractors demanded access to diminishing water supplies, concrete, stone, and sand with little regard to their value as natural resources and their roles in the surrounding ecosystems. Trees were cut for firewood and charcoal, livestock were released to graze eroding slopes, and hunters continued to slaughter migrating birds by the thousands.[82] Several NGOs were developed to meet conservation needs even during the war, and now are mobilizing funds from the financial mechanism of the Convention on Biological Diversity to use protected areas as one means of fostering recovery from the war. Abu-Izzadin identifies at least four ways that the new system of protected areas is promoting peace in Lebanon:

- *Visiting the reserves.* The fragmentation of the country is being repaired by bringing people together from different parts of Lebanon and rein-troducing them to their natural heritage through properly organized and guided tours in the protected areas;
- *Appointing local NGOs.* National reconciliation is promoted by appointing local NGOs to plan, protect, and manage the protected areas, thereby diffusing tensions and minimizing unwanted friction between opposing factions. This measure also helps to ensure that management practices are fully compatible with local political, social, and religious institutions;
- *Bringing institutions together.* Bringing government, NGOs, and scientific institutions together to establish a network of protected areas is expected to enhance national reconciliation;

---

[81] US Department of Defense, "DOD Commander's Guide to Biodiversity" (no date, presumably 1997); US Department of Defense, "Ecosystem Management Policy Directive," issued by the Deputy Under-Secretary of Defense (1994).
[82] Faisal Abu-Izzadin, "Lebanon: The Role of the Protected Areas Project in Promoting Peace," in IUCN, *Parks for Peace Conference Proceedings*, pp. 173–77.

- *Allowing ideas and solutions of different stakeholders to interact.* National reconciliation is being approached from the perspective of people, communities, and institutions, allowing ideas and solutions to be brought together on many different levels through the peaceful activities of nature conservation.[83]

Some countries are also recognizing the possibility of using protected areas designed to conserve biodiversity along their borders as ways of promoting peace.[84] In many countries, boundaries are found in mountainous areas that also tend to be biologically rich because of the great variety of habitats and ecosystem types found within relatively small areas affected by differences in elevation, microclimate, and geological factors. While such ecologically diverse areas are often particularly important for conservation of biodiversity (and thus established as protected areas), they are also frequently sanctuaries in war, especially during civil wars and guerrilla wars.[85]

Given that national frontiers are both especially sensitive areas where conflict is endemic and biological resources are often especially rich, the idea of establishing protected areas on both sides of the border – as so-called "peace parks" – has attracted considerable attention. These parks provide a symbol of the desire of the bordering countries to deal with many of their problems in a peaceful way.[86] It has been found that transboundary protected areas cover well over 1.1 million km^2, representing nearly 10 percent of the total protected area in the world (see Table 14.2).[87] In addition to indicating the importance of transfrontier protected areas, these statistics also demonstrate how much of the world's land area devoted to biodiversity conservation is located in remote frontier areas where risks of war are historically highest.

---

[83] Protected areas foster recovery from war by providing employment to rural people, restoring ecosystems to a productive state, and attracting tourists into remote areas (thereby drawing these areas into the national economy). In the specific case of Lebanon, groups that previously were on opposite sides in the civil war are now working together to re-establish the national parks.

[84] See, for example, John Hanks, "Protected Areas During and After Conflict: The Objectives and Activities of the Peace Parks Foundation," *PARKS* 7 (1997), 11–24.

[85] See, for example, Paul Richards, *Fighting for the Rain Forest: War, Youth, and Resources in Sierra Leone* (Portsmouth, N.H.: Heinemann, 1996); Helen Collinson (ed.), *Green Guerrillas: Environmental Conflicts and Initiatives in Latin America and the Caribbean* (London: Latin American Bureau/US: Monthly Review Press, 1997).

[86] See, for example, Thorsell, *Parks on the Borderline*.

[87] Dorothy C. Zbicz and Michael Greene, "Status of the World's Transfrontier Protected Areas," *PARKS* 7 (1997), 5–10.

War and biodiversity: an assessment of impacts

Table 14.2. *Transfrontier protected areas*

Many protected areas are located on national borders, and some have adjacent protected areas on the other side of the border, forming complexes that could be the focus of collaboration. IUCN calls these (perhaps optimistically) "Parks for Peace."[88] The following is an indication of how widespread and important such areas are.

Continent	Transfrontier protected area complexes	Designated protected areas
Africa	39	110
Asia	31	74
Europe	54	138
North America	10	44
Latin America	35	89
Totals:	169	455

Compiled on the basis of information presented by IUCN (1997).

Although peace parks have probably had relatively little independent effect on international relations, transfrontier cooperation on biodiversity issues has the potential to develop into an important factor in at least regional politics by helping to internalize norms, establish regional identities and interests, operationalize routine international communication, and reduce the likelihood of the use of force.[89]

Conclusions

National and international security can no longer be conceived in narrow military terms. Ethnic conflict, environmental degradation and pollution, and famine leading to civil unrest and massive migrations of refugees, constitute threats to both social stability and the preservation of a productive material base – the planet's biodiversity. Thus, stopping soil degradation and deforestation, or augmenting food production capabilities in deficit areas, can directly and substantially contribute to the security of society, and can help prevent – or at least postpone – armed conflict. Allocating international resources to environmental monitoring and impact assessment, resource management, protection of economically important species, quick response to disasters and accidents, energy conservation, and the

[88] IUCN, *Parks for Peace Conference Proceedings.*
[89] L. Brock, "Peace Through Parks: The Environment on the Peace Research Agenda," *J. Peace Res.* 28 (1991), 407–23.

establishment and management of protected areas along international borders are all highly appropriate activities that will prevent strife and therefore reduce the likelihood of conflicts leading to war. As Thacher put it: "Trees now or tanks later."[90]

Because environmental stress (perhaps better phrased as "biological insecurity") can be a fundamental cause of armed conflict, issues of conserving biodiversity, using biological resources sustainably, and sharing the benefits of such use in a fair and equitable manner – the three objectives of the Convention on Biological Diversity – are critical elements in discussions of national security. Investments in activities to implement these objectives are vital contributions to "biological security," and thus to peace.

[90] Peter Thacher, "Peril and Opportunity: What it Takes to Make our Choice," in J. A. McNeely and K. R. Miller (eds.), *National Parks, Conservation, and Development: the Role of Protected Areas in Sustaining Society* (Washington, D.C.: Smithsonian Institution Press, 1984), pp. 12–14.

INTRODUCTION

JESSICA D. JACOBY

The public health impacts of war often directly correspond to the various ecological consequences described in the previous section. The use of conventional weapons results in impacts such as pollution, depletion of resources, and destruction of vital health-related infrastructure, and frequently causes severe collateral damage to civilian health. In addition, the production, testing, use, and even dismantling of weapons of mass destruction can release deadly toxins with widespread health effects.

Many of the same methodological constraints and scientific uncertainties that impede accurate prediction and assessment of ecological impacts also plague the process of determining the causes and extent of public health damage during war. The nature of the public health discipline also presents unique challenges to achieving accurate assessment and creating successful intervention strategies. The authors in this section address both the health impacts themselves, and reasons and possible solutions for these methodological difficulties.

Jennifer Leaning examines the discipline of public health itself, tracing the history of its relationship with violent conflict, including the more recent, specifically public-health-related challenges presented by many of the conflicts that have taken place since the Cold War. Alastair Hay focuses on the health-related impacts of the use of defoliants during the Vietnam War. Victor Sidel calls attention to the types of environmental and public health damage that result from preparations for war, and broadens the scope of inquiry through an assessment of the ramifications of "militarism" viewed broadly. Finally, David Fidler focuses on the alterations of the human–microbe relationship that result from wartime conditions as the basis for exploring the international legal framework for preventing and mitigating morbidity and mortality in wartime.

As noted above, the causal factors and ultimate expression of the public health impacts of wars are extremely diverse and often not easily distinguishable. The authors in this section analyze the impacts in various ways. Hay offers a detailed account of the studies that initially discovered the teratogenic and carcinogenic properties of dioxin, as well as the ensuing attempts to pinpoint the possible effects on both the military personnel who served during the war and the Vietnamese population itself. He notes that it was not until an accident involving dioxin occurred in Italy that scientific interest and funding for research in this topic boomed, perhaps substantiating Asit Biswas' assertion in the last section that scientists in developed nations display more interest in impacts directly affecting their own countries than impacts that take place in the developing world.

Fidler provides insight into the many ways in which violent conflict facilitates the spread of infectious disease. As he points out, wartime situations give the upper hand to microbial pathogens, which seize opportunities created by the destruction of public health infrastructure, forced population movements in unsanitary conditions, and scarce medical supplies to invade and infect populations with any number of diseases. Fidler also explores the use of biological weapons, which have the specific effect of altering the peacetime human–microbe relationship to the detriment of the population on which they are used.

Leaning echoes Fidler's assertion that war is a root cause of the spread of infectious disease, especially in dislocated populations. She also explores four war-related activities that have "prolonged and pervasive environmental impact with grave attendant consequences for human populations." The first of these is the production and testing of nuclear weapons, which can result at all stages in the exposure of civilian populations to radiation and a vast variety of associated health problems. Sidel's chapter further elaborates on this issue and describes in detail the harms that have resulted in populations exposed to iodine-131 and plutonium in the United States and the former Soviet Union. The second activity that Leaning explores is the aerial and naval bombardment of terrain, which often destroys vital infrastructure such as water treatment plants, denying civilians clean water, promoting waterborne illness, and forcing population movements. The third is the dispersal and persistence of landmines and unexploded ordnance, resulting in widespread dismemberment and loss of life. Finally, she discusses the deliberate and collateral effects of environmental destruction and contamination through the use or storage of military defoliants, toxins, and waste.

Accurate assessment of the causes, scope, and possible remedies for these impacts depends on sound methodologies. As with ecological impacts, the multi-dimensional character of health impacts impedes the sufficiency of any single method. Hay's chapter, through its discrete focus, provides a concrete example of the types of methodological obstacles that the authors have raised throughout this part of the book. There is a recurring problem in these studies with lack of baseline data on the health of those being studied, especially regarding the Vietnamese population. Scientific uncertainties regarding the causes of specific conditions stand in the way of determining the role of defoliants in causing specific maladies. Conducting studies sometimes decades after the incident, often with surrogate measures of exposure, also raises questions of data validity. Finally, complicating lifestyle-related factors, such as smoking, make it difficult to attribute direct cause-and-effect relationships.

Leaning cites the example of Rudolf Virchow, who explored the social and economic causes of the 1848 typhus epidemic in Upper Silesia, to demonstrate some of the issues that have historically plagued public health professionals who attempt to assess and mitigate health issues in the wartime context. She then elaborates on the specific issues arising from the shift over the past decades from traditional warfare to "complex humanitarian emergencies" (CHEs), which are characterized by widespread population distress caused by a number of social, political, and environmental factors. Leaning refers again to lack of baseline data and destruction of necessary infrastructure, but also adds the inability to obtain accurate figures due to frequent population migration, difficulty in cross-cultural translation of information, and the extreme risk posed to relief providers. Further, CHEs themselves are extremely varied, posing the same issues regarding site-specificity as the assessment of ecological damage. Leaning ends this discussion with a call for more thorough investigation of the costs and methods for responding to CHEs.

While other chapters in this volume, including those by Biswas and Leaning, touch upon impacts resulting from preparations for war or military operations other than war, Sidel thoroughly catalogues the impacts of military preparedness, particularly those related to weapons of mass destruction. Here also, lack of baseline data and exposure to compounding factors remain obstacles to accurate assessment. Further, Sidel points out that any attempts to broaden our understanding of the specific effects of these toxins cannot ethically be performed directly on humans, though he does mention cases in which governments have ignored this proscription and conducted tests on unknowing populations. As such, any research in this area has to be the result of inference from either controlled non-human testing, or from observational, rather than experimental, epidemiological studies.

Sidel also explores the implications of a policy of militarism, broadening the context of the environmental consequences of war to include such related activities as economic sanctions against civilian populations, government testing of biological and nuclear weapons, and increased violence in civilian behavior. As Sidel notes, the last of these is most eloquently described by Ricardo Navarro, director of an environmental NGO in El Salvador. Navarro describes the "acquired violent behavior" that results from being exposed over the long term to pervasive belligerence. He observes that it is not restricted to the military that took part in the conflict, but influences the everyday activities of civilians, such as when a driver uses his pistol to demand the right of way at a traffic light.[1] Beyond the threats to physical health that such individuals pose, the psychological well-being of entire cultures may be affected by militarism. In the end, Sidel asserts, all of the environmental and health consequences described in this volume are primarily the result of wars brought on by this militaristic attitude on the part of the aggressor, rather than those fought for legitimate self-defense or national security reasons.

Though Sidel's argument suggests that elimination of war would be the only viable option for completely avoiding the impacts explored here, the law of war provides an existing framework within which it is possible at least to mitigate and assign responsibility and liability for those impacts. Fidler's chapter offers examples of the ways in which the law of armed conflict has been shaped by the need to prevent and control the spread of infectious diseases. His analysis reflects a debate that recurs throughout this volume, the question of whether existing norms are sufficient to address the environmental consequences of war. Fidler offers three areas in which concrete proposals and ongoing activities might improve the current status

---

[1] Ricardo A. Navarro, "The Environmental Consequences of War: The Case of El Salvador," paper presented at the First International Conference on Addressing Environmental Consequences of War, Washington, D.C. (June 1998).

of public health protection during war. First, he notes with approval the International Committee for the Red Cross's current campaign for additional target-based provisions protecting drinking water and sewage treatment infrastructure. He also gives credit to current weapons-based initiatives, such as the one aimed at completing the proposed verification and compliance protocol to the Biological Weapons Convention, and another separate proposal expressly to designate the use of biological weapons as a war crime. Finally, Fidler points to the ICRC's important attempts to create an objective approach for determining whether existing or future weapons are likely to cause "superfluous injury," or "unnecessary suffering," thus categorically banning them from use under international humanitarian law. Some of these proposals would require an entirely new treaty provision, while others are simply an elaboration of what is already inherent in the existing norms. In either case, what is needed most urgently, Fidler argues, is a more comprehensive compliance and enforcement regime to narrow the gap between the law and the actions of belligerents during wartime.

Fidler's argument demonstrates that the public health profession can only serve the law to the extent that the law makes clear what it intends to prohibit. Conversely, as noted in the previous section addressing ecological impacts, effective legal norms rely on sound scientific evidence for effective development and implementation. Lack of baseline knowledge and the need for constant reassessment pose particular difficulties for policymakers attempting to craft sufficiently comprehensive norms, and for implementers seeking closure in a particular matter. In addition, assessment of public health damages during war presents its own challenges. Many of the long-term health impacts, such as those resulting from exposure to released toxins, may not be manifested for decades, complicating such efforts as those undertaken by the UNCC in its attempts to assess and award public health damages in the aftermath of the 1990–91 Gulf War.

Granted, the immediate concerns of survival and the need for rapid humanitarian intervention will continue to take precedence during armed conflict; full-scale epidemiological assessment and effective long-term treatment must necessarily be a lower priority. Nevertheless, development of epidemiological methods specifically geared towards rapid assessment and intervention would be invaluable for health care professionals during war.

15

TRACKING THE FOUR HORSEMEN: THE PUBLIC HEALTH APPROACH TO THE IMPACT OF WAR AND WAR-INDUCED ENVIRONMENTAL DESTRUCTION IN THE TWENTIETH CENTURY

JENNIFER LEANING

Introduction

War marks the experience of every generation to have lived in the twentieth century.[1] Journalists, historians, and demographers have reported its direct effects on human populations, in terms of immediate death and suffering. Reliable estimates suggest that, in the twentieth century, approximately 170 million people lost their lives in all forms of war and politically imposed violence.[2] Other estimates, based on higher casualty figures for episodes of political violence that have not been fully evaluated, would indicate that as many as 270 million people might have died in this same time period from the direct effects of war, political oppression, state-induced famine, and acts of state terror.[3]

Until recently, despite robust precedents set by individual practitioners in the nineteenth century, the public health profession has viewed this tide

---

[1] E. Hobsbawm, *The Age of Extremes: A History of the World, 1914–1991* (New York: Pantheon Books, 1994), pp. 21–53.

[2] Z. Brzezinksi, *Out of Control* (New York: Scribner/Toronto: Maxwell MacMillan Canada, 1993), pp. 3–18.

[3] Carnegie Commission on Preventing Deadly Conflict, "Preventing Deadly Conflict," final report (Washington, D.C.: Carnegie Commission, 1997), p. 11. The references listed refer only to the 100 million war dead; the citation for the figure of 170 million political deaths, according to communication with T. J. Leney, senior associate at Carnegie, was inadvertently omitted in the book and was supplied in: R. J. Rummel, *Death by Government* (New Brunswick, N.J.: Transactions Publishers, 1994).

of death with a silence that is strange, considering that its mission is to
attend to issues of morbidity and mortality in populations. The first
section of this essay looks briefly at the reasons why the profession has
taken considerable time to acknowledge the acute war-caused burden of
morbidity and mortality as a major public health concern.[4] This section
also addresses the particularly relevant public health-related challenges
that have been raised by conflicts since the end of the Cold War.

The second section addresses the main topic of this essay: the indirect
effects of war on human populations, mediated through its destruction of
biological habitat. These indirect effects have received even less systematic
attention from the public health community, evidenced at least in part
by the fact that this study required amassing and sifting data from many
disciplines.[5] An assessment of these indirect effects requires analysis of
factors of potential significance in terms of magnitude or duration of effects
on human populations exposed in specified geographic locations. These
factors have been sought by looking at the use of individual weapon systems,
the results of particular production processes, and the cumulative combined
effects of specified military campaigns.

Based on this inquiry, four activities can be seen as having prolonged
and pervasive environmental impact with grave attendant consequences for
human populations: production and testing of nuclear weapons; aerial and
naval bombardment of terrain; dispersal and persistence of landmines and
buried ordnance; and deliberate and collateral effects of environmental
destruction and contamination, through the use or storage of military
despoliants, toxins, and waste.

A vigorous exploration of the ways in which environmental stress and
resource constraints may contribute to social conflict and the outbreak or
propagation of war has also recently been launched.[6] Discussion of this
topic lies outside the scope of this chapter.

---

[4] R. Rhodes, "Man-Made Death: A Neglected Mortality," *J. Am. Med. Ass'n* 260 (1988), 686–87;
B. S. Levy and V. W. Sidel, *War and Public Health* (New York: Oxford Univ. Press, 1997).
[5] J. Leaning, "War and the Environment: Human Health Consequences of the Environmental
Damage of War," in E. Chivian, M. McCally, H. Hu, and A. Haines (eds.), *Critical Condition:
Human Health and the Environment* (Cambridge, Mass.: MIT Press, 1993), pp. 123–37.
[6] T. F. Homer-Dixon, "On the Threshold: Environmental Change as Causes of Acute Conflict,"
Int'l Security 16 (1991), 76–116; see also Jeffrey A. McNeely, "War and Biodiversity: An
Assessment of Impacts,"chapter 14 in this volume.

The public health approach to war and conflict

The discipline of public health seeks to define, explain, and affect the causes and consequences of population morbidity and mortality. The attention paid by public health practitioners to populations in crisis developed out of the observations of Rudolf Virchow (1821–1902) on the social and economic causes of the typhus epidemic in Upper Silesia in 1848.[7] During this same period in Britain, the practice of public health was advanced by the work of Edwin Chadwick and John Snow, both pioneers in techniques for recording and interpreting patterns of urban deaths.[8] Their horizon of interest was England during a period of great change, yet unscathed by domestic armed conflict. Virchow participated in their tradition, but worked throughout his lifetime on a continent intermittently swept by war and revolution. All three scientists begin their analysis of conditions and causes by counting events and then analyzing them according to the established statistical categories and methods of their time. In many respects, the approach taken by Virchow was the same as that used by Chadwick and Snow: clear definition of events in question; enumeration of these events in a systematic and representative fashion; evaluation of these numerator events in terms of carefully selected, relevant denominators; and development of explanations that fully incorporate the findings and reflect a realistic and sound understanding of underlying political, social, and biological mechanisms.

Because Virchow looked at situations in crisis, which by definition are undergoing rapid change and impose some level of danger and uncertainty on the observor/investigator, his approach differed in two key respects from Chadwick and Snow. These differences involved constraints imposed by time and by data. Virchow was under pressure to report back to the Prussian government regarding the causes of the typhus epidemic; the brittle and unpredictable nature of the political situation required him to accomplish his survey of the area in only two weeks. He was also compelled to work with few baseline demographic records and no comprehensive tally of deaths from the famine, since chronic destitution and population migration had undermined stable record-keeping and, as is almost always the case with severe calamity, the outbreak of epidemic diseases and the

[7] R. Virchow, "The Epidemics of 1848," in L. J. Rather (ed.), *Rudolf Virchow: Collected Essays on Public Health and Epidemiology* (Canton, Mass.: Watson Publishing Int'l, 1985), vol. I, p. 115.
[8] J. V. Pickstone, "Dearth, Dirt and Fever Epidemics: Rewriting the History of British 'Public Health', 1780–1850," in T. Ranger and P. Slack (eds.), *Epidemics and Ideas* (Cambridge: Cambridge Univ. Press, 1992), pp. 125–48.

surge in deaths and dislocation had obliterated the local capacity to maintain ongoing data sets.

Virchow was thus forced to improvise, and in this improvisation lie the seeds of modern epidemiology of war and disaster. Here is how he describes his methods:

> The information I was able to gather during this journey was necessarily incomplete in many respects, and the following report does not claim to be a complete or even adequate description of the epidemic. However, the extraordinary uniformity of the Upper Silesian conditions, the great conformity in the symptomology of the disease, the large number of persons affected simultaneously in the same place, and lastly the exceedingly friendly reception by the local physicians and the willing support of the local authorities, to both of whom I wish to express my heartfelt thanks, made it possible to grasp quite clearly the most essential points despite the short duration of my stay. I would have wished to provide decisive answers to some of the particularly important questions, but the political uprisings that had in the meanwhile broken out made it mandatory for me to participate in the manifestations in the capital. I also knew that in order truly to resolve these questions, I would have to wait for another suitable opportunity, which I did not know would ever arise.[9]

The techniques of obtaining good information in crisis are exemplified in this quote. Issues of access are surmounted by establishing good relations with a wide range of key interlocuters; issues of ascertainment are dealt with by travelling as widely as possible and interviewing as many people as possible (he was working in a time before statistical sampling techniques had been developed); issues of data quality are addressed by applying tests of consistency, association, coherence, and plausibility (reflected in his notions of uniformity, conformity, and simultaneity).

Virchow understood that the value of contemporaneous reporting was twofold: to capture information that might later be dispelled or dissipated, and to allow those who wished to intervene, such as the Prussian government, to do so with the benefit of the most current and precise information possible. To provide information on unstable situations in a time frame when intervention might substantially affect outcome is a daunting task. Yet to wait until relative security and comfort has returned in order to establish a comprehensive retrospective investigation is to run almost

---

[9] R. Virchow, "Report on the Typhus Epidemic in Upper Silesia," in Rather, *Rudolf Virchow*, vol. I, p. 206.

certain risk that much information will have been lost and little can be done to affect the outcome one is now studying.

The impact of Virchow's two-week assessment of the Upper Silesian typhus epidemic was that the world gained a vivid and accurate picture of the root and proximal causes of the spread of this disease through a population, long before the bacteriologic theory of infectious disease was developed. The Prussian government received and acted upon Virchow's very good advice: send food and other supplies to relieve the famine, filth, and overcrowding that underlay the outbreak of the disease.

Although Chadwick and Snow pursued their task in comparative leisure and tranquility and could thus develop more robust and systematic statistical assessments of their findings, they shared with Virchow a fundamental interest in using the information they acquired to shape strategies for positive intervention. The modern approach to sanitation in urban areas can be traced back to their mid-nineteenth-century recommendations to the London Board of Health.

The work of these men contributed greatly to the development of the essential method of twentieth century public health practitioners, known as epidemiology, and defined as "the study of the distribution and determinants of health-related states and events in specified populations and the application of this study to the control of health problems."[10] Viewing public health in this larger context, the notion of "distribution and determinants" can be expanded to include the health effects of environmental change, population growth and migration, war, disaster, political oppression, and civil unrest.[11]

We have had ample opportunity in the twentieth century to establish the closeness and complexity of the temporal and causal relationships between war, famine, and disease. Yet, despite the working tradition of public health in the assessment of the morbidity and mortality of populations, the actual application of the discipline of public health to the study of war and revolution has a relatively short history.[12] Two possible reasons for this lag can be found in the issues of definition and data.

[10] J. M. Last (ed.), *A Dictionary of Epidemiology* (New York: Oxford Univ. Press, 1983); as cited in C. W. Tyler, Jr., and J. M. Last, "Epidemiology," in J. M. Last and R. B. Wallace (eds.), *Public Health and Preventive Medicine* (Norwalk, Conn.: Appleton & Lange, 1992), pp. 11–39.
[11] S. Wing, "Limits of Epidemiology," *Med. & Global Survival* 1 (1994), 74–86.
[12] D. W. Fitzsimmons and A. W. Whiteside, *Conflict, War and Public Health* (Research Institute for the Study of Conflict and Terrorism, 1994), pp. 1–39.

Definition. Public health has conceived of its subject as the assessment of health-related trends in populations. Virchow notwithstanding, definitions of "health-related" have not, until recently, included factors whose root causes lie in political oppression, organized state violence, and war.[13] Furthermore, only in the wars of the twentieth century has the proportion of civilian deaths during war begun to exceed military casualties: 50 percent in the 1950s and 1960s, and over 75 percent in the 1970s and 1980s.[14] The overwhelmingly civilian character of today's wars has forced this topic into the discourse of public health.

Data. Public health has traditionally focused on communicable disease and chronic conditions in relatively stable societies, working from available sources of vital statistics and census data. Absent the usual data elements, attempts at systematic assessment, let alone intervention and evaluation, face daunting obstacles. Refugees and populations targeted by disaster relief programs became the first crisis-based populations to attract significant attention from the public health community, precisely because their needs were acutely visible and the infrastructure of camps and settlements provided comparatively reliable and comprehensive sources of demographic information.[15]

The field of public health is now evolving to encompass the challenges presented by the phenomenon of war, particularly the "new wars," or what the humanitarian relief community terms "complex humanitarian emergencies."[16] The key element in definitions of these events is widespread population distress, caused by a number of social, political, and environmental factors, in a context of collapsing or failed states where warring political or military authorities actively undermine the security and safety of those who are providing relief.[17] Although this element of civilian insecurity has always been present in wars, in recent years this issue has become more frequent, more visible, and more unmanageable.

---

[13] R. M. Garfield, "Epidemiologic Analysis of Warfare: A Historical Review," *J. Am. Med. Ass'n* 266 (1991), 688–92.

[14] Stockholm International Peace Research Institute, *SIPRI Yearbook* (Uppsala: 1989).

[15] Centers for Disease Control, "Famine-affected Refugee and Displaced Populations: Recommendations for Public Health Issues," *Morbidity and Mortality Wkly. Rep.* RR–13 (1992), 41.

[16] M. Kaldor and B. Vashee (eds.), *Restructuring the Global Military Sector, Volume I: The New Wars* (London and New York: Pinter, 1997); United Nations, *Agenda for Development* (New York: 1997).

[17] J. Macrae and A. Zwi (eds.), *War and Hunger: Rethinking International Responses to Complex Emergencies* (London and Atlantic Highlands, N.J.: Zed Books, 1994), p. 21; J. Leaning, "The Bell Tolls," editorial in *Med. and Global Survival* 1 (1994), 122–23.

In terms of prevalence, in 1994 all thirty-two conflicts were internal, waged over issues of territory, minority status, or power.[18] Over 100 million people were directly involved in these conflicts in Afghanistan, Somalia, Sudan, Bosnia, Rwanda, and Chechnya.[19] The term "complex humanitarian emergency" ("CHE") had not been coined at the peak time of conflict, but would also have applied to the long-lasting hostilities that ravaged Mozambique and Angola during the 1970s and 1980s.

Essential features of these wars are mass population dislocation, destruction of community and infrastructure, pervasive insecurity, and gross human rights violations.[20] These features present many difficulties for the public health community in its efforts to assess health needs, evaluate intervention, and develop prevention strategies. These difficulties are briefly discussed below.

ASSESSMENT

Counting numbers of occurrences in key categories of interest is central to supporting efforts to provide relief. Reliable information about the nature and extent of casualties from all causes, the numbers of people in need, and the effectiveness of the local medical response is essential. Yet in the setting of CHEs, gathering such information is technically difficult, politically complex, and often hazardous. There is always the need to balance sound methodology with the timely gathering of information.

As seen in the daily reports from Rwanda/Congo during the three-year period from April 1994 to April 1997, a number of technical questions served as roadblocks to public health policy formulation: What are reliable methods for compiling accurate counts of collections of people, stationary and in motion, or for estimating these numbers? How does one estimate deaths – in transit, in urban warfare, in mass graves? Logistical and managerial questions also keep recurring in these crisis situations, in part because there is scant consensus on what constitutes a "lesson learned," in part because there is no organized process for acquiring and communicating knowledge from past experience in many of these situations, and in

---

[18] F. Jean (ed.), *Populations in Danger 1995* (London: J. Libbey, 1995), pp. 130–31.
[19] S. Hansch, "An Explosion of Complex Humanitarian Emergencies," in Bread for the World Institute, *Hunger 1996: Countries in Crisis* (Silver Spring, Md.: Bread for the World Institute, 1995).
[20] J. Leaning, "Introduction," in J. Leaning, S. Briggs, and L. Chen (eds.), *Humanitarian Crises: The Medical and Public Health Response* (Cambridge, Mass.: Harvard Univ. Press, 1999).

part because people in authority change from one emergency to the next. We are also ignorant about the short- and long-term manifestations and effects of human suffering within and across cultures.

What is needed is an inventory of imaginative new methodologies that can be used for rapid assessments, and then an agreed-upon process through which these methodologies could be evaluated. Discussion is underway within the humanitarian community regarding this need.[21] The information developed through these methodologies would attend to key parameters and metrics, focusing on direct consequences, such as death and injury, and more indirect ones, mediated by factors such as mass migration, food shortages, hunger, and destruction of health services.

REMEDIAL ACTION: EVALUATION OF INTERVENTIONS

In this category, efforts are now underway to develop a standard list of measures of effectiveness, building on work of the US military and the US Centers for Disease Control. These proposed measures for public health are relatively straightforward (crude mortality rates for children under five years old, cause-specific rates for diseases, several malnutrition indicators), although defining the population at risk and obtaining the data on which to base these rates are still major challenges. Other measures relating to security, infrastructure, and economic issues are less well established, and none have been developed for interventions relating to human rights abuses or psychological issues.

The costs of responding to CHEs need to be detailed and evaluated in a much more comprehensive and systematic way than has so far occurred. Reports from major non-governmental organizations and the United Nations would suggest that an increasing share of their development budgets is being channeled to provide emergency relief during CHEs, while confidence in the efficacy of this expenditure is waning.[22] Two lines of analysis serve to undermine this confidence. The first takes a strategic perspective, noting that despite great increases in humanitarian resources devoted to reducing population morbidity and mortality in these crises, the responsible political agents, at the national and international level, have not engaged sufficiently in diplomatic and, if need be, military action

---

[21] F. M. Burkle, K. A. W. McGrady, S. L. Newett et al., "Complex Humanitarian Emergencies: III. Measures of Effectiveness," *Prehospital and Disaster Medicine* 10 (1995), 48–56.

[22] International Federation of Red Cross and Red Crescent Societies, *World Disasters Report 1997* (Oxford: Oxford University Press, 1997).

to bring the crises to an end.[23] The second analysis springs from the recognition that ongoing morbidity and mortality is unacceptably high, despite massive intervention, and embarks on an operational critique: in complex emergencies, access to the affected population is often limited; refugee camp location less than optimal; epidemiologic assessment often inadequate; organizational priorities may compete with population needs; the number of skilled personnel is often insufficient; the deployment of known effective interventions is often uneven; communication and coordination among agencies constitutes a recurrent failure; and institutional memories are poor, thus these same mistakes are repeated.[24]

PREVENTION AND EARLY WARNING

The practice of public health since Virchow has increasingly recognized the social and economic determinants of health and disease as appropriate topics for study and engagement. The political determinants, particularly as expressed through war on civilian populations, have not received formal or sustained attention from the public health community. The task for public health is to contribute towards the advancing of our understanding of the natural history of war, if there be such a thing, and to search for its root causes. What is the relationship between economic and social development and the prevention of war? Can early warning indicators, such as escalating human rights violations or an increasing trade in weapons, be defined and validated? What steps, such as sanctions, designated security zones, or conflict resolution, can be used for mitigation or constraint? The refinement of these questions and the quest for answers can only be undertaken in a multi-disciplinary arena, since the health of populations is only one aspect of the human condition.

The public health effects of war-induced environmental destruction

Two recent factors have converged to make this topic appear more accessible and more relevant to health professionals. First, the development

---

[23] R. Brauman, "Foreword," in Médecins Sans Frontières, *World in Crisis: The Politics of Survival at the End of the 20th Century* (London and New York: Routledge, 1997), pp. xix–xxvi.

[24] World Health Organization, "Consultation on Applied Health Research in Complex Emergencies," final report, EHA–E17/180/1 (Geneva: 1998).

of nuclear, chemical, and biological weapons throughout the Cold War has led to accelerating concern that these massive weapons enterprises are causing extensive environmental degradation and exposing hundreds of thousands, if not millions, of people to unquantified risks of adverse health effects from toxic byproducts.[25] Second, the evolution in conventional military war capabilities and strategies, demonstrated and widely reported during the Gulf War, has underscored the concern that modern technologies of waging war could inflict widespread environmental destruction with potentially significant human health effects.[26]

There remain enormous gaps in our knowledge regarding the effects of past wars and the potential impacts of future ones on the world environment. The following discussion draws attention to a few salient issues that authorities in this area have helped identify.

NUCLEAR WEAPONS PRODUCTION AND TESTING

Nuclear weapons technology, developed during World War II and then expanded as an industrial enterprise of vast scope and complexity in the Cold War societies of the US and the USSR, continues to dominate concerns regarding potential hazards to humans.[27]

Radioactivity in the environment, released in many phases of the full continuum of production and testing processes, poses a serious threat to the health of all biological species, including humans. Assessment of this threat begins with estimates of radiation released (itself a difficult task) and then entails an evaluation of human health risks based on what can be found in epidemiological studies of exposed populations across time. These studies, based on relatively small samples and looking at populations affected by above-ground tests, or living in the vicinity of nuclear weapons production and storage facilities, suggest there is cause for significant concern.[28]

[25] F. Barnaby, "The Spread of the Capability to do Violence: An Introduction to Environmental Warfare," *Ambio* 4 (1975), 178–244.

[26] M. Finger, "The Military, the Nation State, and the Environment," *The Ecologist* 21 (1991), 220–25.

[27] M. Renner, "Assessing the Military's War on the Environment," in L. Brown (ed.), *State of the World 1991* (New York: W. W. Norton, 1991), pp. 132–52.

[28] A. Robbins, A. Makhijani, and K. Yih, *Radioactive Heaven and Earth* (New York: ApexPress/ London: Zed Books, 1991), pp. 34–35, 162; B. Danielsson, "Poisoned Pacific: The Legacy of French Nuclear Testing," *Bull. Atom. Scientists* 46 (1990), 22–34; Center for Defense

AERIAL AND NAVAL BOMBARDMENT

Bombardment of the urban infrastructure that constitutes the environment for a significant fraction of the world's human population has always caused forced dislocation of survivors. The result has been the formation of clusters of refugee populations in situations conducive to the spread of disease, illness, and death from malnutrition, starvation, and marked psychological stress. Throughout much of the twentieth century, since the development of military airpower, the deliberate bombing of civilians was considered outside the codes of war. During World War II, when air power was deployed for the first time as the pivotal military technology, the practice of bombing civilian settlements became increasingly prevalent. Hundreds of thousands of people died as a direct result.[29] The bombardment of cities and destruction of forests, farms, transportation systems, and irrigation networks produced devastating indirect consequences, as well. The number of people who fled but survived far from home, counted as refugees, displaced, or without nationality in the postwar world, was reliably estimated for Europe alone as approximately 40–50 million.[30] Immediate postwar assessments of life support capacities in Europe and Japan documented a number of issues that can be attributed in large measure to aerial bombardment:[31]

Information, "An End to All Nuclear Explosions: The Long Over-due Test Ban," *Def. Monitor* 20(3) (1991), 1–8; J. L. Lyon, M. R. Klauber, J. W. Gardner, and K. S. Udall, "Childhood Leukemias Associated with Fallout from Nuclear Testing," *New Eng. J. Med.* 300 (1979), 397–402; T. E. Hamilton, G. van Belle, and J. P. LoGerfo, "Thyroid Neoplasia in Marshall Islanders Exposed to Nuclear Fallout," *J. Am. Med. Ass'n* 258 (1987), 629–36; T. B. Cochran and R. S. Norris, "A First Look at the Soviet Bomb Complex," *Bull. Atom. Scientists* 47 (1991), 25–31; J. Kitfield, "The Environmental Cleanup Quagmire," *Military Forum* (April 1989), 36–40; D. Coyle et al., *Deadly Defense: Military Radioactive Landfills* (New York: Radioactive Waste Campaign, 1988); Office of Technology Assessment, "Complex Cleanup: The Environmental Legacy of Nuclear Weapons Production," OTA–0–484 (Washington, D.C.: U.S. Government Printing Office, 1991); National Cancer Institute, *Study Estimating Thyroid Doses of I-131 Received by Americans from Nevada Atmospheric Nuclear Bomb Tests* (Washington, D.C.: 1997); see also Victor W. Sidel, "The Impact of Military Preparedness and Militarism on Health and the Environment," chapter 17 in this volume.

[29] A. H. Westing, "Misspent Energy: Munition Expenditures Past and Future," *Bull. Peace Prop.* 16(1) (1986), 9–10.

[30] W. Laqueur, *Europe since Hitler: The Re-birth of Europe* (New York: Penguin Books, 1984), pp. 24–25; M. J. Proudfoot, *European Refugees 1939–1952: A Study in Forced Population Movement* (Evanston, Ill.: Northwestern Univ. Press, 1956), p. 34.

[31] Laqueur, *Europe since Hitler*; D. MacIsaac (ed.), *United States Bombing Survey*, (New York: Garland Press, 1976), 10 vols.

- Widespread housing shortages, particularly in the cities of Germany and Central Europe subjected to Allied bombing, and in Japanese cities, where, in addition to the atomic bombing of Hiroshima and Nagasaki, conventional bombing destroyed much of the housing stock of Tokyo and several other major industrial cities;
- Hunger, if not outright famine, throughout much of Europe and Japan for the first two years after the war, resulting from disruption of transport and distribution systems, as well as from causes less directly attributable to aerial bombardment (loss of manpower, lack of machinery, lack of fertilizer, and heavy declines in livestock); and
- Steep declines in all measures of industrial productivity, resulting from destruction of transport (roads, railways, bridges, harbors, shipping) and communications systems.

This sequence of aerial bombardment, destruction of homes and urban and rural infrastructure, and progressive waves of dislocated or trapped peoples, can be seen in all wars subsequent to World War II. Throughout the fifteen years of the war in Southeast Asia, the US bombardment of Vietnam, Laos, and Cambodia forced approximately 17 million people to become refugees.[32] During the Gulf War, the Allied forces succeeded in crippling urban support systems with less fire-power and more precision, trapping the population of Baghdad in structures that were suddenly rendered useless, in a terrain across which they could no longer communicate or travel.[33] In the new conflicts of the post-Cold War era, marked by sieges of cities, attacks on safe havens, and pulverization of towns to effect ethnic cleansing, millions of people have been forced to flee within or across national borders. In 1997, there were 14 million refugees and an estimated 30 million people displaced within their own countries.[34]

There has not yet been a systematic historical assessment of the longer-term social, economic, and psychological consequences for the refugees of World War II and for all subsequent victims of war-spawned human displacement.

[32] A. H. Westing, *Warfare in a Fragile World: Military Impact on the Human Environment* (London: Taylor & Francis, 1980), p. 94.
[33] W. M. Arkin, D. Durrant, and M. Cherni, *On Impact: Modern Warfare and the Environment. A Case Study of the Gulf War* (London: Greenpeace, 1991); Save the Children, *Iraq Situation Report for Save the Children, UK* (London: 1991); M. G. Renner, "Military Victory, Ecological Defeat," *World Watch* (Jul./Aug. 1991), 27–33.
[34] United Nations High Commissioner for Refugees, http//www.unhcr.ch/February 28, 1998.

LANDMINES

Anti-personnel and anti-tank landmines now litter extensive areas of the earth. It is estimated that as a result of the last fifty years of wars in Europe, Africa, Asia, and Latin America, approximately 100 million landmines are still active and in place worldwide, and another 100 million exist in stockpiles.[35] Almost 400 million have been strewn across continents since World War II, and with the proliferation of civil wars waged by irregular forces, the use and spread of landmines as a preferred method of securing and denying land has accelerated. In March 1999, the Ottawa Landmines Treaty entered into effect, banning the use, production, stockpiling, and transfer of anti-personnel landmines.[36] This major expansion of the applicability of the international law of war represents a significant victory for civil society in its attempts to restrain the means of waging war, in that the treaty was accomplished by a far-flung coalition of grassroots organizations working in concert with committed politicians and diplomats. The task ahead is to monitor compliance with this treaty, accelerate de-mining activities, and expand public awareness. Landmines have been and still are, in many areas, placed without regard to requirements under international law to mark, map, monitor, and remove these weapons. Hence, the majority of the victims of landmine explosions are civilians trying to return home, or once home, trying to reclaim fields, cut wood in forests, or tend herd animals in fields.[37] Many of these domestic rural tasks are directed by children, who are thus affected by these weapons disproportionately. Reliable regional estimates of incident morbidity and mortality are difficult to come by. One frequently cited statistic is that landmines injure or kill approximately 500 people every week.[38] In rural and poor areas, where most of these explosions take place, medical care is often distant and austere. An estimated 50 percent of those injured die outright in

---

[35] Department of Humanitarian Affairs, Mine Clearance and Policy Unit, *Land Mines Facts* (New York: United Nations, 1996).

[36] Convention on the Prohibition of the Use, Stockpiling, Production and Transfer of Anti-Personnel Mines and on Their Destruction (opened for signature in Ottawa on Dec. 3–4, 1997; entered into force, Mar. 1, 1999), reprinted in *I.L.M.* 36 (1997), 1507.

[37] Westing, *Warfare in a Fragile World*, pp. 95–96; E. Stover, *Land Mines in Cambodia: The Coward's War* (Boston, New York: Physicians for Human Rights/Asia Watch, 1991).

[38] C. Giannou, "Antipersonnel Landmines: Facts, Fictions, and Priorities," *BMJ* 315 (1997), 1453–54.

the field, many others die before reaching medical care, and about one-third of the survivors require an amputation.[39]

Landmines accelerate environmental damage through one of four mechanisms:

1. Fear of mines denies access to abundant natural resources;
2. Populations are forced to move preferentially into marginal and fragile environments in order to avoid landmine infested areas;
3. This population movement speeds depletion of biological diversity; and
4. Landmine explosions disrupt essential soil and water processes.

The fear of landmines restricts the use of much arable land throughout the world. The persistence of active mines and unexploded ordnance haunts old battle areas and, despite intensive efforts at clearance and deactivation of these explosive weapons, millions of hectares remain under interdiction in Europe, North Africa, and Asia.[40] In Libya, one-third of the landmass is considered contaminated by landmines and unexploded munitions from World War II.[41] When these mines do explode, in addition to causing serious injury and death to humans, domestic animals, and wildlife, they also shatter soil systems, rip up plant life, and disrupt water flows, all of which accelerates widespread ecosystem disruption. It is with some reason that the US State Department proclaimed in 1993 that landmines are perhaps "the most toxic and widespread pollution facing mankind."

DESPOLIATION, DEFOLIATION, AND TOXIC POLLUTION

Deliberate attempts to damage the environment as a tactic of war against the formal enemy and as a means of instilling terror in the general populace have been described throughout history.[42] In this century, during World

---

[39] R. M. Coupland and R. Russbach, "Victims of Antipersonnel Mines: What is Being Done?" *Med. and Global Survival* 1 (1994), 18–22; Physicians for Human Rights and Human Rights Watch, "Landmines: A Deadly Legacy," a publication of the Arms Project (New York: 1993).

[40] A. H. Westing (ed.), *Explosive Remnants of War: Mitigating the Environmental Effects* (London and Philadelphia: Taylor & Francis, 1985).

[41] K. Sgaier, "Explosive Remnants of World War II in Libya: Impact on Agricultural Development," in Westing, *Explosive Remnants of War*, pp. 33–37.

[42] A. Jones, *The Art of War in the Western World* (New York: Oxford Univ. Press, 1987); C. Royster, *The Destructive War: William Tecumseh Sherman, Stonewall Jackson, and the Americans* (New York: Knopf, 1991).

War II and the Korean War, four instances can be found in campaign reports with relatively little difficulty:

- The 1938 detonation of the Huayuankow dike on the Yellow River by the Kuomintang in an unsuccessful effort to stop the Japanese advance, resulting in the deaths of hundreds of thousands of Chinese;[43]
- The 1944 opening of key dikes in the Netherlands by the Germans in order to ruin 200,000 hectares of agricultural land;[44]
- The 1944 "scorched earth" retreat of the Germans in Norway, destroying villages and mining harbors throughout the northern settlements;[45] and
- The 1953 US bombing of five irrigation dams in North Korea, in order to impede rice production and force the North Koreans to work towards an armistice.[46]

There may be more exhaustive histories of World War II and the Korean War that will bring to light many more instances.

It is generally accepted that one of the most extensive uses of environmental destruction as a sustained aspect of war practice and strategy was the US use of defoliants during the war in Southeast Asia.[47] From 1965–71, the US sprayed 3,640 km^2 of South Vietnam's cropland with herbicides, using a total estimated amount of 55 million kg.[48] The stated rationale was to deny the enemy sources of food and means of cover.[49] This sweeping use of chemicals to destroy farmland, forest, and water sources is unprecedented and the consequences still relatively unknown. Field assessments have been possible only with the granting of access to international teams.[50] The effects on US servicemen, in terms of Agent Orange investigations, have suggested a range of enduring impacts on the civilians and combatants in Vietnam, Cambodia, and Laos.[51]

[43] A. H. Westing (ed.), *Environmental Hazards of War: Releasing Dangerous Forces in an Industrialized World* (London: SAGE Publications, 1990), p. 6.
[44] A. H. Westing, *Weapons of Mass Destruction and the Environment* (London: Taylor & Francis, 1977), p. 54.
[45] D. H. Lund, "The Revival of Northern Norway," *Geographical J.* 109 (1947), 185–97.
[46] Quarterly Review Staff, "The Attack on the Irrigation Dams in North Korea," *Air U. Q. Rev.* 6 (1954), 40–61. [47] Westing, *Warfare in a Fragile World*, p. 79.
[48] *Ibid.* [49] *Ibid.*, pp. 78–90.
[50] G. H. Orians and E. W. Pfeiffer, "Ecological Effects of the War in Vietnam," *Sci.* 168 (1970), 544–54.
[51] R. Harris and J. Paxman, *A Higher Form of Killing: The Secret Story of Gas and Germ Warfare* (London: Chatto & Windus, 1982), pp. 191–94; see also Alastair W. M. Hay, "Defoliants: The Long-term Health Implications," chapter 16 in this volume.

Of the many wars waged since Vietnam, the two-month war in the Gulf during January and February 1991 demonstrates most dramatically the ways in which the technologies of war and industry can be distorted and manipulated to wreak widespread environmental havoc. Early in the war, the Iraqi forces released approximately 10 million barrels of Kuwaiti oil into Gulf waters, causing great stress to an ecosystem already suffering from decades of abuse – from oil spills, the Iraq–Iran war, freighter traffic, and industrial wastes. Scientific assessments of this ecological loss and the catastrophe resulting from the Iraqi firing of more than 600 Kuwaiti oil wells are underway, although constrained by incomplete data and controversy.[52]

Through the creation of large refugee encampments, more recent wars (or CHEs) have been assessed for their potential to inflict harm on the local environment in which the camps are sited. In the cases of the refugee camps that existed in the Great Lakes region in Mozambique, Sudan, and the Afghan–Pakistani border areas from 1994 to 1997, a number of studies are now looking at issues of deforestation, encroachment on vulnerable ecosystems and national parks, water pollution and sanitation degradation, air pollution, and loss of endangered species.[53]

Conclusion

Future work on war and its public health effects must address four main issues: information, threat assessment, vulnerability assessment, and the role of international law.

---

[52] United Nations Environment Program, "Environmental Consequences of the Armed Conflict Between Iraq and Kuwait, an Introductory Report of the Executive Director," UNEP/GC.16/4/Add.1 (1991), 7; A. Carothers, *After Desert Storm: The Deluge* (New York: Greenpeace 1991), pp. 14–17; C. Sheppard and A. Price, "Will Marine Life Survive the Gulf War?" *New Scientist* (Mar. 9, 1991), 36–40; J. Horgan, "Up in Flames," *Sci. Am.* 264 (1991), 17–24; J. Horgan, "Burning Questions," *Sci. Am.* 265 (1991), 17–24; M. L. Wald, "Experts Worried by Kuwait Fires," *N.Y. Times* (Aug. 14, 1991); R. Stone, "Kuwait Quits Smoking," *Sci.* 255 (1992), 1357; T. Y. Canby, "After the Storm," *Nat'l Geographic* 180 (Aug. 1991), 2–32; see also Samira A. S. Omar et al., "The Gulf War Impact on the Terrestrial Environment of Kuwait: An Overview," and Mahmood Y. Abdulraheem, "War-related Damage to the Marine Environment in the ROPME Sea Area," chapters 12 and 13 in this volume.

[53] "Environmentally-induced Population Displacements and Environmental Impacts Resulting from Mass Migration," international symposium report (Geneva: International Organization for Migration, Apr. 21–24, 1996); G. Kibreab, "Environmental Causes and Impact of Refugee Movements: A Critique of the Current Debate," *Disasters* 21 (1997), 20–38.

INFORMATION

Insufficient information exists about effects of war on natural ecosystems, both in the immediate aftermath of war and over the long term. Methods for historical and contemporaneous reporting are incompletely developed and lack robust institutional support. Without improvement in these parameters, assessments of the human impacts resulting from environmental damage of war will also necessarily continue to be fragmentary.

THREAT ASSESSMENT

Escalation in numbers of weapons, elaborations in diverse technologies of destruction and delivery, and widespread proliferation now place the local, regional, and global environment in greater jeopardy than ever before. Nuclear weapons, the most extreme technology, have been shown in careful theoretical studies to be capable, even in limited regional use, of destroying vast sections of the world's environment.[54] Despite the fact that our capacity to contain and mitigate environmental effects of current weapons systems used in war is grossly underdeveloped, the world community continues to permit, and even support, a multiplicity of regional and international arms races.[55]

VULNERABILITY ASSESSMENT

Historical data on destruction of coral reefs during the war in the Pacific and enduring changes in desert terrain from the North African campaign of World War II are faint and isolated hints that fragile environments take a long time to recover from war. Burdened by rapid population growth in many parts of the world, unrestrained settlement, and economic exploitation, regional ecosystems are increasingly threatened and stressed, even in the absence of war.[56] As we continue to encroach upon the margins of our

---

[54] W. Arkin, F. von Hippel, and B. G. Levi, "The Consequences of a 'Limited' Nuclear War in East and West Germany," in J. Peterson (ed.), *The Aftermath: The Human and Ecological Consequences of Nuclear War* (New York: Pantheon Books, 1983), pp. 165–87.

[55] M. Renner, "Budgeting for Disarmament: The Costs of War and Peace," *World Watch Paper* 122 (Washington, D.C.: World Watch Institute, 1994).

[56] T. Ruff, "Ciguatera in the Pacific: A Link with Military Activities," *Lancet* 1 (1989), 201–05; F. W. Oliver, "Dust-storms in Egypt and Their Relation to the War Period, as Noted in Maryut, 1939–1945," *Geographical J.* 106 (1945) 26–49; F. W. Oliver, "Dust-storms in Egypt as Noted in Maryut: A Supplement," *Geographical J.* 108 (1947), 221–26; World Commission on Environment and Development, *Our Common Future* (Oxford and New York: Oxford Univ. Press, 1987).

environment into the twenty-first century, postwar ecological resilience cannot be assumed to be present in all places, particularly within a human time frame.

INTERNATIONAL LAW

In peacetime, public health practitioners often engage in legal and regulatory processes in order to create or enforce specific health protections for the general population or for particular subgroups. The legal and ethical framework within which the medical and public health profession works during wartime is defined by the Geneva Conventions and related documents, such as declarations of the World Medical Association. To those within the medical and public health community who study the evolution of war, important sets of proposals to strengthen or expand upon the ambit of international humanitarian law and regulation relating to war are now attracting close attention:

- The international campaign to abolish nuclear weapons;
- The international campaign to ban landmines;
- The movement to establish a permanent war crimes tribunal;
- The ICRC project to define in operational terms the meaning of the legal description of weapons that cause "superfluous injury and unnecessary suffering";[57]
- Proposals to disseminate respect for the Geneva Conventions among the general population and school-age children worldwide;[58] and
- Proposals to strengthen protection of the environment during war.[59]

These initiatives have grassroots advocates and internationally positioned sponsors. They constitute evidence that civil society is stirring, still in the grip of its old ways of doing business, but increasingly fretful and rebellious. The increasing participation of public health practitioners in this social tumult may well strengthen the profession and lend impetus to the outcome.[60]

---

[57] R. M. Coupland, *The SiRUS Project* (Geneva: ICRC, 1997).
[58] M. Harroff-Tavel, "Promoting Norms to Limit Violence in Crisis Situations: Challenges, Strategies, and Alliances," *Int'l Rev. Red Cross* 332 (1998), 5–20.
[59] F. Barnaby, "The Environmental Impact of the Gulf War," *The Ecologist* 21 (1991), 166–72; A. Toukan, "Humanity at War: The Environmental Price," *PSR Quarterly* 1 (1991), 214–20; M. Nimetz and G. M. Caine, "Crimes Against Nature," *Amicus J.* 13 (1991), 8–10.
[60] W. H. Foege, "Arms and Public Health: A Global Perspective," in Levy and Sidel, *War and Public Health*, pp. 3–11.

16

DEFOLIANTS: THE LONG-TERM
HEALTH IMPLICATIONS

ALASTAIR W. M. HAY

Introduction

Initial concerns about the effects of Agent Orange in Vietnam focused on the herbicide's effects on ecology. In the autumn of 1969, however, the emphasis shifted to health effects. Reports in the Saigon press at that time claimed that an unusually high incidence of birth defects might be related to the herbicide-spraying program.[1] These reports were married with experimental evidence from animal studies showing that one component of Agent Orange (a one-to-one mixture of two herbicides: 2,4-D and 2,4,5-T) caused birth defects in two species of mice and one strain of rat. The animal studies were performed by the Bionetics Research Laboratory on behalf of the United States National Cancer Institute, and they implicated 2,4,5-T as a teratogen (cause of birth deformities).[2] In the face of this evidence, it was no longer possible for the US Department of Defense to claim that there would be no "seriously adverse consequences" of the military use of herbicides in Vietnam; the study signaled the demise of the herbicide-spraying program.

Defoliants had been sprayed over areas that were supposedly sparsely populated in concentrations of 3 gallons per acre – ten times higher than the concentration recommended for users of 2,4,5-T in the US. In addition, occasional intense enemy groundfire would force aircrews to dump 1,000 gallons of herbicides in 30 seconds, rather than the usual 3 to 4 minutes, resulting in even higher concentrations.[3]

---

[1] A. Hay, *The Chemical Scythe: Lessons of 2,4,5-T and Dioxin* (New York: Plenum Press, 1982), p. 264.
[2] *Ibid.*   [3] *Ibid.*

Residual stocks of Agent Orange, stored on Johnson Island in the Pacific, were later analyzed for the presence of contaminants. The samples analyzed contained the extremely toxic 2,3,7,8-tetrachlorodibenzodioxin (dioxin) in concentrations ranging from 0.05 to 47 parts per million (ppm), with an average concentration of 1.91 ppm.[4] With some 11.25 million gallons of Agent Orange having been sprayed in Vietnam, it is estimated that at least 220 to 360 pounds of dioxin were dispersed over the country.[5] In addition, the stocks of Agent Orange sampled were from batches produced in the late 1960s, when the process to manufacture the herbicide had been much improved and dioxin contamination reduced. Had Agent Orange stocks used in the early 1960s been analyzed, they may well have revealed a higher dioxin content.[6]

In 1971, dioxin was confirmed as a cause of birth deformities. Formulations of 2,4,5-T with a low dioxin content (0.5 ppm) were found not to cause malformations in rodents that were affected by the more contaminated 2,4,5-T.[7]

Although the animal evidence was relatively clearcut, the effects of Agent Orange on reproductive outcomes in humans were much less so. There was much disagreement between scientists about the evidence for stillbirths and birth deformities in Vietnam between 1960 and 1969. One interpretation argued that there had been no increase in stillbirths or deformities coincident with the spraying program, while another evaluation argued that an increase had indeed occurred.[8] Both sides acknowledged, however, that the records needed for a true assessment of the evidence were not available. Dislocation of the population, caused by the war and significant under-reporting of cases, limited the possibilities for drawing well-founded conclusions.[9]

---

[4] National Academy of Sciences, "The Effects of Herbicides in South Vietnam," Part A, Summary and Conclusions VII–9 (1974).

[5] *Ibid.*

[6] A. H. Westing, *Ecological Consequences of the Second Indochina War* (Stockholm: Almqvist & Wiksell Int'l, 1976), p. 28.

[7] K. D. Courtney et al., "Teratogenic Evaluation of 2,4,5-T," *Sci.* 168 (1970), 864–66; K. D. Courtney and J. A. Moore, "Teratology Studies with 2,4,5-Trichlorophenoxyacetic Acid and 2,3,7,8-Tetrachlorodibenzo-p-Dioxin," *Toxicology and Applied Pharmacology* 20 (1971), 396–403; G. L. Sparschu et al., "Study of the Teratogenicity of 2,3,7,8-Tetrachlorodibenzo-p-Dioxin in the Rat," *Food & Cosm. Toxicology* 9 (1971), 405–12.

[8] Hay, *The Chemical Scythe.*

[9] *Ibid.*

Table 16.1. *Properties of 2,3,7,8-tetrachlorodibenzo-p-dioxin (dioxin) and 2,4,5-T*

Date	Population	Factors
1970[a]	Birth defects in rats	2,4,5-T with 30 ppm dioxin
1971[b]	Birth defects in rats	Dioxin
1978[c]	Cancers of liver, lung, hard palate, and tongue in rats	Dioxin
1979[d]	Decreased litter sizes; reduced neonatal survival and growth	Dioxin
1980[e]	Cancer promoter	Dioxin

[a] Courtney et al., "Teratogenic Evaluation."
[b] Courtney and Moore, "Teratology Studies."
[c] Kociba et al., "Results of a 2-Year Chronic Toxicity and Oncogenicity Study."
[d] Murray et al., "3-Generation Reproduction Study."
[e] Pitot et al., "Quantitative Evaluation."

The aftermath

In 1976, an accident at a chemical plant near the Italian town of Seveso catapulted dioxin into the news in a far more significant fashion than Agent Orange had. Following the accident at Seveso and the exposure of the local population to dioxin, research on the chemical mushroomed. At the time of writing, there are well over 3,000 scientific publications on dioxin, in addition to numerous books and research monographs.

A brief chronology of the effects dioxin has in animals is shown in Table 16.1. Dioxin, in addition to causing birth deformities, will cause a number of cancers, particularly in the liver and lung of the rat.[10] Female animals exposed to dioxin have smaller litters, and both the survival of their offspring and their subsequent growth are reduced.[11] The principal property of dioxin in the cancer process seems to be that of a cancer promoter, enhancing the cancer process initiated by another agent.[12]

[10] R. J. Kociba et al., "Results of a 2-Year Chronic Toxicity and Oncogenicity Study of 2,3,7,8-Tetrachlorodibenzo-p-Dioxin in Rats," *Toxicology & App'd Pharmacology* 46 (1978), 279–303.
[11] F. J. Murray et al., "3-Generation Reproduction Study of Rats Given 2,3,7,8-Tetrachlorodibenzo-p-Dioxin (TCDD) in the Diet," *Toxicology & App'd Pharmacology* 50 (1979), 241–52.
[12] H. C. Pitot et al., "Quantitative Evaluation of the Promotion of 2,3,7,8-Tetrachlorodibenzo-p-Dioxin of Hepatocarcinogenesis from Diethylnitrosamine," *Cancer Res.* 40 (1980), 3616–20.

Human health effects

Details about the effects of dioxin on human health have been obtained principally from two groups of workers. The first of these are the individuals who have been exposed to dioxin, and sometimes more than one dioxin (there are seventy-five in total), either through poor hygiene in the manufacture of 2,4,5-trichlorophenol (the precursor of 2,4,5-T), or through explosions in chemical reactors. The number of individuals known to be affected in these various incidents is shown in Table 16.2.

DIOXIN EXPOSURE IN AGRICULTURE AND FORESTRY

The second group who have provided details about the health effects of exposure to both 2,4,5-T and dioxin are individuals employed in agriculture and forestry. Numerous investigations have been carried out to determine the incidence of cancer generally, as well as that of certain specific cancers among forestry workers. Two particular types of cancer have been reported to occur more frequently in workers exposed to 2,4,5-T.[13] The first is a cancer of the connective tissue, known as a soft tissue sarcoma; the second is a cancer of the lymph glands, known as non-Hodgkin's lymphoma. Early studies in Sweden carried out by two investigators, Hardell and Eriksson, recorded that individuals with either a soft tissue sarcoma or a non-Hodgkin's lymphoma were much more likely to have been in contact with phenoxyacetic acid herbicides than a matching control group (see Table 16.3).[14] Cancer cases were six times more likely to have been in contact with the herbicides than the controls. All of these results were statistically significant.

Several other investigations in New Zealand and Sweden failed to confirm these earlier findings. Although two investigations in New Zealand, which were of a similar study design to those of Hardell and Eriksson, suggested a slightly increased risk of developing soft tissue sarcoma or non-Hodgkin's lymphoma following exposure to phenoxyacetic acid herbicides,

---

[13] L. Hardell and A. Sandstrom, "Case-controlled Study: Soft-tissue Sarcomas and Exposure to Phenoxyacetic Acids or Chlorophenols," *Brit. J. Cancer* 39 (1979), 711–17; L. Hardell et al., "Malignant Lymphoma and Exposure to Chemicals, Especially Organic Solvents, Chlorophenols and Phenoxy Acids: A Case-controlled Study," *Brit. J. Cancer* 43 (1981), 169–76; M. Eriksson et al., "Soft-tissue Sarcomas and Exposure to Chemical Substances: Case-referent Study," *Brit. J. Indus. Med.* 38 (1981), 27–33. [14] *Ibid.*

Table 16.2. Accidents in chemical plants involving the manufacture of chlorinated phenols

Date	Country	Manufacturer/location	Product	Cause of exposure	Personnel affected
1949	United States	Monsanto/Nitro, West Virginia	TCP	Explosion	228
1949	Federal Republic of Germany	Nordrhein/Westfalen	PCP, TCP	Occupational	17
1952	Federal Republic of Germany	Nordrhein/Westfalen	TCP	Occupational	60
1952–53	Federal Republic of Germany	Boehringer/Hamburg	TCP	Occupational	37
1953	Federal Republic of Germany	BASF/Ludwigshafen	TCP	Explosion	75
1953–71	France	Rhone-Poulenc/Grenoble	TCP	Occupational and explosion	17
1954	Federal Republic of Germany	Boehringer, Ingelheim/ Hamburg	TCP, 2,4,5-T	Occupational	31
1956	United States	Diamond Alkalai/Newark, New Jersey	2,4-D 2,4,5-T	Occupational	29
1956	United States	Hooker/Niagara Falls, New York	TCP	Occupational	Many
1959	Italy	Industrie Chimiche Melegnanesi Saronio/Milan	TCP	Occupational	5
1959	United States	Thompson Hayward/Kansas City, Kansas	TCP	Occupational	–
1960	United States	Diamond Shamrock	TCP	Occupational	Many, 1 fatal

Year	Country	Company/Location	Chemical	Type	Number
1963	Netherlands	Philips-Duphar/Amsterdam	TCP	Explosion	106
1964	USSR		2,4,5-T	Occupational	128
1964	United States	Dow Chemical/Midland, Michigan	2,4,5-T	Occupational	30
1964–69	Czechoslovakia	Spolana	TCP	Occupational	80, 2 fatal
1968	United Kingdom	Coalite and Chemicals Products/Bolsover, Derbyshire	TCP	Explosion	90
1970	United Kingdom	Coalite and Chemicals Products/Hertfordshire	TCP	Occupational	3
1970	Japan		2,4,5-T	Occupational	25
1972	USSR		TCP	Occupational	1
1972–73	Austria	Chemie Worke/Linz, Austria	2,4,5-T	Occupational	50
1974	Federal Republic of Germany	Bayer/Uerdingen	2,4,5-T	Occupational	5
1976	Italy	ICMESA/Meda/Seveso	TCP	Explosion	'000s
1976	United Kingdom	Monsanto/South Wales	PCP	Occupational	–

TCP: 2,4,5-trichlorophenol; PCP: pentachlorophenol; 2,4-D: 2,4-dichlorophenoxyacetic acid; 2,4,5-T: 2,4,5-trichlorophenoxyacetic acid. From Hay, *The Chemical Scythe*.

Table 16.3. *Soft tissue sarcoma (STS) and non-Hodgkin's lymphoma (NHL) in forestry workers*

Date	Country	Population	Agent	Outcome
1979[a]	Sweden	52 patients 208 controls	Phenoxy acids	STS RR: 5.7 (2.9,11.3)
1981[b]	Sweden	169 cases 338 controls	Phenoxy acids Chlorophenols	NHL RR: 6.0 (3.7,9.7)
1981[c]	Sweden	110 cases 219 referents	Phenoxy acids (± dioxins) Chlorophenols	STS RR: 6.8 (2.6,17.3)
1984[d]	New Zealand	82 cases 92 controls	Phenoxy acids Chlorophenols	STS RR: 1.3 (0.6,2.5)
1986[e]	New Zealand	83 cases 168 controls	Phenoxy acids	NHL OR: 1.4 (0.7,2.5)
1986[f]	Sweden	331 cases 1,508 referents	Agriculture Forestry	STS RR: 0.9 (0.8,1.0)
1986[g]	United States	37 cases 133 controls	2,4-D	NHL OR: 6.0 (1.9,19.5) No increase in STS
1988[h]	Sweden	55 cases 330 referents	Phenoxy acids	STS RR: 3.3 (1.4,8.1)
1991[i]	Ten countries	17,372 male and 1,537 female herbicide sprayers or production workers	Phenoxy acids (not all dioxin containing)	STS SMR: 196 For 10–19 year latency, SMR: 606 (165,1552)
1991[j]	Italy	141 cases non-Hodgkin's lymphoma	2,4,5-T and 2,4-D	Incidence rates: Males – 8.8 (7.4,10.4) Females – 5.8 (4.7,7.0)

RR: risk ratio; OR: odds ratio; SMR: standardized mortality ratio; figures in parentheses are 95 percent confidence intervals
[a] Hardell and Sandstrom, "Case-controlled Study."
[b] Hardell et al., "Malignant Lymphoma."
[c] Eriksson et al., "Soft-tissue Sarcomas."
[d] Smith et al., "Soft-tissue Sarcoma."
[e] Pearce et al., "Non-Hodgkin's Lymphoma."
[f] Wiklund and Holm, "Soft-tissue Sarcoma Risk."
[g] Hoar et al., "Agricultural Herbicide Use."
[h] Hardell and Eriksson, "Association between Soft-tissue Sarcomas."
[i] Search et al., "Cancer Mortality."
[j] Vineis et al., "Incidence Rates of Lymphomas."

the results were not significant and may have been a chance finding.[15] A large investigation in Sweden reported that individuals working in the agricultural and forestry sectors were not at increased risk of developing soft tissue sarcoma.[16] In the United States, one investigation suggested that exposure to 2,4-D (the other component of Agent Orange) was associated with an increased risk of non-Hodgkin's lymphoma, but not soft tissue sarcoma.[17] A further study in Sweden, carried out by Hardell and Eriksson in 1988, confirmed their earlier findings that there was indeed an increased risk of developing soft tissue sarcoma with exposure to phenoxyacetic acid herbicides. However, the risk was now only three times greater than for the control group.[18] In this follow-up work, Hardell and Eriksson noted that they had failed to identify an increased risk of soft tissue sarcoma purely on the basis of classifying individuals according to whether they worked in agriculture or forestry. Specific inquiries about the types of chemicals that individuals had worked with were necessary to establish the true risk.[19]

To resolve some of this conflicting evidence, a large cohort study of nearly 19,000 male and female herbicide sprayers and production workers in ten countries was conducted. This study also indicated that the number of deaths from soft tissue sarcomas in individuals exposed to phenoxyacetic acid herbicides was greater than would be expected. Further, it found that for individuals who were exposed ten to nineteen years prior to the investigation, the mortality rate was six times what would be expected.[20] A final study investigating the incidence of non-Hodgkin's lymphoma in association with areas sprayed with 2,4,5-T and 2,4-D recorded higher incidence rates in those areas.[21]

---

[15] A. H. Smith et al., "Soft-tissue Sarcoma and Exposure to Phenoxyherbicides and Chlorophenols in New Zealand," *J. Nat'l Cancer Inst.* 73 (1984), 1111–17; N. E. Pearce et al., "Non-Hodgkin's Lymphoma and Exposure to Phenoxyherbicides, Chlorophenols, Fencing Work and Meat Works Employment: Case-controlled Study," *Brit. J. Indus. Med.* 43 (1986), 75–83.

[16] K. Wiklund and L. E. Holm, "Soft-tissue Sarcoma Risk in Swedish Agricultural and Forestry Workers," *J. Nat'l Cancer Inst.* 76 (1986), 229–34.

[17] S. K. Hoar et al., "Agricultural Herbicide Use and Risk of Lymphoma and Soft-tissue Sarcoma," *J. Am. Med. Ass'n* 256 (1986), 1141–47.

[18] L. Hardell and M. Eriksson, "The Association between Soft-tissue Sarcomas and Exposure to Phenoxyacetic Acid. A New Case Referent Study," *Cancer* 62 (1988), 652–56.   [19] *Ibid.*

[20] R. Search et al., "Cancer Mortality in Workers Exposed to Chlorophenoxyherbicides and Chlorophenols," *The Lancet* 338 (1991), 1027–32.

[21] P. Vineis et al., "Incidence Rates of Lymphomas and Soft-tissue Sarcomas, and Environmental Measurements of Phenoxyherbicides," *J. Nat'l Cancer Inst.* 83 (1991), 362–63.

Table 16.4. *Industrial worker mortality and dioxin exposure*

Date	Population	Factors	Outcome
1987[a]	2,192 Dow Chemical employees	Higher chlorinated phenols – potential exposure to dioxins	Deaths from all or specific cancers no greater than expected
1990[b]	247 BASF employees	Dioxin	All cancer SMR: 117 (80,166) Cancers in workers with chloracne SMR: 139 (87,211)
1991[c]	5,172 US chemical workers	Exposure to dioxin; 4 soft tissue sarcoma (STS) cases	STS SMR: 338 (92,865) Respiratory tract cancer: SMR: 142 (103,192) All cancers SMR: 115 (102,130)

SMR: standardised mortality ratio; figures in parentheses are 95 percent confidence intervals
[a] Ott et al., "Cohort Mortality Study."
[b] A. Zober et al., "Thirty Four Year Mortality Follow-up."
[c] Fingerhut et al., "Cancer Mortality in Workers."

INDUSTRIAL EXPOSURE TO DIOXIN

Results from three of the latest investigations into cancer risk in industrial cohorts of workers exposed to dioxin are shown in Table 16.4. For some 2,000 Dow Chemical employees, deaths from specific cancers, or all cancers combined, are reported to be no greater than expected.[22] Cancer deaths for some 250 German employees at the company BASF, although slightly higher than the norm, are reported to be not significant.[23] However, in a large study of nearly 5,200 United States chemical workers exposed to dioxin at twelve chemical plants, the deaths among workers from soft tissue sarcoma (of which there were only four cases) was three times what would be expected.[24] Deaths from cancer of the respiratory tract were also significantly increased, but it was not possible to exclude a potential contribution from other factors, such as smoking and exposure to differ-

[22] M. G. Ott et al., "Cohort Mortality Study of Chemical Workers with Potential Exposure to the Higher Chlorinated Dioxins," *J. Occupational Med.* 29 (1987), 422–29.
[23] A. Zober, et al., "Thirty Four Year Mortality Follow-up of BASF Employees Exposed to 2,3,7,8-TCDD After the 1953 Accident," *Int'l Archives Occupational & Envtl. Health* 62 (1990), 139–57.
[24] M. A. Fingerhut et al., "Cancer Mortality in Workers Exposed to 2,3,7,8-Tetrachlorodibenzo-p-Dioxin," *New Eng. J. Med.* 324 (1991), 212–18.

Table 16.5. *Birth defects/miscarriages/agriculture*

Date	Country	Population	Factors	Outcome
1979[a]	Arkansas (US)	1,200 cases of cleft lip and/or cleft palate	Computed 2,4,5-T use according to rice acreage	Increased prevalence cleft lip in both *high* and *low* exposure groups; better reporting
1982[b]	New Zealand	Wives of 989 2,4,5-T sprayers and agricultural contractors	Exposure to 2,4,5-T	Birth defects (RR 1.19; CI 0.58–2.45) Miscarriages (RR 0.89; CI 0.61–1.30)
1983[c]	United Kingdom	Women in Oxfordshire and West Berkshire	Birth outcomes Paternal occupation in forestry, agriculture, horticulture	Anencephaly: RR 1.2 Spina bifida: RR 0.8 Cleft lip/palate: RR 0.9

RR: risk ratio; figures in parentheses are 95 percent confidence intervals
[a] Nelson et al., "Retrospective Study."
[b] Smith et al., "Congenital Defects and Miscarriages."
[c] Golding and Sladden, "Congenital Malformations."

ent chemicals. Deaths from all cancers combined were also slightly and significantly increased in these 5,200 men.[25]

BIRTH DEFECTS AND MISCARRIAGES CAUSED BY AGRICULTURAL USE OF 2,4,5-T

Several studies of varying design have investigated the incidence and prevalence of birth defects and miscarriages in communities where there was the potential for exposure to the herbicide 2,4,5-T (details are shown in Table 16.5). In only one of the investigations was there the suggestion of an increased prevalence of cleft palate.[26] However, the increase bore no relation to the use of 2,4,5-T, and the authors considered that the real reason for the increase was better recording or reporting of cases.[27] In two

[25] *Ibid.*
[26] C. J. Nelson et al., "Retrospective Study of the Relationship Between Agricultural Use of 2,4,5-T and Cleft Palate Occurrence in Arkansas," *Teratology* 19 (1979), 377–84.
[27] *Ibid.*

other investigations in New Zealand and the United Kingdom, there were no recorded increases in either birth defects or miscarriages where there was either exposure to 2,4,5-T, or where the father's occupation was in forestry, agriculture, or horticulture.[28]

POPULATIONS EXPOSED TO AGENT ORANGE IN VIETNAM

The effect of exposure to Agent Orange in Vietnam has been assessed by investigating two different populations. The first of these is comprised of the men and women from the United States who served in Vietnam during the war; the second is the Vietnamese population itself.

Health outcomes for US Vietnam veterans

Following the emergence of the evidence from Sweden suggesting an increase in soft tissue sarcoma in forestry workers exposed to 2,4,5-T, investigations were carried out on Vietnam veterans to assess whether their exposure to Agent Orange was associated with a similarly increased risk. Four studies (detailed in Table 16.6) report that service in Vietnam was not associated with an increased risk of developing soft tissue sarcoma.[29] In none of the investigations were there any direct assessments of exposure to Agent Orange. Exposure to the herbicide could only be inferred from surrogate measures, such as the military region in which individuals were located, or their combat unit. In only one of the four investigations was there the suggestion of an increased risk.[30] This increased risk appeared to be in men who served in military region III, an area where the use of Agent Orange was extensive. Five cases of soft tissue sarcoma were recorded in men who served in region III, a figure some eight-and-a-half times what would

---

[28] A. H. Smith et al., "Congenital Defects and Miscarriages Among New Zealand 2,4,5-T Sprayers," *Archives Envtl. Health* 37 (1982), 197–200; J. Golding and T. Sladden, "Congenital Malformations in Agricultural Workers," *The Lancet* 1 (1983), 1393.

[29] P. Greenwald et al., "Sarcomas and Soft-tissues After Vietnam Service," *J. Nat'l Cancer Inst.* 73 (1984), 1107–09; H. K. Kang et al., "Soft-tissue Sarcomas and Military Service in Vietnam: A Case-comparison Group Analysis of Hospital Patients," *J. Occupational Med.* 28 (1986), 1215–18; H. Kang et al., "Soft-tissue Sarcoma and Military Service in Vietnam: A Case-controlled Study," *J. Nat'l Cancer Inst.* 79 (1987), 693–99; Selected Cancers Co-operative Study Group of the Centers for Disease Control, "The Association of Selected Cancers with Service in the US Military in Vietnam. II. Soft-tissue and Other Sarcomas," *Archives Internal Med.* 150 (1990), 2485–92.   [30] Kang et al., "Soft Tissue Sarcoma" (1987).

Table 16.6. *Service in Vietnam and soft tissue sarcoma*

Date	Population	Factors	Outcome
1984[a]	281 cases 411 controls	Vietnam service	OR: 0.53 (0.21, 1.31)
1986[b]	234 cases 13,496 controls	Vietnam service	OR: 0.83 (0.63,1.09)
1987[c]	217 cases 599 controls	Vietnam service Exposure to chemicals	OR: 0.85 (0.54,1.36)
	5 cases	Military Region III	OR: 8.6 (0.77,111.84)
1990[d]	254 cases 1,776 controls	Duration of service	OR: 0.9 (0.5,1.6)

OR: odds ratio; figures in parentheses are 95 percent confidence intervals
[a] Greenwald et al., "Sarcomas and Soft Tissues."
[b] Kang et al., "Soft-tissue Sarcomas" (1986).
[c] Kang et al., "Soft-tissue Sarcoma" (1987).
[d] Centers for Disease Control, "The Association of Selected Cancers. II. Soft-tissue and Other Sarcomas."

be expected.[31] However, given the small number of cases and the lack of statistical significance, a chance observation cannot be ruled out.

There is no evidence that exposure to Agent Orange increased Veterans' risk of developing non-Hodgkin's lymphoma. The three studies reported in Table 16.7 assess this risk. Surrogate measures of exposure to Agent Orange, such as military service, combat region, or specific unit were again used in these assessments.[32] The investigation performed by the Centers for Disease Control on this matter suggested that there was an increased risk of developing non-Hodgkin's lymphoma associated with longer service in Vietnam.[33] However, there was no association between this increased risk and the region in which veterans served, nor with their assessed exposure to Agent Orange.[34]

[31] *Ibid.*
[32] Selected Cancers Co-operative Study Group of the Centers for Disease Control, "The Association of Selected Cancers with Service in the US Military in Vietnam. I. Non-Hodgkin's Lymphoma," *Archives Internal Med.* 150 (1990), 2473–83; N. A. Dalager et al., "Non-Hodgkin's Lymphoma Among Vietnam Veterans," *J. Occupational Med.* 33 (1991), 774–79.
[33] Selected Cancers Co-operative Study Group of the Centers for Disease Control, "The Association of Selected Cancers."
[34] *Ibid.*

Table 16.7. *Service in Vietnam and non-Hodgkin's lymphoma*

Date	Population	Factors	Outcome
1990[a]	1,157 Vietnam veterans 1,776 controls	Duration of service; Units; Military region	OR: 1.47 (1.1,2.0) Increased risk with longer service No association with region; no association with Agent Orange
1991[b]	201 Vietnam era veterans 358 controls	Military service; Region; Combat branch	OR: 1.03 (0.7,1.5)
1991[c]	8,170 Vietnam veterans 7,564 non-Vietnam veterans	Military; Job titles	No association with herbicides (only 7 cases)

OR: odds ratio; figures in parentheses are 95 percent confidence intervals
[a] Centers for Disease Control, "The Association of Selected Cancers. I. Non-Hodgkin's Lymphoma."
[b] Dalager et al., "Non-Hodgkin's Lymphoma."
[c] T. R. O'Brien et al., "Non-Hodgkin's Lymphoma in a Cohort of Vietnam Veterans," *Am. J. Pub. Health* 81 (1991), 758–60.

Birth defects in offspring of Vietnam veterans

The evidence related to birth defects in the children of Vietnam veterans is very difficult to assess. Results of the various investigations into this topic are shown in Table 16.8. A survey of some 8,500 Australian Vietnam veterans found no increase in the risk of children being born with major structural birth defects.[35] In addition, two studies of United States Vietnam veterans, both of which involved over 7,000 soldiers, found that birth defects in the children of the veterans were no greater than expected.[36] In the first of these two investigations, a slightly increased risk of spina bifida occurring was noted; however there was no corresponding increase in the occurrence of anencephaly.[37] These two conditions have a similar embryology link, and are considered to be related defects. The increase

[35] J. W. Donovan, *Case-control Study of Congenital Anomalies in Vietnam Service* (Canberra: Australian Gov't Pub. Service, 1983).
[36] J. D. Eriksson et al., "Vietnam Veterans' Risk for Fathering Babies with Birth Defects," *J. Am. Med. Ass'n* 252 (1984), 903–12; Centers for Disease Control Vietnam Experience Study, "Health Status of Vietnam Veterans. III. Reproductive Outcomes and Child Health," *J. Am. Med. Ass'n* 259 (1988), 2715–19.   [37] Eriksson et al., "Vietnam Veterans' Risk."

Table 16.8. *Birth defects in children of Vietnam veterans*

Date	Population	Factors	Outcome
1983[a]	8,517 Australian Vietnam veterans and controls	Birth outcomes Service in Vietnam	No increased risk structural birth defects
1984[b]	7,133 Vietnam veterans 4,246 controls	Birth outcomes Vietnam service Self-reported exposure to Agent Orange	All defects: RR 0.97 Spina bifida: RR 1.05 Anencephaly: RR 0.89
1988[c]	7,924 Vietnam veterans 7,364 non-Vietnam veteran controls	Service in Vietnam Birth details checked in hospital records	Birth defects odds ratio: Total (1.0) Major (1.1) Minor (1.0) Suspected (0.9)
1988[d]	6,810 US Vietnam Legionnaires	Combat and Agent Orange exposure assessed based on location and military unit	No difficulty in conception; Agent Orange associated with increased miscarriages
1996[e]	NAS/IOM review of published studies	Ranch Hand population	Spina bifida: 3 cases in 792 live births General population rate is 1 case in 2,000 live births

RR: risk ratio

[a] Donovan, *Case-control Study of Congenital Anomalies.*
[b] Eriksson et al., "Vietnam Veterans' Risk."
[c] Centers for Disease Control, "Health Status of Vietnam Veterans. III."
[d] Stellman et al., "Health and Reproductive Outcomes."
[e] Institute of Medicine, *Veterans and Agent Orange.*

in the incidence of spina bifida may, therefore, be a chance finding.[38] In the second of the investigations on the children of US Vietnam veterans, birth details were checked via reference to hospital records; there were no reported increases of birth defects in these children.[39]

A study of some 6,800 US Vietnam Legionnaires recorded an association between Agent Orange exposure and an increase in self-reports of miscarriages; no hospital records were checked. No difficulty in conception was reported by the Legionnaires. As in the other studies, exposure to

[38] *Ibid.*   [39] Centers for Disease Control, "Health Status of Vietnam Veterans. III."

Agent Orange was assessed on the basis of the Legionnaires' military unit and location in Vietnam.[40]

The National Academy of Sciences Institute of Medicine (IOM) has conducted a recent review of birth outcomes for Vietnam veterans.[41] The IOM re-analyzed data from a group of some 900 Operation Ranch Hand Veterans (the Ranch Handers ran the herbicide-spraying program). The IOM reported that there was limited, or suggestive, evidence of an increased risk of spina bifida. Three cases of spina bifida occurred in 792 live births, fathered by the Ranch Handers. For the general population, the rate is one case for every 2,000 live births.

SERVICE IN VIETNAM, MORTALITY AND MORBIDITY

The overall effect of spending time in Vietnam on the health of US servicemen is recorded in a number of investigations detailed in Table 16.9.[42]

Deaths from all causes, and those from accidents and suicides, were higher among Vietnam servicemen generally and among herbicide applicators in particular.[43] Depression and post-traumatic stress disorder were also very common among Vietnam veterans.[44] Vietnam veterans reported additional health problems, although clinical examination on a subset of veterans provided no objective evidence to support these claims of ill-health.[45] A

[40] S. D. Stellman et al., "Health and Reproductive Outcomes Among American Legionnaires in Relation to Combat and Herbicide Exposure in Vietnam," *Envtl. Res.* 47 (1988), 150–74.

[41] Institute of Medicine, National Academy of Sciences, *Veterans and Agent Orange: Update 1996* (1996).

[42] Centers for Disease Control Vietnam Experience Study, "Post Service Mortality Study Among Vietnam Veterans," *J. Am. Med. Ass'n* 257 (1987), 790–95; Centers for Disease Control Vietnam Experience Study, "Health Status of Vietnam Veterans. I. Psychosocial Characteristics," *J. Am. Med. Ass'n* 259 (1988), 2701–7; Centers for Disease Control Vietnam Experience Study, "Health Status of Vietnam Veterans. II. Physical Health," *J. Am. Med. Ass'n* 259 (1988), 2708–14; T. L. Thomas and H. K. Kang, "Mortality and Morbidity Among Army Chemical Corps Vietnam Veterans: A Preliminary Report," *Am. J. Indus. Med.* 18 (1990), 665–73; W. H. Wolfe et al., "Health Status of Air Force Veterans Occupationally Exposed to Herbicides in Vietnam. I. Physical Health," *J. Am. Med. Ass'n* 264 (1990), 1824–31; T. L. Thomas et al., "Mortality Among Women Vietnam Veterans, 1973–1987," *Am. J. Epidemiology* 134 (1991), 973–80; P. Decoufle et al., "Self-reported Health Status of Vietnam Veterans in Relation to Perceived Exposure to Herbicides During Combat," *Am. J. Epidemiology* 135 (1992), 312–31.

[43] Centers for Disease Control, "Post Service Mortality Study;" Thomas and Kang, "Mortality and Morbidity Among Army Chemical Corps."

[44] Centers for Disease Control, "Health Status of Vietnam Veterans. II," 2701–07; Decoufle et al., "Self-reported Health Status."

[45] Centers for Disease Control, "Health Status of Vietnam Veterans. II," 2708–14.

Table 16.9. *Service in Vietnam: mortality and morbidity*

Date	Population	Factors	Outcome
1987[a]	9,324 Vietnam veterans 8,989 US Army controls	Service in Vietnam	Total mortality: 17% higher Accidents/suicides: RR 1.45 (1.08,1.96)
1988[b]		Service in Vietnam	Depression: 2 times higher in Vietnam veterans 15% Vietnam veterans had post-traumatic stress disorder
1988[c]	7,924 US Army Vietnam veterans 7,364 non-Vietnam Army controls	Service in Vietnam	More reported health problems – no objective evidence of these Decreased sperm counts in Vietnam veterans but similar numbers of children
1990[d]	1,000 US Chemical Corp personnel	Herbicide applicators	All deaths: SMR 1.09 Digestive diseases: SMR 2.98 Accidents: SMR 2.0
1990[e]	995 Ranch Hands 1,299 controls	Exposure to Agent Orange	Increased basal cell carcinoma No difference other health measures No previous or current chloracne No difference in three other sun-related skin damage indicators
1991[f]	4,600 female Vietnam veterans 5,300 female veterans – controls	Service in Vietnam	All causes of death: RR 0.93 (1.03,9.86) Pancreatic cancer in Vietnam veteran nurses: RR 3.27 (5 deaths)
1992[g]	7,924 US Army veterans	Perceived exposure to herbicide	Symptoms associated with Post-traumatic stress disorder Inconsistent symptoms for herbicide exposure

RR: risk ratio; SMR: standardized mortality ratio; figures in parentheses are 95 percent confidence intervals
[a] Centers for Disease Control, "Post Service Mortality Study."
[b] Centers for Disease Control, "Health Status of Vietnam Veterans. I."
[c] Centers for Disease Control, "Health Status of Vietnam Veterans. II."
[d] Thomas and Kang, "Mortality and Morbidity Among Army Chemical Corps."
[e] Wolfe et al., "Health Status of Air Force Veterans."
[f] Thomas et al., "Mortality Among Women."
[g] Decoufle, et al., "Self-reported Health Status."

survey of some veterans recorded reduced sperm counts, but no notable differences between the numbers of children fathered by the veterans and their army controls.[46] In a survey of some 995 Ranch Handers, an increase in the skin cancer basal cell carcinoma was recorded. However, there was no reported increase in three other indicators of sun-related skin damage, and no difference in any other measures of health outcome.[47]

Death rates have also been assessed for female Vietnam veterans. Mortality rates for female veterans are no greater than expected, except for death from cancer of the pancreas among nurses who served in Vietnam. The risk of death from pancreatic cancer for these nurses was three times what would be expected.[48] The etiology of pancreatic cancer generally is far from clear, although some studies suggest that it may be related to lifestyle or dietary factors, including fat, alcohol, and coffee consumption. The information available in the study on female Vietnam veterans was insufficient to enable the authors to make any evaluation about factors that were associated with this increased risk of death from pancreatic cancer.[49]

SERVICE IN VIETNAM AND OTHER CANCERS

The association between other cancers, service in Vietnam, and potential exposure to Agent Orange has been assessed in four investigations and is recorded in Table 16.10.[50] For male United States veterans, service in Vietnam is not associated with an increased risk of Hodgkin's disease, nasal cancer, nasopharyngeal cancer, or primary liver cancer.[51] For ground troops, or servicemen sited in III Corps (military region III), there is no increased risk indicated for developing testicular cancer. The ground troops'

---

[46] *Ibid.*   [47] Wolfe et al., "Health Status of Air Force Veterans."

[48] Thomas et al., "Mortality Among Women."   [49] *Ibid.*

[50] Selected Cancers Co-operative Study Group of the Centers for Disease Control, "The Association of Selected Cancers with Service in the US Military in Vietnam. III. Hodgkin's Disease, Nasal Cancer, Nasopharyngeal Cancer, and Primary Liver Cancer," *Archives Internal Med.* 150 (1990), 2495–505; H. M. Hayes et al., "Excess of Seminomas Observed in Vietnam Services US Military Working Dogs," *J. Nat'l Cancer Inst.* 82 (1990), 1042–46; T. A. Bullman et al., "Risk of Testicular Cancer Associated with Surrogate Measures of Agent Orange Exposure Among Vietnam Veterans on the Agent Orange Registry," *Annals of Epidemiology* 4 (1994), 11–16; N. A. Dalager et al., "Hodgkin's Disease and Vietnam Service," *Annals of Epidemiology* 5 (1995), 400–6.

[51] Selected Cancers Co-operative Study Group of the Centers for Disease Control, "The Association of Selected Cancers"; Dalager et al., "Hodgkin's Disease."

Table 16.10. *Service in Vietnam and other cancers*

Date	Population	Factors	Outcome
1990[a]	310 cases with Hodgkin's disease (HD); 48 nasal cancer (NC); 80 nasopharyngeal cancer (NPC); 130 primary liver cancer (PLC).	Service in Vietnam	OR HD: 1.1 OR NC: 0.7 OR NPC: 0.5 OR PLC: 1.2 None significantly different from 1.0
1990[b]	96 US Military working dogs Testicular seminoma	Exposures to herbicides/infections similar to troops; Tetracycline administered regularly to dogs	Testicular seminoma OR: 1.9 (1.2,3.0); Increased testicular dysfunction
1994[c]	97 cases testicular cancer	Surrogate measures of Agent Orange exposure	Navy OR: 2.6 (1.08,6.24) Ground troops OR: 0.46 (0.25,0.86) III Corps OR: 1.1 (0.66,1.84)
1995[d]	283 cases Hodgkin's disease 404 controls	Service in Vietnam	OR: 1.28 (0.94,1.76)

OR: odds ratio; figures in parentheses are 95 percent confidence intervals
[a] Centers for Disease Control, "The Association of Selected Cancers. III."
[b] Hayes et al., "Excess of Seminomas."
[c] Bullman et al., "Risk of Testicular Cancer."
[d] Dalager et al., "Hodgkin's Disease."

possible contact with Agent Orange was assessed on the basis of military unit numbers or location. Navy personnel were at increased risk of developing testicular cancer, with two job categories most at risk: engine men and support equipment technicians. Both jobs involve exposure to fuels such as gasoline, a reported risk factor for testicular cancer.[52]

Dogs that worked for the United States military were also likely to have been exposed to herbicides.[53] The incidence of the cancer testicular seminoma was assessed in ninety-six working dogs. The exposed dogs had a risk of developing the cancer two times the expected rate. An increased

[52] Bullman et al., "Risk of Testicular Cancer."   [53] Hayes et al., "Excess of Seminomas."

prevalence of testicular dysfunction was also noted in these dogs. However, other factors, such as constant doses of the antibiotic tetracycline, could have caused the dysfunction and/or the cancers.[54]

Liver cancer and chronic liver disease

For United States Vietnam veterans, service in Vietnam is not associated with an increased risk of developing primary liver cancer.[55] For the Vietnamese population, however, primary cancer of the liver is a real risk. In 1973, one Vietnamese author suggested that the increase might be attributable to exposure to dioxin from the use of Agent Orange.[56] Other liver disorders, such as chronic hepatitis (inflammation of the liver), were also reported to be ten times more prevalent among subjects who had been directly exposed to herbicides at least a decade previously.[57] At the time of this Vietnamese study, of some 558 cases of chronic hepatitis, none had liver cancer. A further study of some twenty-one Vietnamese subjects with primary liver cancer in 1983 noted that a high proportion had also been exposed to herbicides. Although noting that the sample was small, the author suggested that exposure to dioxin might result in a predisposition to develop cancer of the liver.[58]

Two further surveys have investigated chronic liver abnormalities in either United States veterans of the war or in Vietnamese subjects. Details of these investigations are shown in Table 16.11. Investigation of chronic liver abnormalities in United States veterans suggested that the liver disturbance was more likely to have been caused by a virus or excessive consumption of alcohol, rather than exposure to Agent Orange.[59] A detailed assessment of the evidence from 152 men with primary liver cancer in Vietnam indicated a high risk of developing liver cancer if the individual was positive for the hepatitis B virus. The risk of developing primary cancer of the liver is sixty times greater for individuals with hepatitis B

---

[54] *Ibid.*
[55] Selected Cancers Co-operative Study Group of the Centers for Disease Control, "The Association of Selected Cancers."
[56] T. T. Tung, "Primary Cancer of the Liver in Vietnam," *Chirurgie* 99 (1973), 427–37 (in French).
[57] D. T. Trinh, "Long-lasting Morbid Effects Following Herbicidal Attack," in A. H. Westing (ed.), *Herbicides in War: The Long-term Ecological and Human Consequences* (London and Philadelphia: Taylor & Francis, 1984), pp. 115–17.
[58] D. D. Van, "Herbicide as a Possible Cause of Liver Cancer," in Westing, *Herbicides in War*, pp. 119–21.
[59] C. H. Tamburro, "Chronic Liver Injury in Phenoxyherbicide-Exposed Vietnam Veterans," *Envtl. Res.* 59 (1992), 175–88.

Table 16.11. *Liver cancer and chronic liver disease in Vietnam veterans and the Vietnamese population*

Date	Country	Population	Factor	Outcome
1977[a]	Vietnam	General population	Dioxin exposure	Increase in primary liver cancer
1992[b]	United States	Vietnam veterans	Exposure to Agent Orange; Hepatitis; Alcoholism	Chronic liver abnormalities; viral or alcoholic cause not Agent Orange
1993[c]	Vietnam	152 males with primary liver cancer	Hepatitis B +ve Hepatitis C +ve Alcohol consumption Residence in South Vietnam	Hepatitis B +ve OR: 61.7 (30,128) Hepatitis C +ve OR: 38 (2,1443) Ingestion of alcohol of more than 80g/day OR: 5.1 (1.6,17) Residence in south for longer than 10 years OR: 8.8 (1.9,41)

OR: odds ratio; figures in parentheses are 95 percent confidence intervals
[a] Tung, "Primary Cancer of the Liver."
[b] Tamburro, "Chronic Liver Injury."
[c] Cordier et al., "Viral Infection and Chemical Exposures."

virus infection. For those infected with the hepatitis C virus, the risk of developing primary cancer of the liver is thirty-eight times what would otherwise be expected.[60] Alcohol consumption of more than 80 grams per day also increases the risk of primary cancer of the liver. No direct assessment of exposure to herbicides was available for the 152 patients, other than that reported by the individual cases themselves. Those who stayed in the south of Vietnam after 1960 for military purposes were not at increased risk of developing liver cancer. There was also no evidence of an increased risk for those who reported direct or indirect contact with herbicides. Soldiers who remained in the south for more than ten years after 1960, however, experienced a ninefold increased risk of developing cancer

[60] S. Cordier et al., "Viral Infection and Chemical Exposures as Risk Factors for Hepatocellular Carcinoma in Vietnam," *Int'l J. Cancer* 55 (1993), 196–201.

of the liver.[61] Some other factors in the military environment might explain this increased risk. An interaction between infection with the hepatitis B virus and Agent Orange exposure cannot be ruled out. Exposure to aflatoxins, produced by moulds on foodstuffs in hot moist areas, may also play a part. Aflatoxins are known liver carcinogens and they may act on their own, or together with the hepatitis B virus, to cause liver cancer.[62]

EXPOSURE TO AGENT ORANGE AND
REPRODUCTIVE OUTCOMES IN VIETNAM

Several studies conducted in Vietnam suggest that exposure of one, or in some cases both parents to Agent Orange has a measurable effect on reproductive outcomes. Reported increases have been noted in spontaneous abortions, stillbirths, molar pregnancies, and congenital defects.[63] A review of these studies notes, however, that study design, under-reporting, and the difficulty of establishing exposure to Agent Orange makes interpretation of the available data difficult. For many of the studies these data are, at best, only suggestive of a problem.[64] One study of paternal exposure to herbicides in Vietnam led the authors to suggest tentatively that where the father alone had been exposed to herbicides, there was a greater likelihood that conception would result in a spontaneous abortion. For those pregnancies that went to term, a greater prevalence of children with congenital defects, particularly cleft lip, was observed.[65]

Preliminary evidence from Vietnam suggested that the increased incidence of molar pregnancies might be related to wartime herbicide exposure.[66] Vietnamese doctors had recorded the fact that incidences of molar pregnancies and a cancer of the uterus (choriocarcinoma) had increased sharply since 1976. Hydatidform mole (a condition in which the chorionic villi of the placenta degenerates and the fetus is absorbed) and choriocarcinoma are generally described as gestational trophoblastic disease (GTD). The cause of GTD is unknown. Late maternal age is the most firmly established risk factor, and a higher frequency of prior spontaneous

[61] *Ibid.*   [62] *Ibid.*
[63] A. H. Westing, "Reproductive Epidemiology: An Overview," in Westing, *Herbicides in War,* pp. 141–49.
[64] *Ibid.*
[65] N. Can, "Effects on Offspring of Paternal Exposure to Herbicides," in Westing, *Herbicides in War,* pp. 137–39.
[66] Westing, "Reproductive Epidemiology," pp. 141–49.

abortions is reported in some, but not all, studies. In a further evaluation of GTD in Vietnam, eighty-seven married women, all of whom had recent pathological diagnosis of GTD, were matched with eighty-seven surgical controls.[67] Matching was done by age and area of residence. An increased risk of GTD among Vietnamese women was associated with previous live births, and with women who were involved in the breeding of pigs. A measure of poverty was also associated with the increased risk. There was no association between cumulative Agent Orange exposure, assessed using an index, and the risk of developing GTD. The index for assessing Agent Orange exposure was developed in a study of twenty-seven male subjects; it demonstrates a significant correlation between concentrations of dioxin in fat, and the subjects' assessed exposure to Agent Orange.[68]

Conclusion

The damage to Vietnam's ecology caused by the spraying of Agent Orange is well documented, and still evident. Effects of the herbicide-spraying program on American servicemen and Vietnamese civilians who were exposed to the chemicals is much less clear cut. Evidence from investigations of occupational groups exposed to 2,4,5-T and/or dioxin indicate a risk of developing soft tissue sarcoma. The evidence for other cancers is much less obvious. For most of the industrial populations investigated, assessment of their dioxin and/or 2,4,5-T exposure was much easier. Assessment of 2,4,5-T exposure among agricultural workers is more difficult. Assessing the exposure of United States Vietnam veterans and Vietnamese civilians to the 2,4,5-T and dioxin in Agent Orange is even more problematic. In many cases, the indices of exposure have been extremely crude.

For US military personnel who served in Vietnam, the evidence to date suggests that neither service in Vietnam, nor exposure to Agent Orange, is associated with the types of cancer (soft tissue sarcoma and non-Hodgkin's lymphoma) that have been documented in industrial and agricultural cohorts exposed to 2,4,5-T and dioxin. Service in Vietnam is certainly associated with a higher mortality and risk of accidents, as well as with a higher incidence of post-traumatic stress disorder. These outcomes are

[67] M. C. Ha et al., "Agent Orange and the Risk of Gestational Trophoblastic Disease in Vietnam," *Archives Envtl. Health* 51 (1996), 368–74.
[68] P. Verger et al., "Correlation Between Dioxin Levels in Adipose Tissue: An Estimated Exposure to Agent Orange in South Vietnamese Residents," *Envtl. Res.* 65 (1994), 226–42.

more likely to be the results of engaging in combat than of exposure to Agent Orange.

For chronic liver disease and primary liver cancer, the evidence implicates the hepatitis B virus as the principal problem in Vietnam, rather than exposure to Agent Orange. Infection with the hepatitis B virus increases the likelihood of developing primary liver cancer in Vietnam some sixty-fold. A link between exposure to both the hepatitis B virus and Agent Orange cannot be ruled out, as soldiers who spent ten years in the south of Vietnam are nine times more likely to get primary cancer of the liver than control subjects who were never in the south. However, it could be exposure to another risk factor, such as the liver-cancer-causing agent aflatoxin, which accounts for this increased risk. Further work is required to clarify this picture.

Evidence for an association between exposure to Agent Orange and birth defects both in United States veterans who served in Vietnam, and in Vietnamese soldiers and civilians who were exposed to the herbicide, is still unclear. Several studies of both Australian and US Vietnam veterans suggest that neither paternal service in Vietnam, nor exposure to Agent Orange, is associated with an increased risk of fathering a child with a birth deformity. However, a higher incidence of spina bifida has been recorded among the children of servicemen who were part of the Ranch Hand program. Overall evidence from Vietnam about the risk of spina bifida in association with Agent Orange exposure is still tentative.

More helpful news for the Vietnamese population exposed to herbicides is available on gestational trophoblastic disease. This has been an increasing problem in Vietnam since 1976, but the evidence available now suggests that exposure to Agent Orange is unlikely to be the cause of the increase.

Better tools are now available for assessing the risk of exposure to Agent Orange by way of measuring dioxin concentrations in fat tissue. These concentrations of dioxin in fat provide a cumulative measurement of Agent Orange exposure, and make it possible to incorporate this biological marker of exposure in future investigations in Vietnam.

Some questions about the effect of Agent Orange on the health of the Vietnamese population remain unanswered. There is no information about the incidence of soft tissue sarcoma in the Vietnamese population exposed to herbicides, and it is still far from clear whether Agent Orange has had a measurable effect on the reproductive outcomes of any of the exposed populations. Assessing whether Agent Orange has had an effect on cancer incidence will be much easier than any retrospective investigation of effects on reproductive outcomes.

The available evidence suggests that some of the health problems that were feared as a result of exposure to Agent Orange, including some cancers, have not been realized. As far as liver cancers are concerned, it seems far more likely that agents other than herbicides used during the Vietnam War are to blame for the increased risk. At this juncture, some thirty years after the use of Agent Orange was stopped, it is probably too late to do a further study on birth outcomes related to herbicide exposure. Thus, the evidence is likely to be no better than it is at present; the current picture is far from clear and neither supports, nor refutes, the conclusion that Agent Orange has affected birth outcomes.

17

THE IMPACT OF MILITARY PREPAREDNESS
AND MILITARISM ON HEALTH AND
THE ENVIRONMENT

VICTOR W. SIDEL

Introduction

For the most part, the chapters in this volume address the impacts of the
waging of war on the environment and on health. Several of the other
authors have broadened their considerations to include the environmental
impact of both war and preparations for war. For example, Arthur Westing,
in his discussion of environmental guidelines for armed forces, considers
guidelines for both wartime and peacetime.[1] Asit Biswas, in analyzing
the problem of assessing the long-term environmental consequences of
war, considers the effects of the use of resources by military forces during
both war and peace.[2] These chapters illustrate the difficulties inherent in
attempting to draw artificial distinctions between the environmental consequences of military operations during war and of military operations
during peacetime. While it may be useful in legal analysis to distinguish
environmental and health problems caused by war from those caused by
preparations for war, to those concerned with public health these distinctions have little meaning.[3] This chapter addresses two separate but closely

I am indebted to Howard Frumkin, H. Jack Geiger, Jessica Jacoby, Sergei Kolesnikov, Jennifer
Leaning, Barry Levy, David Rush, Paul Saenger, and Timothy Takaro for providing data and for
suggestions on drafts of this chapter.

[1] See Arthur H. Westing, "In Furtherance of Environmental Guidelines for Armed Forces During
Peace and War," chapter 6 in this volume.
[2] See Asit K. Biswas, "Scientific Assessment of the Long-term Environmental Consequences of
War," chapter 11 in this volume.
[3] Victor W. Sidel and Gurinder Shahi, "The Impact of Military Activities on Development,
Environment and Health," in Gurinder Shahi, Barry Levy, A. Binger, T. Kjellstrom, and Robert
Lawrence (eds.), *International Perspectives in Environment, Development and Health: Toward A
Sustainable World* (New York: Springer, 1997), pp. 283–312.

related topics: the impact on the environment and on health of military preparedness and of militarism itself.

Further, it may at times be difficult to distinguish the health and environmental consequences of some forms of military preparedness from the consequences of war itself. The worst chemical weapons disaster of World War II was caused by the explosion of the US merchant ship *John Harvey*, which was carrying 100 tons of mustard gas during a German bombing raid of Bari, a port on the coast of Italy. More than 1,000 military personnel, and an even larger number of civilians, lost their lives as a result of the explosion.[4] Chemical weapons were not used as instruments of war during World War II, although all the belligerents had stockpiles of these weapons. It would appear to be more useful to ascribe such health and environmental consequences to "military operations," rather than to attempt to distinguish between the consequences of "war" and of "preparation for war."[5]

Military preparedness, and even militarism, may at times be appropriate. Warning the population of a country that their health and safety may be threatened by war and that some sacrifice of their health and environment could be required in order to ensure their security may indeed be necessary. Military preparedness by a nation has long been advocated, particularly by those involved in the military, as a method for preserving peace. In about 375 BC, Vegetius wrote: "Who would desire peace should prepare for war."[6] The Armory of Venice bore the inscription: "Happy is that city which in times of peace thinks of war."[7] And George Washington in his first Inaugural Address intoned: "To be prepared for war is one of the most effectual means of preserving peace."[8] Almost two centuries later he was echoed by his successor, Gerald Ford, who warned: "Weakness invites war."[9] It is rare to find leaders who argue: "Preparation for war invites war."

When the health and safety of a people is not threatened, an excessive level of military preparedness and a shift in priorities that has extraordinarily harmful effects on health and environment justify the use of the word

---

[4] Glenn B. Infield, *Disaster at Bari* (1971).
[5] See, for example, John P. Quinn, Richard T. Evans, and Michael J. Boock, "United States Navy Development of Operational–Environmental Doctrine," chapter 5 in this volume.
[6] Vegetius, *Dei Rei Militari*, Book III, Prologue (circa 375 BC).
[7] Robert Burton, *Anatomy of Melancholy*, Pt. II, Sec. 2 (Amsterdam: Theatrum Orbis Terrarum New York: Da Capo Press, 1621–51).
[8] George Washington, First Annual Address to a joint session of Congress (Jan. 8, 1790).
[9] Gerald R. Ford, Address to a joint session of Congress (Aug. 12, 1974).

"militarism." The dictionary definitions of "militarism" include "a policy of aggressive military preparedness" and "subordination of the civic ideals or policies of a government to the military."[10] The United States, for example, has wide oceans forming its east and west borders and friendly, non-threatening nations forming its north and south borders. The "evil empire" rhetoric of the Cold War, efforts to develop "war fever," such as the campaign to mobilize public opinion to support an attack on Iraq, and even the intensive work by the United States to expand NATO membership and to lead it in bombing Yugoslavia would appear to be evidence of such militarism.

Moreover, efforts to maintain or increase military expenditures in the US appear to be based less on response to actual threats and more on desire for profit on the part of military suppliers, for new or continued jobs on the part of their employees, and for more power for the military–industrial complex. Recent evidence suggests that the Soviet Union, near the end of its existence, was spending a considerable fraction of its gross national product (GNP) on preparation for war.[11] The United States, which has spent a far smaller percentage of its much greater GNP on preparation for war, has for many years been responsible for one-quarter of the world's military spending and now, as other nations reduce their arms expenditures, the figure approaches 40 percent. In fact, the United States now spends more on arms than the amount spent by the next ten nations combined.[12] In any nation, militarism permits assaults on the environment and risks to military personnel and civilians that have little or no basis in national security needs. This chapter documents the environmental and health consequences of the diversion of resources to preparation for war, as well as of some of the more egregious examples of damage resulting from those preparations for war. It examines, in turn, the impact on the environment and on health of the production, testing, stockpiling, and disposal of nuclear and chemical weapons; the production, testing, stockpiling, and disposal of biological and other weapons; and aspects of militarism.

Methodological constraints

Virtually all of the information regarding the impact of military preparedness on the environment documents the nature, and in some cases the

---

[10] *Webster's Third New International Dictionary* (Springfield, Mass.: Merriam-Webster, 1971).
[11] Ruth Leger Sivard, *World Military and Social Expenditures 1996* (Leesburg, Va.: WMSE Publications, 1996), p. 54.   [12] *Ibid.*, p. 11.

quantity, of the toxicants introduced into the ecosystem by activities related to production, stockpiling, testing, and destruction of military weapons. In almost none of these examples, however, is it possible to document health consequences related to these toxicants accurately. Exceptions include, for example, the data on the iodine-131 released by atmospheric nuclear tests and concentrated in the thyroid glands of children, discussed below.[13] The difficulty in documenting the health impact of military and other environmental toxicants lies in quantifying the exposure to humans and in identifying and addressing confounding factors, such as exposure to other toxicants and the physical and health status of the individual prior to exposure. Controlled trials of human exposure to toxicants, military or other, are almost always unethical. As such, the impact of the environmental pollution caused by military preparedness on health will have to be inferred from animal or other non-human evidence, or from observational, rather than experimental, epidemiological studies.[14]

Nuclear weapons and health

NUCLEAR WEAPONS PRODUCTION

Production, stockpiling, testing, and even dismantling of nuclear weapons provide some of the most egregious examples of the impact of military preparedness on the environment. There are over 4,500 Department of Energy (DOE) sites contaminated from these activities in the United States.[15] Production facilities for nuclear weapons, such as those at Feed Materials Production Center (Ohio), Hanford Reservation (Washington), Los Alamos (New Mexico), Rocky Flats (Colorado), Oak Ridge (Tennessee), and Savannah River (South Carolina), are heavily polluted. Epidemiological surveys have suggested that workers involved in the production of the

---

[13] National Cancer Institute, *Estimated Exposures and Thyroid Doses Received by the American People from Iodine-131 in Fallout Following Nevada Atmospheric Nuclear Bomb Test* (Washington, D.C.: National Institute of Health, 1997); Institute of Medicine and National Research Council, *Exposure of the American People to Iodine-131 from Nevada Atomic Bomb Tests: Institute Report and Public Health Implications* (Washington, D.C.: National Institute of Health, 1998).
[14] Jennifer Leaning, "War and the Environment: Human Health Consequences of the Environmental Damage of War," in E. Chivian, M. McCally, H. Hu, and A. Haines (eds.), *Critical Condition: Human Health and the Environment* (Cambridge, Mass.: MIT Press, 1993), pp. 123–37.
[15] Arjun Makhijani, Howard Hu, and Katherine Yih (eds.), *Nuclear Wastelands: A Global Guide to Nuclear Weapons Production and its Health and Environmental Effects* (Cambridge, Mass.: MIT Press, 1995).

weapons, as well as the people in surrounding communities, have been exposed to radiation.[16] Studies performed by the DOE on these hazards have been criticized as grossly inadequate.[17] In June 1999, the DOE settled a lawsuit filed by hundreds of nuclear weapons plant employees in Ohio who alleged that they were exposed to dangerous radiation and not informed about it for years. In July 1999, the DOE formally acknowledged for the first time that nuclear weapons production may have exposed workers in the DOE facilities.[18] Furthermore, the impact of this pollution has been disproportionately concentrated in areas where poor people and people of color live.[19]

Dispersion of these toxicants is an ongoing process. For example, waste storage tanks at Hanford containing millions of gallons of highly toxic processing chemicals and radionuclides are reaching groundwater and flowing towards the Columbia River seven miles away.[20] Spent nuclear fuel at this same facility is at risk of spontaneous combustion due to its component uranium hydrides. Such a fire would spread deadly radionuclides across the agricultural belt of the northwestern United States.[21] In 1998, a tank containing sludge with 62 pounds of plutonium – enough to make twelve nuclear bombs – was found buried outside the facility (see below for a detailed discussion of the health and environmental impacts of plutonium).[22]

Production sites in the former Soviet Union are even more heavily contaminated. These include: Chelyabinsk 65 ("Ozyorsk") in the Urals, where radioactive wastes were dumped into the Techa River and Lake

---

[16] Ibid.; Howard Hu, Arjun Makhijani, and Katherine Yih, Plutonium: Deadly Gold of the Nuclear Age (Cambridge, Mass.: Int'l Physicians Press, 1992); US General Accounting Office, Nuclear Waste: Further Actions Needed to Increase the Use of Innovative Cleanup Technologies, GAO/RCED–98–249 (Washington, D.C., 1998).

[17] H. Jack Geiger, David Rush, David Michaels, Dead Reckoning: A Critical Review of the Department of Energy's Epidemiological Research (Physicians for Social Responsibility, 1992).

[18] "Government Settles Ohio Radiation Lawsuit," Wash. Post (June 11, 1999); Matthew L. Wald, "Work on Weapons Affected Health, Government Admits," N.Y. Times (July 17, 1999).

[19] Gini Egan, "Social Injustices of Nuclear Weapons Development," PSR Health Res. Bull. 4(2) (Fall 1997).

[20] US General Accounting Office, Nuclear Waste: Hanford Reservation Waste Program Needs Cost, Schedule, and Management Changes, GAO/RCED–93–99 (Washington, D.C., 1993); Hanford Advisory Board, "Proceedings of the Hanford Advisory Board" (1998); US Department of Energy, "Budget Hearings for Richland Field Office" (1997); Timothy Takaro, paper delivered at the Physicians for Social Responsibility National Conference, Washington, D.C. (May 1998).

[21] Ibid.

[22] "Hanford Finds Buried Tank of Plutonium," Portland Oregonian (Apr. 21, 1998); also at http://www.oregonlive.com/todaynews/9804/st04202.html.

Karachay; Dimistrovgrad; Tomsk; and Krasnoyarsk.[23] Russian authorities have now admitted to injecting approximately 1 billion curies (a unit of radioactive decay) of radioactive substances underground at both Tomsk and Krasnoyarsk.[24] While the estimate of US dispersion of radioactivity into the environment from nuclear weapons production is approximately 3 million curies, in the former Soviet Union it is approximately 1.7 billion curies.[25]

NUCLEAR WEAPONS TESTS

Atmospheric nuclear tests deposited both short-lived radionuclides (such as iodine-131) and long-lived radionuclides (such as strontium-90) at sites both near and far-removed from the site of testing. The deposits have direct impacts on humans. The deciduous teeth of children, collected in the United States during the late 1950s and early 1960s, showed the deposition of strontium-90. In addition, Bikini Atoll in the Pacific was rendered uninhabitable by US atmospheric tests, and many residents of nearby Rongelap were found to have thyroid tumors, a condition common in people exposed to iodine-131 (I-131).[26]

Indeed, I-131 is considered one of the more dangerous radioactive substances contained in fallout. Cows and goats grazing in fallout areas produce milk with high concentrations of I-131. Once ingested, the I-131, like all ingested iodine, concentrates in the thyroid gland, where it can produce thyroid cancer and thyroid nodules. Young children are the most vulnerable, because children consume more milk than adults and their thyroid glands are smaller. Because I-131 has a half-life of only 8.5 days, human exposure is localized and less diluted in the food chain than is the case with other radioactive elements.[27]

In 1982, the US Congress directed the Department of Health and Human Services (HHS) to assess the iodine-131 exposure of the US population

[23] Makhijani, Hu, and Yih, *Nuclear Wastelands*; Hu, Makhijani, and Yih, *Plutonium*; Aleksandr Yemclyanekov (ed.), *Atom Declassified: Half a Century With the Bomb*, 2nd edn. (1996).

[24] David Rush, paper delivered at the Physicians for Social Responsibility National Conference (May 1998).   [25] *Ibid.*

[26] Anthony Robbins, Arjun Makhijani, and Katherine Yih, *Radioactive Heaven and Earth: The Health and Environmental Effects of Nuclear Weapons Testing In, On, and Above the Earth* (New York: Apex Press/London: Zed Books, 1991).

[27] David Zimmerman, "Thyroid Cancer," in Lewis E. Braverman and Robert D. Utiger (eds.), *The Thyroid* (Philadelphia: Lippincott, 1991), pp. 787–91; Laurence Finberg (ed.), *Saunders Manual of Pediatric Practice* (Philadelphia: W. B. Saunders, 1998).

from the 215 US atmospheric nuclear tests conducted between 1945 and 1962. In essence, Congress mandated that the HHS perform three major tasks:

- develop valid and credible assessment methods that could be used to estimate the thyroid doses of iodine-131 that were received by the US population;
- estimate the total iodine-131 doses the US population received; and
- relate these exposures to the risk of thyroid cancer among the US population.

The study covered some 150 million people who lived in 3,094 counties during the weapons testing period. It was based on an analysis of fallout trajectories, radioactive fallout data from a national network of gum film measuring devices, daily weather data (including wind direction and rainfall throughout the US during the period of testing), dairy farm practices (including seventy-one dairy cow diets), 302 milk consumption rates, and differentiation of fourteen age and sex groups.[28]

In September 1997, almost fifteen years later, the results of the first two tasks were reported by the National Cancer Institute (NCI). Dispersed by the prevailing winds, I-131 had settled in "hot spots" across the country. Exposures varied greatly by geographic region, with high-dose counties downwind of the test site and as far away as Montana and Missouri. Overall, people in the US received an average of 2 rads (radiation absorbed dose), with the inhabitants of some US counties receiving doses of 9–16 rads.[29] In comparison, the mean dose to the US population from cosmic radiation and from naturally occurring background radiation is 0.1 rad annually.[30]

An NCI estimate suggested that I-131 fallout from nuclear weapons tests has caused 10,000 to 75,000 cases of thyroid cancer, but the basis for this estimate has not yet been published. Children, the sector of the population most vulnerable to the fallout's effects, received doses as high as 45 to 100 rads in some counties.[31]

---

[28] H. Jack Geiger, "NCI Study Raises New Concerns About Fallout-related Thyroid Cancer," *Med. & Global Survival* 5 (1998), 8–10. [29] National Cancer Institute, *Estimated Exposures*.
[30] Victor Arena, *Ionizing Radiation and Life* (St. Louis: Mosby, 1971), p. 212.
[31] National Cancer Institute, *Estimated Exposures*; Institute of Medicine and National Research Council, *Exposure of the American People to Iodine-131*; David Rush and H. Jack Geiger, "NCI Study on I-131 Exposure from Nuclear Testing: A Preliminary Critique," *P.S.R. Health Res. Bull.* 4(3) (Winter 1997–98).

The criticisms of these estimates have been both substantive and procedural. On the substance, critics noted that the NCI provided no basis for its thyroid cancer risk estimates and appeared to have ignored evidence from Chernobyl, where thyroid cancer rates have been running ten times higher than expected from conventional calculations, which were based on extrapolation from exposures at Hiroshima and Nagasaki.[32] In Tennessee, health department researchers reported that child thyroid doses in the hundreds of rads were possible in the four counties around Oak Ridge due to fallout alone. North Dakota health department analysts estimated that I-131 in fallout may have increased the rate of thyroid cancer in the state by 5–10 percent.[33]

It is on procedure, however, that the most intense concerns have been raised. The NCI report – and the fifteen-year delay in its completion and release – has been taken as further evidence of a half-century of governmental secrecy and denial of the real dangers of nuclear testing. The American Public Health Association noted that if disclosures of the releases had been made public at the times they occurred, implementation of federal protective action guidelines – including removal of soil, destruction of milk and dairy cows, destruction of contaminated human and animal food, and public education about protective measures – would have been required. Instead, no public warnings were issued (although the Eastman Kodak corporation was warned in advance of some of the tests, to protect its film stocks).[34]

Atmospheric tests in the USSR have caused similar health hazards. The Soviet Academy of Medical Sciences determined in 1989 that residents of Semipalatinsk, near a major test site in Kazakhstan, had experienced excess cancers, genetic diseases, and child deaths because of radiation exposure from pre-1963 atmospheric tests.[35] In 1988, the incidence of cancer was 70 percent above the national average.[36] Kazakh activists claim that life expectancy in the republic has declined by four years over the past two decades, and that the number of people suffering from blood diseases has doubled since 1970.[37]

These impacts are not confined to the two Cold War superpowers. Nuclear tests conducted by France in the 1960s contaminated the islands of Reao,

[32] Rush and Geiger, "NCI Study on I-131."   [33] *Ibid.*
[34] Geiger, "NCI Study"; Rush, P.S.R. paper.
[35] Robbins, Makhijani, and Yih, *Radioactive Heaven and Earth*, pp. 89–104.   [36] *Ibid.*
[37] *Ibid.*

Tureia, Pukarua, and Mangarova, which are to the east and the northeast of the then-French atmospheric nuclear test site on Moruroa Atoll.[38]

Venting of radionuclides into the atmosphere still occasionally occurred in all countries conducting explosive nuclear tests after the tests were moved underground, but with this new procedure most of the radionuclides were deposited underground. The long-lived radionuclides, like plutonium-239, which has a half-life of 23,000 years, will last long enough to leach into the ecosphere through groundwater or other conduits.[39]

NUCLEAR WEAPONS DISPOSAL

Not only does the production, testing, storage, and use of nuclear weapons lead to environmental and health damage, but the process of dismantling the weapons also poses major environmental risks. These risks include: accidents involving, or potential hijacking of, the nuclear weapons during their transport to the site of dismantling; the hazards to the workers during the process of dismantling the weapons; and health and environmental damage associated with the removed components during their transport, storage, and destruction.

In 1989, a committee of the US Senate expressed concern that the Department of Defense had devoted too little money and effort to finding ways to comply with nuclear arms reductions in "an environmentally benign manner."[40] For example, pursuant to the Intermediate-Range Nuclear Forces (INF) Treaty, hundreds of Pershing missiles were burned in the open air or exploded on a test stand at the Pueblo Army Depot in Colorado. These procedures can release clouds of toxic hydrochloric acid when the missiles' solid fuel combines with moisture.[41]

Virtually all of the experience with the disassembly and destruction of nuclear weapons in the United States has been gained over the past decade at the Pantex nuclear weapons facility, located about 17 miles northeast of Amarillo, Texas. The Pantex facility is operated for the US Department of Energy by a contractor, the Mason & Hanger-Silas Mason Co., and is the nation's primary assembly and disassembly plant for nuclear weapons. Prior to 1989, the Department of Energy had considered Pantex to be a relatively clean and safe facility. Since 1989, Pantex has been repeatedly criticized for

---

[38] *Ibid.*, pp. 133–50.   [39] *Ibid.*, pp. 33–48.
[40] "Defending the Environment? The Record of the US Military," *Def. Monitor* 18 (1989), 1–8.
[41] *Ibid.*

its safety and health problems. These problems have included: radiation accidents in 1989 and 1990 resulting in exposure of workers to tritium and depleted uranium; inadequate staffing; insufficient safety training and procedures; and violations in the general worker safety program.[42]

The process of disassembly of nuclear weapons at Pantex was described in detail in a 1993 article in *Popular Science* and a 1994 article in *The New York Times Magazine*.[43] Some of the steps provide room for exposure of dangerous substances to workers, the public, and the environment. For example, weapons are transported to the facility in armored, heavily guarded tractor-trailer trucks. Concerns have been expressed about potential problems such as accidents at railroad crossings and hijacking, but these have not as yet occurred. In addition, the bombs' trigger, or "physics package," consists of the "plutonium pit," a metal orb containing the radioactive material and, surrounding the pit, a spherical shell of chemical high explosives; detonated by computer, the explosives cause the plutonium to implode and nuclear fission to begin. The physics package is dismantled inside a circular, heavily reinforced concrete building overlaid with 17 feet of sand and gravel. In the unlikely event that the chemical explosives detonate, the structure is designed to collapse on itself, trapping the plutonium inside. If any technicians are inside the building at the time of explosion, they too would be trapped inside.

PLUTONIUM

Although plutonium exists naturally in minute quantities bound in uranium-rich deposits, it is primarily a man-made radioactive element produced by irradiating uranium in nuclear reactors. Plutonium has a half-life of over 24,000 years and exists in several physical forms, including metals, oxides (fine powders), residues, and solutions (materials with a lower plutonium content), as well as in the thousands of pits now stored at the Pantex plant.[44] Plutonium was first produced by the scientists of the Manhattan Project in 1942 and is one of the most lethal substances known.

---

[42] US General Accounting Office, *Nuclear Health and Safety: More Attention to Health and Safety Needed at Pantex*, GAO/RCED–91–103 (Washington, D.C., 1991).

[43] Kevin Cameron, "Taking Apart the Bomb," *Popular Science* (Apr. 1993), 64–69, 102–3; Richard Jerome, "Bombs Away! Building the Nuclear Arsenal Was Easy. Now Comes the Hard Part: Taking it Apart," *N.Y. Times Mag.* (Apr. 3, 1994), 46–47.

[44] Cameron, "Taking Apart the Bomb."

Microscopic plutonium particles, when inhaled, will cause cancer with virtual certainty, and new studies indicate new and graver risks of low-level exposure to radiation.[45] Contrary to popular belief, almost all plutonium can be used to produce a nuclear explosive device, a property that makes plutonium one of the most coveted materials of the nuclear age.[46]

The production of plutonium for military purposes has occurred in eight countries. By the end of 1995, it was estimated that military inventories worldwide contained some 270 metric tons of plutonium, in addition to the approximately 180 metric tons that were stockpiled in civilian inventories. Almost 90 percent of the military plutonium can be found in deployed or surplus US and former Soviet nuclear arsenals.[47]

During the nuclear weapons production era, the US Department of Energy continuously recycled its plutonium to be made into pits for nuclear weapons. Since it had never had to store plutonium for any prolonged period of time, when the Department ceased its production of nuclear weapons, much of the plutonium was not packaged adequately for long-term storage.[48] As a result, problems have occurred at many of the sites throughout the Department. For instance, plutonium at some sites was packaged in contact with plastic, which makes the containers susceptible to leaks or ruptures – possibly exposing the workers.

Although the Department of Energy has made some progress in stabilizing its plutonium, the Department is unlikely to meet its May 2002 target date for having all of the plutonium that is not in pits stabilized, packaged, and stored. The Department of Energy sites with the majority of this plutonium have experienced many delays, some due to safety infractions at the sites, and anticipate more in meeting their implementation plan milestones. Given the inherent dangers of plutonium, such delays maintain the high level of risk to workers' health and safety that could be avoided by stabilization and packaging activities. Moreover, because the Department of Energy has not yet finalized the criteria the plutonium must meet to be acceptable for the disposal technologies, it is unclear if current activities to stabilize, package, and store the plutonium will be compatible with the means of converting it for disposal. In addition to its delays in stabilizing and packaging its plutonium that is not in pits, the

---

[45] Hu, Makhijani, and Yih, *Plutonium*.
[46] "Give Us Your Spent Fuel, Your Warheads: Curbing One Nuclear Hazard Creates Another," *US News & World Rep.* (Mar. 20, 1995).   [47] Hu, Makhijani, and Yih, *Plutonium*.
[48] *Ibid.*

Department of Energy is currently storing approximately 10,000 pits in containers that both the Department and the Defense Nuclear Facilities Safety Board believe are not suitable for extended storage, thus risking workers' exposure to plutonium.[49]

Chemical weapons

Among the chemical weapons that have been produced and are now stockpiled in many countries of the world are nerve agents (including sarin, the agent used in the attack in the Tokyo subway system) and mustard gas. These weapons were most recently used in the Iran–Iraq War and in an attack on the Kurdish village of Halabja in Iraq.[50]

In the United States, chemical weapons production and testing was performed at the Edgewood Arsenal (Maryland), Pine Bluff Arsenal (Arkansas), Rocky Mountain Arsenal (Colorado), Tooele (Utah), and Dugway Proving Ground (Utah), among other sites. Production of chemical weapons has led to extensive environmental degradation. A 1968 discharge of nerve gas at the Dugway Proving Ground in Utah caused by unexpected wind conditions killed thousands of livestock. At Dugway, 124 or more hazardous waste sites containing lethal chemicals, radioactive waste, leaking oil tanks, and possibly biological agents have contaminated the site and adjacent public lands, and threatened groundwater and in turn the health of the human population in the area.[51]

Similar pollution occurred in the territory of the former Soviet Union. One example is the city of Dzerzhinsk, 250 miles east of Moscow, the site for decades of chemical weapons production. Dzerzhinsk is reported to have the Earth's highest concentration of dioxin.[52] The life expectancy there at birth is said to be 42 years for men and 47 years for women.[53]

In January 1992, the Chemical Weapons Convention (CWC) was opened for signature in Paris. On April 29, 1997, having been ratified by more than the required sixty-five nations, the CWC entered into force. The provisions of the CWC include a ban on the development, production, acquisition,

---

[49] *Ibid.*   [50] "Chemical Warfare: Return of the Silent Killer," *Time* (Aug. 22, 1998).

[51] Robert Harris and Jeremy Paxman, *A Higher Form of Killing: The Secret Story of Chemical and Biological Warfare* (London: Chatto & Windus, 1982).

[52] For a detailed discussion of the effects of dioxin on human health, see Alastair W. M. Hay, "Defoliants: The Long-term Health Implications," chapter 16 in this volume.

[53] Michael Specter, "The Most Tainted Place on Earth," *N.Y. Times Mag.* (Feb. 8, 1998), 49–52.

stockpiling, transfer, and use of chemical weapons; elimination of all chemical weapons and their production facilities by 2007 (although US military forces are already obligated by US law to do so by 2004); and creation of an Organization for the Prohibition of Chemical Weapons (OPCW) in The Hague to conduct routine and unannounced inspections of companies using precursor chemicals covered by the treaty.[54]

The disposal of chemical weapons required by the CWC is likely to create health and environmental hazards.[55] Russia and the US have the largest stockpiles, with approximately 40,000 and 30,000 tons of weapons respectively.[56] The United States had planned to use incineration as the means of "demilitarizing" its chemical weapons. This method has actually been used at Johnston Island in the Pacific to demilitarize nerve agents shipped there from Okinawa and from NATO forces in Europe. Facilities have been constructed for incineration of stockpiles of chemical weapons at sites in the United States. Russia, on the other hand, plans to use chemical neutralization to dispose of its chemical weapons.[57]

There remains considerable debate regarding the safety of the different methods of disposal of chemical agents.[58] Incineration leads to the decomposition of the chemical agents into small particles, which are released into the atmosphere through tall smokestacks. The proponents of chemical neutralization in Russia contend that it would provide a safer means of disposal, but the Russian method creates a complex organic "soup" that must be mixed with bitumin, a tar-like substance, before disposal in landfills.[59] Scientific and political opposition to the use of these methods

[54] Organization for the Prohibition of Chemical Weapons, *Chemical Disarmament: Basic Facts* (1998); see also Barry Kellman, "The Chemical Weapons Convention: A Verification and Enforcement Model for Determining Legal Responsibility for Environmental Harm Caused by War," chapter 23 in this volume.
[55] S. A. Carnes and A. P. Watson, "Disposing of the US Chemical Weapons Stockpile: An Approaching Reality," *J. Am. Med. Ass'n* 262 (1989), 653–59; D. A. Koplow, "How Do We Get Rid of These Things? Dismantling Excess Weapons While Protecting the Environment," *Nw. U. L. Rev.* 89 (1995), 445–564; Alan H. Lockwood, "The Public Health Effects of the Use of Chemical Weapons," in B. S. Levy and V. W. Sidel (eds.), *War and Public Health* (New York: Oxford Univ. Press, 1997), pp. 84–97.
[56] Ross Ember, "Chemical Weapons Disposal: Daunting Challenges Still Ahead," *Chem. & Eng. News* (Aug. 13, 1990), 10–11.
[57] J. Brooke, "Chemical Neutralization is Gaining in War on Poison Gas," *N.Y. Times* (Feb. 7, 1997).
[58] Henry Condor, US General Accounting Office, "Demilitarization of the Chemical Munitions Stockpile," statement before the Subcommittee on Investigations, House Committee on Armed Services (July 25, 1986).   [59] Ember, "Chemical Weapons Disposal," 19.

must be resolved quickly if the United States, Russia, and other countries are to proceed with timely disposal and meet the deadlines imposed by the CWC.

In short, the implementation of the CWC that began in 1997 and the development of procedures for challenge inspections should ease the environmental and health threats from the development, production, and stockpiling of these weapons, as well as the threat from their use. It will not, however, ease the short-term threat of environmental and health damages from their demilitarization.

Biological weapons

Among the diseases and toxic effects that have been studied for use as biological weapons are the organisms that cause anthrax, plague, smallpox, and tularemia, as well as Marburg virus (closely related to the Ebola virus), and toxins such as aflatoxin and botulinum toxin. The first three of these agents were allegedly part of the strategic arsenal of the USSR, even after the entry into force of the Biological Weapons Convention (BWC) in 1975.[60] Production and testing of biological weapons has taken place in the United States at Fort Detrick (Maryland), Pine Bluff Arsenal (Arkansas), and Dugway Proving Ground (Utah). There has been no documented environmental pollution or large numbers of deaths from the production, testing, or stockpiling of biological weapons in the United States, although during the 1950s three deaths were reported among biological weapons production workers.[61]

It was revealed in 1969 that in the 1950s and 1960s there had been secret experiments at the US Army Dugway Proving Ground involving large-scale field testing of biological warfare agents including tularemia, rocky mountain spotted fever, plague, and Q fever. It is suspected that Q fever and Venezuelan Equine Encephalitis were introduced into Utah's western deserts as a consequence of Army open-air testing. In 1950, US Navy ships in the San Francisco Bay area released large quantities of what was believed to be non-pathogenic, aerosolized *Serratia marcescens* and *Bacillus globigil*

---

[60] Richard Preston, "Annals of Warfare: The Bioweaponeers," *The New Yorker* (Mar. 9, 1998), 52–65; see also David P. Fidler, "War and Infectious Diseases: International Law and the Public Health Consequences of Armed Conflict," chapter 18 in this volume.

[61] Susan Wright (ed.), *Preventing a Biological Arms Race* (Cambridge, Mass.: MIT Press, 1990).

(*Bacillus variant niger*) as simulants to test dispersal efficiency. Subsequent infections and deaths from *Serratia*, particularly among immunologically compromised individuals, were later attributed by some analysts to this release.[62] During the 1950s and 1960s, the US conducted 239 top-secret open-air disseminations of simulants, involving such areas as the New York City subways, the Kittatinny and Tuscarora tunnels on the Pennsylvania Turnpike, and Washington National Airport. All of these potentially dangerous tests were kept secret under "the shroud of national security."[63] In addition, the United Kingdom conducted work on biological weapons at Porton Down. Gruinard Island off the coast of Scotland was contaminated by a test use of anthrax spores conducted by the UK and the US, and parts of the island remain uninhabitable.[64]

Since the unilateral statement by the United States in 1969 that it would no longer produce biological weapons and since the entering into force of the BWC in 1975, further production or testing of "offensive" biological weapons in the US is forbidden. However, "defensive" research is still permitted.[65] This ambiguity has led a number of analysts around the world to believe that the US Army, under cover of its Biological Weapons Defense Program, is actively conducting research that could lead to development of offensive bioweapons.[66]

Production and testing of biological weapons in the USSR is believed to have occurred in Stepnagorsk (Kazakhstan), Obolensk (Moscow Region, Russia), Omutninsk (Kirov Region, Russia), Sergiyev Posad (Moscow Region, Russia), Novosibirsk (Siberia, Russia), Sverdlovsk (Russia), and Rebirth Island (in the Aral Sea). The accidental release of anthrax near Sverdlovsk in the USSR in 1979 was known to have infected over 100 nearby inhabitants, of whom about fifty died.[67] Examination of tissues from some of the victims, recently analyzed in the United States, identified at least four different strains of anthrax in the tissue. Analysts believe the multistrain blend of anthrax being produced at Sverdlovsk was intended to overcome the US vaccine against anthrax.[68]

---

[62] Leonard A. Cole, *Clouds of Secrecy: The Army's Germ Warfare Tests Over Populated Areas* (Savage, Md.: Rowman & Littlefield, 1988).
[63] Harris and Paxman, *Secret Story*; Cole, *Clouds of Secrecy*.
[64] Robert Gould and Nancy D. Connell, "The Public Health Effects of Biological Weapons," in Levy and Sidel, *War and Public Health*, pp. 98–116; Harris and Paxman, *Secret Story*.
[65] See also Fidler, "War and Infectious Diseases."
[66] Wright, *Biological Arms Race*; Preston, "Annals of Warfare."
[67] Preston, "Annals of Warfare."   [68] *Ibid.*

Other weapons systems

Production, testing, and stockpiling of "conventional" weapons also cause pollution. Toxic wastes from weapons production include fuels, paints, solvents, heavy metals, pesticides, PCBs, cyanide, phenols, acids, alkalis, propellants, and explosives. In the United States the military generates between 400,000 and 500,000 tons of toxic materials annually.[69] It is estimated that there are 25,000 toxic military sites nationwide. During fiscal years 1996 and 1997, the US Pentagon budgeted more than $700 million for bringing military construction and repair projects into compliance with environmental laws.[70] Tests of weapons, such as those on the island of Vieques off the coast of Puerto Rico, have left environmental devastation. Research at the University of Puerto Rico has led to estimates that the rate of cancer among the inhabitants of Vieques is 40 percent higher than in the rest of Puerto Rico.[71]

Testing of military equipment and training of those who operate it consumes enormous amounts of non-renewable energy. Worldwide, nearly one-quarter of all jet fuel – 42 million tons per year – was used for military purposes in the late 1980s.[72] The US Department of Defense consumes an amount of fuel equivalent to about 37 million tons of oil a year. The Pentagon uses enough energy in one year to run all of the US mass transit systems for almost fourteen years.[73]

In addition to peacetime military operations on its own territory, the United States operates an array of foreign bases that present many of the same environmental problems. The overseas bases of the Department of Defense include some 800 locations ranging in size from radio relay sites to major airbases. In the Philippines, for example, after the US military departed from Subic Bay and Clark Air Base in 1992 it was revealed that tons of toxic chemicals had been dumped on the ground, into the water, or

---

[69] Michael Renner, "Environmental and Health Effects of Weapons Production, Testing and Maintenance," in Levy and Sidel, *War and Public Health*, pp. 117–35.

[70] For excellent summaries of the military peacetime impact on the economy, see Seth Shulman, *The Threat at Home: Confronting the Toxic Legacy of the US Military* (Boston: Beacon Press, 1992); and Stephen Dycus, *National Defense and the Environment* (Hanover: Univ. Press of New England, 1996).

[71] Associated Press, "Puerto Rico Government Wants Navy Out," *N.Y. Times* Website (Jul. 1, 1999); "Department of Defense Announces Vieques Initiatives," News Release No. 292–99, Office of Assistant Secretary of Defense (June 11, 1999).

[72] Renner, "Environmental and Health Effects."   [73] *Ibid.*

burned in uncontrolled landfills.[74] No US legislation addresses or regulates environmental protection overseas. The current overseas remediation policy, promulgated by the Department of Defense in October 1995, is far weaker than domestic law.[75]

In Russia, military base contamination persists from the period of Soviet military operations. For example, a Russian naval base at Andreyev Bay on the Kola peninsula in the Barent Sea, just 40 km from the Norwegian border, has been termed by the Russian Atomic Energy Minister as having "serious" radiation levels from its use as a dumping ground for nuclear wastes and as a storage site for decommissioned nuclear submarines.[76]

Other consequences of militarism

Three other aspects of environmental and health damage caused by military activities and militarism must be mentioned. The application of economic sanctions may be considered an extension of military activity and militarism. The sanctions imposed on Cuba, virtually unilaterally by the United States, and on Iraq by the United Nations at the insistence of the United States, are examples.[77] These sanctions have denied the societies against which they have been applied the resources necessary to protect their environment and the health of their people. Sanctions often result in shortages of food, medicine, and medical equipment, directly impacting the health of the people in the societies against which the sanctions have been applied.[78] In the case of Iraq, sanctions have denied the resources necessary to repair environmental damage caused by war.

Another consequence of military activities and militarism is described by Ricardo Navarro, the director of Centro Salvadoreno de Tecnologia Apropiada (the Salvadorean Center for Appropriate Technology), an active environmental NGO in El Salvador. Navarro observes the postwar

---

[74] John Lindsay-Poland and Nick Morgan, *Overseas Military Bases and Environment. Foreign Policy in Focus* (1998), pp. 1–4.

[75] *Ibid.*

[76] Bellona Foundation, *The Russian Northern Fleet: Sources of Radiation Contamination*, available at http://www.bellona.no/e/russia/nfl/short.htm.

[77] American Public Health Association, *The Politics of Suffering: The Impact of the US Embargo on the Health of the Cuban People* (1993); Richard M. Garfield, *Morbidity and Mortality Among Iraqi Children from 1990 to 1998: Assessing the Impact of Economic Sanctions* (Fourth Freedom Forum, 1999).

[78] See Richard M. Garfield, "The Health Impacts of Economic Sanctions," in Levy and Sidel, *War and Public Health*, pp. 156–58.

increase in the level of violence throughout El Salvador and attributes it to the fact that people exposed over the long term to militaristic behavior will often use violence as a first means of conflict resolution. [79] A similar phenomenon has been observed in the United States, where military activities and militarism have been factors in the widespread availability of guns to members of the population, including children.[80]

Finally, military activities and militarism have led to experimentation on human beings with little purpose other than military interest and often with inadequate or no informed and voluntary consent by those used as guinea pigs. Examples include the testing of biological weapons over populated areas of the United States and the human experiments using radiation documented in the 1995 report by the President's Advisory Committee on Human Radiation Experiments.[81]

The role of militarism in polluting the environment and destroying life and health includes, of course, not only the impact of excess military preparedness but also the impact of war itself. Much, if not virtually all, of the environmental degradation described in other chapters in this volume was caused by wars brought about by militarism rather than by wars based on the need for self-defense or for national security. The solution to the problem of environmental degradation due to militarism is to make it so costly to nations and their leaders who kill and maim people and despoil the environment by war or preparation for war that they will no longer be able to engage in these self-destructive and immoral practices.

---

[79] Ricardo Navarro, "The Environmental Consequences of War: The Case of El Salvador," paper presented at the First International Conference on Addressing Environmental Consequences of War, Washington, D.C. (June 1998).

[80] B. S. Levy and V. W. Sidel, "The Impact of Military Activities on Civilian Populations," in Levy and Sidel, *War and Public Health*; V. W. Sidel and R. C. Wesley, "Violence as a Public Health Problem," *Social Justice* 22 (1995), 154–70.

[81] Cole, *Clouds of Secrecy*; United States Advisory Committee on Human Radiation Experiments, *The Human Radiation Experiments: Final Report of the President's Advisory Committee on Human Radiation Experiments* (1996).

18

WAR AND INFECTIOUS DISEASES:
INTERNATIONAL LAW AND THE PUBLIC
HEALTH CONSEQUENCES OF
ARMED CONFLICT

DAVID P. FIDLER

Introduction: war as disruption of the human–microbe environment

Much attention has rightly been concentrated on the adverse ecological consequences produced by wartime destruction of the natural environment.[1] Iraq's deliberate attacks on Kuwaiti oil installations serve as dramatic examples of such environmental damage. When we contemplate the environmental consequences of war, we should also be concerned about war-induced disruptions to environmental contexts that encompass more than damage to natural ecosystems. The environmental context that forms the backdrop for this chapter is the complex relationship between humans and pathogenic microbes. One of the most devastating environmental consequences of war is the disruption of the peacetime human–microbe relationship, which produces outbreaks and epidemics of infectious diseases.

Both historical and more recent events prove that armed conflict produces opportunities for pathogenic microbes to spread in human populations. Experts often cite war as a factor contributing to the re-emergence of infectious diseases as a public health problem in the last twenty to thirty years.[2] While warfare clearly plays a role in the current global crisis of emerging infectious diseases, it has always been a situation of microbial opportunity.

A revised version of this chapter was published in David P. Fidler, *International Law and Infectious Diseases* (Oxford: Clarendon Press/New York: Oxford Univ. Press, 1999), pp. 221–44.
[1] See, e.g., Richard J. Grunawalt, John E. King, and Ronald S. McClain (eds.), *Protection of the Environment during Armed Conflict* (Newport, R.I.: Naval War College, 1996).
[2] David P. Fidler, "Return of the Fourth Horseman: Emerging Infectious Diseases and International Law," *Minn. L. Rev.* 81 (1997), 800–1.

The human and microbial world have been interacting since the development of *Homo sapiens*.[3] The long history of human–microbe interaction is punctuated by changes in the relationship that have allowed microbes or humans the opportunity to gain an upper hand.[4] Recent analysis of the global problem of emerging infectious diseases provides a window on the many different kinds of changes that disrupt the human–microbe environment: population growth, urbanization, migration, climatic events, sexual behavior, technological and scientific advances, and war.[5] Such changes alter the natural and/or man-made environments in which humans cope with infectious diseases, and the changes usually produce outbreaks or epidemics of infectious diseases. The lengthy list of factors behind infectious disease outbreaks suggests that the human–microbe environment is complex and delicate.

Although war is not the only type of change that transforms the human–microbe environment, it produces so many opportunities for pathogenic microbes that it has to be considered an extremely effective way to promote microbial traffic and increase human morbidity and mortality.[6] Armed conflict often destroys public health infrastructures, creates scarce medical supplies and services, inflicts wounds susceptible to infection, forces population movements in unsanitary conditions, and generates malnutrition that weakens the human immune system. War favors microbial transmission because it alters the human–microbe environment to the disadvantage of society and human immune systems.

History is full of famous infectious disease outbreaks during armed conflict: the plague of Athens during the Peloponnesian War;[7] the epidemics that devastated the Aztecs and Incas after contact with European *conquistadores*;[8] the typhus epidemic that weakened Napoleon's *Grande Armée* during its advance into and retreat from Russia in 1812;[9] and the 1918–19 influenza pandemic that killed over 20 million people

[3] See, e.g., William H. McNeill, *Plagues and Peoples* (Garden City, N.Y.: Anchor Press, 1977); Frederick F. Cartwright, *Disease and History* (1972); Hans Zinsser, *Rats, Lice and History* (New York: Leventhal & Black Dog Publishers, 1934).

[4] Jared Diamond, *Guns, Germs, and Steel: The Fates of Human Societies* (New York: W. W. Norton & Co., 1997), pp. 193–214 (analyzing changes produced by developments in human food production).   [5] Fidler, "Return of the Fourth Horseman," 785–810.

[6] "Purveyors of Pestilence: Urbanism, War, Trade and Imperialism," in K. F. Kiple (ed.), *Plague, Pox and Pestilence: Disease in History* (New York: Barnes and Noble, 1997), p. 58.

[7] Thucydides, *History of the Peloponnesian War* (Rex Warner trans., London: H. G. Bohn, 1954), pp. 151–56.   [8] Diamond, *Guns, Germs, and Steel*, pp. 210–11.

[9] Zinsser, *Rats, Lice and History*, pp. 161–62; Cartwright, *Disease and History*, pp. 82–112.

worldwide.[10] War and infectious diseases have continued their alliance in more contemporary conflicts as well. In connection with civil wars, the International Committee of the Red Cross (ICRC) observed that "[t]he conflicts fought in the former Yugoslavia, Rwanda, Zaire, Yemen, and Afghanistan and quite a few other parts of the world in 1994 have one point in common: thousands of civilians are suffering from a lack of drinking water and often dying from its consequences – cholera, typhoid, hepatitis and dysentery."[11] The World Health Organization has also called attention to infectious disease problems created by civil wars in various countries, including Sierra Leone, Liberia, and Bosnia.[12] In connection with international armed conflict, the ICRC has expressed concerns about waterborne diseases harming civilian populations during and after the 1990–91 Gulf War.[13] These historical and contemporary examples show that infectious diseases afflict both soldiers and civilians during armed conflict.

In many ways, the international law of armed conflict has been affected by the infectious disease problems that war creates. This chapter analyzes how international law has been developed by states and non-governmental humanitarian organizations to prevent and control the spread of infectious diseases during armed conflict. This body of international legal rules can be divided for analytical purposes into (1) rules that attempt to regulate how force is used; and (2) rules that attempt to minimize the adverse public health consequences in the aftermath of acts of war. The final part of this chapter evaluates the problems that plague this body of international law due to a gap between what the law requires and what still all too frequently happens in times of war.

Throughout, the chapter highlights current initiatives that could address this gap. These include: (1) a proposed verification and compliance

---

[10] Arno Karlen, *Man and Microbes: Diseases and Plagues in History and Modern Times* (New York: Simon & Schuster, 1995), pp. 144–45; see generally Alfred Crosby, *America's Forgotten Pandemic: The Influenza of 1918* (Cambridge and New York: Cambridge Univ. Press, 1989).

[11] International Committee of the Red Cross, "Symposium 'Water in Armed Conflicts': ICRC Steps in to Combat Water-Borne Disease in War Zones" (Nov. 16, 1994), available at http://www.icrc.org/unicc/icrcnews. See also International Committee of the Red Cross, "Water in Armed Conflicts," ICRC Campaign Brochure (Oct. 1994).

[12] World Health Organization, "Threat of Epidemics in Sierra Leone," Press Release WHO/49 (June 23, 1994); World Health Organization, "Yellow Fever Outbreak in Liberia," Press Release WHO/81 (Nov. 15, 1995); World Health Organization, "Disease Outbreaks Reported – Previous Bulletins," available at http://www.who.ch/programmes/emc/oldnews.htm.

[13] International Committee of the Red Cross, "Water in Armed Conflicts: Iraq, Yugoslavia, Rwanda," ICRC Fact Sheet (Oct. 1995); International Committee of the Red Cross, "Water in Iraq," ICRC Special Brochure (July 1996).

protocol to the Biological Weapons Convention; (2) expressly making use of biological weapons a war crime; (3) the ICRC's objective framework for determining whether a weapon causes superfluous injury or unnecessary suffering; (4) the ICRC's calls to strengthen and extend international legal protections from military attacks to water systems and engineers fixing water systems damaged by armed conflict; and (5) the nascent permanent International Criminal Court.

International legal rules on how force is used: regulating weapons and targets

Although not a focus of this chapter, the international legal prohibition on the use of force in international relations[14] forms part of the international law relevant to the control of infectious diseases. Given the powerful alliance between war and infectious diseases, the best approach is to avoid armed conflict. However, the international legal prohibition on war has proven not to have great deterrent effect in the context of international warfare, and it also does not address civil war. International legal rules regulating how force is used exist not only to address legitimate uses of force in self-defense, but also all other situations in which force is used. Such international legal rules regulate (1) what weapons can be used, and (2) what targets can be objects of military attack. Both sets of rules support the objective of controlling outbreaks of infectious diseases during armed conflict.

WEAPONS

Biological weapons

Biological weapons represent a different aspect of the relationship between war and infectious disease because they have the express purpose of altering the normal human–microbe environment in order to gain some military advantage or to spread terror in a population. Much attention has recently been focused on biological weapons in connection with United Nations weapons inspections in Iraq.[15] Concern about biological

---

[14] UN Charter, Art. 2(4).
[15] See, e.g., Raymond A. Zilinskas, "Iraq's Biological Weapons: The Past as Future?" *J. Am. Med. Ass'n* 278 (1997), 418.

weapons is also intense in connection with fears about the possible use of bioweapons by terrorist organizations.[16] Incidences of terrorist interest in biological weapons have been recorded, including the efforts of the Japanese cult Aum Shinrikyo to develop biological weapons, suggesting that fears of terrorist use of biological weapons are well founded.[17] Recently, the National Foundation for Infectious Diseases observed that "[e]xtremist groups worldwide are learning how to use biological agents, such as bacteria, viruses and toxins, to develop weapons and methods of delivery."[18]

Biological weapons raise different public health concerns than conventional weapons because bioweapons introduce virulent pathogens into a war zone or population, as opposed to creating conditions favorable to the spread of microbes that are already part of the natural and human environment. Preparing for a biological weapons attack is very difficult because of the range of potential biological agents that can be used.[19] Detection of biological weapons attacks could prove difficult, given the time between the use of a biological weapon and the actual manifestation of disease.[20] Even when symptoms appear, diagnosis can often be wrong, producing an ineffective course of action and increasing the risk of further transmission.[21]

A related problem appears when the weaknesses of national and international infectious disease surveillance systems are considered, because these systems are the first lines of defense against biological weapons attacks.[22] Vaccinations are available against some biological agents, and antibiotics can cope with some infections produced by exposure to biological agents.[23] But it is simply impossible to prepare troops, let alone

[16] Jonathan B. Tucker, "The Biological Weapons Threat," *Current History* (Apr. 1997), 171; Richard K. Betts, "The New Threat of Mass Destruction," *Foreign Aff.* 77 (1998), 32.
[17] Tucker, "The Biological Weapons Threat," 171; Jeffrey D. Simon, "Biological Terrorism: Preparing to Meet the Threat," *J. Am. Med. Ass'n* 278 (1997), 428; William J. Broad, Sheryl WuDunn, and Judith Miller, "How Japan Germ Terror Alerted the World," *N.Y. Times* (May 26, 1998), A1 and A10.
[18] National Foundation for Infectious Diseases, "Biological Terrorist Attacks and Increasing Antimicrobial Resistance are Growing Global Threats," Press Release (Apr. 14, 1998).
[19] See David P. Franz et al., "Clinical Recognition and Management of Patients Exposed to Biological Warfare Agents," *J. Am. Med. Ass'n* 278 (1997), 399.   [20] *Ibid.*
[21] *Ibid.* (noting that diseases resulting from the use of some biological weapons "are rarely seen in many countries today").
[22] Robert P. Kadlec, Allan P. Zelicoff, and Ann M. Vrtis, "Biological Weapons Control: Prospects and Implications for the Future," *J. Am. Med. Ass'n* 278 (1997), 351.
[23] See Franz et al., "Clinical Recognition," 400.

civilian populations, for all possible biological weapons threats.[24] Even more frightening is the reality that pathogenic microbes can be engineered to be resistant to antibiotics, which in many cases are the only line of defense against certain attacks.[25] If used, some biological weapons agents, such as anthrax, can contaminate the environment and remain a public health menace for years.[26] Without physically touching in any way a country's public health infrastructure, a biological weapons attack can wreak silent and deadly havoc on an army's or civilian population's health and a country's environment.

Unfortunately, interest in the use of disease as an intentional weapon of warfare has been a persistent historical theme.[27] Fortunately, frequent large-scale use of bioweapons has been avoided in international and civil war.[28] The two most extensive biowarfare uses in the twentieth century were the German attempts during World War I to infect livestock and contaminate feed to be exported from neutral countries to Allied forces, and the Japanese use of biological weapons in China during World War II. [29] Many more countries did, however, conduct research on and development of biological weapons during the century, including great powers such as the United States and the Soviet Union.[30]

International legal activity on biological weapons began in 1925 with the Protocol for the Prohibition of the Use in War of Asphyxiating, Poisonous or Other Gases, and of Bacteriological Methods of Warfare (1925 Geneva Protocol),[31] which outlawed the use of biological weapons in warfare. The ban was not, however, absolute. Many states made reservations to the 1925 Geneva Protocol that limited the scope of the ban and

---

[24] Many experts do, however, urge that more be done to prepare civil defense capabilities for biological weapons attacks. See, e.g., Betts, "The New Threat," 36–40; Richard Preston, "Taming the Biological Beast," *N.Y. Times* (Apr. 21, 1998), A25; see also Judith Miller and William J. Broad, "Secret Exercise Finds US Can't Cope with a Biological Terror Attack," *Int'l Herald Trib.* (Apr. 27, 1998), 3.

[25] Kadlec, Zelicoff, and Vrtis, "Biological Weapons Control," 355; Ken Alibek, "Biological Weapons: Russia May Be the Biggest Threat," *Int'l Herald Trib.* (Mar. 28–29, 1998), 6; see also Wendy Orent, "Escape from Moscow," *The Sciences* (May–June 1998), 26, 29–30.

[26] George W. Christopher et al., "Biological Warfare: A Historical Perspective," *J. Am. Med. Ass'n* 278 (1997), 412–13.   [27] *Ibid.*, 412.

[28] Tucker, "The Biological Weapons Threat," 169.

[29] Christopher et al., "Biological Warfare," 413.   [30] *Ibid.*, 413–15.

[31] Protocol for the Prohibition of the Use in War of Asphyxiating, Poisonous or Other Gases, and of Bacteriological Methods of Warfare (June 17, 1925), 44 L.N.T.S. 65 (1929), reprinted in A. Roberts and R. Guelff (eds.), *Documents on the Laws of War*, 2nd edn. (Oxford: Clarendon Press/New York: Oxford Univ. Press, 1989), pp. 137–46.

made compliance conditional on reciprocity. One type of reservation made the ban effective only among states parties to the 1925 Geneva Protocol.[32] Another frequently made reservation stated that the ban would not be effective if a state party violated the 1925 Geneva Protocol by using biological weapons first.[33] The 1925 Geneva Protocol really constituted a treaty prohibiting the first use of biological weapons in warfare between contracting parties.[34]

It is sometimes argued today that customary international law prohibits the use of biological weapons and that the prohibition applies to all states. A later treaty on biological weapons describes them as "repugnant to the conscience of mankind" and bans their development, production, and stockpiling.[35] The less-than-absolute nature of the use prohibition in the 1925 Geneva Protocol suggests, however, that the content of customary international rules on biological weapons might not be clear. Roberts and Guelff argue that the majority position seems to be that international custom prohibits the first use of lethal biological weapons.[36] Less clear, though, is the international legal status of a second use of lethal biological weapons, a first use of non-lethal biological weapons, or a second use of non-lethal biological weapons. Of course, the Biological Weapons Convention (BWC) ban on the development, production, and stockpiling of biological weapons, which seeks "to exclude completely the possibility of bacteriological (biological) agents and toxins being used as weapons,"[37] seems to point to an absolute ban on the use of any biological weapons. After all, Article I of the BWC requires contracting parties "never in any circumstances to develop, produce, stockpile or otherwise acquire or retain" biological agents and weapons designed to use such agents.[38] The BWC does, however, allow contracting parties to develop, produce, stockpile, retain, or otherwise acquire biological agents in types and quantities justifiable "for prophylactic, protective or other peaceful purposes."[39] Perhaps it is not contrary to the BWC, or customary international law, to develop, produce, and use biological weapons in legitimate self-defense. But a number of countries that made reservations to the 1925 Geneva Protocol have

---

[32] See *ibid.*, pp. 144–45.   [33] *Ibid.*
[34] Tucker, "The Biological Weapons Threat," 172.
[35] Convention on the Prohibition of the Development, Production, and Stockpiling of Bacteriological (Biological) and Toxin Weapons and on Their Destruction (Apr. 10, 1972) (Biological Weapons Convention), available at http://www.acda.gov/treaties/bwc2.htm.
[36] Roberts and Guelff, *Documents on the Laws of War*, p. 139.
[37] Biological Weapons Convention, preamble.   [38] *Ibid.*, Art. I.   [39] *Ibid.*

withdrawn or modified them, strengthening the argument that any use of biological weapons violates customary international law.[40]

Further, it might be argued that neither the 1925 Geneva Protocol nor the BWC cover the use of non-lethal biological weapons, which have been made feasible by developments in biotechnology and genetic engineering. While some claim that the whole area of non-lethal weapons "is in its infancy,"[41] other experts have traced a historical pattern of interest in non-lethal weapons, especially chemical weapons, on the part of great powers.[42] Part of this growing field of military strategy involves biological weapons, such as biodegrading organisms that disable systems and non-fatal disease organisms that incapacitate people.[43]

Some experts analyzing non-lethal biological weapons claim that their use would not violate international legal prohibitions on the use of biological weapons. Two United States Air Force officers have argued as follows:

> Although international agreements currently proscribe the use of chemical or biological warfare in water or food supplies, these agreements came at a time when offensive chemical and biological warfare sought to kill the enemy. New forms of chemicals and microbes would not kill; instead they would merely have a temporary effect on the population and conceivably could save lives by averting combat.[44]

Malcolm Dando disagrees, arguing that using bacteria in non-lethal weapons to degrade weapons components or fuel supplies would violate the fundamental reason behind the BWC.[45] These types of arguments clearly raise the need to analyze the development of non-lethal biological weapons more closely from the perspective of international law.[46]

---

[40] Roberts and Guelff, *Documents on the Laws of War*, forthcoming 3rd edn. (noting withdrawals or modifications of reservations to the 1925 Geneva Protocol by Australia, Belgium, Bulgaria, Chile, Czechoslovakia, Ireland, the Netherlands, New Zealand, Romania, Russia, South Africa, Spain, and the United Kingdom).

[41] Jonathan W. Klaaren and Ronald A. Mitchell, "Nonlethal Technology and Airpower: A Winning Combination for Strategic Paralysis," *Airpower J.* (spec. issue 1995), 43.

[42] See, e.g., Malcolm Dando, *A New Form of Warfare: The Rise of Non-Lethal Weapons* (London: Brassey's, 1996).

[43] Klaaren and Mitchell, "Nonlethal Technology," 45 (noting also as non-lethal biological weapons disease-transmitting arthropods that incapacitate people and systems, bioengineering to disable living systems, and behavior-affecting pheromones to disable systems); Dando, *New Form of Warfare*, p. 11.   [44] Klaaren and Mitchell, "Nonlethal Technology," 50.

[45] Dando, *New Form of Warfare*, p. 16.

[46] See, e.g., the successful effort to create international legal rules on another non-lethal weapon, the blinding laser weapon, discussed in Louise Doswald-Beck, "New Protocol on Blinding Laser Weapons," *Int'l Rev. Red Cross* 312 (1996), 272; David P. Fidler, "The International Legal Implications of 'Non-Lethal' Weapons," *Mich. J. Int'l L.* 21 (1999), 51.

A further problem with the international legal prohibitions on biological weapons is that they do not apply directly to non-state actors, such as terrorist organizations. Their development, production, acquisition, and use of biological weapons remains primarily a matter for domestic law. Experts have observed that "[g]lobal domestic legislation to prevent non-state or terrorist biological weapons proliferation has yet to be universally enacted."[47]

While the 1925 Geneva Protocol bans the first use of biological weapons, it does not address the development and manufacture of biological weapons. Many countries that became states parties to the 1925 Geneva Protocol have since engaged in biological weapons research. Ideas to prohibit the development and production of biological weapons received a great boost when the United States unilaterally terminated its offensive biological weapons program in 1969–70.[48] After an extensive review, the United States concluded that biological weapons lacked military utility.[49] This American initiative created a diplomatic environment conducive to addressing the development and production of biological weapons. In 1972, the BWC was opened for signature; it entered into force in 1975.

Perhaps the greatest weakness of the BWC is its lack of verification and compliance provisions. While development, production, and stockpiling are prohibited, the treaty contains no procedures or mechanisms by which a contracting party's compliance with the prohibitions can be verified.[50] The perception that this was a great weakness in the BWC was confirmed by the doubling after 1975 of the number of states that were suspected of having biological weapons capabilities.[51]

Revelations in the early 1990s by the Russian government that the former Soviet Union had indeed developed an extensive biological weapons program – despite being a contracting party and depository state of the BWC – acted as a catalyst for states wanting to strengthen the BWC through a verification regime.[52] Fears about Iraqi biological weapons during the 1990–91 Gulf War also gave proponents of verification mechanisms more fuel for their arguments.[53] In the first half of the 1990s, BWC states parties

[47] Kadlec, Zelicoff, and Vrtis, "Biological Weapons Control," 351.
[48] Christopher et al., "Biological Warfare," 415–16.   [49] Ibid., 415.
[50] Kadlec, Zelicoff, and Vrtis, "Biological Weapons Control," 352.   [51] Ibid., 354.
[52] Ibid.; see also Tucker, "The Biological Weapons Threat," 169–70.
[53] Kadlec, Zelicoff, and Vrtis, "Biological Weapons Control," 354; Tucker, "The Biological Weapons Threat," 170.

moved closer to negotiating a compliance regime for the BWC.[54] In 1995, formal negotiations began on a binding protocol establishing, among other things, a compliance regime.[55] In March 1998, the Ad Hoc Group of States Parties finished their tenth negotiating session.[56] Although little progress has yet been achieved in these protocol negotiations, political pressure is building for BWC states parties to accelerate the negotiations and conclude the protocol by 2000.

In general terms, the international legal regime on biological weapons is comprehensive in that it bans the use, development, production, stockpiling, and other acquisition of such weapons. Yet, fears continue about the threat to public health and national security posed by biological weapons.[57] Such fears build off the reality of biological weapons proliferation in the international system, and the potential of bioterrorism. The negotiations on a compliance protocol are attempting to address bioweapon proliferation. Perhaps the only other way to strengthen the international legal regime against biological weapons is expressly to make the use of any such weapon a war crime in international and civil armed conflicts. It may even be worth consideration to make large-scale uses of biological weapons or uses of genetically altered bioweapons crimes against humanity because of their immediate impacts and the future threats to human health such uses might present.

Such ideas do not, however, tremendously advance international humanitarian law. Use of biological agents in involuntary medical experiments on prisoners of war or civilian internees is already a war crime under international humanitarian law.[58] Using biological weapons against civilian populations would also be a war crime as a violation of the prohibition on attacking civilian targets.[59] Biological weapons attacks against civilian food or water supplies would be a war crime in violation of the prohibition on attacking objects indispensable to the survival of the civilian

---

[54] Kadlec, Zelicoff, and Vrtis, "Biological Weapons Control," 352.   [55] *Ibid.*, 353.

[56] See Procedural Report of the Ad Hoc Group of the States Parties to the Convention on the Prohibition of the Development, Production, and Stockpiling of Bacteriological (Biological) and Toxin Weapons and on Their Destruction, BWC/AD HOC GROUP/40 (Mar. 17, 1998).

[57] Joshua Lederberg, "Infectious Disease and Biological Weapons: Prophylaxis and Mitigation," *J. Am. Med. Ass'n* 278 (1997), 435.

[58] See, e.g., Geneva Convention IV Relative to the Protection of Civilian Persons in Time of War (Aug. 12, 1949), Art. 147, in Roberts and Guelff, *Documents on the Laws of War*, p. 323.

[59] L. C. Green, *The Contemporary Law of Armed Conflict* (Manchester and New York: Manchester Univ. Press, 1993), p. 151.

population.[60] Use of biological weapons may also be prohibited because they cause superfluous injury or unnecessary suffering.[61]

The proposal to criminalize expressly the use of biological weapons would, however, have two positive features for international humanitarian law. First, making biological weapons use a war crime or a crime against humanity would support existing provisions in the laws of war applicable to bioweapons usage. Second, the proposal would force out into the open the emerging questions about the compatibility of non-lethal biological weapons with principles of international humanitarian law.

Neither the compliance regime contemplated in the proposed protocol to the BWC nor the criminalization of biological weapons use would substantially blunt the threat of bioterrorism, against which international law is a limited instrument. Domestic legal developments are needed first and foremost to make bioterrorism more difficult, and domestic public health and medical preparedness will also be important in dealing with bioterrorism.

Conventional weapons

In connection with conventional weapons, the issue concerns whether the effects of certain weapons on the human body produce unnecessary infectious disease morbidity and mortality. All wounds inflicted by conventional weapons can become infected with pathogenic microbes and increase the risk of illness and death. ICRC first aid guidelines for caring for war wounded in the field include protecting wounds by bandaging and treating wounded persons with antibiotics.[62] The question becomes whether it is possible to determine if certain kinds of conventional weapons create more types of infectious disease problems than others, perhaps suggesting that this increased disease risk might constitute "superfluous injury" or inflict "unnecessary suffering," in violation of international

[60] See, e.g., Protocol I Additional to the Geneva Conventions of 12 August 1949, and Relating to the Protection of Victims of International Armed Conflicts (1977), Art. 54, in Roberts and Guelff, *Documents on the Laws of War*, p. 417.
[61] International Committee of the Red Cross, *The SIrUS Project: Towards a Determination of Which Weapons Cause "Superfluous Injury or Unnecessary Suffering"* (1997), p. 24.
[62] International Committee of the Red Cross, *War and Public Health: Handbook on War and Public Health* (1996), p. 226; see also Robin Gray, *War Wounds: Basic Surgical Management* (1994); Robin M. Coupland, *Amputation for War Wounds* (1992), p. 7.

humanitarian law.[63] Traditionally, the application of this rule has focused on specific military technologies, such as exploding or expanding bullets[64] and blinding laser weapons.[65] These weapon-specific approaches are "not based on an objective analysis of the suffering caused by the weapons concerned; such means of warfare were simply deemed 'abhorrent' or 'inhuman.'"[66]

Recently, the ICRC developed an objective approach to determining whether an existing or future weapon causes or is likely to cause superfluous injury or unnecessary suffering. This approach uses four criteria to distinguish between the anticipated effects of conventional weapons and superfluous injury or unnecessary suffering: (1) specific disease, specific abnormal physiological state, specific abnormal psychological state, specific and permanent disability or specific disfigurement; (2) field mortality of more than 25 percent or a hospital mortality of more than 5 percent; (3) Grade 3 wounds as measured by the Red Cross wound classification; and (4) effects for which there is no well-recognized and proven treatment.[67] Criterion 1 involves analyzing specific disease threats as foreseeable effects of weapons.[68] The ICRC states that Criterion 1 would apply to weapons that foreseeably cause injuries – such as gastrointestinal hemorrhage – that require blood transfusions, which can transmit infectious diseases – such as syphilis, hepatitis B, and HIV – in places without reliable blood supplies.[69]

---

[63] See St. Petersburg Declaration Renouncing the Use, in Time of War, of Explosive Projectiles Under 400 Grammes Weight (1868), in Roberts and Guelff, *Documents on the Laws of War*, p. 31; Regulations Respecting the Laws and Customs of War on Land, annexed to the 1907 Hague Convention IV Respecting the Laws and Customs of War on Land, Art. 23(e), in *ibid.*, p. 52; 1977 Protocol I, Art. 35(2), in *ibid.*, p. 409; see also Green, *Contemporary Law of Armed Conflict*, pp. 121–34.

[64] See St. Petersburg Declaration, in Roberts and Guelff, *Documents on the Laws of War*, p. 30; Hague Declaration III Concerning Expanding Bullets (1899), in *ibid.*, p. 40.

[65] Protocol IV on Blinding Laser Weapons to the Convention on Prohibitions or Restrictions on the Use of Certain Conventional Weapons which may be Deemed to be Excessively Injurious or to Have Indiscriminate Effects (Oct. 13, 1995), reprinted in Doswald-Beck, "Blinding Laser Weapons," 299.   [66] ICRC, *The SIrUS Project*, p. 12.

[67] *Ibid.*, p. 23.   [68] *Ibid.*

[69] *Ibid.*, p. 24. McCoubrey and White observe that "[i]n the context of the AIDS epidemic in particular, it may be taken that multiple use, without intervening sterilization, of needles would be potentially culpable." Hilare McCoubrey and Nigel D. White, *International Law and Armed Conflict* (Aldershot: Dartmouth Publishing, 1992), p. 262. The ICRC also applies the four criteria to biological weapons, arguing that Criterion 1 and possibly Criteria 2 and 4 apply to biological weapons. ICRC, *The SIrUS Project*, p. 25. Using these criteria supplements the existing international legal prohibition on the use of biological weapons.

The difficulty in applying the ICRC's objective approach to determining whether a conventional weapon causes superfluous injury or unnecessary suffering in the context of infectious diseases is that all conventional weapons cause wounds that can become badly infected in the absence of prompt and adequate medical treatment. As Dr. Jean-Claude Mulli of the ICRC has observed: "War wounds are always contaminated."[70] Although contamination is not the same thing as infection, contamination is the first step towards the growth of the infectious agent in the wound. Obviously, the larger the wound, the greater the likelihood of infection. Criterion 3's reference to Grade 3 or large wounds, thus, would also be relevant to infectious disease considerations. For example, the large wounds caused by anti-personnel mines raise particular infectious disease dangers and difficulties because when such mines explode "earth, mud and debris are blown into the tissues and into the intermuscular planes."[71] Such infectious disease threats to victims of anti-personnel mines support the argument that such weapons cause superfluous injury or unnecessary suffering.[72] The link between large wounds and infectious diseases in connection with the concept of super-fluous injury or unnecessary suffering is weak, however, because it is simply not known how many people suffering from large wounds suffer unnecessarily because of wound infections.

The ICRC's objective criteria for determining whether a conventional weapon causes superfluous injury or unnecessary suffering are meant to have influence on the design of conventional weapons. As the anti-personnel mine example shows, the war–disease synergy can play a role in the ICRC's criteria, which places infectious disease concerns in the middle of the controversies surrounding weapon design. The ICRC's creation of health-based, objective criteria for determining whether a weapon causes or is likely to cause superfluous injury or unnecessary suffering transforms the war–disease relationship from one in which war produces infectious disease morbidity and mortality to one in which the foreseeability of

---

[70] Jean-Claude Mulli, "Surgical Activities in War Zones: The Experience of the International Committee of the Red Cross (ICRC)," English translation and reprint of Jean-Claude Mulli, "Activités chirurgicales en zones de guerre: l'expérience du Comité International de la Croix-Rouge (CICR)," *Bull. Medicus Mundi Switzerland* 57 (Mar. 1995).

[71] Gray, *War Wounds*, p. 15; see also Coupland, *Amputation*, p. 8.

[72] ICRC, *The SIrUS Project*, p. 20; see also the Convention on the Prohibition of the Use, Stockpiling, Production and Transfer of Anti-Personnel Mines and on Their Destruction (Sept. 18, 1997), preamble, reprinted in *Int'l Rev. Red Cross* 320 (1997), 563–78.

infectious diseases from the effects of conventional weapons works to encourage the development of less harmful weaponry.

TARGETS

International humanitarian law contains the fundamental rule that armed forces may attack only military targets and cannot attack civilian populations or targets.[73] This general rule is supplemented by more specific prohibitions, some of which directly relate to infectious disease control. For example, attacks on "objects indispensable to the survival of the civilian population, such as areas for the production of foodstuffs, crops, livestock, drinking water installations and supplies and irrigation works" are prohibited.[74] Even when these objects support military forces, they may not be attacked if such attack "may be expected to leave the civilian population with such inadequate food or water as to cause its starvation or force its movement."[75]

The general prohibition on attacking civilian populations and targets attempts to preserve, among other things, infrastructure and resources needed to maintain public health for the civilian population. The specific prohibitions on attacking civilian food and water resources seek to prevent malnutrition[76] and the contamination of water supplies through destruction of water systems. Both are long-standing war-generated threats to the human immune system. The rules also aim to prevent civilian populations from being forced into mass movements because such large human migrations always pose infectious disease problems. The ICRC observed that "up to 50 percent of the deaths among displaced populations are caused by waterborne diseases."[77] The reality of the threat of waterborne diseases to persons displaced because of armed conflict was most recently witnessed in the Rwandan refugee camps in Zaire, where approximately 50,000 refugees died from cholera or shigella in the first month of the camps' existence.[78]

---

[73] Green, *Contemporary Law of Armed Conflict*, p. 220.
[74] 1977 Protocol I, Art. 54(2), in Roberts and Guelff, *Documents on the Laws of War*, p. 417; 1977 Protocol II Additional to the Geneva Conventions of 12 August 1949, and Relating to the Protection of Victims of Non-International Armed Conflicts (1977), Art. 17(1), in *ibid.*, p. 456.
[75] 1977 Protocol I, Art. 54(3), in *ibid.*, p. 417; 1977 Protocol II, Art. 14, in *ibid.*, pp. 455–56.
[76] See, e.g., Alain Mourey, "Famine and War," *Int'l Rev. Red Cross* 285 (1991), 549–57.
[77] ICRC, "Water in Armed Conflicts," p. 7.
[78] Mary E. Wilson, "Travel and the Emergence of Infectious Diseases," *Emerging Infectious Diseases* 1 (1995), 41.

Unfortunately, the rules protecting civilians generally and those that support infectious disease control more specifically are frequently violated in both international and civil wars. Generally, civilians have been deliberate targets of warfare throughout the twentieth century, in violation of international humanitarian law. Recent conflicts, such as the one in Bosnia, reveal that civilian populations still suffer grave hardships during armed conflict.[79] Civilians have not fared any better in connection with rules that specifically support infectious disease control. While invading Kuwait, the Iraqis destroyed the local water supply and wastewater and sewage treatment systems.[80] Civil war in the former Yugoslavia crippled water and sanitation systems,[81] and the civil conflict in Rwanda disrupted water supply systems.[82] The ICRC reports that one of the biggest and most frequent problems it confronts in relief work is water-related health threats created by armed conflict, and that "[i]n a growing number of conflicts, water-related problems are reported to cause more casualties than direct injury by weapon."[83]

Part of the recent problem with waterborne diseases flows from the destruction of items necessary for the functioning of a modern water and sanitation system. In the 1990–91 Gulf War, controversy developed in connection with the destruction of Iraqi electricity supplies. The Allied bombing of Iraqi electricity resources created this controversy because, while damaging Iraqi military capabilities, the bombing shut down many important civilian services, including heating, water supplies, water purification, sewage treatment, and medical services, creating suffering in the civilian population.[84] The irony of this situation is that the Allied bombing campaign was, on the whole, very accurate, and yet the electricity targets caused "secondary collateral damage"[85] to civilian populations. The importance of electricity supplies to both military capabilities and civilian services made such supplies both a military and a civilian target. This

[79] See, e.g., International Committee of the Red Cross, "Saving Lives: The ICRC's Mandate to Protect Civilians and Detainees in Bosnia-Herzegovina," Special Brochure (Apr. 1995).
[80] Frank R. Finch, "This Land is Our Land: The Environmental Threat of Army Operations," in Grunawalt et al., *Protection of the Environment*, p. 109.
[81] M. J. Toole, S. Galson, and W. Brady, "Are War and Public Health Compatible?" *The Lancet* 341 (1993), 1193.
[82] International Committee of the Red Cross, "Rwanda," Special Brochure (1994), 8.
[83] ICRC, "Water in Armed Conflicts," p. 2.
[84] William M. Arkin, "The Environmental Threat of Military Operations," in Grunawalt et al., *Protection of the Environment*, p. 122; ICRC, "Water in Iraq," 1.
[85] Arkin, "Environmental Threat," p. 123.

suffering led William Arkin to argue that "[e]lectricity is so important to modern societies that attacks that could have severe effects on the non-combatant population should be prohibited."[86]

The ICRC argues that part of the waterborne disease problem also stems from increasing urbanization and the vulnerability of complex urban water infrastructures to warfare.[87] In its relief work in war zones, the ICRC finds repairing water systems difficult because not only are the systems complex, which demands highly trained engineers to fix them, but also the engineers themselves become targets of military forces.[88] The increasing problems of waterborne diseases in armed conflict have led the ICRC to propose revising international humanitarian law to provide more protection for water resources and some protection for engineers who fix disrupted water systems.[89]

Coping with the adverse public health consequences of war

COMBATANTS

Wounded and sick combatants

The oldest aspects of international humanitarian law involve protecting wounded and sick combatants.[90] International humanitarian law attempts to do this in three ways: (1) by protecting military medical units, personnel, facilities, ships, aircraft, and vehicles from attack;[91] (2) by imposing on

---

[86] *Ibid.*   [87] ICRC, "Water in Armed Conflicts," p. 4.   [88] *Ibid.*, pp. 9–10.

[89] *Ibid.*; see also International Committee of the Red Cross, "Experts Call for Absolute Protection of Water Supplies and Water Engineers During Armed Conflict," ICRC News Release (Nov. 24, 1994).

[90] See, e.g., the 1864 Geneva Convention for the Amelioration of the Conditions of the Wounded and Sick in Armies in the Field, available at http://www.icrc.org/unicc/ihl_eng.nsf.

[91] See 1899 Hague Convention III for the Adaptation to Maritime Warfare of the Principles of the Geneva Convention of 22 August 1864, available at http://www.icrc.org/unicc/ihl_eng.nsf, Arts. 1–3; 1907 Hague Regulations Respecting the Laws and Customs of War, Art. 27, in Roberts and Guelff, *Documents on the Laws of War*, p. 53; 1907 Hague Convention X for the Adaptation to Maritime Warfare of the Principles of the Geneva Convention, Arts. 1–3, available at http://www.icrc.org/unicc/ihl_eng.nsf; 1923 Hague Rules on Aerial Warfare, Art. 25, in Roberts and Guelff, *Documents on the Laws of War*, p. 127; 1949 Geneva Convention I for the Amelioration of the Condition of the Wounded and Sick in Armed Forces in the Field, Art. 19, in *ibid.*, p. 149; 1949 Geneva Convention II for the Amelioration of the Condition of the Wounded, Sick and Shipwrecked Members of the Armed Forces at Sea, Art. 22, in *ibid.*, p. 202; 1949 Geneva Convention IV, Arts. 18, 22, in *ibid.*, pp. 278, 280; 1977 Protocol I, Arts. 12(1), 15(1), 21, 22, and 24, in *ibid.*, pp. 397–402.

belligerent states duties to treat wounded or sick enemy combatants humanely;[92] and (3) by allowing private individuals and relief organizations to provide humanitarian assistance to wounded or sick soldiers.[93] These rules combine to preserve and create opportunities for medical personnel to treat wounded or sick combatants quickly, which contributes to infectious disease control by reducing the vulnerability of wounded and sick combatants to opportunistic infections.

Despite the long heritage of protecting sick, wounded, and shipwrecked combatants in international humanitarian law, the rules protecting wounded and sick combatants have routinely been violated by belligerents in international and civil wars throughout the twentieth century. The same gap between what international humanitarian law requires and what belligerents do in the context of civilian populations appears as well in the area of protection and humane treatment of wounded and sick combatants.

Prisoners of war

International humanitarian law closely regulates the treatment of prisoners of war (POWs) and includes provisions that support infectious disease control. The detaining power has duties towards POWs that deal with providing humane treatment; adequate medical care; sanitary camp facilities; adequate food, water, clothing, and shelter; and active surveillance for infectious diseases.[94] Analogous rules for protecting the health of persons deprived of their liberty for reasons related to a civil war also form part

[92] See 1864 Geneva Convention, Art. 6; 1868 Additional Articles Relating to the Convention of the Wounded in War, Art. 11, available at http://www.icrc.org/unicc/ihl_eng.nsf; 1899 Hague Convention III, Art. 8; 1906 Geneva Convention for the Amelioration of the Condition of the Wounded and Sick in Armies in the Field, Art. 1, available at http://www.icrc.org/unicc/ihl_eng.nsf; 1907 Hague Convention X, Art. 11; 1929 Geneva Convention for the Amelioration of the Condition of the Wounded and Sick in Armies in the Field, Art. 1, available at http://www.icrc.org/unicc/ihl_eng.nsf; 1949 Geneva Convention II, Arts. 3(2) and 12, in Roberts and Guelff, *Documents on the Laws of War*, pp. 195, 198; 1977 Protocol I, Art. 10, in *ibid.*, p. 395; 1977 Protocol II, Art. 7, in *ibid.*, p. 454.

[93] See, e.g., 1864 Geneva Convention, Art. 5; 1906 Geneva Convention, Arts. 5 and 9; 1929 Geneva Convention, Arts. 5 and 9; 1949 Geneva Convention II, Art. 3, in Roberts and Guelff, *Documents on the Laws of War*, p. 195; 1977 Protocol I, Arts. 5(3), 5(4), 8(c), and 17, in *ibid.*, pp. 392, 394, 399; 1977 Protocol II, Art. 18, in *ibid.*, p. 456.

[94] See, e.g., 1907 Hague Regulations Respecting the Laws and Customs of War on Land, Art. 4, in Roberts and Guelff, *Documents on the Laws of War*, p. 48; 1929 Geneva Convention Relative to the Treatment of Prisoners of War, Arts. 2, 10–15, available at http://www.icrc.org/unicc/ihl_eng.nsf; 1949 Geneva Convention III Relative to the Treatment of Prisoners of War, Arts. 13, 15, 25–27, 29–31, in Roberts and Guelff, *Documents on the Laws of War*, pp. 222–23, 227–29.

of international humanitarian law.[95] All these, if obeyed, would foster conditions less favorable to microbial traffic in POW camps.

As with the international humanitarian legal rules on protecting civilian populations and sick and wounded combatants, the rules on POW treatment also have been massively violated in international and civil wars in the twentieth century. Such violations made up parts of the indictments against Nazi and Japanese war criminals after World War II.[96] Combatant and non-combatant prisoners also suffer in civil wars, as illustrated by this description of the Omarska prison camp in Bosnia by the Prosecutor of the International Criminal Tribunal for the Former Yugoslavia:

> Living conditions at Omarska were brutal. Prisoners were crowded together with little or no facilities for personal hygiene. They were fed starvation rations once a day and given only three minutes to get into the canteen area, eat, and get out. The little water they received was ordinarily foul. Prisoners had no changes of clothing and no bedding. They received no medical care.[97]

NON-COMBATANTS

International humanitarian law also regulates the treatment of civilians in occupied territories in connection with international armed conflicts and the treatment of persons deprived of their liberty for reasons related to a civil war. These rules contribute to infectious disease control. The regimes protecting non-combatant health in occupied territories or in the context of civil war are comprehensive, and include the following duties: (1) prohibition on mass forcible transfers of civilian populations, except for evacuations necessary for the security of the civilians – any evacuation must be undertaken in conditions of adequate hygiene, safety, and nutrition;[98] (2) the duty to ensure that the occupied civilian population has adequate clothing, shelter, food, and medical supplies;[99] (3) the duty

---

[95] See 1977 Protocol II, Art. 5(1), in Roberts and Guelff, *Documents on the Laws of War*, p. 451.

[96] See Indictment of the International Military Tribunal, in *Trial of the Major War Criminals Before the International Military Tribunal. Vol. I: Official Documents* (1947), p. 52; *Judgment of the International Military Tribunal for the Far East* (1948), p. 1002.

[97] International Criminal Tribunal for the Former Yugoslavia, Indictment of the Prosecutor of the Tribunal Against Zeljko Meakić and Others, para. 2.5, available at http://www.un.org./icty/13-02–95.htm.

[98] 1949 Geneva Convention IV, Art. 49, in Roberts and Guelff, *Documents on the Laws of War*, p. 288; 1977 Protocol II, Art. 17, in *ibid.*, p. 456.

[99] 1949 Geneva Convention IV, Art. 55, in *ibid.*, p. 290; 1977 Protocol II, Art. 5(1)(b), in *ibid.*, p. 452.

to ensure and maintain medical facilities and services, public health and hygiene in the occupied territory, and measures needed to combat the spread of infectious diseases;[100] (4) the duty to allow relief agencies to provide food, medical supplies, and clothing to inadequately supplied civilian populations;[101] (5) the duty to provide food and sanitary conditions for any persons convicted of criminal offenses;[102] and (6) the duty to provide interned civilian populations with adequate food, sanitary facilities, medical facilities, and active infectious disease surveillance.[103]

International humanitarian rules on treatment of civilians in occupied territories and of persons deprived of their liberty during civil war have not been observed often by belligerents. Civilian populations suffered horribly during occupations by German and Japanese forces during World War II.[104] Civilian suffering has also been an unfortunate characteristic of contemporary civil wars, such as the one in Bosnia, where belligerents inflicted "ethnic cleansing" on certain minority groups. The Prosecutor for the International Criminal Tribunal for the Former Yugoslavia described in many indictments how thousands of Bosnian Muslim and Bosnian Croat civilians were forced into detention camps, where they were subject to inhumane treatment, including murder, torture, rape, inadequate food, insufficient or non-existent medical care, and grossly unhygienic conditions.[105]

War crimes and public health

The depressing lack of compliance with international humanitarian rules that support public health objectives raises questions about punishing those responsible for endangering the health of individuals during times of war. Is there a need to strengthen international humanitarian law to punish individuals who knowingly expose people to infectious disease threats during armed conflicts? Answering this question involves looking at the

[100] 1949 Geneva Convention IV, Art. 56, in *ibid.*, p. 291; 1977 Protocol II, Arts. 5(1)(b) and 5(2)(d)–(e), in *ibid.*, p. 452.
[101] 1949 Geneva Convention IV, Arts. 59–63, in *ibid.*, pp. 292–93; 1977 Protocol I, Arts. 68–71, in *ibid.*, pp. 428–30; 1977 Protocol II, Art. 18, in *ibid.*, p. 456.
[102] 1949 Geneva Convention IV, Art. 76, in *ibid.*, p. 297.
[103] 1949 Geneva Convention IV, Arts. 89–92, in *ibid.*, pp. 301–3; 1977 Protocol II, Art. 5(1)(b), in *ibid.*, p. 452.
[104] See Indictment of the International Military Tribunal, in *Trial of the Major War Criminals*, p. 43; *Judgment of the International Military Tribunal for the Far East*, p. 1031.
[105] See, e.g., Indictment of the Prosecutor of the Tribunal Against Radovan Karadzić and Ratko Mladić, para. 22.

current scope of war crimes and how public health has played a role in the prosecution of war criminals in the past and present.

The concept of a "war crime" has long been sufficiently comprehensive to cover violations of the laws and customs of war that support infectious disease control. The international humanitarian rules that promote public health regulate weapons, target selection, treatment of POWs, and treatment of civilians. Indeed, the Charter of the International Military Tribunal (Nuremberg Charter) covered all but one of these areas, stating that war crimes include violations of the laws or customs of war, such as ill-treatment of civilian populations of or in occupied territory, ill-treatment of POWs, and destruction of civilian objects without military justification.[106] The detailed indictments of the Nuremberg International Military Tribunal and of the International Military Tribunal for the Far East clearly demonstrate that violations of public health related laws of war were considered war crimes. For example, in the Nuremberg Indictment, the Allies charged: (1) in connection with ill-treatment of civilians of or in occupied territories that, "[i]n the concentration camps, the health regime and labor regime were such that the rate of mortality (alleged to be from natural causes) attained enormous proportions";[107] (2) in connection with forced deportations of civilian populations, that "[s]uch deportees were subjected to the most barbarous conditions of overcrowding; they were provided with wholly insufficient clothing and were given little or no food for several days";[108] and (3) in connection with ill-treatment of POWs, that the Nazi defendants "murdered and ill-treated prisoners of war by denying them adequate food, shelter, clothing and medical care and attention."[109] Similar charges can be found in the Indictment of the International Military Tribunal for the Far East.[110]

The 1949 Geneva Conventions III and IV, on POWs and civilians respectively, also underscored that "willfully causing great suffering or serious injury to body or health" represents a grave breach of international humanitarian law.[111] This concept is also used in the 1977 Protocol I.[112] It

---

[106] Charter of the International Military Tribunal, in *Trial of the Major War Criminals*, p. 11.

[107] Indictment of the International Military Tribunal, in *ibid.*, p. 45.   [108] *Ibid.*, p. 51.

[109] *Ibid.*, p. 52.

[110] See Indictment, in *Judgment of the International Military Tribunal for the Far East*, Annex A–6, app. D, pp. 110–14.

[111] 1949 Geneva Convention III, Art. 130, in Roberts and Guelff, *Documents on the Laws of War*, p. 268; 1949 Geneva Convention IV, Art. 147, in *ibid.*, p. 323.

[112] 1977 Protocol I, Art. 11(4), in *ibid.*, p. 396.

is well-established now in international humanitarian law that attacks on civilian populations and on objects indispensable to the survival of the civilian population are war crimes.[113] The indictments of the International Criminal Tribunal for the Former Yugoslavia demonstrate that these war crimes apply in civil conflicts as well.[114]

Thus, neither the war crimes concept nor the prosecution of war criminals ignores the international humanitarian law that supports infectious disease control. Based on this conclusion, there does not appear to be much more that can be done to strengthen international humanitarian law in connection with punishing war criminals guilty of violating the rules on protection of public health during armed conflict. Many advocate strengthening the entire body of international humanitarian law by creating a permanent international criminal tribunal. The Lawyers Committee for Human Rights, for example, has argued that

> most perpetrators of gross human rights abuses and violations of international humanitarian law are not punished by national or international bodies. The time has come to end this impunity by creating a permanent court before which such individuals could be brought to justice. Human rights and the protections guaranteed under international humanitarian law will not be translated into practical behavior unless potential offenders become aware that a price for violations must be paid.[115]

Given that serious violations of international humanitarian law supporting infectious disease control are war crimes subject to the jurisdiction of the proposed International Criminal Court (ICC),[116] perhaps the creation of the ICC can narrow the gap between how the law protects public health and individual lives during warfare and how belligerents destroy public health and individual lives during warfare.

Any enthusiasm for using a permanent international criminal court to ameliorate the adverse public health consequences of armed conflict must, however, be tempered. As noted earlier in this chapter, the war–disease synergy has been powerful historically because of the tremendous

---

[113] See 1977 Protocol I, Art. 85(3)(a)–(d), in *ibid.*, pp. 437–38.

[114] See, e.g., Indictment of the Prosecutor against Zeljko Meakić and Others, para. 2.5; Indictment of the Prosecutor against Radovan Karadzić and Ratko Mladić, paras. 22, 26, 36.

[115] Lawyers Committee for Human Rights, *Establishing an International Criminal Court: Major Unresolved Issues in the Draft Statute* (Aug. 1996), p. 3.

[116] See Rome Statute of the International Criminal Court, UN Doc. A/CONF.183/9 (July 17, 1998), Arts. 6–8.

opportunities armed conflict creates for pathogenic microbes. In fact, the comprehensive set of international humanitarian legal rules that support infectious disease control reflects the enormous public health challenges that any type of warfare creates. As the public health problems experienced in Iraq in the aftermath of the 1990–91 Gulf War suggest, even highly trained and sophisticated armed forces that fight with an eye towards complying with international humanitarian law can cause infectious disease outbreaks.

Another sobering thought is that contemporary warfare often (but not always) occurs in developing countries, where infectious disease control is often non-existent even in peacetime.[117] It is somewhat surreal to expect governments and rebel factions to exhibit sensitivity to public health in war when such sensitivity, and the resources to do something, do not exist in peacetime. This observation points to a tragedy that dwarfs even the war–disease synergy: the everyday condition of public health in developing countries. Infectious diseases remain the world's leading cause of death,[118] and the overwhelming majority of this burden falls on developing countries.[119] According to the Director-General of WHO, infectious diseases are crippling the socio-economic development of many countries and ruining their prospects for a better future.[120]

Ominously, the socio-economic toll of infectious diseases works side-by-side with other forces that lead countries to disintegrate into civil violence and chaos. In much of the world today, pathogenic microbes enjoy many opportunities to spread and infect new hosts and populations, regardless of whether conditions of peace or war prevail. This depressing realization does, however, reinforce why war and pestilence make up two of the four horsemen of the apocalypse.

Conclusion

As history demonstrates, preventing infectious diseases during times of armed conflict is a daunting challenge given the alterations military violence causes in the human–microbe environment. Warfare creates so many opportunities for pathogenic microbes that any response that is less than comprehensive stands little chance of success. As the chapter

---

[117] World Health Organization, *World Health Report 1996: Fighting Disease, Fostering Development* (1996), p. 3.
[118] *Ibid.*, p. 1.   [119] *Ibid.*, p. 9.   [120] *Ibid.*, p. v.

outlines, the body of international legal rules that attempt to prevent and control infectious diseases in times of armed conflict represents a comprehensive framework that addresses weaponry, combatants, and noncombatants. Comprehensiveness is necessary, but not sufficient, because the comprehensive rules are comprehensively violated in virtually every armed conflict. War remains what it has always been: a deadly event for public health.

International legal thinking is not currently frozen in the face of the great public health challenges caused by war. This chapter highlights a number of ideas or initiatives that directly relate to infectious disease control objectives. Of course, governments and NGOs like the ICRC also continue to press for adherence to the comprehensive set of rules that already exist. Whether these new international legal initiatives actually contribute to reducing the virulence of the war–disease synergy remains to be seen. Historical events consistently have treated new developments in international humanitarian law roughly.

The international law that seeks to support public health during armed conflict has so far proven to be no match for the violence and chaos of war. Such a sobering conclusion forces us to understand that the adverse environmental consequences of armed conflict involve not only natural ecosystems, but also the microbial world and the human-made world built to deal with the ever-present threat of pathogenic microbes. While flaming oil rigs darkening the horizon become horrible images of the environmental nightmare of war, greater danger, death, and destruction come from war's stimulation of the world we cannot see.

PART IV

VALUING THE IMPACTS –
ECONOMIC METHODS AND ISSUES

INTRODUCTION

ERIC FELDMAN

Establishing a legal regime to address the environmental consequences of war and elaborating scientific techniques to characterize the specific nature of the damages create a need for economic methods to value these damages and to suggest appropriate compensation measures. This Part of the book surveys existing tools for valuing environmental damages, including ecological and natural resource damages as well as public health damages, and considers possible applications of these tools to the wartime context.

Considerable controversy already surrounds peacetime attempts to define the types of environmental damages that are compensable, the appropriate objectives of compensation, and the economic assessment methods that determine the monetary value of the damages. For this reason, developing compensation measures for wartime environmental damages is a dual challenge for economists, who must choose an appropriate peacetime assessment methodology that also applies to the particular complexities and severe damages arising from armed conflict.

Approaches to assessing environmental damages vary depending on the particular type of damage: ecological, natural resource, or public health impacts; use or non-use values; permanent or temporary losses; and compensation for lost values or restoration of the values – to name just a few of the variables. While damages to natural resources are usually assessed using market-based approaches, many economists believe that ecological and public health damages require other approaches in order to assess non-commercial values fully and yield sums that market-based approaches would otherwise underestimate.

This Part builds on the work of the United Nations Environment Program Working Group of Experts on Liability and Compensation for

Environmental Damage Arising from Military Activities. Meeting in 1995 and 1996, the Working Group focused on the international law aspects of liability and compensation for environmental damage from war, paying particular attention to issues facing the United Nations Compensation Commission (UNCC). The Working Group also considered a variety of valuation methodologies – including contingent valuation, market-based approaches, and other methods – and surveyed how existing methods might apply to specific types of damages. In contrast, the chapters in this Part, all written by economists, draw more heavily on the fundamental principles of economic valuation and consider some of the limitations in applying existing peacetime economic valuation methodologies to wartime environmental damage.

The chapters in this Part consider a range of economic assessment tools, discussing first those applicable to ecological and natural resource impacts (Section A), and then those applicable to public health impacts (Section B). In the first section, Carol Jones discusses restoration-based measures to assess the full social cost of ecological damage, including the interim losses. In the second section, Mark Dickie and Shelby Gerking survey the strengths and weaknesses of a range of methods for assessing public health damages – including cost-of-illness, contingent valuation, and averting behavior – while emphasizing willingness-to-pay (WTP) and willingness-to-accept (WTA) measures of damages. W. Kip Viscusi also surveys existing techniques – the cost-of-illness approach, efforts to estimate WTP values (quality-adjusted life years approach), risk metrics used for the valuation of risk reduction (risk money tradeoffs and the death-risk metric), and the estimation of utility functions – and advocates a cost-of-illness approach for wartime compensation, with WTP measures reserved for situations when deterrence is the goal.

Throughout this Part, there exists some disagreement over the degree to which peacetime economic methods are directly applicable to the wartime context. Viscusi, for example, interprets wartime compensation as a relatively straightforward process that could and should mirror the compensation principles of the US judicial system for other types of damages. In contrast, the other authors describe instances in which certain unique characteristics of wartime damages could complicate or prevent the application of compensation techniques developed for peacetime damages.

One potential challenge in applying peacetime methods to wartime scenarios stems from the sheer scope of wartime damage. As Jones notes, wartime damages may occur both on a large geographic scale and simultaneously to a variety of resources. Consequently, the collective losses resulting from such far-reaching and multiple damage will exceed the sum of individual losses because of the loss of potential substitutes. Furthermore, as Dickie and Gerking suggest, large-scale damage to ecosystems may in turn create synergistic effects between public health and other environmental damages. The authors cite the example of how pollution from petroleum fires in Kuwait led not only to direct public health consequences but also to indirect effects through the pollution's impact on agriculture.

Moreover, war may prolong the time horizon during which damage occurs, which presents an additional challenge in light of the limited ability of current methods to predict and value long-term impacts. War also may hinder attempts to respond to impacts. As both Jones and Dickie and Gerking suggest, ongoing conflict may prevent prompt responses to incidents, postponing remediation until after the war ends and therefore exacerbating damage. In addition, wartime stress on vital physical and economic infrastructure could further forestall the remediation process, while the cost of remediation might increase as a result of changes to wage and price levels during wartime.

More specifically, wartime realities could interfere with various compensation techniques that might otherwise be appropriate in a peacetime context. For example, Dickie and Gerking – and, similarly, Jones – suggest that monetary estimates of damages may be inaccurate as a result of wartime fluctuations in wage and price levels, as well as disruptions in the labor force. Economists attempting to address indirect costs resulting from lost productivity would face the question of whether to use pre- or postwar wages and prices to address these costs.

Wartime pressures also might interfere with survey-based compensation techniques, such as contingent valuation, that rely on hypothetical questions to determine preferences. Such methods may be less effective during high-stress circumstances such as war or its aftermath, when respondents may be so concerned with current realities that they lack the ability or the willingness to think in terms of abstract hypotheticals. Accordingly, arguing in favor of an insurance-based approach to compensation during wartime, Viscusi suggests that survey methods are vulnerable to respondents' "alarmist and irrational" overvaluation of unfamiliar risks associated with armed conflict.

Finally, most of the valuation methodologies have been developed primarily for use in a Western context, and the validity of applying these methodologies to damage sustained by non-Western cultures remains speculative. Different cultural assumptions about damage, especially intangible or aesthetic damage, may lead to a range of culture-specific values. As a result, survey-based compensation techniques may yield extremely low monetary values (because individuals cannot or will not place a monetary value on such damage) or extremely high monetary values (because aesthetic or spiritual value may be placed above standard economic value). Given the international nature of war, established compensation techniques may need to be adjusted to incorporate certain distinct cultural preferences.

While these chapters collectively may suggest uncertainty about compensation for wartime environmental damage, this reflects the nascent stage of research on the subject. The authors in this Part propose a variety of next steps for addressing compensation for damage and furthering the body of research on the subject. Although the authors' analyses are informed by a considerable breadth of economic literature, the cited literature includes only one previous economic assessment of the environmental consequences of war. Even that study, which considered the health effects of air pollution from the 1990–91 Gulf War on the Iranian people, focused on a country located on the periphery of the conflict.[1] Not captured in the case study were the more severe short- and long-term damage and the complex dynamic of simultaneous ecological and public health damage found closer to the heart of the conflict. There remains a need for further research on compensation in countries directly affected by war and the associated damage to competing environmental media and infrastructure.

Two of the concrete proposals in this Part are rooted in existing provisions in US law. Although complete reliance on domestic valuation approaches during wartime may be subject to question, there currently is a dearth of international experience with valuation of environmental damages, much less in a wartime context. At the same time, a wealth of tools and experience has been developed by courts at the national level. These include extensive application of state-of-the-art theories and

[1] M. Rahmatian, "Valuing Reduced Morbidity," mimeo (Department of Economics, California State University–Fullerton, 1997).

methodologies for natural resource and public health damage assessment to the sort of catastrophic damage associated with wartime, including oil spills, deforestation, widespread destruction of wildlife, and immediate and long-term public health impacts from inhalation of herbicides, smoke, and other noxious substances. It is significant that the UNEP Working Group relied on national law "particularly where a general approach could be discerned."[2] It is worth noting, however, that the cultural values assumed in these national methodologies may have limited applicability in other countries.

In the first proposal based on US natural resource damage law, Jones advocates international adoption of a restoration-based approach modeled on the US Oil Pollution Act regulations. This resource compensation (as opposed to monetary compensation) approach considers not only compensation for the replacement of damaged resources and the value of their lost services over time, but also provides compensation for interim losses sustained from the time of the damage until the recovery of original or replacement resources to their "but-for-the-injury" state. As opposed to simplified in-kind replacement approaches, which Jones believes may be unreliable indicators of value, this valuation approach calculates tradeoffs between injured resources and replacement resources. Even so, Jones still questions the degree to which this model would be effective in wartime, given the scope of the damages, and suggests the possible need to revert to monetary compensation for interim losses.

For public health damages, Viscusi, like Jones, believes that compensation approaches should parallel the US legal system. However, he advocates the insurance-based compensation principles favored by the US tort system. By interpreting compensation as a form of insurance rather than deterrence, Viscusi highlights financial (cost-of-illness) methods as the most appropriate tools for compensation and argues that willingness-to-pay measures provide excessive insurance. He suggests that willingness-to-pay measures represent optimal deterrence values, rather than appropriate compensation values, and therefore should be reserved for cases in which deterrence – or prevention of repeated offenses of a similar nature – is the goal. Nevertheless, while potential personal liability for environmental

---

[2] United Nations Environment Program, *Report of the Working Group of Experts on Liability and Compensation for Environmental Damage Arising from Military Activities* (May 17, 1996), para. 20, p. 5 (also asserting that Article 31 of the UNCC Provisional Rules for Claims Procedures allows reliance on national law).

war crimes is likely to remain the greatest deterrent, the threat of civil liability is likely to shape how nations prepare for, enter, and conduct war, particularly as international mechanisms develop to hold nations accountable for their wartime actions.

Viscusi's recommendations contrast with the approach advocated by Dickie and Gerking, underscoring a tension that promises to fuel future research on methods of compensation. Whereas Dickie and Gerking suggest further refinement of the willingness-to-accept approach, Viscusi warns that such survey-based methods might isolate potential sources of irrationality, as respondents could overreact to "novel risks" during wartime, such as new weapon systems and unfamiliar chemical risks. At the same time, Dickie and Gerking, while emphasizing that there exists no single best method for valuing health damages in all situations, regard the cost-of-illness approach favored by Viscusi as a relatively narrow approach that produces lower bound estimates of value.

In two recent and prominent examples of wartime environmental damage, injured nations appear to have sought compensation for the costs of environmental remediation only. In its claims before the UNCC following the 1990–91 Gulf War, the government of Kuwait sought approximately $16.3 billion in compensation for actual and anticipated environmental remediation costs, including associated costs of use or non-use environmental values, environmental assessment, monitoring, and restoration.[3] Kuwait did not file claims for lost use or non-use environmental values, but it reserved the right to assert additional environmental damages. Although the deadline for filing such damages passed in 1997, the UNCC indicated that existing claims can be supplemented. Additionally, other governments may have sought compensation for lost use and non-use harms, but information on these filings remains unavailable due to the confidentiality of the proceedings.

Similarly, in Colombia, more than 700 guerrilla attacks over the course of twelve years caused the spilling of approximately 2 million barrels of

---

[3] Maurice Girgis, "Kuwait's Environmental and Economic Losses: Estimates and Methodologies," paper presented at the First International Conference on Addressing the Environmental Consequences of War, Washington, D.C. (June 1998). Due to a lack of information about the impacts and insufficient remediation technologies, Kuwait delayed submission of two other claims: $16.6 billion for remediating soft mud tidal flats and $11.9 billion for treating public health impacts, including post-traumatic stress disorder.

crude oil that contaminated 2,600 kilometers of Colombian waterways and caused environmental damage totaling $26 million in clean-up costs.[4] In addition, the aquatic impacts extended beyond national borders to Venezuela. Rather than opting to seek compensation for damage to all environmental values, Venezuela reached an agreement with its neighbor whereby Colombia compensates Venezuela for the actual costs of cleaning up downstream contamination in Venezuela. The agreement covers the cost of clean-up, but does not include compensation for environmental or natural resources damages.[5]

Further research will be necessary before the international community will be able to employ fully developed methods for valuing wartime damages. An important step in developing compensation methodologies might be the formation of an international working group of economists specifically to examine issues of wartime environmental damage assessment. This approach would be the economics counterpart to Michael Schmitt's proposal in chapter 3, in which he advocates creation of scientific and legal committees of experts to clarify applicable norms and approaches to preventing, assessing, and redressing wartime environmental damage.[6] This economic committee or working group, likely formed under the auspices of an established international organization, would (1) categorize compensable damages; and (2) work to develop appropriate tools to value these damages. It would complement and continue to build on the work conducted by the UNEP Working Group, with an emphasis on developing and strengthening economic tools for the valuation of wartime damages. Furthermore, the committee would include among its members both natural resource and public health economists to develop the methodologies that are most appropriate for each type of damages.

Whether the goal is deterring wrongful actions or simply compensating for environmental injuries incurred during armed conflict, the chapters

---

[4] Alvaro José Rodríguez, "The Undeclared War for Control Over Natural Resources: Armed Conflict and Environmental Degradation in Colombia," paper presented at the First International Conference on Addressing the Environmental Consequences of War, Washington, D.C. (June 1998).

[5] Personal communication from Leida Y. Mercado, Cornell University, to Eric Feldman, May 27, 1998.

[6] Michael N. Schmitt, "War and the Environment: Fault Lines in the Prescriptive Landscape," chapter 3 in this volume.

that follow confirm that numerous unresolved issues hinder the application of existing valuation tools to the wartime context. The authors identify a number of possible directions for the valuation of future wartime damages. These options include adapting existing peacetime tools, developing entirely new methodologies for use during wartime, or simply curtailing the range of compensable damages. Convening both natural resource and public health economists from all regions of the world to examine these options and develop methodologies would constitute an important first step towards resolving this valuation challenge.

19

<hr>

RESTORATION-BASED APPROACHES TO
COMPENSATION FOR NATURAL RESOURCE
DAMAGES: MOVING TOWARDS CONVERGENCE
IN US AND INTERNATIONAL LAW

CAROL A. JONES

Introduction

In this chapter, I argue that the restoration-based approach to "full compensation" for social losses embodied in the 1996 US Oil Pollution Act regulations provides a valuable new model for other liability regimes designed to protect natural resources in international or national contexts. Though loss or damage by contamination or impairment of the environment is now generally recognized in international liability agreements, the definition of "environmental" or "ecological" damage is still evolving.[1] In addition to the long-standing provision for response costs, the costs of "reinstatement" measures are a central element of compensation for environmental damage in the recent protocols. Some conventions define reinstatement extremely narrowly, limiting it to actual reinstatement of the injured resources; others allow for replacement of the "equivalent", and some allow for monetary compensation when replacement of the equivalent is not possible.

The new measure of damages that has evolved in the United States also relies upon the cost of restoration measures and thereby provides a bridge to the international arena. However, the US measure differs from many

<hr>

[1] Ad Hoc Working Group of Legal and Technical Experts to Consider and Develop a Draft Protocol on Liability and Compensation for Damage Resulting from Transboundary Movements of Hazardous Wastes and their Disposal, UNEP/CHW.1/WG.1/2/Inf.2 (Sept. 15, 1994).

international approaches in that it clearly establishes liability for the two elements of compensation required to make the public "whole": not only (1) restoration or replacement of the injured resources; but also (2) compensation for interim losses during the time period from the injury until the injured resources or their replacements recover to their but-for-the-injury state.

This "full compensation" measure is consistent with a substantial body of law and economics literature that argues that, in order to provide adequate incentives for parties to take precautions to prevent harm to the environment, the responsible parties should bear the full social cost of accidents. Furthermore, a policy that holds responsible parties liable for interim losses will provide incentives for the responsible parties to perform restoration (reinstatement) in a timely manner, because interim losses tend to be larger when restoration is delayed.

Compensation for interim losses was originally conceived in the United States in monetary compensation terms – that is, the amount of money that is required to make the public whole for the loss. However, the statutory restriction that recoveries could only be spent on enhancing or creating natural resources motivated the development of the alternative "resource compensation" approach, in which compensation is provided in the form of resource projects. With this approach, the compensation question becomes: What scale of resource projects is necessary to make the public whole for the interim loss? Natural resource damages are quantified as the costs of a restoration plan designed to return resources to their baseline and to compensate for interim losses.

One advantage of the approach is that, by recovering the costs of compensatory restoration actions rather than the monetary value of the interim losses, the revised format avoids circumstances in which not enough money is collected to implement sufficient compensatory restoration to make the public whole. In addition, the new approach allows trustees to sidestep some of the controversies regarding measurement of monetary compensation, while ensuring that the public is compensated not only for the loss of natural resources but also for the interim losses pending the recovery to baseline conditions of the injured resources or their replacements.

The following section outlines the conceptual framework for the inclusive measure of damages in US regulations, and the section after that compares the US framework to the measure of damages in a variety of international protocols, including the recommendations in the United

Nations Environment Program Report of the Working Group of Experts on Liability and Compensation for Environmental Damage Arising from Military Activities. The next section identifies approaches and methods for measuring restoration-based damages. The final section considers the challenges of implementing a restoration-based approach to value wartime injuries, including simultaneous injuries to multiple resources providing basic life support (air, water, and land for agricultural and other production) over a wide geographical area.

Measures of damages in US laws

In the past two decades, the US Congress has passed several major environmental statutes containing liability provisions that affirm and enhance common law principles of liability for injuries to public natural resources. One set of these statutes, including the Comprehensive Environmental Response Compensation and Liability Act (CERCLA) (Superfund) and the Oil Pollution Act (OPA), focuses on oil and hazardous spills or long-term discharges and establishes prevention and response policies, in addition to the restoration and compensation requirements in the liability provisions. Another set, including the National Marine Sanctuary Act and the Park System Resource Act, establishes protected areas for special resources and mandates the development of resource management plans, which are complemented by liability provisions for injuries to the protected resources from any source.

The innovative liability provisions contained in the statutes designate federal and state resource management agencies and tribal authorities as trustees for the natural resources on behalf of the public, and grant them the authority to recover damages from responsible parties. Further, the US framework provides a clear analytical framework for thinking about the two elements of compensation required to make the public "whole": replacement of the natural assets and compensation for interim losses during the time period from the injury until the injured resources or their replacements recover to their but-for-the-injury state.

As noted above, this "full compensation" measure is consistent with a substantial body of law and economics literature that argues that, in order to provide adequate incentives for firms to take precautions to prevent harm to the environment, the responsible parties should bear the full social cost of accidents.[2] Furthermore, a policy that holds responsible parties liable for interim losses will provide incentives for the responsible parties to restore (reinstate) the injured resources in a timely manner, because interim losses tend to be larger when restoration is delayed.

The most specific language defining the components of the claim appears in the more recent statutes. For example, the OPA specifies the measure of damages as: "(A) the cost of restoring, rehabilitating, replacing, or acquiring the equivalent of, the damaged natural resources ('primary restoration'); (B) the diminution in value of those natural resources pending restoration [of the resource to baseline, but for the injury] ('interim lost value'); *plus* (C) the reasonable cost of assessing those damages."[3] Affirming the resource protection goals of the legislation, Congress mandated that trustees spend all recoveries on actually restoring or acquiring equivalent natural resources.[4]

Figure 19.1 illustrates the relationship between primary restoration and interim losses. Because primary restoration projects may expedite and/or increase the likelihood of recovery, the benefits of projects accrue as reductions in the interim lost value experienced by the public due to resource injuries. In Figure 19.1 the horizontal axis represents time, and the vertical axis represents the value of services provided by an ecosystem affected by a particular release occurring at time t_0 – for example, a spill of no. 6 fuel oil that oils a tidal wetland area. The oiling causes a die-back in the wetland vegetation, in addition to exposing birds, fish, and other animals to oil. On-site ecological services provided by the wetland that may be impaired by the oiling include faunal food and shelter, sediment stabilization, nutrient cycling, and primary productivity. Potentially affected off-site human services, supported by the on-site ecological functions, may include water quality improvements, storm protection and flood control for shoreline properties, as well as birdwatching along the flyway and commercial and recreational fishing.

---

[2] See, e.g., Steven Shavell, *Economic Analysis of Accident Law* (Cambridge, Mass.: Harvard Univ. Press, 1987).

[3] The Oil Pollution Act, 33 U.S.C. § 2706(d). See also the measure of damages for the National Marine Sanctuaries Act, 16 U.S.C. § 1432(6); the Clean Water Act, 33 U.S.C. § 1321(f)(4) and (5); and CERCLA, 42 U.S.C. § 9607(f)(1). See also *Ohio v. Department of Interior*, the D.C. Circuit Court opinion in the litigation over the regulations implementing CERCLA, 880 F.2d, 432, 454 n. 34, 458, 464, 476–78 (D.C. Cir. 1989).

[4] The Oil Pollution Act, 33 U.S.C. § 2706(f).

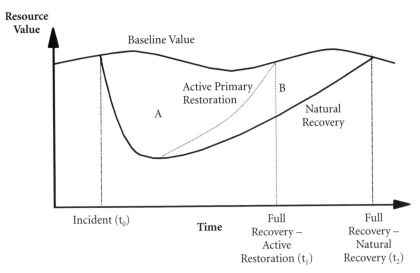

19.1 Relationship between primary restoration and interim lost value

The figure illustrates the case in which the injury site is expected to return to baseline with natural recovery, but active restoration (such as revegetating the wetland) will expedite the return of wetland services to baseline from the time period t_2 to time period t_1. Thus, the interim lost value associated with the natural recovery scenario (areas A+B) is higher than for the scenario with active primary restoration actions (area A only). In natural resource liability provisions in the United States, the conventional economic measure of damages for the interim loss of resources has been the interim lost value incurred by individual members of the public (monetary compensation).[5] In this case, the total measure of damages is the cost of the primary restoration actions that expedite recovery plus the present discounted value of area A in Figure 19.1. Discounting is applied to the streams of past and future losses and gains to take into account the fact that the value of receiving a dollar in one year is less than the value of receiving a dollar today. This measure of damages is particularly appropriate for litigation where individual claimants receive monetary compensation directly – in private tort suits, for example – because it indicates the amount of money necessary to "make whole" the individuals.

---

[5] See 43 C.F.R. § 11.83 (1997); and *Ohio v. Dept. of Interior*, 880 F.2d 432, 464 (D.C. Cir. 1989), *reh'g denied*, 897 F.2d 1151 (D.C. Cir. 1989).

However, as already noted, public trustees in the United States do not have the authority to provide recoveries for natural resource damages directly to individuals; rather, trustees may spend recoveries *only* on enhancing or creating ("restoring, rehabilitating, replacing or acquiring the equivalent of") natural resources.[6] The statutory restriction on the use of the recoveries has motivated the development of an alternative measure for interim losses, "resource compensation," in which compensation for interim losses occurs in the form of compensatory restoration projects. The measure of damages for interim lost services using a resource compensation approach is the cost of the preferred compensatory restoration project(s),[7] where the design and scale of the project(s) are such that they will make the public whole for the interim losses. (Because the scale of the interim losses are determined in part by the choice of primary restoration action(s), the choices of primary and compensatory actions are linked.)

For example, for injuries to a spartina wetland habitat with degraded baseline conditions relative to its potential, it may be possible to implement compensatory restoration actions on-site that achieve ecological and human service levels in excess of baseline. Alternatively, compensatory restoration projects may involve creating or enhancing spartina wetland habitat at a comparable nearby site.

To ensure that the public is fully compensated for the interim losses, the scaling process determines the size of compensatory restoration actions required so that the present discounted value of the gains from the actions will equal the present discounted value of the interim losses. Figure 19.2 illustrates the scaling process for a context in which the injured site was sufficiently degraded that it can sustain additional restoration beyond the pre-incident baseline. (Alternatively, the compensatory restoration project may be performed at another site.) Area C represents the increase in the value of resource services provided by a compensatory restoration project on the same site as the injury. The project will compensate the public for the interim loss if the present discounted value of area C equals the present discounted value of area A.

The regulations promulgated to implement natural resource damage assessments clearly define the measure of damages to include total lost

---

[6] The Oil Pollution Act, 33 U.S.C. § 2706(f).

[7] For a more in-depth discussion of resource compensation as a measure of damages, see C. A. Jones and K. A. Pease, "Restoration-based Measures of Compensation in Natural Resource Liability Statutes," *Contem. Econ. Pol'y* 15 (1997).

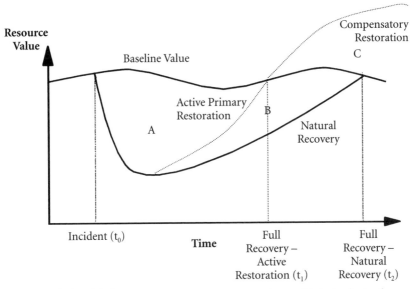

19.2 Relationship between compensatory restoration and interim lost value

value due to the injuries, including both direct use and passive use values.[8] Direct use values may derive, for example, from recreational, commercial, cultural or historical, or other uses of resources. Passive use values may derive from valuing protection of the resource for its own sake (or for direct human uses that are difficult to quantify, such as off-site uses like birdwatching supported by on-site ecological services), for use of the resource by others, or as a bequest to future generations. The regulations also identify a non-exclusive list of valuation methods that may be used.

Measures of damages in international contexts

Most international conventions pertaining to transboundary pollution contain liability provisions for "ecological" or "environmental" damages, in addition to the more traditional damage categories of loss of life or personal injury, lost earnings or profit and property damages, and "reasonable" post-spill clean-up measures. The international provisions and the new OPA regulations appear to be on a path towards convergence with

---

[8] 15 C.F.R. § 990.53(d) and § 990.30.

restoration-based measures of damages; however, the scope of allowable restoration-based damages varies substantially across the different international conventions.

For example, the 1992 Protocols for the two major international conventions addressing oil spills – the 1969 International Convention on Civil Liability for Oil Pollution Damage (CLC) and the 1971 International Convention on the Establishment of an International Fund for Compensation for Oil Pollution Damage (Fund) – extend the definition of pollution damage to include the "costs of reasonable measures of reinstatement actually undertaken or to be undertaken."[9] In this context, reinstatement is generally understood to refer only to reinstatement of the specific types of resources that were injured, though the guidance documents are not explicit.[10] A number of draft conventions have liability schemes comparable to the 1992 Protocols for the international oil spill conventions, including the Draft Convention on Liability and Compensation for Damage in Connection with the Carriage of Hazardous and Noxious Substances by Sea[11] (in preparation since 1984), draft protocols for the 1989 Basel Convention on the Control of Transboundary Movements of Hazardous Wastes and Their Disposal,[12] and the Convention on Civil Liability for Damage Caused During Carriage of Dangerous Goods by Road, Rail and Inland Transport Vessels.[13]

In contrast, several recent conventions or draft conventions have clearer and broader definitions of "ecological damages" that allow replacing damaged components of the environment to provide equivalent compensation

[9] 1992 Protocol to the 1969 International Convention on Civil Liability for Oil Pollution Damage, Art. 2(3).

[10] *See* 1971 International Convention on the Establishment of an International Fund for Compensation for Oil Pollution Damage (Fund), FUND/WGR.7/21, Annex I, p. 4.

[11] Convention on Liability and Compensation for Damage in Connection with the Carriage of Hazardous and Noxious Substances by Sea, IMO LEG 68/11 (March 30, 1993) and IMO LEG 69/3 (May 17, 1993).

[12] 1992 Protocol to the 1969 International Convention on Civil Liability for Oil Pollution Damage, Art. 2(3). In previous versions the draft retained more explicit alternative draft measures of damages, including creation of comparable environment in another area (UNEP/CHW.1/WG.1/4/2); however, they were deleted from the last draft on the grounds that the "issues were mainly dealt with in [the definitions section and the broader liability section] and that forms and modalities could be dealt with under national law."

[13] Convention on Civil Liability for Damage Caused During Carriage of Dangerous Goods by Road, Rail and Inland Transport Vessels (Geneva, Oct. 10, 1989), Intern. Transport Treaties, Suppl. (March 14, 1990).

when measures of reinstatement are not feasible.[14] Further, some draft conventions specifically include the possibility of compensation in monetary or resource terms. For example, the draft protocol for the 1988 Antarctic Convention specifically allows for calculations of lost value as an alternative to reinstatement costs when reinstatement or the introduction of the equivalent of the damaged resources is not possible.[15]

However, all of these provisions lack consistency or at least clarity about the treatment of the interim loss of services pending reinstatement of the same, or replacement with the equivalent of the injured resources. When restoration of the same or equivalent resources is not feasible, compensation for lost services will occur; but when restoration is feasible, there does not tend to be a provision for interim losses. Yet, as noted above, a substantial body of law and economics literature argues that, in order to provide adequate incentives for parties to take precautions to prevent harm to the environment, the responsible parties should bear the full social costs of accidents. The full social costs would include interim losses, which may be quite large.

The clearest statement in international documents of the "full compensation" measure of damages appears in the recommendations of the United Nations Environment Program (UNEP) Working Group of Experts on Liability and Compensation for Environmental Damage Arising from Military Activities,[16] charged with interpreting the liability principles articulated in UN Security Council Resolution 687. The resolution reaffirmed that Iraq was "liable under international law for any direct loss, damage, including environmental damage and the depletion of natural resources, or injury to foreign Governments, nationals and corporations" that occurred "as a result of Iraq's unlawful invasion and occupation

---

[14] See, e.g., the Council of Europe Convention on Civil Liability for Damage Resulting from Activities Dangerous to the Environment (1993), Article 2(8) and (9); the UN Economic Commission for Europe Task Force Guidelines on Responsibility and Liability regarding Trans-boundary Water Pollution (1990); and the draft revisions of the Vienna Convention on Civil Liability for Nuclear Damage (1963).

[15] Draft protocol to the 1988 Antarctic Convention (April 10, 1994), XVIII ATCM/WP.2. See also the measures of damages in the draft articles of the International Law Commission on International Liability for Injurious Consequences Arising out of Acts not Prohibited by International Law, Art. 24(a).

[16] United Nations Environment Program, *Report of the Working Group of Experts on Liability and Compensation for Environmental Damage Arising from Military Activities* (May 17, 1996).

of Kuwait."[17] In setting the criteria for the claims for these damages, the United Nations Compensation Commission Governing Council articulated the following as a non-exclusive set of categories of damages:

(a) Abatement and prevention of environmental damage, including expenses directly relating to fighting oil fires and stemming the flow of oil in coastal and international waters;
(b) Reasonable measures already taken to clean and restore the environment or future measures which can be documented as reasonably necessary to clean and restore the environment;
(c) Reasonable monitoring and assessment of the environmental damage for the purposes of evaluating and abating the harm and restoring the environment;
(d) Reasonable monitoring of public health and performing medical screenings for the purposes of investigation and combating increased health risks as a result of the environmental damage; and
(e) Depletion of or damage to natural resources.[18]

The Working Group of Experts explicitly added an additional category ("Other environmental damage"), citing the judgment of the Permanent Court of International Justice (PCIJ) in the *Chorzów Factory (Indemnity) Case*.[19] In that case, the Court found that reparation for a wrongful act "must, as far as possible, wipe out all the consequences of the illegal act and reestablish the situation which would, in all probability, have existed if that act had not been committed." Specifically, the damages are to be "in kind," but if that is not possible, damages require "payment of a sum corresponding to the value which a restitution in kind would bear."

Thus, the Working Group's additional category ("Other environmental damage") included:

(a) Recoveries for permanent damage to the environment where clean-up or restoration would not be physically possible, reasonable or otherwise feasible, or where clean-up or restoration was not successful; and
(b) recoveries for interim damage pending full clean-up or restoration.[20]

The Working Group report explicitly discusses differing points of view that exist in the international community concerning the appropriateness

---

[17] UN Security Council Resolution 687 (1991), para. E–16.
[18] Decisions of the United Nations Compensation Commission Governing Council, Decision 7, S/AC.26/1991/7/Rev.1 (March 17, 1992), para. 35.
[19] *Chorzów Factory (Indemnity) Case*, 1927 P.C.I.J. (ser. A) No. 17, 47.
[20] UNEP, *Report of the Working Group*, para. 74, p. 20.

of including full compensation for interim lost value (including both lost use and non-use, or "passive use," values) in the claim. The report also considers opposing views regarding the reliability of contingent valuation in valuing non-use values.[21] Contingent valuation is one of the "stated preference methods" referred to below, in which surveys are used to elicit individuals' intentions to purchase goods or to support public programs (for example through tax payments) that are not yet available.

Some of the concerns expressed about monetary compensation measures could be addressed by the adoption of the restoration-based approach to compensation articulated in the OPA regulations. The restoration-based approach deflects some of the public controversy about economic methods, in part because damages to be collected from the responsible parties are the costs of restoration, not the monetized value of interim losses, and in part because the uses of valuation methods are less demanding. As discussed in the next section, in some cases it may not be necessary to conduct valuation studies to determine the appropriate scale of compensatory restoration; alternatively, it may be possible to employ a simplified approach that is analogous to in-kind replacement of lost services with equivalent resources. In cases where valuation studies are conducted, selecting the appropriate scale of compensatory restoration actions generally requires precision only up to the ratio of lost value from injuries to prospective gains in value from resource projects, rather than precision in the absolute dollar amounts of lost value, which is required for calculating monetary compensation.

Approaches and methods in US natural resource liability laws for scaling compensatory restoration

I now consider the process and methods for calculating restoration-based compensation measures under OPA regulations. Under the restoration-based approach, the measure of damages becomes the cost of a restoration plan designed to restore resources to their baseline level and to compensate the public for interim losses from the time of the injury until the injured resources return to their but-for-the-injury levels. The process involves three steps: (1) identifying restoration alternatives; (2) determining the scale of restoration alternatives that would compensate for the

---

[21] *Ibid.*, paras. 78 and 79, pp. 21–22.

interim losses; and (3) selecting the preferred restoration alternative, consisting of primary and compensatory restoration projects.

Compensatory restoration generally involves enhancing resources or providing replacement resources. To ensure that the public is fully compensated for the interim losses, the scaling process determines the size of compensatory restoration actions for which the present discounted value of the gains from the actions equals the present discounted value of the interim losses from the injury (that is, the losses from the time of the injury until the resource returns to its but-for-the-injury state).

The scaling analysis for compensatory restoration actions (as part of a restoration alternative, including primary restoration actions) requires: (1) quantifying the extent and duration of lost services due to the injury, taking into account the primary restoration actions; (2) quantifying services gained for different scales of compensatory restoration actions; and (3) determining the relative value of the lost services due to the injury and the incremental gains in services from restoration actions (for example, the rate at which the public is willing to make tradeoffs between the lost services and the replacement services).

This section will discuss approaches appropriate for calculating resource compensation and identify economic methods for valuing different types of services – both those that are sold on markets and non-marketed services. First, however, I illustrate the concept of resource services, since the type of service being valued generally will determine which valuation method will be appropriate to value it. The concept of services is also critical to establishing restoration goals.

One can view natural resources as natural assets that provide services over time to other natural resources and humans. They are analogous to manufactured assets, such as housing or manufacturing plants and equipment, which also may provide flows of services over an extended time period. Damage to natural resources may interrupt for a time period the flow of ecological and human services (and values) provided by the natural resources. As a result, the public incurs interim losses from the injury. The two major valuation approaches determine either the change in value of the asset or the change in value of the flow of services. Since few resources are sold on a market, generally there are few established asset prices. But economists have developed a variety of strategies to infer the value of non-market service flows. However, a difficulty with this strategy is that for any given resource, it is difficult to articulate all the services it provides.

Returning to the example of wetland habitat to illustrate the concept of resource services, the major categories of ecological services include:[22]

- *Geo-hydrological*: floodwater storage and conveyance, groundwater recharge, pollution assimilation, sediment trapping, and nutrient cycling;
- *Habitat/production*: vegetation products; fishery, fur-bearer, and bird habitat and production; and
- *Ecosystem integrity*: natural open space, micro- and macro-climate regulation, carbon cycling, and biodiversity storehouse to provide resiliency.

Ecological services, in turn, may support direct uses by humans either on-site or off-site, as well as passive uses. For example, the floodwater storage function may provide storm protection for off-site property owners in the flood zone; the pollution assimilation and sediment trapping functions may increase water quality, supporting downstream water uses, such as swimming or municipal drinking water supply; and the habitat function may support birdwatching elsewhere along the flyway.

For the wetland example, major categories of natural resource services to humans include, but are not limited to:[23]

- *Commercial/public or private*: waterway navigation, drinking water, aquaculture, agricultural irrigation, commercial process water, property protection from storms, commercial and subsistence fishing and hunting, timber harvest;[24]
- *Recreational*: beach use/swimming, fishing, boating, wildlife viewing (including birdwatching), and hunting;
- *Cultural/historical*: religious and cultural ritual uses, historical research;

---

[22] For further discussion of wetland ecological services, see G. C. Daily, "Water Quality Improvement by Wetlands," in G. C. Daily (ed.), *Nature's Services* (1997); and V. H. Heywood, "Biodiversity and Ecosystem Functioning: Ecosystem Analyses," in V. H. Heywood (ed.), *Global Biodiversity Assessment* (1995).

[23] See S. Postel and S. Carpenter, "Freshwater Ecosystem Services," in Daily, *Nature's Services*, pp. 195–214, for a discussion of human services resulting from wetlands. See also C. Perrings et al., "Economic Values of Biodiversity," in Heywood, *Global Biodiversity Assessment*, ch. 12.

[24] Note that public sector claimants may recover commercial damages under Section 1002(b)(2)(D) of the OPA, while loss of profits or earning capacity are only recoverable by those experiencing the loss.

- *Health*: reductions in mortality and morbidity – for example, through provision of clean water, air, and foodstuffs (note that natural resource trustees generally are not allowed to claim for health effects – these tend to be private causes of action);
- *Scientific*: research promoting increased productivity in commercial and other activities; and development of life-saving pharmaceuticals; and
- *Passive use*: Species, habitat, and ecosystem protection for existence and for bequest value.

The first five categories of services represent direct uses by humans – for example, the natural resources provide services directly to individuals. The last category, passive use value, captures the fact that individuals may value natural resources independently of direct uses. Individuals may value the services provided to others, or the protection of natural resources for their own sake or as bequests to future generations. For example, the public may value an ecosystem supporting endangered species, even though these species are seldom viewed.

The OPA regulations outline two basic approaches for scaling compensatory restoration projects: the "resource-to-resource" or "service-to-service" approach (a simplified procedure applicable under certain circumstances) and the more general "valuation approach."

SERVICE-TO-SERVICE APPROACH

Service-to-service is analogous to an in-kind trading approach which does not require explicit valuation. Use of this approach presumes an in-kind equivalency between resources and services lost and resources and services to be gained. In this context, the scaling analysis simplifies to selecting the scale of a restoration action for which the present discounted quantity of discounted replacement services equals the present discounted quantity of services lost due to the injury. The use of discounting takes into account the differences in timing.

The judgments required to determine equivalencies for any substitutions across space, time, and species are analogous to those required for various environmental trading programs, including wetlands banks and sulfur dioxide emissions trading. These are also the same kind of judgments that are required for performing benefits transfer of values based in the literature for resource services, such as recreational uses. (Benefits transfer involves the application of existing value estimates or valuation functions developed in one context to address a comparable natural resource valuation question in a different context.) Habitat equivalency analysis, the application of the service-to-service approach to habitat injuries, has been employed in a wide range of US natural resource damage assessment cases, including oil spills, coral reef and seagrass bed groundings, and hazardous waste sites.[25]

Several critical assumptions must apply for the simplified service-to-service approach to be applicable. Because substitutions across space, time, and species are inevitable to some extent, it is essential to employ a common service metric that captures any significant differences in the quantities and qualities of services provided by injured and replacement resources. Further, the changes in resources and services must be sufficiently small that the value per unit of service is independent of the changes in the stock of resources (and of any changes in income or prices of other goods) associated with the losses from the injury and the gains from the compensatory projects after restoration to baseline. Finally, the number of beneficiaries should be roughly comparable for the injury and replacement resources. It is important to note that the second condition, in particular, is unlikely to be met for resources extensively and seriously impaired in a wartime context.

VALUATION APPROACH

Alternatively, the valuation approach to scaling compensatory restoration allows for the use of a variety of economic methods to determine what the appropriate tradeoffs are between gains from the proposed actions and interim losses from the injuries. This discussion focuses on the

---

[25] For applications, see R. C. Bishop, "The Potential Natural Resource Damages from the Asbestos Dump Site in the Dietzman Tract, Great Swamp National Refuge, New Jersey," report prepared for the Department of Interior (1992); R. J. Kopp, "An Analysis of Natural Resource Damages Claimed by the US Government from Dietzman Tract OU–3, Asbestos Dump, Great Swamp National Wildlife Refuge, New Jersey," report prepared on behalf of National Gypsum Company (1992); National Oceanic and Atmospheric Administration (NOAA), "Natural Resource Damage Assessment: M/V *Miss Beholden* Grounding Site Western Sambo Reef, Florida Keys National Marine Sanctuary, March 13, 1993" (1995); R2 and IEc, "Panther Creek Biological Restoration and Compensation Program," report prepared for NOAA (1995); and David Chapman et al., "Blackbird Mine HEA," NOAA Damage Assessment and Restoration Program Technical Paper 97-1 (1997). For an overview of habitat equivalency analysis, see NOAA, Damage Assessment and Restoration Program, Habitat Equivalency Analysis, Policy and Technical Paper Series, No. 95-1 (1997).

"value-to-value" version of the valuation approach, in which the compensatory actions are scaled so that the value gained from the actions is comparable to the value lost from the injuries. In certain circumstances, a variant of the valuation approach may be employed in which the restoration plan is scaled by equating the cost of the restoration plan to the dollar value of losses due to the injury. To apply this procedure, the trustees must judge that the valuation of the lost services is practicable, but valuation of the replacement natural resources or services cannot be performed within a reasonable time frame or at a reasonable cost. These circumstances generally will arise only in the context of spills with limited injuries.[26]

Economic methods for valuing natural resources traditionally have been characterized as either revealed preference or stated preference methods.[27] This section highlights each in turn.

Revealed preference studies infer values based on individuals' behavior, which is construed to reveal their preferences. Included in this set are demand and supply functions for commercially marketed resources, such as water, timber, or fish. It is possible to estimate demand and supply functions from data characterizing the quantity of goods or services purchased at different price levels. When a spill results in a restriction of supply or changes in quality for marketed goods, the models may be used to calculate consumer losses. Market models of demand and supply are employed less frequently than some other methods, because most uses of resources are not bought and sold directly in a market. However, the commercial losses from injury or depletion of supplies of water, timber, or oil, for example, may be valued using this method.

Analogous demand functions can be constructed for non-market goods and services, such as the recreational services provided by resources. Though a recreational trip is a non-market good (for example, without a market price), recreators pay an implicit "price" for use of a site's services through their travel and time costs. Consequently, data on recreators' travel costs and levels of use for different recreation sites can help estimate a travel cost demand function for the recreation sites.

---

[26] Factors to consider in determining whether a time frame or cost is "reasonable" are set forth in 15 C.F.R. § 990.27(a)(2).

[27] For more information about use of the different methods for valuing natural resources, see A. M. Freeman, *The Measurement of Environmental and Resource Values: Theory and Methods* (Washington, D.C.: Resources for the Future, 1993).

From the demand function, it may be possible to calculate the consumer losses due to the closure or impairment of a site or, alternatively, the consumer gains from site improvements. Consumer losses will be measured as the change in consumer surplus that occurs as a result of the change in quality or quantity of resources. Consumer surplus is the consumer analog to profit (or producer surplus) generated by firms. Whereas profit is the excess income received by a firm above what it costs to produce a good, consumer surplus is the additional value received by consumers above what it costs them to acquire a good.

In contrast, stated preference studies determine the value of goods or services based on the results of carefully designed surveys. The surveys present respondents with alternative scenarios describing goods or services and the context in which they will be provided, including price and method of payment. Values are constructed based on the assumption that individuals' preferences can be inferred from statements about the choices they would make among the alternative scenarios offered in the survey.

Because the good does not have to be currently available, these studies are much more flexible than revealed preference methods in that they can value changes in the quality or quantity of resources that are outside the range of current observation. For example, since all Great Lakes fisheries in the United States have fish consumption advisories, these methods can be used to value clean-up of contaminants sufficient to allow removal of the advisories, whereas revealed preference methods cannot. Further, with stated preference methods, it is possible to calculate the total value of goods and services, including both direct use and passive use values.

Some forms of stated preference surveys elicit respondents' intentions to visit recreational sites if changes described in the survey scenario were to occur at the sites. Other forms of stated preference surveys, such as the contingent valuation method, elicit individuals' intentions to purchase goods or to support public programs (through taxes) that are not yet available.

It may be possible to use some stated preference methods, or a combination of stated and revealed preference methods, to elicit direct resource tradeoffs required by the public, as in determining the amount of additional resource projects necessary to compensate for the injury. In particular, various authors have suggested that conjoint analysis, or more broadly, choice experiments, may be well suited for determining resource compensation.[28] These survey-based methods are used to derive the values of particular attributes of goods or services based on individuals' choices between different goods that vary in terms of their attributes or service levels. They have been employed extensively to assist firms in the design of new products, a design problem with some similarities to the problem of designing a restoration plan. Applications of conjoint analysis to environmental or health risk policy issues are beginning to appear in the literature.[29]

Alternatively, another procedure for calculating resource compensation would be to calculate separately the interim loss in value and the gains from alternative restoration projects. Trustees would select the method(s) to employ for the calculations from the set of standard methods for valuing natural resources, as described above.

Implications for environmental damages resulting from war

This section of the chapter considers the challenges of implementing a restoration-based approach to determine compensation for wartime injuries. I consider the implications for determining the costs of restoring resources to baseline, and for determining compensation for interim losses from the time of injury to full recovery of the resources.

During wartime, simultaneous injuries may occur to multiple resources providing basic life support (through air, water, and agricultural land) over a wide geographical area and with an expected long time horizon for recovery. The government may not be able to remediate resources as the

[28] See, for example, M. Mazzotta et al., "Natural Resource Damage Assessment: The Role of Resource Restoration," *Nat. Res. J.* 34 (1994), 153–78; K. E. Matthews et al., "The Potential Role of Conjoint Analysis in Natural Resource Damage Assessments," Triangle Economic Research Technical Working Paper (1996). For surveys of the literature, see D. A. Hensher, "Stated Preference Analysis of Travel Choices: The State of Practice," *Transportation* 21 (1994), 107–33; W. Adamowicz et al., "Combining Revealed and Stated Preference Methods for Valuing Environmental Amenities," *J. Envtl. Econ. & Mgmt.* 26 (1994), 271–92 . W. Adamowicz et al., "An Introduction to Attribute-based State Choice Methods," Advanis, Inc., prepared for NOAA Damage Assessment Center (1998).

[29] See, for example, P. C. Boxall et al., "A Comparison of Stated Preference Methods for Environmental Valuation," *Ecol. Econ.* 18 (1996), 243–53; Christopher Gan and E. Jane Luzar, "A Conjoint Analysis of Waterfowl Hunting in Louisiana," *J. Agric. & Applied Econ.* 25 (1993), 36–45; John Mackenzie, "A Comparison of Contingent Preference Models," *Am. J. Agric. Econ.* 75 (1993), 593–603; and James Opaluch et al., "Evaluating Impacts from Noxious Facilities: Including Public Preferences in Current Siting Mechanisms," *J. Envtl. Econ. & Mgmt.* 24 (1993), 41–59.

injuries occur and prevent or lessen continuing injury processes. Rather, remediation may not occur until after the war is over.

The sheer scope of the environmental damages may militate against the feasibility of complete restoration of resources to their but-for-the-war state in a limited time period. Consequently, the scope of injuries may pose difficulties in implementing a fully restoration-based measure of damages. (This may not be a serious binding constraint since, in any case, the responsible party may not have the financial resources to cover primary restoration, much less compensatory restoration.) In such a context there clearly needs to be a prioritization of projects, focusing first on those pertaining to life support – including clean air, clean water, and the provision of food and energy supplies. As discussed above, several conventions – as well as the Report of the UNEP Working Group – allow for the use of monetary damages, rather than resource compensation, in such a context. However, such a provision is only achievable if the financial resources of the responsible party have not been exhausted by the claim for restoring resources to baseline.

Another major challenge occurs because the society most likely will have sustained major losses to other types of resources critical to creating value, including human resources, basic public and private infrastructure, and private property (produced capital). The changes in all types of resources will combine to affect incomes, prices, and non-market benefits within the society substantially.

The standard approach is to compartmentalize the calculations of damages into the different categories: mortality and morbidity, lost physical capital, lost income, and lost natural resource service flows. However, valuing lost benefit flows separately may miss out on the interaction effects among the individual components. Further complications arise when not all components of losses are compensable, which will generally be the case. The interactions may affect not only the determination of the scale of restoration projects required, but also the costs of restoration. Though market prices generally exist for the costs of restoration, the large scale of resources required in total – across the various injury categories – may lead to subsequent price increases that will be difficult to predict without considering the whole set of demands for compensation. Unless the interdependencies are adequately taken into account, the liability system is unlikely to yield the correct level of compensation overall.

Important interdependencies also may exist among the categories of environmental injuries, which – in a compartmentalized liability system – may be more feasible to consider than the broader effects. The magnitude of wartime injuries is such that environmental goods and services that do not appear to be close substitutes or complements in peacetime may reveal interdependencies at the scale of losses experienced in wartime. For example, the value of the total loss of various ecosystems may be greater than the sum of the losses counted ecosystem-by-ecosystem or service-by-service. To develop valuation models, the challenge is constructing them in a way that incorporates a broader range of interactions across resource services than is standard practice for peacetime.

Further, the various simplified approaches are likely to be unreliable indicators of value. These approaches rely on the assumption that the decrease in supply due to the injury and the increase in supply above baseline as a result of the compensatory restoration project are sufficiently small that the value per unit of service is independent of the changes in supply. Yet, as noted above, as the extent of injuries increases, the value of the last unit lost will be substantially greater than the value of the last unit supplied in the prewar baseline of relative abundance.

Consequently, in wartime the simplified in-kind trading approach discussed in the previous section will not be reliable. Another simplified approach, benefits transfer, will suffer from similar difficulties. As previously noted, benefits transfer involves the application of existing value estimates or valuation functions developed in one context to address a comparable natural resource valuation question in a different context. If there is a major change in the supply of resources and resource services relative to peacetime, the transfer of peacetime values will tend to understate by a substantial margin the value of the losses. The simplified models could serve as a useful starting point for thinking about the problem, but either site-specific valuation studies or further simplification of assumptions will be necessary.

Other challenges can be identified for specific types of models. In stated preference models, it is conventional to forego the more correct willingness-to-accept (WTA) framework for compensation for injuries to resources in which the public has an implicit property right, due to difficulties in eliciting credible WTA responses. Surveys eliciting WTA for foregoing an amenity have a higher incidence of respondents giving protest responses or infinite values. For example, some respondents may reject the implication of "selling" the property right to the resource; altern- atively, because there is no income constraint for WTA, other respond- ents may state amounts that are in excess of their "true" value.[30] Further in the case of eliciting WTA for injuries *after* the injuries have occurred, many responses are likely to contain a "punitive" component that is not consistent with the concept of compensation per se. Consequently, most studies employ a willingness-to-pay (WTP) framework. For example, to value the loss to the public from the interim losses due to the *Exxon Valdez* oil spill, the public was asked how much they would be willing to pay for a plan to prevent a future oil spill of the size of *Exxon Valdez* in Prince William Sound.[31]

Two major issues arise with this substitution. First, it may be very difficult to elicit WTP for the scale of resource injuries caused by a wartime disaster. People will be focused on the war as the origin of such injuries, and on seeking compensation from the responsible parties. Consequently they are likely to reject the concept of paying for any program that could be devised to prevent comparable injuries in the future, as was carried out to elicit WTP to prevent the *Exxon Valdez* oil spill.

Second, in a context of extensive damage to public resources, in tandem with extensive losses of income and other property, WTP is likely to under- estimate seriously the more correct WTA measure. (I make the standard assumption that, on average, an individual's value of the public resources – the willingness-to-pay for increases in the resources – tends to increase with income.) The baseline income level for the WTP elicitation will become the post-wartime level, which may be dramatically lower than the but-for-the-war level. Even if the baseline income level were corrected, in this context the income constraint on WTP is likely to lead to potentially much lower values than WTA, which is not constrained by income. (Note that an analogous issue with substituting WTP for WTA also arises with revealed preference models.)

Large-scale depletion or contamination of natural resources that would be harvested and sold over an extended time period (such as oil or under- ground water supplies) also poses a variety of valuation challenges. The

---

[30] R. C. Mitchell and R. T. Carson, *Using Surveys to Value Public Goods: The Contingent Valuation Method* (Washington, D.C.: Resources for the Future, 1989).

[31] R. T. Carson et al., "A Contingent Valuation Study of Lost Passive Use Values Resulting from the *Exxon Valdez* Oil Spill: Report to the Attorney General of the State of Alaska, vols. 1 and 2" (1992).

UNEP Working Group recommended using the discounted cash flow method to calculate net present value of the loss in asset value because use of the current market price would be quite misleading when the size of the loss was so great that it could only have been expected to have been produced and marketed over a significant time period. However, the Working Group acknowledged that there would be substantial uncertainty in estimating the market prices through time, the choice of production schedule, and the resulting structure of costs through time.[32]

Conclusion

In this chapter I argue that the US restoration-based approach to natural resource damages provides a valuable model for other environmental liability regimes designed to protect natural resources in international or national contexts. Loss or damage by contamination or impairment of the environment is now generally recognized in international liability agreements. Examples range from the International Convention on Civil Liability for Oil Pollution Damage to the Antarctic Convention. In addition to the long-standing provision for post-spill clean-up measures, the predominant concept in the new versions is the costs of resource "reinstatement" measures. However, consensus regarding the appropriate scope of environmental damages is still evolving.

The new US restoration-based approach also relies upon the cost of resource restoration measures, thereby providing a new common point of reference between the United States and the international community provisions. The basic measure of natural resource damages is the costs of implementing a restoration plan, designed to return resources to baseline and to compensate for interim losses.

In the predominant versions of both the international and the US damage measures, damages are to be quantified in financial terms (costs of restoration or reinstatement). This format complies with the most restrictive provisions imposed by some of the international protocols. A major difference, however, is that the US law clearly identifies the two elements of compensation required to make the public "whole": replacement of the injured natural assets or their expected flow of services through time, *plus* compensation for interim losses during the time period from the injury

---

[32] UNEP, *Report of the Working Group*, paras. 82–97.

until the injured resources or their replacements recover to their but-for-the-injury state.

The recommendations of the Report of the UNEP Working Group interpreting UN Security Council Resolution 687 for war damages in Kuwait are consistent with the concept of full compensation. Wartime applications of either the monetary or resource compensation measures, however, will face some difficulties. The sheer magnitude of the environmental damages caused by wartime activities may militate against the feasibility of complete restoration of resources to their but-for-the-war state. Consequently, it may be difficult to implement a fully restoration-based measure of damages. In this case, it may be necessary to revert to monetary compensation of damages for interim losses.

Furthermore, the sheer magnitude of wartime injuries to the human, natural, and produced resources of an economy will pose a number of challenges to applying the various methods for valuing resource or monetary compensation. In recognition of the tremendous changes that occur throughout the economy, it is important to establish a baseline level of resource values in the economy but-for-the-war, as well as the changes from that baseline level due to the war. Further, it is important to take into account interaction effects in damages and costs across injury categories. As a consequence, simplified valuation approaches would not take account of many important dynamics of a wartime context.

20

VALUING PUBLIC HEALTH DAMAGES
ARISING FROM WAR

MARK DICKIE AND SHELBY GERKING

Introduction

Environmental and public health consequences of war recently have
received increased attention in light of circumstances surrounding the
1990–91 Gulf War. During the conflict, which began on August 2, 1990,
Iraq demonstrated its willingness to use environmental destruction as a
weapon of war by setting fire to several hundred oil wells and releasing
millions of gallons of oil into the Persian Gulf. The fires burned for approximately ten months before they could be extinguished, resulting in smoke
clouds that traveled as far as Pakistan and black rains that fell in several
countries of the Middle East.[1] Overall, the damage represents one of the
most serious environmental catastrophes in recorded history, with adverse
effects extending to human health, agricultural productivity, and to the
ecosystem generally.

This chapter surveys available methods of estimating monetary damages to public health that can arise from environmental destruction occurring during wartime. These methods may be applied to evaluating a subset
of environmental claims arising from the 1990–91 Gulf War. Kuwait has

Portions of this chapter rely on material presented in *Handbook for Noncancer Valuation: Review
Draft* (Industrial Economics, Inc., September 1997). Research for that report was funded by the
US Environmental Protection Agency under Contract 68–W6–0061. This chapter does not neces-
sarily reflect the views of the Agency, and no official endorsement should be inferred.

[1] For chemical analyses of the smoke plumes, see K. A. Browning et al., "Environmental Effects
from Burning Oil Wells in the (Persian) Gulf," *Weather* 47(6) (1992), 201–11 (chemical analysis
of the smoke plumes); G. J. Jenkins et al., "Aircraft Measurements of the Gulf Smoke Plume,"
Weather 47(6) (1992), 212–20; W. S. Shaw "Smoke at Bahrain During the Kuwaiti Oil Field
Fires," *Weather* 47(6) (1992), 220–25. For a discussion of the effects on climate, see R. D. Small,
"Environmental Impact of the Fires in Kuwait," *Nature* 350 (1991), 11–12.

submitted five claims to the United Nations Compensation Commission concerning: (1) damage to groundwater resources; (2) damage related to the formation of lakes of oil in the desert; (3) damage to terrestrial resources; (4) damage to marine and coastal resources; and (5) damage to public health. Claims for public health damages seek to recover US $1,457,761,466 in estimated present and future costs of injuries and diseases inflicted on Kuwait's citizens as a result of Iraqi aggression. This figure includes the costs of establishing and operating a data repository or exposure registry for five years; the cost of conducting a human health risk assessment, including evaluation of environmental conditions and health risks to which the Kuwaiti population was exposed; the cost of conducting studies to determine long-term health impacts of the Iraqi aggression; the cost of conducting a long-term clinical monitoring program; the medical expenditures required to treat traumatic injuries caused by mines and ordnance; and costs related to the treatment of diseases arising from the Iraqi aggression.[2]

Methods of health valuation discussed in this chapter have had a long history of application to a broad range of situations involving improvements to or degradation of the environment in the United States and other countries. In addition, they have been applied to estimate values of both morbidity and mortality. Despite extensive use over the past thirty years, however, these methods and the resulting estimates of monetary benefits or damages still are highly controversial. At one extreme, some people believe that it is simply inappropriate to value health in monetary terms. Additionally, there is no single, universally accepted method for computing monetary values of changes in health status, and the same method in the hands of different investigators often produces divergent estimates.

Special problems in applying public health valuation methods to situations involving war only increase the level of uncertainty associated with damage estimates. For example, environmental damages (e.g., from oil well and refinery fires and from marine pollution) can be exacerbated in situations where armed forces may prevent giving them prompt attention. Resulting damages to public health arise involuntarily, both in the country under attack and in countries not directly participating in the conflict. Public health problems can arise indirectly when the ecosystem is damaged on a broad scale. Petroleum fires, for example, result in air pollution

---

[2] Public Authority for Assessment of Compensation for Damages Resulting from Iraqi Aggression (PAAC), *Oil and Environmental Claims Bulletin* (1997), 15.

that has detrimental consequences for public health both directly and indirectly through its effects on agriculture. Monetary costs for use in constructing damage estimates may be difficult to establish if economic infrastructure is stretched, causing wages and other prices to change sharply. Also, because some public health problems would exist had peace been maintained, it may be difficult to establish precisely the number of cases of particular diseases or deaths attributable to war.

The following section of this chapter presents the conceptual background that lies behind making monetary estimates of health damages. The next section describes available methods for making these assessments and suggests how they might be applied in situations in which environmental damages arise from war. This section also presents illustrative monetary health damage estimates that were developed in previous studies of environmental hazards. It is important to underscore the idea that these estimates are only suggestive and may or may not be applicable to the particular damages arising from war.

Background

Economists often define the benefits or damages associated with changes in health status as monetary equivalents of changes in well-being. In economic theory, an individual's well-being depends on consumption of goods and services, health status, and other environmental characteristics. Typically, dollar equivalents of changes in well-being are measured by willingness-to-pay or willingness-to-accept compensation. Willingness-to-pay (WTP) for health is the largest amount of money an individual would voluntarily forego to obtain an improvement (or to avoid a decrement) in health. Willingness-to-accept (WTA) compensation is the smallest amount of money that would be accepted as compensation to forego an improvement (or endure a decrement) in health. In either case, the focus is on a tradeoff between health and money that would leave a person's overall level of well-being unchanged.

Although WTP and WTA both measure monetary equivalents of changes in well-being, they are not identical concepts because they adopt different reference points.[3] WTP measures what a person would pay for better health, while WTA measures what an individual would have to be

---

[3] For a recent discussion of the WTP–WTA disparity, see T. C. Brown and R. Gregory, "Why the WTA–WTP Disparity Matters," *Ecol. Econ.* 28 (1999), 323–25.

paid to endure worse health. A person's WTP cannot exceed income; WTA has no upper limit and would be at least as large as WTP. The difference between the two measures is likely to be small for small changes in health, but there may be large differences for large changes in health. As discussed by Carson and Mitchell,[4] however, the choice between using WTP and WTA is a question of property rights. WTP is used when the public is responsible for paying to avoid pollution of a public resource, and WTA is used when the public must be compensated for tolerating pollution of a public resource. In other words, WTA is the most appropriate choice when current law or outcomes of adjudication confer property rights to the environment on those exposed involuntarily to contamination. Thus, WTA is perhaps the more relevant of the two valuation concepts when assessing environmental and public health damages from war. The remainder of this chapter, however, focuses more heavily on WTP because it turns out to be less problematic to quantify and because it has been used more frequently in the health valuation literature. Nevertheless, much of the discussion would apply equally to the WTA measure and research continues to refine this approach to health valuation.

In general, WTP depends on two factors: preferences and opportunities. Preferences represent the strength of desires for or perceptions about how health, market goods and services, and other features of the environment affect well-being. Preferences usually are taken as given and no judgments are made about whether one set of preferences is "better" than another. Opportunities refer to the means available to satisfy preferences and are determined by prices, money income, and time. To see how the two concepts fit together, consider a person who has a strong desire for good health and another person who has a weaker desire for good health. If each person faces the same opportunities, the first presumably would be willing to pay more to avoid air pollution episodes. This comparison, however, is deceptively simple because both preferences and opportunities can differ greatly between people. For example, differences can be related to age, gender, schooling, pre-existing health impairments, or other personal characteristics.

Measurement of WTP often is based on the premise that actual behavior reveals preferences. In particular, there are two basic methods available for

---

[4] R. T. Carson and R. C. Mitchell, "Contingent Valuation and the Legal Arena," in R. J. Kopp (ed.), *Valuing Natural Assets: The Economics of Natural Resource Damage Assessment* (Washington, D.C.: Resources for the Future, 1993).

measuring WTP for health. One method is called "revealed preference" because it infers WTP by linking health to a related market good. For example, if two acetaminophen tablets relieve one headache and provide no other benefit, anyone buying acetaminophen must value the last headache relieved at no less than the price of two tablets. Revealed preference is most easily appreciated when applied to goods traded in markets, but it also has application when valuing changes in health.

The second method is called "stated preference" because it relies on individuals' statements about how they would behave in a hypothetical situation, or how much a hypothetical change in health is worth to them. For example, survey respondents might be asked whether they would be willing to pay $25 to eliminate one day of a particular acute respiratory symptom.

Measuring WTP for health in an environmental context presents at least four specific problems that arise no matter whether the revealed preference or stated preference approach is used. First, when environmental quality changes, there are several health-related impacts on well-being; it is easy to overlook one or more of these, resulting in an underestimate of the value of health. Health effects may consist of several specific symptoms, but may also include anxiety, pain, suffering, and other aspects that are difficult to describe precisely. Second, the health of one person may affect the well-being of another, suggesting that the focus on each individual's WTP for his or her own health may be too narrow in many cases. Parents are concerned about the well-being of their children, and people are often concerned about others outside their own household. Third, health effects of exposure to environmental contamination may be immediate or delayed, making it important to consider how the timing of health effects influences WTP. For example, WTP today to avoid a specific health effect would be lower the farther into the future it is expected to occur. Fourth, environmental contamination may not cause specific health effects with certainty, but rather may increase the risk of poor health. Uncertainty can make estimating WTP for health quite complex for several reasons including the fact that scientific assessments of environmental risks are seldom congruent with people's risk beliefs.

Health valuation methods

Before reviewing specific methods for estimating WTP for health, it is useful to distinguish between types of health outcomes that can arise from environmental hazards. Differences in the kind and degree of health effects can influence both the magnitude of the WTP estimate as well as the choice of a valuation method. Illness or morbidity either can be short-term (acute) or long-term (chronic), and mortality can occur immediately or at a later time. Both common sense and economic theory predict that WTP to avoid a mild, short-term symptom that is easily relieved is smaller than WTP to avoid a severe, long-lasting impairment that has no known cure. Besides differences in duration and severity, WTP to avoid adverse health effects also can depend on characteristics of people affected (i.e., age, income, and prior health status) and on the context in which the health effects occurred (i.e., whether hazards are imposed or borne voluntarily). Additionally, some methods are better suited to valuing morbidity effects, while others are more applicable in valuing mortality effects.

Regardless of the health aspect to be valued, however, health outcomes stand as an intermediate link between environmental change and economic value. There is a clear distinction in disciplines between estimating dose-response functions for environmental exposures and resulting health effects, and estimating WTP of affected individuals for avoiding those health effects. This distinction suggests two general approaches to health effects measurement for valuation.[5] The common approach is to value health effects, while taking an assessment of the pollution–health link as given. An alternative (and more complex) approach is to incorporate the environment–health relationship into a more comprehensive model of economic behavior. Both approaches are discussed below in the context of specific methods for valuing health outcomes.

COST-OF-ILLNESS METHOD

The cost-of-illness method measures direct and indirect costs of morbidity and premature mortality. This method is closely related to the human capital approach to mortality valuation, which focuses on the present discounted value of earnings lost and is sometimes used in legal proceedings involving wrongful death. Direct costs include the value of goods and services used to treat, rehabilitate, and accommodate ill or impaired individuals.

[5] M. Dickie et al., "Improving Accuracy and Reducing Costs of Environmental Benefit Assessments: Reconciling Averting Behavior and Contingent Valuation Benefit Estimates of Reducing Symptoms of Ozone Exposure," Draft Report to the Office of Policy, Planning and Evaluation, US Environmental Protection Agency (1987).

Indirect costs reflect the value of foregone productivity, most often measured as foregone earnings. The total cost of illness is the sum of direct and indirect costs.[6] The relative size of direct and indirect costs may vary by impairment as well as by estimation approach. Indirect costs account for about 60 percent of the total cost of illness in the United States, according to Cooper and Rice, counting losses from both morbidity and premature mortality.[7] The share of total costs attributable to morbidity-induced indirect costs alone is about 22 percent. For the major impairments studied by Hartunian et al. – cancer, coronary heart disease, stroke, and motor vehicle injuries – indirect costs account for about 70 percent of the total, again counting both morbidity and mortality losses.[8]

Link to health valuation theory

The main theoretical issue concerning use of the cost-of-illness approach is that the method measures ex post costs rather than either WTP or WTA. A number of researchers have examined the theoretical relationship between WTP and cost-of-illness or human capital measures of value. Studies of mortality valuation have concluded that foregone earnings from premature death are a lower bound on WTP-based values of statistical lives.[9] The comparison of the cost-of-illness and WTP-based morbidity values is not as straightforward, but most authors agree that under plausible conditions an individual's cost of illness is a lower bound on WTP.[10] The main reason is that the cost-of-illness method does not account for elements of WTP such as pain and suffering, defensive expenditures, lost leisure time, and potential altruistic benefits. Additionally, it does not

---

[6] Standard references on cost-of-illness methodology include D. P. Rice, "Estimating the Cost of Illness," *Health Econ. Series*, Public Health Service, Washington, D.C. (1966); B. S. Cooper and D. P. Rice, "The Economic Cost of Illness Revisited," *Soc. Security Bull.* (1976), 21–36; D. P. Rice et al., "The Economic Cost of Illness: A Replication and Update," *Health Care Financing Rev.* 39 (1985), 61–81; N. S. Hartunian, C. N. Smart, and M. S. Thompson, *The Incidence and Economic Costs of Major Health Impairments* (Lexington, Mass.: Lexington Books, 1981); T. Hu and F. H. Sandifer, *Synthesis of Cost-of-Illness Methodology: Part 1*, Report to the National Center for Health Services Research, Department of Health and Human Services (1981).

[7] Cooper and Rice, "The Economic Cost of Illness."

[8] Hartunian et al., *The Incidence and Economic Costs.*

[9] B. C. Conley, "The Value of Human Life in the Demand for Safety," *Am. Econ. Rev.* 66(1) (1976), 45–55; W. B. Arthur, "The Economics of Risks to Life," *Am. Econ. Rev.* 71(1) (1981), 54–64.

[10] W. Harrington and P. R. Portney, "Valuing the Benefits of Health and Safety Regulation," *J. Urban Econ.* 22 (1987), 101–12; Mark C. Berger, "Valuing Changes in Health Risks: A Comparison of Alternative Measures," *S. Econ. J.* 53 (1987), 977–84.

account for the fact that civilians may suffer wartime illness costs involuntarily. A related theoretical problem affecting the cost-of-illness method is that, especially for minor impairments, individuals exercise considerable choice over the amount of medical care and work loss they experience. The cost-of-illness method in effect measures the costs of these choices, rather than the dollar equivalent of the loss in well-being caused by the illness itself.

Methodological problems

The most serious methodological problems affecting the cost-of-illness approach concern the measurement of the value of lost production. Key difficulties include: (1) accounting for the full impact of chronic illness on earnings; (2) choosing an appropriate wage rate to apply to lost work time; and (3) valuing time spent in unpaid work.

Morbidity can affect earnings in three distinct ways. A chronic or acute illness can cause a person to miss regularly scheduled work time. A chronic illness also may limit job options, causing a person to work in a job with fewer regularly scheduled hours. Extreme cases of this second effect are the complete withdrawal from the workforce of a disabled person and the lost productivity of a person who dies prematurely. Finally, any restrictions on job opportunities caused by chronic impairment may result in a lower rate of pay per hour worked. These distinctions are important because some measures of work loss count only hours missed from a person's schedule, evaluated at the hourly wage. While this would be appropriate for most cases of acute illness, it would not capture long-term effects of chronic illness on usual hours or wages.

Even in peacetime, the choice of a wage rate to apply to time lost from work raises difficult issues. Wages are closely linked to education and age or work experience, as well as to gender and other demographic characteristics. Incidence rates of many health impairments also vary markedly by these same characteristics. If wage rates applied to lost work time do not match the demographic distribution of illness, indirect cost estimates will be inaccurate indicators of actual earnings loss. For example, more educated persons earn higher wages and tend to be healthier, suffering fewer days of work loss than less-educated, lower-paid workers. Most cost-of-illness studies do not control for effects of schooling on wages and work loss, leading to possible overestimates of foregone earnings. Choosing appropriate wage rates to apply during and after a war presents additional complications. Because of disruptions in the labor market, some people may work in exchange for goods, rather than money. Also, monetary problems experienced during wartime may lead to wage and price controls or, in extreme cases, hyperinflation. Consequently, an important issue to consider is whether to use pre- or postwar wages and prices in assessing indirect costs from lost productivity.

More practical problems arise for measuring foregone productivity of persons not employed in paid work, such as homemakers and those who may have lost jobs because of war. Some studies do not value the time of people not in the labor force. A more common approach is to apply the same wage rate used for comparable, employed persons. Another approach that has been applied when estimating the lost productivity of homemakers is to add up the cost of hiring out all services that typically were performed. In the case of persons not in the labor force because of wartime disruptions, the situation is more complex. On the one hand, the prewar wage rate could be used, but another approach would be to use the pre- or postwar wage rate earned by a hypothetical individual with similar schooling, work experience, and other labor market characteristics.

Data collection and analysis

Costs of illness usually are measured either on a prevalence or an incidence basis. Prevalence-based measures assign costs of all existing cases of an illness to the year in which the costs are incurred and typically follow some variation of the methodology set out by Rice.[11] Incidence-based measures assign the present value of all costs of illness – from onset to recovery or death – to the year of onset and follow a methodology similar to that of Hartunian et al.[12] There is little difference between prevalence-based and incidence-based costs for short-term illnesses, but the differences increase with the duration of the illness. Usually, prevalence costs exceed incidence costs unless incidence is rising rapidly, and the difference is larger for indirect than for direct costs. Both approaches, however, rely on market cost and wage data. As emphasized above, wartime disruptions to the economy may result in difficult choices concerning which data to use.

---

[11] Rice, "Estimating the Cost of Illness."
[12] Hartunian et al., *The Incidence and Economic Costs.*

In any case, prevalence- and incidence-based approaches have different data requirements and different degrees of aggregation. Prevalence costs are often computed from aggregate data. Total health care expenditures are divided into several categories such as hospital care, services of physicians and other health care professionals, nursing home care, drugs and medical supplies, and non-personal health care services. Expenditures in each category are then allocated to specific diseases, and a direct cost of a disease is found by summing over expenditure categories. Indirect costs are typically estimated by applying a monetary value to the duration of restricted activity. For example, Cooper and Rice apply mean earnings by age and gender to work loss days for employed people and use a market-cost approach to value homemakers' bed disability days.[13]

The incidence-cost approach, on the other hand, estimates direct and indirect costs for each year of illness, weighted by the probability that an individual would survive each year, and computing the present discounted value of this stream of costs. Direct costs are built up from actual costs incurred by patients. Surprisingly little data, however, exists on the costs of treating specific illnesses over time, even for major impairments. As a result, direct illness costs are often estimated from data presented in literature reviews or from information obtained from medical experts. Indirect costs are computed using estimates of the duration of impairment and the earnings differential attributable to the disability. In principle, this approach will include all sources of lost earnings among impaired, employed individuals, including shorter work schedules and lower wages. However, data on earnings losses for chronic impairments are quite sparse. Two other practical problems with this approach involve the choice of a discount rate and forecasting future direct and indirect costs.

CONTINGENT VALUATION

Contingent valuation approaches are stated preference methods for directly eliciting an individual's valuation of a hypothetical commodity, usually using survey research methods. The method was first proposed by Ciriacy-Wantrup and was first applied years later by Davis.[14] Early work

---

[13] Cooper and Rice, "The Economic Cost of Illness."

[14] S. V. Ciriacy-Wantrup, "Capital Returns from Soil-Conservation Practices," *J. Farm Econ.* 29 (1947), 1181–96; R. K. Davis, "The Value of Outdoor Recreation: An Economic Study of the Maine Wood," PhD thesis, Harvard University (1963).

often focused on valuing recreation benefits[15] and air quality, visibility or aesthetic environmental preferences,[16] but assessments of a whole range of values relevant to public policy, including values for avoided morbidity and mortality, currently use the method. Contingent valuation methods have been used to value avoidance of respiratory and other symptoms of air pollution exposure, avoidance of asthma-related illness,[17] reductions in skin cancer risk,[18] and reductions in risk of death from job-related hazards.[19] The method also has been used to estimate values of minor symptomatic discomforts experienced by Iranian people because of air pollution problems caused by the 1990–91 Gulf War.[20] Moreover, it could be used to value other types of public health damage arising from war, such as diseases that have a long latency period (i.e. cancer) as well as risk of premature death.

For example, in Rahmatian's study,[21] data measuring contingent values were obtained from 100 residents of Tehran. A questionnaire was developed to collect data on symptom frequency and severity as well as steps taken to avoid exposure to air pollutants in the previous month. Values for seven individual symptoms were developed: (1) cough; (2) shortness of breath; (3) eye irritation; (4) headache; (5) chest pain; (6) sore throat; and (7) asthma. Respondents were asked to state their maximum willingness to pay to avoid these symptoms on a per symptom per day basis. Mean values of symptoms avoided per day ranged from 18,390 rials for coughing to 40,510 rials for an asthma attack. Median values of willingness to pay for symptoms avoided were roughly 70 percent of the mean values, indicating a tendency for some respondents to provide relatively large bids.

---

[15] See R. Bishop and T. Heberlein, "Measuring Values of Extramarket Goods: Are Indirect Values Biased?" *Am. J. Agric. Econ.* 61 (1979), 926–30; C. Ciecchetti and V. K. Smith, "Congestion, Quality Deterioration, and Optimal Use: Wilderness Recreation in the Spanish Peaks Primitive Area," *Soc. Science Res.* 2 (1973), 15–30; J. Hammack and G. Brown, *Waterfowl and Wetlands: Toward Bioeconomic Analysis* (Washington, D.C.: Resources for the Future, 1974).

[16] See D. S. Brookshire et al., "The Value of Public Goods: A Comparison of Survey and Hedonic Approaches," *Am. Econ. Rev.* 72 (1982), 165–77; Randall et al., "Bidding Games for Evaluation of Aesthetic Environmental Improvement," *J. Envtl. Econ. & Mgmt.* 1 (1974), 132–49.

[17] R. D. Rowe and L. G. Chestnut, *Oxidants and Asthmatics in Los Angeles: A Benefits Analysis*, Report to the Office of Policy Analysis, US Environmental Protection Agency (Washington, D.C., 1985).

[18] M. Dickie and S. Gerking, "Formation of Risk Beliefs, Joint Production and Willingness to Pay to Avoid Skin Cancer," *Rev. Econ. & Stat.* 78(3) (1996), 451–63.

[19] S. Gerking et al., "The Marginal Value of Job Safety: A Contingent Valuation Study," *J. Risk & Uncertainty* 1(2) (1988), 185–200.

[20] M. Rahmatian, "Valuing Reduced Morbidity," mimeo (Department of Economics, California State University–Fullerton, 1997).   [21] *Ibid.*

Contingent valuation is quite controversial, especially when applied to estimate passive-use values (the value of knowing that a resource exists, as opposed to the value of actively using it). But the method has been accepted by the US government for use in estimating certain types of benefits, including values of recreation areas and oil spills.[22] The potential controversy in using values from survey methods (such as contingent valuation) makes it particularly important to seek plausibility checks for these estimates.

Link to valuation theory

The contingent valuation method can measure either WTP or WTA (depending on how the valuation question is asked), and so is consistent with economic theory. If respondents understand the commodity to be valued and answer questions truthfully, the method yields estimates of either measure of value. The method is quite flexible; for example, valuation questions can ask for household WTP, or even for the WTP an individual may have for others outside of the household. Contingent valuation appears to be the only method capable of capturing these altruistic benefits. Also, contingent valuation potentially captures the full set of effects of illness on individual well-being. In situations involving risks, the method can elicit ex ante values, although many contingent valuation studies have estimated ex post values instead.

Methodological problems

Although the contingent valuation method sets out to find the theoretically correct measure of economic benefit, many economists doubt that the measures obtained actually correspond to individuals' true WTP.[23] The main objections to contingent valuation center on the hypothetical nature

---

[22] See R. Mitchell and R. T. Carson, *Using Surveys to Value Public Goods: The Contingent Valuation Method* (Washington, D.C.: Resources for the Future, 1989) (a standard reference on contingent valuation); R. G. Cummings et al. (eds.), *Valuing Environmental Goods: An Assessment of the Contingent Valuation Method* (Totowa, N.J.: Rowman & Allanheld, 1986); D. J. Bjornstad and J. R. Kahn, *The Contingent Valuation of Environmental Resources: Methodological Issues and Research Needs* (Cheltenham, UK and Brookfield, Vt.: Edward Elgar, 1996) (a comprehensive review of the method); P. A. Diamond and J. A. Hausman, "Contingent Valuation: Is Some Number Better Than No Number?" *J. Econ. Persp.* 8(4) (1994), 45–64 (a decidedly less sympathetic evaluation).

[23] Diamond and Hausman, "Contingent Valuation."

of the transaction. Because a respondent does not have to pay the amount stated, there may be little incentive to answer carefully. Most economists agree that strategic responses to contingent valuation questions are not a serious problem,[24] but some economists argue that the responses do not reflect stable preferences with the generally accepted properties. For example, researchers have expressed concern that contingent valuation responses are "insensitive to scope" and are unduly sensitive to the sequencing of alternatives to be valued.[25] Insensitivity to scope, for example, would occur if the WTP to avoid five symptoms was no larger than the WTP to avoid one of them. This effect is also known as "embedding" of values. Sequencing problems would imply that the values of individual symptom avoidance were unduly sensitive to the order in which the symptoms were presented to the respondents for valuation.

Other economists have suggested that related problems arise because people do not know precisely their own preferences. Whereas contingent valuation usually assumes that people "know their own minds," van Kooten et al. argue that preferences might be better treated from a fuzzy set perspective.[26]

Another criticism of contingent valuation involves the unfamiliarity of the valuation task. Respondents may not understand the commodity to be valued the way researchers intend, and respondents almost certainly lack experience paying for a commodity not normally traded in markets.[27] For example, respondents have never directly purchased relief from illness or reductions in health risk. This criticism is particularly apt for efforts to

---

[24] See Cummings et al., *Valuing Environmental Goods*; A. M. Freeman III, *The Measurement of Environmental and Resource Values: Theory and Methods* (Washington, D.C.: Resources for the Future, 1993).

[25] See W. Desvousges et al., "Measuring Natural Resource Damages with Contingent Valuation: Tests of Validity and Reliability," in J. Hausman (ed.), *Contingent Valuation: A Critical Assessment* (1993), 91–164; P. A. Diamond et al., "Does Contingent Valuation Measure Preferences? Experimental Evidence," in Hausman, *Contingent Valuation*, 41–89; K. C. Samples and J. R. Hollyer, "Contingent Valuation of Wildlife Resources in the Presence of Substitutes and Complements," in R. L. Johnson and G. V. Johnson (eds.), *Economic Valuation of Natural Resources: Issues, Theory and Applications* (Boulder: Westview Press, 1990), 177–92.

[26] See G. van Kooten et al., "Fuzzy Measures for a Fuzzy Concept: A New Approach to Nonmarket Valuation," mimeo (CentER, Tilburg University, 1999).

[27] See B. Fischoff and L. Furby, "Measuring Values: A Conceptual Framework for Interpreting Transactions with Special Reference to Contingent Valuation of Visibility," *J. Risk & Uncertainty* 1(2) (1988), 147–84; D. W. Schkade and J. W. Payne, "How People Respond to Contingent Valuation Questions: A Verbal Protocol Analysis of Willingness to Pay for Environmental Regulation," *J. Envtl. Econ. & Mgmt.* 26(1) (1994), 88–109.

value health risks, especially for low probability illnesses, because of the apparent difficulties people have in understanding risk information.

Critics have proposed other reasons why contingent valuation responses may not reflect WTP or WTA. Respondents may express a general attitude about a commodity on a dollar scale only because that is the scale the survey offers, or they may report a high value to obtain a "warm glow" from contributing to a worthy project such as environmental improvement.[28] They may state a WTP because they assume that, by virtue of the survey, the commodity surely has some value. Furthermore, willingness to pay may be influenced by the choice of payment vehicle (i.e., hypothetical tax, referendum bid, higher utility bills, or higher prices of other goods). On the other hand, proponents of contingent valuation argue that well-designed studies provide reliable information about WTP. These economists believe that contingent valuation responses reflect stable preferences, in accordance with economic theory, and often correspond closely to value measures inferred from actual behavior.[29] Practitioners generally try to eliminate, minimize, or test for known sources of bias or imprecision through careful survey design and data analysis.

Data collection and analysis

The contingent valuation method generally is implemented using a survey that collects relevant information about respondents' personal characteristics, attitudes concerning the commodity to be valued, and valuation information. The three key components of contingent valuation are: (1) a description of the commodity to be valued, such as the symptoms to be avoided or the health risk to be reduced or presented; (2) a method of hypothetically paying for the commodity; and (3) a method of eliciting WTP or WTA.

The two major techniques used to elicit valuations are the "open-ended" and "referendum" approaches. Two other methods, "contingent behavior" and "contingent ranking," are used less frequently.[30] Early research

---

[28] See Diamond and Hausman, "Contingent Valuation"; D. Kahneman and J. L. Knetsch, "Valuing Public Goods: The Purchase of Moral Satisfaction," *J. Envtl. Econ. & Mgmt.* 22(1) (1992), 57–70.

[29] W. M. Hanemann, "Valuing the Environment through Contingent Valuation," *J. Econ. Persp.* 8(4) (1994), 19–43; Mitchell and Carson, *Using Surveys to Value Public Goods*; and V. K. Smith, "Arbitrary Values, Good Causes and Premature Verdicts," *J. Envtl. Econ. & Mgmt.* 22(1) (1992), 71–89.   [30] See Freeman, *The Measurement of Environmental and Resource Values.*

typically used open-ended questions of the form "What is the most you would be willing to pay for . . . ?" Respondents might circle a dollar figure from a set of values on a payment card or they might simply state a value. A variant of this approach is the "bidding game" in which the interviewer suggests an initial dollar amount. If the respondent indicates a willingness to pay that amount, successively higher values are suggested until a value the respondent would be unwilling to pay is reached. If the respondent was unwilling to pay the original amount, lower values are suggested until one the respondent would be willing to pay is reached.

In principle, the open-ended approach directly elicits each respondent's maximum WTP. But respondents appear to find it difficult to answer this type of question, as evidenced by high rates of non-response, zero responses, or implausibly large values.[31] These problems may arise because people rarely have to decide the most they would pay for something; most purchases involve a simpler decision of whether to buy an item at a posted price. In consequence, many researchers now favor the referendum approach, in which respondents are asked whether they would be willing to pay a specific amount.[32] A disadvantage of this method is that it yields less information per response: a "yes" reveals a lower bound, and a "no" reveals an upper bound to WTP. A related valuation method that has attracted recent interest is conjoint analysis, in which respondents rank suites of hypothetical options having various amenities and prices. Individual's rankings are then used to assess the marginal value of a characteristic.[33]

Regardless of value elicitation procedure, considerable attention must be paid to questionnaire design. A particularly important issue is that respondents must understand the commodity, believe that the level of the commodity could be changed as described in the survey, and view the method of making payment as plausible. When contingent valuation is used to assess WTP for commonly occurring health symptoms, most respondents probably have a clear understanding of the commodity. Respondents, however, would presumably be less familiar with rare diseases, and might be less able to express meaningful values for avoiding them.

---

[31] *Ibid.*   [32] Hanemann, "Valuing the Environment."
[33] See V. K. Smith, "Pricing What is Priceless: A Status Report on Non-Market Valuation of Environmental Resources," in H. Folmer and T. Tietenberg (eds.), *The International Yearbook of Environmental and Resource Economics 1997/1998: A Survey of Current Issues* (Cheltenham, UK, and Northampton, Mass.: E. Elgar, 1997).

Another issue involves the type of sampling to be used. Most researchers naturally prefer some form of random sampling, with a sample size large enough to support precise estimation of values and detailed analysis from subgroups of interest. Nevertheless, some contingent valuation studies have employed small, convenience samples. Additionally, in-person interviews often are preferred over telephone and mail surveys. In-person interviews allow researchers to maintain greater control over the information presented to respondents and permit use of more complex survey designs with follow-up questions that depend on answers given previously. However, in-person surveys generally are more costly and may be susceptible to "interviewer effects" in which respondents' answers are inadvertently influenced by the person collecting the data.

AVERTING BEHAVIOR

The averting behavior method is a revealed preference approach used to infer WTP from actions taken to prevent or to mitigate adverse health outcomes of pollution. Averting behavior can take several forms, including: (1) the purchase of a durable good, such as an air purifier or water purifier; (2) the purchase of a non-durable good such as bottled water or a service such as medical care; or (3) a change in daily activities, such as staying indoors. Thus, averting actions may be intended to avoid exposure to environmental contamination, or to mitigate the health effects of exposure.

The theory linking averting behavior to WTP originated in the 1970s and early 1980s,[34] with continued development in recent years.[35] The first empirical applications concerned cleaning activities to reduce soiling damages from air pollution, but the focus quickly turned to health damages. The most frequent empirical application has involved actions taken to avoid contaminated water supplies.[36] Other applications have investigated individuals' efforts to avoid potential hazardous waste

[34] H. Hori, "Revealed Preferences for Public Goods," *Am. Econ. Rev.* 65 (1975), 978–91; P. N. Courant and R. C. Porter, "Averting Expenditure and the Cost of Pollution," *J. Envtl. Econ. & Mgmt.* 8(4) (1981), 321–29.
[35] B. W. Bresnahan and M. Dickie, "Averting Behavior and Policy Evaluation," *J. Envtl. Econ. & Mgmt.* 29(3) (1995), 378–92.
[36] C. W. Abdalla et al., "Valuing Environmental Quality Changes Using Averting Expenditures: An Application to Groundwater Contamination," *Land Econ.* 68(2) (1992), 163–69; W. Harrington et al., "The Economic Losses of a Waterborne Disease Outbreak," *J. Urban Econ.* 25(1) (1989), 116–37.

contamination,[37] to reduce radon concentrations in the home,[38] or to reduce asthma or angina symptoms.[39] Researchers also have examined use of medical care to offset effects of air pollution exposure.[40] The averting behavior method incorporates the WTP aspect, unlike the cost-of-illness approach, because individuals are able to choose medical care to alleviate the illness most effectively. In addition, researchers have investigated the use of air conditioners to reduce air pollution exposure,[41] reductions in time spent outdoors on days of poor air quality,[42] and precautions taken to reduce the risk of skin cancer.[43]

Link to health valuation theory

The averting behavior method is based on generally accepted economic theory and the revealed preference approach. It accounts for all of the effects of health on individual well-being, including altruism towards other household members if averting actions are taken jointly (for example, if everyone in the household drinks bottled water). The theory of averting behavior predicts that a person would take protective action as long as the perceived benefit exceeds the cost. If there is a continuous relationship between defensive action and health improvement, then in theory the individual will continue to avert until the cost just equals his WTP for the health improvement. For example, if substituting a gallon of bottled water for a gallon of tap water yields a risk reduction of one in 5 million at a cost of $1, the individual will purchase bottled water until

[37] V. K. Smith and W. Desvousges, "The Generalized Travel Cost Model and Water Quality Benefits: A Reconsideration," *S. Econ. J.* 52 (1985), 371–81.
[38] J. Akerman et al., "Paying for Safety: Voluntary Reduction of Residential Radon Risks," *Land Econ.* 67 (1991), 435–46; J. K. Doyle et al., "Protective Responses to Household Risk: A Case Study of Radon Mitigation," *Risk Analysis* 11 (1991), 121–34; V. K. Smith et al., "Do Risk Information Programs Promote Mitigating Behavior?" *J. Risk & Uncertainty* 10(3) (1995), 203–21.
[39] L. G. Chestnut et al., *Heart Disease Patients' Averting Behavior, Costs of Illness, and Willingness to Pay to Avoid Angina Episodes*, Final Report to the Office of Policy Analysis, US Environmental Protection Agency (1998).
[40] M. L. Cropper, "Measuring the Benefits from Reduced Morbidity," *Am. Econ. Ass'n Papers & Proc.* 71(2) (1981), 235–40; S. Gerking and L. R. Stanley, "An Economic Analysis of Air Pollution and Health: The Case of St. Louis," *Rev. Econ. & Stat.* 68(1) (1986), 115–21; M. Dickie and S. Gerking, "Willingness to Pay for Ozone Control: Inferences from the Demand for Medical Care," *J. Envtl. Econ. & Mgmt.* 21(1) (1991), 1–16.
[41] M. Dickie and S. Gerking, "Valuing Reduced Morbidity: A Household Production Approach," *Southern Econ. J.* 57 (1991), 690–720.
[42] B. W. Bresnahan et al., "Averting Behavior and Urban Air Pollution," *Land Econ.* 73(3) (1997), 340–57.   [43] Dickie and Gerking, "Formation of Risk Beliefs."

his WTP for a one in 5 million risk reduction just equals $1. Thus, WTP for a small change in health or health risk is inferred from two pieces of information: (1) the cost of the averting good; and (2) its effectiveness, as perceived by the individual, in reducing risk or improving health.

Measuring WTP for large changes, using revealed preference methods, is generally more difficult than estimating marginal WTP. Bartik showed that under certain conditions, averting costs are a lower bound on non-marginal WTP.[44] For example, a person who avoids drinking contaminated tap water by spending $20 a month on bottled water is willing to pay at least $20, though perhaps not exactly $20, to avoid the contamination. Several studies have used averting expenditures to estimate a lower bound on WTP to avoid contaminated water. Empirical efforts to estimate the exact WTP for a non-marginal change, rather than simply to bound it, require complex theoretical and econometric methods.[45]

Additionally, the averting behavior method appears to be better suited to measuring WTP, rather than WTA. As previously indicated, this method focuses on identifying voluntary actions that people take to improve health or reduce risk of diseases in the face of environmental threats. As a result, the averting behavior method may be less able to capture the involuntary nature of public health hazards arising from war.

Methodological problems

Although the basic theory is straightforward, several strict conditions must be imposed to estimate WTP using the averting behavior method.[46] One problem relating to catastrophic wartime public health damages is that it may be difficult to identify a good or goods that would be effective in improving health. Also, as mentioned previously in a related context, prices of goods that can be used to ameliorate public health problems may be dramatically altered in wartime situations. An additional complication involves isolating WTP for a health improvement from the values of other services provided by a good. For example, use of air conditioning may

[44] T. J. Bartik, "The Estimation of Demand Parameters in Hedonic Price Models," *J. Pol. Econ.* 95(1) (1987), 81–88.

[45] Dickie and Gerking, "Willingness to Pay for Ozone Control"; M. D. Agee and T. D. Crocker, "Parental Altruism and Child Lead Exposure: Inferences from the Demand for Chelation Therapy," *J. Hum. Res.* 31(3) (1996), 677–91.

[46] See T. J. Bartik, "Evaluating the Benefits of Non-marginal Reductions in Pollution Using Information on Defensive Expenditures," *J. Envtl. Econ. & Mgmt.* 15 (1988), 111–27.

reduce symptoms from exposure to air pollution, but the main reason for running the air conditioner, presumably, is to cool the house. Disentangling the value of health from other values associated with taking averting action can be quite complicated.

A related difficulty is that many averting actions do not have an easily observed market price to use in computing their costs. A person may stay indoors to avoid air pollution, for example, but it is difficult to assign a cost to this action. No corresponding monetary price exists for time spent indoors. Furthermore, since time spent indoors may not constitute entirely lost time and given that wartime situations can have dramatic effects on prices, there may be no compelling reason to use the wage rate.

Even when the cost of averting action is clear, the perceived benefit of the action may be difficult to infer. A person's choice of averting behavior, and thus the value revealed by his actions, is based on his perception of the resulting health effects. Individuals' perceptions about health risks, however, may differ from the assessments made by experts. Also, implementation of the averting behavior method may require detailed and expensive surveys to elicit individuals' perceptions of the effects of behavior on health risks.

Finally, averting behavior often involves a discrete choice of whether to take an action, rather than a decision about the level of a continuous variable. For example, a person decides whether or not to purchase an air or water purifying system. Discrete choices by themselves do not directly reveal WTP, but only bound it. It is possible to use discrete choice data to estimate the exact WTP by applying complex methods,[47] but most researchers either ignore the issue or simply use averting expenditures to bound WTP.

Data collection and analysis

Most applications of the averting behavior method use surveys to collect data on averting actions taken, their costs, and perhaps on the actual or perceived health effects. Information on respondents' health status, attitudes, and socio-economic characteristics generally is also obtained. In many cases, surveys have been timed to occur during or immediately after incidents such as temporary water contamination. During or immediately

---

[47] *Ibid.*

after a war, surveys may not be practical. Consequently, surveys may have to rely on recollections of respondents, even though people may have difficulty in accurately recalling perceptions and events that occurred at a very stressful time.

OTHER METHODS OF HEALTH VALUATION

While the cost-of-illness, contingent valuation, and averting behavior methods have been the most widely used for valuing environmental morbidity and risk of mortality, other methods have been used less frequently. Three of these methods – hedonic wage, risk–risk tradeoffs, and health-state indexes – are described below for completeness.

Hedonic methods

Hedonic methods are based on the idea that goods and services often can be viewed as bundles of characteristics. A useful application to environmental and health valuation arises when these methods are applied to the labor markets, where wages reflect the economic value of characteristics of workers and jobs. According to the theory, employers must pay higher wages to attract workers to jobs viewed as more dangerous or less pleasant than alternative occupations. Application of the theory requires that careful consideration be given to the many factors causing wages to differ. For example, while neurosurgery is less dangerous than logging, the differences in compensation for these occupations are probably better explained by differences in the amounts of specialized education, training, and experience required to perform the job. In practice, studies that adopt this approach must carefully control for these factors that affect compensation for employment in order to isolate the "wage-risk premium" demanded by workers to compensate for choosing a more risky occupation.

There have been two main applications of the hedonic-wage method to environmental valuation.[48] One of these matches workers' wages to characteristics of their location, such as crime rates, climate, or average air

[48] Reviews of the theory and empirical results can be found in W. L. Fisher et al., "The Value of Reducing Risks of Death: A Note on New Evidence," *J. Pol'y Analysis & Mgmt.* 8(1) (1989), 88–100; T. R. Miller, "The Plausible Range for the Value of Life: Red Herrings Among the Mackerel," *J. Forensic Econ.* 3(3) (1990), 17–39; W. K. Viscusi, "The Value of Risks to Life and Health," *J. Econ. Literature* 31 (1993), 1912–46; and W. K. Viscusi, *Fatal Tradeoffs: Public and Private Responsibilities for Risk* (New York: Oxford Univ. Press, 1992).

pollution concentrations, to estimate implicit prices for these character-istics. The second application is more closely linked to health: it involves estimating the tradeoff between wages and risk of death or injury on the job. Estimated wage–risk tradeoffs underlie many calculations of the "value of a statistical life." After controlling for differences in education and experience of workers, and other characteristics of their jobs, the wage decrease associated with a small reduction in job risk reflects the marginal WTP for reduced risk. Statistical life values established in a labor market context may carry over to a broader range of situations involving environ-mental hazards and risk of death.

Wage–risk tradeoffs have been applied to value reduced risk of death, with several extensions to value risks of non-fatal injuries. Many economists regard estimated wage–risk tradeoffs as the most successful application of the economic theory of health valuation. Unfortunately, wage-risk effects of environmental contamination are quite different from the types of injuries occurring on the job. It would be difficult, for example, to infer the value of an avoided asthma attack from the wage–death risk relationship. The risk–risk tradeoff method, however, offers one way of linking wage–risk tradeoffs to the valuation of serious illnesses.

Risk–risk tradeoffs

The risk–risk tradeoff method considers individuals' decisions about tradeoffs they would be willing to make between two different risks – for example, the risk of death and the risk of contracting a chronic disease. In the first application of the method, Viscusi et al. presented people with a hypothetical choice between residence in two cities, which differed in the risk of a fatal automobile accident and a relatively severe risk of chronic bronchitis.[49] The authors used an interactive computer program to pre-sent alternative combinations of the risks until reaching the point where an individual's response implied indifference between a death risk of one magnitude and a chronic bronchitis risk of another magnitude. For example, the median rate of tradeoff was 0.32, indicating that the median respondent viewed chronic bronchitis as about one-third (0.32) as adverse as a fatal automobile accident.

---

[49] W. K. Viscusi et al., "Pricing Environmental Health Risks: Survey Assessments of Risk–Risk and Risk–Dollar Tradeoffs for Chronic Bronchitis," *J. Envtl. Econ. & Mgmt.* 21(1) (1991), 32–51.

The risk–risk approach is based on respondents' statements rather than their actual behavior and so is potentially susceptible to many of the criticisms leveled at the contingent valuation (CV) method. A possible advantage of the risk–risk approach over CV, however, is that it may be easier for respondents to make tradeoffs between two risks than between risk and money, as they would have to do if CV were applied to value chronic bronchitis. A major disadvantage of the method is that it does not yield WTP estimates; but it offers an obvious chance to link morbidity valuation to wage–risk tradeoffs. For example, Viscusi et al. apply a $2 million value of a statistical life to the median bronchitis–death risk tradeoff to estimate a value per statistical case of severe chronic bronchitis of $640,000.[50] The risk–risk method would appear to be a promising area for further valuation research, but there have been few applications to date.

Health-state indexes

Another set of methods has been used by health economists to evaluate individuals' preferences for different health outcomes. The idea behind these methods is to construct a scale or index which ranks health outcomes in terms of how adverse individuals believe them to be. Often, the extreme points on the scale are "perfect health" and "immediate death," but some applications allow for health outcomes that might be viewed as worse than death. These methods do not yield estimates of WTP, but are quite informative about individuals' views of different illnesses and may be useful in benefits transfer.

There are three main approaches to constructing health-state indexes. The "standard gamble" approach is similar to the risk–risk method and relies heavily on expected utility theory. A respondent might be presented with two situations: (1) the certainty of having chronic bronchitis; or (2) a risky prospect involving, say, a 10 percent chance of death and 90 percent chance of perfect health. The idea is to find the risk of death that the respondent thinks is just as adverse as having chronic bronchitis with certainty. Thus, respondents are not making tradeoffs between risk of death and risk of chronic bronchitis, as in the risk–risk approach, but between risk of death and certain chronic bronchitis.

---

[50] *Ibid.*

A second approach is the "time-tradeoff" method, which asks respondents to trade years of life in full health against years of life with a chronic ailment. For example, a respondent might be asked to compare a given remaining life span in full health to a longer life span with chronic bronchitis. Finding the number of years that makes the respondent indifferent gives an alternative measure of the adversity of chronic bronchitis relative to perfect health and to death.

The third approach is the "rating scale" method, in which respondents are asked to score different health outcomes on a numerical scale, such as a one-to-ten scale. If immediate death is assigned a value of one, and full health the value ten, then the ranking of a given impairment indicates how adverse it is relative to the two extremes. Analyses often compress the scale to lie in the zero–one interval.

Each of these methods provides potentially useful information about individual preferences over different health outcomes. An obvious question is whether the three methods would yield similar results. It appears that, at a minimum, the three indexes rank health outcomes in the same order. But whether each method would yield the same measure of the adversity of a disease is not quite as clear. Triangle Economic Research cites evidence that consistent results are obtained from all three of the methods, but other authors have found differences.[51]

More importantly, it is not clear whether the ranking of health outcomes obtained by health-state indexes would match the ranking obtained by knowing individuals' WTP for various health effects. As discussed by Johansson, health-state indexes rely on much more restrictive assumptions about the nature of individual preferences than are normally made in WTP studies.[52] For example, the time-tradeoff method assumes that chronically ill individuals are willing to trade a constant proportion of their remaining life years for better health, regardless of their current age and life expectancy. Restrictive assumptions about the substitution of income for health and the discounting of future health effects also are implicit in health-state indexes.

---

[51] P. Dolan et al., "Valuing Health States: A Comparison of Methods," *J. Health Econ.* 15 (1996), 209–31.

[52] P. Johansson, *Evaluating Health Risks: An Economic Approach* (Cambridge and New York: Cambridge Univ. Press, 1995).

Illustrative values

Acute and chronic exposures to environmental contaminants can cause a broad range of adverse health effects. Tables 20.1 and 20.2 present values of specific health effects taken from the recent valuation literature. These values are provided for illustration only; figures presented may or may not be relevant to assessing public health damages arising from war. These figures were assembled from US EPA documents, academic journal articles, and various private sector reports. Table 1 presents estimates of monetized health effects drawn from US EPA.[53] Table 2 draws additional estimates of benefits from symptom reduction from Weitzel.[54]

More specifically, Table 20.1 shows values for a number of symptoms thought to be associated with various types of pollutants together with monetized values and an indication of the method used to obtain them. Symptom benefit estimates are not always comparable because the units in which they were measured differed between studies cited. In any case, stated preference methods, including contingent valuation and risk–risk tradeoffs, place comparatively higher values on chronic bronchitis and much lower values on less serious health problems such as acute bronchitis, acute asthma, and upper and lower respiratory symptoms. The cost-of-illness method, on the other hand, appears to assign relatively lower values to closely related illnesses as compared with stated preference methods. For example, while risk–risk tradeoffs value chronic bronchitis as $260,000 per case (for a case of average severity), cost-of-illness values for chronic obstructive respiratory disease and general respiratory illness are $8,100 per case and $6,100 per case, respectively. This outcome illustrates the tendency of cost-of-illness to produce lower values than methods that estimate WTP.

Table 20.2 contrasts mean and median values for a number of pollution-related symptoms obtained in a number of studies using contingent valuation. Median values are always lower, often very much lower, than mean values. This result illustrates the tendency found in some studies for the distribution of bids to exhibit a long right-hand tail. In other words, a few very large bids sometimes have a substantial influence on the mean. This

[53] US Environmental Protection Agency, "The Benefits and Costs of the Clean Air Act, 1970 to 1990," Draft Report to the United States Congress (1997).

[54] D. L. Weitzel, *Economic Valuation of Environmental Health Benefits: A Review of the Literature*, Report to the Washington State Department of Ecology (1990).

Table 20.1. *Monetized health effects associated with criteria air pollutants*

Monetized health effects	Valuation technique used			Mean benefit estimate (1990 dollar values)	Relevant studies
	Contingent valuation	Cost of illness	Other		
Chronic bronchitis			X	$260,000 per case	Viscusi et al. (1991)
Lost IQ points			X	$2,500 per IQ point	Schwartz (1994)
			X	$3,400 per IQ point	Salkever (1995)
Incidence of IQ <70		X		$42,000 per case	Kakalik et al. (1981)
Hypertension		X		$680 per case per year	Krupnick and Cropper (1989)
Strokes		X		$200,000 per case (males) $150,000 per case (females)	Taylor et al. (1996)
Coronary heart disease		X		$52,000 per case	Wittels et al. (1996)
Ischemic heart disease		X		$10,300 per case	Elixhauser et al. (1993) Abt Associates Inc. (1992)
Congestive heart failure		X		$8,300 per case	Elixhauser et al. (1993) Abt Associates Inc. (1992)
Chronic obstructive pulmonary disease		X		$8,100 per case	Abt Associates Inc. (1992)
Pneumonia		X		$7,900 per case	Elixhauser et al. (1993) Abt Associates Inc. (1992)
General respiratory illness		X		$6,100 per case	Elixhauser et al. (1993) Abt Associates Inc. (1992)

Table 20.1. (cont.)

Monetized health effects	Valuation technique used			Mean benefit estimate (1990 dollar values)	Relevant studies
	Contingent valuation	Cost of illness	Other		
Acute bronchitis	X			$45 per case	Neumann et al. (1994)
Acute asthma	X			$32 per case	Rowe and Chestnut (1986)
Acute respiratory symptoms	X			$18 per case	Neumann et al. (1994) Pope et al. (1995) Schwartz et al. (1994)
Upper respiratory symptoms	X			$19 per case	Neumann et al. (1994) Pope et al. (1995)
Lower respiratory symptoms	X			$12 per case	Neumann et al. (1994) Schwartz et al. (1994)
Shortness of breath	X			$5.30 per day	Ostro et al. (1995)
Work loss days			X	$83 per day	US Department of Commerce (1992)
Mild restricted activity days	X			$38 per day	Tolley et al. (1986)

Source: US EPA, The Benefits and Costs of the Clean Air Act, 1970–1990 (October 1997).

Table 20.2. *Benefit estimates for reductions in morbidity resulting from changes in air quality (value of one-day reduction in symptoms)*

Symptom (severity)	Source study	Benefit per day (1995 dollar values)	
		Median value	Mean value
*Asthma attack (moderate)	Rowe and Chestnut (1985)	—	$58.12
*Cannot breathe deeply	Dickie et al. (1987)	$1.42	$1,616.13
Chest tightness	Dickie et al. (1987)	$7.09	$1,153.57
*Coughing/sneezing (minor)	Loehman (1979)	$11.34	$110.58
Drowsiness	Tolley (1986)	$21.26	$44.53
Eye irritation	Tolley (1986)	$17.72	$39.31
Head congestion (minor)	Loehman (1979)	$8.51	$73.72
Headache	Tolley (1986)	$28.35	$56.85
Nausea	Tolley (1986)	$24.81	$71.28
*Pain on deep respiration	Dickie et al. (1987)	$4.96	$1,352.63
*Shortness of breath (severe)	Loehman (1979)	$25.52	$180.04
Sinusitis	Tolley (1986)	$19.85	$49.69
Throat irritation	Dickie et al. (1987)	$4.25	$21.26
Wheezing	Dickie et al. (1987)	$2.84	$82.22

Ailments marked with an asterisk (*) indicate decrements in lung function, as measured by reductions in FVC or FEV_s.

Source: D. Weitzel, *Economic Valuation of Environmental Health Benefits: A Review of the Literature*, prepared for the Washington State Department of Ecology, December 31, 1990.

problem is exacerbated in studies where respondents state their willingness to pay, rather than their willingness to pay a posted price, and where the survey design allowed very large bids to occur. In the studies cited, mean values for symptom avoidance were at least twice as large as median values. Additionally, Dickie et al. report symptoms for which mean values were many times greater than median values (for example, inability to breathe deeply, chest tightness, and pain on deep respiration).[55]

Conclusion

This chapter has presented an overview of strengths and weaknesses of alternative methods of placing monetary values on human mortality and morbidity. It considered three methods at length: (1) cost-of-illness;

[55] Dickie et al., "Improving Accuracy and Reducing Costs."

(2) contingent valuation; and (3) averting behavior. Although the cost-of-illness method is frequently applied, it is generally thought to underestimate the amount of money a person might voluntarily give up in order to enjoy better health because values associated with pain and suffering and other difficult-to-measure aspects of illness are ignored. The contingent valuation method, on the other hand, attempts to measure the broader and more theoretically correct concept of health value, but whether it actually does so is a controversial question. The method's detractors question whether people answer hypothetical questions carefully enough and whether they fully comprehend the questions asked. Proponents of the method suggest that these and other potential weaknesses can be overcome through appropriate survey design and data analysis. The averting behavior method also attempts to measure a theoretically correct concept of value; however, data needed for implementation are often difficult to obtain. This chapter also described other less frequently applied valuation methods such as hedonic methods, risk–risk tradeoffs, and health-state indexes.

The discussion emphasizes that there is no single, best method to use in all situations to place values on aspects of human health. Additionally, valuing human health damages arising from war only compounds the uncertainties because many special problems may arise. As outlined in the introduction, wartime situations sometimes prevent giving even severe environmental problems prompt attention. There may be important synergistic effects between public health damages and other types of environmental damages (i.e., petroleum fires in Kuwait have deleterious consequences for public health both directly and indirectly through their effects on agriculture). Estimates of wages and prices needed to value damages may be difficult to establish because local economies do not function normally during wartime.

Nevertheless, a few guiding principles emerge that may be useful in estimating monetary values associated with war-related public health damages. Perhaps the most obvious is to regard cost-of-illness measures as lower bound estimates of value. Out-of-pocket costs and lost work time, although difficult to estimate, reflect a narrower approach to measuring damages than would, for example, contingent valuation or averting behavior. Additionally, greater attention should be focused on willingness-to-pay and willingness-to-accept measures of damages. Moreover, although these two concepts are closely related theoretically, willingness-to-accept estimates may be the more appropriate of the two when estimating damages to public health arising from war. The reference point used to construct willingness-to-accept estimates is what affected persons should be paid to tolerate involuntarily pollution of a public resource, compensation that would leave them just as well off as before. Compensation required has no upper bound and, partly as a result, willingness-to-accept estimates are generally larger than willingness-to-pay estimates, and sometimes by a wide margin. However, willingness-to-accept estimates have been employed less frequently in a public health context than willingness-to-pay estimates. Consequently, it might be useful to pursue as a methodological goal the further refinement of the willingness-to-accept approach in the context of estimating monetary damages of war-related public health problems.

21

VALUING THE HEALTH CONSEQUENCES OF WAR

W. KIP VISCUSI

Introduction

Wars often involve major health consequences for thousands of individuals. Those affected include the combatants from the countries engaged in the conflict, armed forces from other nations, and citizenry. These groups also could include individuals far removed from the conflict if, for example, chemical exposures from the combat situation led to genetic damage that harmed the offspring of a combatant.

This chapter addresses how adverse consequences resulting from war should be valued from the standpoint of compensation. In undertaking this analysis, I will make the assumption that compensation is appropriate. In some instances involving war, providing compensation may strike one as being quite odd. For example, one would not think that a nation that launched an aggression would seek financial compensation for the injuries to the soldiers who were killed in such a conflict. What I will assume, then, is that there has been a determination that compensation is warranted, and the remaining issue is how such compensation should be set.

This subject in a generic sense has been the focus of a considerable literature in economics. How one should set compensation will depend in large part on the purpose one is trying to achieve through such compensation. In particular, is the intent to insure the losses of the accident victim or to provide deterrence? The principal message of this chapter is that the standard objective in compensatory legal contexts should be an insurance function so that compensation for economic loss should be the guiding principle determining the value of the adverse health consequences of wars.

The valuation of health outcomes is not a straightforward proposition. We are generally dealing with issues much more complex and of a different dimension than financial costs alone. Risks to individual health often are unpleasant to confront. To some, valuing losses to individual health may appear to be outside the realm of usual economic analysis. However, over the past several decades, a considerable literature in economics has developed in an effort to enable analysts to think sensibly about these issues and to place meaningful empirical estimates on health outcomes.

This chapter will consider how one should approach the valuation of the health-related effects of wars. The nature of the inquiry will necessarily be limited by current knowledge, much of which is associated with the valuation of health outcomes in contexts in which these values already play a prominent role in government policy. The chief example is, of course, the extensive literature on the value of life. The fact that these examples will not encompass all health outcomes that are possibly influenced by wars does not imply that the economic methodology is restrictive. Rather, this literature indicates how one can successfully address these questions and what methodological mechanisms are available for people to resolve the often difficult valuation problems for health effects.

The first section will introduce the principal methodological concerns, primarily focusing on what should be the guiding principle for setting damages: should it be society's willingness to pay for risk reduction or the present value of the financial losses? This section will also address practical techniques that are frequently used in the medical decisionmaking context, such as the focus on quality-adjusted life years. The second section explores how market-based evidence often has been used to assess the implicit value of life and job-related injuries. Since explicit or implicit market trades do not always exist for every health outcome of interest, it is often necessary to utilize surveys to elicit the appropriate willingness to pay values, and these are the subject of the third section. The fourth section indicates how such survey results can be used to assess the underlying utility functions pertaining to different health states. One potential difficulty for health loss assessments is that these risks do not arise from choices and may be tainted by irrational behavior. Some of the more salient irrationalities are the subject of the final section.

Economic principles for valuing health risks from war

COMPENSATION PRINCIPLES

Determining the appropriate value of compensation for the adverse health effects of war depends in large part on the purpose of such compensation. In the US legal system, the basic principle for accident compensation is that of insurance.[1] In particular, the intent of such compensation is to restore the economic loss associated with the accident.

As a practical matter, this approach leads to the following kinds of compensation. In the case of a wrongful death, the value of compensation is the present value of the decedent's lost earnings net of the share of these earnings that would have been devoted to the decedent's consumption. In the case of non-fatal injuries, the value of the compensation is the present value of the lost earnings plus the present value of the medical costs. Courts often supplement these amounts by some value for pain and suffering compensation, but these levels on average are around the same magnitude as the value of the attorneys' fees, thus enabling the injured person to be made whole financially, after attorneys' fees are deducted.

In this chapter, I adopt the point of view that these same economic principles for damages applied in US tort law should also be applicable for determining the value of appropriate compensation for injuries due to wars. To the extent that the objective is insurance and compensation of accident victims, the standard economic methodology of determining financial losses is appropriate.

One alternative approach is to ask how much an individual would need to be compensated to be made whole after the adverse health effect. In the case of a person killed or catastrophically injured in war, no amount of money may suffice to make that individual as well off as they would have been had they remained healthy. This concept consequently leads to a potentially unbounded level of compensation even for an individual person.

The more general concept adopted by economists is the value of society's willingness to pay for risk reduction. Much of this chapter will focus on this concept, which is widely employed throughout the US government

---

[1] For a discussion of the insurance and deterrence roles of accident compensation, see S. Shavell, *Economic Analysis of Accident Law* (1987); A. M. Polinsky, *An Introduction to Law and Economics*, 2nd edn. (Cambridge, Mass.: Harvard Univ. Press, 1989); W. K. Viscusi, *Reforming Products Liability* (Cambridge, Mass.: Harvard Univ. Press, 1991).

to value the health benefits of reducing risk. It is important to note, however, that this concept pertains to the optimal deterrence value for preventing injuries, not the appropriate compensation value for transferring income to people after they are injured. If, for example, one were to use this willingness-to-pay measure to compensate people injured in wars, the result would be excessive compensation from the standpoint of insurance. The reasons for this difficulty will be apparent upon further exploration of the source of these willingness-to-pay figures.

Within the US court system, there have been attempts to use these willingness-to-pay measures to set a value for human life and health. This effort has come under the general heading of "hedonic" damages. This approach to setting damages is generally viewed with disrepute and has been widely rejected in jurisdictions throughout the country.[2]

THE WILLINGNESS-TO-PAY MEASURE

The deterrence value of the health outcomes associated with wars is no different in character from valuing any other public policy outcome. What matters is society's willingness to pay for the benefit generated by this effort. In the case of wars, the typical outcome will be an increase in societal risk levels due to the conflict. As a result, the value of society's willingness to pay to avoid the marginal increases in risk that will occur is the appropriate deterrence measure.

In making this deterrence tally, one consequently should not equate the economic costs of war with financial costs alone. The effects on hospital fees, out-of-pocket medical expenses, and earnings of those affected by wars are, of course, among the potential consequences that should be valued. However, these items reflect only a partial tally of the overall effects. Many of the most severe impacts will be the ramifications for individual well-being. Even though individual health is generally not treated explicitly in markets, changes in risk to health can be valued and should be an explicit component of any deterrence value assessment of wars.

The valuation amounts that are pertinent are those associated with the preferences of those at risk. Thus, the matter of interest is society's willingness to avoid the risks from wars. We are not concerned with the assessments

---

[2] See J. O. Ward and T. R. Ireland (eds.), *The New Hedonics Primer for Economists and Attorneys*, 2nd edn. (Tucson, Ariz.: Lawyers & Judges Pub. Co., 1996), pp. 413–30 for a comprehensive review of the case law pertaining to hedonic damages.

of politicians, generals, physicians, or other experts, but rather with the preferences of the people who will be directly affected by the outcomes. To obtain these assessments, it is necessary to acquire information with respect to individual preferences in the target population, rather than to rely upon expert panels or government officials to make these judgments.

In situations in which economists assess valuations of small risks, the phraseology "value of life" often appears. The genesis of this terminology is as follows. Consider the case where the good being valued is a reduction in mortality risk, such as one in 10,000. Let there be some associated willingness to pay for this risk reduction, such as $500. In such an instance, a group of 10,000 individuals would be collectively willing to pay $5 million to avert one statistical death. As a result, the "value of life" in this instance would be $5 million. What is being valued here is a statistical life rather than a certain death.

Society's valuation of a certain health outcome, whether it be death or some other health effect, may be quite different. Few of us would knowingly face a certain probability of death for a fixed reward such as $5 million. However, such certain adverse outcomes are not the matter in question. The consequences of wars are also lotteries, given that the effects are probabilistic. We do not know in advance who will be affected adversely or favorably by these efforts. What is needed is the value of the statistical lives, statistical illnesses, and other expected health effects that will result from these efforts. In this regard, utilization of value-of-life estimates as well as similar valuations for other health outcomes is appropriate.

These estimates generalize lives of different length and quality, health outcomes of different severity, and other potential health conditions. The appropriate value is the pertinent willingness to pay for the associated risk reduction. Formulating this issue, however, is much more straightforward than placing an explicit dollar value on the answer. Subsequent sections of this chapter will detail how evidence from the market and from surveys can be utilized to resolve issues such as this.

QUALITY-ADJUSTED LIVES

The length of life that is at risk may vary depending on the particular ailment involved, whom it affects, and the lag time before the health impacts become apparent. Research by Viscusi, Hakes, and Carlin provides estimates of the quantity-adjusted values of these different health risks, as well as the cost per quantity-adjusted health risk prevented for a variety of government regulations.[3] For example, efforts that address acute accident risks tend to have a greater health effect than those that reduce health hazards, such as cancer.

Within the medical economics field, a variation of this methodology has also been employed. Zeckhauser and Shepard,[4] for example, proposed that a quality-adjusted life year (QALY) measure be used.[5] In particular, when one values life, one values heterogeneous commodities. One cares about the length of life that is at stake as well as the quality of that life. The concept that the quality and duration of life is of consequence is certainly a legitimate concern. Often, however, the degree of information available does not permit full refinement of values to reflect all of these differences.

The use of some kind of QALY approach is not necessarily inconsistent with the traditional value-of-life literature. For example, the same kinds of job risk studies that have been used to estimate the implicit value of life also have been employed to estimate the quantity-adjusted value of life, where the life years at risk reflect the quality of life likely to be experienced by a typical worker.[6]

In practice, the quality-adjusted life year approach has been associated with various pragmatic techniques for obtaining an assessment of the QALY value associated with different health outcomes. As a result, generating the QALY value often requires imposing strong assumptions. The typical approach is to ask what proportion of the individual's future lifetime when healthy would the person be willing to sacrifice in return for obtaining a particular specified health improvement. This approach may provide a health index, but it is not a direct valuation of the willingness to pay associated with a small risk reduction. Moreover, as shown by Johannesson et al., such an approach does impose severe restrictions.[7]

---

[3] W. K. Viscusi et al., "Measures of Mortality Risks," *J. Risk & Uncertainty* 14(3) (1997), 213–33.

[4] R. J. Zeckhauser and D. Shepard, "Where Now for Saving Lives?" *Law & Contemporary Problems* 39 (1976), 5–45.

[5] Specific estimates that operationalize this concept for quantity-adjusted values of life are reported in W. K. Viscusi, *Fatal Tradeoffs: Public and Private Responsibilities for Risk* (New York: Oxford Univ. Press, 1992); W. K. Viscusi and M. Moore, "Rates of Time Preference and Valuations of the Duration of Life," *J. Pub. Econ.* 38(3) (1989), 297–317.

[6] The first examples of this quantity-adjusted value of life approach appear in M. Moore and W. K. Viscusi, "The Quantity-Adjusted Value of Life," *Econ. Inquiry* 26(3) (1988), 369–88; Viscusi and Moore, "Rates of Time Preference."

[7] M. Johannesson et al., "A Note on QALYs, Time Tradeoff, and Discounting," *Med. Decision Making* 14(2) (1994), 188–93.

Adopting their notation, the risk-neutral QALY equates the utility U(Q,T) of some health state Q with associated number of life years available T as being equal to some function that reflects the quality of the health state V(Q) multiplied by the number of years of life remaining, or

$$U(Q,T) = V(Q)T.$$

This approach embodies three principal assumptions. First, the various life years Q are assumed to be utility-independent. This is a very strong assumption in that it implies that the shape of the utility function for life years is the same for all health states. Moreover, the degree of risk aversion is assumed to be the same for all health states. Since the effect of many adverse health effects, such as paraplegia, cancer, and other severe illnesses, is to alter the structure of individual preferences greatly, this assumption is unlikely to be borne out in practice for many health outcomes of interest. This independence assumption also implies that the standard gamble quality weighting term V(Q) does not vary with the number of years that will be spent in the health state, whereas in practice there may be an important variation of this type.

The second major assumption associated with this approach is that a constant proportional tradeoff is assumed by the model. In particular, the proportion of remaining life that one would be willing to sacrifice in return for some specified quality improvement is assumed to be independent of the amount of remaining life. In practice, one would not expect this assumption to hold. One implication of this formulation is that individual utility functions for life years will display constant proportional risk aversion, which constitutes another restrictive assumption.

The third principal assumption embodied in the standard formulation is that individuals are risk-neutral over life years. Thus, having four life years for sure is viewed as being equivalent to a 50–50 chance of eight life years remaining or zero life years. Such a linear utility function is unlikely to be a plausible shape, although the formulation can be generalized to incorporate the potential for risk aversion.

Discounting is also a potential concern. Years of life far into the distant future are likely to receive a lower weight than more immediate life years at risk. The QALY format can be generalized to incorporate discounting by eliciting the percentage amount of the discounted number of life years that the individual views as being equivalent to a particular health consequence. Although one can reformulate the QALY model in this

discounted manner, most implementations of the analysis do not incorporate such flexibility.

There has also been an increasingly substantial literature with other
approaches to assessing QALY values.[8] This includes literature on health-
year equivalents as well as a variety of techniques for assessing QALY
amounts. All such techniques should be viewed as approximations to the
more fundamental objective of eliciting the willingness to pay for the
associated risk reduction explicitly.

Risk–money tradeoffs

The most prevalent approach to valuing health risks in the literature has
been an examination of wage–risk tradeoffs. These are values for prevention, not compensation after the fact. Using data on worker wages and
linking these data to worker characteristics and job characteristics, including job risks, economists have estimated the wage premiums that workers
receive for risk.

The underlying theoretical basis is indicated in Figure 21.1. Firms have
offer curves FF and GG, where these represent the different isoprofit lines
for the firm. At a high risk level in each case, the firm can offer a higher
wage rate and still maintain the same level of profitability. The outer enve-
lope of these offer curves is the market opportunities frontier facing workers in terms of their best available wage–risk combinations. On the supply
side of the market, workers have a constant expected utility locus, such as
is illustrated by EU_1 and EU_2 for two different workers. The worker's objective is to be on the highest constant expected utility locus possible, or as far
in the upper left direction, where this expected utility locus will be tangent
to the available market opportunities. In the case illustrated, worker 1 will
select job risk p_1 and an associated wage rate of $w_1(p_1)$.

The wage equation estimates will ascertain the wage–risk tradeoff
locus given by XX in Figure 21.1. In the case in which a linear relationship between wages and risks is estimated, economists in effect estimate
the average local rate of tradeoff for the set of workers in the sample.
These tradeoffs, which are based on the tangency of the expected utility
locus with the market opportunity set, consequently represent both the

---

[8] The pivotal contribution to this literature is Zeckhauser and Shepard, "Where Now for Saving
Lives?"

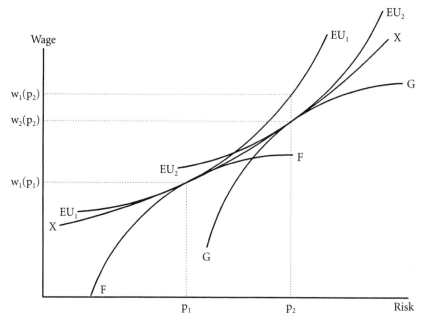

21.1 Market process for determining compensating differentials

willingness-to-pay and the willingness-to-accept amount for very small risks. It is not appropriate to extrapolate these amounts to larger risk changes. For example, a risk increase from p_1 to p_2 would require that the worker be compensated at a level of $w_1(p_2)$ rather than the lower amount of $w_2(p_2)$ that would be pertinent based on the estimated market risk tradeoff. Thus, the estimated market curve XX will lie below the constant expected utility locus and will be tangent only at a single point.

The market tradeoff locus consequently provides very limited information regarding risk–money tradeoffs, as it only pertains to a local neighborhood. Through the use of various interaction terms, such as those involving age, union status, and other personal characteristics, it is possible to estimate differences in tradeoff rates. However, since these tradeoffs reflect the simultaneous interaction of labor supply and labor demand, each of which may depend on these characteristics, market-based evidence is not ideal for making refined judgments regarding the heterogeneity of tradeoff values.

The overall implication of these studies is that, on average, the estimated rates of tradeoff based on labor market studies tend to cluster in the range of $3 million to $7 million per statistical life (in 1990 prices).[9] Over-all, labor market evidence alone is not sufficient to resolve all the pertinent issues with respect to the valuation of risks. Although it offers the advantage of being based on actual choices being made involving real threats to individual well-being, it has important limitations as well. Perhaps most salient is that the job risks involved, which include acute accidents and in some cases non-fatal on-the-job injuries, do not span all of the risk outcomes of interest. Within the domain of health outcomes, government policymakers often have to value illnesses, such as chronic bronchitis, and other causes of death, such as cancer, which may be viewed quite differently from immediate deaths.

Moreover, there are many risks, such as environmental risks, that may not be reflected accurately even in terms of implicit market prices. Although one could undertake property value studies to investigate environmental amenities in much the same manner as labor economists have done for job risks, these market experiments are not perfectly controlled. It is often impossible to disentangle the wide variety of influences at work. These difficulties pertain to the labor market studies as well and may have contributed at least in part to the disparity in the value-of-life estimates across different studies.

Use of market data also presupposes that individuals understand the risks they face. Thus, the analyses are typically based on an assumption that the objective measures of the risk and the subjective risk assessments that drive behavior are identical. To the extent that one wishes to move beyond this assumption and incorporate a measure of the subjective risk assessment, then a more extensive survey is needed.[10]

Perhaps the most fundamental limitation of the labor market studies is that even if one elicits the subjective risk perception value and perfectly controls for all the individual and job characteristics driving wages, the scope of the questions that can be answered is very limited. Only a narrow range of health outcomes can be addressed – far fewer than are needed to

---

[9] See Viscusi, *Fatal Tradeoffs*; W. K. Viscusi, "The Value of Risks to Life and Health," *J. Econ. Literature* 31(4) (1993), 1912–46 for a review.

[10] Studies that have incorporated subjective risk assessment values include W. K. Viscusi, *Employment Hazards: An Investigation of Market Performance* (Cambridge: Harvard Univ. Press, 1979); W. K. Viscusi and C. O'Connor, "Adaptive Responses to Chemical Labeling: Are Workers Bayesian Decision Makers?" *Am. Econ. Rev.* 74(5) (1984), 942–56; J. Hersch and W. K. Viscusi, "Cigarette Smoking, Seatbelt Use, and Differences in Wage–Risk Trade-Offs," *J. Hum. Res.* 25(2) (1990), 202–27.

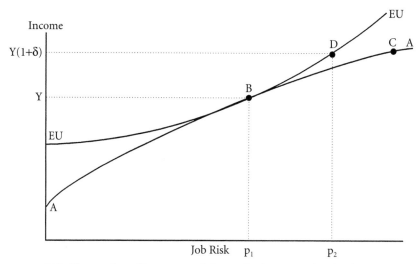

21.2 The market offer curve and the worker's expected utility locus

assess the health consequences of war. The only tradeoffs that can be examined are the local tradeoff rates pertaining to averages across some broad population group. Finally, any attempt to refine these tradeoff levels for different population subgroups is impeded by the aforementioned difficulty of disentangling the interaction of labor demand and labor supply factors, given that the econometric analysis estimates only the locus of market equilibrium, and does not consider either labor demand or labor supply separately. (Structural estimation techniques potentially could be of some assistance in this regard, but to date they have not been.)

The first attempt to go beyond the hedonic labor market studies of risk was a study by Viscusi and O'Connor, which utilized a survey approach to value changes in job risk.[11] The survey structure can best be discussed with reference to Figure 21.2. The sample of workers consisted of 335 workers at four different chemical plants. The first piece of pertinent information elicited from the respondents was their baseline job risk p_2 at their current job, where this was indicated using a linear risk scale in which there was a single job risk anchor, the average worker injury rate. (A 1990 study by Hersch and Viscusi modifies this approach by using a series of discrete boxes to indicate the risk level and by including multiple risk reference points. In each case, the risk reference point pertains only to job hazards.)

[11] Viscusi and O'Connor, "Adaptive Responses to Chemical Labeling."

Table 21.1. *Summary of value of life estimates based on survey evidence*

Author (year)	Nature of risk	Implicit value of life ($ millions)
Acton (1973)	Improved ambulance service, post-heart attack lives	0.1
Jones-Lee (1976)	Airline safety and locational life-expectancy risks	15.6
Gerking, deHaan, and Schulze (1988)	Job fatality risk	3.4 willingness to pay 8.8 willingness to accept
Jones-Lee (1989)	Motor vehicle accidents	3.8
Miller and Guria (1991)	Traffic safety	1.2
Viscusi, Magat, and Huber (1991)	Automobile accident risks	2.7 (median) 9.7 (mean)

Note: All values in December 1990 US dollars.
Source: W. K. Viscusi, "The Value of Risks to Life and Health," *J. Econ. Literature* 31(4) (1993), Table 6.

The survey also elicits the baseline wage or salary amount Y so that the starting point B can be observed. After acquiring this information, subjects received one of four different hazard warning labels and were told that this chemical would replace the chemicals with which they were then working on the job. They were then asked to assess their new risk level (p_2) and were asked what percentage wage increase they required to work with this new chemical.

Thus, the survey establishes two points along a constant expected utility locus, B and D, which provides different information than does market-based evidence. For small increases in risk, this tradeoff will be identical to the marginal tradeoff at point B. However, for larger risk increments, the average risk tradeoff for BD will exceed that at the point of tangency with EU at point B. Moreover, once one has knowledge of two or more points along a constant expected utility locus, it will be possible to estimate the structure of individual utility functions, as will be indicated below.

Surveys have been used to value not only job-related outcomes but other health consequences as well. Table 21.1 summarizes the survey results pertaining to estimates of the value of life. The first two studies appearing in Table 21.1 are based on relatively small samples and should be regarded as being very exploratory in nature. The latter four studies are more extensive and yield implicit value of life estimates of the same order of magnitude as those found by the labor market studies. The main exception is the lowest mean value of life in the Miller and Guria study, but since this sample pertains to New Zealand, for which the average income level is lower, one would expect to obtain lower value of life estimates.[12] In addition, it is noteworthy that the classes of health outcomes, including motor vehicle accidents and death due to heart attack, also can be broadened to analyze differences in the value of life depending on how one dies as opposed to simply death itself.

For the most part, the studies in Table 21.1 utilize either an interview approach similar to the one used by Viscusi and O'Connor[13] or a relatively straightforward contingent valuation approach in which respondents indicate how much they would be willing to pay for different kinds of improvements in public safety efforts that will lead to improved safety. The main exception is that Viscusi, Magat, and Huber utilize an interactive computer program in which respondents are presented with pairwise comparisons of different areas in which they could live, where these areas differ in terms of their automobile accident fatality risk and their cost of living.[14] Respondents indicate which of the two areas they prefer, and the program revises these options until indifference is achieved. The observed rates of tradeoff at this point of indifference are then used to determine the implicit value of life.

Table 21.2 indicates how this methodology can be extended to analyze non-fatal health risks. The methodology can address a broad range of classes of injuries, including illnesses, a wide variety of health consequences from different household chemicals, and health outcomes from broader environmental exposures including nerve disease, lymphoma, and chronic bronchitis. Thus, these studies can greatly expand the scope of the outcomes that can be addressed.

The 1987 study by Berger et al.[15] is perhaps the main exception in that this study does not focus on probabilistic outcomes but rather willingness

---

[12] T. Miller and J. Guria, "The Value of Statistical Life in New Zealand," Report to the Ministry of Transport, Land Transportation Division.

[13] Viscusi and O'Connor, "Adaptive Responses to Chemical Labeling."

[14] W. K. Viscusi, W. A. Magat, and J. Huber, "Pricing Environmental Health Risks: Survey Assessments of Risk–Risk and Risk–Dollar Tradeoffs for Chronic Bronchitis," *J. Envtl. Econ. & Mgmt.* 21(1) (1991), 32–51.

[15] M. C. Berger et al., "Valuing Changes in Health Risks: A Comparison of Alternative Measures," *Southern Econ. J.* 53(4) (1987), 967–84.

Table 21.2. *Summary of valuations of non-fatal health risks*

Author (year)	Nature of risk	Value of health outcome
Viscusi and O'Connor (1984)	Job injury of sufficient severity to be reported to US Bureau of Labor Statistics	$13,810–$17,761
Mark Berger et al. (1987)	Certain outcome of one day of various illnesses	$98 (coughing spells), $35 (stuffed up sinuses), $57 (throat congestion), $63 (itching eyes), $183 (heavy drowsiness), $140 (headaches), $62 (nausea)
Viscusi and Magat (1987)	Bleach: chloramine gassings, child poisonings; Drain opener: hand burns, child poisonings	$1.78 million (bleach gassing), $0.65 million (bleach poisoning), $1.60 million (drain opener hand burns), $1.06 million (drain opener and child poisoning)
Viscusi, Magat, and Huber (1987)	Morbidity risks of pesticide and toilet bowl cleaner; valuations for 15/10,000 risk decrease to zero	Insecticide: $1,504 (skin poisoning), $1,742 (inhalation), $3,489 (child poisoning); Toilet bowl cleaner: $1,113 (gassing), $744 (eye burn), $1,232 (child poisoning)
Viscusi, Magat, and Forrest (1988)	Insecticide inhalation–skin poisoning, inhalation–child poisoning	Inhalation–skin poisoning: $2,538 (private), $9,662 (NC altruism), $3,745 (US altruism); Inhalation–child poisoning: $4,709 (private), $17,592 (NC altruism), $5,197 (US altruism)
Evans and Viscusi	Morbidity risks of pesticides and toilet bowl cleaner; utility function estimates of risk values. T values pertain to marginal risk–dollar tradeoffs, and L values pertain to monetary loss equivalents.	Insecticide: $761 (T), $755 (L) (skin poisoning); $1,047 (T), $1,036 (L) (inhalation–no kids); $2,575 (T) (inhalation–children) $1,748 (L); $3,207 (T), $2,877 (L) (child poisoning); Toilet bowl cleaner: $633 (T), $628 (L) (eye burn); $598 (T), $593 (L) (gassing–no kids); $717 (T), $709 (L) (gassing–children); $1,146 (T), $1,126 (L) (child poisoning)
Magat, Viscusi, and Huber (1991)	Environmental risk of non-fatal nerve disease, fatal lymphoma, non-fatal lymphoma	$1.6 million (nerve disease), $2.6 million (non-fatal lymphoma), $4.1 million (fatal lymphoma)
Viscusi, Magat, and Huber (1991)	Environmental risk of severe chronic bronchitis morbidity risk	0.32 fatality risk of $904,000 risk–risk; $561,000 risk–dollar
Krupnick and Cropper (1992)	Environmental risk of severe chronic bronchitis morbidity risk	$496,800–$691,200 (median)

Source: W. K. Viscusi, "The Value of Risks to Life and Health," *J. Econ. Literature* 31(4) (1993), Table 7, with additions by the author.

to pay to alleviate certain outcomes in which particular days are going to be spent with health symptoms, such as a sore throat. Otherwise, the studies focus on risk–money tradeoffs of various kinds. Further, all six studies in which I collaborated involve different kinds of pairwise comparisons, where the attributes of the options are manipulated until indifference is achieved. The 1992 Krupnick and Cropper study[16] administered the Viscusi, Magat, and Huber survey to a different sample and consequently adopts an identical methodology. In almost all cases, the pairwise comparisons involve a choice of two different products or a decision to move to one of two different regions, where the two attributes of each option include risk and monetary components.

Some of these studies also use what can be termed risk–risk tradeoffs in that instead of trading off combinations of health risks and money, the pair of attributes for each of the options pertains to risk. For example, a region may be characterized by an automobile accident fatality rate and a cancer death rate due to environmental air pollution exposures. Respondents then consider different options and continue to do so until achieving indifference, where the ultimate objective is to establish an automobile death risk equivalent to the health outcome such as cancer. Use of this risk–risk approach avoids the utilization of a monetary metric in the survey, and some of the advantages of this method will be discussed below. In conjunction with existing estimates of the implicit value of life, it is possible to convert these risk–risk estimates into risk–money tradeoffs. Alternatively, one can incorporate such a risk–money tradeoff into the survey, as was the case in these studies.

The death risk metric

A major class of concerns pertains to the metric used to assess the valuation of the risk reduction. Although it is convenient to use the familiar monetary metric, this metric often offends the sensitivities of non-economists and may seem a bit inappropriate to respondents who are less comfortable with the idea of making such tradeoffs. Another approach that can be utilized is to use a risk metric in which two different classes of risk are traded off.

[16] A. J. Krupnick and M. L. Cropper, "The Effect of Information on Health Risk Valuations," *J. Risk & Uncertainty* 5(1) (1992), 29–48.

Although the risk–money tradeoff approach is the most common, it is also possible to use other metrics to value risk. For example, an approach used to value cancer, nerve disease, and chronic bronchitis has utilized reference lotteries involving automobile accident risks. Thus, instead of giving respondents pairwise choices involving money and health outcomes, the outcome pairs involve automobile accident deaths and the risk in question. Should one then choose to convert an automobile accident death risk metric to a monetary metric, one can either use automobile accident–money tradeoffs elicited within the survey or else use implicit value-of-life estimates based on the literature.

Moreover, in some contexts, it is not necessary to make such a conversion. Policy analyses in which the critical concern is the cost per life saved do not require the establishment of a benefit value, as one can simply compare the cost-per-life saved amount with various reference points for policy acceptability. In the standard benefit–cost case, this reference point would be the implicit value of life, but few government agencies in the United States other than the US Department of Transportation appear to be constrained in this manner.[17] Wars also involve a range of health effects that can be converted to death risk equivalents.

The use of the death lottery metric has a variety of practical advantages. Most important is that it avoids the explicit presentation of money–risk tradeoffs to respondents. Many policymakers and, indeed, many respondents may be averse to making tradeoffs between cost of living and lives saved or similar kinds of choices. Use of two different risk attributes can alleviate these specialized sensitivities. Wholly apart from the special problems posed by outcomes such as life and health, this approach presents subjects with commodities that may be more comparable. As a result, it may be easier for respondents to conceptualize tradeoffs since the nature of the commodities is much more similar.

A particularly important benefit of utilizing risk–risk tradeoffs is that this approach may be less prone to criticisms that respondents are dealing with hypothetical interview currency. In situations in which respondents are asked their willingness-to-pay amounts for risk reduction, there may

---

[17] The low value of life for regulations issued by the US Department of Transportation relative to other agencies is exemplified in the cost-per-life-saved statistics reported in Viscusi et al., "Measures of Mortality Risks." See also the data presented in S. Breyer, *Breaking the Vicious Circle: Toward Effective Risk Regulation* (Cambridge, Mass.: Harvard Univ. Press, 1993).

be a tendency to exhibit substantial willingness to pay that may not in fact be evidenced once confronted with real choices.

Hypothetical expenditures are not bound by the same rigid budget constraints as actual expenditures. Use of two different risk attributes makes both of the consequences involved pertinent to the respondents' well-being, and they are likely to elicit more honest and meaningful answers than would be yielded through hypothetical contingent valuation currencies.

The final studies listed in Table 21.2 indicate the implications of these risk–risk tradeoffs for several different environmental risks. Nerve disease, fatal lymphoma, and non-fatal lymphoma are all associated with implicit values of more than $1 million per statistical health outcome.[18] Severe cases of chronic bronchitis are less highly valued, as they are tantamount to roughly one chance in three of death.[19] In contrast, cancer is viewed as being tantamount to death by the respondents.

By utilizing two different risk tradeoffs, it is also possible to normalize the denominators associated with the risks being faced. It may be that the risks in question are truly rare events, of the order of one in a million. Respondents can then be asked what the equivalent automobile accident risk per 1 million would be, thus enabling them to focus on the relative severity of the two different health outcomes involved as opposed to attempting to comprehend the subtleties of the small probabilities being presented to them.

Although there has been much less experience with the risk–risk approach than with the various risk–money contingent valuation methodologies, the technique does offer substantial potential advantages, particularly in contexts in which respondents will be better able to deal with the risk tradeoffs in a more meaningful manner.

Estimation of utility functions

Knowing the shape of individual utility functions for the particular attributes of interest would put one in a good position to assess the deterrence values for a wide variety of health risks associated with war. It would be

---

[18] W. A. Magat et al., "The Death Risk Lottery for Health Risks: Cancer and Nerve Disease," Duke Working Paper (1991), forthcoming in *Mgmt. Science*.

[19] See W. K. Viscusi et al., "Pricing Environmental Health Risks: Survey Assessments of Risk–Risk and Risk–Dollar Tradeoffs for Chronic Bronchitis," *J. Envtl. Econ. & Mgmt.* 21(1) (1991), 32–51; Krupnick and Cropper, "The Effect of Information on Health Risk Valuations."

possible to analyze local rates of tradeoff, substantial changes in risk, and a wide variety of other questions regarding how people value risk and how these valuations differ across the population.

Perhaps the greatest benefit of utilizing surveys rather than market data is that one is not restricted to addressing the narrow set of questions that can be answered using available market evidence. Hedonic wage and price studies focus on the market equilibria represented by the set of tangencies between individual offer curves and the available opportunity sets. In the job market case, one observes average rates of tradeoff between risk and wages. For property values, one can estimate average rates of tradeoff between property values and environmental amenities. However, the use of surveys enables one to trace out the entire character of the constant expected utility locus sketched in Figure 21.2. Indeed, by asking the individual multiple questions, one can identify more than two points on a constant expected utility locus and thus ascertain the character of individual preferences.

A series of studies with William Evans[20] examines many survey situations involving consumers and workers. Using a survey on more than one price–risk combination or wage–risk combination along a constant expected utility locus, the studies estimate the character of individual utility functions pertinent to the problem.

In the case of job accidents, for which the risk is likely to alter the character of individual utility functions, we have estimated state-dependent utility functions. These have included functions for which no specific functional form has been assumed, as we have taken first-order and second-order Taylor's series approximations to general utility functions. In addition, we have also obtained estimates assuming a specific logarithmic functional form for the utility functions. In each case, it is possible not only to estimate average shapes of utility functions across a population, but also to let the parameters of the utility function vary with the individual characteristics. The key parameters can be made dependent on demographic attributes such as individual age, education,

---

[20] See W. K. Viscusi and W. Evans, "Utility Functions that Depend on Health Status: Estimates and Economic Implications," *Am. Econ. Rev.* 80(3) (1990), 353–74; W. Evans and W. K. Viscusi, "Estimation of State-Dependent Utility Functions Using Survey Data," *Rev. Econ. & Stat.* 73(1) (1991), 94–104; W. Evans and W. K. Viscusi, "Utility-Based Valuations of Health," *Am. J. Agric. Econ.* 73(5) (1991), 1422–27; W. Evans and W. K. Viscusi, "Income Effects and Value of Health," *J. Hum. Res.* 28(3) (1993), 497–518.

sex, and similar attributes. Thus, not only does this formulation enable one to estimate the character of utility functions, but it also enables one to distinguish the heterogeneity in preferences, whereas market evidence on heterogeneity compounds the influence of heterogeneity in supply and heterogeneity in demand.

In the case of consumer risks, the consequences have often been so minor that it is unlikely that the adverse outcomes alter the structure of utility functions. Using this approach, it is impossible to test formally whether utility functions alter in character or whether the adverse outcome can be treated as a monetary loss equivalent. Thus, this technique enables one to explore the implications of different outcomes for the structure of individual preferences, which is often of substantial interest in its own right.

In the case of risks that entail losses that might be potential objects of government insurance, as in the case of workers' compensation or court-provided product liability awards, the structure of utility functions is clearly of paramount interest. If the marginal utility of income substantially decreases as a result of an accident, then it will not be optimal to replace the income loss. Individuals who suffer brain damage, for example, experience a very low level of utility, but transfers to them may do little to enhance their welfare once the basic medical care has been provided.

In the case of job market risks, we have found that because of the adverse effects of job injuries on individuals' ability to derive welfare from expenditures, the optimal replacement rate for job-related income losses is 0.85. In contrast, for minor consumer product injuries that individuals view as being tantamount to a drop in income, the optimal replacement rate is equal to the monetary equivalent value of the loss.[21]

This same kind of issue would be pertinent to other damages, including health losses from wars, if the objective were to provide optimal social insurance. Moreover, if the objective is to restore individual levels of utility, adverse effects on the structure of utility functions and the marginal utility derived from income also should be taken into account. The procedure that we have developed enables one to distinguish the particular factors that are at work and the extent of their influence.

Knowledge of individual utility functions enables one to address all of the fundamental issues pertaining to valuation, and we have done so in our consumer- and job-related examples. Thus, it is possible to analyze local

---

[21] Viscusi and Evans, "Utility Functions that Depend on Health Status."

rates of tradeoff, not only at the current level of risk, but also if the base risk level is altered. Higher base risk levels increase the implicit value of injury, but the extent of the variation is an empirical question that must be resolved through exploration of the character of individual preferences.

Similarly, one can analyze marginal rates of willingness to pay and willingness to accept based on the character of individual utility functions, thus avoiding the distortion of these responses through the explicit use of a willingness-to-accept survey methodology. Along the same lines, one can assess the valuation of non-marginal risk changes and explore risk valuations for risk changes other than those specifically addressed in the survey instrument. The effect of individual income and other personal attributes on the heterogeneity of risk valuation can also be resolved through explicit estimation, thus making it possible specifically to link findings to the populations of interest. For example, the estimated income elasticity of the implicit value of job injuries is approximately 1.0.[22]

In short, the use of survey data to estimate utility functions makes it possible to assess individual utility functions and to answer all the risk valuation questions that may be on our evaluation agenda. As a consequence, surveys should not be viewed as simply a mechanism to replicate or augment market-based data, but rather as a much more powerful approach for expanding the scope of inquiry.

Sources of potential irrationality

Although there should be little difference between small changes in risk that represent risk increases rather than risk decreases, in practice there is often substantial asymmetry in the way these risks are treated. It is important to isolate the pertinent tradeoff values free of possible irrational responses that may taint them. In the case of pharmaceutical regulation by the Food and Drug Administration, for example, researchers have suggested that the agency behaves as if its objective is to minimize type II errors, which are the risks arising from approving a defective new drug, while at the same time accepting very substantial type I errors, which are the risks that could have been averted if the drugs had been approved earlier.[23] The

---

[22] *Ibid.*

[23] The respective role of the errors is discussed by H. G. Grabowski and J. M. Vernon, *The Regulation of Pharmaceuticals: Balancing the Benefits and Risks* (Washington, D.C.: American Enterprise Institute, 1983).

drug lag in the United States that accounts for prescription drugs being approved more rapidly in Europe has averted potential disasters, such as the effects of the drug Thalidomide, which led to birth defects in Europe. The FDA, however, never approved this drug for use by pregnant women in the United States. The usual case is that prescription drugs are approved more quickly in Europe, making it possible for these citizens to benefit from drugs such as beta blockers before US patients can take them.[24] These instances are not isolated examples. Among the many drugs ultimately approved in the United States and which were approved earlier in the United Kingdom are Somatotropin, Danazol, and Propranolol. Similarly, drugs that led to major adverse reactions in Europe before being withdrawn include the following drugs that were never approved in the United States: Practolol (severe conjunctivitis), Aminorex (pulmonary hypertension), and Benziodarone (jaundice).[25]

Similarly, events that reduce mortality rates by 1/100,000 are likely to be viewed as less consequential than those that generate an increased mortality risk of 1/100,000. Although the risks involved are very small, there may be an asymmetry in society's value of the two risk changes, even though there should not be.

From an economic standpoint, there should be very little difference between the willingness-to-pay and the willingness-to-accept values for small changes in risk. There may be some small discrepancy. One source of differences is the role of income effects, since an individual's willingness to pay for risk reductions will be a decreasing function of one's income level. Willingness-to-accept values will also be higher than willingness-to-pay values because this change is associated with the increasing risk, where this change involves an increase in the probability that a state of the world in which there is a lower marginal utility of income will occur. Consequently, the opportunity cost of the resources has diminished. These influences are unlikely to be substantial, however, for very small risks.

---

[24] For further discussion of these and other drugs that were approved earlier for use in Europe, see the US General Accounting Office, "FDA Drug Approval – A Lengthy Process that Delayed the Availability of Important New Drugs," HRD–80–64 (May 28, 1980), p. 68.

[25] For further discussion of drugs that led to adverse reactions in other countries but were never approved in the United States, see the US Congress House Subcommittee on Science, Research, and Technology, "The Committee on Science and Technology, Report on the Food & Drug Administration's Process for Approving New Drugs," 96th Congress, First Session, 1980.

Table 21.3. *Valuation of incremental risk reductions for household chemicals*

	Incremental willingness to pay (dollars/bottle) for risk decreases of 5/10,000 from different starting risks			
	Insecticide		Toilet bowl cleaner	
Starting risk (injuries/10,000 bottles)	Inhalation–skin poisoning	Inhalation–child poisoning	Gassing–eyeburn	Gassing–child poisoning
15	1.04	1.84	0.65	0.99
10	0.34	0.54	0.19	0.24
5	2.41	5.71	0.83	0.99

Source: W. K. Viscusi et al., "An Investigation of the Rationality of Consumer Valuations of Multiple Health Risks," *Rand J. Econ.* 18(4) (1987), 475.

The discrepancies that have been observed between willingness to pay and willingness to accept are starkly different from what one would expect based on rational economic models. Consider the results that were revealed in a study of consumer-product risks by Viscusi, Magat, and Huber (1987). In that study, we gave consumers an opportunity to purchase successive reductions in various risks associated with household chemicals. The baseline risk value was a risk of various injury types of 15/10,000. Consumers then had the opportunity to purchase successive reductions of the risk in 5/10,000 increments by paying a higher price for the product. Table 21.3 provides a summary of these willingness-to-pay values for risk reductions. Consumers' willingness to pay for risk reduction diminishes with successive purchases of risk reductions, as one would expect. However, consumers have a willingness to pay that reflects a substantial premium for the final risk reduction that leads to complete elimination of the risk. Thus, there is evidence of certainty premiums as individuals are willing to pay an unusually large amount of money to be assured of safety of the product.

One might also expect that if consumers were faced with risk increases of the order of 5/10,000 there would be a willingness-to-accept value comparable to the willingness-to-pay values for risk reductions of 5/10,000. Respondents confronted with this choice refused to give any finite response that would induce them to purchase the product after the risk had increased in this manner. As a result, the survey was reworded so that the risk increase was only 1/10,000.

Table 21.4. *Response to risk increases of 1/10,000 for pairs of product risks*

Injury pair	Percentage for whom product is too risky to purchase	Mean value ($/bottle) of positive responses
Insecticide		
Inhalation–skin poisoning	77.2	2.86
Inhalation–child poisoning	68.1	3.19
Toilet bowl cleaner:		
Eyeburns–gassing	61.5	5.52
Gassing–child poisoning	74.3	1.28

This question asked subjects what price discount they would require on the new product to accept an additional risk of 1/10,000 for both injuries, starting with risks of 15 injuries per 10,000 bottles sold for both injuries. See W. K. Viscusi et al., "An Investigation of the Rationality of Consumer Valuations of Multiple Health Risks," *Rand J. Econ.* 18(4) (1987), 477.

Consumer reactions to this risk change are indicated in Table 21.4. As can be seen, the consumers who were willing to name a finite price for accepting a risk increase indicated that they needed a much higher level of compensation for this risk increase that was five times smaller than the risk decrease that they were purchasing in the previous manipulation. For the willingness-to-pay amount, the implicit value of the health outcome involved was only $420 for the injury pair inhalation–skin poisonings, whereas the comparable implicit value of the health outcome generated by the willingness-to-accept values was $28,600. This divergence in values by a factor of more than sixty reflects an asymmetry in the way in which risks are treated.

For wars, the main implication is that people are likely to be particularly averse to risking changes that imply that an increase in the risk level has occurred from their accustomed risk amount. What consumers may be reacting to is the fact that they are now facing an unaccustomed risk that they did not previously encounter, whereas many more familiar risks may be of much larger magnitude. Willingness-to-accept amounts will overstate the deterrence value of reducing risks to war.

A variety of explanations have been put forth to explain this phenomenon. What is noteworthy about these explanations is that they all involve departures from rational expected utility maximization. In one study, Viscusi, Magat, and Huber term this phenomenon the "reference risk effect," whereby individuals have reference risk levels.[26] Once these risk levels are disturbed through policy shifts, consumers will react in an alarmist manner, as was indicated above.

More generally, these kinds of phenomena reflect differences in attitudes towards errors of commission and errors of omission. Errors of commission, whereby a new risk is initiated through a war or other instances, tend to be viewed quite adversely. In contrast, errors of omission, such as the failure to take action to save lives, tend to be less highly valued. The errors of commission tend to involve identified lives at risk, whereas errors of omission impose costs on statistical lives. Since the statistical lives at risk are not a well-organized lobbying group, the losses to them are less visible and receive less attention.

The question then becomes: what should be the role of government policy in the presence of these various forms of irrational behavior? One might argue that the role of the government in a democratic society is to promote the preferences of its citizens. However, in the case of irrational choices, it makes little sense to foster programs that simply institutionalize the irrationalities that are displayed in our private choices. A more sensible approach would be to maximize the expected utility of the citizenry in the manner in which they would choose if they fully understood the risks that were present and could act upon them in a rational manner. Thus, we would not jettison the legitimate differences in tastes that people had, but biases in risk perception and similar anomalies in behavior should not become the driving force for government action. Alarmist and irrational responses to novel risks, in particular, pose a threat to innovations that may promise to yield much greater expected health benefits to the public than the associated costs that may be based on unfounded fears.

A similar kind of bias in decisionmaking may arise with respect to ambiguous risks. As the Ellsberg paradox[27] demonstrated, individuals would prefer to have a precise opportunity to win a prize rather than have an imprecise chance in which the subjective probability was the same but the odds were uncertain. Viscusi, Magat, and Huber later generalized this phenomenon to the loss situation.[28] That article showed that, when facing

---

[26] W. K. Viscusi et al., "An Investigation of the Rationality of Consumer Valuations of Multiple Health Risks," *Rand J. Econ.* 18(4) (1987), 465–79.

[27] See D. Ellsberg, "Risk, Ambiguity and the Savage Axioms," *Q. J. Econ.* 75 (1961), 643–69.

[28] W. K. Viscusi et al., "Communication of Ambiguous Risk Information," *Theory & Decision* 31(2/3) (1991), 159–73.

ambiguous environmental risks, individuals displayed ambiguity aversion as they would be willing to incur a higher mean risk level if doing so could provide them with a choice that had a smaller degree of risk ambiguity associated with it. From the standpoint of subjective expected utility maximization, the precision of the probabilistic judgments should not enter. However, in practice, when facing the prospect of losses imprecisely understood probabilities tend to be avoided.

The implications of this result for wars are similar, in spirit, to the implications of the willingness-to-pay/willingness-to-accept discrepancy. Novel risks, such as those that arise through new weapon systems or chemical exposures, will tend to be less precisely understood. People consequently will tend to overvalue these risks relative to more familiar risks that have been more precisely identified. Once again, the role of the government should be to act upon the best information regarding these risk judgments rather than to be deterred by the presence of imprecision.

Conclusion

Establishing the appropriate economic principles for wars is relatively straightforward. If the objective is compensation, as in the case of the US tort system, the basic principles for compensation should follow those used by the judicial system. In the case of wrongful death, the appropriate compensation is the present value of lost earnings less the decedent's consumption. For non-fatal injuries, the present value of lost earnings plus medical expenses should be the guide.

Situations in which the objective is not insurance but rather deterrence would require a different methodology, such as that now used to value the health-enhancing effects of government regulations. However, it is difficult to envision situations in which these deterrence values would be applied in war contexts, except to judge liability. In setting compensation, it would not be appropriate to use these amounts since they would provide for excessive insurance of the individuals who were being compensated. An alternative approach if the objective is to provide deterrence is to use the willingness-to-pay measures to set the appropriate level of the total economic damages, part of which will be paid in compensation and the rest of which will be a fine paid to the state. That approach will yield efficient deterrence and also will not provide excessive insurance for the victims of wars.

The appropriate measure for deterrence is society's willingness to pay for the changes in risk that result from these wars. A variety of approaches have emerged in an effort to estimate these willingness-to-pay values. The literature pertaining to quality-adjusted life years is a frequently employed approach in the medical decisionmaking literature. However, the usual empirical implementation of this framework imposes very severe restrictions on the character of individual preferences across health states that are unlikely to hold generally.

Since the appropriate matter of interest is society's willingness to pay for small variations in risk, there is no barrier to eliciting these values explicitly. In some instances market evidence is instructive. In others, survey data can be used to obtain individual valuations of the risks involved. This effort is also not necessarily a trivial proposition, as any such undertaking must adequately convey to respondents the nature of the health outcomes and the character of the tradeoff so that they can think about these issues in a sensible manner and give reasonable responses. If the deterrence values for health outcomes of wars become important, undoubtedly there will be an emerging body of work undertaken to address these concerns. At present, the literature is dominated by studies targeted at efforts in policy areas where implicit values of life and health now provide the basis for policy judgments, as in the case of health, safety, and environmental regulations.

Although the empirical techniques for estimating these values undoubtedly will continue to undergo development and further refinement, even current methodologies can shed considerable light on pertinent health effect assessment issues. In many cases simply avoiding the most extreme policy errors is most important. In particular, one should not fall prey to the potential irrationalities that often impede choices in these areas, such as excessive attention to risks of commission as opposed to risks of omission. Rather, policies should focus on all risk consequences in a manner that reflects the preferences the citizenry would express if they were fully informed and could make rational choices with respect to these risks.

PART V

PROSPECTS FOR THE FUTURE

INTRODUCTION

JAY E. AUSTIN

As will be discussed in detail in the Epilogue to this volume, the 1999 Kosovo conflict showed the inadequacy of existing legal mechanisms for hearing and evaluating allegations of wartime environmental damage. Among other things, Yugoslavia's International Court of Justice lawsuit against the ten NATO countries alleged breaches of "the obligation not to cause considerable environmental damage," "the obligation not to cause far-reaching health and environmental damage," and "the obligation not to use prohibited weapons."[1] Taken purely on their face, these charges – epitomized by the NATO bombing of the Pancevo petrochemical complex and the use of depleted uranium – could plausibly have triggered provisions of the Geneva Conventions, Protocol I, and customary international law, all of which were cited in the petition. Yet they suffered the same fate as Yugoslavia's other assertions of legal violations: the ICJ, limited by its consent-based system of jurisdiction, declined to address the merits of the case.

The question remains how, even in the wake of justifiable outrage about Serbia's own clear violations of law, the consequences of NATO actions also might be examined, judged, and if necessary redressed. At the same time that the International Criminal Tribunal for the Former Yugoslavia handed down its historic indictment of President Slobodan Milošević, a coalition of Greek, Canadian, and US lawyers was petitioning the Tribunal to investigate the legality of NATO's bombing campaign and to indict NATO leaders, including President Bill Clinton and Prime Minister

---

[1] E.g., *Legality of Use of Force (Yugo. v. US)*, Application Instituting Proceedings (Apr. 29, 1999), available at http://www.icj–cij.org/icjwww/idocket/iyus/iyusapplication/iyus_application_19990428.html.

Tony Blair.[2] Once the health and environmental impacts of the Pancevo bombing became known, Serb lawyers considered the possibility of filing civil damage suits against the United States.[3] Neither strategy is likely to have widespread success – the former for political reasons, the latter due to issues of sovereign immunity and venue. In the absence of permanent legal fora that are specifically authorized to adjudicate claims of wartime environmental damage, the only recourse is to Security Council action, as in the Gulf War, or to ad hoc fact-finding missions, such as the UN Balkan Task Force of experts from UNEP, NGOs, and national governments sent to investigate postwar conditions in Kosovo. As discussed in Parts II and III, such efforts are complicated by legal ambiguities and scientific uncertainty. To take just one example, in the immediate aftermath of a conflict, it is exceedingly difficult to predict which environmental damage will prove to be "long-term," much less how that phrase will be applied by a court or tribunal.

This Part focuses on new and emerging legal regimes for preventing, investigating, and sanctioning wartime environmental damage. The authors share the goal of strengthening international institutions or creating new ones in order to clarify the rules of engagement, reach speedy and accurate determinations of when they are violated, and hold the responsible states or individuals accountable. For the most part, their proposals are within the immediate reach of the international community, requiring adoption of modest extensions to the law of war, increased use of existing institutions, and defining the role of the nascent International Criminal Court. But they also point beyond the current horizon, and towards more ambitious agendas, such as Richard Falk's call for an "ecocide convention" or the broad proposals to establish an International Court of the Environment.

On the prevention side, Richard Tarasofsky offers an analysis and critique of the IUCN's Draft Convention on the Prohibition of Hostile Military Activities in Protected Areas. This Draft Convention, which is reproduced here in full, is the first attempt at an area-based system of wartime environmental protection. As such, it descends from a long line of law-of-war treaties that restrict entire areas or categories of targets, such as

---

[2] Alexander Cockburn, "If Slobo, Why Not Bill?" *The Nation* (June 21, 1999).

[3] Uli Schmetzer, "Serbs Allege NATO Raids Caused Toxic Catastrophe," *Chicago Trib.* (July 8, 1999). Interestingly, the reverse tactic also has been attempted, with Kosovar Albanians filing a civil suit against Milošević and members of his government in a US court. Raymond Bonner, "Civil Action Accuses Yugoslavs of War Crimes," *N.Y. Times* (May 26, 1999), A12.

the 1954 Hague Convention for the Protection of Cultural Property. The Draft Convention would require designating, in advance of conflict, "non-target" areas in which no hostile military activities would be permitted, subject to certain clearly defined exceptions. Such a regime is largely aimed at deterring harmful activity, but it also has the advantage of establishing bright-line rules that would make it easier to discover, prove, and sanction violations. Towards this end, the Draft Convention also provides for compliance monitoring by UN-supervised expert missions, compulsory arbitration of inter-party disputes, and the possibility of referral to the International Court of Justice.

Another novel approach, from a weapons-based rather than a target-based perspective, is outlined by Barry Kellman, a leading expert on the Chemical Weapons Convention. Kellman examines the verification and enforcement provisions of the CWC, which he describes as "the most intrusive and most information-demanding international weapons control agreement." As a non-proliferation treaty, the CWC is as much concerned with allegations of weapons production (including production of precursor chemicals) as with allegations of actual use. Nonetheless, its detailed, stringent inspection regime not only is a major step towards the elimination of chemical agents, but it also could serve as the model for any future ban on weapons – for example, depleted uranium – that might similarly be deemed excessively harmful to civilian health or the natural environment. Even more intriguing, Article X of the CWC creates an innovative program of investigation and assistance in response to alleged use of chemical weapons, including a voluntary fund established by the states parties. As discussed in Part II, a comparable fund dedicated to wartime environmental response could provide resources for timely expert inspections like the UNEP-led effort in Kosovo.

Indeed, deploying such investigative capability may not require drafting a new treaty. Jean-Marie Henckaerts of the International Committee for the Red Cross observes that Article 90 of Protocol I established a little-used International Fact-Finding Commission to investigate grave breaches and serious violations of the Protocol or the Geneva Conventions, and that Article 91 may allow the Commission's findings to serve as a basis to hold states liable for compensation. Henckaerts thus argues that the Commission could be employed to look into allegations of wartime environmental damage that violates Protocol I, in particular the Article 35(3) prohibition against "widespread, long-term and severe damage to the natural environment." The drawback is that states must make an express declaration recognizing the Commission's competence, either as a general matter or on a case-by-case basis. Since barely a third of the 154 signatories to Protocol I have made a general declaration, the Commission suffers from the same jurisdictional weaknesses as the ICJ. Acknowledging this, Henckaerts also notes that the United Nations could exercise its authority under Article 89 of the Protocol and Chapter VII of the UN Charter to authorize the Commission directly to investigate a specific conflict, which would provide an alternative or supplement to other ad hoc UN mechanisms such as the UNCC or the Balkan Task Force.

The question of the appropriate role of the United Nations – in particular the Security Council – in addressing environmental damage is a theme that runs throughout this Part. Henckaerts's hope is that the UN will come to rely on the Commission's expertise and to incorporate its fact-finding mandate into future Security Council resolutions. Similarly, the IUCN Draft Convention would require the Security Council to include a list of designated protected areas in every resolution dealing with armed conflict; Tarasofsky raises the interesting legal issue of whether a treaty other than the UN Charter technically can "require" the Security Council to take action. Both proposals echo Falk's recommendation, spelled out in Part II, that the UN General Assembly pass a resolution that would generalize the liability principles of Security Council Resolution 687 and make them apply prospectively to future conflicts.

Of course, Security Council action also can obstruct the investigation of allegations, especially when they are made against a permanent member of the Council. One of the most promising institutions for addressing wartime environmental damages, the International Criminal Court, has been controversial precisely because of its proposed independence from the Security Council. The United States, which opposed the ICC almost from the beginning, has continued to push for changes that would require the Security Council to approve ICC prosecutions[4] – an ironic stance, given the US government's equally fervent contention that Security Council approval was not needed to initiate hostilities in Kosovo. The broad debate about creation of the Court and the scope of its jurisdiction in reality is a debate about the future of international humanitarian law.

---

[4] E.g., Paul Lewis, "US to Seek to Alter Plan for Pursuing War Crimes," *N.Y. Times* (July 25, 1999), A12.

While any discussion of environmental protection is merely a footnote to this larger debate, it nonetheless is worth considering how a fully empowered International Criminal Court could become a tool for deterring and punishing wanton environmental destruction during wartime.

Article 8 of the Rome Statute that created the ICC gives the Court jurisdiction over "war crimes in particular when committed as a part of a plan or policy or as part of a large-scale commission of such crimes." Among a long list of enumerated offenses is Article 8(2)(b)(iv), which prohibits "widespread, long-term and severe damage to the natural environment which would be clearly excessive in relation to the concrete and direct overall military advantage anticipated." The inclusion of environmental crimes within the Court's purview was supported by international environmental and humanitarian organizations, including the ICRC, and thus was relatively uncontroversial. Nevertheless, the delegates considered four alternative formulations of varying stringency, including the possibility of having no prohibition against environmental damage at all, before settling on the provision quoted.

As Henckaerts points out, the final language of Article 8(2)(b)(iv) borrows from Articles 35(3) and 55 of Protocol I. The two pacts share the same threshold for environmental damage, and the same lack of clarity. The crucial terms "widespread," "long-term," and "severe" are not defined in the Rome Statute, and will need to be fleshed out by the Court, which must apply and enforce treaty language that until now has only been the subject of academic discussion. Article 8(2)(b)(iv) also shares another important limitation of Protocol I: it applies only to international conflicts, not to civil wars or other internal strife. The Rome delegates considered the option of including identical environmental protection language in Article 8(2)(e), which defines war crimes in non-international settings, but declined to do so.

Although the Rome drafters clearly took the Protocol I prohibition against "widespread, long-term and severe" environmental harm as their starting point, they qualified it by requiring that it be balanced against "the concrete and direct overall military advantage anticipated." This language, taken from Articles 51 and 57 of Protocol I dealing with civilian casualties, imports the principle of proportionality into the ICC's definition of environmental war crimes, and allows military objectives to be offered as a defense against charges of environmental damage, even intentional damage, as long as that damage is outweighed by the expected military gain.

Indeed, the Rome Statute's version of proportionality is more forgiving than Protocol I's, requiring that the damage be "clearly excessive" rather than just "excessive." Henckaerts, who views the ICC's jurisdiction over individuals as an ideal complement to the International Fact-Finding Commission's jurisdiction over states, worries that the Court's hybrid standard could prove difficult to apply in practice.

Finally, unlike Protocol I, which prohibits both intentional environmental damage and damage that "may be expected," Article 8(2)(b)(iv) contains a strict *mens rea* element, requiring that the offender "intentionally launch[ed] an attack in the knowledge" that it would result in the proscribed level of harm. Thus, to be found guilty of an environmental war crime, an ICC defendant must both have intended the action and known the consequences of that action for the environment. Such an intent requirement may be considered appropriate for assigning criminal responsibility, and is consistent with the other crimes defined in the Rome Statute. However, this insistence on specific intent, coupled with the Court's focus on war crimes that are committed as part of a larger "plan or policy," could further hamper the prosecution of environmental cases.

Given these limitations on the International Criminal Court's authority over environmental war crimes, some observers have recommended going further. In his chapter, Mark Drumbl criticizes the Rome Statute's high threshold of widespread, long-term, and severe damage, which he argues could be lowered to " 'harm' more generally." Drumbl also questions the strict intent requirement, arguing that it could encourage military commanders to engage in willful ignorance about the consequences of their actions on the environment. He suggests that the Court should construe these limitations narrowly to criminalize a broader range of actions, and also assert jurisdiction over violations of other international laws and customs, including Protocol I, that prohibit merely reckless or negligent environmental damage.

However, it would be difficult for the Court to relax both the threshold of damage and the intent requirement while remaining within its present mandate. Generally, criminal law can punish a malicious state of mind that results in little or no damage, as in the crime of attempt, or it can punish a more benign state of mind that results in especially severe damage, as in criminal environmental law. It seems unlikely that the countries that acceded to the Rome Statute intended to let their military officers be prosecuted for any action, committed with any state of mind, that causes any environmental damage whatsoever.

Another refinement, noted by both Drumbl and Henckaerts, would be to establish an environmental remediation fund from the fines and forfeitures collected by the ICC. Under Article 79 of the Rome Statute, it is conceivable that any penalties assessed from environmental war crimes could be earmarked for restoration of the affected environment. However, as the Kuwait example suggests, the magnitude of wartime damage typically is so great that it is extremely unlikely to be remedied from the resources, even the pooled resources, of individual defendants. Further, to the extent that charges of environmental war crimes are ancillary to other serious charges, the concern for using the trust fund to aid human victims doubtless will take priority over addressing environmental harm.

Realistically, the ICC's emphasis on genocide and other grave violations of human rights will continue to occupy most of its attention, and it is questionable whether defendants who seem to be undeterred by the sanctions of humanitarian law will be swayed by the added threat of prosecution for environmental crimes. Nevertheless, Article 8(2)(b)(iv) has rekindled interest in more far-reaching initiatives. Drumbl cites approvingly the various efforts to champion a "Fifth Geneva Convention" on the environment, a treaty that defines "ecocide" as a crime, or an "International Court of the Environment" that would serve as a forum for environmental claims. These proposals differ widely in their approach and underlying philosophy. Some are specific extensions of the law of war to cover a more clearly defined set of environmental war crimes, while others seek to elevate violations of international environmental law to the level of human rights violations, whether or not they occur in wartime. The latter proposals generally also seek to expand standing, so that complaints could be brought by NGOs and individuals as well as states, and to expand jurisdiction, so that complaints could be brought against governments, corporations, and other legal persons in addition to natural persons. A new institution embodying some combination of these reforms arguably could supplement or complement the ICC.

At the same time, it is important to keep in mind the difference between these two related but distinct objectives: extending the international community's jurisdiction over environmental war crimes versus creating a more pervasive international role in environmental regulation. Some of the mechanisms discussed by Drumbl and Kellman blur this distinction; Kellman observes that the CWC, with its focus on weapons precursors, aspires to be a "regulatory scheme for the global chemical industry." This intersection of the law of war and environmental law is a reflection of the increasingly indistinct boundaries between war and military operations other than war; between declared international war and internal conflict, guerrilla warfare, or terrorism; or, for that matter, between war and large-scale peacetime industrial operations that are equally capable of "ecocide."

A key premise of this book is that the two legal regimes have many policy goals in common, and that each has much to learn from the history and experience of the other. But clearly, not all of the legal mechanisms that have evolved in one context will prove to be applicable in both, and to apply the highly specialized model of war crimes tribunals to all environmental damage would be to criminalize the whole of international environmental law. One lesson from the controversy surrounding the ICC is that political support for reforms will continue to depend on clarifying and maintaining thoughtful distinctions between wartime and peacetime activities and damages; between government, military, corporate, and individual actors; between international and domestic procedures for adjudicating responsibility; and between criminal liability, civil liability, and the respective bases and penalties for each.

22

PROTECTING SPECIALLY IMPORTANT AREAS DURING INTERNATIONAL ARMED CONFLICT: A CRITIQUE OF THE IUCN DRAFT CONVENTION ON THE PROHIBITION OF HOSTILE MILITARY ACTIVITIES IN PROTECTED AREAS

RICHARD G. TARASOFSKY

Introduction

The creation of protected natural areas has long been an important conservation tool. Protected areas serve to preserve ecosystems, landscapes, and biological processes. Virtually every country in the world has domestic legislation creating protected areas, and several international environmental treaties require their creation.[1] It is axiomatic that armed conflict can potentially harm these areas, especially since perpetuity and integrity are necessary attributes for achieving the overall conservation objectives. As leading authority Arthur Westing puts it:

> Damage to protected natural areas in times of war can take the form of site disruption (through the expenditure of high-explosives, including the emplacement of mines, the expenditure of chemical weapons, the use of tracked and other vehicles, the setting of wildfires, the releasing of impounded waters, the construction of fortifications, the establishment of bivouacs, etc.), or it can be directed at specific components of the flora or fauna (through the cutting of trees, the hunting of wildlife, fishing, etc.). Damage to the infrastructure of a protected natural area can also occur, including the death and injury of personnel.[2]

In light of what is at stake, it is useful to inquire into what protection the law affords to these areas during armed conflict and to explore possibilities for strengthening this protection.

---

[1] For a survey, see C. de Klemm and C. Sine, *Biological Diversity Conservation and the Law* (Gland, Switzerland: IUCN, 1993), pp. 141ff.

[2] Arthur H. Westing, "Protecting Natural Areas and the Military," *Envtl. Conservation* 19 (1992), 232.

International law provides protection to certain areas during armed conflict. Examples include the 1972 Convention for the Protection of the World Cultural and Natural Heritage (World Heritage Convention)[3] and the 1954 Hague Convention for the Protection of Cultural Property in the Event of Armed Conflict,[4] both of which are administered by UNESCO. However, the effectiveness of these instruments is open to question. The former does not contain any mechanism for ensuring implementation during armed conflict;[5] and the latter, while containing detailed provisions for armed conflict, does not have a very wide scope in practice.[6]

The customary international law principles of military necessity, humanity, and proportionality may, in certain circumstances, operate so as to protect certain areas from damage in specific conditions.[7] However, there are several difficulties in relying purely on these principles. They are so fraught with vagaries and uncertainties that they may not provide sufficient guidance to the commander on the ground. Indeed, by their nature, it is often only possible to evaluate the legality of particular actions on an ex post facto basis – after the possibly irreversible environmental damage has occurred. There is neither an institutionalized way to protect such areas in a strategic manner, nor a mechanism by which to evaluate particular actions.

Calls to develop the international law of armed conflict further so as to protect the environment better have come from many quarters, including the academic literature[8] and Principle 24 of the Rio Declaration on Environment and Development.[9] Seeking to strengthen the international legal protection of specially important sites, the International Union for the Conservation of Nature (IUCN) Commission on Environmental Law (CEL) and the International Council on Environmental Law (ICEL) initiated development of a Draft Convention on the Prohibition of Hostile Military Activities in Protected Areas (annexed to this chapter). The idea of the Draft Convention grew out of several meetings of experts, including con-

---

[3] Convention for the Protection of the World Cultural and Natural Heritage (1972), Arts. 6(1) and 6(3).

[4] Hague Convention for the Protection of Cultural Property in the Event of Armed Conflict (1954).

[5] See W. D. Verwey, "Protection of the Environment in Times of Armed Conflict: In Search of a New Legal Perspective," *Leiden J. Int'l L.* 8 (1995), 15.

[6] See Wolfgang Burhenne, "The Prohibition of Hostile Military Activities in Protected Areas," *Envtl. Pol'y & L.* 27 (1997), 373.

[7] Richard G. Tarasofsky, "Legal Protection of the Environment During International Armed Conflict," *Netherlands Ybk. Int'l L.* (1993), 17ff.

[8] See, e.g., the literature surveyed in Glen Plant, *Environmental Protection and the Law of War* (1992).   [9] Rio Declaration on Environment and Development (1992), Principle 24.

sultations sponsored by IUCN–CEL and ICEL in Munich and Amsterdam in 1991 and 1992, as well as the 1992 World Parks Congress in Caracas. The World Conservation Congress endorsed the concept in 1996.[10]

The Draft Convention seeks to establish a mechanism whereby the UN Security Council provides "safe area" protection to specially important sites. It builds on the principles of the international law of armed conflict by clearly designating areas where the overall interests of humanity should predominate over military ones. This chapter seeks to describe and critique this initiative.

Overview of the Draft Convention

The object and purpose of the Draft Convention is stated in the preamble. The first paragraph recognizes the value of the work done by international organizations within and outside the United Nations in protecting natural and cultural heritage during armed conflict. One such organization is UNESCO, which administers the treaties mentioned above.

The second paragraph expresses the conviction that the legal means for protecting important areas during armed conflict are not yet strong enough to provide full protection for such sites.

The third paragraph expresses the need to bring about the prohibition of all hostile military activities into, out of, or affecting internationally protected areas in all circumstances. This Draft Convention creates one such mechanism, limited to prohibiting such activities in important protected areas designated in accordance with the procedures set out.

The fourth paragraph emphasizes the potential for the UN Security Council, acting under Chapter VII of the UN Charter, to implement the provisions of this instrument. As will be expanded upon below, the heart of the Draft Convention is Article 2, which provides for listing by the Security Council of areas to be protected. These areas are then deemed "non-target" areas during armed conflict.

The final paragraph of the preamble is based on recent experience, and recognizes that regional arrangements and agencies play a key role in relation to maintaining international peace and security. The Declaration on the Enhancement of Cooperation between the United Nations and Regional Arrangements or Agencies in the Maintenance of International

---

[10] For the history of this initiative, see Burhenne, "Prohibition of Hostile Military Activities."

Peace and Security,[11] referred to in the text, builds on Chapter VIII of the UN Charter.

Article 1 sets forth the definitions, which define the scope of the Draft Convention. The Draft Convention applies to "protected areas," defined as those which meet certain qualifying criteria. It must be emphasized that the Draft Convention does not seek to cover all areas that States decide to place under protection, but only those that are of "outstanding international significance" from any one of the listed points of view. Such areas may be terrestrial or marine. They may include those so designated under international agreements or programs.

Article 2 is key. It creates the mechanism whereby the UN Security Council designates protected areas as non-target areas. This listing is meant to ensure that these sites do not become the targets of military activities, either directly or indirectly by attacks aimed outside the area but with the intent of causing harm to the sites. The protection provided by the listing is temporary, lasting only for the duration of the particular armed conflict. It is important to note that the protection provided by the Draft Convention only becomes available to those protected areas the UN Security Council places on its list; listing under an international agreement or program alone does not entitle such an area to protection until the Security Council so determines. Naturally, an area that already has internationally recognized status may have a better chance of being designated.

In designated areas, all hostile military activity is prohibited. This protection is not, however, absolute. Article 3 provides that protected status can be lost if the state party in whose territory the area is located uses it for military purposes.

Article 4 expressly anticipates partnerships between international organizations and non-governmental organizations (NGOs), operating under the supervision of the United Nations. Should cases of non-compliance be discovered, provision is made for follow-up action. Article 5 calls for widespread dissemination of the Draft Convention. Article 6 provides for meetings of the parties, to take place at the request of at least one state party. The purpose of these meetings is to review the implementation of the Convention.

---

[11] Declaration on the Enhancement of Cooperation between the United Nations and Regional Arrangements or Agencies in the Maintenance of International Peace and Security, annex to UN General Assembly Resolution 49/57 (Dec. 9, 1994).

Article 7 provides for inter-state dispute settlement. It establishes compulsory arbitration at the request of any state that is party to the dispute. In the event that agreement is not reached on the organization of the arbitration, the Draft Convention allows any of the disputants to submit the matter to the International Court of Justice in accordance with its Statute.

Evaluation

In this author's view, this initiative has considerable merit. Focusing on only those sites that are determined to be internationally important not only has the advantage of being more feasible than seeking to provide legal protection to all protected areas, but it also builds on existing international agreements and programs. Agreements in the conservation realm include the 1971 Convention on Wetlands of International Importance Especially as Waterfowl Habitat[12] and the 1972 World Heritage Convention;[13] an example of a relevant international program is that for Biosphere Reserves, administered by UNESCO. Areas designated under international agreements might also include those agreed to be "demilitarized zones" in accordance with Article 60 of the 1977 Additional Protocol I to the Geneva Conventions of 1949,[14] which meet the listed criteria. The Draft Convention in no way interferes with the exercise of rights and obligations under these treaties, including their applicability during armed conflict. Rather, the effect of the Draft Convention is to strengthen their effectiveness during armed conflict.

Article 2 is the central innovation in the Draft Convention. By including this paragraph in the text, the Parties to the Convention assert not only that it is appropriate to enlist the Security Council in this effort, but that the Security Council may usefully take further action to ensure that the Draft Convention is effectively implemented. The legal basis cited is Chapter VII of the UN Charter, entitled "Action With Respect to Threats to the Peace, Breaches of the Peace, and Acts of Aggression," which defines the obligations and entitlements of the Security Council to act where it determines such conditions to exist. Under this Chapter, the Security

---

[12] Convention on Wetlands of International Importance Especially as Waterfowl Habitat (1971), Art. 2.   [13] World Cultural and Natural Heritage Convention, Arts. 1–6.

[14] Additional Protocol I to the Geneva Conventions of August 12, 1949, and Relating to the Protection of Victims of International Armed Conflicts (June 8, 1977; entered into force, Dec. 7, 1978), 16 *I.L.M.* (1977), 1391.

Council is provided with a range of possible actions in response to a situation of armed conflict, from recommending or deciding provisional measures,[15] measures not involving use of armed forces,[16] and measures relying on armed action.[17] Moreover, by not specifying whether the armed conflict in question is international or non-international, the Draft Convention appears to cover both cases.

That the Security Council has a key role to play in environmental protection during armed conflict should not be surprising, given the increasingly recognized linkage between environment and security and the strong mandate provided to the Security Council under Article 24(1) of the UN Charter.[18] The requirement that every resolution adopted by the Security Council in response to armed conflict include a list of internationally protected areas may help ensure that preservation of these sites remains high on the international agenda.

The basic technique used in the Draft Convention is similar to that used by the Security Council in its recent practice. During the conflict in Bosnia and Herzegovina, the Security Council declared a number of "safe areas" that were meant to be free from armed attacks or other hostile acts that would endanger the well-being or safety of the inhabitants.[19] The declaration of such areas was followed by extension of the mandate of the UN Protection Force in order to enable it to "deter acts against safe areas" and to act "in self-defence, to take the necessary measures, including the use of force, in reply to bombardments against the safe areas by any of the parties or to armed incursion into them."[20]

The central purpose of the Draft Convention is to ensure that areas that are of special importance to humanity are protected. By making this protection conditional on not using the area for military gain, the Draft Convention seeks to balance military and humanitarian interests. This tradeoff is similar to the scheme established by Article 60 of Additional

---

[15] UN Charter, Art. 40.   [16] Ibid., Art. 41.   [17] Ibid., Art. 42.
[18] Ibid., Art. 24(1), which provides, "In order to ensure prompt and effective action by the United Nations, its Members confer on the Security Council primary responsibility for the maintenance of international peace and security, and agree that in carrying out its duties under this responsibility the Security Council acts on their behalf." In addition, Article 25 provides, "The members of the United Nations agree to accept and carry out the decisions of the Security Council in accordance with the present Charter."
[19] UN Security Council Resolutions 819 and 824 (1993); see also Report of the Secretary-General Pursuant to Resolution 844 (1993), S/1994/555 (May 9, 1994).
[20] UN Security Council Resolution 836 (1993).

Protocol I, according to which if a state uses a protected area for specified military purposes, the protected status shall be revoked.

Making the protection conditional effectively gives the state of whose territory the protected area is a part a veto over whether to accept the protection. This is appropriate, in that a state should not be deprived of its legitimate right of self-defense unless it so chooses. The importance of the right of self-defense has been recently reaffirmed by the International Court of Justice, which stated the following:

> [T]he Court is of the view that the issue is not whether the treaties relating to the protection of the environment are or are not applicable during an armed conflict, but rather whether the obligations stemming from these treaties were intended to be obligations of total restraint during military conflict. The Court does not consider that the treaties in question could have intended to deprive a State of the exercise of its right of self-defence under international law because of its obligations to protect the environment. Nonetheless, States must take environmental considerations into account when assessing what is necessary and proportionate in the pursuit of legitimate military objectives. Respect for the environment is one of the elements that go to assessing whether an action is in conformity with the principles of necessity and proportionality.[21]

Further, by creating a means for independent monitoring of compliance by expert missions, the Draft Convention has a greater chance of success. As seen above, follow-up action in the event of non-compliance would most likely be through the Security Council, either directly as the sending body, or arising out of recommendations made to it by the sending body. Deeming the members of the mission to be UN personnel within the meaning of the cited instrument helps provide for their protection.

Finally, although seemingly self-evident, the provision calling for dissemination and study of the Draft Convention is useful. The obligations contained in the Draft Convention must be made known to relevant decisionmakers, from the senior commander down to the field soldier. The importance of ensuring wide dissemination and study of the obligations of the law of armed conflict has increasingly been recognized.[22]

---

[21] *Legality of the Threat or Use of Nuclear Weapons*, Advisory Opinion of the International Court of Justice (July 8, 1996), para. 30.

[22] See, e.g., UN General Assembly Resolution 49/50 (Dec. 9, 1994), in relation to Guidelines for Military Manuals and Instructions on the Protection of the Environment in Times of Armed Conflict. The Guidelines have been published as an annex to UN Doc. A/49/323 (1994).

As experience in implementing and applying the Draft Convention is gathered, it may become necessary to have an intergovernmental review of implementation. But the idea of making this review discretionary is useful. In so doing, no new international bureaucracies or permanent bodies are created.

Suggestions for improvement

Further work is expected to be done on the Draft Convention. The following are some suggestions for its improvement. Beginning with the least important, the Draft is not as clearly written as it might be. Further drafts should clear up some of the stylistic editorial ambiguities.

Another modest improvement would be to clarify the role of NGO members of the expert missions. While it is laudable that the Draft Convention provides for independent verification of compliance, it is unlikely that states will agree to provide such personnel with full UN protection unless some discipline is placed on their activities. This is not a difficult area conceptually – the suggestion is that further thought must be given to the operational aspects.

Further, the powerful force of the compulsory arbitration provision in Article 7, as currently drafted, is defeated by the optional character of the remedy – possibly going to the ICJ – in case the venue for arbitration is not agreeable. This effectively allows the defending state to delay the proceedings indefinitely. One possible change would be to provide for an initial compulsory arbitration, on the question of the arbitration venue, by the UN Secretary-General or another independent body nominated by the Security Council.

The role of the Security Council is the most interesting, but also the most legally challenging component of the Draft Convention. It is virtually unprecedented for a treaty (other than the UN Charter itself) to *require* the Security Council to do something; and as a matter of law it is unclear whether this is possible. An alternative might be to require the parties to the Convention to *request* that the Security Council make the designations. Similarly, it may be infeasible to expect the Security Council to develop a list of protected areas with every resolution it passes. This too might require some softening so as to increase acceptance of the Convention.

Finally, the Draft Convention does not set forth a procedure for how the Security Council should determine which protected areas to include on its list. By not stipulating this, the Security Council is afforded maximum flexibility to devise the procedure most appropriate to the circumstances. In most cases, however, it would be preferable that states having jurisdiction over the area or relevant international bodies nominate areas meeting the aforementioned criteria for listing by the Security Council. These nominations may need to be evaluated by experts to determine whether they in fact meet the requisite criteria. It would then be up to the Security Council to make the political decision whether to include them on its list. Although it might not be appropriate to predetermine what procedure the Security Council should employ when making its designations, it might be appropriate for further versions of the Draft Convention to provide an indicative list of possible procedures, including the one just described.

Annex

Draft Convention on the Prohibition of Hostile Military Activties in Internationally Protected Areas (prepared by the IUCN Commission on Environmental Law and the International Council of Environmental Law)

The States Parties to the present Convention,

Recognising the value of the work done by the competent international organizations both within and outside the United Nations system in dealing with the questions of protection of cultural or natural heritage in times of armed conflicts,

Convinced of the need to further develop international rules relating to armed conflicts to ensure full protection, during such conflicts, of protected areas within the scope of the present Convention,

Convinced further that the rules of international law should establish viable mechanisms for bringing about complete prohibition of all hostile military activities into, out of, or affecting any internationally protected areas in all circumstances, pending the earliest possible termination of an armed conflict,

Mindful of the powers and functions of the Security Council of the United Nations under Chapter VII of the Charter, and of the role the Council could play in adopting appropriate resolutions, in the exercise of such powers and functions, implementing, *inter alia*, the rules contained in the articles set forth below,

Mindful also of the important role the regional arrangements or agencies can play under Chapter VIII of the Charter, in implementing the present Convention, in conformity with the procedures established under the 1994 United Nations cooperation declaration,

Have agreed as follows:

Article 1
Use of terms

For the purposes of the present Convention:

(a) "protected areas" means natural or cultural area [*sic*] of outstanding international significance from the points of view of ecology, history, art, science, ethnology, anthropology, or natural beauty, which may include, *inter alia*, areas designated under any international agreement or intergovernmental programme which meet these criteria; and

(b) "United Nations cooperation declaration" means the Declaration on the Enhancement of cooperation between the United Nations and Regional Arrangements or Agencies in the Maintenance of International Peace and Security, annexed to the General Assembly resolution 49/57, adopted on 9 December 1994.

Article 2
Designation of internationally protected areas

1. Each resolution adopted by the Security Council to take action under Chapter VII of the Charter, in response to a situation of armed conflicts, shall include a list of the relevant internationally protected areas, thereby designated as non-target areas in which all hostile military activities shall not be permitted during the armed conflict in question.

2. The same rule shall apply to the regional arrangements or agencies when taking appropriate actions in the exercise of their functions under Chapter VIII of the Charter, in conformity with the United Nations cooperation declaration.

Article 3
Loss of the status of internationally protected areas

Any internationally protected area as defined in article 1 for designation pursuant to article 2 of the present Convention, shall cease to enjoy such protection when the State Party in whose territory the area is situated:

(a) maintains military installations of any kind within [- - -] of the area in question,

(b) decides to use the area in question to carry out any military activities during an armed conflict.

Article 4
Measures for monitoring compliance with the protection of the designated areas

1. The Security Council, or the regional arrangement or agency as appropriate, shall send expert missions to monitor compliance with the provisions of the present Convention.

2. Competent United Nations organs, programmes and bodies, its specialised agencies or the International Atomic Energy Agencies as well as non-governmental

international organisations, may also send expert missions to monitor compliance with the provisions of the present Convention, as part of the United Nations operation.

3. The expert missions shall report any cases of non-compliance to the sending body which shall take necessary actions to ensure effective implementation of the present Convention.

4. Members of the expert missions performing the functions described in this article shall be considered as United Nations personnel within the meaning of article 1 of the Convention on the Safety of United Nations and Associated Personnel, annexed to the General Assembly resolutions 49/59, adopted on 9 December 1994.

Article 5
Dissemination
The States Parties undertake to disseminate the present Convention as widely as possible and, in particular, to include the study thereof, as well as pertinent provisions of the relevant international instruments.

Article 6
Review meetings
At the request of one or more States Parties, and if approved by a majority of States Parties, the Secretary-General of the United Nations shall convene a meeting of the States Parties to review the implementation of the present Convention, and any problems encountered with regard to its application.

Article 7
Dispute settlement
1. Any dispute between two or more States Parties concerning the interpretation or application of this Convention which is not settled by negotiation shall, at the request of one of them, be submitted to arbitration. If within six months from the date of the request for arbitration the parties are unable to agree on the organization on [*sic*]the arbitration, the dispute may be submitted to the International Cournt of Justice by any of the parties by application in conformity with the Statute of the Court.

Article 8
Signature
This Convention shall be open for signature by all States, until [- - -], at United Nations Headquarters in New York.

Article 9
Ratification, acceptance or approval
This Convention is subject to ratification, acceptance or approval. Instruments of ratification, acceptance or approval shall be deposited with the Secretary-General of the United Nations.

Article 10
Accession
This Convention shall be open for accession by any State. The instruments of accession shall be deposited with the Secretary-General of the United Nations.

Article 11
Entry into force
1. This Convention shall enter into force thirty days after [- - -] instruments of ratification, acceptance, approval or accession have been deposited with the Secretary-General of the United Nations.
2. For each State ratifying, accepting, approving or acceding to the Convention after the deposit of the [- - -] instrument of ratification, acceptance, approval or accession, the Convention shall enter into force on the thirtieth day after the deposit by such State of its instrument of ratification, acceptance, approval or accession.

Article 12
Authentic texts
The original of this Convention, of which the Arabic, Chinese, English, French, Russian and Spanish texts are equally authentic, shall be deposited with the Secretary-General of the United Nations, who shall send certified copies thereof to all States.

23

THE CHEMICAL WEAPONS CONVENTION: A VERIFICATION AND ENFORCEMENT MODEL FOR DETERMINING LEGAL RESPONSIBILITY FOR ENVIRONMENTAL HARM CAUSED BY WAR

BARRY KELLMAN

Introduction

When warfare was envisaged as Napoleonic battalions or German Panzer units traversing Europe, no serious conceptual difficulties attended the detection and identification of environmental consequences. Even in the modern era, battle scars inflicted by artillery and gunfire raise only trifling new problems in this regard. And when considering nuclear weapons, it is ironic that an exemplary virtue of their use would be the ease of detecting at least the direct environmental damage from their detonation.

But a more insidious form of warfare is moving into a preeminent role on the international stage: chemical and biological weapons (CBW). Chemical weapons may be defined primarily as nerve agents, which are closely related to toxins – inanimate poisonous substances produced by living organisms. Biological weapons may be defined as living organisms that infect their victims, causing incapacitation and often death; some can spread to other living entities, even those not initially attacked.[1] Unlike ordnance, these weapons are dispersed as a difficult-to-detect aerosol; moreover, unlike ordnance, the injurious effects of these weapons typically linger far beyond their initial use. Measured by their capability to contaminate soil and water and hence despoil an ecosystem for a prolonged period, the environmental harms caused by CBW exceed the damage caused by most explosive munitions. In terms of assigning responsibility, the invisibility of chemical or biological agents, combined with their long-lasting and

---

[1] See Barry Kellman, "Bridling the International Trade of Catastrophic Weaponry," *Am. U.L. Rev.* 43 (1994), 762–63.

noxious effects, complicates the task of building a legal regime to assess those harms.

One other consideration further confounds the determination of liability and assessment of damages from these weapons: they have not typically been deployed in battle but have been targeted against civilians, and there is every indication that future use will follow the same pattern.[2] These weapons have limited battlefield utility due to the unpredictability and unmanageability of disseminating deadly agents, the ability of attacked troops to defend themselves (either through protective equipment or through inoculation), and these weapons' obvious inability to destroy matériel.

But against civilians, concentrated and exposed and often unaware, or against critical environmental resources that are similarly exposed, chemical and biological agents are devastating. Saddam Hussein correctly calculated that chemical weapons could decimate Iranian troops and squelch Kurdish resistance. From the perspective of an enemy seeking, for whatever reason, to inflict deadly horror that shreds a nation's social fabric, it is difficult to imagine a more effective tool.

Best of all from this warped perspective, chemical and biological weapons are easy to make and to use, and determining who is responsible and holding them liable is nearly impossible. Consider the possibility of a car driven through an urban area at night with a trunk containing a tank of anthrax disseminating from a small nozzle. By dawn, the tank would be empty and the car would be far away; only the disease would remain. Analogously, a helicopter could spray deadly agents over an enemy's food supply; the effects might not be as immediate as fire or bombing, but those effects would last longer and could affect the entire population, and responsibility could be difficult to assess. In some of the most likely sites for warfare today, such as the Middle East and the Indian subcontinent, poisoning of rivers on which entire populations depend offers nightmarish opportunities for a belligerent during wartime.

Thus, the question that this chapter addresses may be phrased as follows: What international legal mechanisms may be developed and applied to determine liability and assess damages if non-destructive but highly lethal agents are used in war, causing widespread environmental consequences?

---

[2] See Sam Nunn, "Terrorism Meets Proliferation: A Post-Cold-War Convergence of Threats," *The Monitor* (Spring 1997), 1.

This is a profoundly new and difficult question, and there are no very good answers.

Some incomplete and imperfect guidance may be obtained from the Chemical Weapons Convention (CWC).[3] The CWC is one of the most recent and most far-reaching multilateral treaties to eliminate an entire category of weapons of mass destruction and prevent their production or proliferation. For the first time, nations have agreed not only to foreswear the use of a weapon, thus spelling the end of chemical weapons' legitimacy as a military armament, but to eliminate that weapon's very existence. Moreover, the CWC's extensive verification regime offers the capability of monitoring a weapon's continued non-production, signifying a quantum leap in international disarmament initiatives. It must be admitted, however, that the central thrust of the CWC is the prevention of chemical weapons proliferation; it is not explicitly designed to offer legal mechanisms for determining liability if those weapons are used.

In three important respects, the CWC may hint at mechanisms that merit serious attention in connection with liability for environmental harm: (1) elaborate mechanisms to monitor and track critical precursors of agents; (2) investigations of alleged use; and (3) legal assistance modalities. The next section of this chapter briefly summarizes the CWC. The following section discusses these three mechanisms, identifies the benefits offered and their inherent limitations, and suggests how these mechanisms could be strengthened in future international agreements.

Overview of the Chemical Weapons Convention

The CWC has three principal objectives. First, it specifies illegality without qualification or condition: the use of chemical weapons[4] is absolutely

---

[3] Convention on the Prohibition of the Development, Production, Stockpiling and Use of Chemical Weapons and on Their Destruction (Jan. 13, 1993), *I.L.M.* 32 (1993), 800 (entered into force April 29, 1997). As of early 1998, the CWC had 106 states parties and over 60 non-ratifying signatories.

[4] "Chemical weapons" are defined as toxic chemicals and their precursors, except where intended for not-prohibited purposes, as long as the types and quantities are consistent with such purposes; munitions and devices specifically designed to cause death or other harm through the toxic properties of toxic chemicals which would be released as a result of employment of such munitions and devices; and any equipment specifically designed for use directly in connection with the employment of munitions and devices. *Ibid.*, Art. II, para. 1.

prohibited. No state party may use chemical weapons nor engage in any military preparations for such use; nor may a state party develop, otherwise acquire, stockpile, or retain chemical weapons, nor transfer them or assist anyone to engage in prohibited conduct.[5] In this regard, the CWC follows a long tradition of efforts to control the methods of warfare and contributes to the international law of armed conflict by codifying substantive limits of permissible conduct in wartime.

Second, the CWC requires that existing chemical weapon stockpiles and production facilities be declared and destroyed, subject to environmental, health, and safety constraints, beginning within two years and completed not later than ten years after the CWC takes effect.[6] Each state party may destroy its weapons and facilities however it chooses, so long as the destruction can be verified.[7] Although the overwhelming majority of states parties have not had national chemical weapons programs and do not possess stockpiles, the CWC's obligations pertaining to destruction of chemical weapons and production facilities are crucial to the Convention's disarmament objectives. The CWC specifies: (1) the principles and methods of destruction of chemical weapons; (2) order of destruction and destruction deadlines; (3) destruction plans; and (4) verification of destruction.

Third, and for purposes of this chapter most important, the CWC seeks to verify that states parties do not initiate or resume chemical weapons production and storage. Verifying non-production of chemical weapons is the core of the CWC; even states parties with no chemical weapons to destroy must comply with the verification measures. Within this elaborate and multi-faceted verification regime are aspects that may be relevant to the determination of liability for environmental consequences of war.

This section of the chapter depicts the CWC generally, surveying: (1) the organization it establishes; (2) its restrictions on chemical activities; (3) its verification regime (in broad terms); (4) its requirements for national implementation; and (5) its compliance mechanisms. Readers familiar with the Convention's basic operations may wish to skip immediately to the next section, where discussion of this chapter's thesis is more directly resumed.

---

[5] *Ibid.*, Art. I, para. 1(b). This prohibition can abide no reservations. *Ibid.*, Art. XXII.
[6] *Ibid.*, Art. IV, para. 6.
[7] *Ibid.*, Verification Annex, pt. IV, paras. 13–14; pt. V, paras. 11, 44(a).

THE ORGANIZATION FOR THE PROHIBITION OF
CHEMICAL WEAPONS

The Organization for the Prohibition of Chemical Weapons (OPCW) is an independent international body that will monitor the production capabilities and activities of CWC states parties to oversee the accomplishment of the CWC's objectives. Its principal organ, the Conference of States Parties, supervises CWC operation, enacts procedural rules, assesses compliance, and resolves issues about the CWC's scope. The Executive Council administers day-to-day activities, including supervising verification. Members are elected for two-year terms by the Conference based on equitable geographic distribution; some seats in each region are designated for nations with the largest chemical industries. The Technical Secretariat consists of a Director-General appointed for a four-year term; inspectors; and requisite scientific, technical, and other personnel. It carries out verification measures and performs functions delegated to it by the Conference and the Council, including monitoring and inspecting facilities that could relate to illegal chemical weapons production.[8]

PRODUCTION AND TRADE RESTRICTIONS

Regulated chemicals that could be made into chemical weapons are listed on three "schedules" that roughly correspond to the relative ease of making a prohibited substance from them. Schedule 1 chemicals primarily include chemical weapons agents. Schedule 2 chemicals are immediate precursors of weapons agents. Schedule 3 chemicals are also weapons precursors, yet these chemicals also have more legitimate commercial uses. While each state party may produce and use toxic chemicals for legitimate commercial purposes, they must ensure that these chemicals are not used for purposes prohibited by the CWC.[9]

The lethal Schedule 1 chemicals that present the greatest risk to the CWC's objectives and purpose may be produced only in limited quantities at specific types of facilities. A state party cannot produce, acquire, retain, or use these chemicals outside the territories of states parties, and cannot

---

[8] See generally *ibid.*, Art. VIII.   [9] *Ibid.*, Art. VI, para. 1.

transfer such chemicals outside its territory except to another state party and according to several restrictions.[10]

The CWC also restricts transfers of chemicals. Any transfer of weapons agents or their precursors among states parties must be for purposes not prohibited by the CWC. Schedule 1 chemicals are subject to the most severe transfer restrictions. They may be transferred only to another CWC state party and only for research, medical, pharmaceutical, or protective purposes; they may not be retransferred. Both the transferring and receiving states parties must notify the Technical Secretariat of each transfer of scheduled chemicals not less than thirty days before any transfer. Furthermore, each state party must make annual declarations regarding transfers during the previous year. For each Schedule 1 chemical that has been transferred, the declaration must identify the chemical and specify the quantity, recipient, and purpose.[11]

Chemicals listed on Schedule 2 may only be transferred to or received from states parties. This restriction went into effect in early 2000, three years after the CWC entered into force. During the interim, each state party had to require an end-use certificate for transfers of these chemicals to states not party to the CWC.[12] Finally, export restrictions of precursor chemicals listed on Schedule 3 apply only to transfers made to states not party to the CWC. For these transfers, each state party must adopt measures to ensure that the transferred chemicals are only used for purposes not prohibited under the CWC[13] and obtain a certificate to this effect from the receiving state. States parties must also "review their existing national regulations in the field of trade in chemicals in order to render them consistent with the object and purpose of the CWC."[14]

VERIFICATION

The CWC throws a pervasive net over a broad array of chemical activities. Its approach was initially modeled on the Nuclear Non-Proliferation

[10] *Ibid.*, Verification Annex, pt. VI, paras. 8–12.
[11] *Ibid.*, Verification Annex, pt. VI, paras. 3–6.
[12] *Ibid.*, Verification Annex, pt. VII, paras. 31–32.
[13] *Ibid.*, Verification Annex, pt. VIII, para. 26.
[14] *Ibid.*, Art. XI, para. 2(e). It should be noted that since 1985 the "Australia Group" has played an important role in coordinating export controls on fifty-four chemicals and dual-use equipment important to the development and spread of chemical weapons. Since the CWC's conclusion, the twenty-six members of the Australia Group have agreed to review controls on exports to signatory states.

Treaty's[15] approach to nuclear proliferation, but the CWC differs in important respects. Whereas controlling nuclear proliferation is based on a tight
accounting of nuclear materials,[16] chemical weapons control cannot successfully adopt a similar strategy because chemical weapons are derived
from substances that are used by legitimate commercial facilities. To be
effective, verification of chemical weapons non-production must be pushed
"upstream," from complete weapons systems to their component parts
and precursors, to critical raw materials and processing technologies. The
existence of dynamic and diversified global chemical industries, whose
production could be readily converted to lethal chemical weapons agents,
requires more extensive verification procedures than those for nuclear
weapons.

Accordingly, users and possessors of scheduled chemicals must report
information to their national government, which must in turn report that
data to the OPCW. Facilities that so report, and only those facilities, are
subject to routine inspection to verify the accuracy of their declarations. A
more intrusive challenge inspection scheme is available if there are doubts
about a state party's compliance.

Declarations

Each state party must make initial and annual declarations regarding any
facility that produces, acquires, consumes, uses, or stores a scheduled
chemical. In addition, declarations must be made regarding facilities that
manufacture organic chemicals beyond certain threshold quantities. The
information to be declared varies with the schedule triggering the declaration. More detailed information must be provided about Schedule 1
chemicals and related facilities than about Schedule 2 chemicals, and more
about Schedule 2 chemicals than about Schedule 3 chemicals. For example, declarations regarding Schedule 1 chemicals and related facilities
include a considerable amount of detailed information about the chemicals and related facilities, while declarations regarding Schedule 2 and

---

[15] Treaty on the Non-Proliferation of Nuclear Weapons (July 1, 1968), *I.L.M.* 7 (1968), 809, 21
U.S.T. 483, T.I.A.S. No. 6839, 729 U.N.T.S. 161 (entered into force Mar. 5, 1970), which has
over 175 states parties. See generally D. Gualtieri and Barry Kellman, "Advancing the Law of
Weapons Control – Comparative Approaches to Strengthen Nuclear Non-Proliferation,"
Mich. J. Int'l L. 16 (1995), 1029.

[16] See generally, William Epstein, "Indefinite Extension – With Increased Accountability," *Bull.
Atom. Sci.* (July 1995), 27.

Schedule 3 chemicals and related facilities focus on aggregate national data, on plant sites, and on past production of these chemicals that were used for chemical weapons purposes. Similarly, declarations of Schedule 2 chemicals and related facilities must include the quantities of Schedule 2 chemicals produced or consumed at each plant site, whereas Schedule 3 declarations only require identification of plant sites that produce these chemicals.

An impressive innovation of the CWC is the attention given to protection of confidential information. The OPCW will require only the minimum amount of information necessary to carry out its responsibilities, and will establish a stringent regime governing the handling of confidential information, including agreements and regulations specifying what information states parties must provide.[17] Confidential information will be securely stored at the OPCW – or, in some cases, with the state party – in a way that precludes identification of the facility to which the information pertains.[18] The Director-General, inspectors, and other staff members must not disclose any confidential information that they have acquired in the course of their duties.[19]

Routine inspections

The Technical Secretariat will conduct routine inspections of chemical facilities to verify the accuracy of declarations and compliance with CWC obligations. The inspected state party must ensure the inspection team's

[17] The CWC denotes information as confidential: (1) if the state party so designates it; or (2) if, in the judgment of the Director-General, the unauthorized disclosure of the information could cause damage to the state party to which it refers (including private interests that the state party represents) or to the mechanisms implementing the CWC. The level of sensitivity of confidential data is to be established based upon criteria categorized in a classification system that must be applied uniformly. Chemical Weapons Convention, Confidentiality Annex, paras. 1–2.

[18] *Ibid.*, Confidentiality Annex, para. 2. Such documents include initial and annual reports and declarations, general reports on verification activities, and other information provided in compliance with the CWC. *Ibid.*, Confidentiality Annex, para. 2(A)(2)(b)(i)–(iii). The exceptions are: (1) general information on CWC implementation; (2) information released with the express consent of the state party to which the information refers; and (3) confidential information released by the OPCW pursuant to agreed procedures which ensure that release only occurs in strict conformity with the needs of the CWC. *Ibid.*, Confidentiality Annex, para. 2(A)(2)(c)(i)–(iii).

[19] *Ibid.*, Confidentiality Annex, paras. 6–7. This obligation continues even after the end of their functions. Also, staff members must sign individual secrecy agreements with the Technical Secretariat covering the period of their employment and five years thereafter. *Ibid.*, Confidentiality Annex, para. 9.

safe conduct to the inspection site within twelve hours from its arrival at the point of entry.[20] Inspectors must have unimpeded access to the inspection site and may choose the items to be inspected. Most inspections will be of Schedule 2 facilities that will be covered by facility agreements, negotiated between the state party and the OPCW, that enumerate the inspectable areas. The OPCW has elaborated model facility agreements for each type of declared facility.[21] As a rule, access will include elements of the common infrastructure of the plant site directly associated with the declared activities related to the scheduled chemicals.[22] While the inspection team must timely and effectively discharge its functions, inspections should cause the least possible inconvenience or disturbance to the state party and the inspected facility. Moreover, the inspection team must not operate the facility, must avoid unnecessary interference or delay to its operation, and must avoid affecting its safety.[23]

Inspectors may interview any facility personnel in the presence of the inspected state party's representatives to establish necessary facts. The inspection team may inspect documents and records that they deem relevant to the conduct of their mission. Inspectors can also demand that representatives of the inspected state party or the inspected facility take photographs.[24] If the inspection team requests access to other parts of the facility not covered by the facility agreement, access to these areas must be granted according to a clarification procedure that obligates the inspected state party to provide the inspection team with enough information to

---

[20] *Ibid.*, Verification Annex, pt. II, paras. 22–25, 35–36.

[21] See OPCW Report, "Generic Text Elements for Model Facility Agreements"; OPCW Report, "Discussion Paper Prepared by the Secretariat: Facility-Specific Sections of the Model Facility Agreement."

[22] The areas to be inspected may include: (1) areas where feed chemicals (reactants) are delivered or stored; (2) areas where manipulative processes are performed upon the reactants prior to addition to the reaction vessels; (3) feed lines as appropriate from the areas referred to in subparagraph (a) or subparagraph (b) to the reaction vessels together with any associated valves, flow meters, etc.; (4) the external aspect of the reaction vessels and ancillary equipment; (5) lines from the reaction vessels leading to long- or short-term storage or to equipment further processing the declared Schedule 2 chemicals; (6) control equipment associated with any of the items under subparagraphs (a) to (e); (7) equipment and areas for waste and effluent handling; (8) equipment and areas for disposition of chemicals not up to specification. Chemical Weapons Convention, Verification Annex, pt. VII, para. 28.

[23] *Ibid.*, Verification Annex, pt. II, paras. 38–41, 45. Taking into account the guidelines developed and approved by the Conference of States Parties, the Technical Secretariat must develop detailed procedures on conducting inspections for inclusion in the inspection manual. *Ibid.*, Verification Annex, pt. II, para. 42.   [24] *Ibid.*, Verification Annex, pt. II, paras. 47, 48.

clarify the ambiguity,[25] including providing access to areas of declared facilities that raise ambiguities.[26] Moreover, all states parties must cooperate with the OPCW in the exercise of all its functions and in particular provide assistance to the Technical Secretariat.

Before conducting inspections, the OPCW and the state party must negotiate facility agreements for certain declared facilities that include detailed and specific arrangements regarding confidentiality issues. Each state party may take measures it deems necessary to protect confidentiality so long as it fulfills its obligations to demonstrate compliance. During inspections (both routine and challenge), a state party may indicate to the inspection team sensitive equipment, documentation, or areas that are unrelated to the inspection's purpose.[27] Moreover, the inspection team must fully respect procedures designed to protect sensitive installations and to prevent the disclosure of confidential data. The inspection report must contain only facts relevant to the CWC and must be handled in the same manner as any other CWC confidential information.

Challenge inspections

The CWC provides progressively stronger steps for a state party to resolve doubts as to another state party's compliance, up to and including a "challenge inspection." States parties should first engage in direct consultation and cooperation. If requested, a state party must, within ten days, provide information to satisfy another state party's concerns. In addition, a state party may ask the Executive Council to request clarification of another state party or have the Director-General establish a group of experts. If doubts remain, a state party may request a special session of the Executive Council or, after sixty days, a special session of the Conference of States parties, to resolve the situation.[28]

Independent of these consultation procedures, each state party may request an on-site challenge inspection, conducted by an inspection team designated by the Director-General, of any location in the territory or

---

[25] *Ibid.*, Verification Annex, pt. II, para. 51. Issues that cannot be resolved will be brought to the attention of the Technical Secretariat, and the ambiguity will be noted in the final inspection report.   [26] *Ibid.*, Art. VIII, para. 37.

[27] *Ibid.*, Confidentiality Annex, para. 13.

[28] Any such efforts to resolve doubts do not affect the requesting state party's rights and obligations, including the right to request a challenge inspection. *Ibid.*, Art. IX, paras. 2–7.

under the jurisdiction or control of a state party.[29] Only a CWC state party (not the OPCW) can initiate a challenge inspection. The requesting state party must provide "all appropriate information on the basis of which the concern has arisen,"[30] including specification of the CWC's relevant provisions and identification of the site to be inspected. It may send an observer if the inspected state party agrees.[31] The challenge inspection may be stopped only if three-quarters of the Executive Council deem the request frivolous (the concerns are minor irregularities or excessively technical), abusive (the concerns are artificial or intended to harass), or clearly beyond the scope of the CWC challenge inspection provisions.[32] The requested state party may not refuse the inspection.

After at least twelve hours' notice of the inspection team's arrival, the inspected state party must transport the inspectors to the site's perimeter within twenty-four hours if the site is a declared facility, thirty-six hours if it is an undeclared facility. The CWC contains an intricate process to determine the inspected site's final perimeter.[33] Upon arrival, the inspection team may secure the site and begin perimeter activities including: identifying vehicular exits, making traffic logs, taking photographs, video-recording exits and exit traffic, using appropriate monitoring instruments, and taking samples. These procedures may continue for the inspection's duration, but may not unreasonably hamper or delay the facility's normal operation.[34]

While challenge inspections are relatively unconstrained, the inspection team may only seek sufficient relevant facts to clarify the non-compliance concerns. It should conduct the inspection in the least intrusive manner possible, proceeding to more intrusive procedures only as it deems necessary.[35] The inspected state party must make every reasonable effort to demonstrate its compliance with the CWC. Access must be granted to the greatest degree, "taking into account any constitutional obligations [the state party] may have with regard to proprietary rights or searches and

[29] *Ibid.*, Art. IX, para. 8. [30] *Ibid.*, Verification Annex, pt. X, para. 4(d).
[31] A refusal to allow an observer will be recorded in the final report. The observer has the same rights of access to the inspection site as the inspection team, and may make recommendations as to the conduct of the inspection. *Ibid.*, Art. IX, para. 12; *ibid.*, Verification Annex, pt. X, paras. 53–56. The observer is also entitled to basically the same privileges and immunities as well as amenities as members of the inspection team. *Ibid.*, Verification Annex, pt. II, para. 16.
[32] *Ibid.*, Art. IX, para. 17. See also Walter Krutzsch and Ralf Trapp, *A Commentary on the Chemical Weapons Convention* (Dordrecht and Boston: M. Nijhoff, 1994), pp. 189–91.
[33] Chemical Weapons Convention, Verification Annex, pt. X, paras. 8, 16–21.
[34] *Ibid.*, Verification Annex, pt. X, paras. 23–31.
[35] *Ibid.*, Verification Annex, pt. X, paras. 44–45.

seizures."[36] The inspection team and the inspected state party will negotiate the extent of access, the performance of activities, and the provision of
information. For declared facilities with facility agreements, access must
be unimpeded within the agreed boundaries. For declared facilities without facility agreements, access will be negotiated according to the CWC's
general inspection guidelines.[37]

"Managed access" is an important process for limiting the scope of challenge inspections so that an inspected state party may protect sensitive
equipment, information, or areas not related to chemical weapons. Such
measures may include: (1) removal of sensitive papers from office spaces;
(2) shrouding sensitive displays, stores, and equipment; (3) shrouding
sensitive equipment, such as computer or electronic systems; (4) logging
off computer systems and turning off of data-indicating devices; (5)
restriction of sample analysis to detect the presence or absence of chemicals listed in Schedules 1, 2, and 3 or appropriate degradation products;
(6) using random selective access techniques whereby the inspectors may
select a given percentage or number of buildings of their choice to inspect;
and (7) in exceptional cases, giving only individual inspectors access to certain parts of the inspection site. The inspected state party must reasonably
demonstrate that protected objects are not used for purposes related to the
possible non-compliance concerns raised in the inspection request.[38]

The inspection must be completed within eighty-four hours unless the
inspected state party agrees to an extension, and the inspection team and
the observer must leave the inspected state party's territory in the minimum time possible.[39] The inspection team must prepare a report summarizing its activities and findings as to the compliance concerns that
prompted the request and, within thirty days, circulate that report to the
requesting state party, the Executive Council, and the inspected state

---

[36] These limitations may not be invoked to conceal evasion of CWC obligations, nor to engage in
prohibited activities; if invoked, the inspected state party must provide reasonable alternative
means to clarify the possible non-compliance concern that generated the challenge inspection.
Ibid., Verification Annex, pt. X, para. 41.

[37] *Ibid.*, Verification Annex, pt. X, para. 51. Regardless of negotiated limitations, if the inspection
team finds evidence of non-compliance, it will not be bound to the managed access agreement.
Ibid., Verification Annex, pt. X, para. 47. See Krutzsch and Trapp, *Commentary*, p. 491.

[38] This may be accomplished by means of, *inter alia*: (1) partial removal of a shroud or environmental protection cover, at the discretion of the inspected state party; (2) a visual inspection of
the interior of an enclosed space from its entrance; or (3) other methods. Chemical Weapons
Convention, Verification Annex, pt. X, paras. 48–50.

[39] *Ibid.*, Verification Annex, pt. X, paras. 57–58.

party. The Executive Council must then determine if any non-compliance has occurred and may take further appropriate actions to ensure CWC compliance or make specific recommendations to the Conference.[40]

Article VII of the CWC requires each state party to implement the Convention, including empowerment of a "National Authority" to serve as a liaison with the OPCW and other states parties. Moreover, each state party must enact penal legislation to prohibit legal and natural persons in its territory or under its control from undertaking activities prohibited by the CWC. The term "prohibited activities" is undefined, but most likely includes the obligations of Article I, paragraphs 1 and 5, which prohibit the development or use of chemical weapons or riot control agents as a method of warfare. It is left for each state party to decide whether penal sanctions could apply to additional conduct, such as producing Schedule 1 chemicals in excess of the CWC's limitations, transferring chemicals to a state in contravention of the CWC's obligations, or obstructing verification activities. Also left to each state party to decide is the meaning of the term "penal" as well as the penalties that might result from a violation.

NON-COMPLIANCE

In cases where the Executive Council has requested the state party to redress a situation and the state party has failed to do so within the specified time, the Executive Council is authorized to consult with the states parties involved. Failing that, the Conference may restrict or suspend a state party's rights and privileges under the CWC until it conforms to its obligations. The CWC does not specify possible sanctions for violations of specific obligations, giving flexibility to the Conference to react as it deems appropriate in a specific case. However, a state party may not be deprived of its membership.

Where the state party's action threatens the object and purpose of the Convention, collective measures may be recommended. This could include withholding from the malefactor any relevant exports of chemicals, technical equipment, and scientific or technical know-how. Yet, the prerogatives

---

[40] *Ibid.*, Art. IX, paras. 22–25.

of the United Nations Security Council must be respected, as collective action may proceed only in conformity with international law. The Conference may bring cases of particular gravity to the United Nations, which presumably can respond in any way authorized by the United Nations Charter.[41]

Mechanisms for ascertaining harm and determining liability

As the preceding description should clarify, the CWC is designed to prevent proliferation of chemical weapons; it does not directly focus on detection, identification, and ascertainment of environmental harm caused by the use of chemical weapons. Yet, amidst this detailed regulatory effort, the CWC's mechanisms are relevant in three ways to the use of catastrophic weaponry[42] generally, not just chemical weapons. First, the CWC establishes an investigatory capability to respond to cases where a state alleges that chemical weapons have been used. Second, the CWC's extensive data-collection obligations suggest the rudiments of a system for tracking chemicals, thus enabling identification of agents used to harm the environment. Third, the CWC links to broader mutual legal assistance capabilities by requiring states to cooperate with regard to investigating activity that contravenes the Convention's prohibitions. All three of these mechanisms can perhaps enlighten a discussion of how to determine liability and assess damages for environmental harm caused by war.

INVESTIGATIONS OF ALLEGED USE

Currently, the international community does not have an established response system to investigate situations where catastrophic weapons are used or are alleged to have been used. If a state believes that it has been attacked, or that some other state has been attacked, its only options for international assistance or investigation entail after-the-fact requests to

---

[41] See generally *ibid.*, Art. XII; *ibid.*, Art. VIII, paras. 2, 36.
[42] The term "catastrophic weaponry" refers to nuclear (including radiological), chemical, and biological weapons, as well as ballistic missiles. The distinction between these weapons and "conventional weapons," although inexact, is based on the idea that these weapons signify total, as opposed to limited, war. Other weapons can be restricted to battlefield use and are primarily designed to overpower an adversary's military force; catastrophic weapons would necessarily devastate civilian populations. See Kellman, "Bridling the International Trade of Catastrophic Weaponry," 755.

allied states or to international relief agencies. The after-the-fact nature of these requests presents two overlapping problems: (1) what arrangements will govern the scope of entry and access and the conduct of investigations by foreign officials and personnel? and (2) how can the sophisticated technological capabilities needed to detect environmental harm be amassed and organized, in exigent circumstances, and brought to the site of an alleged weapons use?

The implications of these problems should be understood. When national law enforcement officials identify environmental harm caused by weapons use, that harm must be analyzed and traced. However, most nations lack both the equipment and expertise necessary to do the job proficiently. Some states, even if victimized, object to foreign inspection of damaged territory, especially near national security installations. Many states demand that outside scientists and technicians seek diplomatic permission to undertake tests within their territory; obtaining that permission may take precious time, complicating and prolonging the investigation and allowing the trail to grow cold. Transporting test samples from the point of seizure to a testing facility (assuming one exists) wastes even more time and risks theft or loss of the material in transit. A mobile testing unit that could be flown rapidly to wherever an attack is alleged would enable technicians to pursue an investigation more efficiently, but no such unit exists.[43]

Article X of the CWC provides an instructive, albeit incomplete, model of an international agreement to respond to alleged weapons use. Before there is any allegation of use, each state party must either: (1) contribute to a voluntary assistance fund established by the Conference of the States Parties; (2) conclude an agreement with the OPCW concerning the procurement upon demand of assistance; or (3) declare the kind of assistance it might provide in response to an OPCW request.[44] As more than 100 states parties fulfill this obligation, a reservoir of resources should be available to respond when necessary.

If chemical weapons are used, or if a state party believes that chemical weapons have been used or are threatened to be used, that state party may request assistance and protection against such use or threat of use. The request should include the following information: (a) the state party on

---

[43] See generally Barry Kellman and D. Gualtieri, "Barricading the Nuclear Window – A Legal Regime to Curtail Nuclear Smuggling," *U. Ill. L. Rev.* (1996), 667.

[44] Chemical Weapons Convention, Art. X, para. 7.

whose territory chemical weapons were allegedly used; (b) the point of entry or other safe routes of access; (c) location and characteristics of areas where chemical weapons were allegedly used; (d) when chemical weapons were allegedly used; (e) types of chemical weapons believed to have been used; (f) the extent of alleged use; (g) characteristics of possible toxic chemicals; (h) effects on humans, animals, and vegetation; and (i) a request for specific assistance if possible.[45] Upon receipt of the request, the Director-General must inform the Executive Council and all states parties and, within twelve hours, dispatch emergency assistance or request states parties that have volunteered to so dispatch.

Within twenty-four hours of such a request, the Director-General must initiate an investigation. An inspection team consisting of inspectors already designated for challenge inspections must be dispatched at the earliest opportunity, taking into account their safety.[46] Making use of trained inspectors solves various problems. Such individuals do not have to familiarize themselves with the tasks needing to be performed, nor with the legal restrictions that may constrain their ability to conduct an inquiry. Such persons do not have to be gathered, as they are already in a single location (The Hague) and can be immediately sent to the affected destination. They are already familiar with the equipment that they will need to use, which should be the best available. Moreover, if these designated inspectors lack a capability or expertise that the Director-General believes is needed, the CWC authorizes the Director-General to place additional selected experts on the inspection team.[47]

The Convention specifies inspectors' powers and scope of responsibility, obviating the need to negotiate terms and conditions when a situation arises. The objective of the investigation is to establish relevant facts as well as the type and scope of supplementary assistance and protection needed.[48] Upon their arrival, the inspection team may be briefed by representatives of the inspected state party. Thereupon, those inspectors "shall have the right of access to any and all areas which could be affected by the alleged use of chemical weapons." Specified areas of access include hospitals and refugee camps.[49] In addition, the inspection team has the right to collect samples that it considers necessary, and may request assistance

---

[45] *Ibid.*, Verification Annex, pt. XI, paras. 3, 5.   [46] *Ibid.*, Verification Annex, pt. XI, para. 9.
[47] *Ibid.*, Art. X, paras. 8, 9.   [48] *Ibid.*, Verification Annex, pt. XI, paras. 8–13.
[49] *Ibid.*, Verification Annex, pt. XI, para. 15.

from the inspected state party, which must cooperate under the inspectors' supervision. These samples include: "toxic chemicals, munitions and devices, remnants of munitions and devices, environmental samples (air, soil, vegetation, water, snow, etc.) and biomedical samples from human or animal sources (blood, urine, excreta, tissue, etc.)."[50] The inspection team may also interview and examine persons affected by or eyewitness to the alleged use of chemical weapons, as well as medical personnel who have treated affected persons; inspectors are granted access to medical histories and may participate in autopsies.[51]

The Convention provides that the investigation will be completed within seventy-two hours unless additional time periods of seventy-two hours are needed. At the end of each seventy-two-hour period, interim reports must be submitted to the Executive Council. These reports should indicate any urgent need for assistance and summarize the investigation's factual findings. Of specific relevance, the report should identify "any impurities or other substances," or any other information that "might serve to identify the origin of any chemical weapons used."[52]

Within twenty-four hours after receiving an investigation report, the Executive Council must decide, by simple majority, whether to instruct the Technical Secretariat to provide supplementary assistance. When so decided, the Director-General must provide assistance immediately in cooperation with the requesting state party, other states parties, and relevant international organizations. If immediate action is indispensable on behalf of victims of chemical weapons use, the Director-General must pursue emergency measures, using resources the Convention makes available for such contingencies.[53]

TRACKING WEAPONS AGENTS TO DETERMINE RESPONSIBILITY

If weapons use causes environmental harm, and if investigation of such use reveals what specific agents caused that harm, then there should be some mechanism to trace those agents back to their source. Clearly, to undertake that task on an ad hoc basis is nearly impossible; if all that investigators know is the nature of a lethal agent, how will it be possible to identify its source? This is a profoundly difficult question that undermines any

---

[50] *Ibid.*, Verification Annex, pt. XI, paras. 16–17.   [51] *Ibid.*, Verification Annex, pt. XI, para. 21.
[52] *Ibid.*, Verification Annex, pt. XI, para. 26.   [53] *Ibid.*, Art. X, paras. 10, 11.

discussion of the efficacy of a court or other legal forum to hold perpetrators accountable. Obviously, a legal system of accountability is only as effective as its ability to identify potentially culpable parties. As asserted above, modern weapons and nearly undetectable dissemination methods complicate that process of identification. Indeed, for agents that are entirely fungible, such as typical anthrax, there may be no solution to this problem, and identification of the perpetrators may have to depend on other mechanisms.

For chemical agents that are more uniquely designed as weapons, however, it is possible to envision a tracking system capable of guiding an investigation from the point of use to the site of the agents' production, and thereby to the state or person that is responsible for the attack. Significant quantities of information would be required, and that information would have to enable experts to make fine distinctions among similar items. The premise of such a system is that if an investigator comes across evidence of weapons use that has caused significant environmental harm, that evidence may contain a "fingerprint" – a unique characteristic that would enable laboratory technicians to identify its source. If so, then allocation of responsibility would require the existence of an information repository able to match that fingerprint.

No such information repository currently exists. Yet, the comprehensive declaration requirements of the CWC suggest a relevant capability. Each chemical facility in a CWC state party capable of producing weapons precursors must identify the chemicals it uses and provide detailed information about the facility itself. Declarations of Schedule 1 facilities, those of greatest concern to the Convention, must include equipment inventory, detailed diagrams, and the volume of reaction vessels in production lines. For less-sensitive Schedule 2 and 3 chemicals, information must be provided that identifies each plant site, its activities, and its production capacity.

In addition, a tagging and tracking system should include the capability to track critical agents and weapons in transit. Again, the CWC provides something of a model. With regard to Schedule 1 chemicals, both transferring and receiving states parties must notify the Technical Secretariat of each transfer at least thirty days in advance. Further, each state party must make annual declarations regarding transfers of Schedule 1 chemicals during the previous year, identifying the chemical and specifying the quantity, recipient, and purpose.[54] Unfortunately for purposes of this discussion,

---

[54] *Ibid.*, Verification Annex, pt. VI, paras. 3–6.

no specific notification requirements apply to transfers of Schedule 2, Schedule 3, or other chemicals or equipment. For Schedule 2 chemicals, initial and annual declarations must aggregate the total amount of imported and exported chemicals.[55] Initial and annual declarations of Schedule 3 chemicals must include aggregate national data for the previous year's imports and exports.[56]

The CWC falls considerably short of a comprehensive regulatory scheme for the global chemical industry that would enable investigators to trace substances back to their source of production, and it may not even be the best example among arms control agreements. The most highly evolved tracking system is that of the International Atomic Energy Agency (IAEA) with its capability of detecting "nuclear signatures" – indications from samples of reprocessed nuclear material that suggest the reactor that produced that material. It is a characteristic of nuclear materials that they can be tagged (chemically or isotopically), and a record of these unique characteristics is partially maintained by the IAEA. Moreover, it is physically possible to implant distinguishable attributes at safeguarded nuclear facilities. Some experts have suggested that the IAEA should compile records of all fissile-material processing facilities, including those located in the nuclear weapons states, in order to help law enforcement authorities more readily identify nuclear material.[57]

The CWC deals with materials that are far less able to be tagged than nuclear materials, but it throws a far broader net over the global chemical industry and movement of materials and equipment. Between the CWC and the NPT, there may emerge the outlines of a tracking system for determining liability for environmental harm caused by war. If the international community decided that having a capability to trace weapons agents from production to use was a high priority, a system could be envisaged that combines the precision of the NPT's technical information with the breadth of the CWC's reporting requirements, and that feeds all of this information into a repository for law enforcement officials. In combination with the investigatory authority discussed above in cases of alleged use, an integrated tracking system may enable officials at least to identify where a lethal agent was produced, which information should aid in the identification of who is responsible for the attack.

---

[55] *Ibid.*, Verification Annex, pt. VII, para. 1 (aggregate national data); pt. VII, para. 8 (each declared plant site).   [56] *Ibid.*, Verification Annex, pt. VIII, para. 1.
[57] See Mark Hibbs, "Which Fissile Fingerprint?" *Bull. Atom. Sci.* (May/June 1995), 10.

LEGAL ASSISTANCE MODALITIES

The third part of this discussion focuses on the capability of law enforcement officials to cooperate with their counterparts in other states. The previous discussion has suggested that if the environment is harmed by the use of modern weapons, especially weapons whose source and user are difficult to detect, then to determine responsibility requires immediate investigatory authority combined with an information repository to make use of discovered evidence. With that information, the next step involves traditional law enforcement techniques to identify suspects, whether states or persons, and to compile sufficient evidence of their culpability to substantiate a charge of criminality.

Yet, many states' police forces are ill-accustomed to undertaking international investigations, especially in connection with the use of weapons in armed conflict. Limitations associated with the failings of domestic law enforcement in addressing international criminality have been identified in the context, *inter alia*, of combatting the illegal narcotics trade and money laundering. One mechanism to overcome such limitations is to strengthen international police capabilities pursuant to an agreement that regularizes interactions among police in the field and overcomes the unpredictability and inadequacies inherent in domestic enforcement techniques.

Modalities of inter-state cooperation in penal matters can help states agree on law enforcement priorities and interact effectively despite differences among their legal systems and the limitations that sovereignty places on criminal law enforcement. These typically involve obligations of a state to authorize its judicial, law enforcement, and administrative bodies to provide assistance in both criminal and administrative matters to their counterparts in other states. The objective of such authorization is to enable the final steps of an investigation – identification of perpetrators, apprehension, and prosecution – to proceed on a transnational basis as efficiently as a domestic investigation could proceed, without unnecessary interference from diplomatic roadblocks of claims of sovereignty. The task, in the context of this discussion, is to consider how to employ these modalities to acquire information about the environmental consequences of war caused by catastrophic weapons.

In this regard, note should be taken of the CWC's inclusion of a requirement to expedite effective international legal cooperation through provision of mutual legal assistance. Article VII, which requires that states enact penal legislation, also requires that "[e]ach State Party shall cooperate with other States Parties and afford the appropriate form of legal assistance."[58] With this obligation, the CWC unites principles of international criminal and administrative law enforcement with arms control. Using the various forms of legal assistance in criminal and administrative matters, states parties may be better able to investigate suspected weapons activities. Because states parties will be required to provide legal assistance to every other state party, each will have access to information located in other countries.

If this CWC obligation is given its full meaning, each state party will be required to provide information relating to facially non-criminal but suspect activities of persons or entities within its jurisdiction, including disclosing information it possesses, conducting searches, examining sites or objects, taking evidence or statements from persons, effecting service of judicial papers, and providing relevant documents such as financial or business records. In addition to mutual legal assistance, the forms of legal cooperation most immediately relevant to CWC implementation are immobilization and forfeiture of illicit proceeds, extradition, and recognition of foreign penal and administrative judgments.

This obligation of the CWC addresses the problem of criminal weapons segmentation by suggesting the application of powerful law enforcement modalities to discover and prosecute clandestine weapons activities. Using the various forms of legal assistance in criminal and administrative matters, states parties may be better able to investigate suspected CWC violations. Because other states parties will be required to provide legal assistance, each will have access to information located in other countries. Effective obstruction of the chemical weapons trade will demand advancement of these modalities to acquire information and, where necessary, prosecute those who violate non-proliferation obligations or actually use prohibited weaponry.

It should be noted, however, that the obligation contained in CWC Article VII is both brief and vague, mirroring language in previous arms

---

[58] Chemical Weapons Convention, Art. VII, para. 2.

control agreements that have, to date, not realized the promise of serious international law enforcement cooperation.[59] Moreover, it seems likely that mutual legal assistance will be more relevant to the investigation of weapons use by criminals than their use by states in war. Yet even with these qualifications, the increasing reference to, and hopefully employment of, mutual legal assistance techniques can offer greater capabilities to identify wrongdoers and hold them accountable.

Conclusion

The Chemical Weapons Convention is certainly the most intrusive and most information-demanding international weapons control agreement. Measured by the scope of its obligations, it suggests a substantial step forward in international regulation of state and private activity. Yet, the CWC is designed to prevent proliferation; accordingly, it has definite limits as a model for determining legal responsibility for environmental harm caused by actual use during war.

Cognizant of those limitations, this discussion has asserted that the Convention's usefulness for such determination entails three mechanisms: properly authorized investigations of an alleged use and the harm inflicted, carried out promptly and with sufficient technical expertise; informational capabilities for tracking evidence that is gathered by such investigations; and mutual legal assistance obligations that enable states to cooperate with one another in apprehending and prosecuting those responsible. The CWC offers a strong model for the first mechanism; a vague model, but probably among the best existent, for the second mechanism; and an as-yet-undefined obligation that may someday serve as a model for the third mechanism.

Perhaps more than anything else, the CWC suggests the need for enhanced international law enforcement authority. This need will become all the greater if the concerns about the use of catastrophic weapons turn out to be justified. As consideration is given to the environmental

---

[59] See, e.g., the Convention on the Physical Protection of Nuclear Material (Mar. 3, 1980), *I.L.M.* 18 (1979), 1419 (entered into force Feb. 8, 1987). Notably, both the Physical Protection Convention and the CWC lack some of the stronger mutual legal assistance provisions contained in other international treaties, especially concerning drug trafficking, which are themselves quite incomplete. See generally M. Cherif Bassiouni, "Critical Reflections on International and National Control of Drugs," *Denv. J. Int'l L. & Pol'y* 18 (1990), 311.

devastation that modern war can cause, to say nothing of its human devastation, it is manifestly clear that the web of international law must, of necessity, be strengthened. The mechanisms that have been developed to address weapons proliferation do not offer ideal answers, but these mechanisms may offer a basis for expansion. In view of the threats our age confronts and the consequences of failing to address them, it is difficult to imagine a more compelling undertaking.

24

INTERNATIONAL LEGAL MECHANISMS FOR
DETERMINING LIABILITY FOR ENVIRONMENTAL
DAMAGE UNDER INTERNATIONAL
HUMANITARIAN LAW

JEAN-MARIE HENCKAERTS

Introduction

International humanitarian law contains a number of rules that provide
legal protection for the environment during armed conflict.[1] A violation
of these rules can give rise to two types of responsibility under international law: state responsibility and individual responsibility.[2] According to
the principles of state responsibility, the injured state is entitled to request
"full reparation, in the form of restitution in kind, compensation, satisfaction and assurances and guarantees of non-repetition."[3] According to the
principles of individual responsibility, on the other hand, a person who is
found to be guilty of a crime under international law can be criminally
sanctioned. The determination of either form of responsibility usually
requires fact-finding.

---

[1] These rules have been summarized in the "Guidelines for Military Manuals and Instructions on
the Protection of the Environment in Times of Armed Conflict," *Int'l Rev. Red Cross* 36 (1996),
231. In 1994, the Guidelines were submitted to the UN General Assembly, which invited all
states to give due consideration to the possibility of incorporating the Guidelines into their military manuals. GA Res. 49/50 (Dec. 9, 1994). The Guidelines were published as an annex to UN
Doc. A/49/323 (1994). See also Hans-Peter Gasser, "For Better Protection of the Natural
Environment in Armed Conflict: A Proposal for Action," *Am. J. Int'l L.* 89 (1995), 637.
[2] See, e.g., Christopher Greenwood, "State Responsibility and Civil Liability for Environmental
Damage Caused by Military Operations," in Richard J. Grunawalt, John E. King, and Ronald S.
McClain (eds.), *Protection of the Environment During Armed Conflict* (Newport, R.I.: Naval War
College, 1996), pp. 395–415; Michael Bothe, "Criminal Responsibilities for Environmental
Damage," in *ibid.*, pp. 473–78.
[3] International Law Commission, Draft Articles on State Responsibility, pt. 2, Art. 42, in Report
of the International Law Commission on the Work of its Forty-Eighth Session, UN Doc.
A/51/10 (1996), p. 141.

The notions of fact-finding, state responsibility, and reparation exist under general international law, and as such could be applied to violations of international humanitarian law. In order to determine responsibility and assess damages, parties to a conflict could resort to any of the means available under the UN Charter for the peaceful settlement of disputes: "negotiation, enquiry, mediation, conciliation, judicial settlement, resort to regional agencies or arrangements, or other peaceful means of their own choice."[4]

It is interesting to note, however, that the notions of fact-finding, state and individual responsibility, and reparation are specifically restated in humanitarian law. In combination with the substantive humanitarian law rules that protect the environment, such as rules on targeting and the more specific prohibition against causing widespread, long-term, and severe damage to the natural environment,[5] humanitarian law offers some reasonable prospects for determining responsibility, assessing damages, and awarding compensation.

Among the various mechanisms that exist specifically to enforce humanitarian law, this chapter considers in depth two that could become particularly relevant for assessing and determining responsibility for environmental damage. These are: (1) the International Fact-Finding Commission established pursuant to Article 90 of the 1977 First Additional Protocol to the Geneva Conventions of August 12, 1949 (Protocol I); and (2) the International Criminal Court to be established in accordance with its Statute adopted in Rome in July 1998. Other mechanisms of a similar nature also exist on an ad hoc level, and some of these are mentioned where appropriate.

The International Fact-Finding Commission

STRUCTURE, POWERS, AND OPERATION OF THE COMMISSION

In an effort to secure the guarantees that Protocol I affords to victims of armed conflict, and to promote enforcement by individual states, Article 90 provides for the establishment of an International Fact-Finding

---

[4] UN Charter, Art. 33.
[5] For a critical appraisal of the present substantive law, see Adam Roberts, "The Law of War and Environmental Damage," chapter 2 in this volume; Michael N. Schmitt, "War and the Environment: Fault Lines in the Prescriptive Landscape," chapter 3 in this volume; Michael N. Schmitt, "Green War: An Assessment of the Environmental Law of International Armed Conflict," *Yale J. Int'l L.* 22 (1997), 1.

Commission.[6] The Commission was officially constituted in 1991 as a permanent body whose primary purpose is to investigate allegations of grave breaches and serious violations of international humanitarian law. It is an important mechanism to ensure that international humanitarian law is implemented and respected during times of armed conflict.

The Commission is composed of fifteen individuals elected by those states that have recognized its competence. Commissioners act in their personal capacity, and do not represent the states of which they are nationals. Each must be of high moral standing and acknowledged impartiality. Elections occur every five years, and states have an obligation to ensure that the Commission reflects an equitable geographic representation. The Commission is authorized to: "(i) enquire into any facts alleged to be a grave breach or other serious violation of the Geneva Conventions or Protocol I; (ii) facilitate through its good offices, the restoration of an attitude of respect for the Conventions and Protocol I."[7]

The principal task of the Commission is to inquire into facts. It only investigates whether the alleged conduct has occurred. It functions as an investigative body, not as a court or judicial tribunal, and does not issue any judgment or address questions of law in relation to the facts it has established. Further, the Commission's inquiry must involve grave breaches or serious violations of the treaties; it does not investigate minor violations. There is no doubt, however, that willful and wanton destruction of the environment or causing widespread, long-term, and severe damage to the environment are such serious violations. This conclusion is supported not only by the language of Protocol I, but also by the subsequent inclusion of these violations of humanitarian law in the list of war crimes over which the International Criminal Court has jurisdiction, as discussed below.[8]

---

[6] See generally, "The International Fact-Finding Commission," fact sheet prepared by the Advisory Service on International Humanitarian Law of the International Committee of the Red Cross (ICRC), available on the ICRC website at http://www.icrc.org. The Commission's own website, located at http://www.ihffc.org, contains commentaries on the legal provisions governing the Commission, the Rules of the Commission, a Model Declaration, and a bibliography. See also Erich Kussbach, "The International Humanitarian Fact-Finding Commission," *Int'l & Comp. L.Q.* 43 (1994), 175; Françoise Hampson, "Fact-Finding and the International Fact-Finding Commission," in Hazel Fox and Michael A. Meyer (eds.), *Armed Conflict and the New Law: Effecting Compliance* (London: British Institute of International & Comparative Law, 1993), vol. II, p. 53.

[7] Protocol I, Art. 90(2)(c).

[8] Rome Statute of the International Criminal Court, UN Doc. A/CONF.183/9 (July 17, 1998), Art. 8.

The Commission is also authorized to facilitate an "attitude of respect" for the Conventions and Protocol. Generally, this means that the Commission may, in addition to communicating its conclusions on points of fact, put forth observations and suggestions to promote compliance with the treaties among the opposing parties. Further, while the Geneva Conventions and Protocol I are only directly applicable to international armed conflicts, the Commission has expressed its willingness to investigate violations of humanitarian law occurring in non-international armed conflicts, provided that the parties consent to its inquiry.[9]

In order for the Commission to begin an inquiry, there must be a request for it to do so. Only states or the parties to a conflict have the capacity to make such a request. Private individuals, organizations, or other representative bodies do not have such authority, nor does the Commission have the power to act upon its own initiative. Generally, an inquiry is not conducted by the entire Commission. Unless otherwise agreed, inquiries are conducted by a chamber consisting of seven commissioners – five current members of the Commission and two ad hoc appointees. Each side to the conflict selects one ad hoc member. However, none of the members of the chamber can be nationals of a party involved in the conflict.[10]

During the course of the investigation, the opposing parties are invited to assist the chamber and to present, as well as challenge, evidence. In addition, the chamber is authorized to conduct its own search for information. All evidence is fully disclosed to the parties and to those States that may be otherwise concerned, which have the right to comment upon it.[11] Based upon the findings of the chamber, the Commission submits a report to the parties. The report contains the Commission's findings on issues of fact as well as any recommendations it considers appropriate. The Commission does not disclose its conclusions publicly unless requested to do so by all parties to the conflict.[12]

Administrative expenses of the Commission are covered by those states that have recognized the Commission's competence in advance, as well as through voluntary contributions. The costs of an actual inquiry are borne by the parties involved. A party requesting an inquiry must advance the necessary funds to cover the expenses of the investigative chamber. Fifty

---

[9] See, e.g., Frits Kalshoven, "Protocol II, the CDDH and Colombia," in Karel Wellens (ed.), *International Law: Theory and Practice* (The Hague and Boston: M. Nijhoff, 1998), p. 597.
[10] Protocol I, Art. 90(3)(a). [11] *Ibid.*, Art. 90(4). [12] *Ibid.*, Art. 90(5).

percent of this advance must be reimbursed by the party that is the object of the investigation. The Commission has indicated that there is considerable flexibility concerning the financing of inquiries. Consequently, other financial arrangements may be made by agreement.

RECOGNIZING THE COMMISSION'S COMPETENCE

One of the primary characteristics of the Commission is that it may conduct an investigation only with the consent of the parties involved. A state does not recognize the Commission's competence simply by signing or ratifying Protocol I; the state must indicate its consent separately. A state may make a one-time declaration, in advance of any armed conflict, and recognize the Commission's competence continually, or it may consent solely on a temporary basis for the investigation of a particular dispute. In this respect, the consent regime of the Commission closely resembles that of the International Court of Justice.

By making an advance declaration, a state authorizes the Commission to conduct an investigation in conflicts between itself and another state that has made the same declaration. If a conflict involves parties that have not made declarations, a state is not bound by its previous consent, but must reaffirm the Commission's competence if it becomes the subject of a complaint. A state cannot have an inquiry imposed upon it unless the state requesting the inquiry has also recognized the Commission's authority.

In conflicts between states that have made advance declarations, no additional approval is required for the Commission to act other than the request for an investigation. Such a request does not have to come from a party to the conflict. It may come from a state that has made a declaration, but is not involved in the hostilities. Thus, by accepting the Commission's competence by declaration, a state consents to an inquiry on an ongoing basis, and in return it obtains the right to request an inquiry in conflicts between other declaring states.

An advance declaration can be made when signing, ratifying, or acceding to Protocol I or at any subsequent time. There is no standardized format for the declaration; however, it must unambiguously announce that the government recognizes the competence of the International Fact-Finding Commission as set out in Article 90 of Protocol I. The declaration must be submitted to the depository, the government of the Swiss

Confederation. The Swiss Confederation has drafted a model declaration of recognition that states are free to utilize.[13]

Alternatively, a party to an armed conflict that has not made a declaration in advance may subsequently accept the Commission's competence on a temporary, ad hoc basis. Any party to a conflict may request the Commission to conduct an inquiry. If a non-consenting party is the object of a complaint, the Commission will forward the allegation to that party and ask it to consent to the investigation. If consent is refused, the Commission will be barred from conducting an inquiry. If consent is granted, the inquiry procedure will begin. In these instances, the request for an inquiry can come only from a party to the conflict. It is important to emphasize that this form of recognition is limited to the investigation of the complaint and does not amount to a permanent acceptance of the Commission's competence.

The Geneva Conventions and Protocol I oblige states to "respect" and "ensure respect" for their provisions. The International Fact-Finding Commission is an important mechanism in achieving these objectives. By recognizing the Commission's competence, on a permanent or ad hoc basis, a state contributes significantly to the implementation of international humanitarian law and the ensuring of its respect during periods of armed conflict. Consequently, by its declaration of recognition, a state takes an important step in securing the fundamental guarantees provided by international humanitarian law, including those relating to the environment.

USE OF THE COMMISSION FOR SERIOUS VIOLATIONS AGAINST THE ENVIRONMENT

Since the Commission is a viable, existing option for neutral fact-finding, it could very well be used for fact-finding concerning wartime environmental damage. While most of its members are lawyers, the Commission could, of course, rely on outside technical experts to assist it in this respect. In addition, the findings of the Commission could be used by the parties to the conflict to settle questions of liability and compensation.

In this respect, it is significant that Article 90 of Protocol I is immediately followed by a provision dealing with precisely these questions. Article

---

[13] This model declaration is available on the Commission's website, http://www.ihffc.org.

91 states that: "A Party to the conflict which violates the provisions of the Conventions or of this Protocol shall, if the case demands, be liable to pay compensation. It shall be responsible for all acts committed by persons forming part of its armed forces."[14] The phrase "if the case demands" simply refers to the requirement that, for the obligation to pay compensation to exist, there must also be a finding of actual loss or damage, and a finding that restitution in kind or restoration of the situation existing prior to the violation is not possible. It does not refer to any subjective judgment by the parties as to whether compensation would be desirable or appropriate.[15]

Unfortunately, however, to date the Commission has not been seised.[16] The reason for this seems to be states' unwillingness to accept independent outside fact-finding and "the reluctance of states, including those which have accepted the Commission's competence, to invoke its services in view of the fact that it may have to deal with issues as sensitive as the applicability of the Conventions, and the characterization of particular acts as 'grave breaches' or 'serious violations.'"[17] It is quite significant, therefore, that more than twenty years after the adoption of Protocol I, only fifty-five states (out of 154 party to Protocol I) have made a declaration accepting the competence of the Commission. However, there has been a significant increase in the number of declarations since the beginning of the nineties. Since 1996, for example, eight new states have made such a declaration: Colombia, Argentina, Tajikistan, Paraguay, Laos, Greece, the United Kingdom, and Ireland.[18] As the list of states that have made a declaration under

[14] Protocol I, Art. 91.
[15] See Yves Sandoz et al. (eds.), *International Committee of the Red Cross, Commentary on the Additional Protocols of 8 June 1977 to the Geneva Conventions of 12 August 1949* (Geneva: M. Nijhoff for ICRC, 1987), p. 1056, para. 3655.
[16] A training chamber was organized in Stockholm in September 1998 that allowed the Commission to test its procedures in a fictional conflict. For more information see the Commission's website, http://www.ihffc.org. See also Fredrik A. Holst, "The International Humanitarian Fact-Finding Commission after its First Exercise – A Body Ready to Act in the Name of International Humanitarian Law?" *Allgemeine Schweizerische Militärzeitschrift*, no. 3, (Mar. 1999).
[17] Adam Roberts, "The Laws of War: Problems of Implementation in Contemporary Conflicts," in European Commission, *Law in Humanitarian Crises: How can International Humanitarian Law be Made Effective in Armed Conflicts?* (Lanham, Md.: Office for the Official Publications of the European Communities, 1995), vol. I, pp. 13 and 36.
[18] The others, in chronological order, are: Sweden, Finland, Norway, Switzerland, Denmark, Austria, Italy, Belgium, Iceland, The Netherlands, New Zealand, Malta, Spain, Liechtenstein, Algeria, Russia, Belarus, Ukraine, Uruguay, Canada, Germany, Chile, Hungary, Qatar, Togo, United Arab Emirates, Slovenia, Croatia, Seychelles, Bolivia, Australia, Poland, Bosnia-Herzegovina, Luxembourg, Rwanda, Madagascar, Macedonia, Brazil, Guinea, Bulgaria, Portugal, Namibia, Slovakia, Cape Verde, Czech Republic, Romania, and Mongolia.

Article 90 of Protocol I becomes longer, the prospects for the actual use of the Commission become greater. As pointed out above, in conflicts between states that have made advance declarations, no additional approval is required for the Commission to act other than the request for an investigation.

In the current situation, where states appear hesitant or unwilling to resort voluntarily to consent-based fact-finding, a possible solution would consist of fact-finding imposed by the international community, followed by a determination of liability, the assessment of damages, and the payment of compensation. The international community could adequately be represented by the United Nations, and in particular the Security Council, which could have the authority to impose such measures under Chapter VII of the United Nations Charter. Since the Security Council is often seised of wartime situations and Chapter VII is often declared applicable in this type of situation, this approach is not simply theoretical.

Protocol I in effect contemplates this option of enforcing humanitarian law through the United Nations and on the basis of the UN Charter. Indeed, Article 89 provides: "In situations of serious violations of the Conventions or of this Protocol, the High Contracting Parties undertake to act, jointly or individually, in co-operation with the United Nations and in conformity with the United Nations Charter."[19] The sequence of Articles 89, 90, and 91 of Protocol I highlights the existence of various mechanisms to address serious violations of humanitarian law: in case of serious violations, the United Nations should be seised (Article 89); the International Fact-Finding Commission is available (Article 90); and compensation should be paid for all violations (and a fortiori for serious violations) (Article 91).

An example of such ad hoc Security Council action occurred in the wake of the Iraqi invasion of Kuwait. In that context, the Security Council set up the United Nations Compensation Commission (UNCC) as a subsidiary organ under Chapter VII of the United Nations Charter.[20] The UNCC adjudicates claims submitted by victims, physical persons, companies or States, who have suffered "any direct loss, damage, including environmental damage . . . or injury . . . as a result of Iraq's unlawful invasion and

---

[19] Protocol I, Art. 89.

[20] See generally Sonja Boelaert-Suominen, "Iraqi War Reparations and the Laws of War: A Discussion of the Current Work of the United Nations Compensation Commission with Specific Reference to Environmental Damage During Warfare," *Austrian J. Pub. & Int'l L.* 50 (1996), 225.

occupation of Kuwait."[21] In order to establish the veracity of claims and to assess the actual damage, the Commission engages in fact-finding. The Commission then determines the compensation to be paid and instructs the Compensation Fund set up for this purpose to pay out compensation to the victims. It is a good example of damage assessment by technical experts who sit on the Compensation Panels of the UNCC, sometimes assisted by outside consultants.[22] However, as a model for establishing liability it is of more limited use, since the Security Council mooted the liability question by determining from the outset that Iraq is liable under international law for any direct loss, damage, or injury resulting from its aggression.

In at least one other notable instance, the Security Council opted for ad hoc fact-finding arrangements when it established the Commission of Experts to examine and analyze information on the commission of war crimes in the former Yugoslavia, which preceded the establishment of the International Criminal Tribunal for the Former Yugoslavia.[23] Whereas the Security Council set up new organs in the two aforementioned instances, in the future it could rely on an existing body, the International Fact-Finding Commission, to carry out fact-finding missions relating to serious violations of humanitarian law, including those against the environment. Since no consent-based use has so far been made of the International Fact-Finding Commission, this potentially could be a more successful approach for putting the Commission in business.

Given that the Security Council seems to prefer ad hoc arrangements, it could rely on the International Fact-Finding Commission on an ad hoc basis. In this case, the activities of the Commission would not be based on Article 90 of Protocol I, but on the powers of the Security Council under the United Nations Charter. Constituted in this way, the Commission would share the advantages of ad hoc arrangements identified by Adam Roberts:

> it is not necessary for individual states to initiate the process; states or other entities can be investigated irrespective of whether they have accepted the competence of the Commission; the relevant body of law to be applied can be identified separately in each instance, and can thus be appropriate to the

[21] UN Security Council Res. 687 (Apr. 8, 1991), *I.L.M.* 30 (1991), 847, para. 16.
[22] See Robert O'Brien, "The Challenge of Verifying Corporate and Governmental Claims at the United Nations Compensation Commission," *Cornell Int'l L. J.* 31 (1997), 1.
[23] UN Security Council Res. 780 (Oct. 6, 1992), *I.L.M.* 31 (1992), 1476, 1477, para. 2.

particular conflict and the facts alleged; the range of problems and situations which can be investigated is therefore greater, since it is not limited to clear cases of international armed conflict; there are fewer obstacles to publication of the outcome of an investigation; and the fact-finding process can be linked to action in the form of prosecutions.[24]

The question remains, of course, why the Security Council would rather call upon the Commission than set up another ad hoc arrangement of its own choice and design. One could hope, however, that once the Commission gets an opportunity to carry out its work, it would prove to be truly expert with regard to violations of humanitarian law, so that it would become the obvious choice on fact-finding with regard to violations of this part of international law that is of particular relevance for the work of the Security Council.

The International Criminal Court (ICC)

INTRODUCTION

International humanitarian law sets out detailed rules aimed at protecting the victims of armed conflict and restricting the means and methods of warfare. It also establishes mechanisms to ensure that these rules are respected. In particular, humanitarian law holds individuals responsible for serious violations of humanitarian law that they commit, or order others to commit. It requires that those responsible for serious violations be prosecuted and punished as criminals. The serious violations of humanitarian law that require criminal sanction are termed war crimes.[25]

The concept of war crimes is a concept of customary international law. It requires states to try and punish members of their own armed forces who commit such crimes, as well as anyone else who commits such crimes on national territory or on territory under national control. In addition, international law establishes universal jurisdiction for war crimes, in the sense that states even have jurisdiction to try war criminals with whom they do not have the ordinary jurisdictional connections mentioned above – although they have no obligation to do so.

---

[24] Roberts, "The Laws of War," p. 37.
[25] See generally International Committee of the Red Cross, "Penal Repression: Punishing War Crimes," fact sheet prepared by the ICRC Advisory Service on International Humanitarian Law, available at http://www.icrc.org.

When most of humanitarian law was codified in the four Geneva Conventions of 1949 and Protocol I of 1977, certain of the most serious war crimes were specifically listed as "grave breaches" and specific obligations were attached to them. But other war crimes continued to exist outside the framework of these treaties. The basic difference is that states have to try or extradite anyone who is accused of grave breaches, whereas for war crimes not amounting to grave breaches, this obligation is limited to the crimes committed by one's own troops or on one's own territory.

Thus, the essence of the grave breaches regime is that the perpetrators must be punished. In that respect, humanitarian law requires states to take the following specific action in relation to grave breaches. First, the Geneva Conventions and Protocol I do not set out specific penalties, nor do they create a tribunal to try offenders. Instead, they expressly require states to enact criminal legislation prohibiting and punishing grave breaches – either by adopting a separate law or by amending existing laws. Such legislation must cover all persons, regardless of nationality, who commit grave breaches or order them to be committed, including instances where violations result from a failure to act when a legal duty to act exists. It also must cover acts committed both within and outside the territory of the state.

Second, states are also required to search for persons accused of grave breaches and either to bring them before their own courts or to hand them over for trial in another state – to "try or extradite." Third, as applicable to all war crimes, a state must require its military commanders to prevent, suppress, and take action against those under their control who commit grave breaches. Fourth, states must assist each other in connection with criminal proceedings relating to grave breaches. States are required to fulfill these obligations in times of peace and in times of armed conflict. In order to be effective, the above measures must be adopted before grave breaches have the opportunity to occur.

Grave breaches include "the extensive destruction of property, not justified by military necessity and carried out unlawfully and wantonly,"[26] and "the launching of an indiscriminate attack affecting civilian objects in the knowledge that such attack will cause excessive damage to civilian objects."[27] They do not include the causing of "widespread, long-term and

[26] Geneva Convention I, Art. 50; Geneva Convention II, Art. 51; Geneva Convention IV, Art. 147.
[27] Protocol I, Art. 85(3)(b).

severe damage to the environment."[28] The causing of such damage is still a
serious violation of customary international law constituting a war crime,
and hence may be tried by any state under the principle of universal jurisdiction; but it does not rise to the level of a grave breach.

The advantage of having a list of grave breaches is that they are thus
defined and codified. It was less clear, until recently, which other serious
violations of humanitarian law constitute war crimes that also have to be
criminally sanctioned. There were some indications in other treaties, for
example, the revised Mines Protocol to the 1980 Conventional Weapons
Convention,[29] which requires states to impose penal sanctions against
those killing or injuring civilians in violation of the Protocol. But it was
not clear, for example, whether serious violations of the 1977 Second
Additional Protocol to the Geneva Conventions of August 12, 1949
(Protocol II), relating to non-international armed conflicts, constituted
war crimes under international law. The adoption of the Statutes of the
International Criminal Tribunals for the Former Yugoslavia and Rwanda,
followed by the enactment of criminal legislation in a number of countries
to punish violations of the Geneva Conventions and Protocol II that apply
to non-international armed conflict, then paved the way for the Statute of
the International Criminal Court to include a considerable list of war
crimes committed in non-international armed conflict.[30] This Statute is
also an authoritative restatement of existing war crimes under international law. As a result, not only grave breaches are now codified, but all
other war crimes as well.

ESTABLISHMENT OF THE ICC

Given that the primary means of prosecution of war crimes through
national courts has largely failed, the need for international action became
apparent many years ago. Ever since the end of World War II, the United
Nations has considered the idea of establishing a permanent international
criminal court at various times. After a number of failed efforts, in 1993

---

[28] See Geneva Convention IV, Art. 147; Protocol I, Art. 85.
[29] Protocol on Prohibitions and Restrictions on the Use of Mines, Booby-Traps and Other
Devices (Protocol II to the 1980 Convention), as amended on May 3, 1996, UN Doc.
CCW/CONF.I/16, Art. 14(2).
[30] This evolution is described in a number of essays by Professor Theodor Meron, brought
together in Theodor Meron, *War Crimes Law Comes of Age* (Oxford: Clarendon Press/New
York: Oxford Univ. Press, 1999).

and 1994 it set up two ad hoc tribunals to punish serious violations of international humanitarian law committed, respectively, in the former Yugoslavia and Rwanda. Starting in 1994, there were a series of negotiations to establish a permanent court that would have jurisdiction over serious international crimes, including war crimes, regardless of where they were committed. These negotiations ultimately led to the adoption of the ICC Statute in July 1998 in Rome. This accomplishment, the culmination of years of effort, shows the resolve of the international community to ensure that those who commit serious international crimes do not go unpunished. The Statute will enter into force once it is ratified by sixty states.

Under Article 8 of the Statute, the ICC has jurisdiction over war crimes, including most of the serious violations of international humanitarian law mentioned in the 1949 Geneva Conventions and their 1977 Protocols, whether committed during international or non-international armed conflicts. One of the war crimes over which the ICC has jurisdiction is the "intentional launching of an attack in the knowledge that such an attack will cause widespread, long-term and severe damage to the natural environment which would be clearly excessive in relation to the concrete and direct overall military advantage anticipated."[31] While in the draft statute this war crime was defined for both international and non-international armed conflicts, the final statute only defines it for international armed conflicts.[32]

Articles 35 and 55 of Additional Protocol I similarly outlawed any attack that causes "widespread, long-term and severe damage."[33] The ICC Statute adds a proportionality test, requiring that such damage be "clearly excessive" in relation to the concrete and direct overall military advantage anticipated, before it can constitute a war crime over which the ICC has jurisdiction. The reason why these two conditions were put together is not clear, because the idea behind Protocol I was to introduce an objective criterion that made the subjective test of proportionality redundant and inapplicable – if damage to the environment was widespread, long-term, and severe, it would automatically be considered disproportionate and therefore illegal. With respect to the current text of the ICC Statute, it seems plausible to conclude that if widespread, long-term, and severe

[31] Rome Statute, Art. 8(2)(b)(iv).
[32] See Draft Statute for the International Criminal Court, UN Doc. A/CONF.183/2/Add.1 (Apr. 14, 1998), pp. 16 and 24. [33] Protocol I, Arts. 35 and 55.

damage to the environment is caused, there is at least a strong presumption that such damage would also be disproportionate. Indeed, it is difficult to think of any concrete and direct military advantage that would justify widespread, long-term, and severe damage to the environment.

However, the difficulty with the criterion of widespread, long-term, and severe damage is that it is not well defined, even though it was meant to be an objective criterion. It gives little guidance to those who have to decide on an attack, given that it is difficult to foresee, for example, whether damage will be long-term without waiting a few decades to assess the impact. At any rate, it is a threshold that fortunately is not likely to be reached very often. It is not even clear, for example, whether the damage caused to the environment in Kuwait and neighboring countries during the 1990–91 Gulf War qualifies as widespread, long-term, and severe. It is clear, however, that the requirement of widespread, long-term, and severe damage excludes the more common environmental damage that may be local, short-term, and less severe.

But even if the damage caused does not meet this high threshold, it does not mean the attack was legal. It is likely that the general proportionality test that military commanders have to apply at all times in fact offers greater protection to the environment, even though it is a subjective test. And there are other rules that offer protection to the environment even though the "environment" as such is not mentioned. For example, the environment is usually considered a civilian object, and as such cannot be destroyed outright; and collateral damage to civilian objects has to be proportionate.

Thus, other war crimes over which the ICC has jurisdiction are potentially more relevant with regard to damage to the environment. These are: (1) "the extensive destruction of property, not justified by military necessity and carried out unlawfully and wantonly"; (2) "the intentional directing of attacks against civilian objects which are not military objectives"; and (3) "disproportionate collateral damage to civilian objects."[34] The criminalization of these acts is, in fact, much more relevant for more common damage to the environment. In addition, the Statute prohibits the use of poison and poisoned weapons, as well as the use of chemical weapons.[35]

---

[34] Rome Statute, Arts. 8(2)(a)(iv), 8(2)(b)(ii), 8(2)(b)(iv).
[35] *Ibid.*, Arts. 8(2)(b)(xvii), 8(2)(b)(xviii). There are only a few provisions concerning certain weapons whose use is prohibited under various existing treaties, and these do not apply with respect to non-international armed conflicts.

All of these war crimes are defined solely for international armed conflict, and this is certainly a serious gap. The only war crime defined for non-international armed conflict that could be potentially relevant is the "destruction of the property of an adversary unless such destruction be imperatively demanded by the necessities of the conflict."[36] The extension to non-international armed conflict of at least some of the war crimes relevant for protection of the environment could be discussed at the Review Conference of the Statute. This Review Conference, according to Article 123 of the Statute, is to be convened seven years after the entry into force of the Statute in order to consider any amendments to the Statute, including to the list of war crimes. The Review Conference, whenever it will take place, will provide an excellent opportunity to review the shortcomings of the Statute and to adopt amendments in light thereof.

Also interesting, however, is that Article 75 on reparations to victims gives the Court the authority to "establish principles relating to reparations to, or in respect of, victims, including restitution, compensation and rehabilitation. On this basis, in its decision the Court may, either upon request or on its own motion in exceptional circumstances, determine the scope and extent of any damage, loss and injury to, or in respect of, victims and will state the principles on which it is acting."[37] This could become very important with regard to illegal attacks affecting the environment and would require fact-finding by the Court in this context; Article 54 provides that the Prosecutor may conduct on-site investigations of alleged crimes. The definition of "victims" as used in Article 75 also could raise some interesting questions.

Furthermore, Article 75 provides that the Court may make an order directly against a convicted person specifying appropriate reparations to, or in respect of, victims, including restitution, compensation, and rehabilitation. Where appropriate, the Court may order that the award for reparations be made through the Trust Fund provided for in Article 79, as follows:

1. A Trust Fund shall be established by decision of the Assembly of States Parties for the benefit of victims of crimes within the jurisdiction of the Court, and of the families of such victims.

[36] *Ibid.*, Art. 8(2)(e)(xii). [37] *Ibid.*, Art. 75.

2. The Court may order money and other property collected through fines or forfeiture to be transferred, by order of the Court, to the Trust Fund.
3. The Trust Fund shall be managed according to criteria to be determined by the Assembly of States Parties.[38]

This article would be particularly relevant for illegal attacks on the environment, because the damage caused by such attacks would probably be beyond anyone's personal budget.

In sum, the ICC could become a very relevant mechanism for establishing individual criminal responsibility. Its jurisdiction would include certain attacks on the environment, some of which would apply to both international and non-international armed conflicts; its Prosecutor would have fact-finding powers; and the Court itself could award damages to victims to be paid through the Trust Fund.

JURISDICTION OF THE ICC

As soon as a state becomes a party to the Rome Statute, it accepts the jurisdiction of the ICC with regard to the crimes over which the ICC has jurisdiction. Under Article 25 of the Statute, the Court has jurisdiction over individuals and not states. The ICC may exercise its jurisdiction at the instigation of the Prosecutor or a state party, provided that the state on whose territory the crime was committed or the state of which the person accused of the crime is a national is bound by the Statute. Moreover, a state that is not a party to the Statute may make a declaration to the effect that it accepts the Court's jurisdiction.

Under the collective security framework of Chapter VII of the United Nations Charter, the Security Council may refer a situation to the Prosecutor for investigation. It may also request that no investigation or prosecution commence or proceed for a renewable period of twelve months. The exercise of jurisdiction by the ICC over war crimes can be further limited under Article 124 of the Statute. This provision allows a state, on becoming a party to the Statute, to declare that it does not accept the jurisdiction of the Court for a period of seven years with respect to war crimes that have allegedly been committed by its own nationals or on its own territory.

---

[38] *Ibid.*, Art. 79.

NATIONAL ENFORCEMENT SYSTEMS AND THE ICC

As discussed above, under the 1949 Geneva Conventions and Protocol I, states must prosecute persons accused of grave breaches before their own national courts or extradite them for trial elsewhere. Nothing in the ICC Statute releases states from their obligations under existing instruments of international humanitarian law or under customary international law. Further, states party to other instruments of international humanitarian law are still required to enact implementing legislation giving effect to their obligations under those instruments. By virtue of the principle of complementarity, the jurisdiction of the ICC is intended to come into play only when a state is genuinely unable or unwilling to prosecute alleged war criminals over which it has jurisdiction. To benefit from this principle, states will need to have adequate legislation enabling them to prosecute such criminals.

ENSURING THE ICC'S EFFECTIVENESS

In order to bring the ICC into existence and make it effective, states will need to ratify the Rome Statute as soon as possible, since universal ratification is essential to allow the Court to exercise its jurisdiction effectively and whenever necessary. Ideally, states would refrain from making use of the opt-out clause of Article 124 of the Statute. Once the Statute is ratified, states should carry out a thorough review of their national legislation to ensure that they can take advantage of the complementarity principle on which the ICC is founded and try individuals under their own legal systems for offenses that fall within the Court's jurisdiction. States should assist each other and the ICC in connection with proceedings relating to crimes that come within the Court's jurisdiction. This likewise will require the enactment or amendment of legislation to ensure any necessary transfer of those accused of such crimes. In short, the establishment of the International Criminal Court is a further step towards the effective punishment of persons responsible for committing serious international crimes. But states need to ratify the ICC Statute so that these persons cease to enjoy impunity.

Conclusion

In conclusion, it appears that in the framework of humanitarian law the Security Council and the ICC have the potential of becoming two powerful organs to perform the tasks under consideration here, namely determining liability and assessing damages. The Security Council, however, is an organ whose action or inaction frequently depends on factors other than law. It remains to be seen whether, and to what extent, the ICC will succeed in becoming as independent and effective as many have advocated. If it becomes an independent and effective court, it could potentially become the most important mechanism to deal with serious violations of international humanitarian law, including those against the environment.

25

WAGING WAR AGAINST THE WORLD: THE NEED TO MOVE FROM WAR CRIMES TO ENVIRONMENTAL CRIMES

MARK A. DRUMBL

When two elephants fight, it's always the grass that gets hurt.[1]

Introduction

Over the past century, the international community has shown considerable concern for the humanitarian consequences of war. Examples of this concern include the adoption of the four 1949 Geneva Conventions on the law of war,[2] public condemnation of the use of landmines, and the creation of non-partisan international criminal tribunals in the former Yugoslavia and Rwanda.[3] Negotiations have established a permanent International Criminal Court, principally designed to adjudicate genocide and crimes against humanity.[4]

The international community has been more hesitant in accounting for the environmental consequences of war. This reluctance exists notwithstanding the severity of military damage to the environment, often intentionally inflicted. In a sense this is no surprise. Modification and desecration of the natural environment is seen by many as a strategic

---

An earlier version of this essay appeared in *Fordham Int'l L.J.* 21 (1998), 122.

[1] African proverb, cited in Ben Jackson, *Poverty and the Planet* (1990), p. 150.
[2] The 1949 Geneva Conventions are reprinted in consolidated form in Adam Roberts and Richard Guelff (eds.), *Documents on the Laws of War*, 2nd edn. (Oxford: Clarendon Press/New York: Oxford Univ. Press, 1989), pp. 377–85.
[3] The International Criminal Tribunal for the Former Yugoslavia was created by UN Security Council Resolution 808 of February 22, 1993; the International Criminal Tribunal for Rwanda was created by UN Security Council Resolution 955 of November 8, 1994.
[4] Rome Statute of the International Criminal Court, UN Doc. A/CONF.183/9 (July 17, 1998).

mechanism to safeguard state sovereignty. In large part, such activity remains permissible because there is no definitive or readily enforceable code of conduct governing what warring parties can and cannot do to the environment. All the international community has been able to negotiate are scattered collateral references in a variety of treaties and conventions. At most, these references provide some definitional parameters as to what constitutes unacceptable treatment of the environment in times of war. These are summarized in the next section of this chapter, with special attention to the definition of environmental war crimes in the treaty that created the new International Criminal Court.

Notwithstanding the often limited and ambiguous scope of these definitions, they do provide a starting point for more protracted discussion. One immediate task will be to consider whether these references should be consolidated into a single document or treaty, and this is addressed in the third section. A more daunting task, a brief overview of which is provided in the fourth section, is developing an actual institutional mechanism to ensure compliance with these standards, to deter deviation therefrom, and to allocate responsibility for wrongdoing. More specifically, the fifth section considers the ability of the International Criminal Court to perform such a task. The chapter concludes that the Court may not be particularly well suited to sanction environmentally destructive behavior, and that other, broader standards and institutions should be considered.

The environment and war: what standards have we negotiated so far?

Environmental protection is heralded as a laudable goal by a broad variety of international agreements.[5] Only a small subset of these demonstrate any consensus on what constitutes acceptable or unacceptable use of the environment as a tool of war. It is only recently that the international community has made tentative inroads into contemplating the prosecution of those who engage in unacceptable use of the environment during wartime. In this latter regard, the Rome Statute of the International Criminal Court is important.

---

[5] There are over 900 international agreements that purport to protect the environment. See Edith Brown Weiss, "Strengthening National Compliance with International Environmental Agreements," *Envtl. Pol'y & L.* 27 (1997), 297.

Under the Rome Statute, intentional infliction of harm to the environment may constitute a "war crime."[6] However, Article 8, which defines "war crimes," limits the jurisdiction of the International Criminal Court to "war crimes in particular when committed as a part of a plan or policy or as part of a large-scale commission of such crimes."[7] To this end, there is an immediate question whether isolated incidents will even fall within the purview of the Court. A more important limitation, however, is the fact that prohibiting harm to the natural environment is only explicitly mentioned once in the entire Rome Statute. In this regard, Article 8(2)(b)(iv) prohibits "[i]ntentionally launching an attack in the knowledge that such attack will cause incidental loss of life or injury to civilians or damage to civilian objects or widespread, long-term and severe damage to the natural environment which would be clearly excessive in relation to the concrete and direct overall military advantage anticipated."[8]

The negotiation history of Article 8(2)(b)(iv) merits a brief review. The draft version of the Rome Statute[9] – which served as the basis for the final negotiations – listed three other options along with the language that was eventually adopted in Article 8(2)(b)(iv). The three rejected options were: (1) "intentionally launching an attack in the knowledge that such attack will cause incidental loss of life or injury to civilians or damage to civilian objects or widespread, long-term and severe damage to the natural environment which is not justified by military necessity"; (2) "intentionally launching an attack in the knowledge that such attack will cause incidental loss of life or injury to civilians or damage to civilian objects or widespread, long-term and severe damage to the natural environment"; and (3)

---

[6] Article 5(1)(c) vests the Court with jurisdiction over "war crimes." Article 5(1)(d) and (2) also creates jurisdiction over "crimes of aggression." However, the definition of this term is not provided; in fact, the Rome Statute leaves it to the parties to define this term in the future.

[7] Rome Statute, Art. 8(1).

[8] *Ibid.*, Art. 8(2)(b)(iv). In other places, Article 8 prohibits as a "war crime" conduct that may be collaterally related to the well-being of the natural environment, or have some other ancillary connection. Examples include Article 8(2)(a)(iv), which prohibits extensive destruction and appropriation of property not justified by military necessity and carried out unlawfully and wantonly. Article 8(2)(b) prohibits other serious violations of the laws and customs applicable to international armed conflict, many of which – such as prohibitions of intentional attacks against civilian objects, buildings, property, or means of sustenance – have some bearing on "environmental" damage broadly defined.

[9] Draft Statute for the International Criminal Court, UN Doc. A/CONF.183/2/Add.1 (Apr. 14, 1998), section B(b) to the "War Crimes" section of Part 2. The Draft Statute is available at http://www.un.org/icc.

"no paragraph" (in other words, no prohibition on intentionally inflicting widespread, long-term and severe damage to the natural environment). In the end, the provision that was adopted was a compromise and, from an environmental perspective, occupies a middle ground. However, as discussed below, it shares with the first option the important limitation that global environmental integrity can be made secondary to national security interests.

As adopted, Article 8(2)(b)(iv) triggers numerous interpretive concerns. By way of overview, there are three principal components to the language of Article 8(2)(b)(iv): (1) the actual physical act – or *actus reus* – which consists of inflicting "widespread, long-term and severe damage" to the natural environment; (2) the mental element – or *mens rea* – namely, that the infliction of this harm must be done intentionally and with knowledge that the attack will create such damage; and (3) a justification element, which allows "military advantage" to operate as a defense to criminal wrongdoing even if both the physical and mental elements are found.

THE PHYSICAL ELEMENT: WIDESPREAD, LONG-TERM, AND SEVERE DAMAGE

A successful prosecution under the Rome Statute will, first and foremost, have to show that the accused launched an attack which caused "widespread, long-term and severe damage to the natural environment." Of great importance is that all three elements must be proven conjunctively. The language of "widespread, long-term and severe" is derived from other international agreements relating to the use of the environment in times of war, for example Article I of the 1977 United Nations Convention on the Prohibition of Military or Any Other Hostile Use of Environmental Modification Techniques[10] ("ENMOD") and the 1977 Additional Protocol

---

[10] Convention on the Prohibition of Military or Any Other Hostile Use of Environmental Modification Techniques (Dec. 10, 1976; entered into force, Oct. 5, 1978), 31 U.S.T. 333, which prohibits engagement "in military . . . environmental modification techniques having widespread, long-lasting or severe effects as the means of destruction, damage, or injury to any other State Party." This convention focuses on the use of the environment as a weapon – as a result, wanton destruction of the environment occurring as a byproduct of a military campaign might not fall within its parameters. Some of the activities prohibited by the ENMOD Convention amount to outrageous behavior not within the military capability of most nations: for example inducing earthquakes and tidal waves, or activating quiescent volcanoes. These activities may not be real threats, and the ENMOD prohibitions may be more apparent than real.

I to the 1949 Geneva Conventions[11] ("Protocol I"). Given its derivation, it may be that the Rome Statute does not advance environmental concerns beyond the progress made in these prior documents. In fact, by providing that all three elements conjunctively must be shown to exist, this language regresses from the wording of the ENMOD Convention, which bases responsibility disjunctively on proof of any one of these three characteristics.

What exactly do "widespread," "long-term," and "severe" mean? The Rome Statute is silent on this point. Some interpretive guidance can be provided by the work of the Geneva Conference of the Committee on Disarmament (CCD) Understanding[12] regarding the application of these terms in the ENMOD Convention. This additional work was necessary because the text of the ENMOD Convention also does not define its terms. The CCD Understanding provides as follows: "'widespread': encompassing an area on the scale of several hundred square kilometers; 'long-term': lasting for a period of months, or approximately a season; 'severe': involving serious or significant disruption or harm to human life, natural and economic resources or other assets."[13]

Regrettably, the interpretive value of the CCD Understanding is curtailed by the fact that it stipulates that it is limited to the ENMOD Convention and is not intended to prejudice the interpretation of similar terms if used in another international agreement.[14] Further interpretive guidance may be obtained from commentaries on Protocol I, especially since the language of this Protocol is, like the Rome Statute, conjunctive in nature. Yet from an environmental perspective, the prohibitions in Protocol I are even more circumscribed than those of ENMOD.

---

[11] Additional Protocol I to the Geneva Conventions of August 12, 1949, and Relating to the Protection of Victims of International Armed Conflicts (June 8, 1977; entered into force, Dec. 7, 1978), *I.L.M.* 16 (1977), 1391. Article 35(3) prohibits "methods or means of warfare which are intended, or may be expected, to cause widespread, long-term and severe damage to the natural environment." Article 55 states that: "Care shall be taken in warfare to protect the natural environment against widespread, long-term and severe damage. This protection includes a prohibition on the use of methods or means of warfare which are intended or may be expected to cause such damage to the natural environment and thereby to prejudice the health or survival of the population. Attacks against the natural environment by way of reprisals are prohibited."

[12] Understanding I of the Conference of the Committee on Disarmament, reprinted in Roberts and Guelff (eds.), *Documents on the Laws of War.*

[13] *Ibid.*   [14] *Ibid.*

For example, "long-term" has been interpreted as meaning "lasting for decades."[15]

It will be important to develop a similar memorandum of understanding under the Rome Statute in which the scope of "widespread," "long-term," and "severe" is spelled out. In doing so, it may be necessary to go beyond the language of the ENMOD Convention. For starters, the "widespread" and "long-term" principles attempt to ascribe temporal and geographic limitations on environmental harm which, for the most part, does not know such boundaries. As the planet constitutes a single ecosystem, environmental degradation of one part of the earth inevitably affects the entire planet.[16] On another note, a narrow interpretation of the "severe" requirement might mean that damage to an isolated section of the global commons whose natural resources have not yet been valued by global financial markets could escape punishment, notwithstanding its biodiversity or ecological importance. The anthropocentric limitation of "severe" damage to that which affects human life and human consumption of natural resources underscores a more general shortcoming with the existing framework of environmental protection during wartime – namely, that this protection is not geared to protecting the environment per se, but, rather, humanity's need to make use of it.

In the end, it may be preferable to reduce the threshold of responsibility not to "widespread, long-term and severe" harm, but instead to "harm" more generally. The amplitude of the harm would inform sentencing principles, rather than culpability. Such a paradigm shift would focus on the environment itself as the victim of the harm, not only humanity. Given the fact that such constrained language has woven its way into the Rome Statute, it will be necessary for environmental public interest groups to involve themselves in any litigation in order for the Court to arrive at an informed and environmentally sensitive decision. This involvement would require quite a turnaround, given the limited presence of environmental public interest groups at the negotiation of the Rome Statute. The question – by now academic – is whether a greater presence of such groups

---

[15] Jozef Goldblat, "The Mitigation of Environmental Disruption by War: Legal Approaches," in Arthur H. Westing (ed.), *Environmental Hazards of War: Releasing Dangerous Forces in an Industrialized World* (London and Newburg Park: SAGE Publications, 1990), p. 52.

[16] Lynn Berat, "Defending the Right to a Healthy Environment: Toward a Crime of Geocide in International Law," *B.U. Int'l L.J.* 11 (1993), 347 n. 102.

at the negotiations could have resulted in the integration of stronger provisions safeguarding the environment.

Criminal behavior is evaluated not only on the actual physical act, but also on the mindset of the criminal when that act was committed. In the case of Article 8(2)(b)(iv), criminal sanctions will only fall upon the most invidious offender: the individual who *knows* that his or her behavior *will cause* widespread, long-term, and severe damage to the environment and, notwithstanding proof of this knowledge, still commits the act with the full *intention* of causing such damage. Proof that someone did not know that the act would lead to "widespread, long-term, and severe" damage would, under the present wording, be sufficient to absolve that individual. In this respect, the language of Article 8(2)(b)(iv) is very narrow, declining to extend liability for negligently or carelessly inflicting environmental damage.

Greater detail as to the intentions of the negotiating parties emerges from footnotes in the Draft Rome Statute. These footnotes reinforce the conclusion that a significant mental element generally is required to establish culpability. The negotiators "accept that it will be necessary to insert a provision . . . which sets out the elements of knowledge and intent which must be found to have existed for an accused to be convicted of a war crime."[17] An accused's actions are to be evaluated in light of the "relevant circumstances of, and information available to, the accused at the time."[18] Given this defense, it will be important to educate military and political officials in both developing and developed nations as to the environmentally harmful effects of certain types of warfare, and to disseminate technologies to avoid reliance on such strategies in the first place.

In this regard, the work of the International Committee of the Red Cross (ICRC) can play a pivotal role. The ICRC has published a document entitled "Guidelines for Military Manuals and Instructions on the Protection of the Environment in Times of Armed Conflict," which is "[i]ntended as a tool to facilitate the instruction and training of armed forces in an often neglected area of international humanitarian law: the protection of the natural environment. The Guidelines['] . . . sole aim is to contribute

---

[17] Draft Statute, n. 9.   [18] *Ibid.*

in a practical and effective way to raising awareness . . . [T]hey are an instrument for dissemination purposes."[19] The United Nations General Assembly invited all states to disseminate these Guidelines widely and to give due consideration to the possibility of incorporating them into their military manuals.[20]

The Guidelines state that they are drawn from existing international legal obligations and, as such, constitute a baseline of *ius commune* among nations.[21] They provide in relevant part that "destruction of the environment not justified by military necessity violates international humanitarian law" and that "under certain circumstances, such destruction is punishable as a grave breach of international humanitarian law."[22] Article III(11) echoes the language of ENMOD and Protocol I, prohibiting "methods of warfare which are intended, or may be expected, to cause widespread, long-term and severe damage to the natural environment and thereby prejudice the health or survival of the population."[23] More detailed rules are provided in Article III(9), which covers numerous issues ranging from barring incendiary weapons in forested regions to precluding the use of naval mines.[24] It is these rules that translate often vague international norms into daily practice.

Ultimately, it is to be hoped that the Guidelines could constitute the level of objective knowledge imputed to all military and civilian leaders and agents for purposes of determining culpability under international criminal legislation. It is also hoped that they will be taken into account as new weaponry is developed. In this latter regard, Article IV(18) of the Guidelines is particularly important: "In the study, development, acquisition or adoption of a new weapon, means or method of warfare, states are under an obligation to determine whether its employment would, in some or all circumstances, be prohibited by applicable rules of international law, including these providing protection of the environment in times of armed conflict."[25] The international community ought to consider developing a

[19] International Committee of the Red Cross, "Guidelines for Military Manuals and Instructions on the Protection of the Environment in Times of Armed Conflict," *Int'l Rev. Red Cross* 36 (1996), 230–37, published as an annex to UN Doc. A/49/323 (1994), and available at http://www.icrc.org/unicc/icrcnews.nsf/8. See also Louise Doswald-Beck (ed.), *San Remo Manual on International Law Applicable to Armed Conflicts at Sea* (Cambridge and New York: Cambridge Univ. Press, 1995) for a restatement of the law applicable to armed conflicts at sea. Many of the principles in the *San Remo Manual* are encapsulated in the general provisions of the ICRC Guidelines. [20] See UN GA Res. 49/50 (Dec. 9, 1994), Art. 11.
[21] ICRC Guidelines, Art. I(1). [22] *Ibid.*, Art. III(8). [23] *Ibid.*, Art. III(11).
[24] *Ibid.*, Art. III(9). [25] *Ibid.*, Art. IV(18).

permanent body to ensure that these investigations are undertaken, and the results adhered to.

In short, unless this or some other level of objective knowledge is read into the Rome Statute's intentionality requirement, individuals who choose not to inform themselves that their actions are deleterious for the environment might be able to use their ignorance as a full defense. The failure to incorporate an objective element into the Rome Statute's environmental war crimes provision also represents a step backwards, insofar as Protocol I had grounded responsibility not on intentional environmental damage, but simply on a reasonable expectation that environmental damage could occur.[26]

THE JUSTIFICATION ELEMENT: PROOF OF MILITARY ADVANTAGE

Under the Rome Statute, even if there is intentional, widespread, long-term, and severe damage to the natural environment, liability will be found only if this damage is "clearly excessive in relation to the concrete and direct overall military advantage anticipated."[27] This limitation on culpability traces its roots to the doctrine of "military necessity," a long-standing customary principle which has, in the past, often been used to mitigate or eliminate responsibility for grievous breaches of humanitarian standards. In short, "military necessity" is "[a] subjective doctrine which 'authorizes' military action when such action is necessary for the overall resolution of a conflict, particularly when the continued existence of the acting state would otherwise be in jeopardy."[28] In other words, "[w]hen the existence . . . of a state stands in unavoidable conflict with such state's treaty obligations, the latter must give way, for the self-preservation and development . . . of the nation are the primary duties of every state."[29]

"Military necessity" is a slippery slope that historically has justified a broad array of environmentally destructive conduct. For example, the 1907 Hague Convention's environmental protection provisions have been largely eroded by the doctrine of military necessity. Florencio Yuzon relates the following example:

---

[26] Protocol I, Arts. 35(3), 55. [27] Rome Statute, Art. 8(2)(b)(iv).
[28] Mark J. T. Caggiano, "The Legitimacy of Environmental Destruction in Modern Warfare: Customary Substance over Conventional Form," *B.C. Envtl. Aff. L. Rev.* 20 (1993), 496.
[29] Burleigh Cushing Rodick, *The Doctrine of Necessity in International Law* (New York: Columbia Univ. Press, 1928), p. 44.

In the Second World War, the German General Lothar Rendulic adopted a scorched earth policy in Norway in order to evade advancing Russian troops. General Rendulic ordered the evacuation of all inhabitants in the province of Finmark, and destroyed all villages and surrounding facilities. The Nuremberg Military Tribunal charged General Rendulic with wanton destruction of property, but later acquitted him on the basis that military necessity justified his actions in light of the military situation as he perceived it at the time.[30]

Although one step removed from a blanket exemption for "military necessity," Article 8(2)(b)(iv)'s use of "military advantage" shares many of these same drawbacks. More pointedly, however, there also are concerns as to the effectiveness of the specific language arrived at by the negotiating parties in Article 8(2)(b)(iv). First, although the article establishes a "proportionality" test, requiring that the environmental damage must be "clearly excessive" in relation to the military advantage, no guidelines, definitions, or examples are provided. In fact, "the addition of the word 'clearly' . . . in the definition of collateral damage is not reflected in any existing legal source."[31] Thus, initial decisions by the International Criminal Court will be important in setting the scope for "excessive," and from this judicial discretion there emerges a risk that a very high threshold will be required.

The factual element of the proportionality test is also unclear. Since proof that an action is "clearly excessive" is required in order to find someone guilty, and since the onus of proof rests with the Prosecutor, what types of data and evidence will have to be marshaled? Secondly, the adjectival terms "concrete," "direct," and "overall" are vague and, for the most part, fairly novel in the international legal context. Once again, it is unclear what meaning will be ascribed to these qualifying terms. Finally, the military advantage needs simply to be "anticipated." It is unclear by whom and according to what standards this anticipation is to be judged. Does there need to be an objective element to the anticipation, or can the belief be

---

[30] Ensign Florencio J. Yuzon, "Deliberate Environmental Modification through the Use of Chemical and Biological Weapons: 'Greening' the International Laws of Armed Conflict to Establish an Environmentally Protective Regime," *Am. U. J. Int'l L. & Pol'y* 11 (1996), 815.

[31] Request from the Governments of Belgium, Costa Rica, Finland, Hungary, the Republic of Korea, South Africa and the Permanent Observer Mission of Switzerland to the United Nations Regarding the Text prepared by the International Committee of the Red Cross on Article 8, paragraph 2(b)(i), (ii), (iii), (iv), (v), (vi), (vii), (ix), (xi), and (xii) of the Statute, UN Doc. PCNICC/1999/WGEC/INF.2/Add.1 (July 30, 1999), p. 29 (hereinafter Preparatory Commission Request).

unrealistic? As with the intentionality requirement, if the notion of military advantage remains subjective in the mind of the military or political leader under the circumstances in which the tactical decision was made, then the defense could be widely available. In order to curtail misuse of the defense, it will be important to establish some objective standards as to when the military advantage of an attack may justify widespread, long-term, and severe damage to the natural environment.

More profoundly, the time may have come to question whether humanity's recourse to aggression to settle national or local disputes ought ever to trump environmental integrity. This would involve a reinterpretation of the interaction between international environmental law and international humanitarian law. Certain practices – such as genocide and torture – have been deemed illegal by the international community to the extent that they can never be undertaken, even if essential to defend national sovereignty. Why should intentional environmental desecration not be similarly proscribed?

APPLICATION OF ARTICLE 8(2)(B)(IV)

The international community's decision to criminalize the willful infliction of "widespread, long-term and severe damage to the natural environment" is cause for limited celebration, considerable disappointment, and some concern. The disappointment flows from the fact that the defined conduct is already "prohibited" by virtue of Protocol I and the ENMOD Convention. Nonetheless, it was an important step for the international community to actually criminalize such conduct, and the Rome Statute does provide a more viable mechanism – the International Criminal Court – to prosecute and punish it.

But as we have seen, it is unclear how difficult it will be to prove "widespread, long-term and severe damage," and proof will be rendered more problematic by the fact that the provision appears to be conjunctive, which may denude it of much practical effect. Additionally, the offense could possibly be interpreted as requiring a very significant level of knowledge, intentionality, and harm. If specific intent is required, then behavior could no longer be sanctioned on an objective basis, and ignorance of the law could serve as a defense. This would be less than desirable, as environmental education and transparency of knowledge would be discouraged. Requiring direct knowledge of the environmental war crime may also create some tension with Article 28's evaluation of command responsibility along objective standards.[32] If intention is required for the offense, then it may prove difficult to hold a commander liable for subordinates' activities not known to the commander at the time. The wording of Article 8(2)(b)(iv) appears to preclude a commander's liability for environmental destruction that the commander "should have known" about but did not, even if this ignorance is due to wanton disregard.

Equally important, the environmental war crimes provisions of the Rome Statute do not apply to internecine, as opposed to inter-state, conflicts. Article 8(2)(c) and (e), which lists the types of war crimes punishable within internal armed conflicts, omitted "widespread, long-term and severe harm to the environment" from the list, though the Draft Statute included proposed language that would have paralleled Article 8(2)(b)(iv). Basic principles of treaty interpretation provide that this omission is deliberate and evinces a desire not to punish environmental desecration when committed in an internal conflict. Further limitations on the application of the entire Rome Statute to internal conflicts are found in Article 8(2)(f), which provides that it:

> applies to armed conflicts not of an international character and thus does not apply to situations of internal disturbances and tensions, such as riots, isolated and sporadic acts of violence or other acts of a similar nature. It applies to armed conflicts that take place in the territory of a State when there is protracted armed conflict between governmental authorities and organized armed groups or between such groups.[33]

In sum, nations appear even less willing to support objective standards of criminal behavior in internal conflicts than in international conflicts. This is a major limitation. Recent events in Rwanda and the former Yugoslavia underscore that the environment will suffer even in the event of a civil war. Insurgency and counter-insurgency guerrilla civil wars have a particularly devastating effect on local environments. Insurgents often use tropical forests as home bases and hiding grounds; counter-insurgency forces often respond by slashing and burning forests and by polluting rivers, viewing both as legitimate theaters of operations. Given the current dearth of standards in this area, the development of international law applicable to internal conflicts should be a top priority for policymakers.

---

[32] Rome Statute, Art. 28.   [33] *Ibid.*, Art. 8(2)(f).

On the other hand, one of the major successes of the Rome Statute is that it creates an institution to actually punish the conduct it prohibits. However, from the environmental point of view, the extent to which these environmental war crimes will receive the Court's attention is uncertain, given the broad array of other crimes to which it will have to direct its energies. Article 8(2)(b)(iv) constitutes only one provision out of dozens in the Statute. Environmental crimes are not raised as independent crimes; at most, they constitute an add-on in narrowly circumscribed areas.[34] This limits the possibility for future growth and application within and outside of the context of military conflict.

OTHER PROVISIONS

Article 8 of the Rome Statute also criminalizes the use of certain weapons that have destructive effects on both humanity and the natural environment. Prohibited practices include employing poison or poisoned weapons (Article 8(2)(b)(xvii)), and employing asphyxiating, poisonous, or other gases, and all analogous liquids, materials, or devices (Article 8(2)(b)(xviii)). Many of these weapons are already prohibited by other international agreements.[35] Nonetheless, this codification within the International Criminal Court will likely provide a more viable mechanism to enforce compliance than those presently contemplated in these other agreements.

The list of enumerated war crimes in Article 8(2)(b) appears to be exhaustive. The article defines as a war crime "other serious violations of the laws and customs applicable in international armed conflict, within the established framework of international law, namely, any of the following

---

[34] See the opening language to Article 5 of the Rome Statute, where the jurisdiction of the International Criminal Court is set out. The International Criminal Court is not given any jurisdiction to address environmental crimes standing by themselves.

[35] See, e.g., Convention on Prohibitions or Restrictions on the Use of Certain Conventional Weapons which may be Deemed to be Excessively Injurious or to Have Indiscriminate Effects, 35 UN GAOR, 35th Sess., UN Doc. A/CONF. 95/15 (Oct. 27, 1980), *I.L.M.* 19 (1980), 1523; Protocol for the Prohibition of the Use in War of Asphyxiating, Poisonous or Other Gases, and of Bacteriological Methods of Warfare (June 17, 1925), 26 U.S.T. 571; Convention on the Prohibition of the Development, Production and Stockpiling of Bacteriological (Biological) and Toxin Weapons and on their Destruction (Apr. 10, 1972), 26 U.S.T. 583; Convention on the Prohibition of the Development, Production, Stockpiling and Use of Chemical Weapons and on Their Destruction (Jan. 13, 1993), *I.L.M.* 32 (1993), 800.

acts," of which it then lists many, including Article 8(2)(b)(iv).[36] Discussions following the signing of the Rome Statute indicated that the use of the term "namely" likely implies exclusivity. This means that there would be limited opportunity for judicial interpretation to reach beyond the enumerated war crimes. Although Article 21 of the Rome Statute provides that the Court shall apply, "where appropriate, applicable treaties and the principles and rules of international law, including the established principles of the international law of armed conflict,"[37] this residual jurisdiction appears to be curtailed in the case of war crimes. Without the flexibility to go beyond the four corners of the enumerated categories of crimes under Article 8(2)(b), the Court may not be able to do justice to developments in international environmental law.

This is a lost opportunity given that, in the interplay between environmental integrity and military action in the "established principles of the international law of armed conflict," there are a number of important pre-existing conventions. These give rise to a corpus of principles, both international agreements and international practices, that constitute customary international law. Some of these principles go beyond the categories of conduct expressly proscribed by the Rome Statute. As a result, if and when environmentally related litigation begins under the International Criminal Court, it will be important to raise the following international treaty provisions – in addition to Protocol I and the ENMOD Convention – in any environmental war crimes trial, and to argue that they should in fact form part of the Court's residual jurisdiction.

Some of the listed treaties have not yet been universally ratified, and this may constitute an impediment to full protection of the environment in times of armed conflict. However, in some cases the number of signatories is sufficiently large to substantiate the argument that the content of the agreement constitutes customary international law.[38]

- The World Charter for Nature,[39] Principle 5, states that "Nature shall be secured against degradation caused by warfare or other hostile activities."

---

[36] Rome Statute, Art. 8(2)(b).   [37] *Ibid.*, Art. 21(1)(b).

[38] For example, 147 states are party to Protocol I to the 1949 Geneva Conventions, and 139 states are party to Protocol II to the 1949 Geneva Conventions. See "Five Years After Rio," Written Statement at the United Nations General Assembly, Nineteenth Special Session (June 23–27, 1997), available at http://www.icrc.org/unicc/icrcnews.nsf/5.

[39] GA Res. 37/7, UN GAOR, 37th Sess., 48th plen. mtg. (1982).

- The Rio Declaration,[40] Principle 24, states that "Warfare is inherently destructive of sustainable development. States shall therefore respect international law providing protection for the environment in times of armed conflict and cooperate in its further development, as necessary."
- The International Law Commission's Draft Articles on State Responsibility[41] create a limited basis for criminalizing intentional environmental harms. Article 19(3)(d) provides that an international crime may result from, *inter alia*, a serious breach of an international obligation of essential importance for the safeguarding and preservation of the human environment, such as those prohibiting massive pollution of the atmosphere or of the seas. This is one of the few international agreements prior to the Rome Statute that demonstrated a willingness to criminalize environmental degradation.
- The International Law Commission's Draft Code of Crimes Against the Peace and Security of Mankind,[42] Article 20, employs some familiar language in recognizing certain environmental crimes as "war crimes":

  (i) extensive destruction ... of property, not justified by military necessity and carried out unlawfully and wantonly; (ii) employment of poisonous weapons or other weapons calculated to cause unnecessary suffering; (iii) wanton destruction of cities, towns or villages, or devastation not justified by military necessity; and (iv) in the case of armed conflict, using methods or means of warfare not justified by military necessity with the intent to cause widespread, long-term and severe damage to the natural environment and thereby gravely prejudice the health or survival of the population and such damage occurs.

- The 1907 Hague Regulations,[43] Article 23(g), states that it is prohibited "to destroy or seize the enemy's property, unless such destruction or seizure be imperatively demanded by the necessities of war." This is one

[40] Rio Declaration on Environment and Development, UN Doc. A/CONF.151/5Rev.1, *I.L.M.* 31 (1992), 874.
[41] Shabtai Rosenne (ed.), *International Law Commission's Draft Articles on State Responsibility* (Dordrecht and Boston: M. Nijhoff, 1991).
[42] GA Res. 97, UN GAOR, 33rd Sess., Supp. No. 45, p. 220, UN Doc. A/33/45 (1978), as amended by GA Res. 151, UN GAOR, 42nd Sess., Supp. No. 49, p. 292, UN Doc. A/42/49 (1987). In the negotiations for the International Criminal Court, some negotiators suggested that the Draft Code of Crimes Against the Peace and Security of Mankind should be used in the creation of the International Criminal Court. See United Nations Press Release GA/L/3015 (Nov. 5, 1996).
[43] Regulations Respecting the Laws and Customs of War on Land, annexed to the Convention Respecting the Laws and Customs of War on Land (Oct. 18, 1907), 36 Stt. 2277, 1 Bevans 631, Art. 23(g).

of the earliest suggestions that there are limits on what a warring party can do to "property." Although not explicitly mentioned, the natural environment can be considered to constitute "property," although it is unclear whether the natural environment within the global commons would fall within the notion of "property."

- The 1949 Geneva Convention IV,[44] Article 53, states that "any destruction by the occupying power of real or personal property belonging individually or collectively to private persons, or to the State, or to other public authorities, . . . is prohibited, except when such destruction is rendered absolutely necessary by military operations." As with the Hague Regulations, this provision is limited by the military necessity defense and is inapplicable to the global commons. Additionally, this provision requires the destruction to occur within a nation that is actually occupied by another; indiscriminate aerial bombing in which enemy forces are not occupying the other nation's territory would fall outside its scope.
- Resolution 687 of the UN Security Council,[45] adopted in the aftermath of the 1990–91 Gulf War, made Iraq accountable for "any direct loss, damage, including environmental damage and the depletion of natural resources . . . as a result of Iraq's unlawful invasion and occupation of Kuwait." This is an important precedent upon which to ground civil liability for environmental destruction. The creation of the United Nations Compensation Commission to value damages and assess liability is also an important step in implementing responsibility for environmental wrongdoing during wartime.

In sum, these fragments, together with the express pronouncements in the Rome Statute, provide some definitional guidelines as to the permissible use of the environment during wartime. Unfortunately, they create a "...current international legal framework [that] is vague and unenforceable in environmental matters."[46] The background to and the language of the Rome Statute reveal a stagnation in the drive to sanction the use of the environment as a tool of war. Consideration should be given to developing ways of going beyond this language.

[44] 75 U.N.T.S. 287 (Aug. 12, 1949).
[45] UN SCOR Res. 687, UN SCOR, 2981st mtg., p. 7, UN Doc. S/RES/687 (1991).
[46] Jessica E. Seacor, "Environmental Terrorism: Lessons from the Oil Fires of Kuwait," *Am. U. J. Int'l L. & Pol'y* 10 (1995), 523.

Consolidating the fragments: towards the crime of ecocide

Some commentators have suggested making it a crime recklessly or intentionally to harm the environment, both within and outside the context of war.[47] This crime, labeled "geocide" or "ecocide" – the environmental counterpart of genocide – would be enshrined in a single international convention. The legal theory of ecocide is as follows: significantly harming the natural environment constitutes a breach of a duty of care, and this consists, at the least, in tortious or delictual conduct and, when undertaken with willfulness, recklessness, or negligence, ought to constitute a crime. Defining the crime to encompass negligent or willfully blind conduct is particularly important; as we have seen, proof of intentionality can be difficult to establish. In this regard, lessons can be learned from the domestic context. In North America, environmental wrongdoing normally is prosecuted on a negligence standard. Absent legislative intervention to couch environmental destruction as a "civil offense," positioned between criminal and public welfare law, it would be difficult for the law to serve as a deterrent to individuals who misuse the natural environment.

Given these lessons from domestic law, we ought to re-evaluate the merit of collapsing environmental wrongdoing within a criminal context such as the ICC, which is primarily geared to prosecute violators of humanitarian law on a strict intentionality basis. Pressing policy considerations of preserving the integrity of the environment for future generations argue in favor of attaching liability for environmental infractions at a lower standard. As a result, it would be important for the effectiveness of any ecocide provision to capture not only the *mens rea* standard of criminal law, but also negligence, reasonable foreseeability, willful blindness, carelessness, and objective certainty standards, many of which animate tort law and civil liability. By way of example, under a willful blindness standard, the nonfeasance of the authorities who maintained the nuclear reactors involved in the Chernobyl disaster could be prosecuted as ecocide. Lynn Berat concludes that "[t]here is substantial evidence that although

---

[47] See, e.g., Richard A. Falk, "Environmental Disruption by Military Means and International Law," in Arthur H. Westing (ed.), *Environmental Warfare: Technical, Legal and Policy Appraisal* (London and Philadelphia: Taylor & Francis, 1984), pp. 33–51; Seacor, "Environmental Terrorism"; Berat, "Defending the Right to a Healthy Environment"; Caggiano, "Legitimacy of Environmental Destruction"; Yuzon, "Deliberate Environmental Modification"; Mark Allan Gray, "The International Crime of Ecocide," *Cal. W. Int'l L.J.* 26 (1996), 215.

Soviet scientists and governmental officials were aware that the Soviet nuclear power plant design was flawed and had the potential for causing unmitigated disaster, they persisted in maintaining old plants and built new ones without design modification."[48]

It is also important to ground the *actus reus* not in the existence of "widespread, long-term and severe" damage, but simply in the existence of damage per se. If consensus is obtained on this latter point, Florencio Yuzon points out that "[in] an international crime of environmental destruction, the quantum of proof that is necessary, or the threshold of damage that must occur, is relatively low compared to ENMOD and Protocol I where higher thresholds of damage must be met . . . Any damage, regardless of the degree . . . would automatically render the State and/or its military, criminally liable."[49] On this theory, the extent of the damage, together with the pervasiveness of the mental element, would only inform sentencing principles. If enforcement authorities are given sufficient discretion in terms of sentencing, then a broader liability provision can not only be effective, but also respect shared notions of fundamental justice.

The jurisdiction of an international ecocide tribunal would be based on the transboundary nature of environmental destruction, together with its cumulative and pernicious effects on the global commons. However, any international tribunal ought to be guided by the principles of complementarity in its relationships with national courts. In negotiating jurisdiction, it is important for an Ecocide Convention to apply equally to natural persons, legal persons, and public authorities as well as states.[50] State responsibility is particularly crucial in order for civil damages and restitution to be viable remedies, as discussed below.

Unfortunately, some commentators have focused only on the definition of ecocide, concluding that "enforcement provisions and machinery . . . presently lie within the realm of theory."[51] As a result, much of the existing literature is limited to discussion of definitional issues. Any right, however, is but theoretical without a remedy; there can be no crime without punishment. Thought must be given to how ecocide could be enforced, and which organizations could be optimally suited to engage in this enforcement. There is some academic work in this area, though it is not as prevalent as in

---

[48] Berat, "Defending the Right to a Healthy Environment," 345.
[49] Yuzon, "Deliberate Environmental Modification," 841.
[50] See, e.g., Richard Falk, *Revitalizing International Law* (Ames: Iowa State Univ. Press, 1989), p. 189.
[51] Gray, "The International Crime of Ecocide," 217.

the definitional area.[52] The goal of this chapter is to provide some broad brushstrokes in this area, so as to ground future debate and discussion.

Although there may be a nascent international consensus that state responsibility for destruction of the environment is *ius cogens*, it is unclear whether the international community would be prepared to criminalize such destructive behavior, when undertaken in the context of armed conflict, beyond the contours suggested by the Rome Statute. What is clear, however, is that by failing to try to do so, the international community is shirking responsibility for one of the principal factors threatening the integrity of the planet for future generations. Although the concept of ecocide may sound utopian within the context of the present framework of reference, this framework needs to be challenged. After all, the notion of what is politically realistic is, and has always been, essentially elastic.

Enforcement at a crossroads: ecocide within an International Environmental Court or within a permanent International Criminal Court?

As suggested above, collapsing environmental crimes within the permanent International Criminal Court might not be the most effective way to prosecute such crimes. One overarching problem is that the International Criminal Court is principally designed to punish and deter genocide and crimes against humanity per se. As we have seen, environmental offenses are basically ancillary offenses, and might get lost in the shuffle. An example of this is in Rwanda, where the environmental destruction of the internecine conflict – which has been ongoing since 1994 – is significant. The Rwandan civil war has seen two national parks landmined,[53] endangered species poached, agricultural lands rendered barren to coerce migration of persecuted peoples, and systematic resettlement exhausting moderate lands – specifically in eastern Congo – of their agricultural capacities. The ad hoc International Criminal Tribunal for Rwanda has made no mention of these issues in its proceedings or in any of the

[52] See, e.g., J. Amedeo Postiglione, "A More Efficient International Law on the Environment and Setting Up an International Court for the Environment Within the United Nations," *Envtl. L.* 20 (1990), 321.

[53] Paradoxically, there is a correlation between the placing of landmines and increased biodiversity, owing to the fact that mines limit human encroachment. See Jeffrey A. McNeely, "War and Biodiversity: An Assessment of Impacts," chapter 14 in this volume.

mandates it has authorized; the domestic war crimes prosecutions that are occurring in Rwanda also have been very reticent in the area of environmental crimes. It may be that environmental concerns will become similarly neglected within the context of an International Criminal Court. The fact that environmental war crimes have received such little attention in the work of the Preparatory Commission sessions presages this neglect. The Preparatory Commission intends to "ensure the formulation of generally acceptable elements of crimes on Article 8, as part of a complete set of elements for all crimes, laid down in the [Rome] Statute."[54] Thus far, specific discussion of the environmental war crime provision has been very limited.[55] In fact, Article 8(2)(b)(iv) remains peripheral to the ongoing discussions. There is no indication that, as work progresses on the establishment of the Court, the environmental war crime will be able to attract the attention it requires in order to be effectively implemented.

Another limitation is the fact that the Court can only address environmental crimes committed by military forces actively engaged in hostilities. There thus appears not to be any jurisdiction to sanction the environmental insecurity created by armed forces in the testing of weapons or in the mobilization of forces. Nor is there jurisdiction to supervise any disarmament or decommissioning process.

---

[54] Preparatory Commission for the International Criminal Court, Second Session, July 26 to Aug. 13, 1999, http://www.un.org/law/icc/prepcomm/prepjul.htm (visited Oct. 18, 1999).

[55] See *ibid*. The Working Group on the Elements of Crimes regularly meets during the Preparatory Commission sessions. So far, it has considered the elements of some of the war crimes enumerated in the Rome Statute. It has divided the war crimes provisions into nine clusters based on "the possible commonality of their elements." Article 8(2)(b)(iv) is clustered with Article 8(2)(b)(v) (attacking or bombarding, by whatever means, towns, villages, dwellings or buildings which are undefended and which are not military objectives); (ix) (intentionally directing attacks against buildings dedicated to religion, education, art, science, or charitable purposes, historic monuments, hospitals, and places where the sick and wounded are collected, provided they are not military objectives); and (xxiv) (intentionally directing attacks against buildings, material, medical units, and transport, and personnel using the distinctive emblems of the Geneva Conventions in conformity with international law). So far, several discussion papers have been proposed by the Working Group on the Elements of Crimes. No discussion paper has been prepared for Article 8(2)(b)(iv). The official website for the Preparatory Commission addresses this gap in the following manner: "there was not sufficient time for the Coordinator to prepare discussion papers on the elements of all the provisions of war crimes." *Ibid*. Of the twenty-three national government proposals submitted to the Working Group on the Elements of Crimes, only a handful made mention of Article 8(2)(b)(iv). See Rome Statute of the International Criminal Court, List of documents issued at the second session of the Preparatory Commission, http://www.un.org/law/icc/prepcomm/julaug/docs2nd.htm (visited Oct. 19, 1999). Only one of these proposals gave thorough treatment to Article 8(2)(b)(iv). See Preparatory Commission Request, n. 31 above.

Magistrates and judges on the International Criminal Court likely will not have expertise in the areas of environmental law, policy, or science. This can heighten the transaction costs of proceeding judicially with environmental cases, as well as produce ineffective jurisprudence. For example, in the International Court of Justice decision on the Danube dispute between Hungary and Slovakia,[56] the judges had to be educated in the environmental science aspects of the dispute.[57] Although there is much to be gained from educating jurists on environmental issues, this can involve significant time as well as financial costs, which a specialized tribunal could avoid. Were environmental crimes to be litigated in a separate courtroom that only addressed ecocide and related infractions, there could be a greater guarantee of an appropriate level of scientific expertise.

Another critical limitation on the effectiveness of the Rome Statute is the fact that China, India, Russia, and the United States are not signatories; further, the "opt-out" provision, which allows even signatory countries to reject the Court's jurisdiction over war crimes for the first seven years of its existence, may also become a significant limitation. Clearly, there are many reasons why these nations chose not to sign on.[58] Some concerns relate to Article 15's allocation to the Prosecutor of a certain degree of independence; for example, the United States wished to have the option to veto the Prosecutor's decision to charge any American citizen.[59] More broadly, some dissenters wished the United Nations or Security Council to have control over the Court's docket. Other concerns relate to fears that soldiers will be prosecuted for activities resulting out of "international policing" activities.[60] It is interesting to consider whether these same issues

---

[56] *Case Concerning the Gabcíkovo–Nagymaros Project (Hungary/Slovakia)*, No. 92, General List (Sept. 25, 1997).

[57] The International Court of Justice has had only limited experience with environmental matters, although it has taken some very important decisions, such as the *Nuclear Tests Cases (Australia v. France)*, 1974 I.C.J. 253; and *Military and Paramilitary Activities In and Against Nicaragua (Nicaragua v. United States)*, 1986 I.C.J. 16. It also has created an Environmental Chamber with a view to playing a more proactive role in resolving environmental disputes. The principal impediments to the effectiveness of the International Court of Justice in adjudicating ecocide are: (1) the requirement that both litigants consent to the jurisdiction of the Court, which is impractical in an ecocide context; and (2) the Court's lack of jurisdiction to hear disputes involving individuals.

[58] See Alessandra Stanley, "US Dissents, but Accord is Reached on War-Crime Court," *N.Y. Times* (July 18, 1998).

[59] "Permanent War Crimes Court Approved," *N.Y. Times* (July 17, 1998).

[60] Stanley, "US Dissents"; see also Paul Koring, "US Qualms Over World Court Called Groundless," *The Globe & Mail* (July 24, 1998), A8.

would affect the negotiation of an Ecocide Convention, and if so, whether the effect would be as notable. In any event, what is clear is that the law of war crimes in general is such a thorny area in which to obtain meaningful consensus that segregating environmental war crimes from other types of war crimes may in fact facilitate consensus-building in the environmental arena.

There should be multilateral negotiations to develop an Ecocide Convention that would independently address environmental concerns. The Convention could be enforced by a permanent or, at first, ad hoc, International Environmental Court. In the past, many proponents of prosecuting international environmental crimes have focused on domestic courts as enforcers. For example, the ICRC Guidelines emphasize that "domestic legislation and other measures taken at the national level are essential means of ensuring that international law protecting the environment in times of armed conflict is indeed put into practice."[61] Instead, an international tribunal could settle issues of extraterritoriality, as well as fulfill a policing role in the areas of the global commons. It also could ensure some level of environmental protection for the citizens of nations whose domestic courts fail to sanction ecocide and other environmental crimes. However, it is clear that any International Environmental Court will have to operate in conjunction with national tribunals. Principles of complementarity between national and international adjudicators, which are now being developed in the area of genocide, also will have to be implemented in the environmental context.

Recent scholarship in the area of international relations shows that conventions with strict liability and rigorous enforcement measures are difficult to negotiate and even more difficult to enforce, especially when no uniform consensus exists.[62] The trick lies in utilizing more effective, and often gradual, methods to stimulate agreement. Discussions related to ecocide might be more effective if undertaken within a framework negotiation, as was the case in another urgent area of environmental concern, climate change. Instead of focusing on immediately creating unambiguous rules and strict liability, an attempt ought to be made to negotiate consensus around mutually acceptable standards which, through ongoing negotiations, can eventually be distilled into rules. Arguably, the failure of

---

[61] ICRC Guidelines, Art. I(2).
[62] Abram Chayes and Antonia Handler Chayes, *The New Sovereignty* (Cambridge, Mass.: Harvard Univ. Press, 1995).

previous attempts to codify environmental war crimes, such as the "Fifth Geneva Convention on the Protection of the Environment in Time of Armed Conflict," can be attributed to an overly radical stance.[63]

Such negotiations should involve not only states, but also NGOs, transnational public interest advocates, trade organizations, and other such groups. Thought should be given to establishing a managing secretariat, along with an adjudicative body. The managing secretariat is especially important since it can make decisions between official meetings of the parties, act in an administrative capacity, suggest policy alternatives, and engage in follow-up investigations.[64] As a result, the Ecocide Convention would not simply be a criminal statute, but also an organization designed to enhance awareness and develop methods to maximize incentives not to engage in environmentally pernicious military initiatives in the first place. It can also, drawing from the United Nations Compensation Commission, be involved in valuing environmental damage and perfecting methods of assessment.

What punishment?

Penalties are geared to deter misconduct, provide restitution for the aggrieved, voice condemnation, and offer some rehabilitation for the convicted. These essential principles ought to guide those accused of ecocide or any subset of environmental war crimes. Here again, Part 7 of the Rome Statute offers the most contemporary compilation of the international community's thinking on how international crimes ought to be punished. The punishment provisions of the Rome Statute contain two limitations on the effectiveness of Article 8(2)(b)(iv).

First, the jurisdiction of the Court is limited to natural persons. This makes it impossible to find any institutional or state liability in cases where

---

[63] See Hans-Peter Gasser, "For Better Protection of the Natural Environment in Armed Conflict: A Proposal for Action," *Am. J. Int'l L.* 89 (1995), 639. More promising framework approaches have had an inchoate development in the Conference of Experts on the Use of the Environment as a Tool of Conventional Warfare (Ottawa, July 1992), and previously at the International Council of Environmental Law (Munich, Dec. 1991).

[64] See Simon Lyster, "Effectiveness of International Regimes Dealing with Biological Diversity from the Perspective of the North," in Oran R. Young, George J. Demko, and Kilaparti Ramakrishna (eds.), *Global Environmental Change and International Governance* (Hanover/ Dartmouth College: Univ. Press of New England, 1996), pp. 214–16. See also Patricia Birnie, "Regimes Dealing with the Oceans and All Kinds of Seas from the Perspective of the North," in *ibid.*, pp. 83–92.

it is difficult to prove that the actions of one or more specific individuals accounted for the environmental destruction.

Second, and more important, the sentencing provisions are based on imprisonment, fines, and forfeiture of the proceeds of the crime.[65] There does not appear to be much ability for the Court to compel restitution, remediation, civil liability, or otherwise to clean up the environmental harm. Without the Court being able to order such remedies, the curative nature of punishment for causing "widespread, long-term and severe" damage to the natural environment is limited at best. Although there is discussion in Article 79 of the Rome Statute about transferring any fines and assets collected to a trust fund for the benefit of victims of the crime,[66] this does not directly address the situation where it is the natural environment directly, and humanity only indirectly, that bears the loss of the crime.

As a result, there is cause for concern that environmental crimes will not only be poorly cognizable under the International Criminal Court, but also that the punishments for wrongdoing will not address the unique nature of these crimes. This is a further argument in support of an Ecocide Convention, administered by its own Secretariat and enforced by its own Court. It is important for such a Court to be empowered to decide on both criminal as well as civil matters. In order for the decisions of this Court to be implemented and executed, it would have to be given jurisdiction over natural and legal persons in all nation-states, together with governments themselves. It would also be important for this Court to be given injunctive powers to stop violations from happening and to arrest future breaches. The International Criminal Court does not appear to have such a capacity. This is another reason why it may not be well suited to adjudicate environmental crimes.

However, more proactive methods also need to be developed. After all, any finding of ecocide operates only on an ex post facto basis – the environmental harm has already occurred. What is more important is to provide incentives not to act in environmentally threatening ways in the first place. Examples include the creation of economic disincentives to producing environmentally destructive weaponry, technology transfers to assist developing countries to pursue national security interests in a more environmentally friendly manner, and financial assistance mechanisms. One

---

[65] Rome Statute, Art. 77.   [66] *Ibid.*, Art. 79.

option that should be considered is the creation of an international insurance scheme, funded from international contributions or taxes, to carry out environmental clean-up as a stopgap measure until liability can be conclusively determined.[67] Linkages to trade and investment should be developed so as to create disincentives for peddling and manufacturing the more environmentally injurious military technology.

One final linkage that is of considerable importance involves international peacekeeping or peace-enforcement forces. These could be given a mandate to ensure environmental, as well as humanitarian, protection. Allotting international forces a "green-keeping" mandate could help integrate international environmental norms into internecine conflict. By way of example, were UN involvement in Somalia to have had a "green-keeping" mandate, then practices of deforestation and assaults on water purity – commonplace in the conflict – could have been addressed. Ultimately, the prevention of ecocide cannot be disaggregated from the fact that environmental scarcity and resource depletion are often the cause of military conflict.[68] In this fashion, the Rwandan conflict was partly precipitated by demand for arable land.[69] As a result, equipping nations to engage in proper environmental management and sustainable development could have the collateral benefit of mitigating military aggression in the first place.

Conclusion: going beyond military conflict

The concept of ecocide ought not to be restricted to actual war. In fact, it could apply to the pre-deployment and post-deployment phases of armed forces activity.[70] Drawing distinctions between these phases and overt military conflict is a somewhat artificial exercise. For example, capturing

[67] See David Caron, "The Place of the Environment in International Tribunals," chapter 9 in this volume; Jeffrey G. Miller, "Civil Liability for War-Caused Environmental Damage: Models from United States Law," chapter 10 in this volume.

[68] See McNeely, "War and Biodiversity."

[69] On the relationship between agricultural land-use and the Rwandan genocide, see Guenthar Baechler, "Rwanda: The Roots of Tragedy, Battle for Elimination on an Ethno-Political and Ecological Basis," in Guenthar Baechler and Kurt R. Spillman (eds.), *Environmental Degradation as a Cause of War* (1996), vol. II, pp. 461–502; M. A. Drumbl, "Rule of Law Amid Lawlessness: Counseling the Accused in Rwanda's Genocide Trials," *Colum. Hum. Rts. L. Rev.* 29 (1998), 545.

[70] See Victor W. Sidel, "The Impact of Military Preparedness and Militarism on Health and the Environment," chapter 17 in this volume.

pre-deployment military activity could oblige a nation to face international ecocide charges for development, testing, and detonation of nuclear devices, clearly an issue of importance – and one that could prove quite a barrier to obtaining international consensus on an ecocide treaty. Post-deployment liability would cover activities such as the decommissioning of weapons – for example, Russian attempts to decommission nuclear submarines in the Arctic, which are currently being carried out with insufficient financial and human resources, and which thus constitute a serious threat to the environment.[71]

Ecocide also could apply in times of peace. Environmental crime – most notably trade in endangered species, hazardous wastes, and ozone-depleting substances – already constitutes an underground market estimated at $20 billion annually.[72] Peacetime infractions of this nature ought also to be prosecuted within the rubric of an International Environmental Court. In the longer run, a Prosecutor's office attached to the Court could receive a mandate to investigate allegations of such transboundary environmental crimes.[73]

On another note, the forces of international financial expansion also wreak havoc on the environment.[74] International criminal sanctions could constitute a powerful device to mitigate the unsustainable and environmentally destructive effects of these market forces. Particularly troubling examples are the ongoing forest fires in the Amazon basin and in Indonesia. In both cases, there is compelling evidence that these fires had been deliberately set by enterprises seeking to clear the forests for economic development.[75] The effects on the environment are clear: immediate destruction, a reduced ability for ecosystem regeneration, and contribution to global warming. This destruction also has immediate effects on humanity: through death and disability owing to the effects of asthma and smog-related illnesses, and, in the case of the Indonesian fires, creating smoke and haze that may have induced a plane crash in Sumatra

---

[71] See Lakshman D. Guruswamy and Jason B. Aamodt, "Nuclear Arms Control: The Environmental Dimension," *Colo. J. Int'l Envtl. L.* 10 (1999), 267.

[72] "8 Countries Agree to Fight Environmental Crime," *N.Y. Times* (Apr. 6, 1998), 4.

[73] *Ibid.*

[74] McNeely contends that market forces may ultimately destroy more biodiversity than military forces. McNeely, "War and Biodiversity."

[75] John C. Klotz, "Scorched-Earth Policy is Intolerable," *National Law Journal* (Nov. 17, 1997), A17, col. 3. For the Indonesian context, see Randy Lee Loftis, "The Tropics are on Fire," *Toronto Star* (June 6, 1998), C6.

that took the lives of 234 people.[76] Such conduct ought to fall within an Ecocide Convention and be sanctioned by an International Environmental Court. It remains an open question whether such conduct could be conjunctively sanctioned by the International Criminal Court. If so, an entente of understanding would have to be developed between the two courts to avoid situations of double jeopardy and overlapping jurisdiction.

[76] Klotz, "Scorched-Earth Policy Is Intolerable."

EPILOGUE

The Kosovo Conflict: a case study of unresolved issues

CARL E. BRUCH AND JAY E. AUSTIN

This volume has highlighted ways in which the community of nations has sought to limit and redress wartime environmental damage. Over the past few decades, great strides have been made in developing the relevant legal norms, as well as the necessary scientific and economic tools; and international institutions capable of investigating and enforcing these provisions are emerging. The history of the law of war thus far has been a matter of incremental development in response to the horrors of previous conflicts. This patchwork quilt of legal prescriptions and institutions suffers from a wide variety of unresolved issues related to preventing, assessing, remediating, and determining responsibility and liability for environmental damage from armed conflict. The controversy over the 1999 Kosovo conflict, including the decision of the International Court of Justice, highlights many of these gaps and presents a number of challenges for the international community. Further, it raises questions of how well the existing legal framework and institutions can adapt to new advances in high-technology warfare.

The Kosovo situation implicates the most serious crimes against humanity: genocide and ethnic cleansing. This Epilogue focuses on a small subset of issues, specifically the environmental consequences of the conflict. It does not attempt to weigh these environmental consequences against the humanitarian imperatives motivating the NATO action. At the same time, even if the reasons for going to war are just and legal, the law of war requires separate consideration of the conduct of the war. And while this book lays out various reasons for considering and addressing the environmental consequences of conducting war, it acknowledges that conflicts such as Kosovo usually entail a much broader range of humanitarian concerns.

647

At the outset, the Kosovo conflict was primarily a low-intensity internal conflict, like the vast majority of armed conflicts in the world today. Few binding international norms apply in these situations, and while the international community fretted about the reported humanitarian (and some environmental) impacts, there was little agreement on an appropriate response. The primary international agreement applying to internal conflicts such as Kosovo is the 1977 Additional Protocol II to the 1949 Geneva Conventions. While Protocol II does not address environmental damage directly, the wells poisoned by Serb soldiers and militia members[1] arguably violated Article 13, which protects the civilian population, and Article 14, which protects objects indispensable to the survival of the civilian population, including "drinking water installations and supplies."

Once NATO was involved, the conflict became international, and the applicable legal regime shifted. An irony of these circumstances is that the stricter environmental norms of the international law-of-war regime applied primarily to the NATO forces. As in the 1990–91 Gulf War, the US military took the lead in the 78-day bombing campaign that ensued. And as in the Gulf War, US military lawyers provided real-time advice regarding targeting and choice of weapons in Kosovo.[2] The US military has incorporated environmental norms into their operational and law-of-war handbooks, and NATO has started to follow suit, at least for peacetime operations. Yet, while these military commands may well have operated in accordance with their handbooks, aspects of the Kosovo bombing campaign raise serious questions about the application and adequacy of the environmental and other norms contained in the handbooks.

For example, in making targeting decisions, military commanders balance the military necessity of destroying the target against the civilian and environmental impacts. In the 1990–91 Gulf War, this balancing sometimes led to potential targets being "scrubbed" from the list. In Kosovo, however, the effectiveness of this process came into question. The tragic bombing of the Chinese Embassy has been attributed to the strong demand imposed by the US State Department seeking potential targets,

---

[1] R. Jeffrey Smith, "Poisoned Wells Plague Towns All Over Kosovo," *Wash. Post* (Dec. 9, 1998), A30 (citing an estimate of thousands of poisoned wells).

[2] See Michael Ignatieff, "The Virtual Commander: How NATO Invented a New Kind of War," *The New Yorker* (Aug. 2, 1999), 30, 33–34; see also Carl Bruch, "Law (and Lawyers) on the Battlefield," *Envtl. Forum* (Nov./Dec. 1998), 34.

and the lack of adequate time or desire to review those targets.[3] This and other bombings of civilians and civilian objects eventually were admitted to be in error.

On the other hand, the deliberate and repeated bombing of the Pancevo fertilizer, oil refinery, and petrochemical plant complex, located a mere 16 km from Belgrade, raises more troubling concerns about the very nature of the balancing test. According to NATO, in addition to making products for civilian consumption, the Pancevo complex supplied gasoline and other essential materials to the Serb army, and thus was a legitimate military target.[4] In all, NATO bombed more than eighty industrial facilities, with some of the most severe environmental impacts occurring at Pancevo and Novi Sad.[5]

While it is not known what advance intelligence NATO commanders had about Pancevo, or what environmental damage they projected would result from the strikes, initial assessments indicated that the bombing released approximately 1,500 tons of vinyl chloride (a known carcinogen), 15,000 tons of ammonia, 800 tons of hydrochloric acid, 250 tons of liquid chlorine, 100 tons of mercury, and significant quantities of dioxin (a carcinogenic and mutagenic industrial byproduct that is also found in Agent Orange).[6] The poisonous gases appear to have doubled the rate of miscarriages over that of the previous year, caused widespread human illness, contaminated food crops and fish stocks, and caused unknown long-term damage to human health and the environment.[7] Additionally, some of the reported contamination and public health problems appear to be the result of bombing water and sewage treatment facilities. The impacts are not confined to the immediate area: the facility's location near the Danube River led to contamination downstream, with reports of oil slicks and other war-related contamination coming from as far away as the Danube Delta and the Black Sea port of Odessa, Ukraine.

---

[3] See, e.g., Ignatieff, "The Virtual Commander," 34.

[4] Chris Hedges, "Serbian Town Bombed by NATO Fears Effects of Toxic Chemicals," *N.Y. Times* (July 14, 1999), A1, A10.

[5] "Chemicals Leaking into Water, Soil as Result of NATO Airstrikes in Yugoslavia," *Int'l Env't Rep.* 22 (July 7, 1999), 586; see also Regional Environment Center for Central and Eastern Europe (REC), *Environmental Impact of the Yugoslavia Conflict: Preliminary Findings* (June 1999), available at http://www.rec.org/REC/Announcements/yugo/contents.html, sec. 7.5 (detailing 105 industrial targets in Yugoslavia).

[6] Hedges, "Serbian Town Bombed," A1, A10; see also REC, *Environmental Impact*, sec. 4.

[7] E.g., Hedges, "Serbian Town Bombed," A1.

It is unclear whether international politics will permit an objective evaluation of the decisions to bomb Pancevo or other industrial targets in Yugoslavia. But what nations say about their wartime actions contributes to the development of customary international law. In justifying the decision to bomb the complex, NATO asserted that "Pancevo was considered to be a very, very important refinery and strategic target, as important as tactical targets inside Kosovo."[8] This remarkable statement underscores the vagueness and inherent manipulability of the existing law-of-war provisions limiting wartime environmental damage, and the difficulty in trying to make them universally applicable. The complex calculations that factor into the balancing test cannot, and should not, be reduced to the number of times the target's importance is prefixed with the word "very." As Michael Schmitt observes, however, there is no universal metric for assessing the relative weight of the countervailing interests.[9]

If NATO's decision violated applicable international law, then the thorny issue arises of how responsibility, and possibly liability, should be determined. Alternatively, the NATO countries could be absolved of responsibility and liability on the theory that they were responding to Serbian aggression in Kosovo that violated international law. If NATO conducted its balancing assessment correctly, and the decision to bomb Pancevo was in fact legal, then the resulting human and environmental damage raises some grave questions about the adequacy of the existing norms, as well as the institutions available to determine responsibility and liability for violating these norms.

Potential responsibility of the NATO countries

During the height of the NATO bombing campaign, Yugoslavia filed a case before the International Court of Justice, requesting the Court to declare the bombing illegal and to order an immediate cessation of the campaign. Since the ICJ has jurisdiction to hear cases against nations only, Yugoslavia filed separate complaints against the ten NATO countries involved in the bombing, including claims of environmental war crimes.[10] However, because two countries – the United States and Spain – do not recognize the

---

[8] *Ibid.*, A10 (quoting an unnamed NATO spokeswoman).
[9] Michael N. Schmitt, "War and the Environment: Fault Lines in the Prescriptive Landscape," chapter 3 in this volume.
[10] E.g., *Legality of Use of Force (Yugo. v. US)* (1999), found at http://www.icj-cij.org/icjwww/idocket/iyus/iyusframe.htm; see also the Introduction to Part IIA of this volume.

compulsory jurisdiction of the ICJ and had not consented to jurisdiction in the case at hand, the Court held that it manifestly lacked jurisdiction against them; it also found that it lacked prima facie jurisdiction against the other eight countries.[11] As a result, the Court dismissed the cases against Spain and the United States, and continued to examine whether it had jurisdiction over the other eight nations, denying the requested injunction until it had resolved jurisdictional issues. Cessation of hostilities would have mooted the request for injunctive relief, but not necessarily the declaration of legality or illegality.

If the ICJ had jurisdiction, it remains an open question whether it would have found a violation of law-of-war norms, including environmental norms. Yugoslavia's environmental claims were vague and only loosely grounded in applicable law. This analysis explores various applicable law-of-war provisions that the ICJ might have considered had it reached the merits of the environmental claims, particularly as applied to the bombings at Pancevo and elsewhere.

As discussed at length in Parts II and V, the starting point for wartime environmental damage in international conflicts is the 1977 Additional Protocol I to the 1949 Geneva Conventions.[12] Protocol I sets an objective threshold, prohibiting "widespread, long-term and severe damage to the natural environment" regardless of the military objective.[13] Unlike other provisions of Protocol I and international humanitarian law, once this threshold is met, there is no exception for military necessity.[14] The extent to which these different provisions apply to the United States or other NATO countries is unclear. The environmental provisions of Protocol I have yet to be applied by an international tribunal, and the United States has not ratified Protocol I. Nevertheless, the United States has acknowledged that many of the provisions of Protocol I reflect customary international law, and the United States and other NATO countries have incorporated many of them into their military manuals.[15]

---

[11] E.g., *Legality of Use of Force.*

[12] Protocol Additional to the Geneva Conventions of August 12, 1949, and Relating to the Protection of Victims of International Armed Conflicts (June 8, 1977; entered into force, Dec. 7, 1978), reprinted in *I.L.M.* 16 (1977), 1391.   [13] *Ibid.*, Arts. 35(3) and 55.

[14] See Schmitt, "War and the Environment."

[15] E.g., John P. Quinn et al., "United States Navy Development of Operational–Environmental Doctrine," chapter 5 in this volume; Arthur H. Westing, "In Furtherance of Environmental Guidelines for Armed Forces During Peace and War," chapter 6 in this volume (also noting incorporation of environmental norms into NATO's guidelines for armed forces during peacetime).

The difficulty is that "widespread, long-term and severe" remains undefined. At Pancevo, Novi Sad, and other facilities, the clouds of toxic chemicals, contaminated waterways, and soiled earth may well have had, and continue to have, severe health and environmental impacts. Some of the known contaminants, such as mercury and dioxin, retain their toxicity indefinitely and bioaccumulate. Much of Pancevo's contamination was focused in the municipal area – Serbian officials estimate that the bombing of Pancevo endangered 70,000 people[16] – but it appears that significant quantities of the various toxic materials also moved into and down the Danube River. The question is whether this contamination is sufficient to trigger the environmental provisions of Protocol I. Since, as discussed by Schmitt, these provisions have yet to be applied in practice, the scope of the terms "widespread" and "severe" remains uncertain; and if, as some commentary suggests, "long-term" is to be "measured in decades," this prong of the test also might not be satisfied. From an initial examination of the matter, though, the ICJ could entertain a colorable claim that the bombing of Pancevo violated Articles 35(3) and 55 of Protocol I.

The ICJ also could have considered Article 56 of the Protocol, which protects "works and installations containing dangerous forces . . . even where these objects are military objectives." However, paragraph 2 provides that this protection ceases if such a facility is used "in regular, significant and direct support of military operations." A refinery, fertilizer, and petrochemical complex contains a variety of dangerous forces, particularly explosive and toxic elements, whose release could and did cause severe health damage to the surrounding civilian population. However, the facility's asserted contribution to the Serb military, if proven, would curtail the protections of Article 56. Even so, Article 57 requires that "those who plan or decide upon attack shall take all feasible precautions in the choice of means and methods of attack with a view to avoiding, and in any event to minimizing, incidental loss of civilian life, injury to civilians and damage to civilian objects."[17] The question remains whether direct bombing of Pancevo was necessary or whether other options existed, such as cutting off supplies or delivery routes from the facility, particularly given the availability of laser-guided precision missiles.

---

[16] REC, *Environmental Impact*, sec. 3.1.
[17] Protocol I, Art. 57(2)(a)(ii); see also Art. 56(3) (providing that citizens are entitled to the protections of Article 57, notwithstanding any military objective of the installation that might cancel the protection of Article 56(1)).

The ICJ also would have examined the NATO bombing campaign in light of the Protocol I prohibition on indiscriminate attacks. These are attacks "which employ a method or means of combat the effects of which cannot be limited as required by this Protocol, and consequently . . . are of a nature to strike military objectives and civilians or civilian objects without distinction."[18] Protocol I specifically prohibits as indiscriminate "an attack which may be expected to cause incidental loss of civilian life, injury to civilians, damage to civilian objects, or a combination thereof, which would be excessive in relation to the concrete and direct military advantage anticipated."[19] Again, NATO's assertion that the anticipated "very, very important" military advantage outweighed the incidental human and environmental loss highlights the subjective nature of this decision, as well as the lack of meaningful criteria for evaluating it.

The United States and NATO rest their decision on the "dual-use" exemption contained in various provisions of Protocol I: although Pancevo may have been a civilian facility, once it started producing gasoline and other products for the Yugoslav military, it became a legitimate target. Thus, while Article 52 of Protocol I prohibits attacks on civilian objects and "strictly" limits attacks to military objectives, paragraph 2 permits attacks on "those objects which by their nature, location, purpose or use make an effective contribution to military action and whose total or partial destruction, capture or neutralization, in the circumstances ruling at the time, offers a definite military advantage." As discussed above, Article 56, which prohibits attacks on installations containing "dangerous forces," includes a similarly explicit exemption. In addition to justifying the attacks on the Pancevo complex, NATO and the United States invoked the dual use exemption to justify controversial attacks on other civilian infrastructure, including power plants and sewage treatment facilities, as well as television and other media facilities.

While the dual-use exemption explicitly applies to the various humanitarian provisions, including the rule of discrimination, again there is no similar exemption for the environmental provisions of Articles 35(3) and 55. Once the environmental damage is "widespread, long-term and severe," there is no exemption for military necessity. It may be that the damage in Kosovo is not "widespread, long-term and severe" under international law, in which case resort to the other humanitarian protections is

---

[18] *Ibid.*, Arts. 51(4), 51(4)(c).   [19] *Ibid.*, Art. 51(5)(b).

necessary. However, if the long-term assessments of the environmental impacts of the Kosovo conflict – particularly the "hot spots" identified by the UN Balkans Task Force[20] – indicate long-term and severe but not "widespread" ecological and public health damage, the dual-use exemption as utilized in the Kosovo conflict could eviscerate the law-of-war protections for human health and the environment.

Weapons choice and tactics in the Kosovo campaign also raise issues of discrimination. For instance, as Richard Falk notes, the political decision to minimize the risk of NATO casualties by conducting high-altitude bombing came at the expense of civilian deaths on the ground.[21] Unexploded cluster bombs continue to cause civilian casualties, although NATO countries did commit money and personnel to removing unexploded ordnance.[22] Charges that NATO forces used depleted-uranium munitions, which are chemically toxic and persist in the environment, could raise similar issues.[23] The bombing campaign saw the first use of graphite bombs to short-circuit power lines and collapse Serbia's electric power system,[24] raising questions of targeting civilian infrastructure but also of whether this weapon caused less environmental damage than conventional explosives.

Yugoslavia also asserts that NATO wrongfully targeted various national parks and other protected areas.[25] These areas may enjoy some measure of protection in wartime, for instance under the 1954 Cultural Property Convention and the 1972 World Heritage Convention. Richard Tarasofsky points out, however, that these conventions are limited during wartime,

---

[20] E.g., Steven Erlanger, "Team Finds NATO Bombing Left Few Environmental Woes," *N.Y. Times* (July 28, 1999), A6.

[21] Richard Falk, "The Inadequacy of the Existing Legal Approach to Environmental Protection in Wartime," chapter 4 in this volume; see also Richard Falk, "Reflections on the War," *The Nation* (June 28, 1999), 11, 12 (asserting that the bombing of civilian infrastructure was a "grave violation of the laws of war"); see also David Rieff, "The Precarious Triumph of Human Rights," *N.Y. Times Magazine* (Aug. 8, 1999), 37, 41.

[22] E.g., Michael Dobbs, "A War-Torn Reporter Reflects," *Wash. Post* (July 11, 1999), B1 (estimating 11,000 unexploded bomblets, and exploring the issue of indiscriminate warfare); "US to Pledge $500 Million," United Press International (July 26, 1999) (detailing funds to be used for clearing landmines and unexploded ordnance, among other humanitarian assistance volunteered by the United States for Kosovo); Katharine Q. Seelye, "World Leaders Join in a Drive to Aid Balkans," *N.Y. Times* (July 31, 1999), A1; see also "NATO Pledges to Retrieve Jettisoned Bombs to Eliminate Potential Environmental Risk," *Int'l Env't Rep.* 22 (May 26, 1999), 464–65.

[23] E.g., Arlene Getz, "Toxic Bombs?" *Newsweek.com* (April 29, 1999), available at http://newsweek.com/nw-srv/tnw/today/ps/pso1we_1.htm; but see Erlanger, "NATO Bombing," A6 ("initial findings [of the UN Balkan Task Force] did not show any increased level of radioactivity from . . . depleted uranium, as was feared").

[24] E.g., REC, *Environmental Impact*, sec. 4.1.5.   [25] E.g., *ibid.*, sec. 4.1.4.

and advocates a clear delineation and designation of protected areas that would be off-limits to wartime activities. However, even under the Draft IUCN Convention that Tarasofsky analyzes, protection for a designated area is waived when the area is put to military use.[26] The protected areas bombed in Yugoslavia do not appear to be pristine areas, and may well have included legitimate military targets.

It is interesting to note that NATO's actions in Kosovo were significantly less expansive and destructive than those of the United States and its allies in the 1990–91 Gulf War. There, Coalition forces devastated Iraqi factories and refineries following the same dual-use justification; dropped millions of cluster bombs, leaving an estimated 1.2 to 1.5 million unexploded bomblets in the Gulf (more than 100 times the number estimated in Kosovo), that have so far killed more than 1,600 people; and littered the desert with an estimated 320 tons of depleted uranium.[27] In light of the much greater environmental and human impacts of the 1990–91 Gulf War, impacts in Kosovo have more of the character of isolated incidents.

Nevertheless, if the damage at Pancevo and elsewhere in Yugoslavia were held to be widespread, long-term, and severe, then the NATO countries would appear to be responsible despite the previous practice. However, as in the Gulf War, while scientific assessments proceed, there is little international support for any serious consideration of legal responsibility for the NATO countries. Yet, if the law of war is to maintain its legitimacy and universal applicability, and not become just something imposed ad hoc by victors, the international community needs to undertake a credible examination of whether and to what extent NATO's actions comported with the international law of war.[28]

Potential responsibility of the Yugoslav government

Alternatively, the international community or a legal tribunal could declare that the Yugoslav government is responsible and liable for all

---

[26] Richard G. Tarasofsky, "Protecting Specially Important Areas during International Armed Conflict: A Critique of the IUCN Draft Convention on the Prohibition of Hostile Military Activities in Protected Areas," chapter 22 in this volume (Art. 3 of the Draft Convention).

[27] E.g., Dan Eggen, "NATO 'Duds' Keep Killing in Kosovo," *Wash. Post* (July 19, 1999), A1, A15.

[28] See generally Rieff, "Precarious Triumph," 38 (noting that with respect to international human rights generally, "some advocates have begun to fear that in the future Western Governments may be willing to uphold principles only where economically unimportant countries like Serbia or Burma are concerned").

damages, from both its actions and NATO actions, on the basis that it engaged in aggressive warfare in Kosovo. This argument would parallel UN
Security Council Resolution 687, which held Iraq liable for all "direct loss,
damage, . . . or injury . . . as a result of Iraq's unlawful invasion and occupation of Kuwait."[29] The Governing Council of the United Nations Compensation Commission interpreted this to include "any loss suffered as a
result of military operations or threat of military action by either side,"[30]
apparently reasoning that since Iraq's aggression necessitated the Allied
invasion, Iraq should be liable for its consequences as well. By analogy,
Serbia could be held liable for all damages resulting from NATO's humanitarian intervention in Kosovo, including the environmental damage at
Pancevo and elsewhere, as well as the environmental damages resulting
from the hundreds of thousands of refugees and displaced people.[31]

Still open for resolution, and unaddressed by the precedent set by the
UN Security Council or the UNCC decisions, is whether there truly would
or should be limits on liability for "*any* loss suffered as a result of military
operations or threat of military action *by either side.*" Under the UNCC
regime, Iraq evidently could also be held liable for the consequences of the
Coalition's decision to use armor-piercing depleted-uranium munitions
in the 1990–91 Gulf War, even though many countries consider depleted
uranium to be an inhumane weapon due to its long-lasting impacts.[32] But
it seems unlikely that there would be no limits whatsoever to Iraq's liability
for the actions of Coalition forces in liberating Kuwait. To take an extreme
example, if Coalition forces had decided to drop a nuclear bomb on
Baghdad or Kuwait City, it is doubtful that the international community
would have held Iraq liable for such an action, even if it was for the express
purpose of compelling Iraq to withdraw from Kuwait.

Moreover, the law of war applies to all combatants, not just aggressors.
Violation of the rules governing entry into war (*ius ad bellum*) cannot justify a violation of the rules governing the conduct of war (*ius in bello*). Any

---

[29] UN Security Council Res. 687 (Apr. 8, 1991), reprinted in *I.L.M.* 30 (1991), 847.
[30] UNCC Governing Council Decision 7, S/AC.26/1991/7/Rev.1 (Mar. 17, 1992), para. 6(a).
[31] See Seth Borenstein, "UN to Probe Claims of Harm to Environment," *San Jose Mercury News* (May 16, 1999) (citing Michael Diederich as asserting that Yugoslavia is responsible for any ecological damage); REC, *Environmental Impact* (detailing "major" environmental impacts of refugees in Kosovo, Albania, and Macedonia, as well as Serbia and Montenegro; impacts include felling trees, polluting water sources, loss of habitat, and generation of waste).
[32] Rosalie Bertell, "Gulf War Veterans and Depleted Uranium," paper prepared for the Hague Peace Conference (May 1999), available at http://prop1.org/2000/du/99du/9905du.hague.htm.

other scenario would encourage nations to escalate responses and violate the carefully negotiated proscriptions, each claiming that the other side's actions justified their response or absolved them of responsibility. The UNCC Governing Council decision necessarily (and implicitly) assumes that none of the actions by the Coalition forces violated the law of war. The issue in Kosovo then becomes whether a particular NATO action, such as the bombing of the Pancevo complex, violated the law of war.

There are difficulties, however, in drawing too close a parallel between the 1990–91 Gulf War and the conflict in Kosovo. First, the former was indisputably an international conflict, and Iraq violated numerous international law provisions in invading Kuwait, particularly those forbidding aggressive warfare between states.[33] In contrast, Serbia's actions in Kosovo remained a non-international conflict and, from the Serb perspective, an internal police action, until NATO entered into the fray on humanitarian grounds. Nevertheless, Serbia arguably violated the peremptory norm against genocide and committed other grave breaches of international law. As a result, the escalating human rights violations in Kosovo over the last decade could justify international intervention, and be grounds for subsequently holding Yugoslavia criminally and civilly liable for all consequences of the war, including environmental consequences.

From a practical standpoint, however, holding Yugoslavia civilly liable would serve only to absolve NATO nations of any liability. Kosovo is a semi-autonomous republic of Yugoslavia, and enforcing any judgment against Yugoslavia or against Serbia – the dominant republic in Yugoslavia and the seat of the government responsible for most of the atrocities in Kosovo – would entail significant manipulation of internal Yugoslav politics. It would be surprising if the international community would want to enter into the fray of setting priorities for remediating environmental damage. For example, it has been suggested that one of the reasons Milošević did not act immediately on damage in Pancevo is that it is an opposition stronghold.[34] Furthermore, Yugoslavia likely would be unable to compensate the injured parties, including downstream countries. As in most internal conflicts where the combatants have poured resources into sustaining a long drawn-out conflict on their own soil, Yugoslavia would be an insolvent defendant.

[33] E.g., UN Charter, Art. 2, para. 4. [34] See Hedges, "Serbian Town Bombed," A10.

Inadequacy of international institutions

Most allegations of Serb atrocities will be handled by the pre-existing International Criminal Tribunal for the Former Yugoslavia, as evidenced by that body's indictment of President Slobodan Milošević for war crimes. On the other hand, if the United States and NATO are alleged to have violated the law of war, there are many practical limitations in adjudicating their responsibility and trying to hold them liable, particularly for environmental damage. The greatest limitation would be finding a forum that is receptive to such a petition. The most natural venue would be the International Court of Justice, but, as discussed, the ICJ held that it lacked jurisdiction over the parties.

If the ICJ had found jurisdiction, it remains an open question not only whether it would have found a violation of Protocol I, but also whether it could have – in addition to enjoining the bombing campaign – applied Article 91 of Protocol I, which provides that states party to the Protocol or the Geneva Conventions "shall, if the case demands, be liable to pay compensation." The United States is party to the Geneva Conventions, but not to the Protocols. And, as discussed in Part V, other international institutions are politically unlikely to entertain such a claim, and seeking redress in domestic courts is similarly problematic.

If the United States and other NATO countries are actually responsible for violating the law of war, yet are not held liable, then the existing legal norms become subject to the assertion that they are simply "victor's justice" enshrouded in the cloak of legitimacy. In Part II, Richard Falk highlighted the lack of parity in applying comparable law-of-war proscriptions in the Vietnam War and the 1990–91 Gulf War, depending primarily on whether the country conducting the environmental warfare was the United States or its opponent. While the environmental damage in Kosovo is significantly less than in these previous two wars, a credible examination of NATO actions in Kosovo is necessary to maintain the legitimacy of the law-of-war regime, as well as to clarify the scope of norms at issue, such as which weapons are "inhumane" and what is the scope of the dual-use exemption.

In sum, the same legal issues raised by the Kosovo conflict will continue to arise as other humanitarian emergencies compel armed international intervention. Unless acceptable conduct is explicitly and specifically detailed and the standards applied equally to all sides, conduct of these humanitarian efforts will remain of questionable legality, and could threaten the overall legitimacy of the international law-of-war regime.

Assessing the environmental impacts in Kosovo

Throughout the Kosovo conflict, NATO maintained tight control of information regarding the bombing campaign. The little information about the environmental impacts that reached the West came from Serb sources, who had a strong incentive to exaggerate the damages wrought on them. Thus, it became clear early on that something had happened at Pancevo, but it was unclear exactly what the damage was, whether it was justified, and what mitigation steps could be taken to stem the impacts.[35]

Once the hostilities ceased, the United Nations established a Balkans Task Force (BTF) to investigate the possible environmental impacts of the conflict. The BTF included personnel from UNEP – which also played a prominent role in performing the initial assessment of the environmental impacts of the 1990–91 Gulf War[36] – as well as from non-governmental organizations and from governments.[37] International investigative organizations such as the BTF can lend credibility to the findings, due to their independence and accumulated expertise in assessing the environmental consequences of war. In order for such independent investigative organizations to function properly, they need to be able to mobilize quickly: in Kosovo, a UNEP needs assessment team surveyed the situation while hostilities wound down, and the BTF conducted a preliminary investigation a month after hostilities ceased.[38]

---

[35] Seth Borenstein and Barry Shlachter, "Pollution Alleged amid Airstrikes," *San Jose Mercury News* (May 9, 1999) (describing the lack of reliable information regarding environmental impacts); Borenstein, "UN to Probe Claims" (quoting a UNEP official as saying: "We urgently need clear, detailed and credible information on the impacts").

[36] See, e.g., United Nations Environment Program, "Environmental Consequences of the Armed Conflict between Iraq and Kuwait: Report of the Executive Director" (16th Sess., agenda item 4), UNEP/GC.16/4/Add.1 (1991); United Nations Environment Program, Response to the Environmental Emergency Created by the Gulf War: Lessons to be Learned from the UN Response to the Environmental Crisis in the ROPME Region (undated memorandum; on file with the *Stanford Journal of International Law*).

[37] Susan Ladika, "UN Groups, NGOs Trying to Coordinate Data-Gathering on Environmental Damage," *Int'l Env't Rep.* 22 (May 26, 1999), 464; Borenstein, "UN to Probe Claims" (noting use of remote-sensing in assessing the damages in Kosovo).

[38] See, e.g., Ladika, "UN Groups," 464; see also "Chemicals Leaking," 586 (describing the initial UN needs assessment mission of May 16–27, 1999).

Even with such organized efforts, and even with experience from assessing the impacts of the Gulf War fresh in the minds of the international community, it is likely that the environmental and health impacts in Kosovo will be difficult to assess and predict. As discussed in Part III, a major problem with such assessments is that the baseline environmental conditions are uncertain, and it is difficult to discern which contamination is due to wartime actions and which is pre-existing, or even caused by the Serbs during the conflict.[39] Assessment of immediate impacts in Kosovo was hampered by a lack of adequate medical and environmental technology, aggravated by nine years of economic sanctions and the brief war.[40] In neighboring countries, inadequate or non-existent monitoring facilities complicated assessments of transboundary pollution.[41] Around Pancevo, doctors have seen a dramatic rise in skin rashes, cardiopulmonary ailments, and miscarriages,[42] but the scientific (and thus legal) proof of direct causation is lacking. In fact, notwithstanding the heavy press coverage about the severity of the environmental damage from bombing the Pancevo complex, as well as other industrial facilities, the BTF initially reported that their preliminary investigation revealed "no ecological catastrophe," only some hot spots.[43]

The long-term health and ecological impacts of the Kosovo conflict are even more problematic.[44] Cancers usually take years, if not decades, to

---

[39] Erlanger, "NATO Bombing," A6; see also Borenstein and Shlachter, "Pollution Alleged" (citing "unconfirmed reports that Serbian authorities might have added to the problem by deliberately dropping more crude [oil] into the Danube, apparently to spur anti-NATO sentiment in such downstream countries as Romania and Bulgaria").

[40] E.g., REC, *Environmental Impact*, sec. 1.2.2 ("very inadequate monitoring facilities and resources" in most countries).   [41] E.g., *ibid.*, secs. 3.2 (Albania), 3.5 (Romania).

[42] E.g., Hedges, "Serbian Town Bombed," A1; "Poisonous Reminders Linger in Serbia Weeks after War's End," *Deseret News* (July 25, 1999), available at http://www.desnews.com/cgi-bin/libstory_reg?dn99&9907260207.

[43] See, e.g., Edmund L. Andrews, "Kosovo Damage Seems Less than Feared," *N.Y. Times* (July 14, 1999), A10; Erlanger, "NATO Bombing," A6. But see REC, *Environmental Impact*, sec. 1 (stating that the "environment in the whole territory of Yugoslavia was affected"; although the REC found that "there is no evidence of a large-scale ecological catastrophe," it noted "very severe" pollution around targeted industrial complexes); *ibid.*, sec. 4.3 (finding "no measurable effects on the [Danube] river from the war" and no significant air or soil impacts in Bulgaria).

[44] E.g., William Booth, "A Ghost City of Mixed Poisons," *Wash. Post* (July 21, 1999), A15; Borenstein and Shlachter, "Pollution Alleged" (describing "danger of long-term contamination of reservoirs and underground waters" and potential health hazards of depleted uranium); REC, *Environmental Impact*, sec. 1.2.1 (possible contamination of foodstuffs will require research and monitoring, but this may prove difficult in "those countries that have shown an inability or unwillingness to present results of general pollution"); *ibid.*, sec. 5 (detailing a number of potential long-range impacts arising from the wartime environmental damage).

appear, and a lack of baseline information can make it difficult to deter-mine statistical increases or otherwise distinguish wartime impacts from peacetime "lifestyle-related" impacts. After more than twenty-five years, the long-term health impacts of Agent Orange in Vietnam remain unclear, as discussed by Alastair Hay in Part III. Similarly, in addition to the cases of asthma and emphysema already evident, other expected impacts of the burning oil wells in Kuwait are likely to take many more years to manifest themselves, and even then it will be difficult to discern which are wartime impacts. If the impacts in Kosovo prove to be largely localized, it may be easier to determine the health impacts by searching for "clusters" of certain diseases around these hot spots. Ecological impacts also will be difficult to predict: in previous wars, impacts often have been under- or over-predicted, due in part to the difficulties of assessing long-term impacts of nonlinear ecological systems. Adding to the predictive difficulties, Yugosla-via has a different climate from the Persian Gulf and Vietnam. Thus, the experiences of assessing ecological impacts of the wars in these regions have limited applicability to Yugoslavia.[45]

In order to improve assessments of the environmental impacts of war, the scientific community needs to develop scientific indicators of environ-mental harm (as discussed by Schmitt), methodologies for measuring those indicators, and baseline environmental data against which to com-pare the contemporary measurements. The baseline ecological and public health data are the most problematic, as most wars are now conducted in developing countries that do not have the necessary technological and professional resources. This is particularly important because economic development itself – for example, in Kuwait or Kosovo – impacts the envir-onment, and it becomes difficult to discern the damage subsequently caused by war. The attempts by scientists to gather data on the local and transnational environmental impacts of the Kosovo conflict, even in the midst of the conflict, are a useful first step in characterizing the impacts, although the background data is still lacking.[46] Postwar efforts in both Kuwait and Kosovo are establishing a comprehensive environmental profile, which is necessary for characterizing future impacts, setting an upper bound on certain damages, and providing valuable modeling data.

[45] See Erlanger, "NATO Bombing" (mentioning aspects of Yugoslavia's climate that differ from the Persian Gulf or Vietnam, but that could help ameliorate the environmental damage).
[46] See generally, REC, *Environmental Impact*.

Valuing the environmental impacts in Kosovo

Even after the ecological and health impacts have been estimated, the economic value of those impacts may be difficult to determine. As discussed in Part IV, war introduces many difficulties in applying traditional peacetime valuation methodologies. Determining the economic value of the impacts in Kosovo is of limited utility, however, as it is unlikely that a forum will ever be called upon to adjudicate the damages. Formal compensation from the United States is unlikely, considering how cautiously the United States approached compensating China for the admittedly wrongful bombing of the Chinese embassy.[47] In fact, the United States asserted that because the US bore most of the responsibility and costs of conducting the Kosovo campaign, Europe should shoulder the majority of reconstruction costs.[48]

Even without a formal mechanism for assigning liability, developing appropriate methodologies would assist in prioritizing remediation of environmental damages. The Kosovo conflict introduces factors that could affect the valuation methodologies in ways that other recent high-profile armed conflicts have not. There, nine years of internal conflict and economic sanctions reduced the infrastructure for mitigating and remediating environmental damages, affecting common Western assumptions about the availability of resources for addressing the damages. Moreover, as in the 1990–91 Gulf War, countries not involved in the conflict incurred environmental damages: Romania, Bulgaria, and Ukraine suffered potential damages to the Danube River, and Hungary and Macedonia observed elevated air pollution. While formal redress for these countries is improbable, informal compensation may be available through political channels, and reliable estimates of any damage would be useful for this purpose.[49]

---

[47] E.g., John Pomfret, "US, China Discuss Bomb Damages," *Wash. Post* (July 17, 1999), A15 (describing US concerns about using the word "compensation" due to its potential acknowledgment of legal fault, opting for "humanitarian payments"); Seth Faison, "US to Pay China for Embassy Bombing," *N.Y. Times* (July 31, 1999), A5.

[48] E.g., Andrews, "Kosovo Damage Seems Less than Feared," A10.

[49] Seelye, "World Leaders" (describing funds allocated by the United States and other countries for the purpose of, among other things, "compensat[ing] neighboring countries that housed refugees or suffered economic harm").

Conclusion

In preparing for the 1998 Conference in Washington, the Environmental Law Institute received a proposal from personnel in the Croatian Ministry of Defense for a paper on "Chemical Warfare Without Chemical Weapons." It modeled the potential consequences of a 1995 attack on a fertilizer plant in Croatia; while the actual attack did not cause any environmental damage, the authors maintained that it could have killed or poisoned tens of thousands of people, contaminated waters, impacted forests and agriculture, and harmed wildlife. It took only four more years for this scenario to be realized, in Pancevo, Novi Sad, and elsewhere in Serbia.

How does the law of war, which has focused so much attention on grave topics such as genocide and weapons of mass destruction, deal with such a prosaic, yet potentially horrifying result? Many gaps and issues remain. From a purely environmental perspective, Kosovo presses the international community to reconsider the norms applicable to internal armed conflicts and to humanitarian intervention efforts. Internal armed conflicts represent the overwhelming number of ongoing conflicts, and the international community has realized that internal conflicts often cause regional instability, in addition to untold human suffering. Kosovo is a classic example, with the real threat of genocide. Yet, the international efforts to ameliorate the human suffering and restore stability entailed wartime tactics that caused severe environmental harm and weapons that some in the international community label inhumane, or even as contravening the international law of war. Kosovo also compels examination of the practice of targeting civilian infrastructure, even where it has a potential military application or contribution.

An international effort is necessary to answer the questions left unresolved by the existing norms: Is depleted uranium an inhumane weapon? Is civilian infrastructure a legitimate target when it contributes to the war effort? How much must it contribute? At least as important, the international community must move towards a coherent, consistently applied set of norms. Institutional reforms, such as those suggested in Part V, are a step in this direction.

Perhaps the most thorny issue facing the international community is how to apply the norms against powerful nations: for example, the United States in Vietnam; Russia in Chechnya; China in Tibet; and Western allied forces (including the US, France, and the UK) in the 1990–91 Gulf War and Kosovo. While the international community held German General Alfred Jodl criminally liable for scorched earth tactics in World War II, and held Iraq civilly liable for environmental damages in the 1990–91 Gulf War, applying these norms against the winning side is much more difficult, especially in a political climate with a single military superpower.

Much progress has been made in establishing norms and institutions to prevent, assess, and redress wanton environmental damage from armed conflict. The challenge lies not only in clarifying the legal norms and developing the necessary institutions and scientific and economic tools, but also in developing the political initiative to apply these prescriptions equally and universally. Over 100 years old, the Martens Clause provides that where the law of war does not address a particular case, we should look to "the rule of the principles of the law of nations, as they result from the usages established among civilized peoples, from the laws of humanity, and the dictates of the public conscience." Surely, the laws of humanity and the dictates of the public conscience also demand equal application of these provisions.

INDEX

Index